Microsoft®

EXCEL 97

Step by Step

Other titles in the *Step by Step* series:

*Microsoft Access 97 Step by Step
*Microsoft Excel 97 Step by Step, Advanced Topics
*Microsoft FrontPage 97 Step by Step
 Microsoft Internet Explorer 3.0 Step by Step
 Microsoft Office 97 Integration Step by Step
*Microsoft Outlook 97 Step by Step
*Microsoft PowerPoint 97 Step by Step
 Microsoft Team Manager 97 Step by Step
 Microsoft Windows 95 Step by Step
 Microsoft Windows NT Workstation version 4.0 Step by Step
*Microsoft Word 97 Step by Step
*Microsoft Word 97 Step by Step, Advanced Topics

Step by Step books are also available for the Microsoft
Office 95 programs.

* These books are approved courseware for Certified Microsoft
  Office User (CMOU) exams. For more details about the CMOU
  program, see page xvii.

Microsoft®

EXCEL 97

Step by Step

Microsoft *Press*

PUBLISHED BY
Microsoft Press
A Division of Microsoft Corporation
One Microsoft Way
Redmond, Washington 98052-6399

Copyright © 1997 by Catapult, Inc.

Library of Congress Cataloging-in-Publication Data
Microsoft Excel 97 step by step / Catapult, Inc.
        p.   cm.
    Includes index.
    ISBN 1-57231-314-5
    1. Microsoft Excel (Computer file)   2. Business--Computer
programs   3. Electronic spreadhseets.   I. Catapult, Inc.
HF5548.4.M523M51575   1997
005.369--dc20   96-38988
                                                            CIP

Printed and bound in the United States of America.

1 2 3 4 5 6 7 8 9   WCWC   2 1 0 9 8 7

Distributed to the book trade in Canada by Macmillan of Canada, a division of Canada Publishing Corporation.

A CIP catalogue record for this book is available from the British Library.

Microsoft Press books are available through booksellers and distributors worldwide. For further information about international editions, contact your local Microsoft Corporation office. Or contact Microsoft Press International directly at fax (425) 936-7329.

Intel and Pentium are registered trademarks of Intel Corporation. IBM is a registered trademark of International Business Machines Corporation. AutoSum is a trademark, and Microsoft, Microsoft Press, MS-DOS, PivotTable, PowerPoint, Windows, Windows NT, and Visual Basic are registered trademarks of Microsoft Corporation.

Other product and company names mentioned herein may be the trademarks of their respective owners.

Companies, names, and/or data used in screens and sample output are fictitious unless otherwise noted.

For Catapult, Inc.
Managing Editor: Diana Stiles
Writer: Julia Kelly
Project Editor: Armelle O'Neal
Technical Editor: John Cronan
Production/Layout Editor: Jeanne Hunt
Indexer: Julie Kawabata

For Microsoft Press
Acquisitions Editor: Casey D. Doyle
Project Editors: Laura Sackerman, Ina Chang

Part No. 097-0001852

Catapult, Inc. & Microsoft Press

Microsoft Excel 97 Step by Step has been created by the professional trainers and writers at Catapult, Inc., to the exacting standards you've come to expect from Microsoft Press. Together, we are pleased to present this self-paced training guide, which you can use individually or as part of a class.

Catapult, Inc., is a software training company with years of experience in PC and Macintosh instruction. Catapult's exclusive Performance-Based Training system is available in Catapult training centers across North America and at customer sites. Based on the principles of adult learning, Performance-Based Training ensures that students leave the classroom with confidence and the ability to apply skills to real-world scenarios. *Microsoft Excel 97 Step by Step* incorporates Catapult's training expertise to ensure that you'll receive the maximum return on your training time. You'll focus on the skills that can increase your productivity the most while working at your own pace and convenience.

Microsoft Press is the book publishing division of Microsoft Corporation. The leading publisher of information about Microsoft products and services, Microsoft Press is dedicated to providing the highest quality computer books and multimedia training and reference tools that make using Microsoft software easier, more enjoyable, and more productive.

Table of Contents

Table of Contents

Table of Contents

Making an embedded chart into a chart sheet, see Lesson 9, page 150

Formatting markers with fill effects, see Lesson 9, page 146

Scaling printed charts, see Lesson 10, page 165

Adding a secondary axis, see Lesson 9, page 153

Naming sheets, see Lesson 2, page 30

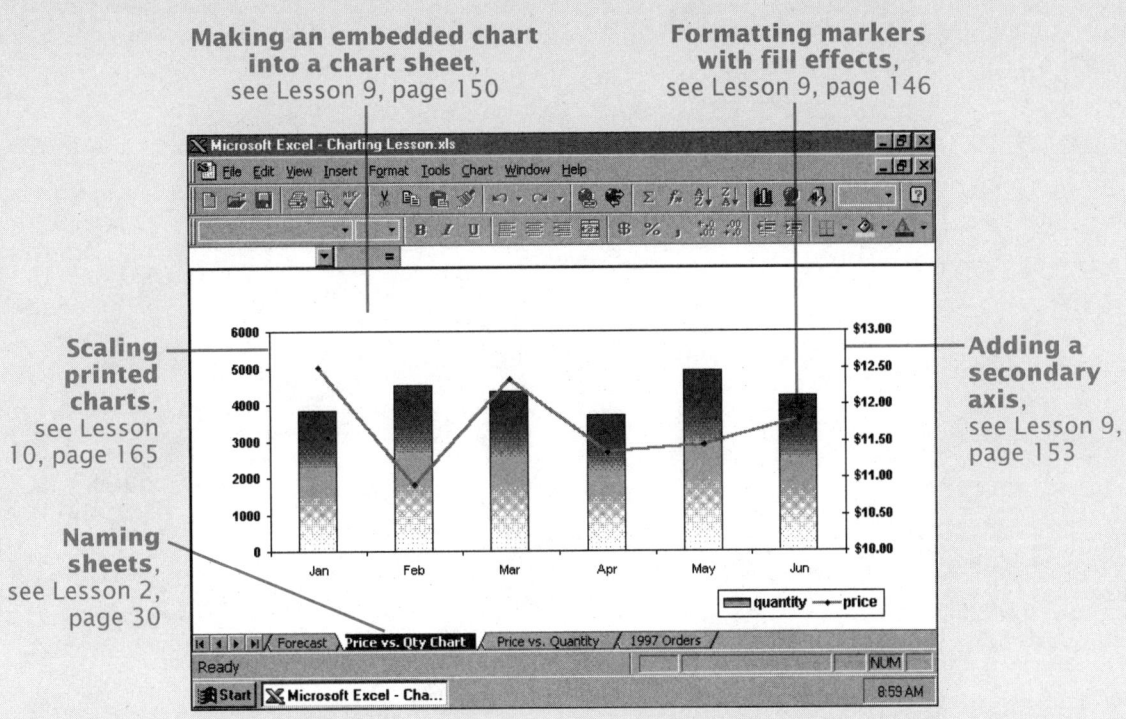

Selecting functions from the function list, see Lesson 3, page 53

Sharing a workbook, see Lesson 12, page 184

Writing formulas using the Formula palette, see Lesson 3, page 53

Highlighting revisions, see Lesson 12, page 187

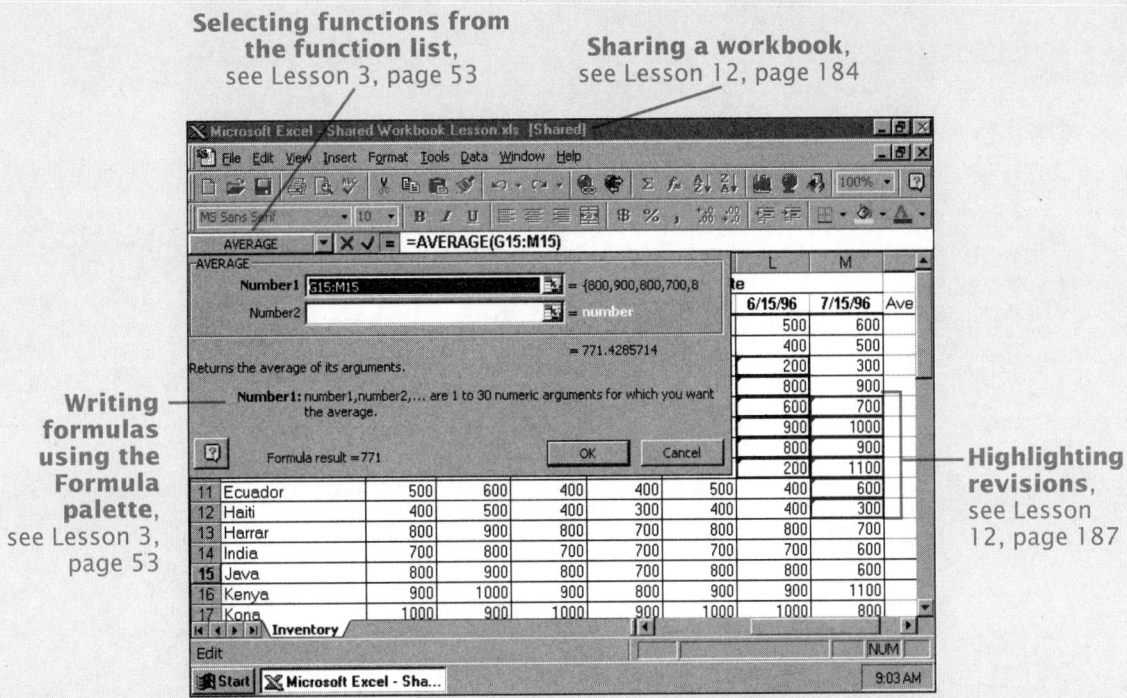

*Quick*Look Guide

Filtering records, see Lesson 6, page 100

Writing formulas with AutoSum, see Lesson 3, page 48

Undoing multiple actions, see Lesson 1, page 16

Performing quick calculations with AutoCalculate, see Lesson 6, page 103

Writing a SUBTOTAL formula, see Lesson 6, page 104

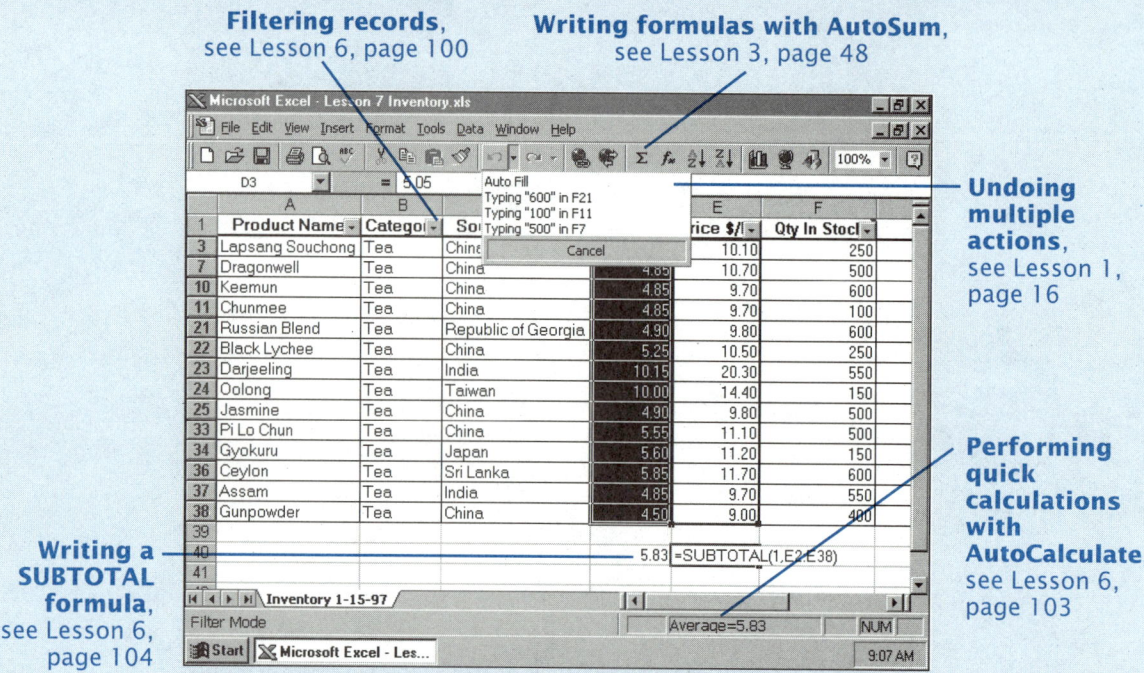

Applying conditional number formatting, see Lesson 5, page 89

Copying worksheets by dragging and dropping, see Lesson 5, page 87

Arranging multiple workbooks in multiple windows, see Lesson 5, page 85

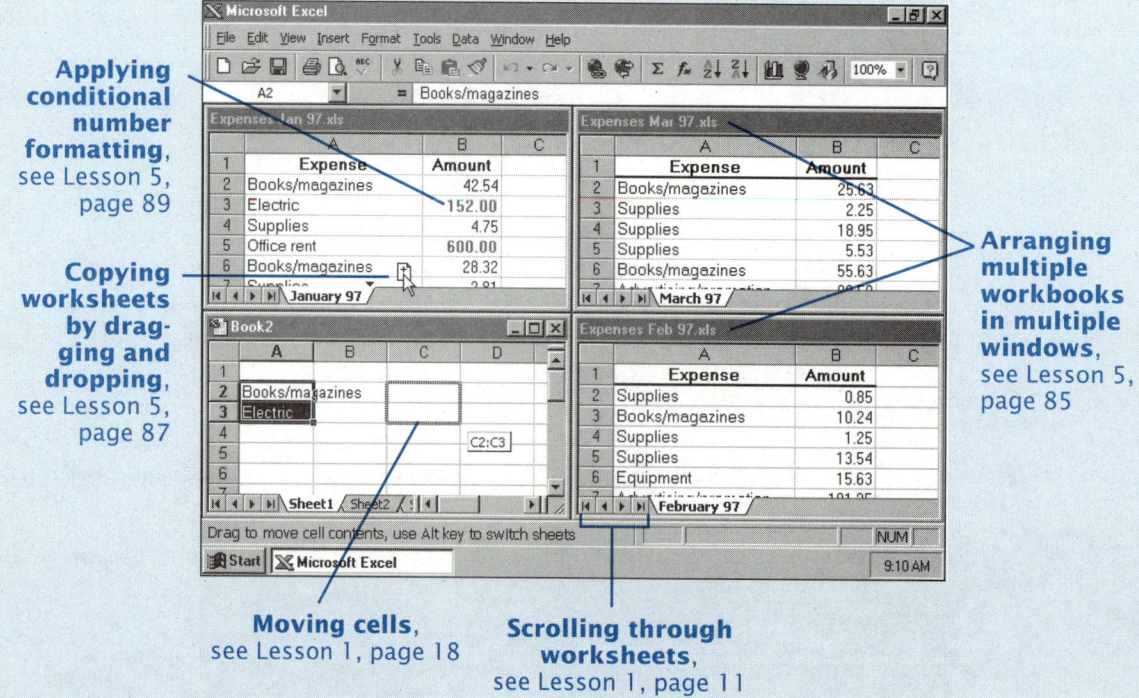

Moving cells, see Lesson 1, page 18

Scrolling through worksheets, see Lesson 1, page 11

Creating PivotTables,
see Lesson 8, page 129

Creating embedded charts,
see Lesson 9, page 145

Grouping dates into months,
see Lesson 8, page 130

Applying AutoFormats,
see Lesson 8, page 132

Getting help from the Office Assistant,
see Lesson 1, page 8

Viewing a worksheet in Page Break Preview,
see Lesson 10, page 159

Changing page printing order,
see Lesson 10, page 161

Changing page breaks by dragging,
see Lesson 10, page 159

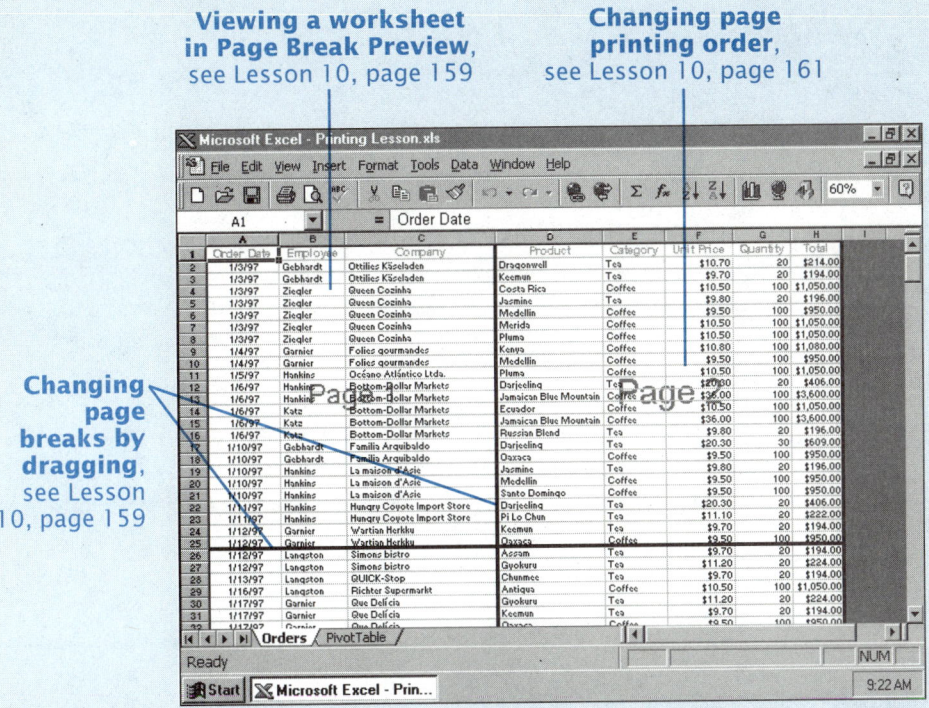

Applying custom number formatting, see Lesson 4, page 66

Writing formulas using worksheet labels, see Lesson 3, page 51

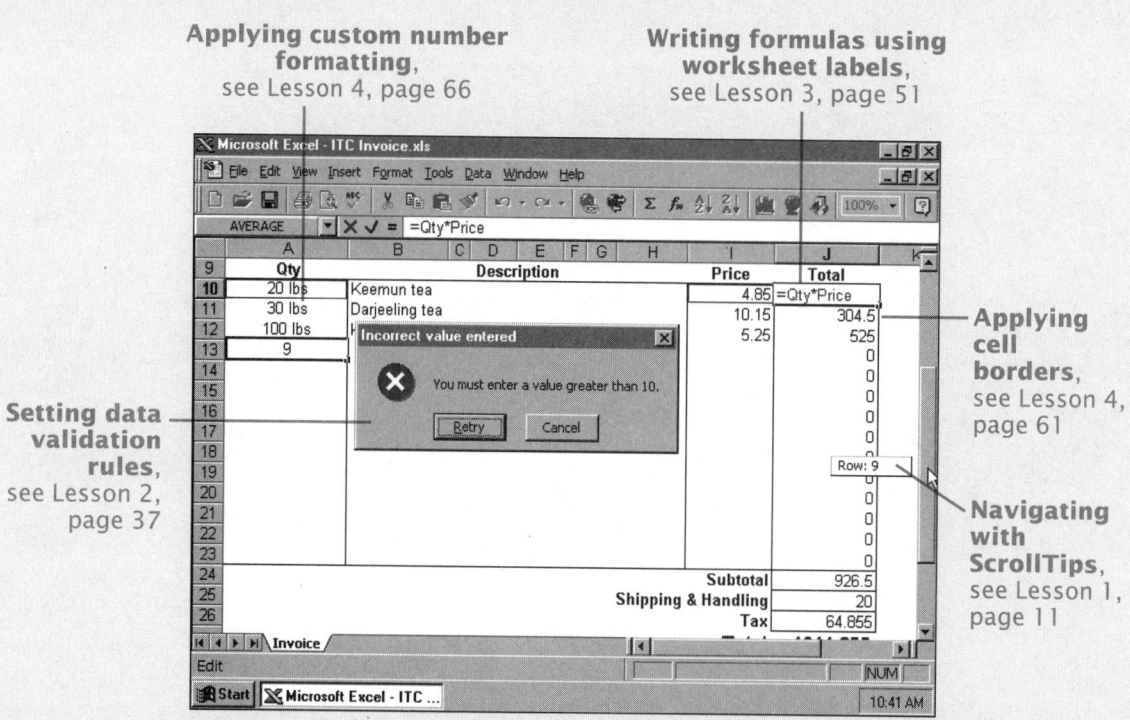

Setting data validation rules, see Lesson 2, page 37

Applying cell borders, see Lesson 4, page 61

Navigating with ScrollTips, see Lesson 1, page 11

Hiding and showing details, see Lesson 7, page 114

Creating automatic subtotals, see Lesson 7, page 112

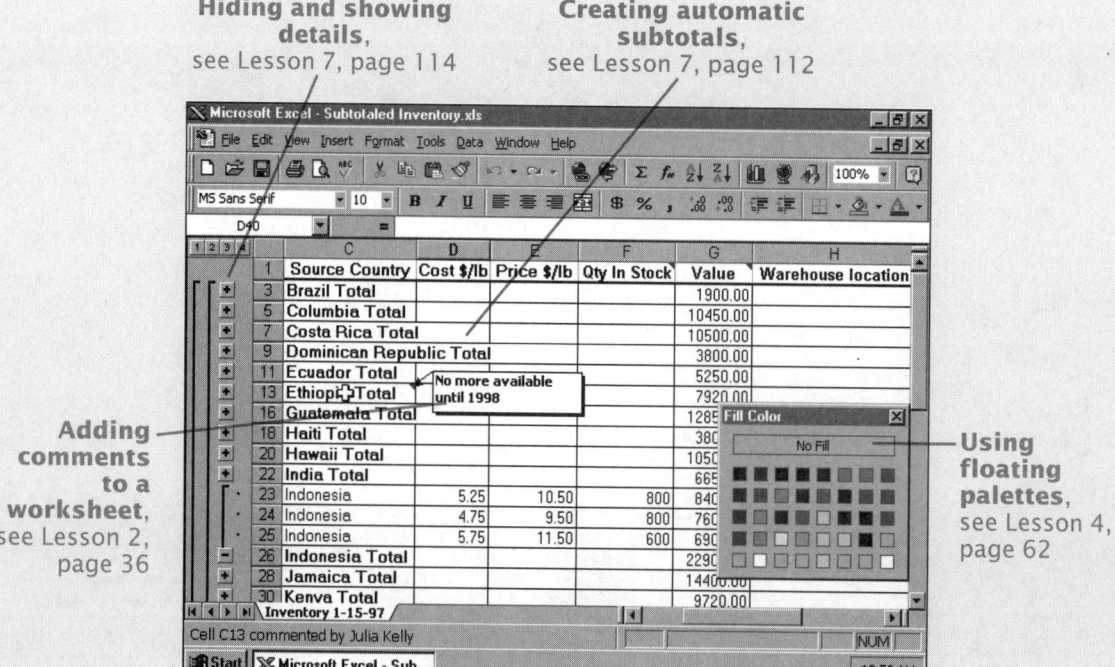

Adding comments to a worksheet, see Lesson 2, page 36

Using floating palettes, see Lesson 4, page 62

Finding Your Best Starting Point

Microsoft Excel is a powerful spreadsheet program that you can use to efficiently store and work with lists of data, calculate numbers, and create reports and charts. With *Microsoft Excel 97 Step by Step*, you'll quickly and easily learn how to use Microsoft Excel to get your work done.

 IMPORTANT   This book is designed for use with Microsoft Excel 97 for the Windows 95 and Windows NT version 4.0 operating systems. To find out what software you're running, you can check the product package or you can start the program, click the Help menu at the top of the screen, and then click About Microsoft Excel. If your product is not compatible with this book, a Step by Step book for your program is probably available. Please visit our World Wide Web site at http://mspress.microsoft.com/ or call 1-800-MSPRESS for more information.

Finding Your Best Starting Point in This Book

This book is designed for readers learning Microsoft Excel for the first time and for more experienced readers who want to learn and use the new features in Microsoft Excel 97. Use the following table to find your best starting point in this book.

If you are	Follow these steps

New...

to computers

to graphical (as opposed to text-only) computer programs

to Windows 95 or Windows NT

1 Install the practice files as described in "Installing and Using the Practice Files.

2 Become acquainted with the Windows 95 or Windows NT operating system and how to use the online Help system by working through Appendix A, "If You're New to Windows 95, Windows NT, or Microsoft Excel."

3 Learn basic skills for using Microsoft Excel by working sequentially through Lessons 1 through 4. Then, you can work through Lessons 5 through 13 in any order.

Switching...

from Lotus 1-2-3

from QuattroPro

from Microsoft Works

1 Install the practice files as described in "Installing and Using the Practice Files."

2 Learn basic skills for using Microsoft Excel 97 by working sequentially through Lessons 1 through 4. Then, you can work through Lessons 5 through 13 in any order.

Upgrading...

from Microsoft Excel for Windows 95

1 Learn about the new features in this version of the program that are covered in this book by reading through the following section, "New Features in Microsoft Excel 97."

2 Install the practice files as described in "Installing and Using the Practice Files."

3 Complete the lessons that cover the topics you need. You can use the table of contents and the *Quick*Look Guide to locate information about general topics. You can use the index to find information about a specific topic or a feature from a previous version of Microsoft Excel.

Referencing...

this book after working through the lessons

1 Use the index to locate information about specific topics, and use the table of contents and the *Quick*Look Guide to locate information about general topics.

2 Read the Lesson Summary at the end of each lesson for a brief review of the major tasks in the lesson. The Lesson Summary topics are listed in the same order as they are presented in the lesson.

Certified Microsoft Office User Program

The Certified Microsoft Office User (CMOU) program is designed for business professionals and students who use Microsoft Office 97 products in their daily work. The program enables participants to showcase their skill level to potential employers. It benefits accountants, administrators, executive assistants, program managers, sales representatives, students, and many others. To receive certified user credentials for a software program, candidates must pass a hands-on exam in which they use the program to complete real-world tasks.

The CMOU program offers two levels of certification: Proficient and Expert. The following table indicates the levels available for each Microsoft Office 97 program. (You can find out more about the certification levels by visiting the CMOU program World Wide Web site at http://www.microsoft.com/msoffice/train_cert/)

Software	Proficient level	Expert level
Microsoft Word 97	✔	✔
Microsoft Excel 97	✔	✔
Microsoft Access 97		✔
Microsoft PowerPoint 97		✔
Microsoft Outlook 97		✔
Microsoft FrontPage 97		✔

Microsoft Press offers the following books in the *Step by Step* series as approved courseware for the CMOU exams:

Proficient level:
Microsoft Word 97 Step by Step, by Catapult, Inc. ISBN: 1-57231-313-7
Microsoft Excel 97 Step by Step, by Catapult, Inc. ISBN: 1-57231-314-5

Expert level:
Microsoft Word 97 Step by Step, Complete Course, by Catapult, Inc., and Russell Borland. ISBN: 1-57231-579-2
Microsoft Excel 97 Step by Step, Complete Course, by Catapult, Inc., and Reed Jacobson. ISBN: 1-57231-580-6
Microsoft Access 97 Step by Step, by Catapult, Inc. ISBN: 1-57231-316-1
Microsoft PowerPoint 97 Step by Step, by Perspection, Inc. ISBN: 1-57231-315-3
Microsoft Outlook 97 Step by Step, by Catapult, Inc. ISBN: 1-57231-382-X
Microsoft FrontPage 97 Step by Step, by Catapult, Inc. ISBN: 1-57231-336-6

Candidates may take exams from any participating CMOU-Approved Certification Test Center, or participating schools, corporations, or employment agencies. To find the CMOU Test Center nearest you, call 1-800-933-4493.

To become a candidate for certification, or for more information about the certification process, please visit the CMOU program World Wide Web site at http://www.microsoft.com/msoffice/train_cert/ or call 1-800-933-4493 in the U.S.

New Features in Microsoft Excel 97 .

The following table lists the major new features in Microsoft Excel 97 that are covered in this book. The table shows the lesson in which you can learn how to use each feature. You can also use the index to find specific information about a feature or a task you want to perform.

To learn how to	See
Get help with specific procedures from the Office Assistant	Lesson 1 and Appendix A
Enter lists of data in a worksheet efficiently using AutoReturn	Lesson 1
Undo multiple actions and redo multiple undone actions	Lesson 1
See the range reference where dragged cells will be dropped using ScreenTips	Lesson 1
Write formulas using the Formula palette	Lesson 1
Select formulas from the formula list in the Name box	Lesson 1
See which cells a formula refers to by looking at the color-coded cell references in a formula	Lesson 1
Use the new interface to name a worksheet	Lesson 2
Add worksheet comments with an automatic user name	Lesson 2
Ensure entry of valid data using data validation	Lesson 2
Use worksheet labels in formulas	Lesson 3
Use conditional number formatting to apply cell formatting that changes depending on the value in the cell	Lesson 5
Open a file using Microsoft Outlook	Lesson 6
Apply new fill effects to chart elements	Lesson 9
Switch an embedded chart to a chart sheet and vice versa	Lesson 9
View a worksheet's page layout using Page Break Preview	Lesson 10
Set and change page breaks easily using Page Break Preview	Lesson 10
Track changes and review revisions made to a shared workbook	Lesson 12
Print a history of changes made to a shared workbook	Lesson 12
Work with other Microsoft Office 97 programs	Lesson 13

Corrections, Comments, and Help

Every effort has been made to ensure the accuracy of this book and the contents of the practice files CD-ROM. Microsoft Press provides corrections and additional content for its books through the World Wide Web at:

http://mspress.microsoft.com/mspress/support/

If you have comments, questions, or ideas regarding this book or the practice files CD-ROM, please send them to us.

Send e-mail to:
mspinput@microsoft.com

Or send postal mail to:
Microsoft Press
Attn: Step by Step Series Editor
One Microsoft Way
Redmond, WA 98052-6399

Please note that support for the Microsoft Excel 97 software product itself is not offered through the above addresses. For help using Microsoft Excel 97, you can call Microsoft Excel 97 Technical Support at (425) 635-7070 on weekdays between 6 A.M. and 6 P.M. Pacific time.

Visit Our World Wide Web Site

We invite you to visit the Microsoft Press World Wide Web site. You can visit us at the following location:

http://mspress.microsoft.com/

You'll find descriptions for all of our books, information about ordering titles, notices of special features and events, additional content for Microsoft Press books, and much more.

You can also find out the latest in software developments and news from Microsoft Corporation by visiting the following World Wide Web site:

http://www.microsoft.com/

We look forward to your visit on the Web!

Installing and Using the Practice Files

The CD-ROM included with this book contains practice files that you'll use as you perform the exercises in the book. For example, when you're learning how to filter a list of data, you'll open one of the practice files—an inventory list—and then practice different filtering methods. By using the practice files, you won't waste time creating the samples used in the lessons—instead, you can concentrate on learning how to use Microsoft Excel 97. With the files and the step-by-step instructions in the lessons, you'll also learn by doing, which is an easy and effective way to acquire and remember new skills.

IMPORTANT Before you break the seal on the practice CD package, be sure that this book matches your version of the software. This book is designed for use with Microsoft Excel 97 for the Windows 95 and Windows NT version 4.0 operating systems. To find out what software you're running, you can check the product package or you can start the program, and then on the Help menu at the top of the screen, click About Microsoft Excel. If your product is not compatible with this book, a Step by Step book matching your program is probably available. Please visit our World Wide Web site at http://mspress.microsoft.com/ or call 1-800-MSPRESS for more information.

Install the practice files on your computer

Follow these steps to install the practice files on your computer's hard disk so that you can use them with the exercises in this book.

 NOTE If you are new to Windows 95 or Windows NT, you might want to work through Appendix A, "If You're New to Windows 95, Windows NT, or Microsoft Excel," before installing the practice files.

If you don't know your username or password, contact your system administrator for assistance.

Close

1 If your computer isn't on, turn it on now.

2 If you're using Windows NT, press CTRL+ALT+DEL to display a dialog box asking for your username and password. If you are using Windows 95, you will see this dialog box if your computer is connected to a network or is configured for user profiles.

3 Type your username and password in the appropriate boxes, and then click OK. If you see the Welcome dialog box, click the Close button.

4 Remove the Microsoft Excel 97 Step by Step Complete Course CD-ROM from its envelope.

5 Insert the CD-ROM in your computer's CD drive.

6 On the taskbar at the bottom of your screen, click the Start button.

The Start menu appears.

7 On the Start menu, point to Settings, and click Control Panel.

8 In Control Panel, double-click the Add/Remove Programs icon.

9 On the Install/Uninstall tab, click Install, and then follow the directions on the screen.

The Setup program window opens with recommended options preselected for you. For best results in using the practice files with this book, accept these preselected settings.

10 When the files have been installed, remove the CD-ROM from your drive and replace it in its envelope.

A folder called Excel SBS Practice has been created on your hard disk, and the practice files have been put in that folder.

Microsoft
Press
Welcome

Excel
Camcorder
Files

NOTE In addition to installing the practice files, the Setup program has created two shortcuts on your Desktop. If your computer is set up to connect to the Internet, you can double-click the Microsoft Press Welcome shortcut to visit the Microsoft Press Web site. You can connect to the Web site directly at http://mspress.microsoft.com/

You can double-click the Excel Camcorder Files shortcut to display a document with links to audiovisual demonstrations of how to do a number of tasks in Excel. You can also copy these files from the *Microsoft Excel 97 Step by Step* Camcorder files Web page. You can connect to the Web site directly at http://mspress.microsoft.com/mspress/products/340/

Using the Practice Files

Each lesson in this book explains when and how to use any practice files for that lesson. When it's time to use a practice file, the book will list instructions for how to open the file. The lessons are built around scenarios that simulate a real work environment, so you can easily apply the skills you learn to your own work. For the scenarios in this book, imagine that you're the office manager for the Island Tea & Coffee Company, a small company that imports and sells gourmet coffees and teas from around the world.

The screen illustrations in this book might look different than what you see on your screen, depending on how your computer has been set up. To help make your screen match the illustrations in this book, please follow the instructions in Appendix B, "Matching the Exercises."

For those of you who like to know all the details, here's a list of the files for this book included on the CD-ROM:

Filename	Description
Lesson 1	
Customer List	A list of the Island Tea & Coffee Company's customers
Lesson 2	
No practice file	This lesson begins with a new workbook

Filename	Description
Lesson 3	
03 Lesson	A copy of the partially completed workbook from Lesson 2 (or you can open the workbook you saved at the end of Lesson 2, ITC Invoice)
Lesson 4	
04 Lesson	A copy of the partially completed workbook from Lesson 3 (or you can open the workbook you saved at the end of Lesson 3, ITC Invoice)
Review & Practice 1	
No practice file	This Review & Practice begins with a new workbook
Lesson 5	
Expenses Jan 97	An Island Tea & Coffee Company expenses list for January 1997
Expenses Feb 97	An Island Tea & Coffee Company expenses list for February 1997
Expenses Mar 97	An Island Tea & Coffee Company expenses list for March 1997
Lesson 6	
Lesson 6 Inventory	An inventory list for practicing filtering data
Lesson 7	
Lesson 7 Inventory	An inventory list for practicing subtotaling
Inventory Report.doc	A short Microsoft Word document you'll paste a subtotaled Microsoft Excel list into
Review & Practice 2	
R&P 2	Expenses lists for four employees, and a long list that combines all four expenses lists
Lesson 8	
1996order.txt	A text file containing a list of 1996 sales information
Lesson 9	
Current Orders	A workbook with two short lists and a PivotTable of sales figures for practicing charting

Filename	Description
Lesson 10	
1997 Orders	A long list of 1997 sales orders, a PivotTable, and a chart, for practicing printing
Review & Practice 3	
1996exp.txt	A text file containing a list of 1996 expenses
Lesson 11	
1997 Budget	The Island Tea & Coffee Company 1997 budget
Lesson 12	
Shared Inventory List	An inventory history, containing monthly inventory figures for six months
Lesson 13	
Sales Analysis.doc	Microsoft Word document, containing sales analysis
Sales Report.xls	Microsoft Excel document, containing sales data
Review & Practice 4	
R&P 4	A list of the expenses for the 2nd quarter of 1997, and a consolidation of the same list
SUAA Newsletter	A short Microsoft Word file that you'll paste into a Commentary.doc worksheet
Appendix C	
Price list	A price list of available goods

Need Help with the Practice Files?

Every effort has been made to ensure the accuracy of this book and the contents of the practice files CD-ROM. If you do run into a problem, Microsoft Press provides corrections for its books through the World Wide Web at:

http://mspress.microsoft.com/mspress/support/

We also invite you to visit our main Web page at:

http://mspress.microsoft.com/

You'll find descriptions for all of our books, information about ordering titles, notices of special features and events, additional content for Microsoft Press books, and much more.

Deleting the Practice Files

Use the following steps when you want to delete the shortcuts added to your Desktop and the practice files added to your hard drive by the Step by Step Setup program.

1   If any windows are covering the shortcuts on your Desktop, use the right mouse button to click an unoccupied area of the taskbar at the bottom of your screen, and then click Minimize All Windows.

2   On the Desktop, click the Microsoft Press Welcome shortcut icon, hold down CTRL, and click the Excel Camcorder Files shortcut icon. Then press DELETE.

   If you are prompted to confirm the deletion, click Yes. The Desktop shortcut icons are removed from your computer.

3   Click the Start button, point to Settings, and click Control Panel.

4   In Control Panel, double-click the Add/Remove Programs icon.

5   To remove the practice files for *Microsoft Excel 97 Step by Step*, on the Install/Uninstall tab, select Excel 97 Step By Step.

6   Click Add/Remove, and then click Yes.

7   To remove the practice files for *Microsoft Excel 97 Step by Step, Advanced Topics*, on the Install/Uninstall tab, select Excel 97 Step By Step, Advanced Topics.

8   Click Add/Remove, and then click Yes.

9   To remove the Camcorder files, on the Install/Uninstall tab, select Excel 97 Step By Step, Camcorder Files.

10 Click Add/Remove, and then click Yes.

   All practice files on your computer are now deleted.

Conventions and Features in This Book

You can save time when you use this book by understanding, before you start the lessons, how instructions, keys to press, and so on, are shown in the book. Please take a moment to read the following list, which also points out helpful features of the book that you might want to use.

 NOTE If you are unfamiliar with Windows 95, Windows NT, or mouse terminology, see Appendix A, "If You're New to Windows 95, Windows NT, or Microsoft Excel."

Conventions

- Hands-on exercises for you to follow are given in numbered lists of steps (1, 2, and so on). An arrowhead bullet (▶) indicates an exercise with only one step.
- Text that you are to type appears in **bold**.
- A plus sign (+) between two key names means that you must press those keys at the same time. For example, "Press ALT+TAB" means that you hold down the ALT key while you press TAB.

The following icons identify the different types of supplementary material:

	Notes labeled	Alert you to
	Note	Additional information for a step.
	Tip	Suggested additional methods for a step or helpful hints.
	Important	Essential information that you should check before continuing with the lesson.
	Troubleshooting	Possible error messages or computer difficulties and their solutions.
	Warning	Possible data loss and tell you how to proceed safely.
	Demonstration	Skills that are demonstrated in audio-visual files available on the Microsoft Excel 97 Step by Step Complete Course CD-ROM and on the World Wide Web.

Other Features of This Book

- You can learn how to use other Microsoft products, such as Outlook and FrontPage, with Excel by reading the shaded boxes throughout the book.

- You can learn about techniques that build on what you learned in a lesson by trying the optional "One Step Further" exercise at the end of the lesson.

- You can get a quick reminder of how to perform the tasks you learned by reading the Lesson Summary at the end of a lesson.

- You can quickly determine what online Help topics are available for additional information by referring to the Help topics listed at the end of each lesson. To learn more about online Help, see Appendix A.

- You can practice the major skills presented in the lessons by working through the Review & Practice sections at the end of each part.

- You can view audiovisual demonstrations of how to perform some of the more complicated tasks in Excel. Double-click the Excel Camcorder Files shortcut that was created on your Desktop when you installed the practice files for this book, or use your Web browser to connect to http://mspress.microsoft.com/mspress/products/340/. The page that opens contains full instructions for viewing the demonstration files.

Accomplishing Basic Tasks

Part
1

Lesson

1

Working in the Excel Environment

Estimated time
45 min.

In this lesson you will learn how to:

- Open and save a workbook file.
- Navigate through a workbook and a worksheet.
- Enter, edit, and delete data.
- Use AutoComplete and AutoCorrect to speed data entry.
- Move and copy cells and sheets.
- Write and edit simple formulas.

The basic working environment in Microsoft Excel is a workbook file that can contain one or more worksheets. A worksheet is similar to an accountant's ledger, with numbers, text, and calculations lined up in columns and rows. But, unlike in an accountant's ledger, when you type the numbers in Microsoft Excel, the program performs the calculations for you.

With Microsoft Excel, it's easy to enter information into a worksheet, and then change, delete, or add to the information. You don't need to worry about entering your data perfectly or completely the first time; you can always edit it later. You can arrange multiple worksheets within a workbook (for example, you might place all the worksheets for a single client or a single project into one workbook), and then name them so that you can locate the information you need quickly.

In this lesson, you'll learn how to work with worksheets and workbooks; open, save, and close a workbook; and enter and edit data in a worksheet. You'll also

3

learn how to work more efficiently by using features like AutoComplete and AutoCorrect to do some of your work for you, and by writing simple formulas.

Starting the Lesson

If you have not yet started Microsoft Excel or installed the Excel SBS Practice files, refer to "Installing and Using the Practice Files," earlier in this book.

In the following exercises, you'll open the practice file called Customer List, and then save the file with a different name, Lesson 01. This process creates a duplicate of the practice file, which you can work on and modify during the lesson. The original file, Customer List, will remain unchanged and will be used again later in this book.

Open a workbook

Open

1 On the Standard toolbar, click the Open button.

The Open dialog box appears. In this dialog box, you select the folder and the document you want to open. The box labeled Look In shows the folder that is currently selected.

Look In Favorites

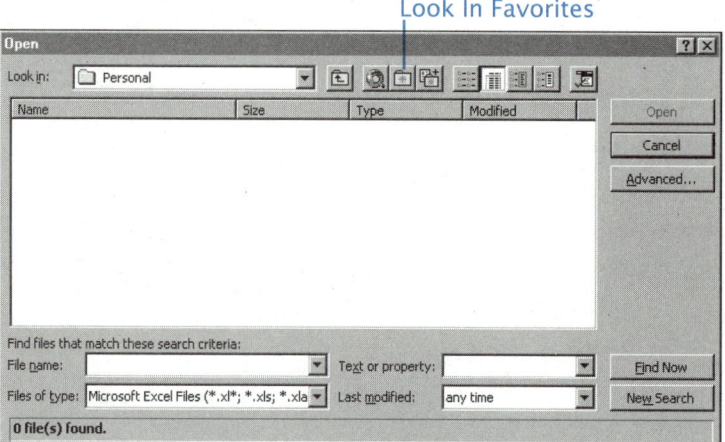

2 Click the Look In Favorites button.

The names of all folders and files that are contained within the selected folder are listed.

3 Be sure that the Excel SBS Practice folder appears in the Look In box. Scroll the window, if necessary.

4 Double-click the folder named Excel SBS Practice.

The list of practice files appears.

5 In the file list, double-click the Customer List file.

The Open dialog box closes, and the Customer List file appears in the document window.

Save the practice file with a new name

When you save a practice file, you give it a name and specify where you want to store it. For each file you use in this book, you'll usually save it in the Excel SBS Practice folder with a new name so that the original practice file will remain unchanged.

IMPORTANT   For the purposes of this book we have elected to show the file extensions. To match the illustrations in this book, click the Start button, point to Programs, and then click Windows Explorer. On the View menu, click Options. On the View tab, clear the Hide MS-DOS File Extension For File Types That Are Registered check box. Click OK.

1   On the File menu, click Save As.

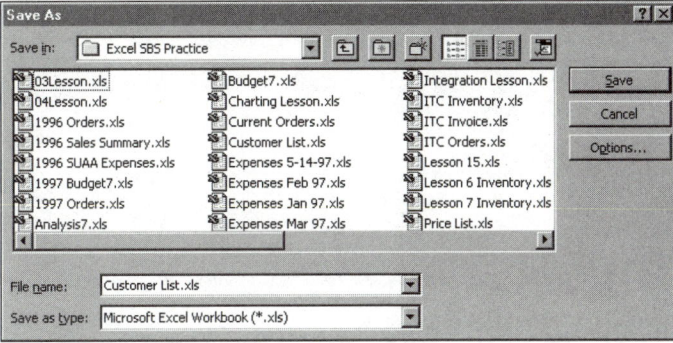

2   Be sure that Excel SBS Practice appears in the Save In box.

If the Excel SBS Practice folder does not appear, repeat steps 2 through 4 of the previous exercise to select the folder.

3   In the File Name box, type **Lesson 01**

4   Click the Save button or press ENTER to close the dialog box and save the file.

Getting Around in a Workbook

In Microsoft Excel, files are called *workbooks*. Workbooks can contain multiple worksheets, as well as chart sheets. You'll learn more about charts and chart sheets in Lesson 9, "Charting to Assess Trends and Relationships." In this lesson, you'll learn about moving around in a worksheet as well as in a workbook that contains worksheets.

Moving Around in a Workbook

The practice file you opened in the previous exercise contains customer information for the Island Tea & Coffee Company. The first worksheet, as shown in the following illustration, contains a list of customer names and addresses, and the remainder of the worksheets are blank. You can select different sheets in a workbook by clicking the Sheet tabs (also called "tabs") that are located at the bottom of each sheet. You can use the Sheet tab scroll buttons to bring hidden sheet tabs into view so that you can select them. The selected sheet is called the *active* sheet.

Sheet tab
scroll buttons   Sheet tabs

Additionally, you can select several sheets at a time, even if they are non-adjacent sheets, and enter the same data on all the active sheets at once. This is particularly useful if you need to set up several worksheets that are identical in some respect (for example, adding common labels to a monthly report).

Select worksheets in a workbook

In this exercise, you select different sheets in the workbook.

1   Click the Sheet tab labeled Sheet2.

   Sheet2 becomes the active sheet.

2   Click the tab labeled Customers.

Last Tab Scroll

3 Click the Last Tab Scroll button.

The sheet tabs scroll so that you can see the last tab in the workbook, which is Sheet10. The Customers sheet is still the active sheet.

4 Click the tab labeled Sheet10.

Sheet10 becomes the active sheet.

5 Use the right mouse button to click a Sheet tab scroll button.

A shortcut menu appears, listing the names of all the sheets contained in the workbook.

6 On the shortcut menu, click Customers.

The Customers sheet becomes the active sheet.

Select several worksheets at once

In this exercise, you select several sheets at the same time. All the selected sheets become active and, if you enter data in one of the sheets, the data is automatically entered in all of the other active sheets.

To select a group of non-adjacent sheets, hold down CTRL while you click the Sheet tabs.

1 Click the tab for Sheet2.

2 Hold down SHIFT and click the Sheet4 tab.

Sheet2, Sheet3, and Sheet4 are all selected and active. The word [Group] appears in the title bar next to the filename.

3 Use the right mouse button to click the Sheet2 tab.

4 On the shortcut menu, click Ungroup Sheets.

Only Sheet2 remains active.

Ask the Office Assistant for help

If you want to know more about moving around in worksheets, you can enlist help from the Office Assistant.

An Introduction to the Office Assistant

While you are working with Microsoft Office 97, an animated character called the *Office Assistant* pops up on your screen to help you work productively. As you work, you can ask the Office Assistant questions by typing your question, then clicking Search. The Office Assistant then shows you the answer to your question.

You will sometimes see a light bulb next to the Office Assistant—clicking the light bulb displays a tip about the action you are currently performing. You can view more tips by clicking Tips in the Office Assistant balloon. In addition, the Office Assistant is tailored to how you work—after you master a particular skill, the Office Assistant stops offering tips.

You can close any Office Assistant tip or message by pressing ESC.

— Clippit, an Office Assistant, in action

The Office Assistant appears in the following situations:

Office Assistant

- When you click the Office Assistant button on the Standard toolbar.
- When you choose Microsoft Excel Help on the Help menu or press F1.
- When you type certain phrases.

The Office Assistant is a shared application—any settings that you change will affect the Office Assistant in other Office 97 programs. You can customize the Office Assistant in two ways. You can:

Determine under what circumstances you want to see the Office Assistant

You can use the right mouse button to click the Office Assistant and click Options to open the Office Assistant dialog box. You can then define when you want the Office Assistant to appear, and what kind of help you want it to offer.

Change your Office Assistant character

You can use the right mouse button to click the Office Assistant and click Options to open the Office Assistant dialog box. Click the Gallery tab.

Lesson 1: Working in the Excel Environment

IMPORTANT If the Office Assistant appears, click the Start Using Microsoft Program option. If the User Name dialog box appears, fill in your name and initials, and then click OK. In the Office Assistant, click the Close button.

For the purposes of this book, the Office Assistant will not appear in the illustrations. If you want to match the illustrations, any time the Office Assistant appears, use the right mouse button to click the Office Assistant, and then click Hide Assistant. If you want to leave Office Assistant on top to help guide you, but it is in your way, simply drag it to another area on the screen.

1 Click the Office Assistant button.

2 In the What Would You Like To Do area, type **Learn about moving around in a worksheet**, and then click Search.

3 Click the Change Options For Entering And Editing Data topic.

4 Read the Help topic, and then click the Close button in the Help window.

Close

Moving Around in a Worksheet

Column headers are also referred to as column letters. Row headers are also referred to as row numbers.

A worksheet consists of *columns* and *rows*. Columns run vertically and are identified by letters, called *column headers*, which run across the top of a worksheet. Rows run horizontally and are identified by numbers, called *row headers*, which run down the left side of a worksheet. The intersection of a row and a column is called a *cell*. Cells are identified according to their positions in the rows and columns. The combination of the column letter and row number for a cell is called the *cell reference*. For example, the cell reference for the cell located in column A and row 1 is A1.

9

When you select a cell by clicking it, that cell becomes the *active cell* and you can enter data in it. The active cell is surrounded by a heavy border. The cell reference for the active cell appears in the Name box, on the left side of the formula bar, and the corresponding row and column headers become bold and raised. You can also change the active cell by pressing the ENTER key, the TAB key, or the arrow keys.

Scroll bars appear on the right and bottom side of the worksheet, and are used to view different parts of a worksheet quickly when it contains more information than can be displayed on one screen. When you change the view of a worksheet using the scroll bars, the active cell does not change; only your view of the worksheet changes. You can only see a small portion of your worksheet in the Microsoft Excel window (an entire worksheet is 256 columns by 65536 rows), but the scroll bars help you to move around quickly to view any part of the worksheet.

In the following exercises, you'll learn how to select cells and view worksheets.

Select cells on a worksheet

In this exercise, you practice moving around in a worksheet and selecting data.

1 Click the Customers sheet tab to select it.

2 Click the cell at the intersection of column B and row 2.

Cell B2 is selected.

B2		=	Alfreds Futterkiste	
	A	B	C	D
1	Customer ID	Company Name	Contact Name	Contac
2	ALFRE	Alfreds Futterkiste	Maria Anders	Sales Represen
3	ANATR	Ana Trujillo Emparedados y helados	Ana Trujillo	Owner
4	ANTON	Antonio Moreno Taquería	Antonio Moreno	Owner

Because it is the active cell, B2 is surrounded by a heavy border. The cell reference, B2, appears in the Name box, and the headers for column B and row 2 are bold and raised. The contents of the cell appear in the formula bar.

3 Press the down arrow key.

The active cell is now B3.

4 Press CTRL+HOME.

The active cell moves to the beginning of the worksheet, cell A1.

To drag, point to the first cell, then hold down the mouse button as you move the pointer, and release when the pointer is over the last cell.

5 Drag from cell A1 to cell C3.

A rectangular *range* of cells is selected.

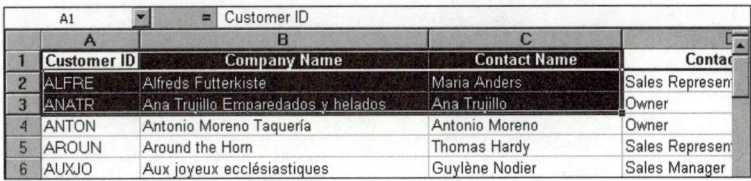

Cell A1 is the active cell within the selected range, and the headers for the range (columns A through C and rows 1 through 3) are highlighted.

6 Press ENTER repeatedly.

The active cell moves around within the selected range.

Pressing the TAB key will also move the active cell around within a selected range, from left to right instead of top to bottom.

7 Click cell A5.

Cell A5 becomes the active cell and the range A1 to cell C3 is no longer highlighted.

8 Move the mouse over the bottom border of the cell until the pointer becomes a white arrow, and then double-click the bottom border of the cell.

Double-click this border.

3	ANATR	Ana Trujillo Empa
4	ANTON	Antonio Moreno T
5	AROUN	Around the Horn
6	AUXJO	Aux joyeux ecclé
7	BERGL	Berglunds snabbl

The active cell moves to the bottom of the list of data (cell A119 is selected).

9 Double-click the top border of the active cell.

The active cell moves to the top of the list (cell A1 is selected).

View different areas of the worksheet

You can use the scroll bars to see different areas of your worksheet. In this exercise, you move around your worksheet to familiarize yourself with its different areas.

1 Move the mouse pointer over the vertical scroll box (the box that moves within the vertical scroll bar), and press and hold down the mouse button.

A ScrollTip appears that contains the number of the row at the top of your worksheet window (Row: 1).

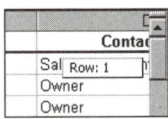

2 Drag the scroll box downward as far as it will go.

The ScrollTip displays the number of the row that will be visible at the top of your worksheet window when you release the mouse button.

3 Release the mouse button.

You can now see the data at the end of the list.

4 Drag the horizontal scroll box until the ScrollTip reads Column: D, then release the mouse button.

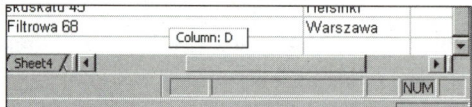

Column D is the leftmost visible column in the worksheet.

5 Press CTRL+HOME to return to cell A1, the first cell of the worksheet.

Display helpful tips

In addition to ScrollTips, there are ScreenTips to help you identify buttons on the toolbars, and comments to add extra information to your worksheet. You'll learn how to add comments to cells in your worksheet in Lesson 2, "Setting Up a Worksheet."

If the ScreenTips do not appear, use the right mouse button to click a toolbar, and then click Customize. Click the Options tab, and then select the Show ScreenTips On Toolbars check box.

1 Move the pointer over any tool on a toolbar.

A ScreenTip will appear below the pointer and will display the name of the button.

If comment indicators do not appear, on the Tools menu, click Options. On the View tab, click the Comment Indicator Only option button.

2 Move the pointer over cell A1.

A comment appears and displays information entered by the workbook's author. A cell containing a comment is identified by a small red triangle in its upper right corner.

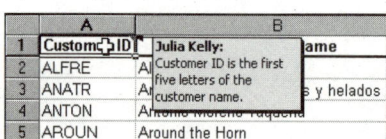

Entering and Editing Data

You can enter text, numbers, and formulas into any cell on a worksheet. When you enter data, Microsoft Excel recognizes it as either text, a date, a number that can be calculated, or a formula. You can also edit or delete anything that you have entered. Whatever you type appears in both the active cell and the formula bar, and can be edited in either location.

Entering Data

Entering data is simple. You first select the cell in which you want the information to appear, type the text or numbers you want, and then press ENTER or TAB to enter what you typed. You can also press an arrow key or click another cell to enter typed information.

You can cancel an entry before you enter it (for example, if you entered it in the wrong cell or misspelled it) by pressing ESC. If you make a mistake while typing, you can use the BACKSPACE key to undo the mistake.

When you first create a worksheet, you'll start by typing in your data. After a while, your worksheet will start to fill up with information, and you might not be able to see all your data on your screen. When you are revising a large worksheet, you can make your editing tasks easier by controlling what you can see on the worksheet.

For example, the customers list is too long to see in one window, so when you enter data at the bottom of the list, you can't see the column headings at the top of the list. You can *freeze* the first row (the row with the column headings) so that it remains visible regardless of where you are working in the list.

Another way to make your editing tasks easier and speed up data entry is by using AutoComplete to type recurring entries in a column. For example, in the customers list, contact titles are repeated for many customers. AutoComplete can save you time by entering these repeated entries for you.

Freeze panes to keep column headings visible

In this exercise, you freeze row 1 so that the column labels will remain visible while you enter new data at the bottom of the list.

If you select cell B2, both row 1 and column A will be frozen.

1 On the Customers sheet, click cell A2.

2 On the Window menu, click Freeze Panes.

The top row, row 1, is frozen. You can scroll down the worksheet, and row 1 will remain in view.

Enter text

A new customer of the Island Tea & Coffee Company needs to be added to the customers list. In this exercise, you enter the Company Name, Contact

Name, and Contact Title of the new customer. Microsoft Excel recognizes text entries as text, and aligns them automatically on the left side of the cell.

1   Click cell B1.

2   Double-click the bottom border of cell B1 to move quickly to the last entry in the column.

   The cell containing the last entry in the Company Name column is selected.

3   Click cell B120.

4   Type **Hanari Carnes**, then press TAB.

   The new company name is entered, and the next cell on the right is selected.

5   Type **Mario Pontes**, and then press TAB.

   The new contact name is entered, and the next cell on the right is selected.

6   Type **Ac**

   AutoComplete has guessed, based on the closest match to previous entries in the D column, that you want to enter Accounting Manager and has inserted it for you.

118	Matti Karttunen	Owner/Marketing Assistant	Keskuskat
119	Zbyszek Piestrzeniewicz	Owner	ul. Filtrowa
120	Mario Pontes	Accounting Manager	
121			
122			

7   Press ENTER to complete the entry.

   A feature called AutoReturn returns the active cell to the next cell in which you have started to type—in this case cell B121, the next company name.

TIP In a column of repeated entries, such as the Contact Title column, you can use the right mouse button to click the cell, and then click the Pick From List command on the shortcut menu. A list of all entries available in the column will appear. You can then click the entry you want to enter in the cell.

Enter numbers

In this exercise, you practice entering numbers on a blank worksheet. You enter numbers the same way you enter text: type the number, then press ENTER. Microsoft Excel recognizes numbers and aligns them automatically on the right side of the cell.

1 Click the tab for Sheet2.

Sheet2, a blank worksheet, is the active sheet.

2 In cell B2, type **12**, then press ENTER.

The value 12 is entered in cell B2, and B3 becomes the active cell.

3 In cell B3, type **100**, then press ENTER.

The value 100 is entered in cell B3, and B4 becomes the active cell. Your screen should look similar to the following illustration.

Making Changes

You can change or edit data in a worksheet by deleting the data, typing a new entry over an existing entry, or changing a few characters in an entry. In the following exercises, you will change data, then practice undoing and redoing deletions and entries.

Delete data

To delete an entry and leave the cell blank, click the cell, and then press DELETE.

1 Click cell B3, type **200**, and then press ENTER.

Your new entry replaces your previous entry.

2 Double-click cell B2.

The data contained in cell B2 is ready to be edited.

3 Click between the 1 and the 2 to place the insertion point there, and then press BACKSPACE to erase the 1.

4 Type **5**, then press ENTER.

Cell B2 now contains the number 52.

Undo a previous action

▶ Click the Undo button on the Standard toolbar.

The change you just made to cell B2 is undone, and the value is 12 again.

Undo several previous actions

Undo

1 Point to the Undo button on the Standard toolbar, and then click the down arrow that appears on the right side of the button.

A list of recent actions appears.

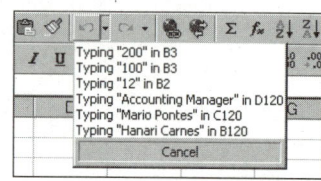

2 Drag down the list of actions until the first three actions are highlighted, and then release the mouse button.

Your last three actions are undone. All the numbers you entered in Sheet2 are deleted.

Redo previous actions

Redo

1 Point to the Redo button on the Standard toolbar, and then click the down arrow that appears on the right side of the button.

A list of recently undone actions appears.

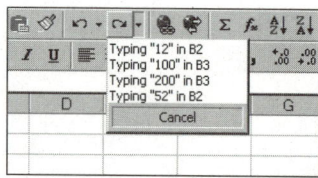

2 Click the fourth action in the list.

All of the actions you had undone in the previous exercise are redone. The number in cell B2 is 52, and the number in B3 is 200.

Making Corrections Using AutoCorrect

To turn off AutoCorrect, on the Tools menu, click AutoCorrect, and then clear the Replace Text As You Type check box.

AutoCorrect corrects typing mistakes for you as you type. You don't have to do anything extra, and you might not even be aware that you made a mistake and that it was corrected. AutoCorrect includes an extensive list of commonly misspelled words, but you can customize it by adding your own words to the list. You can also customize AutoCorrect to insert long words or phrases when you type a short abbreviation or acronym.

To undo an AutoCorrect change without turning off AutoCorrect, click the Undo button as soon as the AutoCorrect change is made.

In the following exercises, you will see how AutoCorrect works, and then customize AutoCorrect to insert the company name, Island Tea & Coffee, when you type the acronym "itc."

Correct commonly misspelled words

1 Click cell B14.

2 Type **teh** followed by a space, type **adn**, and then press ENTER.

When you press SPACEBAR or ENTER, the spelling of the word you just typed is corrected.

Customize AutoCorrect to type long words

1 On the Tools menu, click AutoCorrect.

The AutoCorrect dialog box appears.

2 In the Replace box, type **itc**

3 In the With box, type **Island Tea & Coffee**

If you have more words to add to the list, click Add, add the desired acronyms and terms, and then click OK to close the dialog box when you are finished.

4 Click OK.

5 Click cell B14.

6 Type **itc**, and then press ENTER.

Island Tea & Coffee is entered in the cell.

Rearranging a Worksheet by Moving and Copying Cells

Sometimes you might enter information in the wrong cells, or you might want to enter the same information in three different places in a workbook. Instead of deleting and re-entering the information, or entering the same information several times, you can move or copy it easily. In the following exercise, you will practice moving and then copying cells.

NOTE Although what you will be doing in the following exercises is commonly referred to as "moving" and "copying" cells, you are actually moving and copying the entries in cells, rather than the cells themselves.

Move cells to a new location on the same worksheet

In this exercise, you move cells by dragging them to another location on your worksheet.

1 On Sheet2, select the B2:B3 range.

2 Point to a border of the selection, and then hold down the mouse button while you drag the selected range to cells D2:D3.

While you drag the selected cells, a tip appears next to the pointer to tell you what range of cells your selection is in.

	A	B	C	D	E	F
1						
2		52				
3		200				
4						
5				D2:D3		

3 When the D2:D3 range is selected, release the mouse button.

The cells are moved to the D2:D3 range.

Move cells to a different worksheet

Dragging cells to move them works well when you are moving the cells short distances on the same worksheet, but if you want to move cells to a different area of the worksheet or to another worksheet, using the toolbar buttons is easier.

Cut

Paste

1   On Sheet2, verify that the D2:D3 range is still selected.

2   On the Standard toolbar, click the Cut button.

    A moving border appears around the cut selection.

3   Select Sheet3.

4   On Sheet3, select cell B2, and then click the Paste button.

    The cut cells are pasted onto Sheet3. The upper-left corner of the cut selection is pasted into the cell you selected on the new sheet.

Copy cells to another location on the same worksheet

There are many ways to copy cells. In this exercise, you practice two of the easiest methods.

1   On Sheet3, verify that the B2:B3 range is selected.

2   Point to a selection border, and then hold down CTRL while you drag the selection to the F2:F3 range.

    While you are dragging the selection, a small plus sign (+) appears next to the pointer to tell you that you are dragging a copy of the selection.

	A	B	C	D	E	F	G	H
1								
2		52						
3		200						
4							F2:F3	
5								

3   Release the mouse button, and then release CTRL.

    The cells are copied to a new location.

4   Select the B2:B3 range.

5   Point to a selection border, and then use the right mouse button to drag the selection to the C7:C8 range.

    A shortcut menu appears after you release the right mouse button.

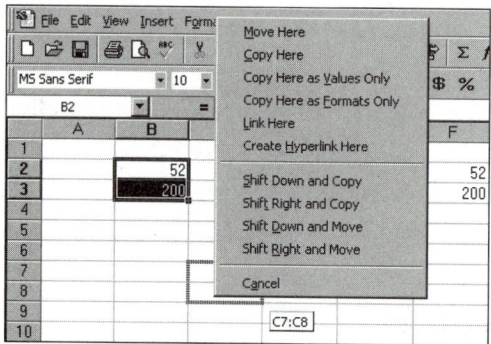

6 On the shortcut menu, click Copy Here.

The cells are copied to the new location.

Move cells to a different worksheet

As with moving cells, dragging cells to copy them works well when you copy the cells across short distances on the same worksheet, but if you want to copy cells to another area of the worksheet or to another worksheet, using the toolbar buttons is easier.

1 On Sheet3, select the range F2:F3.

2 On the Standard toolbar, click the Copy button.

A moving border appears around the copied selection.

Copy

3 Select Sheet2.

4 On Sheet2, select cell C4, and then click the Paste button.

Paste

The copied cells are pasted onto Sheet2. The upper-left corner of the copied selection is pasted into the cell you selected on the new sheet.

Rearranging a Workbook by Moving and Copying Sheets

Now you know how to move and copy cells in a workbook, but suppose you want to rearrange your workbook by moving or copying an entire sheet. This is even simpler than moving and copying cells. In the following exercises, you rearrange your workbook by moving a worksheet, and then copying it.

Move a sheet to a new location in the same workbook

In this exercise, you move Sheet2 behind Sheet3.

1 Click the Sheet2 tab.

2 Drag the Sheet2 tab to the right, until the small triangle appears on the right of the Sheet3 tab. Your screen should look similar to the following illustration.

3 Release the mouse button.

Sheet2 is now behind Sheet3 in the workbook.

Copy a sheet in the same workbook

Suppose you have spent time creating a worksheet, and would like to re-use it as a starting point for another worksheet. Instead of recreating the worksheet, you can just make a copy of it. In this exercise, you create a copy of Sheet2.

1 Click the Sheet2 tab.

2 Hold down CTRL while you drag the Sheet2 tab to the right.

3 When the small triangle appears on the right of the Sheet2 tab, release the mouse button, and then release CTRL.

Sheet2 is now copied, and the copy is named Sheet2 (2).

 NOTE You will learn about moving or copying sheets between workbooks in Lesson 5, "Consolidating Multiple Lists."

Writing Simple Formulas

Microsoft Excel was specifically created to calculate numbers. You can place raw data (numbers) in a worksheet, and then tell Microsoft Excel how to calculate the numbers to give you the results you want. You tell Microsoft Excel how you want the numbers calculated by writing a formula. In its simplest form, a formula might be used to add two numbers together. One of the main advantages of using a powerful spreadsheet program like Microsoft Excel is that you can insert a formula in a cell and have it perform a calculation on values that are in other cells. For example, you can enter a formula in a cell to total the values in another range of cells, such as the cells above the formula. Regardless

You'll learn more about the Formula Palette in Lesson 3. of what numbers you place in the specified range, the correct total will appear in the cell containing the formula.

You can perform calculations with your data using arithmetic operators (such as +, -, and *) and with *functions*, which are built-in formulas. Microsoft Excel comes with hundreds of functions that you can use in formulas to save you time. For example, there are functions that calculate the periodic payment on a loan or annuity (the PMT function), the standard deviation based on a sample (the STDEV function), and the square root of a number (the SQRT function). The Formula Palette makes it easy to write formulas that use these and other functions.

In Microsoft Excel, all formulas begin with an equal sign (=). After the equal sign, you type the formula, and then press ENTER. After the formula has been entered, the cell will display the results of the calculation. You can easily edit the formula to change any part of it.

In the following exercises, you will practice writing and editing simple formulas.

Write a simple formula

In this exercise, you write a formula to add two numbers.

1 On Sheet2, select cell E4.

2 Type =**52+200**, and then press ENTER.

The formula is entered in the cell, and the result of the addition appears.

3 Select cell E4.

The formula appears in the formula bar, and the result appears in the cell.

E4		▼	=	=52+200	
	A	B	C	D	E	F
1						
2						
3						
4			52		252	
5			200			

4 Select cell E5.

5 Type =, and then click cell C4.

The cell reference is entered in the formula.

SUM		▼ X ✓	=	=C4	
	A	B	C	D	E	F
1						
2						
3						
4			52		252	
5			200		=C4	
6						

6 Type +, click cell C5, and then press ENTER.

The formula, which adds the contents of cells C4 and C5, is entered in the cell. The result of the addition appears in the cell.

7 Click cell C4, type **100**, and then press ENTER.

The formula in cell E5 displays the result of the addition.

 NOTE You can also write formulas that use a combination of cell references and numbers. For example, you can write a formula that calculates a sales tax of 7% on a price by multiplying .07 times a cell reference.

Edit an existing formula

You can edit a formula by selecting the cell that contains it, and then making changes in the formula bar. You can also double-click the cell and make changes to the formula directly in the cell. In this exercise, you change the operator, and then modify a reference in the formula.

1 Double-click cell E5.

Cell E5 is opened for editing. The cell references in the formula and the cells that are referred to are color-coded to help you see which cells the formula refers to.

2 Select the plus sign (+) by dragging the insertion point over it, type an asterisk (*), and then press ENTER.

The formula multiplies the two cells and displays the result of the multiplication.

3 Double-click cell E5, and then double-click the reference to cell C5 in the formula.

The reference to cell C5 is selected.

SUM	▾	✕ ✓ =	=C4*C5		
	A	B	C	D	E	F
1						
2						
3						
4			100		252	
5			200		=C4*C5	
6						

4 Click cell E4, and then press ENTER.

The formula now multiplies the value in cell C4 by the value in cell E4. The result is 25200.

 NOTE If you'd like to build up on the skills you learned in this lesson, you can do the One Step Further. Otherwise, skip to "Finish the Lesson."

One Step Further: Creating a Form to Enter Data Easily

In this lesson, you entered data in the Customers sheet by typing text directly in the cells, but it can be time-consuming to move from cell to cell in a worksheet, and you might enter data in the wrong cells. Sometimes it's easier to enter data in a form because you don't have to scroll around in the worksheet or move from cell to cell. By using a form, you can make certain that you're entering the right data in the right place. You can create a data form quickly for any worksheet.

1   Select the Customers sheet, and be sure that a cell within the customer list table is selected.

2   On the Data menu, click Form.

A data entry form is created for the Customers sheet. The column headings in the worksheet become field names on the left side of the form. The form opens with the first record in the worksheet showing.

3   On the data form, click New.

The form displays a new blank record, and you can enter data for a new customer. You can move from box to box in the data form by pressing TAB.

4   When you are finished using the data form, click Close.

Finish the lesson

1   On the File menu, click Save.

2   To continue to the next lesson, on the File menu, click Close.

3   If you are finished using Microsoft Excel for now, on the File menu, click Exit.

Lesson Summary

To	Do this	Button
Open a file	On the Standard toolbar, click the Open button. Locate the folder that contains the file you want to open, and then double-click the filename.	
Save a file with another name	On the File menu, click Save As. Open the folder in which you want to save the file, type the new name in the File Name box, and then click Save.	
Select a worksheet	Click the sheet tab.	
Select multiple worksheets	Click the sheet tab for the first worksheet you want to select, hold down SHIFT, and then click the sheet tab for the last worksheet you want to include (hold down CTRL to select non-adjacent sheets).	
Select a cell	Click the cell.	
Select a range of cells	Hold down the mouse button and drag from one corner to the opposite diagonal corner of the range you want.	
Enter data	Select a cell. Type the data, and then press ENTER or select another cell.	
Freeze panes	Select a cell immediately below or to the right of the row or column, and then, on the Window menu, click Freeze Panes.	
Change data	Select the cell containing the data you want to change. Type the new data, and then press ENTER or select another cell.	
Delete data	Select the cell (or range of cells) containing the data you want to delete, and then press DELETE.	

To	Do this	Button
Undo an action	On the Standard toolbar, click the Undo button. To undo several actions, click the Undo down arrow, and then select the actions you want to undo.	
Redo an undone action	On the Standard toolbar, click the Redo button. To redo several undone actions, click the Redo down arrow, and then select the actions you want to redo.	
Customize AutoCorrect	On the Tools menu, click AutoCorrect. Type the misspelled word or the acronym in the Replace box, type the correct spelling or long phrase in the With box, and then click OK.	
Move cells	Drag a cell or range of cells by its border.	
Copy cells	Hold down CTRL while you drag a cell or range of cells by its border.	
Move a worksheet	Drag the sheet tab.	
Copy a worksheet	Hold down CTRL while you drag the sheet tab.	
Write a formula	Type =, type the rest of the formula, and then press ENTER.	
Edit a formula	Double-click the cell containing the formula. Select the part of the formula you want to change, type your changes, and then press ENTER.	

For online information about	On the Help menu, click Contents And Index, click the Index tab, and then type
Opening and saving files	opening, files; documents, saving
Using workbooks	workbooks
Using worksheets	worksheets
Selecting cells	selecting, cells
Changing data	changing data
Entering formulas	entering formulas
Using data forms	data forms

Setting Up a Worksheet

In this lesson you will learn how to:

■ Add a keyword to a file to quickly find it later.

■ Name a worksheet.

■ Delete worksheets.

■ Set column widths.

■ Add comments to a worksheet to document it.

■ Control data entry with Data Validation.

■ Print a worksheet.

Estimated time
30 min.

In the next few lessons, you'll learn how to perform many basic Microsoft Excel tasks while creating a template. Templates are great time-savers. When you open a copy of a template, such as the invoice template you are about to create, all the labels, formulas, and formatting are in place and ready for you to build upon. You simply enter your new data and change any formatting that you want, and you're finished.

To find the templates supplied with Microsoft Excel, on the File menu, click New.

To create a template, you can use any workbook that contains formatting and data that you use repeatedly, such as a time sheet, a weekly task list, an inventory form, an order form, or a tax-estimation worksheet, and then simply save your workbook as a template, as you'll do later in this book.

In this lesson, you'll create a new workbook and build the structure of the Island Tea & Coffee Company invoice. You'll add and position text entries, add

27

instructions for users, set data validation rules so that only the appropriate data can be entered in specific cells, and then you'll preview and print a copy of the new (unfinished) invoice. This invoice, which you'll continue to build in Lessons 3 and 4, will be the basis for the template that you'll create in Lesson 4.

NOTE Although you are starting to build your template in this lesson, you won't save your workbook as a template until the end of Lesson 4, when the template has been completed with formulas and formatting. Until then, the file you work on will be a workbook file like any other.

Setting Up a New Workbook

The first task in setting up a workbook is to open a new workbook and save it with a name that makes sense to you and that will remind you of its contents. Next, you can add a keyword to the file properties (file properties include such things as the title, author, subject, date saved, and so on) so that, in the future, you can find the file quickly by searching for the keyword.

The invoice template that you will be creating will only require one worksheet. In the following exercises, you will open and save a new workbook, name the worksheet that will become the invoice, and then delete all the remaining worksheets in the workbook.

Open a new workbook

Microsoft Excel opens with a new, unsaved workbook ready for you to start using. If you have already been working in Microsoft Excel, however, you might need to open a new workbook to use in this lesson.

If you need to open a new workbook, follow this exercise. If you have just started Microsoft Excel and a new, blank workbook is already open, skip to the next exercise, "Save a new workbook."

New

▶ On the Standard toolbar, click the New button.

A new workbook appears. It will display an unsaved workbook name, such as Book1 or Book2, in the title bar.

Save a new workbook

You are ready to start working on your invoice template. The first step is to save your workbook under a name that describes its contents. In this exercise, you name the new workbook "ITC Invoice" and save it in the Excel SBS Practice folder.

Save

1 On the Standard toolbar, click the Save button.

The Save As dialog box appears.

2 In the Save As dialog box, click the Look In Favorites button.

The Favorites folder appears in the Save In box. The Excel SBS Practice folder appears in the list of folders and files.

3 Double-click the Excel SBS Practice folder.

Excel SBS Practice appears in the Save In box, and the names of the practice files appear in the file list.

4 In the File Name box, drag over the default book name to select it, and then type **ITC Invoice**

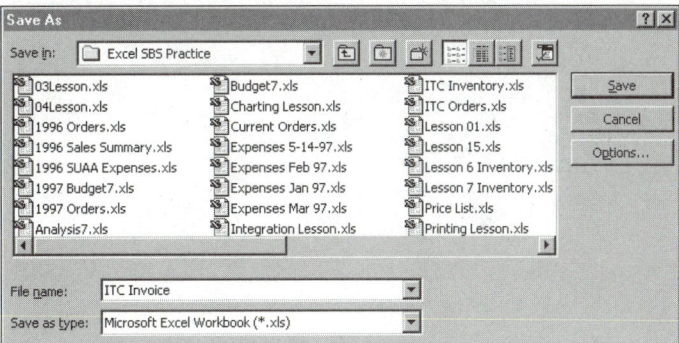

5 Click Save.

The file is saved with the name ITC Invoice in the Excel SBS Practice folder. The new file name, ITC Invoice, appears in the title bar.

Add a keyword to easily find the file later

The Island Tea & Coffee Company creates many files in the course of conducting business, and it can be tedious to find the specific file or files you need among hundreds of filenames in a list. Microsoft Excel speeds up the process by letting you search for specific files based on *file properties.*

You can add as many file properties as you want.

There are many file properties you can base your search on, including title, author, date last saved, or subject. Some properties, such as date last saved and author, are automatically recorded as file properties, but others, like subject and keyword, must be specifically entered before you can use them in a file search. For example, if you create monthly budget workbooks, you can add the keyword "budget" to each of those files. Later, you can search for the keyword "budget," and Microsoft Excel will find all the files that have that keyword as a file property.

In this exercise, you add the keyword "invoice" to your invoice worksheet. When you create a template from this worksheet, all copies of the template will contain this keyword.

1 On the File menu, click Properties.

The Properties dialog box appears.

2 On the Summary tab, click in the Keywords box, type **invoice**, then click OK.

3 On the Standard toolbar, click the Save button.

The new keyword is saved with the file.

Save

Name a worksheet

If a workbook contains several sheets, the sheet names (on the sheet tabs) are important for identification purposes. Even if, as in this case, there will only be one sheet in the workbook, the sheet name is important because it might be used in formulas and it provides the default header for the printed page.

You can easily give your worksheets names that make more sense than "Sheet1." In this exercise, you name the invoice worksheet "Invoice."

1 Double-click the Sheet1 tab.

The sheet name is highlighted.

2 Type **Invoice**, and then press ENTER.

The sheet is renamed "Invoice."

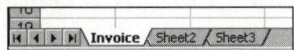

Delete unnecessary sheets to streamline your workbook

By default, new workbooks contain three worksheets. If you don't need the extra sheets, you can streamline your workbook by deleting them—you can always add worksheets later if you need them. In this exercise, you delete the two extra worksheets you won't be needing.

1 Click the Sheet2 tab, hold down SHIFT, and then click the Sheet3 tab.

Sheet2 and Sheet3 are selected.

2 Use the right mouse button to click one of the selected tabs.

A shortcut menu appears.

3 Click Delete.

A message box appears, prompting you to confirm the deletion of the worksheets.

4 Click OK.

The extra sheets are deleted.

 TIP If you need to insert a worksheet, use the right mouse button to click a sheet tab, click Insert on the shortcut menu, and then double-click the Worksheet icon.

Building a Template

Your invoice template will be a standard form that the Island Tea & Coffee Company sales staff can fill out online, print, and then mail or fax to customers along with their orders.

You will create the invoice template in stages. First, you'll build the structure of the invoice by entering labels on the worksheet and arranging them to create a useful layout on the invoice printed page. Then, you'll add formulas to the template so that calculations are automatic, and finally, you'll apply formatting to the template for a professional appearance.

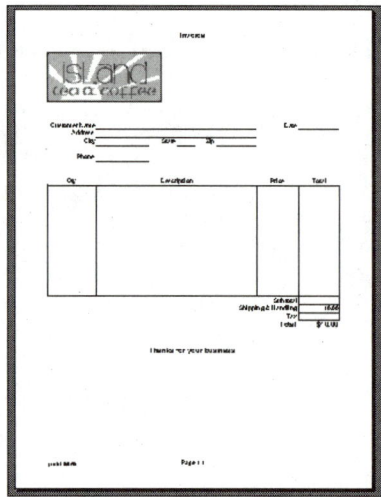

Entering Data to Build the Invoice

In the following exercises, you'll enter text labels that will identify the cells where the sales staff will enter data.

Enter labels for the customer information cells

In this exercise, you enter labels for the customer information cells.

1 In cell A1, type **Customer Name**, and then press ENTER.
2 In cell I1, type **Date**, and then press ENTER.
3 In cell A2, type **Address**, and then press ENTER.
4 In cell A3, type **City**, and then press ENTER.
5 In cell D3, type **State**, and then press ENTER.
6 In cell G3, type **Zip**, and then press ENTER.
7 In cell A5, type **Phone**, and then press ENTER.

Enter labels for the order information area

In this exercise, you enter labels for the order information area.

1 In cell A8, type **Qty**, and then press ENTER.

2 In cell B8, type **Description**, and then press ENTER.

3 In cell I8, type **Price**, and then press ENTER.

4 In cell J8, type **Total**, and then press ENTER.

Your worksheet should look similar to the following illustration.

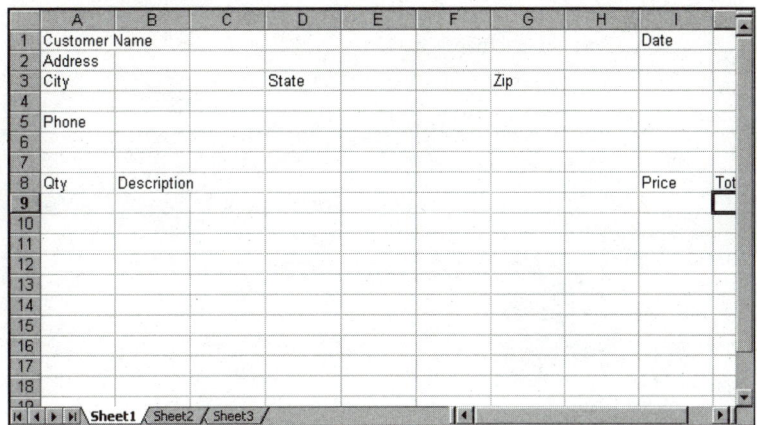

Enter labels for the subtotal and total area

In this exercise, you enter labels for the subtotal/total area.

1 In cell I23, type **Subtotal**, and then press ENTER.

2 In cell I24, type **Shipping & Handling**, and then press ENTER.

3 In cell I25, type **Tax**, and then press ENTER.

4 In cell I26, type **Total**, and then press ENTER.

Enter a farewell note at the bottom of the invoice

In this exercise, you enter a cheerful closing sentence.

➤ In cell A29, type **Thanks for your business!**, and then press ENTER.

Your worksheet should look similar to the following illustration.

Arranging the Labels

In the following exercises, you will align the labels and set column widths so that the invoice layout makes the best use of the printed page space.

Align text entries for effective use of available space

By default, Microsoft Excel aligns text entries on the left side of the cell. However, you can modify the alignment. In this exercise, you change label alignment to create a better page layout.

Align Right

1 Select cells A1 through A5, and then click the Align Right button on the Formatting toolbar.

The entries in cells A1 through A5 are aligned to the right.

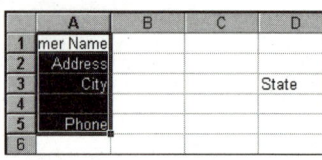

2 Select cells I23 through I26, and then click the Align Right button on the Formatting toolbar.

The entries in cells I23 through I26 are aligned to the right.

3 Select cell D3, hold down CTRL and select cells G3 and I1, and then click the Align Right button on the Formatting toolbar.

The entries in cells D3, G3, and I1 are aligned to the right.

Center

Merge And Center

4 Select cell A8, hold down CTRL and select cells I8 and J8, and then click the Center button on the Formatting toolbar.

The entries in cells A8, I8, and J8 are centered.

5 Select cells B8 through H8, and then click the Merge And Center button on the Formatting toolbar.

The entry in cell B8 is centered across all the selected cells.

TIP To indent text from the left without aligning it on the right of the cell, use the right mouse button to select the cell, and then click Format Cells. On the Alignment tab, under Horizontal, select Left (Indent). Under Indent, select a number of character widths to indent by, and then click OK.

Set column widths to space entries

In this exercise, you set column widths to make the best use of space on the invoice page.

1 Drag the right border of the column A header until the entry in cell A1 fits within the cell.

As you drag, a tip appears indicating the column width.

	B8	Width: 14.57	=	Desc
	A		B	
1	mer Name			
2	Address			

2 Drag the right column border to manually change the column width based on the following table.

You can set multiple columns to the same width by selecting multiple columns before setting the column width. (Use CTRL to select non-adjacent columns.)

Column	Width
B	16
C	2
D	5
E	5
F	2
G	3
H	12

3 Use the right mouse button to click column I.

Column I is selected, and a shortcut menu appears.

4 Click Column Width.

The Column Width dialog box appears.

5 Type 12, and then click OK.

Column I width is set to a width of 12.

6 Repeat steps 3 through 5 to change the width for column J.

Your worksheet should look similar to the following illustration.

Column width is the number of characters (in the default font) that fit in a cell in the column.

35

	A	B	C	D	E	F	G	H	I	J
1	Customer Name								Date	
2	Address									
3	City			State			Zip			
4										
5	Phone									
6										
7										
8	Qty			Description					Price	Tota
9										
10										
11										

7 On the Standard toolbar, click Save.

Save

 NOTE If you want to delete a column or a row, use the right mouse button to click the column header, and then, on the shortcut menu, click Delete. If you want to insert a column or a row, use the right mouse button to click the column to the right of which you want to insert the new column or the row under which you want to insert the new row, and then, on the shortcut menu, click Insert.

Documenting the Template for Other Users

Your invoice will be used by several sales people at Island Tea & Coffee Company. You can ensure that it is used correctly by adding helpful instructions and data validation to the worksheet. Data validation can prevent the entry of inaccurate data (for example, entering text in a cell that should contain a number value), or allow the entry of any type of data but display an error message if an inappropriate data type is entered. This allows you to maintain control over the usefulness of the data.

Add an instruction in a comment

A simple way to insert the current date in a cell is to press CTRL+; and then press ENTER. You can help your co-workers by sharing this tip with them in a comment. In this exercise, you add a comment to the date cell.

1 Select cell J1.

2 On the Insert menu, click Comment.

A comment box, surrounded by a hatched border and containing your user name, appears on the worksheet.

3 Type the instruction **Enter CTRL+; to insert the current date**, and then click outside the comment box.

The comment is entered in the cell. You can read the new comment by holding the mouse pointer over the cell.

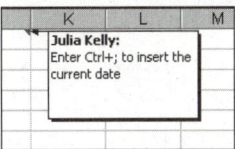

Control data entry with data validation

Sometimes it's critical that the correct type of data is entered in a cell. For example, at Island Tea & Coffee Company, products are sold by the pound, with a 10-pound minimum order per item. You can ensure that quantities in an invoice meet these requirements by adding data validation to the cells in the Qty column. In this exercise, you add data validation to the Qty cells.

1 Select cells A9 through A22.

2 On the Data menu, click Validation.

The Data Validation dialog box appears.

3 Click the Allow down arrow, and then click Whole Number.

4 Click the Data down arrow, and then select Greater Than Or Equal To.

5 In the Minimum box, type **10**

6 Click the Error Alert tab, and then verify that the Style box reads Stop.

7 In the Title box, type **Invalid Entry**, and then, in the Error Message box, type **You must enter a whole number greater than 10.**

8 Click OK.

9 Select cell A16, type **9**, and then press ENTER.

An error message appears containing the text you entered in the Data Validation dialog box.

10 Click Retry, type **10**, and then press ENTER.

11 Select cell A16, and then press DELETE to delete the entry.

12 Save your work.

Printing a Copy Quickly

In the following exercises, you will preview your worksheet and print a single copy of it.

Preview the worksheet to see it before you print it

No matter how quickly you need to print a document, it is always a good idea to preview it before you print. Previewing saves time and paper by allowing you to find and fix small errors before sending the worksheet to the printer. It also gives you a clear view of the layout of the printed page.

IMPORTANT You must have a printer set up and configured to work with Windows 95 before you can use Print Preview.

Print Preview

To print worksheet gridlines, click Page Setup on the File menu, and then select the Gridlines check box on the Sheet tab.

1 On the Standard toolbar, click the Print Preview button.

The Preview window appears, letting you see what the worksheet will look like when you print it. By default, worksheet gridlines are not printed.

2 Move the mouse pointer over the preview page so that the pointer takes the shape of a magnifying glass, and then click.

A close-up of the area you clicked appears.

3 Click the page again.

The full-page preview appears again.

4 Click Close.

Your worksheet reappears.

Print a quick copy

You can use the Print button to quickly print a single copy of the active worksheet, using the default print settings.

Print

➤ On the Standard toolbar, click the Print button.

Your worksheet is sent to the printer.

 NOTE If you'd like to build up on the skills you learned in this lesson, you can do the One Step Further. Otherwise, skip to Finish the Lesson.

One Step Further: Adding a Graphic to a Worksheet

Considering that the invoice will be sent to customers, it needs to look professional and attractive. One way to improve its appearance is to add the company logo to the invoice.

In this exercise, you first insert the logo picture, and then resize the row in which it was pasted to accommodate the picture.

1 Use the right mouse button to click the row 1 header.

Row 1 is selected and a shortcut menu appears.

2 On the shortcut menu, click Insert.

A new row is inserted at the top of the worksheet, above the selected row.

3 Select cell A1.

4 On the Insert menu, point to Picture, and then click From File.

The Insert Picture dialog box appears.

5 In the Look In box, locate the Excel SBS Practice folder, and then double-click the Logo file.

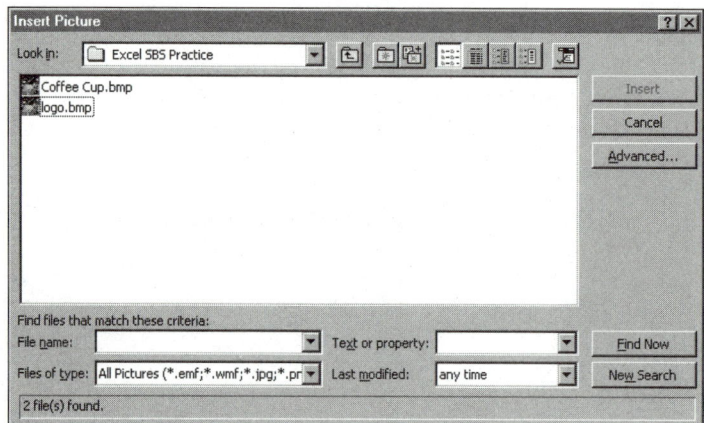

The Island Tea & Coffee Company logo is pasted into the worksheet, with the upper-left corner of the picture in the upper-left corner of the worksheet. The "handles" on the sides and corners of the picture indicate that the picture is selected, and that you can move or resize it.

6 Use the right mouse button to click the graphic, and then, on the short-cut menu, click Format Picture.

7 Click the Properties tab, select the Don't Move Or Size With Cells option button, and then click OK.

8 Move the pointer between the headers for rows 1 and 2 until the pointer becomes a two-headed arrow, and then drag the header border downward until it is taller than the picture (about 110).

Your worksheet should look similar to the following illustration.

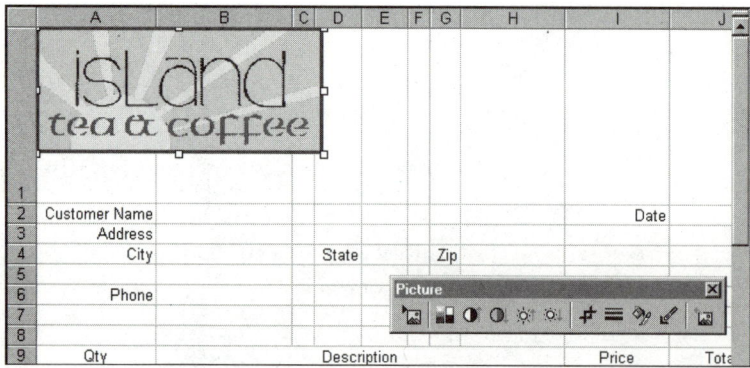

9 Save your work.

Finish the lesson

1 To continue to the next lesson, on the File menu, click Close.

2 If you are finished using Microsoft Excel for now, on the File menu, click Exit.

Lesson Summary

To	Do this	Button
Add a file property	On the File menu, click Properties. On the Summary tab, enter the properties you want, and then click OK.	
Name a worksheet	Double-click the sheet tab, type the new name, and then press ENTER.	
Delete a worksheet	Use the right mouse button to click the appropriate sheet tab, and then, on the shortcut menu, click Delete. Click OK in the message box to confirm the deletion.	
Align cell entries on the right	Select the cells, and then, on the Formatting toolbar, click the Right Align button.	
Center cell entries	Select the cells, and then, on the Formatting toolbar, click the Center button.	
Center a label across columns	Enter the label in the leftmost cell of the selection you want to center across. Select all the cells you want to center across, and then, on the Formatting toolbar, click the Merge And Center button.	
Set column width	Use the right mouse button to click the column header, and then click Column Width. Type a width, and then click OK.	
Add a comment to a cell	On the Insert menu, click Comment. Type your comment text, and then click outside the comment box.	

To	Do this	Button
Set data validation	Select the cells to be validated. On the Data menu, click Validation. Select the validation criteria, and then click OK.	
Preview a worksheet	On the Standard toolbar, click the Print Preview button.	
Print a worksheet	On the Standard toolbar, click the Print button.	

For online information about	On the Help menu, click Contents And Index, click the Index tab, and then type
Adding file properties	files, properties
Entering comments	comments, adding
Validating data	data validation
Printing	printing

Writing Formulas

Estimated time
30 min.

In this lesson you will learn how to:

- Find files using a keyword.
- Write formulas to calculate data.
- Name cells.
- Use names and labels in formulas.

As you work through lessons 2, 3, and 4, you are learning basic and important Microsoft Excel tasks while creating a template. In this lesson, you will learn to write formulas in Microsoft Excel by adding formulas to a partially built invoice that is going to become a template. The advantage of creating and using a template is that the time-consuming work of setting up the worksheet is done only once. To use a template, you open a copy of it, and then enter your current data. There is no need to write formulas to calculate totals because the formulas are already in place in the template worksheet.

If you completed Lesson 2 and the One Step Further exercise, you can continue working with the file you previously saved.

In the following exercises, you will add formulas to the invoice to calculate the item totals, subtotal, sales tax, and grand total automatically. You will also learn how to name cells, and then write formulas using names and labels.

To begin this lesson, you locate and open the 03Lesson.xls file in the Excel SBS Practice folder.

Finding Files Using File Properties

As time goes by and the number of Island Tea & Coffee Company invoice files increases, it becomes easier to have Microsoft Excel find the invoice files by searching for file properties that they have in common, rather than looking through folders to find them.

Whether you plan on using your own file or use the 03Lesson.xls file, you need to first locate the file.

Search for a file using a keyword

In this exercise, you search for the invoice keyword to find and open the ITC Invoice file.

Open

1 On the Standard toolbar, click the Open button.

2 Click the Look In down arrow, and then select the letter icon for your hard disk (usually C:).

   Microsoft Excel will search the entire hard disk.

3 Click Advanced.

   The Advanced Find dialog box appears.

4 In the lower part of the Advanced Find dialog box, click the Property down arrow, and then scroll down and select Keywords.

5 Make sure that Includes Words appears in the Condition box, and then type **invoice** in the Value box.

6 Click Add To List.

   The keyword is added to the Find Files That Match These Criteria list at the top of the dialog box.

7 Select the Search Subfolders check box.

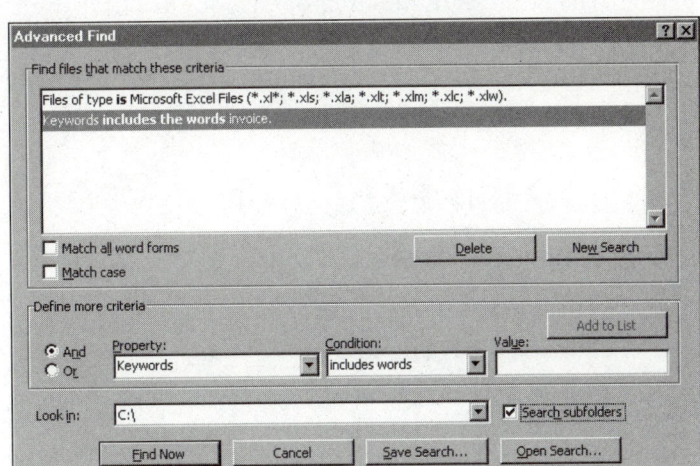

8 Click Find Now.

The results of the search appear in the Open dialog box.

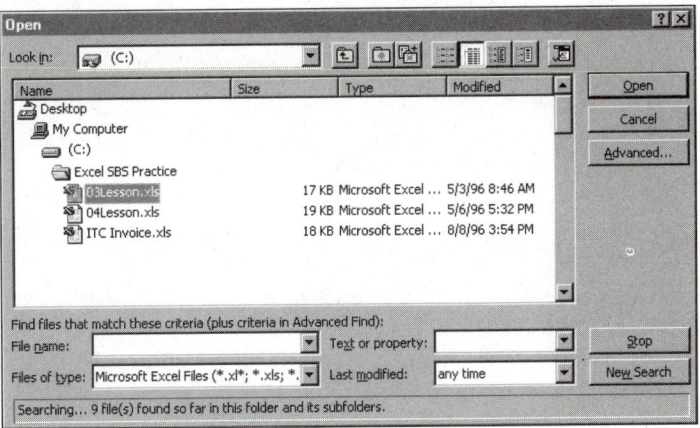

9 Double-click the 03Lesson file. (If you did Lesson 2, you can double-click the ITC Invoice file.)

The file opens.

Save the file with a new name

If you did not do Lesson 2, you need to save the 03Lesson file as ITC Invoice. If you opened the ITC Invoice file in the last exercise, you can skip this exercise.

1   On the File menu, click Save As.

The Save As dialog box opens. Be sure that the Excel SBS Practice folder appears in the Save In box.

2   Double-click in the File Name box, and then type **ITC Invoice**

3   Click Save, or press ENTER.

Adding Calculation Formulas

In the following exercises, you will write formulas to automate the calculations in your invoice. You will first create formulas that compute the total amount for each item in the order, and then add formulas that calculate the order subtotal, sales tax, and grand total.

Add mock data to test the formulas as you write them

When you write a formula, you can tell if it is written correctly by checking the accuracy of the result it displays. In this exercise, you enter a few items of mock data so that you can instantly verify that your formulas were written correctly by checking the results that are immediately displayed.

1   Select cell A10.

2   Type **20**, press TAB, type **Keemun Tea**, and then press ENTER.

When you press ENTER, AutoReturn returns the active cell to the beginning of the next row in your list.

3   Repeat step 2 to enter orders of 30 pounds of Darjeeling Tea and 100 pounds of Kona Coffee.

4   Select cell I10.

5   Type **4.85**, and then press ENTER.

6   Repeat step 5 to enter the price per pound of the Darjeeling Tea (10.15) and the Kona Coffee (5.25).

Your screen should look similar to the following illustration.

	A	B	C	D	E	F	G	H	I	J
2	Customer Name								Date	
3	Address									
4	City			State			Zip			
5										
6	Phone									
7										
8										
9	Qty			Description					Price	Tota
10	20	Keemun tea							4.85	
11	30	Darjeeling tea							10.15	
12	100	Kona coffee							5.25	
13										
14										

Write a formula to compute an item total

In this exercise, you write a formula that calculates an item total by multiplying the quantity ordered by the price.

1 Select cell J10.

2 Type =, click cell A10, type *, click cell I10, and then press ENTER.

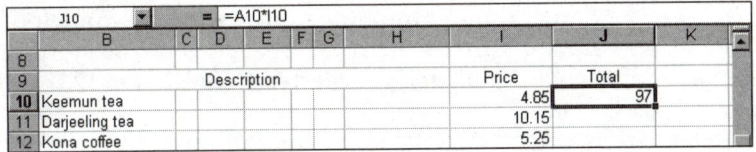

Copy the formula to other cells using AutoFill

All of the cells in the Total column need to use the formula you just wrote. Copying cells one by one can be tedious, but AutoFill provides an easy and quick alternative. It allows you to copy the formula into a range of adjacent cells and automatically adjust the cell references to new cells, so the results will be accurate in all the new formulas. In this exercise, you use AutoFill to quickly copy the formula you created in the previous exercise into additional cells.

1 Select cell J10.

2 Move the mouse pointer over the small black box, also called *fill handle*, located in the lower right corner of the active cell, until the pointer becomes a black cross shape.

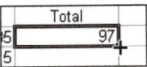

In Lesson 4, you will apply formatting to hide the zeroes.

3 Drag the fill handle down to cell J23, and then release the mouse button.

The formula is copied into cells J11 through J23. Cells J13 through J23 display zeroes because Microsoft Excel will interpret the blank cells from A13 to A23 and I13 to I23 as having a value of zero.

Add a SUM formula to calculate the order total

In this exercise, you write a formula that adds up the total price of items ordered. You use AutoSum to write the formula quickly.

AutoSum

If the AutoSum range isn't correct, simply drag the correct range before pressing ENTER.

1 Select cell J24.

2 On the Standard toolbar, click the AutoSum button.

AutoSum inserts a formula that uses the SUM function, displays a moving border around the range Microsoft Excel anticipates you want to add up, and inserts the range reference in your formula. In this case, the range AutoSum has selected (J10 through J23) is correct.

Price	Total
4.85	97
10.15	304.5
5.25	525
	0
	0
	0
	0
	0
	0
	0
	0
	0
	0
	0
Subtotal	=SUM(J10:J23)
& Handling	
Tax	

3 Press ENTER.

The result of the SUM formula, 926.5, appears in the subtotal cell.

Calculate sales tax

The Island Tea & Coffee Company must charge 7% tax on all orders, and you want the invoice to calculate the tax automatically. In this exercise, you write a formula that calculates tax based on the subtotal cell.

In Lesson 4, you'll apply formatting to display the result as dollars and cents, with two decimal places.

1 Select cell J26.

2 Type =, click cell J24, type ***.07**, and then press ENTER.

The tax formula is entered.

=J24*0.07						
D	E	F	G	H	I	J
						0
					Subtotal	926.5
					Shipping & Handling	
					Tax	64.855
					Total	

3 Save your work.

Using Cell Names and Labels to Make Formulas Easier to Understand

All the formulas you've written so far are correct and functional, but when you read them, it's not immediately clear which values are being calculated. You can identify specific cells and ranges more clearly by giving them *names*, and then use those names instead of cell references when you write formulas. For example, the formula: =Price*Qty is instantly understandable, whereas =A16*I16 might not be so clear.

In the following exercises, you will name some of the cells in the invoice, and then write formulas using the new names.

Name cells to use in formulas

In this exercise, you name the Subtotal, Shipping & Handling, and Tax cells.

You can also use row and column labels in your formulas, without having to name the cells first.

1 Select the range I24 through J26.

This range contains the Subtotal, Shipping & Handling, and Tax labels and data cells. Be sure to select both the cells that include labels and the cells that include data.

2 On the Insert menu, point to Name, and then click Create.

The Create Names dialog box appears. The Left Column check box is selected because Microsoft Excel recognizes labels are located in the left column of the selected range.

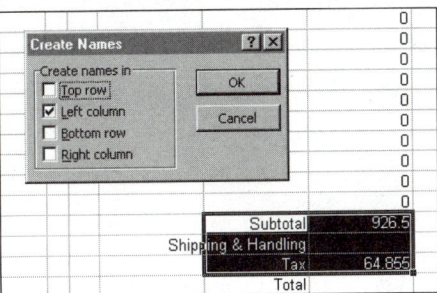

3 Click OK.

Cells J24 through J26 are named with the labels in cells I24 through I26.

4 On the formula bar, click the Name Box down arrow.

The names you created are listed.

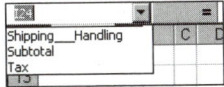

5 Click Subtotal.

The cell named Subtotal is selected.

Write a formula using cell names

In this exercise, you write a formula in the Total cell that sums the named cells.

1 Select cell J27, and type =

The Functions list replaces the Name Box list.

2 On the Functions list, click SUM.

The Formula palette appears to help you write the SUM formula. The Number 1 box is highlighted.

3 Click cell J24, named Subtotal.

The cell name is inserted in the Number 1 box.

4 Press TAB, click cell J25 (named Shipping___Handling), press TAB, and then click cell J26 (named Tax).

The cell names are inserted in the Formula palette.

Spaces and ampersands (&) are not allowed in cell names, so Microsoft Excel changes Shipping & Handling to Shipping ___Handling when it creates the cell name.

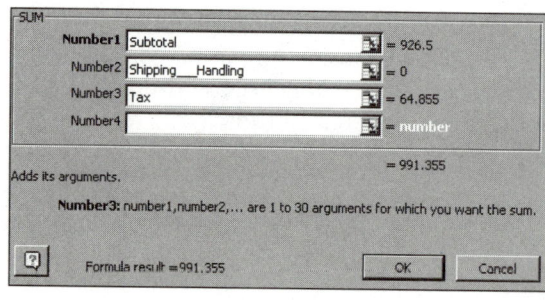

5 Click OK.

The SUM formula is entered in the Total cell. It is now easy to discern which cells are being calculated because you can read their names in the formula.

Use labels in formulas

When cells have identifying labels nearby, you can often write clear formulas using those labels instead of cell references and instead of naming the cells. Using labels is quicker than using names because you don't have to perform the extra steps required to name cells. But there are instances in which using names is more efficient than using labels. For example, if you need to include the label of a range of cells in a formula, you must drag the whole range, but if the range is named you can simply insert its name. Also, you can name a non-contiguous range of cells, but you cannot label it; or, you might set up your worksheet so that the labels are too far away from the data to be recognizable to Microsoft Excel as labels.

In the ITC Invoice worksheet, Microsoft Excel automatically recognizes the labels for the Qty and Price columns. When you type a label into your formula, Microsoft Excel knows which cell to calculate. In this exercise, you rewrite your total price formula using labels.

1   In cell J10, type **=Qty*Price**, and press ENTER.

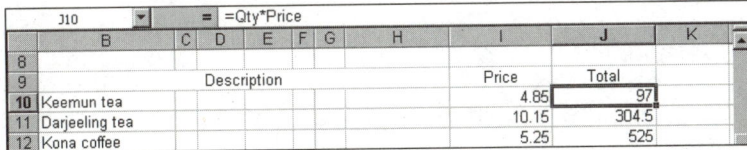

Your new formula with labels is clearer than the old formula with cell references. In addition, if you change the label in the worksheet (for example, if you change Qty to Quantity in cell A10), the formula will change automatically to use the new label.

2   Use AutoFill to copy the new formula in cells J11 through J23.

3   Save your work.

NOTE   If you'd like to build up on the skills you learned in this lesson, you can do the One Step Further. Otherwise, skip to "Finish the Lesson."

One Step Further: Calculating a Specific Cost

You want to automate the calculation of the shipping charge for an order so that you do not have to look up the charge manually each time you fill out an invoice. In this section, you write a formula that sums the total weight of the order (in the Qty column), and then applies a lower shipping charge for orders under 50 pounds and a higher shipping charge for orders of 50 pounds or more.

51

In order to write your formula properly, you will have to use an IF function, a *logical* function that evaluates whether a mathematical statement is true or false. If the mathematical statement is true, the IF formula returns one value; if the statement is false, the IF formula returns another value.

An example of an IF formula is =IF(A3<5,100,350). This equation means that if A3 is less than 5, the value returned will be 100; if A3 is 5 or higher than 5, the value returned will be 350.

A function is a calculation tool that a formula can use; a formula is a mathematical equation that begins with an equal sign and returns a calculated value.

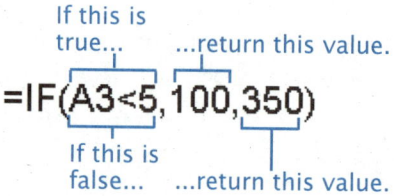

In the following exercises, you will write an IF formula that determines a shipping charge ($10 or $20) based on the order weight (less than 50 pounds, or 50 pounds and up). The IF formula will determine the order weight by using a *nested* SUM function. A nested function is a function within another function; in this case, the SUM function will be contained within the IF function. Microsoft Excel will calculate the SUM function first, and then the IF function will be calculated using the result of the SUM function.

Name the Qty range

In this exercise, you name the range of cells in the Qty column because a name is more efficient than a label when you're summing a range of cells.

1   Select the range A10 through A23.

2   On the formula bar, click in the Name Box.

The cell reference is highlighted.

3   Type **Pounds**, and then press ENTER.

The new name appears in the Name Box. Be sure you press ENTER before you click another cell.

Calculate the shipping cost using a named cell

In this exercise, you write the formula that determines the shipping charge.

1   On the formula bar, click the Name Box down arrow, and then click Shipping___Handling.

The cell named Shipping___Handling becomes the active cell.

2   Type =, and then click the Name Box down arrow, which is now called the Functions down arrow since you've begun to write a formula.

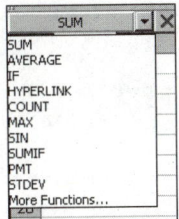

3   In the Functions list, click IF.

The Formula palette opens up to help you write the IF formula. The insertion point is in the Logical_Test box, which is the first of the three *arguments*, or components, required by the IF function.

4   Type **sum(Pounds)<50**, and then press TAB.

The sum(Pounds)<50 statement is entered in the Formula palette as well as in the formula, and the insertion point moves to the Value_If_True box. The nested function, SUM(Pounds), has been inserted into the IF formula.

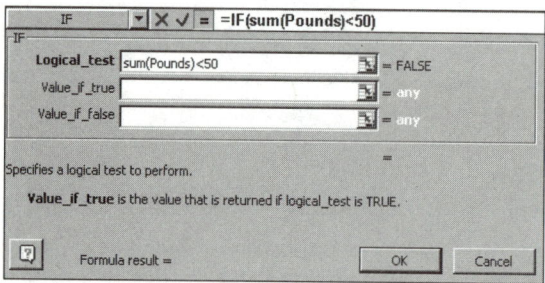

5   In the Value_If_True box, type **10**, and then press TAB.

6   In the Value_If_False box, type **20**, and then click OK.

The IF formula that calculates a shipping & handling charge based on the weight of the order is entered in the Shipping___Handling cell.

Shipping___Handling ▼				=	=IF(SUM(Pounds)<50,10,20)			
	B	C D	E	F G	H	I	J	K
24						Subtotal	926.5	
25						Shipping & Handling	20	
26						Tax	64.855	
27						Total	1011.355	

7   Save your work.

TROUBLESHOOTING   When you type a function name, such as SUM, be sure to type it in lowercase. This is a good way to check whether you've typed the function name correctly; if you have spelled it correctly, it will be converted to uppercase when you enter the formula. If you get an error message and the function name is still lowercase, check the spelling.

Finish the lesson

1   To continue to the next lesson, on the File menu, click Close.

2   If you are finished using Microsoft Excel for now, on the File menu, click Exit.

Lesson Summary

To	Do this	Button
Search for a file based on a keyword	Click the Open button, then select your hard disk or a folder to search. Click the Advanced button, select Keywords in the Property box, and then type the keyword in the Value box. Click Add To List, and then select the Search Subfolders check box. Click Find Now.	
Copy cells using AutoFill	Drag the fill handle down to the last cell you want to include, and then release the mouse button.	
Sum a range using AutoSum	Click the cell where you want to insert the SUM formula, and then click the AutoSum button. Define the range you want to sum by dragging, and then press ENTER.	Σ
Create cell names using labels in adjacent cells	Select a range that includes the cells to be named and the cells containing the name labels. On the Insert menu, point to Name, then click Create. Be sure the correct label location is checked, and then click OK.	
Use names in formulas	Click the named cell to insert in the formula.	
Use labels in formulas	Type the data label in the formula.	
Write a formula using the Formula palette	Type =, then select a function name from the Functions list. Click cells to paste them into the Formula palette boxes, and then click OK when you are finished.	

For online information about	On the Help menu, click Contents And Index, click the Index tab, and then type
Searching files	searching
AutoFill	autofill
Naming cells	naming, cells
Cell labels (in formulas)	labels in formulas
IF function	IF worksheet function

Formatting Your Worksheet for a Professional Look

Estimated time
45 min.

In this lesson you will learn how to:

- Format cells.
- Create, apply, and change styles.
- Format numbers.
- Create a custom number format.
- Create custom headers and footers.
- Save a workbook as a template.

Now that you have automated the calculations in your invoice using formulas, you are ready to start formatting the invoice page to make it look professional. Formatting also allows you to make your worksheet easier to read and group data visually, for example. You can format fonts, cell borders, and cell shading, as well as the way numbers are displayed. You can create styles, which are packages of formatting attributes, to save you time in the future when you want to change the formatting of a group of cells. You can also create headers and footers that print on every page, and include codes that automatically print the current date or number of pages in the printed document. After you finish formatting your invoice worksheet, you'll save it as a template so that Island Tea & Coffee Company employees can easily open a copy of the invoice and fill it out.

Open a file and save it with a new name

As you begin this lesson, one of your co-workers has partially formatted your invoice worksheet for you. But he has been called away on other business, and has asked you to complete the invoice formatting.

Open

1 On the Standard toolbar, click the Open button.

2 In the Open dialog box, click the Look In Favorites button.

3 In the file list, double-click the Excel SBS Practice folder, and then double-click the 04Lesson file.

The Open dialog box closes, and the 04Lesson file appears in the document window.

4 On the File menu, click Save As.

The Save As dialog box opens. Be sure that the Excel SBS Practice folder appears in the Save In box.

5 In the File Name box, type **ITC Invoice**

6 Click the Save button or press ENTER.

Save

If a dialog box appears asking you confirm that you want to replace the existing file, click Yes.

Formatting Cells

In the following exercises, you will practice formatting with fonts and learn how to use styles to save time when changing cell formatting. You will also practice formatting borders and cell shading, as well as setting page margins so that the invoice fits in the center of a single page.

Format fonts

A co-worker at Island Tea & Coffee Company has formatted part of the invoice worksheet for you, but didn't complete the job. You need to format the remaining labels to make the worksheet look professional enough to be sent out to customers. In this exercise, you change the font for one of the labels, and then apply the new formatting to other labels.

1 Select cell A9.

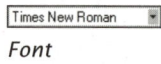

Font

2 On the Formatting toolbar, click the Font down arrow, and then select Times New Roman.

Font Size

3 On the Formatting toolbar, click the Font Size down arrow, and then select 12.

Bold

4 On the Formatting toolbar, click the Bold button.

Your screen should look similar to the following illustration.

A9		=	Qty							
	A	B	C	D	E	F	G	H	I	J
8										
9	**Qty**				Description				Price	Tot
10	20	Keemun tea							4.85	
11	30	Darjeeling tea							10.15	
12	100	Kona coffee							5.25	
13										

Format Painter

5 With cell A9 still selected, on the Standard toolbar, double-click the Format Painter button.

The mouse pointer takes the shape of the Format Painter button face. Until you click the Format Painter button again to turn it off, the formatting from cell A9 will be applied to every cell you click.

6 Click cell B9, then cell I9, and then cell J9.

The new formatting is applied to all the selected cells.

7 On the Standard toolbar, click the Format Painter button to turn it off.

Your screen should look similar to the following illustration.

	A	B	C	D	E	F	G	H	I	J
8										
9	**Qty**	**Description**							**Price**	**Tot**
10	20	Keemun tea							4.85	
11	30	Darjeeling tea							10.15	
12	100	Kona coffee							5.25	
13										

Create styles by example

Applying formatting is a simple procedure, but if you have to apply the same formatting to several worksheets it can become quite tedious. Suppose you have several worksheets in a workbook that all have the same types of labels (such as titles and subtitles), and you need to change the formatting of all the labels. You can save a lot of time by applying a *style* instead of reapplying the formatting: you can simply change the style definition instead of reformatting each individual cell.

A style is a collection of formatting attributes such as font, font size, bold, italic, cell shading, or color, and is simple to create, apply, and change. When you apply a style to a cell, all of the formatting attributes contained in the style are applied to the cell. When you change a formatting attribute in a style (for example, you might change the font from Times New Roman to Tahoma), the attribute is automatically changed in all cells to which the style has been applied.

59

All Island Tea & Coffee Company documentation that will be seen by customers has to be approved by the Marketing manager. Considering that the Marketing manager will most likely request formatting changes, you have decided to set up the invoice formatting using styles to speed up future modifications. If you need to change the formatting later, you can simply redefine the style and the changes will be reflected in all the cells to which that style has been applied. In this exercise, you create a style based on existing cell formatting, and then apply the style to several cells.

1 Select cell A9.

You can remove an attribute from a style definition by clearing the appropriate check box in the Style dialog box.

2 On the Format menu, click Style.

The Style dialog box appears, and the Style Name box is highlighted. The dialog box lists the attributes associated with the style shown in the Style Name box.

3 In the Style Name box, type **Label**, and then click OK.

The formatting applied to cell A9 is now available as a style named Label.

4 Click cell B9, and then hold down CTRL and click cells I9 and J9.

The three remaining information labels are selected.

5 On the Format menu, click Style. Click the Style Name down arrow, select Label, and then click OK.

The Label style is applied to all four information labels.

Merge And Center

6 Select cells B9 through H9, and then click the Merge And Center button.

The Description text is centered, and the Label style continues to be applied.

Change a style definition

You have just received the formatting changes requested by the Marketing manager. In this exercise, you change the font in the labels by simply modifying the Label style definition.

1 Click cell A9.

2 On the Format menu, click Style.

The Style dialog box appears.

3 On the Style dialog box, click Modify.

The Format Cells dialog box appears.

4 Click the Font tab, select Arial in the Font list, and then 10 in the Size list.

5 Click OK, and then click OK again.

All of the labels on the worksheet are reformatted. Your screen should look similar to the following illustration.

	A	B	C	D	E	F	G	H	I	J
8										
9	Qty			Description					Price	Tot
10	20	Keemun tea							4.85	
11	30	Darjeeling tea							10.15	
12	100	Kona coffee							5.25	
13										

Apply borders

Right now, your invoice is full of information that is not easily identifiable. In order to make the invoice more usable for the other employees of the Island Tea & Coffee Company and more readable for your customers, you decide to break the page into clearly defined areas. In this exercise, you apply borders to visually separate different areas of information.

TIP You can quickly select a range of cells by typing the range reference in the Name Box, and then pressing ENTER. For example, if you want to select the range A22 through A35, you can type **A22:A35** in the Name Box, and then press ENTER. The range will be selected.

1   Select cells A10 through A23, and then hold down CTRL and select cells B10 through H23, I10 through I23, and J10 through J23.

The ranges containing order information are selected. You can select each range individually and place a border around it, but you can also save time by selecting all of the individual ranges that you want to place borders around as if they were non-adjacent, using the CTRL key, and placing borders around each of the ranges all at once.

Borders

2   On the Formatting toolbar, click the Borders down arrow.

The Borders palette appears.

3   Click the top border of the Borders palette, and then drag it onto the worksheet.

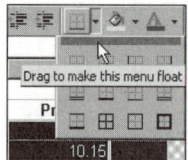

The Borders palette "floats" on the worksheet, which means it can be placed anywhere that is convenient, rather than being docked at one edge of the document window.

4   Click the Outline border button.

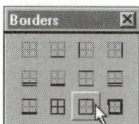

An Outline border is applied to each of the selected ranges.

5   Select cells J24 through J26, and then click the outline-and-inside border button.

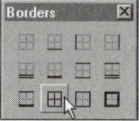

6 On the Borders palette, click the Close button.

Your worksheet should look similar to the following illustration.

	B	C	D	E	F	G	H	I	J	K
13									0	
14									0	
15									0	
16									0	
17									0	
18									0	
19									0	
20									0	
21									0	
22									0	
23									0	
24								Subtotal	926.5	
25								Shipping & Handling	20	
26								Tax	64.855	
27								**Total**	**1011.355**	
28										

Apply shading

In order to ensure that your colleagues at the Island Tea & Coffee Company will not be entering information in cells that contain formulas, you decide to format them differently. Considering that one of the company's internal formatting conventions is that information is not entered into shaded cells, you elect to follow this convention. In this exercise, you apply shading to the cells that contain formulas as a visual reminder to users not to enter information in those cells.

Fill Color

You can also drag the Fill Color palette onto the worksheet.

1 Select cells J10 through J27.

2 On the Formatting toolbar, click the Fill Color down arrow, and then click the palest blue color.

Your screen should look similar to the following illustration.

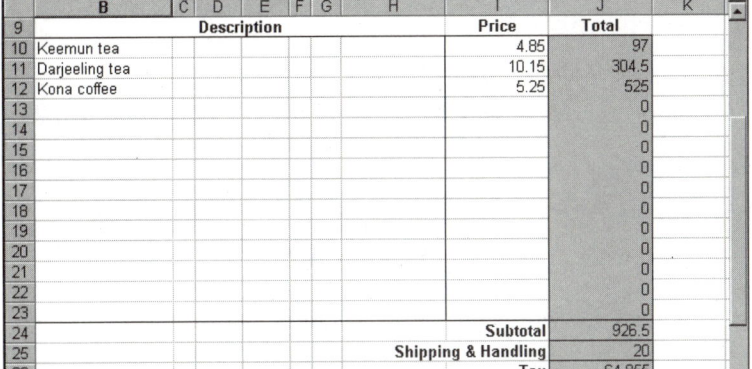

	B	C	D	E	F	G	H	I	J	K
9				Description				Price	Total	
10	Keemun tea							4.85	97	
11	Darjeeling tea							10.15	304.5	
12	Kona coffee							5.25	525	
13									0	
14									0	
15									0	
16									0	
17									0	
18									0	
19									0	
20									0	
21									0	
22									0	
23									0	
24								Subtotal	926.5	
25								Shipping & Handling	20	
26								Tax	64.855	

63

Set page margins

Before printing your invoice, you preview it to make sure that it all fits on one page. In this exercise, you change the page margins so that the entire invoice fits on a single page, center the invoice on the printed page, and preview the invoice.

1 On the File menu, click Page Setup.

   The Page Setup dialog box appears.

2 Click the Margins tab.

3 Double-click in the Left box, and then type .5

4 Double-click in the Right box, and then type .5

5 In the Center On Page area, select the Horizontally check box, and then click Print Preview.

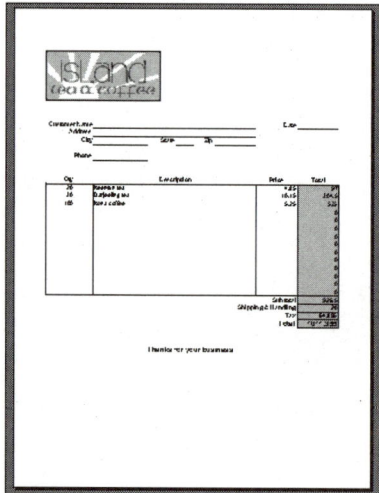

6 Click Close.

7 Save your work.

   Your screen should look similar to the following illustration.

Formatting Numbers

Number formatting determines the display of number values, and such formatting takes effect only when a cell contains a number. By default, all the cells in a worksheet use the General number format, in which extra zeroes on the right of the decimal point are left out, all calculated decimal places are shown, and numbers are aligned on the right. For example, in column J, the formula results look like "general numbers" rather than dollars and cents.

You are now ready to finalize your invoice by formatting the numbers. In the following exercises, you will format the cells located in the Total column to display numbers as prices, remove the extra zeroes in the Total column, and format the Qty column to display numbers with the suffix "lbs," as in "100 lbs."

Format numbers to look like prices

In order to have the number formatting in the invoice look like product prices, you need to modify the formatting of the Total column. In this exercise, you format numbers in the Total column to have two decimal places and a thousands separator.

1 Select cells I10 through J26.

2 Use the right mouse button to click the selection, and then, on the shortcut menu, click Format Cells.

The Format Cells dialog box appears.

3 Click the Number tab.

4 In the Category list, select Number, verify that the number in the Decimal Places box is 2, and then select the Use 1000 Separator (,) check box.

5 Click OK.

All the numbers in the Totals column are rounded to two decimal places, and extra zeroes are displayed to fill out the two decimal places on the right of the decimal point.

6 Select cell I10, and then hold down CTRL and click cells J10, J24, and J27.

7 Use the right mouse button to click any one of the selected cells, and then, on the shortcut menu, click Format Cells.

8 On the Number tab, select the category Currency, then click OK.

Your screen should look similar to the following illustration.

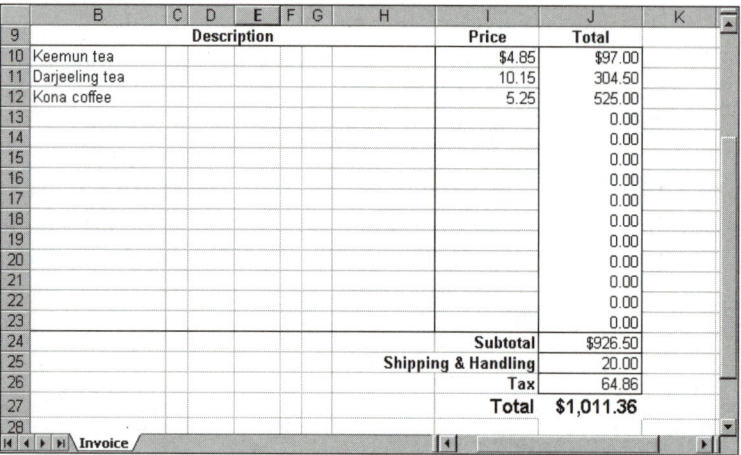

	B	C	D	E	F	G	H	I	J	K
9								Price	Total	
		Description								
10	Keemun tea							$4.85	$97.00	
11	Darjeeling tea							10.15	304.50	
12	Kona coffee							5.25	525.00	
13									0.00	
14									0.00	
15									0.00	
16									0.00	
17									0.00	
18									0.00	
19									0.00	
20									0.00	
21									0.00	
22									0.00	
23									0.00	
24								Subtotal	$926.50	
25							Shipping & Handling		20.00	
26								Tax	64.86	
27								Total	$1,011.36	
28										

Invoice

Format numbers using a custom number format

You need to include the suffix "lbs" after entries in the Qty column. This is to make sure that the employees of the Island Tea & Coffee Company using the invoice know to enter quantities in pounds in this column, and to make it clear to customers that the amount of each order is measured in pounds. In this exercise, you format the numbers in the Qty column to include the "lbs" text suffix.

1 Select cells A10 through A23, use the right mouse button to click the selection, and then, on the shortcut menu, click Format Cells.

2 In the Category list, click Custom.

3 In the Type box, select the entry, then type **0 "lbs"**

Be sure you type a zero, not the letter O.

4 Click OK.

The Custom number format is applied, and saved as a Custom format that you can apply again later.

	A	B
9	**Qty**	
10	20 lbs	Keemun tea
11	30 lbs	Darjeeling tea
12	100 lbs	Kona coffee
13		
14		

 NOTE A custom format is similar to a style. A style encompasses many aspects of a cell's formatting, including the number format; a custom number format is like any other number format. In fact, you can create a style that includes your new custom number format.

Turn off zeroes

The formulas located in the Totals column that don't have data to calculate are displaying values of zero, and that might be confusing to future users and to customers. In this exercise, you turn off the zero values display.

1 On the Tools menu, click Options.

The Options dialog box appears.

2 Click the View tab, clear the Zero Values check box, and then click OK.

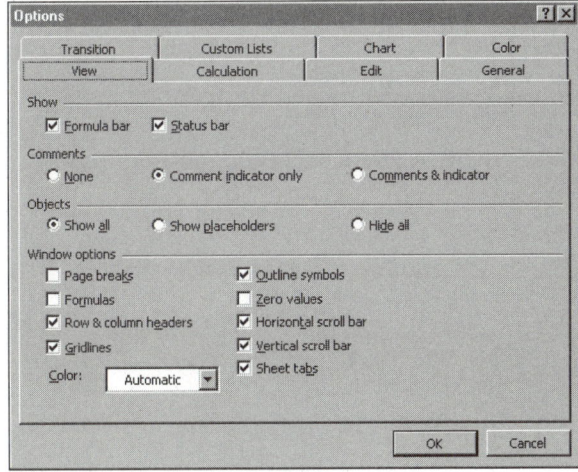

The extraneous zero values on the worksheet are hidden.

Creating Custom Headers and Footers

By default, Microsoft Excel creates no headers or footers, but you can easily create and customize the header and/or the footer, if you want.

Create a custom header

After looking at the ITC invoice in the Print Preview window, you decide that it needs a custom header. In this exercise, you create a custom header to match the rest of the invoice.

1 On the File menu, click Page Setup.

The Page Setup dialog box appears.

2 Click the Header/Footer tab.

3 Click Custom Header.

The Header dialog box appears.

Font button

4 In the Center box, type **Invoice**, double-click the text to select it, and then click the Font button.

The Font dialog box appears

5 In the Font Style box, select Bold, and in the Size box, select 12, and then click OK.

The Font dialog box closes.

6 In the Header dialog box, click OK.

The Header dialog box closes. You can see the changes to your header in the Header/Footer tab.

Create a custom footer

In order to track each invoice more easily, you decide to add useful information in the footer. In this exercise, you create a footer that will display the print date as well as the individual page number and number of pages on each invoice page.

1 On the Header/Footer tab, click Custom Footer.

2 In the Left Section box, type **printed**

3 Press SPACEBAR, and then click the Date button.

Date button

4 Select all the text in the Left Section box, and then click the Font button.

The Font dialog box appears.

5 Select 8 in the Size box, and then click OK.

The Font dialog box closes.

6 In the Center Section, type **Page**, and then press SPACEBAR.

7 Click the Page button, press SPACEBAR, type **of**, and then press SPACEBAR.

8 Click the Pages button, press SPACEBAR, and then type **Pages**

Page button

Pages button

The Page and Pages codes will automatically appear, and print the individual page number and the total number of pages in the invoice, for example, "Page 1 of 2."

9 Click OK to close the Footer dialog box, and then click OK to close the Page Setup dialog box.

Saving Your Workbook as a Template to Re-Use It Easily

Now that you are finished building the ITC invoice, you are ready to save it as a template. In the following exercises, you will delete the mock data you inserted during the creation of the invoice and save the workbook as a template.

Delete the mock data

▶ Select cells A10 through I12, and then press DELETE.

The mock data is deleted and the formula cells are cleared, but the important formatting work that you've done remains. The Shipping & Handling value remains because the cell contents are based on the result of the formula you created in Lesson 3, "Writing Formulas."

Save a workbook as a template

Your invoice is now ready to be saved as a template. In this exercise, you save the workbook as a template.

1 On the File menu, click Save As.

2 In the Save As Type box, select Template.

The filename automatically changes to ITC Invoice.xlt.

3 In the Save In box, locate the Spreadsheet Solutions folder.

4 Click Save.

The workbook is saved as a template in the Spreadsheet Solutions folder.

5 On the File menu, click Close.

Open a copy of the template

The template is complete and available to any Island Tea & Coffee Company employee who has access to your templates folder. In this exercise, you verify that your invoice opens correctly and looks the way you want.

1 On the File menu, click New.

2 Click the Spreadsheet Solutions tab.

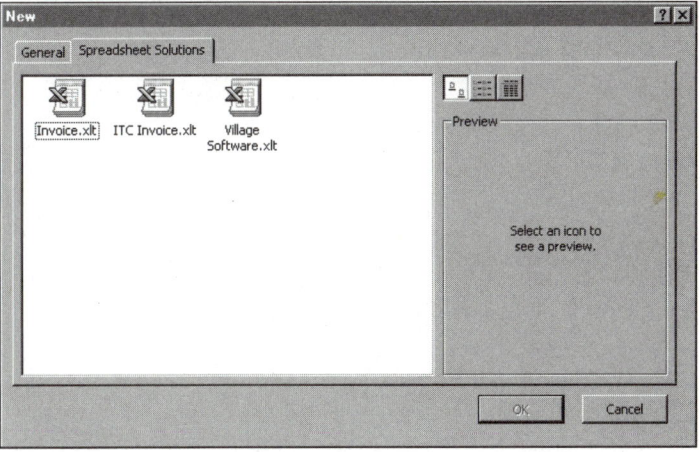

3 Double-click the ITC Invoice icon.

A copy of your invoice, temporarily named ITC Invoice1, opens and is ready to be filled out and saved with a permanent name.

4 Close the ITC Invoice File. If prompted to save, click No.

If You Have Microsoft FrontPage...

If you have Microsoft FrontPage, you can place a link to your template in a Web page on the company intranet. Then, the rest of the Island Tea & Coffee Company employees will be able to open your Web page, click the hotlink you created to the invoice template, and open copies of the template on their computers.

 NOTE If you'd like to build on the skills you learned in this lesson, you can do the One Step Further. Otherwise, skip to "Finish the Lesson."

One Step Further: Editing the Template

During the Marketing manager's final review of the invoice, she suggested that the shading added to the formula cells in column J should not appear on the customer copy. But you still want to keep the shaded cells on the ITC invoice template to help the Island Tea & Coffee Company employees fill out the invoice properly. Fortunately, Microsoft Excel allows you to prevent the shading from being printed.

Open the template

If you need to make changes to your template (for example, add more formulas or modify the formatting), you should open the template itself rather than a copy of the template. In this exercise, you open the template.

1 On the File menu, click Open, and then locate the Spreadsheet Solutions folder.

2 Double-click the ITC Invoice file.

The template opens, rather than a copy. The name in the title bar is ITC Invoice.

Select black and white printing

You don't want the shaded cells to be printed on the copies that you mail or fax to customers. In this exercise, you set the worksheet to print in black and white, with no shades of gray except in the graphic so that your customers will not see the cell shading.

1   On the File menu, click Page Setup.

The Page Setup dialog box appears.

Print Preview

2   Click the Sheet tab.

3   Select the Black And White check box, and then click OK.

4   On the Standard toolbar, click the Print Preview button.

Your worksheet should look similar to the following illustration.

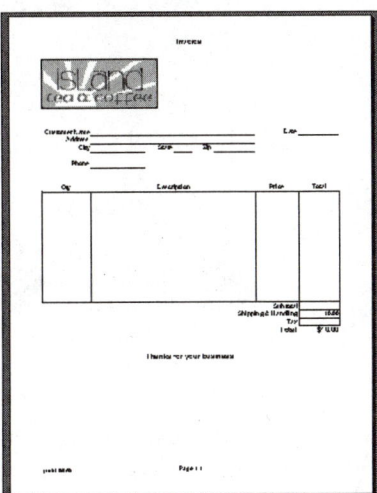

5   Click Close, and then save your work.

Finish the lesson

1   To continue to the Review and Practice, on the File menu, click Close.

2   If you are finished using Microsoft Excel for now, on the File menu, click Exit.

Lesson Summary

To	Do this	Button
Format font for typeface, size, or formatting (such as bold, italic or underline)	Select cells, and then click the appropriate buttons on the Formatting toolbar.	
Copy formatting	Select a cell that contains the formatting you want to apply to other cells, and then double-click the Format Painter button.	
Create a style by example	Select a cell that contains all the formatting attributes you want to include in the style, and then, on the Format menu, click Style. Type a new style name, and then click OK.	
Apply a style	Select cells you want to apply the style to, and then, on the Format menu, click Style. Select the style you want in the Style Name box, then click OK.	
Change a style definition	On the Format menu, click Style. Select the style to change in the Style Name box, and then click Modify. Change the style attributes as needed, and then click OK twice.	
Apply borders	Select cells to be formatted. On the Formatting toolbar, click the Borders down arrow, and then click the appropriate border button.	
Drag a palette away from the toolbar to make it float on the worksheet	Drag the palette by its top border onto the worksheet.	
Apply shading	Select cells to be formatted. On the Formatting toolbar, click the Fill Color down arrow, and then click a color.	
Set page margins	On the File menu, click Page Setup. Click the Margins tab, and then set the margins.	

To	Do this
Format numbers	Select the cells containing the numbers you want to format, and then use the right mouse button to click one of them. On the shortcut menu, click Format Cells, click the Number tab, select a Category, and then set the appropriate formatting options for the category.
Hide zero values on the worksheet	On the Tools menu, click Options. On the View tab, clear the Zero Values check box.
Create custom headers and footers	On the File menu, click Page Setup. Click the Header/Footer tab, and then click the Custom Header or Custom Footer button. Type and format headers and footers in the Header and Footer dialog boxes.
Save a workbook as a template	On the File menu, click Save As. In the Save As Type box, select Template, and then click Save.
Open a copy of a template	On the File menu, click New. Click the tab representing the folder where you stored your template, and then double-click the template icon.

For online information about	On the Help menu, click Contents And Index, click the Index tab, and then type
Formatting worksheets	**formatting cells**
Styles	**styles**
Headers and footers	**headers; footers**
Templates	**templates**

Review & Practice

You will review and practice how to:

**Estimated time
20 min.**

- Name and delete worksheets.
- Enter labels and formulas.
- Format cells.
- Apply borders.
- Add comments.
- Save a workbook as a template.

Before you move on to Part 2, in which you will learn about and practice consolidation, subtotaling, and filtering, you can practice the skills you learned in Part 1 by working through the steps in this Review & Practice section.

Scenario

The State University Alumni Association (SUAA) is a non-profit organization that conducts fundraising activities. As the office manager, you've been asked to help standardize and streamline the accounting system by creating a time-sheet template for the Alumni Association's employees.

Part

1

77

Step 1: Open a File and Enter Labels

You first need to set up your timesheet. In this step, you start a new workbook, delete any extra sheets, and then enter labels. You also add a keyword that will help users find the timesheet.

1 Open a new workbook, and then save it as SUAA Timesheet.

2 Delete all but one sheet.

3 Rename the remaining sheet with the place holder text **Your Name Here**

4 Enter **Monday** in cell B1, and then AutoFill the weekday names across to cell F1.

5 Enter the following labels into cells A2 through A9:

Dates
Tasks
Telephone contacts
Answer mail
Organize events
Update computer
Administrative tasks
Vacation

6 In cell A16, enter **Total hours**

7 Add the keyword **timesheet** to the workbook's file properties. (Hint: On the File menu, click Properties.)

For more information about	See
Opening a new file	Lesson 1
Saving files	Lesson 1
Deleting sheets	Lesson 2
Naming sheets	Lesson 2
Entering data	Lesson 1
Using AutoFill	Lesson 3
Adding keywords	Lesson 2

Step 2: Format the Worksheet and Add Borders

Now that you have entered the labels, you are ready to format your timesheet. In this step, you format the labels and apply borders to the cells where users will enter their daily hours for each task.

1 Format cells B1 through F1 as centered and bold, and format cells B2 through F2 as centered.

2   Format cell A2 ("Dates") and cell A16 ("Total hours") as bold and aligned right, and cell A3 ("Tasks") as bold and centered.

3   Apply inside-and-outside borders to cells B3 through F15.

For more information about	See
Formatting cells	Lesson 4
Applying borders	Lesson 4

Step 3:   *Write Formulas and Add Instructions*

Now that your timesheet looks the way you want, you need to make it functional. In this step, you add formulas and helpful instructions to the timesheet, and then save the workbook as a template.

1   In cell B16, use AutoSum to write a SUM formula that adds up cells B3 through B15.

2   Use AutoFill to copy the SUM formula to cells C16 through F16.

3   In cell A1, add the comment **Be sure to replace the sheet name with your name.**

4   In cell B2, add the comment **To enter the current date, press** CTRL+;

5   In cell A10, add the comment **Enter other tasks as necessary.**

6   Adjust the width of each column so that its contents are displayed.

7   Save the workbook as a template in the Spreadsheet Solutions folder.

Your finished template should look similar to the following illustration.

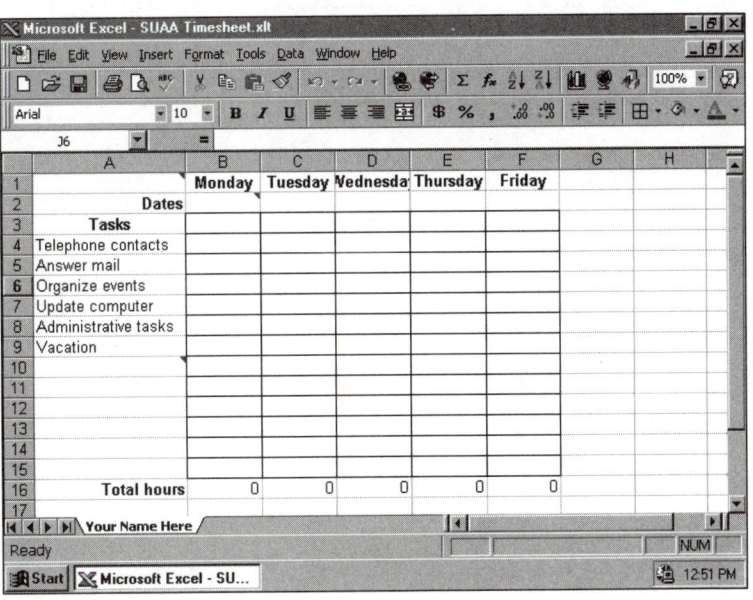

79

For more information about	See
AutoSum	Lesson 3
Adding comments	Lesson 2
Saving a workbook as a template	Lesson 4

Finish the Review & Practice

1 To continue to the next lesson, on the File menu, click Close.

2 If you are finished using Microsoft Excel for now, on the File menu, click Exit.

Organizing and Summarizing Your Data

Consolidating Multiple Lists

Estimated time
30 min.

In this lesson you will learn how to:

- Open multiple files at the same time.
- Work with a group of files displayed in multiple windows.
- Move worksheets between workbooks.
- Consolidate detailed data into a summary.
- Create a conditional number format to make specific values stand out.
- Use a built-in Microsoft Excel template to automate the consolidation process.

In its most basic form, data consists of a series of detailed information (for example, lists of expenses, individual sales records, item quantities in an inventory, or results from scientific experiments). To make this information useful in a decision-making process, data must be organized and summarized. Microsoft Excel provides several ways to summarize details, including the Consolidate command, the Subtotals command, and PivotTables. Usually, one method is more appropriate than the others in specific situations.

At the Island Tea & Coffee Company, expenses are entered in a Microsoft Excel workbook as they are incurred. Due to personnel shifts at the beginning of the year, the January, February, and March expenses lists were recorded by various employees in three different workbooks. Each list consists of two columns: a column of text labels and a column of amounts. One of your tasks as office manager is to organize the three monthly expenses lists into a quarterly summary.

In this case, the best method of summarizing the quarterly expenses is to use the Consolidate command. Consolidation is the easiest method to learn and quickest to perform; it also works best on simple lists that contain a single column of text labels on the left side of the list (as your monthly expenses lists do). Consolidation combines all like items into a single totaled item; for example, all the Supplies entries will be combined into a single Supplies total. One of the advantages of using consolidation is that you can consolidate data stored in different worksheets and workbooks; one of the drawbacks is that the resulting consolidated summary will not provide any details. In the case of the quarterly expenses summary, the lack of details isn't an issue, so you will use the Consolidate command. You will learn about the Subtotals command in Lesson 7, and about creating PivotTables in Lesson 8.

Opening and Arranging a Group of Files

For a demonstration of how to open multiple files, double-click the Excel Camcorder Files shortcut on your Desktop or connect to the Internet address listed on page xxiii.

The Island Tea & Coffee Company employees who kept the expenses lists during the first quarter of 1997 have saved those files with the keyword "expenses." You can use the keyword to locate the files quickly, and then open all three at once.

In the following exercises, you will practice opening a group of expenses files by searching for a common keyword, and then opening all of them at once. You will also practice arranging the files in multiple windows so that you can see all the files and work with them more easily.

Open a group of files that share a keyword

The monthly expenses data has been entered in three different worksheets by various employees. In this exercise, you locate and open the three monthly expenses files.

Open

1   On the Standard toolbar, click the Open button.

2   In the Open dialog box, click the Look In Favorites button.

3   In the file list, double-click the Excel SBS Practice folder.

4   Click Advanced.

5   Click the Property down arrow, and then scroll down and select Keywords.

6   Be sure that Includes Words appears in the Condition box, and then type **expenses** in the Value box.

7   Click Add To List, and then click Find Now.

    The results of the search appear in the Open dialog box.

8 Click Expenses Feb 97, then hold down CTRL and click Expenses Jan 97 and Expenses Mar 97, and finally click Open.

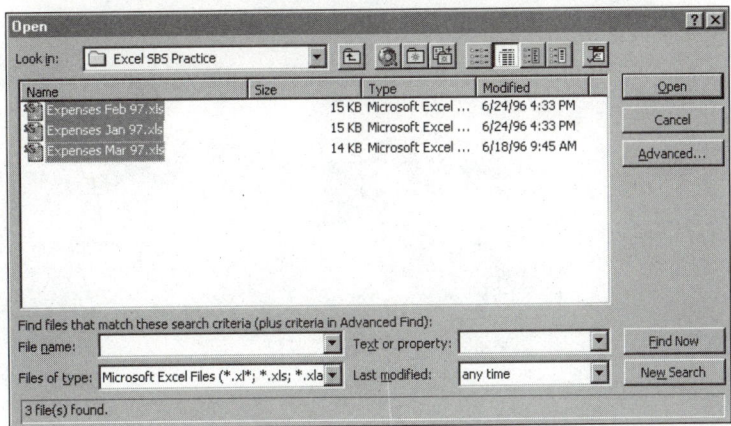

The three expenses files are opened.

Arrange windows to get a better view of your workbooks

For a demon-stration of how to arrange files displayed in multiple win-dows, double-click the Excel Camcorder Files shortcut on your Desktop or connect to the Internet address listed on page xxiii.

The name of any open Microsoft Excel workbook is listed at the bottom of the Window menu; each workbook can be displayed by selecting its name from the list. But, if you need to move rapidly between workbooks, or drag and drop sheets between workbooks, it's more efficient to display all of the workbooks at the same time. You can put each workbook in its own window, and arrange the windows in a convenient manner.

In this exercise, you arrange the windows containing the expenses files, add a new workbook, and then rearrange the windows to display it.

1 Click the Window menu.

The three open workbooks are listed at the bottom of the menu.

2 On the Window menu, click Arrange.

The Arrange Windows dialog box appears.

3 Under Arrange, click the Horizontal option button, and then click OK.

The workbooks are arranged in horizontal windows, and you can see the sheet tabs for each workbook.

New

4 On the Standard toolbar, click the New button.

A new workbook appears on top of the arranged windows.

5 On the Window menu, click Arrange.

6 Under Arrange, click the Tiled option button, and then click OK.

The four open workbooks are arranged in windows in a tiled configuration. You can use any configuration option you wish, as long as you can easily see the sheet tabs.

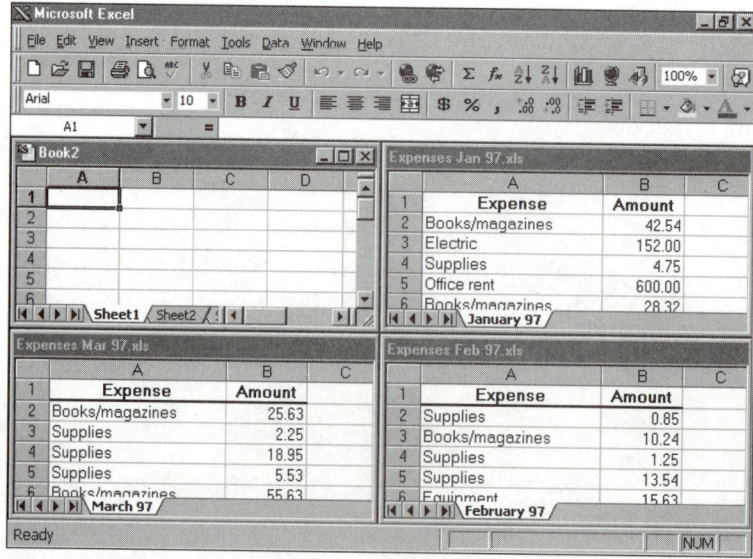

Consolidating Data from Several Worksheets

Now that you have the three expenses files open, you can drag copies of these worksheets into the new workbook where you will perform the consolidation.

 NOTE Even though you can consolidate ranges that are located in different workbooks, it will be easier to learn about consolidation if all the partial lists are in the same workbook. When you consolidate ranges from different workbooks, you must either add the ranges from each separate workbook (if the workbooks are open) or remember the filenames and references so you can type them into the Consolidate dialog box (if the workbooks are closed).

In the following exercises, you will copy sheets from three files into a new workbook, and then consolidate them in a single worksheet.

Copy sheets into a single workbook

Now that you have created the workbook in which the consolidation will take place and arranged the windows so that they are all visible, you are ready to compile the worksheets in your newly created workbook. In this exercise, you copy the three expenses worksheets in the new workbook in preparation for the consolidation.

1 Click in the Expenses Jan 97 workbook window to make it active.

To move a worksheet to another workbook rather than copying it, drag the sheet tab without holding down CTRL.

2 Hold down CTRL and drag the January sheet tab from the Expenses Jan 97 workbook to the new workbook, placing the sheet tab to the right of the last sheet in the workbook.

The January worksheet is copied into the new workbook.

3 Repeat steps 1 and 2 to drag the February and March sheet tabs from the expenses workbooks to the new workbook, placing each to the right of the previous sheet tab.

All three worksheets have been copied into the new workbook. Your screen should look similar to the following illustration.

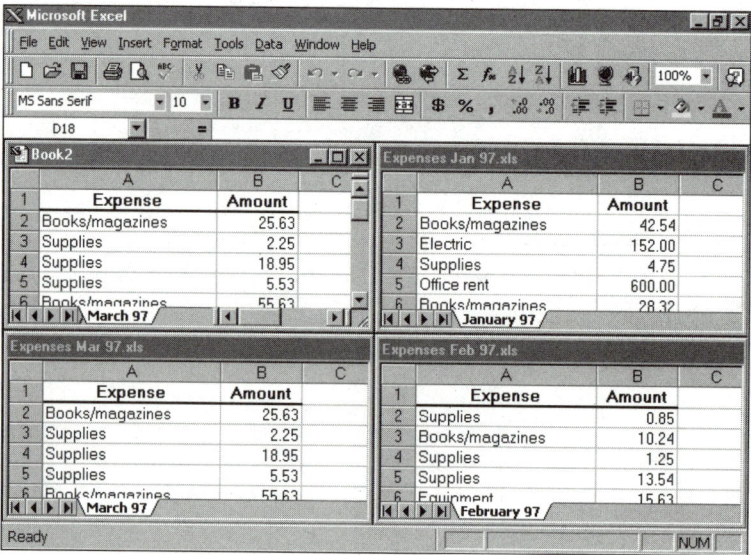

4 Close the Expenses Jan 97, Expenses Feb 97, and Expenses Mar 97 workbooks.

5 Double-click the title bar of the new workbook.

The new workbook is maximized.

6 Save the new workbook as **Quarterly Expenses**

Consolidate data into a single list

You're ready to consolidate the three monthly expenses lists into one quarterly summary. In this exercise, you consolidate the partial lists into a single summary list.

1 In the Quarterly Expenses workbook, change the name of the Sheet1 sheet to **First Qtr 1997**

2 On the First Qtr 1997 sheet, click cell A1, and then, on the Data menu, click Consolidate.

3 In the Consolidate dialog box, be sure that the Function box contains Sum, and then click in the Reference box, if necessary.

4 Select the January 97 sheet, and then drag to select the entire table (cells A1 through B20).

The selected reference appears in the Reference box.

5 In the Consolidate dialog box, click Add.

The range reference is added to the All References box.

6 Repeat steps 4 and 5 to add the February 97 and March 97 sheets (cells A1 through B17).

Your dialog box should look similar to the following illustration.

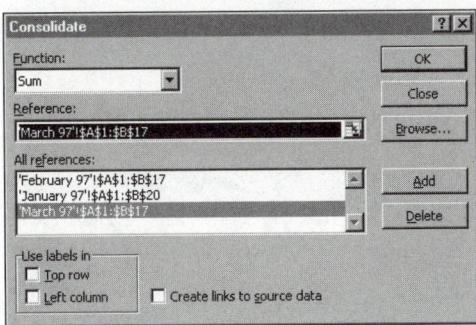

7   Under Use Labels In, select the Top Row and Left Column check boxes, and then click OK.

The three monthly lists are consolidated in the First Qtr 1997 sheet. Your consolidated list should look similar to the following illustration.

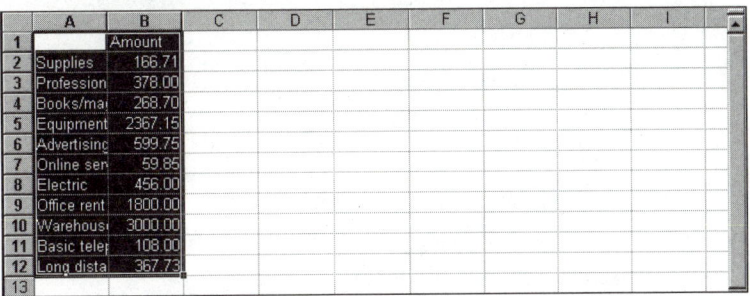

Creating a Conditional Number Format

One of the managerial concerns at the Island Tea & Coffee Company is to keep an eye on quarterly expenses that exceed $2000. When you present the expenses summary, management likes to have any quarterly expense that exceeds $2000 pointed out or highlighted in some way.

Instead of picking out the excessive expenses manually (and running the risk of missing some), you can easily format numbers that are above a specific value to be displayed in a different color, font, or other format, so they stand out and can be easily located.

Create a number format that depends on the value in the cell

In preparation for the quarterly management meeting, you have to format the quarterly expenses summary. In this exercise, you apply a *conditional format* (a format that appears only if the cell value meets certain conditions) to the Amount column so that any entries above 2000 appear in red.

1   In the First Qtr 1997 sheet, select column B by clicking the column letter.

2   On the Format menu, click Conditional Formatting.

The Conditional Formatting dialog box appears.

3   Under Condition 1, verify that Cell Value Is appears in the first drop-down list box.

4   In the second drop-down list box, select Greater Than.

The two right-most boxes become a single box.

5   In the right-most box, type **2000**

You have entered a *condition*, or qualifying value, which tells Microsoft Excel to apply a special format to cells that contain a number that is more than 2000.

6   Click Format.

7   In the Format Cells dialog box, be sure that the Font tab is selected, and then, in the Font Style list, select Bold.

8   In the Color list, select red, and then click OK.

The Conditional Formatting dialog box appears again, and should look similar to the following illustration.

9 Click OK.

Your worksheet should look similar to the following illustration.

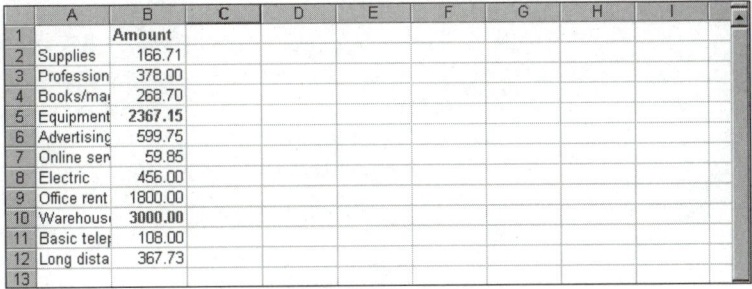

10 Save and close the workbook.

 TIP You might want to add a comment to the worksheet that explains what the formatting means.

Using a Built-in Template to Automate Data Collection

As you learned in the previous series of exercises, you can manually consolidate data in separate lists. You can also automate the collection of data in a single list by using one of the built-in templates that come with Microsoft Excel.

One of the templates that Microsoft Excel provides is an Expense Statement template. All of the automation work is already done for you, and all that remains to be done is to customize the template for the Island Tea & Coffee Company. When you or your co-workers create and save workbooks based on the Expense Statement template, the data entered in each workbook is automatically copied to a *linked*, or attached, *database*. The term database in Microsoft Excel is just another term for list; it's simply a worksheet with data organized into *records*, or rows, and *fields*, or columns. A list has column labels, and no blank rows or columns within it. For example, each expenses list you consolidated in the previous exercise is a database.

When you need to see the collected list of expenses from all the Expense Statement workbooks, you simply open the database workbook, where the data from each Expense Statement has been copied. The linking and automation is carried out by the Template Wizard.

 IMPORTANT You must have the Template Wizard With Data Tracking add-in installed to perform the following exercises. If you do not see the Template Wizard command on your Data menu, click Add-ins on the Tools menu. If you do not see Template Wizard With Data Tracking in the list of available add-ins, you will need to install it from the disk by using Custom Installation. To do this, click Start, point to Settings, and then click Control Panel. Click the Add/Remove Programs icon, select Microsoft Office 97, and then click Add/Remove. Insert the Microsoft Office 97 CD-ROM, and then click Add/Remove in the Microsoft Office 97 Setup dialog box. Select Microsoft Excel and click Change Option. Select the Spreadsheet Templates and Add-Ins, click Change Options, and be sure that Expense Statement Template and Template Wizard With Data Tracking are selected, respectively. Click OK, and then follow the prompts to install the two components.

Create an expenses template that collects data automatically

After having consolidated three expenses lists into one, you decide to automate the data collection process to save time in the future. In this exercise, you open the built-in Expense Statement template and modify it.

1 On the File menu, click New.

2 In the New dialog box, click the Spreadsheet Solutions tab, and then double-click the Expense Statement icon.

   A copy of the Expense Statement, named Expense Statement1, opens and contains a special toolbar and a worksheet.

3 Click the Customize Your Statement sheet tab.

4 Click in the Type Company Information Here section, and fill in the company information as follows:

Company Name	**Island Tea & Coffee Company**
Address	**123 Any Street**
City	**Bigtown**
State	**WA**
Zip Code	**99999**
Phone Number	**800-555-6666**
Fax Number	**800-555-7777**

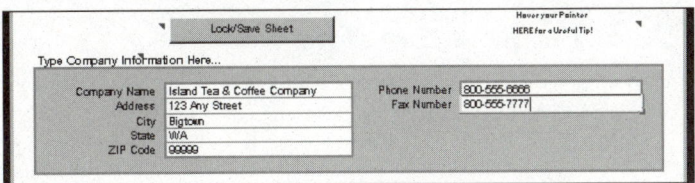

*For more infor-
mation about
the Template
Wizard Data-
base, click Tem-
plate Help on
the Expense
toolbar.*

Print Preview

5 In the section titled Specify Default Expense Statement Information Here, look at the entries in the Common Database box and in the Template Wizard Database box—these boxes tell you that the Microsoft Excel Library folder is where you will find the database of expenses later, and that the name of the database is expdb.xls.

To use a database other than the default expdb.xls, you will need to create it using the Template Wizard.

6 Click the Expense Statement sheet tab.

7 On the Standard toolbar, click the Print Preview button.

The Select Employee and Customize buttons won't print, nor will the shading in the total cells. Your screen should look similar to the following illustration.

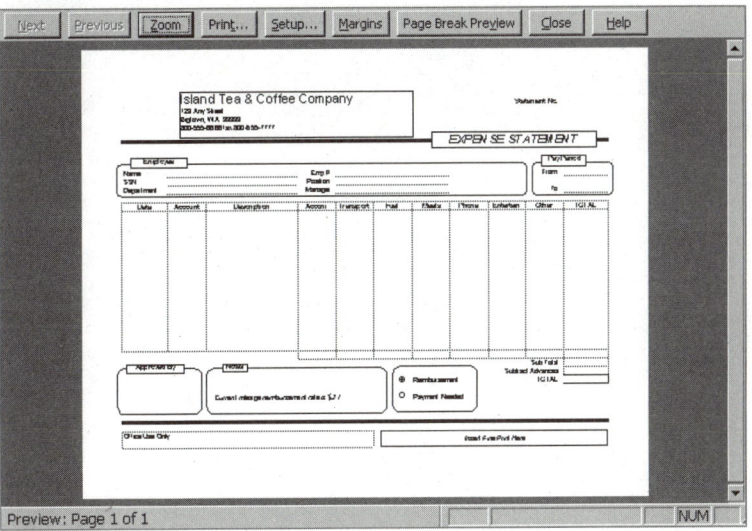

8 Close the Print Preview window, and then click the Customize button in the upper right corner of the expense statement.

The Customize Your Statement sheet appears.

93

Save the new template

Now that your new company template is customized, you can save it in the Spreadsheet Solutions folder so that it will always be available to you, along with all the other built-in Microsoft Excel templates.

 TIP To make the template available to all of your co-workers, be sure to save it in a folder that is accessible to every computer on the company intranet. You might want to store the template in a network location that is accessible by all users in your group. Then, you can have them create a shortcut icon to the folder or template in their Templates folder.

1 At the top of the worksheet, click the Lock/Save Sheet button to protect and then save the template you created.

The Lock And Save Sheet button becomes the Unlock This Sheet button after you click it, and vice versa.

2 In the Lock/Save Sheet dialog box, be sure that the Lock And Save Template option button is selected, and then click OK.

3 In the Save Template dialog box, double-click the Spreadsheet Solutions folder.

4 Select the current filename, type **ITC Expenses**, and then click Save.

5 Read the informational dialog box that appears, and then click OK.

6 On the File menu, click Close.

The template is saved and closed.

 NOTE If you want to further customize your template at a later time, you can click the Open command on the File menu, then navigate to the Spreadsheet Solutions folder (in the Templates folder, in the Microsoft Office folder) and open the template file. Click the Customize button in the upper right corner of the statement to show the Customize Your Statement sheet. Then, click the Unlock This Sheet button, make your changes, and when you're done, click the Lock/Save Sheet button to save your changes.

Test the new expenses template

Before you make the template available to your co-workers, you decide to test it. In this exercise, you try the new template and capture the information in the database.

1 On the File menu, click New.

2 In the New dialog box, double-click the ITC Expenses icon.

A copy of the ITC Expenses template, named ITC Expenses1, opens.

3 Enter the required information (such as your name) in the appropriate locations, and then enter the following expense information:

Date	Description	Accom	Transport	Meals
5/12/97	meeting in Boston	129.00	78.00	36.85
5/13/97	meeting in Boston	129.00	78.00	42.94

The formulas that are built into the shaded cells calculate your totals automatically. Your expense statement should look similar to the following illustration.

Date	Account	Description	Accom	Transport	Fuel	Meals	Phone	Entertain	Other
5/12/97		meeting in Boston	$129.00	$78.00		$36.85			
5/13/97		meeting in Boston	$129.00	$78.00		$42.94			

Capture Data In A Database

4 On the Expense toolbar, click the Capture Data In A Database button.

5 In the Create And Interact With Database dialog box, be sure that the Update Existing Database option button is selected, and then click OK.

6 In the Template File–Save To Database dialog box, be sure that the Create A New Record option button is selected, and then click OK.

7 On the File menu, click Save, and then in the Template File–Save To Database dialog box, be sure that the Continue Without Updating option is selected, and finally click OK.

The Save As dialog box appears.

8 Be sure that the Excel SBS Practice folder is in the Save In box, name the file Expenses 5-14-97, and then click Save.

9 Close the workbook.

Look at the expenses database

Now you can check the new expenses database to be sure that your template is saving entries properly. The databases that are created automatically are saved by default in the Microsoft Excel Library folder.

NOTE The template and database that are created by the Template Wizard will only collect a single record of data from each expense statement that you create and save. If you need to compile a list of details instead of a list of totals, a better approach would be to use a *shared workbook*, a workbook that you make available on the company intranet so that all employees can enter details about their expenses into the same list. You'll learn about shared lists in Lesson 12, "Sharing Your Workbooks with Others."

1 On the File menu, click Open.

2 In the Open dialog box, locate your Microsoft Office folder, double-click your Excel folder, and then double-click the Library folder.

The Template Wizard has given your expenses database the default name of expdb, which is the default database for the built-in Expense Statement template.

3 Double-click the expdb file to open it.

The expenses total from your expense statement has been entered in the expdb database. Every time you create and save a copy of the expenses statement, a new record will be created in the database.

4 Close the database.

 NOTE If you'd like to build up on the skills you learned in this lesson, you can do the One Step Further. Otherwise, skip to "Finish the Lesson."

One Step Further: Adding Employee Names to the Expense Statement Template

You might have noticed the Select Employee button in the Employee information area of the Expense Statement template. You can modify the list that appears when you click the Select Employee button so that the Island Tea & Coffee Company employee information appears instead of sample information. Then, each employee can click his or her own name in the list and all the information is automatically filled in.

 IMPORTANT Be sure that no templates or copies of templates are open when you start this exercise.

1   On the File menu, click Open, locate the Microsoft Office folder, double-click the Excel folder, double-click the Library folder, and then double-click the Common file.

2   In the Common file, click the Employee Info sheet tab.

    The Employee Info worksheet contains employee information provided as an example by Microsoft Excel.

3   Delete the sample data and add the following records to the Employee Info worksheet:

	Paul Garnier	**Mark Davis**
SSN	222-22-2222	333-33-3333
Emp #	5	6
Position	Shipping	Clerical
Region	US	US
Department	Warehouse	Management
Manager	Barbara Lang	Barbara Lang

4   Save and close the Common file.

5   Open a copy of the ITC Expenses template.

6   On the Expense Statement worksheet, click the Select Employee button.

    The Select An Employee dialog box appears, with the names you added to the Common file.

7   Select Mark Davis, and then click OK.

    All of Mark Davis' employee information is entered in the expense statement automatically.

Finish the lesson

1   To continue to the next lesson, on the File menu, click Close (do not save the workbook).

2   If you are finished using Microsoft Excel for now, on the File menu, click Exit.

Lesson Summary

To	Do this
Open a group of files	In the Open dialog box, hold down CTRL and click multiple files. Click Open.

To	Do this
Arrange multiple windows	On the Window menu, click Arrange, select a type of arrangement, and then click OK.
Copy a sheet between workbooks	Hold down CTRL and drag a sheet tab from one workbook to another.
Consolidate lists into a single list	On the Data menu, click Consolidate. Click in the Reference box, select a worksheet containing a list, select the list by dragging, and then click Add. Repeat these steps for each list you want to include in the consolidation. Select the Use Labels In Top Row and Left Column check boxes, and then click OK.
Create a conditional number format	Select the cells to be formatted, and then, on the Format menu, click Conditional Formatting. Select cell value conditions, select the desired formatting, and then click OK.
Customize a built-in template	On the File menu, click New. In the New dialog box, click the Spreadsheet Solutions tab, and then double-click the template you want. Click the Customize sheet, customize the template, click the Lock/Save Sheet button, and then save the template in the Spreadsheet Solutions folder.
Open a database created using the Template Wizard	On the File menu, click Open. Locate the Library folder (in the Excel folder in the Microsoft Office folder), and then double-click the database that is linked to your template.

For online information about	On the Help menu, click Contents And Index, click the Index tab, and then type
Arranging multiple windows	**arranging windows**
Moving and copying sheets	**moving sheets in workbook** *or* **copying, sheets**
Consolidating data	**consolidating data**
Using templates and databases	**templates**

Filtering to Find Specific Information

Estimated time
30 min.

In this lesson you will learn how to:

- Filter a list to find specific information.
- Find totals and averages quickly using AutoCalculate.
- Calculate sets of filtered records using the SUBTOTAL function.

As the office manager for the Island Tea & Coffee Company, one of your responsibilities is to keep the inventory updated. For that reason, your co-workers often call you when they want to know what's in stock. You can easily answer their questions by using a few simple filtering techniques on your inventory list. Filtering allows you to quickly find and bring up information matching the criteria you set.

Your list is composed of records, or rows, and fields, or columns. All of the records in a list have the same information fields (for example, each record has a Product Name field, a Source Country field, a Warehouse Location field, and so on). Each field in a list provides a specific type of information (for example, the Source Country field contains the source country information for each record).

When you filter a list, you define conditions known as *criteria* that are shared by the subset of records you want to locate. For example, all of the records for products that come from Mexico share the criterion Source Country = Mexico, and all of the records for products that have a per pound price less than $10 share the criterion Price $/lb < 10. You can also filter your list using multiple criteria, such as all products from Mexico with prices less than $10 per pound.

Open an existing file

You have been asked to find out if some specific items are in stock. In order to perform the most accurate search possible, you need to open the current inventory list. In this exercise, you open the most up-to-date inventory file.

Open

1 On the Standard toolbar, click the Open button.

2 In the Open dialog box, click the Look In Favorites button.

3 In the file list, double-click the Excel SBS Practice folder.

4 Double-click the Lesson 6 Inventory file.

> ### If you have Microsoft Outlook, you can open the file this way
>
> If you have Microsoft Outlook, you can open Microsoft Excel and the Lesson 6 Inventory file by using the following procedure.
>
> **1** In the Microsoft Outlook Open dialog box, in the Folders list, click the Other Folders button.
>
> **2** In the Other Folders list, click the Favorites icon.
>
> **3** In the Favorites list, double-click the Excel SBS Practice folder.
>
> **4** Double-click the Lesson 6 Inventory file.

Filtering to Display a Set of Related Records

Filtering allows you to display only the records that share specific *criteria*, or field values. With Microsoft Excel, the easiest way to filter records in a list is to use AutoFilter. When you turn on AutoFilter, *filter arrows*, which look like down arrows, will appear next to the column headings in your list. You click an arrow to display a list of the values in that field, and then select a value to use as a criterion or condition for filtering the list. After you have selected a criterion, the filter arrow for that field and the row numbers for the filtered records appear in blue to provide a quick reminder of which field you filtered on.

Find a subset of items quickly using an AutoFilter

One of your co-workers needs to find out if the Island Tea & Coffee Company offers any coffees from Mexico. In this exercise, you filter the inventory list to locate coffees imported from Mexico, and then you remove the filter.

1 Select cell C7.

You could select any cell in your list. Microsoft Excel will then select the entire contiguous range of cells.

2   On the Data menu, point to Filter, and then click AutoFilter.

Filter arrows appear next to your column headers.

Filter arrows

	A	B	C	D	E	F	
1	Product Name	Category	Source Country	Cost $/l	Price $/l	Qty In Stock	War
2	Antigua	Coffee	Guatemala	5.25	10.50	500	
3	Blue Mountain	Coffee	Jamaica	28.00	36.00	400	
4	Bourbon Santos	Coffee	Brazil	4.75	9.50	200	
5	Celebes	Coffee	Indonesia	4.75	9.50	800	
6	Chanchamayo	Coffee	Peru	5.25	10.50	600	
7	Coatepec	Coffee	Mexico	5.25	10.50	900	
8	Coban	Coffee	Guatemala	4.75	9.50	800	
9	Costa Rica	Coffee	Costa Rica	5.25	10.50	1000	
10	Ecuador	Coffee	Ecuador	5.25	10.50	500	
11	Haiti	Coffee	Haiti	4.75	9.50	400	

3   Click the Source Country filter arrow column heading (in cell C1).

An alphabetical list of all the source countries appears.

	A	B	C	D	E	F	
1	Product Name	Category	Source Country	Cost $/l	Price $/l	Qty In Stock	War
2	Antigua	Coffee	(All)	5.25	10.50	500	
3	Blue Mountain	Coffee	(Top 10...)	28.00	36.00	400	
4	Bourbon Santos	Coffee	(Custom...) Brazil	4.75	9.50	200	
5	Celebes	Coffee	China	4.75	9.50	800	
6	Chanchamayo	Coffee	Columbia	5.25	10.50	600	
7	Coatepec	Coffee	Costa Rica Dominican Republic	5.25	10.50	900	
8	Coban	Coffee	Ecuador	4.75	9.50	800	
9	Costa Rica	Coffee	Ethiopia	5.25	10.50	1000	
10	Ecuador	Coffee	Guatemala Haiti	5.25	10.50	500	
11	Haiti	Coffee	Hawaii	4.75	9.50	400	
12	Harrar	Coffee	India	4.95	9.90	800	
13	India	Coffee	Indonesia Jamaica	4.75	9.50	700	
14	Java	Coffee	Japan	5.25	10.50	800	
15	Kenya	Coffee	Kenya	5.40	10.80	900	
16	Kona	Coffee	Mexico Peru	5.25	10.50	1000	
17	Medellin	Coffee	Columbia	4.75	9.50	1100	

You can copy and paste the filtered records into another worksheet for further reference or manipulation, or into an e-mail message to your co-worker.

4   Click Mexico.

All the records for products from Mexico remain in view, and all other records are hidden.

5   To remove the filter, click the Source Country filter arrow (in cell C1), and then scroll to the top of the list and click All.

The filter is removed and all the records are displayed.

You can remove filtering from a list either by removing the specific criterion that you set, or by turning off the AutoFilter.

Find the seven lowest-priced coffees

One of the sales representatives of the Island Tea & Coffee Company wants to know what the seven lowest-priced coffees are, and what quantities of each are available. In this exercise, you filter your inventory list to find the seven lowest-priced coffees.

AutoFilter's Top 10 feature only works in numeric fields.

1 Click the Category filter arrow (in cell B1), and then click Coffee.

All the teas are hidden and only the coffees appear.

2 Click the Price $/lb filter arrow (in cell E1), and then click Top 10.

The Top 10 AutoFilter dialog box appears.

3 In the leftmost list box, select Bottom.

4 In the center list box, select 7, and then click OK.

The seven lowest-priced coffees are filtered. In fact, the filtered list contains nine entries because the nine lowest-priced coffees have the same price.

5 Click the Price $/lb filter arrow, and then click All.

6 Click the Category filter arrow, and then click All.

The filter is removed and all the records are displayed.

Filter data using multiple criteria with a custom AutoFilter

One of your co-workers in the Marketing department is creating a new ad campaign, and he wants to know which products are priced between $10 and $15 per pound. In this exercise, you create and then use a custom filter to quickly bring up the list requested by your colleague.

1 Click the Price $/lb filter arrow (in cell E1), and then click Custom.

The Custom AutoFilter dialog box appears.

2 In the upper-left list box, click Is Greater Than.

3 In the upper-right list box, type **10**

4 Be sure that the And option button is selected.

5 In the lower-left list box, click Is Less Than.

6 In the lower-right list box, type **15**

The dialog box should look similar to the following illustration.

7 Click OK.

Products with prices higher than $10 per lb but lower than $15 per lb are in view, and all other products (those with prices $10/lb or less and those with prices $15/lb or more) are hidden.

Calculating Filtered Sets of Records

After you have filtered the records you need, you might want to manipulate them further. For example, you might have several fields in a list that need to be summed or averaged, and you might need to perform the same calculations on several different filtered subsets of records; or, you might want to average both price and cost for products from different countries. There are specific functions, such as SUBTOTAL, that are very useful when trying to calculate filtered data quickly.

In the following exercises, you will also learn about AutoCalculate, a Microsoft Excel feature that performs calculations without written formulas.

Calculate a total using AutoCalculate

Your list is currently filtered to show the records for products priced between $10 and $15 per pound. Your colleague in Marketing also wants to know what the average price is. In this exercise, you find out what the average price of the coffees in the $10 to $15 range is.

1 Select cells E2 through E38, and then look at the AutoCalculate box on the status bar.

	A	B	C	D	E	F	
9	Costa Rica	Coffee	Costa Rica	5.25	10.50	1000	
10	Ecuador	Coffee	Ecuador	5.25	10.50	500	
14	Java	Coffee	Indonesia	5.25	10.50	800	
15	Kenya	Coffee	Kenya	5.40	10.80	900	
16	Kona	Coffee	Hawaii	5.25	10.50	1000	
18	Merida	Coffee	Venezuela	5.25	10.50	700	
19	Mocha	Coffee	Yemen	5.75	11.50	800	
21	Pluma	Coffee	Mexico	5.25	10.50	400	
23	Sumatra	Coffee	Indonesia	5.75	11.50	600	
26	Black Lychee	Tea	China	5.25	10.50	250	
27	Ceylon	Tea	Sri Lanka	5.85	11.70	600	
31	Lapsang Souchong	Tea	China	5.05	10.10	250	
32	Oolong	Tea	Taiwan	10.00	14.40	150	
35	Dragonwell	Tea	China	5.35	10.70	500	
37	Gyokuru	Tea	Japan	5.60	11.20	150	
38	Pi Lo Chun	Tea	China	5.55	11.10	500	
39							

Inventory 1-15-97

19 of 37 records found   Sum=208.00   NUM

AutoCalculate box

Your AutoCalculate box might look different from the illustration if a different function was previously selected.

2 Use the right mouse button to click the AutoCalculate box, and then click Average.

The selected cells are averaged. Only the visible records (those not hidden by the filter) are averaged, and the hidden records are ignored.

Calculate filtered sets of records using the SUBTOTAL function

In preparation for an upcoming sales meeting, your manager asks you to compare the average costs and average prices of products from each different country. In this exercise, you filter your inventory to first locate the country of origin for each product, and then average their prices using the SUBTOTAL function.

1 Click the Price $/lb filter arrow (in cell E1), and then click All.

The previous filter is removed.

2 Click the Source Country filter arrow (in cell C1), and then click China.

Your list only shows products from China.

	A	B	C	D	E	F	
1	Product Name ▾	Categoi ▾	Source Country ▾	Cost $/l ▾	Price $/l ▾	Qty In Stocl ▾	Wai
26	Black Lychee	Tea	China	5.25	10.50	250	
29	Jasmine	Tea	China	4.90	9.80	500	
30	Keemun	Tea	China	4.85	9.70	600	
31	Lapsang Souchong	Tea	China	5.05	10.10	250	
34	Chunmee	Tea	China	4.85	9.70	100	
35	Dragonwell	Tea	China	5.35	10.70	500	
36	Gunpowder	Tea	China	4.50	9.00	400	
38	Pi Lo Chun	Tea	China	5.55	11.10	500	
39							

3 Select cell D41.

4 On the Standard toolbar, click the AutoSum button, and then press ENTER.

AutoSum

The SUBTOTAL formula for a sum is entered. If a range is filtered, the AutoSum button enters a SUBTOTAL formula; if the range is not filtered, the AutoSum button enters a SUM formula.

5 Double-click the cell containing the formula.

The formula is ready for editing.

6 Select the first argument in the parentheses to the left of the first comma: the number 9 in this case.

Arguments provide the information that tells the function what data to calculate and what operations to perform. Arguments are contained within parentheses and separated by commas. The first argument in the SUBTOTAL function indicates which function should be used in the sub-total calculation. A "9" represents the SUM function, but you want to use the AVERAGE function, which is represented by a "1." Your formula should look similar to the following illustration.

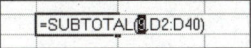

```
=SUBTOTAL( D2:D40)
```

7 Type **1**, and then press ENTER.

Your SUBTOTAL formula calculates an average of the filtered cells in the Country Source field.

> **NOTE** For your easy reference, the SUBTOTAL function arguments are as follows: 1=AVERAGE, 2=COUNT, 3=COUNTA, 4=MAX, 5=MIN, 6=PRODUCT, 7=STDEV, 8=STDEVP, 9=SUM, 10=VAR, and 11=VARP. To learn more about these functions, you can ask the Office Assistant for help.

8 Select cell D41, and then drag its fill handle to cell E41.

The SUBTOTAL formula is copied to cell E41.

9 Change the filter criterion to India.

The average cost and price of products imported from India appear.

	A	B	C	D	E	F	
1	Product Name	Category	Source Country	Cost $/l	Price $/l	Qty In Stock	Wai
13	India	Coffee	India	4.75	9.50	700	
25	Assam	Tea	India	4.85	9.70	550	
28	Darjeeling	Tea	India	10.15	20.30	550	
39							
40							
41				6.5833333	13.166667		
42							

10 On the Data menu, point to Filter, then click AutoFilter.

The AutoFilter is removed.

11 On the File menu, click Save.

> **NOTE** If you'd like to build on the skills you learned in this lesson, you can do the One Step Further. Otherwise, skip to "Finish the Lesson."

One Step Further: Summing Up a Set of Records Without Filtering

You can use the SUMIF function to calculate a sum of values for specific records. The SUMIF function sums cells that meet conditions you specify, without having to filter the list first.

Your manager wants to quickly find out the total quantity of tea that is in stock. In this exercise, you write a SUMIF formula to rapidly produce the answer.

Calculate the quantity of tea in stock

1 Select cell I2, and then click the equal sign in the formula bar.

The Formula palette appears, and the Name Box becomes a Formula list.

2 Click the Formula list down arrow, and then click SUMIF.

The Formula palette expands to help you write your SUMIF formula. You might need to drag it out of your way when you select cells on the worksheet.

3 Click in the Range box, and then click the column B header to select the entire column.

"B:B" appears in the Range box.

4 In the Criteria box, type **"tea"** (be sure you include the quotation marks).

5 Click in the Sum_Range box, and then click the column F header to select the entire column.

6 Click OK.

The sum of pounds of tea in stock, 5700, appears in cell I2.

7 Save your work.

Finish the lesson

1 To continue to the next lesson, on the File menu, click Close.

2 If you are finished using Microsoft Excel for now, on the File menu, click Exit.

Lesson Summary

To	Do this
Turn AutoFilter on and off	Select a cell in the table that you want to filter. On the Data menu, point to Filter, then click AutoFilter.
Select filter criteria	Use the filter arrows to select filtering criteria.
Remove a filter criterion	In the column header, click the filter arrow for the criterion you want to remove, and then click All.
Filter the ten highest or lowest values	In the column header, click Top 10, and then in the Top 10 AutoFilter dialog box, select Top or Bottom.
Filter using multiple criteria	Click any filter arrow, and then click Custom.
Select an AutoCalculate function	Use the right mouse button to click the AutoCalculate box, and then click the function you want.
Calculate filtered records using the SUBTOTAL function	Turn on AutoFilter, and then select a cell at least one row beneath the last cell in the field you want to calculate. On the Standard toolbar, click the AutoSum button, and then edit the first argument as appropriate.

For online information about	On the Help menu, click Contents And Index, click the Index tab, and then type
Using AutoFilter	**autofilter**
Filtering records	**filters, overview** *or* **filters, in lists**
The SUBTOTAL function	**subtotal worksheet function**

Sorting and Subtotaling to Organize Your Data

Estimated time
30 min.

In this lesson you will learn how to:

■ Sort a list by several categories.

■ Subtotal an entire list of data at one time.

■ Use a subtotal outline to show only the level of detail you want.

As the office manager for the Island Tea & Coffee Company, one of your responsibilities is to present the current inventory to the management team for analysis. Management wants the data they see to be summarized in a logical way. For example, you might need to sort the inventory so that products are arranged by category, and then by source country within each category, and then by value within each source country. To make the inventory more useful to management, you need to add subtotals to the Cost, Price, and Value fields so that they can evaluate and compare meaningful data rather than details.

In this lesson, you'll learn how to quickly sort a list of data, add subtotals to the list, and modify worksheet outlines to summarize the details the way you want.

Open an existing file

One of your monthly tasks is to summarize the current inventory before it's presented to management. In this exercise, you open the current inventory file.

Open

1   On the Standard toolbar, click the Open button.

2 In the Open dialog box, click the Look In Favorites button.

3 In the file list, double-click the Excel SBS Practice folder.

4 Double-click the Lesson 7 Inventory file.

Save the file with a new name

1 On the File menu, click Save As.

The Save As dialog box opens. Be sure the Excel SBS Practice folder appears in the Save In box.

2 In the File Name box, type **Subtotaled Inventory**, and then click Save.

Sorting a List of Information

Before you can subtotal the details in your inventory, you have to sort the details into logical groups because the subtotaling only works with sorted data. You begin by selecting a cell within the list that you want to sort, and then use column labels to define how you want to sort your data. You can sort your inventory by any column in the list. The column that you sort by is called a *sort key*; you can sort by more than one key.

Management wants your final inventory report to show summaries of stock value by category (coffee or tea) and by country within each category. Furthermore, they want to see the value of stock on hand sorted from highest to lowest within each summary group. With the requirements for this final report in mind, you'll begin by sorting the data into groups.

Sort the inventory list

In this exercise, you sort your inventory list by category, then by country, and finally by value so that all of the coffees will be grouped together, followed by all of the teas.

1 Select any cell within the inventory list.

2 On the Data menu, click Sort.

3   Click the Sort By down arrow, and then click Category.

Your data will be sorted by Category, and the categories will be listed in alphabetical order.

4   Click the first Then By down arrow, and then click Source Country.

5   Click the second Then By down arrow, and click Value; then, click the Descending option button next to the second Then By box, and finally click OK.

Your worksheet should look similar to the following illustration.

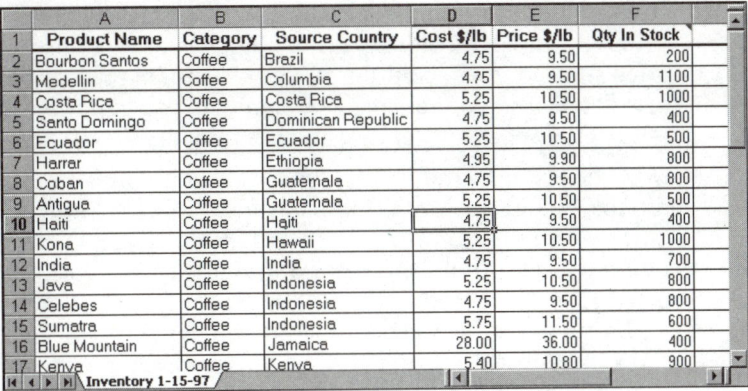

	A	B	C	D	E	F
1	Product Name	Category	Source Country	Cost $/lb	Price $/lb	Qty In Stock
2	Bourbon Santos	Coffee	Brazil	4.75	9.50	200
3	Medellin	Coffee	Columbia	4.75	9.50	1100
4	Costa Rica	Coffee	Costa Rica	5.25	10.50	1000
5	Santo Domingo	Coffee	Dominican Republic	4.75	9.50	400
6	Ecuador	Coffee	Ecuador	5.25	10.50	500
7	Harrar	Coffee	Ethiopia	4.95	9.90	800
8	Coban	Coffee	Guatemala	4.75	9.50	800
9	Antigua	Coffee	Guatemala	5.25	10.50	500
10	Haiti	Coffee	Haiti	4.75	9.50	400
11	Kona	Coffee	Hawaii	5.25	10.50	1000
12	India	Coffee	India	4.75	9.50	700
13	Java	Coffee	Indonesia	5.25	10.50	800
14	Celebes	Coffee	Indonesia	4.75	9.50	800
15	Sumatra	Coffee	Indonesia	5.75	11.50	600
16	Blue Mountain	Coffee	Jamaica	28.00	36.00	400
17	Kenya	Coffee	Kenya	5.40	10.80	900

Inventory 1-15-97

Sorting on more than three keys

You may occasionally have a more complex list of data that you need to sort on more than three keys. For example, you might have an extensive company personnel list that you need to sort by division, then by department within each division, then by position within each department, and then by last name within each position. The Sort dialog box makes it easy to sort on up to three keys, but in order to sort on four keys, you will need to run the Sort command twice.

The trick to sorting on four keys is the order in which you run the sorts. The major sort key (which in this personnel list example would be the division) should be run in the second sort procedure; you sort the minor keys (by department, then by position, then by last name) first, and then you sort a second time by division only.

Summarizing Data with Subtotals

In Lesson 5, you summarized details by using the Consolidate command, which allowed you to consolidate detailed data from multiple lists but created a summary that contained no details. In this lesson, you will learn to summarize details by using the Subtotal command, which will summarize only a single list but will create a summary that includes details that you can show or hide.

When you want to summarize a list that has multiple columns (or fields) of text entries, such as the Island Tea & Coffee Company inventory, subtotaling is better than consolidation. Subtotaling will include all of the text fields and can create subtotals for groups within each text field; for example, you can create subtotals for each category and for each source country. In addition, the subtotaled summary will contain all of the detailed data as well as allow you to show any details that you choose. For example, you can show the details for all the teas but not the coffees, or for the products from China but not from other countries.

Now that your Island Tea & Coffee Company inventory list has been sorted into groups, you can subtotal those groups so that the management team can quickly find the summary information it needs. You can use the Subtotal command to add subtotals to the groups you choose, without having to manually insert rows for the subtotals or write formulas. The Subtotal command also adds outlining to your worksheet so that you can easily decide how much detail to show in your inventory report.

Calculate subtotals in a detailed list

Now that your inventory list has been sorted in preparation for subtotaling, you can organize the presentation of the information it contains. In this exercise, you create subtotals that sum the value of stock on hand for each source country.

1 Select any cell within the inventory list.

2 On the Data menu, click Subtotals.

   The Subtotal dialog box appears.

3 Click the At Each Change In down arrow, and then click Source Country.

4 Click the Use Function down arrow, and then click Sum.

5 In the Add Subtotal To box, select the Value check box, and then scroll through the list to be sure that all the other check boxes are cleared.

6 Be sure that the Replace Current Subtotals and Summary Below Data check boxes are selected.

   Your dialog box should look similar to the following illustration.

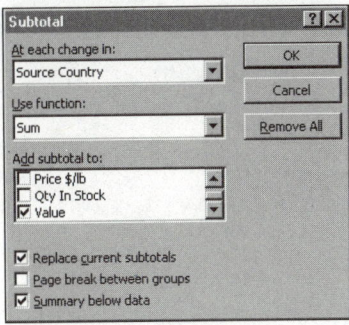

7 Click OK.

Subtotals are added to your worksheet in the Value field, and captions are added to the Source Country field. Your worksheet should look similar to the following illustration.

		A	B	C	D	E	F
	1	**Product Name**	**Category**	**Source Country**	**Cost $/lb**	**Price $/lb**	**Qty In Stock**
	2	Bourbon Santos	Coffee	Brazil	4.75	9.50	20
	3			**Brazil Total**			
	4	Medellin	Coffee	Columbia	4.75	9.50	110
	5			**Columbia Total**			
	6	Costa Rica	Coffee	Costa Rica	5.25	10.50	100
	7			**Costa Rica Total**			
	8	Santo Domingo	Coffee	Dominican Republic	4.75	9.50	40
	9			**Dominican Republic Total**			
	10	Ecuador	Coffee	Ecuador	5.25	10.50	50
	11			**Ecuador Total**			
	12	Harrar	Coffee	Ethiopia	4.95	9.90	80
	13			**Ethiopia Total**			
	14	Coban	Coffee	Guatemala	4.75	9.50	80
	15	Antigua	Coffee	Guatemala	5.25	10.50	50
	16			**Guatemala Total**			
	17	Haiti	Coffee	Haiti	4.75	9.50	40

Inventory 1-15-97

Add a second level of subtotals

Management wants to see a summary of stock value by product as well as by country, so you need to create a second level of subtotals. The trick to creating multiple levels of subtotals is to create them in the proper order. In this case, you want the smaller subtotals (by Source Country) to be nested in the larger subtotals (by Category). To do this, you need to create the larger subtotals first, and then the nested subtotals. In this exercise, you first remove the subtotals you created in the previous exercise, and then create subtotals for each category, and then for each source country within each category.

1 On the Data menu, click Subtotals.

2 In the Subtotal dialog box, click Remove All.

The subtotals and outlining are removed.

3 On the Data menu, click Subtotals.

113

4 Click the At Each Change In down arrow, and then click Category.

5 Be sure that the Use Function box contains Sum and that the Value check box is the only check box selected under Add Subtotal To, and then click OK.

The Category field is subtotaled. Subtotals have been added for the Coffee and Tea categories, and a Grand Total field has been added to the bottom of the list.

6 On the Data menu, click Subtotals.

7 Click the At Each Change In down arrow, and then click Source Country.

8 Be sure that the Use Function box contains Sum, and that the Value check box is the only check box selected under Add Subtotal To.

9 Clear the Replace Current Subtotals check box, and then click OK.

Subtotals for the Category and Source Country groups are calculated and displayed on your worksheet in the Value field, and captions are added to the Source Country field. Grand totals have been added at the bottom of the list. Your worksheet should look similar to the following illustration.

	Product Name	Category	Source Country	Cost $/lb	Price $/lb	Qty In Sto
1						
2	Bourbon Santos	Coffee	Brazil	4.75	9.50	
3			Brazil Total			
4	Medellin	Coffee	Columbia	4.75	9.50	1
5			Columbia Total			
6	Costa Rica	Coffee	Costa Rica	5.25	10.50	1
7			Costa Rica Total			
8	Santo Domingo	Coffee	Dominican Republic	4.75	9.50	
9			Dominican Republic Total			
10	Ecuador	Coffee	Ecuador	5.25	10.50	
11			Ecuador Total			
12	Harrar	Coffee	Ethiopia	4.95	9.90	
13			Ethiopia Total			
14	Coban	Coffee	Guatemala	4.75	9.50	
15	Antigua	Coffee	Guatemala	5.25	10.50	
16			Guatemala Total			
17	Haiti	Coffee	Haiti	4.75	9.50	

Inventory 1-15-97

Show and hide levels of detail to display only the information you want

One of the advantages of using the Subtotal command is that it allows you to manipulate the level of detail showing in the summary by clicking the outline buttons that appear next to your worksheet.

The new column that appeared to the left of your worksheet contains the outline buttons that you can use to hide and show details. The outline level buttons across the top of the new column (the buttons that are numbered) allow you to show a specific level of summary details—for example, the Level 1 button changes the worksheet display so that only the grand total level is shown and all other details and subtotals are hidden. The buttons next to each subtotal row allow you to hide and show the details for each specific subtotal. By clicking the outline buttons, you can show only the details that you want; for example, you can show subtotals for each country, but show the details only for Guatemala.

Outline level buttons

	A	B	C	D	E
	Product Name	Category	Source Country	Cost $/lb	Price $/l
2	Bourbon Santos	Coffee	Brazil	4.75	9.5
3			Brazil Total		
4	Medellin	Coffee	Columbia	4.75	9.5
5			Columbia Total		
6	Costa Rica	Coffee	Costa Rica	5.25	10.5

Hide Detail button

The Island Tea & Coffee Company management team only wants to see summary-type information, so you can take advantage of the Microsoft Excel outlining feature to quickly hide or show different levels of detail. In this exercise, you practice hiding and showing details, and then set up the final detail for your inventory report.

1 Click the Level 2 outline button.

Your worksheet changes to show only the sum of stock value for each product category. Each category summary row has a Show Detail button to its left.

	A	B	C	D	E
1	Product Name	Category	Source Country	Cost $/lb	Price $/l
43		Coffee Total			
64		Tea Total			
65			Grand Total		
66		Grand Total			
67					

Show Detail button

2 Click the Show Detail button for Tea Total.

Show Detail

The outline expands to show the totals for each source country in the Tea category.

	A	B	C	D	E
1	Product Name	Category	Source Country	Cost $/lb	Price $/l
43		Coffee Total			
44	Keemun	Tea	China	4.85	9.7
45	Pi Lo Chun	Tea	China	5.55	11.1
46	Dragonwell	Tea	China	5.35	10.7
47	Jasmine	Tea	China	4.90	9.8
48	Gunpowder	Tea	China	4.50	9.0
49	Black Lychee	Tea	China	5.25	10.5
50	Lapsang Souchong	Tea	China	5.05	10.1
51	Chunmee	Tea	China	4.85	9.7
52			China Total		
53	Darjeeling	Tea	India	10.15	20.3
54	Assam	Tea	India	4.85	9.7
55			India Total		
56	Gyokuru	Tea	Japan	5.60	11.2
57			Japan Total		
58	Russian Blend	Tea	Republic of Georgia	4.90	9.6

Inventory 1-15-97

3   Click the Level 3 outline button.

The worksheet shows both Category and Source Country totals. This is the level of detail you will include in your inventory report to management. Your worksheet should look similar to the following illustration.

1 2 3 4		B	C	D	E	F	G
+	30		Kenya Total				9720.00
+	34		Mexico Total				20300.00
+	36		Peru Total				6300.00
+	38		Tanzania Total				9500.00
+	40		Venezuela Total				7350.00
+	42		Yemen Total				9200.00
–	43	Coffee Total					173290.00
+	52		China Total				31340.00
+	55		India Total				16500.00
+	57		Japan Total				1680.00
+	59		Republic of Georgia Total				5880.00
+	61		Sri Lanka Total				7020.00
+	63		Taiwan Total				2160.00
–	64	Tea Total					64580.00
–	65		Grand Total				237870.00
	66	Grand Total					237870.00
	67						

Inventory 1-15-97

4   On the File menu, click Save.

If you want to apply outlining without using automatic subtotals

If you have data that already contains manual subtotals or that you don't want to apply subtotals to, you can still apply outlining. First, you need to determine which rows or columns should be grouped so that they can be hidden and shown together.

1   Select the rows or columns that you want to combine into one outline detail group. Do not include subtotals in the group, or they will be hidden when you hide the group details.

2   On the Data menu, point to Group And Outline, and then click Group.

The group is outlined and a Hide Detail symbol appears at the left side of the worksheet. To hide the group of details, click the Hide Detail symbol.

3   Repeat steps 1 and 2 for each group you want to outline.

4   To remove the outlining, select all the rows or columns in the group, and, on the Data menu, point to Group And Outline, and then click Ungroup.

Hide Detail

Lesson 7: Sorting and Subtotaling to Organize Your Data

NOTE If you'd like to build on the skills you learned in this lesson, you can do the One Step Further. Otherwise, skip to "Finish the Lesson."

One Step Further: Pasting a Subtotaled Summary into a Microsoft Word Document

In order to facilitate the review of the information from the inventory list, you decide to paste it in the inventory report, which is a Microsoft Word document. This way, the management team will be able to open the Microsoft Word document and read the report without having to use Microsoft Excel.

IMPORTANT In order to perform the following exercise, you'll need to have Microsoft Word 97 installed on your computer.

1 Start Microsoft Word, and then open the Inventory Report file, located in the Excel SBS Practice folder.

You can switch between programs by clicking the buttons on the taskbar at the bottom of your screen.

2 Switch to Microsoft Excel, and on the inventory worksheet, select the range B1 through G66 (this range includes all the data contained in the Category through Value fields).

3 On the Edit menu, choose Copy.

4 Switch to Microsoft Word, and be sure that the insertion point is at the end of the document.

5 On the Edit menu, click Paste.

A picture of the selected range from the Subtotaled Inventory workbook is pasted into the Inventory Report document.

6 On the File menu, click Save.

7 Close Microsoft Word.

Finish the lesson

1 To continue to the Review & Practice, on the File menu, click Close.

2 If you are finished using Microsoft Excel for now, on the File menu, click Exit.

117

Lesson Summary

To	Do this
Sort data by up to three keys	Select a cell within the list you want to sort, and then, on the Data menu, click Sort. In the Sort By and Then By boxes, select the fields you want to sort by, and then click OK.
Sort data by more than three keys	Sort first by the keys you want to be nested, and then sort again by the major key.
Add subtotals	Select a cell within the list you want to subtotal, and then, on the Data menu, click Subtotals. In the At Each Change In box, select the field you want to create subtotals for. In the Use Function box, select the type of calculation you want the subtotal to perform. In the Add Subtotal To box, select the fields that you want calculated, and then click OK.
Remove subtotals	On the Data menu, click Subtotals. Click Remove All.
Create a second level of subtotals	Create the major level of subtotals first, and then create the second level of subtotals using the same procedure, but clear the Replace Current Subtotals check box before running the second level of subtotals.
Hide details in an outline	Click a Hide Detail button or a low number outline button.
Show details in an outline	Click a Show Detail button or a high number outline button.

For online information about	On the Help menu, click Contents And Index, click the Index tab, and then type
Sorting data	sorting, lists
Subtotaling data	subtotals, automatic *or* automatically, calculating subtotals

Part
2

Review & Practice

Estimated time
20 min.

You will review and practice how to:

- Consolidate lists.
- Filter and sort a detail list.
- Subtotal a list and define the level of detail to present.

Before you move on to Part 3, which covers PivotTables, charting, and printing, you can practice the skills you learned in Part 2 by working through the steps in this Review & Practice section. You will practice consolidating, filtering, sorting, and subtotaling expenses lists.

Scenario

You have been asked to organize the lists of business-related expenses that are kept by the permanent and volunteer staff of the State University Alumni Association for tax purposes. Four lists have already been copied into a single workbook. You will create two summaries, which will each have a different purpose: one will be a consolidated list for a quick reference to item totals, and the other will be a subtotaled list containing specific details that can be used to track down over-expenditures. You will also filter the detailed list to take a look at specific information.

Step 1:   Consolidate expenses lists

A co-worker has previously copied four expenses lists into a file named SUAA
Expenses. The expenses lists are on the worksheets named Katz, Loren, Tanner, and Edmund (the employees' names). In this step, you will consolidate the
multiple expenses lists into one.

1   Locate and open the practice file named R&P 2, and then save it as
SUAA Expenses

2   Select the Sheet1 worksheet and use the Consolidate command to consolidate the lists on the Katz, Loren, Tanner, and Edmund worksheets.
(Hint: Because the Consolidate command looks for text labels in the leftmost column, consolidate only columns B through E in each list.)

3   Adjust the column widths in the consolidated table so that the entries are
easy to read, and then save the workbook.

Your consolidated summary should look similar to the following
illustration.

	A	B	C	D	E	F	G	H
1		Vendor	Purpose	Amount				
2	Office Supplies			$13.70				
3	Tax preparation			$59.46				
4	Telephone Charges			$203.73				
5	Office Equipment			$568.60				
6	Travel			$47.20				
7	Legal and Professional Services			$91.60				
8	Books/Publications			$322.19				
9								
10								

For more information about	See
Consolidating lists	Lesson 5

Step 2:   Filter the detail list

In this step, you will filter the worksheet named Big List because one of your co-
workers needs to quickly find out what the total books and publications expenses are to include that information in a presentation he is giving.

1   Select the Big List worksheet.

2   Turn on the AutoFilter.

3   In the Category field, select the Books/Publications criterion.

4 Select the cells in the Amount field, and then look at the AutoCalculate sum (Hint: Be sure that AutoCalculate is set to the SUM function).

Your AutoCalculate sum should be 322.19.

5 Turn off the AutoFilter.

For more information about	See
Filtering data	Lesson 6

Step 3: Sort and subtotal the detail list by tax categories

In this step, you will sort and subtotal the Big List worksheet list so that it is ready for the association's accountant.

1 In the Big List worksheet, select a cell within the list, and sort the list first by Category, then by Vendor, and finally by Date.

2 Subtotal the list by Category only.

3 Show the second-level details. (Hint: Only the Category subtotals and Grand Total should show.)

Your finished worksheet should look similar to the following illustration.

		A	B	C	D	E	F
	1	Date	Category	Vendor	Purpose	Amount	
	10		Books/Publications Total			$322.19	
	12		Legal and Professional Services Total			$91.60	
	20		Office Equipment Total			$568.60	
	26		Office Supplies Total			$13.70	
	28		Tax preparation Total			$59.46	
	40		Telephone Charges Total			$203.73	
	45		Travel Total			$47.20	
	46		Grand Total			$1,306.48	
	47						

For more information about	See
Sorting data	Lesson 7
Subtotaling data	Lesson 7

Finish the Review & Practice

1 To continue to the next lesson, on the File menu, click Close.

2 If you are finished using Microsoft Excel for now, on the File menu, click Exit.

Presenting Your Data to Others

Creating PivotTables to Summarize Data

Estimated time
30 min.

In this lesson you will learn how to:

- Import a text file.
- Create a PivotTable.
- Modify a PivotTable.
- Update a PivotTable.

In Part 2, you learned how to summarize data by using consolidation and sub-totaling, and you saw the strengths and weaknesses of each method. In this lesson you will learn how to create and use PivotTables as a data presentation tool. A *PivotTable* combines the best of consolidation and subtotals, and goes well beyond both of those tools to give you greater flexibility of presentation. When you create a PivotTable, you can organize data stored in multiple worksheets or workbooks as well as show or hide any details you want. Additionally, you can modify the PivotTable presentation by changing the layout or the level of detail shown without having to recreate the PivotTable—you can change the presentation "on the fly" by simply dragging items to new locations on your worksheet.

At the Island Tea & Coffee Company, your manager has requested a summary of last year's sales data. She wants the data summarized in three ways: monthly sales totals by each employee, for a comparison of monthly performances over the past year; quarterly sales totals in each product category, coffee or tea, for each individual employee; and average quarterly sales of each product.

You can create all of these summaries by creating a single PivotTable, and then manipulating it to show what you want.

The sales data for 1996 was assembled by another employee using his laptop computer; to keep the size of the database to a minimum, he entered the data in a text file. A text file is the simplest type of data file and can be opened by most programs, including Microsoft Excel. You will begin the task of creating the 1996 sales presentation by importing the data from the text file into a workbook.

Open a new workbook

If you have just started Microsoft Excel, you will already have a new, unsaved workbook open. If not, follow this procedure to open a new workbook.

New

▶ On the Standard toolbar, click the New button.

A new workbook appears. You do not need to save it yet.

Getting External Data into a Workbook

To import a text file, you simply open it. Opening a text file in Microsoft Excel automatically starts the Text Import Wizard, which guides you through the process of selecting a *delimiter* and formatting the columns of data. A delimiter is a character, like a space, a tab, or a comma, that separates fields of data in a database. For example, to create a tab-delimited database of names and addresses, you would separate each field by a tab character. The tab characters *parse*, or separate, each field in a record (such as first name or last name) into its own column in the database.

The Text Import Wizard usually detects the delimiter automatically, and allows you to select the data format for each field in the database. The default data format is General, which works fine for most data—Microsoft Excel will recognize dates as dates, numbers as numbers that can be calculated, and text as text; however, if you have a field of numbers that are not supposed to be calculated, such as zip codes, you need to format that field as text, or Microsoft Excel will delete leading zeroes (for example, 07654 will become 7654), and you will lose the integrity of the data.

Import a text file

The text file database of 1996 sales was passed along to you with the information that it is a tab-delimited text file with a header row. In this exercise, you import the text file into a workbook, and then verify that the tab delimiters are set properly.

Open

1 On the Standard toolbar, click the Open button, and locate the Excel SBS Practice folder.

2 In the Open dialog box, click the Files Of Type down arrow, and then select Text Files.

The names of all the text files contained in the folder are listed.

3 Double-click the 1996 Orders.txt file.

The Text Import Wizard appears.

4 Since you have been told that the text file is tab-delimited and has a header row, be sure that the Delimited option button is selected and that the Start Import At Row box shows 1, and then click Next.

5 In the Step 2 dialog box, verify that the Tab Delimiters check box is selected.

By looking at the Data Preview box, you can tell that Tab is the correct delimiter, because the data is parsed into columns.

127

6 Click Next.

7 In the Step 3 dialog box, under Column Data Format, be sure that the General option button is selected, and that all of the column titles in the top row of the sample in the Data Preview box read "General."

8 Click Finish.

The text file data is imported, and the worksheet name is automatically changed to the text file name. Your worksheet should look similar to the following illustration.

	A	B	C	D	E	F	G	H	I
1	Order Date	Employee	Company	Product	Category	Unit Price	Quantity	Total	
2	1/1/96	Ulrich	MEREP	Chancham	Coffee	9.5	100	950	
3	1/1/96	Ulrich	MEREP	India	Coffee	8.6	100	860	
4	1/4/96	Langston	SAVEA	Chancham	Coffee	9.5	100	950	
5	1/4/96	Langston	SAVEA	Chunmee	Tea	8.7	20	174	
6	1/4/96	Langston	SAVEA	Gunpowde	Tea	8.1	20	162	
7	1/5/96	Hankins	ERNST	Keemun	Tea	8.7	20	174	
8	1/5/96	Hankins	ERNST	Kenya	Coffee	9.7	100	970	
9	1/6/96	Hankins	BERGL	Ecuador	Coffee	9.5	100	950	
10	1/6/96	Hankins	BERGL	Harrar	Coffee	8.9	100	890	
11	1/6/96	Hankins	BERGL	Pi Lo Chur	Tea	10	20	200	
12	1/6/96	Hankins	BERGL	Tanzania	Coffee	8.6	100	860	
13	1/6/96	Garnier	REGGI	Keemun	Tea	8.7	20	174	
14	1/6/96	Garnier	REGGI	Medellin	Coffee	8.6	100	860	
15	1/7/96	Hankins	BERGL	Java	Coffee	9.5	100	950	
16	1/7/96	Hankins	BERGL	Kenya	Coffee	9.7	100	970	
17	1/8/96	Langston	RICAR	Black Lych	Tea	9.5	20	190	

1996 Orders

Save the new workbook

Save

1 On the Standard toolbar, click the Save button.

2 In the Save As Type box, select Microsoft Excel Workbook, and then save the workbook in the Excel SBS Practice folder as 1996 Sales Summary.

Creating a Dynamic Summary with a PivotTable

To quickly and efficiently review last year's sales, your manager has asked you to generate three summaries of the 1996 sales data. In the following exercises, you'll create the monthly sales totals summary for each employee in 1996, and then format the table.

Create a PivotTable to summarize data for easy analysis

The first step toward creating the summary report is to organize the records that are currently contained in the workbook. In this exercise, you create a PivotTable that includes Order Date and Employee data.

For a demonstration of how to create and use a PivotTable, double-click the Excel Camcorder Files shortcut on your Desktop or connect to the Internet address listed on page xxiii.

1 Click any cell in the list, and then, on the Data menu, click PivotTable Report.

The PivotTable Wizard appears.

2 Be sure that the Microsoft Excel List Or Database option button is selected, and then click Next.

The Step 2 dialog box shows the range Microsoft Excel has selected as the data for the PivotTable.

3 Click Next.

The Step 3 dialog box appears.

The white boxes in the middle of the dialog box form a PivotTable layout diagram. You drag the buttons located on the right side of the dialog box, which are labeled with the field names from the data list, to create your PivotTable.

4 Drag the Order Date field button to the Row box in the layout diagram.

5 Drag the Employee field button to the Column box in the layout diagram.

6 Drag the Total field button to the Data box in the layout diagram.

The Total field button becomes a Sum Of Total button when you drop it in the Data box. Your dialog box should look similar to the following illustration.

7 Click Next.

8 In the Step 4 dialog box, be sure that the New Worksheet option button is selected, and then click Finish.

Your worksheet should look similar to the following illustration.

	A	B	C	D	E	F	G	H	I
1	Sum of Total	Employee							
2	Order Date	Davis	Garnier	Gebhardt	Hankins	Katz	Langston	Newbert	Ulrich
3	1/1/96								1810
4	1/4/96						1286		
5	1/5/96				1144				
6	1/6/96		1034		2900				
7	1/7/96				1920				
8	1/8/96						1242		2580
9	1/11/96						1810		
10	1/12/96				1810				
11	1/13/96		1920				2292		
12	1/14/96		1036						
13	1/15/96	260					1316		
14	1/18/96		1316						
15	1/19/96		950	3240					
16	1/20/96								
17	1/21/96						1070		

Sheet1 / 1996 Orders /

Group PivotTable dates by month

The PivotTable Wizard has arranged the information in the layout you se-lected, but it shows every detail. Since your manager requested a summary report, you need to organize and condense the level of detail. In this exercise, you group dates by month for a more meaningful and easy-to-read summary.

1 Use the right mouse button to click any cell in the Order Date column.

2 On the shortcut menu, point to Group And Outline, and then click Group.

The Grouping dialog box appears.

3 Be sure that Months is selected in the By list, and then click OK.

Your worksheet should look similar to the following illustration.

	A	B	C	D	E	F	G	H	I
1	Sum of Total	Employee							
2	Order Date	Davis	Garnier	Gebhardt	Hankins	Katz	Langston	Newbert	Ulrich
3	Jan	4222	8240	3422	11014		11176	1226	4390
4	Feb	6806	9664	4144	4892	1900	3992	4276	2002
5	Mar	5128	2014	3756	8456	1230	6608	1214	6322
6	Apr	7078	3814	7142	5110	2930	9252	1900	7106
7	May	10448	2976	2428	8716	3136	8404	6680	
8	Jun	12440	8596	2790	950		10960	2586	2160
9	Jul	6066	3210	2760	2542	1520	10960	5644	3020
10	Aug	16540	7485	10078	9170	1304	4660	174	
11	Sep	10200	11098	5260	4892	860	10950	5851	9699
12	Oct	1682	1211	2437	15533	8839	10341	950	7543
13	Nov	13474	4271	9083	14967	5521	13963	2023	5148
14	Dec	15016	7116	3812	12146	6280	16282	26176	4215
15	Grand Total	109100	69695	57112	98388	33520	117548	58700	51607
16									
17									

Sheet1 / 1996 Orders /

TROUBLESHOOTING If you are unable to group dates in a PivotTable, it is most likely because the dates are not formatted properly and Microsoft Excel does not recognize them as dates. To fix this, change the format of the Date field in the source data to a Date format, and then, on the Data menu, click Refresh PivotTable.

Apply an AutoFormat to the PivotTable

Your PivotTable is now a concise summary, so it is time to make it more appealing by formatting it. In this exercise, you apply an AutoFormat to the PivotTable for a professional look.

1 Select any cell within the PivotTable.

2 On the Format menu, click AutoFormat.

The AutoFormat dialog box appears.

3 In the Table Format list, scroll down and select List 1, and then click OK.

The List 1 AutoFormat is applied to your PivotTable. Your worksheet should look similar to the following illustration.

	A	B	C	D	E	F	G	H	Ul
1	Sum of Total	Employee							
2	Order Date	Davis	Garnier	Gebhardt	Hankins	Katz	Langston	Newbert	
3	Jan	4222	8240	3422	11014		11176	1226	
4	Feb	6806	9664	4144	4892	1900	3992	4276	
5	Mar	5128	2014	3756	8456	1230	6608	1214	
6	Apr	7078	3814	7142	5110	2930	9252	1900	
7	May	10448	2976	2428	8716	3136	8404	6680	
8	Jun	12440	8596	2790	950		10960	2586	
9	Jul	6066	3210	2760	2542	1520	10960	5644	
10	Aug	16540	7485	10078	9170	1304	4660	174	
11	Sep	10200	11098	5260	4892	860	10950	5851	
12	Oct	1682	1211	2437	15533	8839	10341	950	
13	Nov	13474	4271	9083	14967	5521	13963	2023	
14	Dec	15016	7116	3812	12146	6280	16282	26176	
15	Grand Total	109100	69695	57112	98388	33520	117548	58700	
16									
17									

Sheet1 / 1996 Orders /

Format the numbers in the PivotTable

The numbers in the data section of the PivotTable are not very intuitive. In this exercise, you apply formatting that shows that the numbers represent dollars.

For a demonstration of how to format numbers in a PivotTable, double-click the Excel Camcorder Files shortcut on your Desktop or connect to the Internet address listed on page xxiii.

1 Use the right mouse button to click any cell containing a number within the data portion of the table.

2 On the shortcut menu, click Field.

The PivotTable Field dialog box appears.

3 Click the Number button.

The Format Cells dialog box appears, but it contains only number formatting options.

4 In the Category list, click Currency.

5 In the Decimal Places box, change the value to 0.

6 Verify that $ is selected in the Symbol box, and then click OK.

7 In the PivotTable Field dialog box, click OK.

The first summary your manager requested is complete, and ready to be printed. Your worksheet should look similar to the following illustration.

	A	B	C	D	E	F	G	H	
1	*Sum of Total*	Employee							
2	Order Date	*Davis*	*Garnier*	*Gebhardt*	*Hankins*	*Katz*	*Langston*	*Newbert*	*U*
3	Jan	$4,222	$8,240	$3,422	$11,014		$11,176	$1,226	
4	Feb	$6,806	$9,664	$4,144	$4,892	$1,900	$3,992	$4,276	
5	Mar	$5,128	$2,014	$3,756	$8,456	$1,230	$6,608	$1,214	
6	Apr	$7,078	$3,814	$7,142	$5,110	$2,930	$9,252	$1,900	
7	May	$10,448	$2,976	$2,428	$8,716	$3,136	$8,404	$6,680	
8	Jun	$12,440	$8,596	$2,790	$950		$10,960	$2,586	
9	Jul	$6,066	$3,210	$2,760	$2,542	$1,520	$10,960	$5,644	
10	Aug	$16,540	$7,485	$10,078	$9,170	$1,304	$4,660	$174	
11	Sep	$10,200	$11,098	$5,260	$4,892	$860	$10,950	$5,851	
12	Oct	$1,682	$1,211	$2,437	$15,533	$8,839	$10,341	$950	
13	Nov	$13,474	$4,271	$9,083	$14,967	$5,521	$13,963	$2,023	
14	Dec	$15,016	$7,116	$3,812	$12,146	$6,280	$16,282	$26,176	
15	**Grand Total**	$109,100	$69,695	$57,112	$98,388	$33,520	$117,548	$58,700	$!
16									
17									

Sheet1 / 1996 Orders /

Modifying the Data Displayed in a PivotTable

The second summary your manager asked for is a quarterly sales totals summary, sorted by category and individual employees. You need to add the Category field to the PivotTable, and change the date grouping from months to quarters. You will also create Page fields in the upper-left corner of the PivotTable for the Employee data so that individual summaries can be displayed.

Add another field to the PivotTable and change the date grouping

To create a quarterly sales summary by category, you need to add the Category field to the PivotTable and re-group the order dates into quarters. In this exercise, you add the Category field to the PivotTable and switch the Order Date data to a quarterly summary.

For a demonstration of how to group dates in a PivotTable, double-click the Excel Camcorder Files shortcut on your Desktop or connect to the Internet address listed on page xxiii.

1 Use the right mouse button to click any cell within the PivotTable.

2 On the shortcut menu, click Wizard.

Step 3 of the PivotTable Wizard appears.

3 Drag the Category field button to the Row box of the layout diagram.

Your Step 3 dialog box should look similar to the following illustration.

133

4   Click Finish.

Your worksheet should look similar to the following illustration.

	A	B	C	D	E	F	G	H	I
1	Sum of Total		Employee						
2	Order Date	Category	Davis	Garnier	Gebhardt	Hankins	Katz	Langston	New
3	Jan	Coffee	$3,800	$7,350	$3,240	$7,400		$9,140	
4		Tea	$422	$890	$182	$3,614		$2,036	
5	Jan Total		$4,222	$8,240	$3,422	$11,014		$11,176	$1
6	Feb	Coffee	$4,282	$7,318	$3,194	$3,374	$1,900	$2,580	$3
7		Tea	$2,524	$2,346	$950	$1,518		$1,412	
8	Feb Total		$6,806	$9,664	$4,144	$4,892	$1,900	$3,992	$4
9	Mar	Coffee	$4,770	$1,840	$2,850	$7,630	$970	$5,340	$1
10		Tea	$358	$174	$906	$826	$260	$1,268	
11	Mar Total		$5,128	$2,014	$3,756	$8,456	$1,230	$6,608	$1
12	Apr	Coffee	$6,520	$3,640	$6,410	$4,570	$2,670	$8,700	$1
13		Tea	$558	$174	$732	$540	$260	$552	
14	Apr Total		$7,078	$3,814	$7,142	$5,110	$2,930	$9,252	$1
15	May	Coffee	$9,670	$2,610	$1,900	$8,190	$2,760	$7,270	$8
16		Tea	$778	$366	$528	$526	$376	$1,134	
17	May Total		$10,448	$2,976	$2,428	$8,716	$3,136	$8,404	$8

Sheet1 / 1996 Orders

5   In the Order Date column, use the right mouse button to click any month cell.

Both of the rows for the month cell you click will be automatically selected; for example, if you click March (cell A9), rows 9 and 10 will both be selected.

6   On the shortcut menu, point to Group And Outline, and then click Group.

7   In the By list, click Months to clear it, click Quarters to select it, and then click OK.

   ・ Your screen should look similar to the following illustration.

	A	B	C	D	E	F	G	H	I
1	*Sum of Total*		Employee						
2	Order Date	Category	*Davis*	*Garnier*	*Gebhardt*	*Hankins*	*Katz*	*Langston*	*Newl*
3	Qtr1	Coffee	$12,852	$16,508	$9,284	$18,404	$2,870	$17,060	$5
4		Tea	$3,304	$3,410	$2,038	$5,958	$260	$4,716	$1
5	**Qtr1 Total**		$16,156	$19,918	$11,322	$24,362	$3,130	$21,776	$6
6	Qtr2	Coffee	$27,620	$14,470	$11,100	$13,710	$5,430	$25,610	$10
7		Tea	$2,346	$916	$1,260	$1,066	$636	$3,006	
8	**Qtr2 Total**		$29,966	$15,386	$12,360	$14,776	$6,066	$28,616	$11
9	Qtr3	Coffee	$30,950	$18,910	$16,000	$13,580	$2,760	$22,890	$9
10		Tea	$1,856	$2,883	$2,098	$3,024	$924	$3,680	$1
11	**Qtr3 Total**		$32,806	$21,793	$18,098	$16,604	$3,684	$26,570	$11
12	Qtr4	Coffee	$23,920	$9,550	$10,220	$38,230	$18,300	$35,990	$28
13		Tea	$6,252	$3,048	$5,112	$4,416	$2,340	$4,596	$3
14	**Qtr4 Total**		$30,172	$12,598	$15,332	$42,646	$20,640	$40,586	$29
15	**Grand Total**		$109,100	$69,695	$57,112	$98,388	$33,520	$117,548	$58
16									
17						·			

Sheet1 / 1996 Orders /

Create page fields

One of the goals of this summary is to show the sales totals for each employee. In this exercise, you create Page fields for individual employees so that the PivotTable can show data for one employee at a time.

For a demonstration of how to show data on separate pages in a PivotTable, double-click the Excel Camcorder Files shortcut on your Desktop or connect to the Internet address listed on page xxiii.

1 Use the right mouse button to click any cell within the PivotTable.

2 On the shortcut menu, click Wizard.

The Step 3 dialog box appears.

3 In the layout diagram, drag the Employee button from the Column box to the Page box, and then click Finish.

Your worksheet should look similar to the following illustration.

	A	B	C	D	E	F	G	H	I
1	Employee	(All) ▼							
2									
3	*Sum of Total*								
4	Order Date	Category	*Total*						
5	Qtr1	Coffee	$110,500						
6		Tea	$25,172						
7	**Qtr1 Total**		$135,672						
8	Qtr2	Coffee	$125,370						
9		Tea	$12,026						
10	**Qtr2 Total**		$137,396						
11	Qtr3	Coffee	$137,060						
12		Tea	$18,435						
13	**Qtr3 Total**		$155,495						
14	Qtr4	Coffee	$185,870						
15		Tea	$31,839						
16	**Qtr4 Total**		$217,709						
17	**Grand Total**		$646,272						

Sheet1 / 1996 Orders /

To the right of the Employee button in the PivotTable is a list that shows All, and the data shown in the PivotTable is the summary data for all employees. You can show the data for an individual employee by selecting his or her name from the drop-down list.

4 Click the Employee down arrow, and then click Davis.

Davis' sales data for 1996 appears in the PivotTable. Your worksheet should look similar to the following illustration.

	A	B	C	D	E	F	G	H	I
1	Employee	Davis ▾							
2									
3	*Sum of Total*								
4	Order Date	Category	*Total*						
5	Qtr1	Coffee	$12,852						
6		Tea	$3,304						
7	Qtr1 Total		$16,156						
8	Qtr2	Coffee	$27,620						
9		Tea	$2,346						
10	Qtr2 Total		$29,966						
11	Qtr3	Coffee	$30,950						
12		Tea	$1,856						
13	Qtr3 Total		$32,806						
14	Qtr4	Coffee	$23,920						
15		Tea	$6,252						
16	Qtr4 Total		$30,172						
17	Grand Total		$109,100						

Sheet1 / 1996 Orders /

Change the PivotTable view

For a demonstration of how to change a PivotTable's presentation, double-click the Excel Camcorder Files shortcut on your Desktop or connect to the Internet address listed on page xxiii.

In your PivotTable, the Order Date data is displayed in rows; this presentation is called a *row orientation*. The data contained in the Category column is also displayed in a row orientation, but the Employee names appear in a *page orientation*, since the data for each employee is summarized individually (as if it were on its own page).

Having both the Order Date and the Categories data presented in a row orientation is cumbersome to read. In this exercise, you change the presentation of the Order Date data from row to *column orientation* so that the data for each quarter is displayed in a separate column.

1 Drag the Order Date button up and to the right of the Sum Of Total label (so it's over cell B3).

As you drag the button to different areas of the worksheet, the mouse pointer icon will change to indicate what will happen to the data orientation when you drop the button. The following icon shapes appear depending on where the mouse pointer is.

Row orientation   Remove

Column orientation   Page orientation

2 When the mouse pointer looks like the Column Orientation icon, release the mouse button.

The second summary your manager requested is complete and ready to be printed. Your worksheet should look similar to the following illustration.

	A	B	C	D	E	F	G	H
1	Employee	Davis						
2								
3	Sum of Total	Order Date						
4	Category	Qtr1	Qtr2	Qtr3	Qtr4	Grand Total		
5	Coffee	$12,852	$27,620	$30,950	$23,920	$95,342		
6	Tea	$3,304	$2,346	$1,856	$6,252	$13,758		
7	Grand Total	$16,156	$29,966	$32,806	$30,172	$109,100		
8								
9								

3 Save the workbook.

Showing Average Sales by Product

The third summary your manager requested was a presentation of the average sales of each product by quarter. You can quickly and easily create this summary in the existing PivotTable by removing the Category and Employee fields, adding the Product field, and changing the summary function from Sum to Average.

Remove data from the PivotTable

In this exercise, you remove the Category and Employee fields from the PivotTable.

For a demonstration of how to change a PivotTable's presentation, double-click the Excel Camcorder Files shortcut on your Desktop or connect to the Internet address listed on page xxiii.

1 On the worksheet, drag the Category button away from the PivotTable until the mouse pointer looks like the Remove icon, and then release the mouse button.

The Category data is removed from the PivotTable.

2 Repeat step 1 to remove the Employee data from the PivotTable.

Add a new field to the PivotTable and change the summary function

To create a summary of average sales by product by quarter, you need to add a new field. In this exercise, you add the Product field to the PivotTable, and change the summary function from Sum to Average.

1 Use the right mouse button to click any cell in the PivotTable, and then click Wizard.

2 In the Step 3 dialog box, drag the Product field button to the Row box in the layout diagram.

3 Double-click the Sum Of Total button.

The PivotTable Field dialog box appears.

4 In the Summarize By list, select Average, and then click OK.

In the Step 3 dialog box, the Sum Of Total button becomes the Average Of Total.

5 Click Finish.

The PivotTable has been changed to show a summary of average quarterly sales by Product. The Grand Total column shows the average for the year. Your worksheet should look similar to the following illustration.

	A	B	C	D	E	F	G
1							
2							
3	Average of Total	Order Date					
4	Product	Qtr1	Qtr2	Qtr3	Qtr4	Grand Total	
5	Antigua	$950	$950	$950	$1,017	$967	
6	Assam	$174	$174	$232	$274	$225	
7	Black Lychee	$190	$190	$222	$297	$228	
8	Bourbon Santos	$860	$860	$860	$885	$869	
9	Celebes	$871	$860	$860	$883	$871	
10	Ceylon	$457	$210	$263	$333	$321	
11	Chanchamayo	$696	$950	$950	$990	$892	
12	Chunmee	$375	$174	$226	$277	$274	
13	Coatepec	$678	$950	$950	$964	$900	
14	Coban	$777	$860	$860	$905	$838	
15	Costa Rica	$928	$950	$950	$979	$951	
16	Darjeeling	$347	$366	$366	$582	$420	
17	Dragonwell	$382	$192	$240	$299	$265	

Sheet1 / 1996 Orders /

Refreshing Data and Showing Details

Refresh the PivotTable data

One of the sales people, Mr. Langston, calls to tell you there is a mistake in the data that was sent out: he actually sold 400 lbs of Antigua coffee, worth $4200, in his 12/15/96 order. You need to first make the change in the underlying database, and then refresh the PivotTable to include the correction in the summary.

You can find this record rapidly by using AutoFilter and filtering on the employee name, the product name, or the date.

1 Select the 1996 Orders worksheet, and select cell G773 (Langston's Antigua order on 12/15/96).

2 Change the amount in cell G773 to 400, and the amount in cell H773 to 4200.

3 Select Sheet1 (the PivotTable worksheet), and then use the right mouse button to click any cell in the PivotTable.

4 On the shortcut menu, click Refresh Data.

The PivotTable data is updated, and the average sale amount of Antigua coffee for the fourth quarter has increased to $1542. Your worksheet should look similar to the following illustration.

	A	B	C	D	E	F	G
1							
2							
3	*Average of Total*	Order Date					
4	Product	*Qtr1*	*Qtr2*	*Qtr3*	*Qtr4*	*Grand Total*	
5	Antigua	$950	$950	$950	$1,542	$1,098	
6	Assam	$174	$174	$232	$274	$225	
7	Black Lychee	$190	$190	$222	$297	$228	
8	Bourbon Santos	$860	$860	$860	$885	$869	

Show the details underlying a specific calculation

After a quick review of the summary reports you compiled, your manager decides to take a closer look at the data for the Jamaican Blue Mountain coffee sales in the fourth quarter. She wants to see the specific details used to calculate the fourth quarter average. You can generate this information quickly by doing a *drilldown*. A drilldown creates a new worksheet that lists all the records used to calculate a PivotTable figure.

In this exercise, you do a drilldown to extract the requested information.

You can sort the Product column alphabetically by selecting a cell in the column, and then clicking the Sort Descending button on the Standard toolbar.

1 Double-click the Qtr4 figure for Jamaican Blue Mountain.

A new worksheet is added to the workbook, containing a list of detailed information on the sales of Jamaican Blue Mountain coffee for the fourth quarter. Your screen should look similar to the following illustration.

	A	B	C	D	E	F	G	H
1	Order Date	Employee	Company ID	Product	Category	Unit Price	Quantity	Tot
2	12/19/96	Newbert	RICAR	Jamaican Blue Mountain	Coffee	36	100	36
3	12/13/96	Newbert	SUPRE	Jamaican Blue Mountain	Coffee	36	100	36
4	12/8/96	Davis	ALFRE	Jamaican Blue Mountain	Coffee	36	100	36
5	12/2/96	Newbert	LILAS	Jamaican Blue Mountain	Coffee	36	100	36
6	11/22/96	Langston	WELLI	Jamaican Blue Mountain	Coffee	32.4	100	32
7	11/18/96	Katz	KONIG	Jamaican Blue Mountain	Coffee	32.4	100	32
8	11/2/96	Hankins	LEHMA	Jamaican Blue Mountain	Coffee	32.4	100	32
9	10/14/96	Katz	WARTI	Jamaican Blue Mountain	Coffee	32.4	100	32
10	10/13/96	Langston	ISLAN	Jamaican Blue Mountain	Coffee	32.4	100	32
11	10/11/96	Katz	QUICK	Jamaican Blue Mountain	Coffee	32.4	100	32

Sheet2 / Sheet1 / 1996 Orders

2 Save the workbook.

> **NOTE** If you'd like to build on the skills you learned in this lesson, you can do the One Step Further. Otherwise, skip to "Finish the Lesson."

One Step Further: Creating Page Reports for Distribution to Individuals

In preparation for performance reviews, your manager asks you to compile a report of average quarterly sales by employee, broken down by product. You can do this by using the current PivotTable and adding Employee data in a page orientation, and then creating separate worksheets for each employee's average quarterly sales by product.

In this exercise, you create printable page reports for each employee.

1   On the worksheet containing the PivotTable, use the right mouse button to click any cell in the PivotTable.

2   On the shortcut menu, click Wizard.

3   In the Step 3 dialog box, drag the Employee field button to the Page box, and then click Finish.

    The Employee button appears in a page orientation in the PivotTable.

4   Use the right mouse button to click any cell in the PivotTable.

5   On the shortcut menu, click Show Pages.

6   In the Show Pages dialog box, click OK.

    A new worksheet for each employee is added to the workbook. Each new worksheet contains a PivotTable that summarizes the employee's quarterly sales by product.

7   Save your workbook.

Finish the Lesson

1   To continue to the next lesson, on the File menu, click Close.

2   If you are finished using Microsoft Excel for now, on the File menu, click Exit.

Lesson Summary

To	Do this	Button
Import a text file	On the Standard toolbar, click the Open button. In the List Files Of Type box, select Text Files, and then open the text file. Using the Text Import Wizard, select a delimiter, select the column formatting you want, and then click Finish.	
Create a PivotTable	Select any cell in the data list. On the Data menu, click PivotTable Report. Follow the steps in the Wizard, and arrange the data by dragging the field buttons and placing them appropriately in the layout diagram.	
Group dates	Use the right mouse button to click a date cell, and then, on the shortcut menu, point to Group And Outline and click Group. Select the date grouping that you want, and then click OK.	
Apply an AutoFormat	Select any cell in the PivotTable. On the Format menu, click Auto-Format. Select a Table Format, and then click OK.	
Format PivotTable numbers	Use the right mouse button to click any cell in the data portion of the table. On the shortcut menu, click Field. In the PivotTable Field dialog box, click Number, and then select a number format for the data. Click OK twice.	
Add a new field	Use the right mouse button to click any cell in the PivotTable. On the shortcut menu, click Wizard, and then in the dialog box, drag the field button for the data you want to add into the layout diagram. Click Finish.	

To	Do this	Button
Create page fields	Use the right mouse button to click any cell in the PivotTable. On the shortcut menu, click Wizard. Drag the field button for the data you want in the Page field into the Page box in the layout diagram, and then click Finish.	
Change data orientation	In the PivotTable, drag a field button to a new orientation position. Drop the field button when the mouse pointer icon changes to the correct shape for the data orientation you want.	
Remove data	In the PivotTable, drag a field button away from the PivotTable. Drop the field button when the mouse pointer takes the shape of the Remove icon.	✖
Change the summary function	Use the right mouse button to click any cell in the PivotTable. On the shortcut menu, click Wizard. Double-click the button in the Data box in the layout diagram. In the PivotTable Field dialog box, select a new summary function in the Summarize By list, click OK, and then click Finish.	
Refresh data	Use the right mouse button to click any cell in the PivotTable. On the shortcut menu, click Refresh Data.	
Show underlying details	In the PivotTable, double-click the data cell for which you want to find additional information.	

For online information about	On the Help menu, click Contents And Index, click the Index tab, and then type
Importing data	importing data
Creating PivotTables	pivottables, creating
Modifying PivotTables	pivottables, adding and removing fields
Updating PivotTables	pivottables, updating

Charting to Assess Trends and Relationships

Estimated time
30 min.

In this lesson you will learn how to:

- Create a chart.
- Customize a chart.
- Make a chart format re-usable.
- Create a trendline.

A worksheet can help you calculate precise numbers, trends, and changes over time, but it can be difficult to grasp the overall meaning of numbers and trends just by looking at figures. A chart, on the other hand, creates a visual presentation of data and its relationship to other data so that the overall meaning can be grasped very quickly.

You can easily create and customize charts in Microsoft Excel by using the Chart Wizard. You can also save the formatting of the chart you create, and then re-use it in other charts. Charts can be *embedded* on the worksheet next to your data; they can also appear on a *chart sheet*. A chart sheet is a sheet in a workbook that contains only a chart. You can easily make an embedded chart into a chart sheet, or a chart sheet into an embedded chart, depending on what you prefer at any point in time.

Other features, such as trendlines and secondary axes, make charted data even more useful. A trend in a series of data, such as monthly sales for a year, can be calculated and used to forecast sales; you can show that trend and forecast in the chart by using a trendline. Data series that are related but are on different number scales, for example volume sold (in thousands of pounds) and price per pound (in dollars per pound), can be displayed on the same chart by using a secondary axis for the second number scale. This enables you to relate sales volume to sales price in a direct and meaningful manner.

At the Island Tea & Coffee Company, your manager has asked you to generate two documents based on the current sales orders for 1997, which run through June: monthly sales performances for the entire company and for each employee, and a sales forecast for the next six months based on sales since January 1997. The data needed to produce these documents is currently stored in a PivotTable and in multiple worksheets.

Open an existing file

You keep the current orders data in a workbook named Current Orders. In this exercise, you open the Current Orders file.

Open

1   On the Standard toolbar, click the Open button.
2   In the Open dialog box, click the Look In Favorites button.
3   In the file list, double-click the Excel SBS Practice folder.
4   Double-click the Current Orders file.

Save the file with a new name

1   On the File menu, click Save As.

    The Save As dialog box opens. Be sure the Excel SBS Practice folder appears in the Save In box.

2   In the File Name box, type **Charting Lesson**, and then click Save.

Presenting Data Graphically with Charts

Your manager at the Island Tea & Coffee Company has asked for a chart of the company's sales by category for each month this year. A PivotTable has been created on the PivotTable sheet (based on the 1997 Orders worksheet) to show this data. After you create the chart, you'll customize it by changing the color of the Tea series to a two-color fade, and changing the column markers in the coffee series into picture markers of stacked coffee cups.

Create a chart

Now that you have opened your current orders list, you are ready to start charting it. In this exercise, you create an embedded column chart based on the data in the PivotTable.

For a demonstration of how to create an embedded chart based on a PivotTable, double-click the Excel Camcorder Files shortcut on your Desktop or connect to the Internet address listed on page xxiii.

1 Select the PivotTable sheet.

2 Use the right mouse button to click a cell within the PivotTable, point to Select, and if the Enable Selection command looks pushed in, click it.

3 Select cells C10 through A4 by dragging from cell C10 up and left to cell A4 so that the Order Date button stays in the PivotTable.

4 On the Standard toolbar, click the Chart Wizard button.

The Chart Wizard appears.

5 In the Step 1 dialog box, be sure that Column is selected in the Chart Type list, and then click Next.

6 In the Step 2 dialog box, be sure that the Columns option button is selected, and then click Next.

7 In the Step 3 dialog box, on the Titles tab, click in the Chart Title box, type **Current Orders by Category**, and then click Next.

8 In the Step 4 dialog box, be sure that the As Object In option button is selected and that the list reads PivotTable, and then click Finish.

The new chart is created in the middle of the worksheet. Your worksheet should look similar to the following illustration.

Chart Wizard

145

Customize a chart to match specific requirements

Now that you have created your embedded chart, you need to format it according to the Island Tea & Coffee Company standard. In this exercise, you customize the formatting of your chart.

For a demonstration of how to customize charts, double-click the Excel Camcorder Files shortcut on your Desktop or connect to the Internet address listed on page xxiii.

1   If you do not see handles around the edges of your chart, point to an empty area of the chart background, and then, when the ChartTip shows Chart Area, click the chart.

Handles appear around the edges of the chart showing that it is selected, and the Name box shows Chart Area.

2   Drag the corner handles of the chart until cells B3 through I16 are covered by the chart to make it larger and easier to see.

3   Point to the gray area behind the data markers (the plot area), and when the ChartTip shows Plot Area, double-click.

The Format Plot Area dialog box appears.

4   Under Area, click the None option button, and then click OK.

The plot area background color disappears.

5   Double-click one of the data markers in the Tea series.

The Format Data Series dialog box appears.

If you have trouble selecting a chart element, select any element, and then press an arrow key to cycle through all the elements in the chart.

6   On the Patterns tab, click the Fill Effects button.

The Fill Effects dialog box appears.

7   On the Gradient tab, under Colors, click the Preset option button; under Preset Colors, select Daybreak; under Shading Styles, be sure that Horizontal is selected; and under Variants, select the upper-right box.

8 Click OK to close the Fill Effects dialog box, and then click OK again to close the Format Data Series dialog box.

Your chart should look similar to the following illustration.

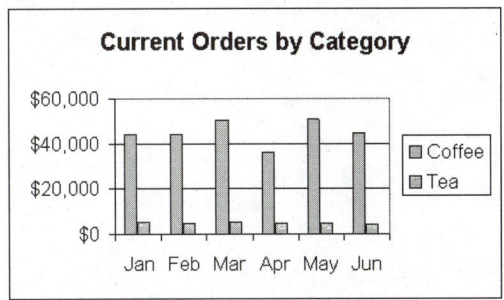

Add picture markers to a series

Before printing your chart, you need to finish bringing it up to the Island Tea & Coffee Company formatting standard. In this exercise, you make the data markers for the coffee series look like stacked coffee cups.

1 Double-click one of the data markers in the Coffee series.

The Format Data Series dialog box appears.

2 On the Patterns tab, click the Fill Effects button.

3 In the Fill Effects dialog box, click the Picture tab, and then click Select Picture.

The Select Picture dialog box appears.

4 In the Excel SBS Practice folder, double-click the Coffee Cup file.

The clipart picture appears in the Fill Effects dialog box.

5 Under Format, click the Stack option button, and then click OK.

6 In the Format Data Series dialog box, click OK.

Your completed chart should look similar to the following illustration.

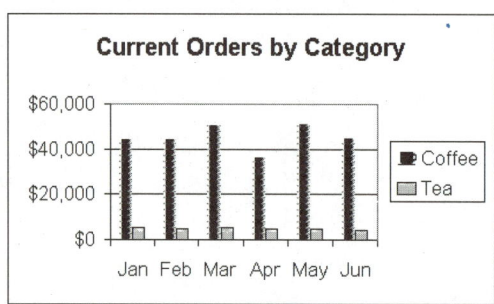

Draw your own markers

Another way to customize a chart is to draw your own markers using Microsoft Excel's drawing tools.

Using the drawing tools, you can draw objects of any shape in both worksheets and charts. You can replace markers in a chart with an object you draw—you can replace an entire series, or just a single marker to make it stand out. You can even draw an object and give it a shadow or a 3-D effect.

Before you print the chart, you decide to experiment with its look—you want to replace the Tea series markers with a drawn object of your own.

1 Use the right mouse button to click a toolbar, and then click Drawing.

The Drawing toolbar appears.

Oval

2 On the Drawing toolbar, click the Oval button.

The mouse pointer becomes a crosshair.

3 Drag the crosshair pointer diagonally on the chart or the worksheet to draw a circular object.

The object can be either circular or oblong.

4 Make the object approximately 1 inch in diameter.

When you release the mouse button, the object is selected and has handles around it.

Fill Color

5 While the object is selected, on the Formatting toolbar, select a red color from the Fill Color button palette.

The drawn object is colored red.

3-D

6 On the Drawing toolbar, click the 3-D button.

A shortcut menu of 3-D shapes appears.

7 Click the shape in the lower right corner (3-D Style 20).

The drawn object takes on a 3-D shape.

Copy

8 While the object is still selected, on the Standard toolbar, click the Copy button.

9 In the chart, click a Tea series marker.

The entire Tea series is selected.

10 On the Standard toolbar, click the Paste button.

The Tea series markers take on the shape of your drawn, 3-D object.

Paste

To replace a single marker, click the marker twice (do not double-click), and then paste the drawn object.

11 Click the object you drew, and then press DELETE.

The drawn object is deleted, and your chart has custom-drawn markers in it.

12 Close the Drawing toolbar.

Undo the changes

You decide that you don't like the drawn-object markers in this particular chart, so you undo the changes you made.

Undo

➤ On the Standard toolbar, click the down arrow next to the Undo button, and undo actions until the Tea series markers are in their original form.

Print the chart

IMPORTANT In order to complete this exercise, you'll need to be connected to a printer.

Before distributing the chart for further review, you decide to show it to your manager. In this exercise, you print a copy of the chart.

Print

➤ Click the chart to select it, and then, on the Standard toolbar, click the Print button.

Create and print different charts by changing the PivotTable

Your manager also wants to see monthly sales by category for each employee. In this exercise, you create the new charts, and then print one of them. But first, you have to be able to identify whose data is in each chart. The simplest way is to extend the range of data included in the chart so that the cell containing the employee name is included.

Chart Wizard

1 Click in the chart, and then click the Chart Wizard button.

2 Click Next, and in the Step 2 dialog box, in the Data Range box, change $A$4 to $A$1, and then click Finish.

The chart is updated, but the legend is too large at the current font size.

Font Size

3 In the chart, click the legend, and then on the Formatting toolbar, in the Font Size box, select 9.

The legend fits neatly into the chart area.

4 Click the PivotTable Page down arrow (cell B1), and then select Davis.

Davis' data appears in the PivotTable, and the chart is automatically updated to display the PivotTable data.

5 On the Standard toolbar, click the Print button.

Print

Make an embedded chart into a chart sheet (and vice versa)

The embedded chart is convenient because it streamlines the process of generating charts for each employee. But, since the PivotTable you want to experiment with is large, the embedded chart is in your way. In this exercise, you convert the embedded chart into a chart sheet so that it remains functional but is off the worksheet.

1 Use the right mouse button to click in the chart area.

2 On the shortcut menu, click Location.

The Chart Location dialog box appears.

3 Click the As New Sheet option button, and then click OK.

The embedded chart is moved onto a separate chart sheet.

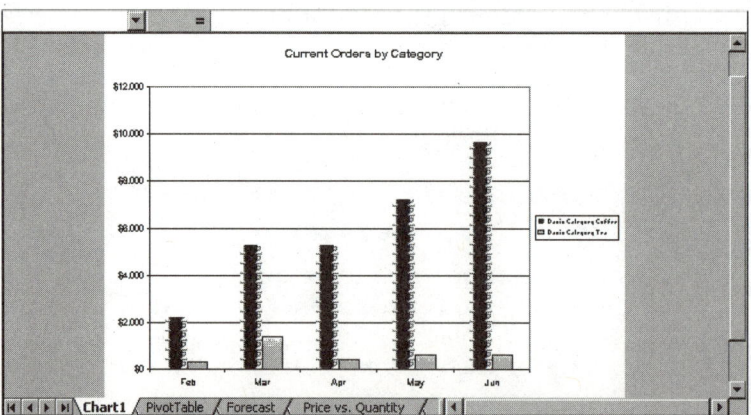

You can rename, move, copy, and delete a chart sheet in the same way that you would a worksheet.

Making a Chart Format Re-Usable

Even though customizing your chart was easy, it would be even easier in the future if you could reapply the Island Tea & Coffee Company custom formatting to any chart without having to perform the individual formatting steps. You can save your chart formatting by making it into a custom chart type, and then simply reapply it whenever you create a new chart.

Create a custom chart type

Because you formatted your chart based on the Island Tea & Coffee Company guidelines, you decide to save the settings for future use. In this exercise, you create a custom chart type and remove the chart title so that it doesn't become part of the custom chart type formatting.

1 Click the chart title, and then press DELETE.

2 On the Chart menu, click Chart Type.

3 Click the Custom Types tab.

4 Under Select From, click User-Defined, and then click Add.

5 In the Name box, type **ITC Standard**, and in the Description box, type **Company standard chart format**, and then click OK.

The new chart type is added to the Chart Type list. The next time you run the Chart Wizard, you can click the User-Defined option button, and then select your custom chart type on the Custom Types tab in the Step 2 dialog box.

6 Click OK.

Forecasting Trends

One of the charts your manager requested is a six-month sales forecast based on the sales data for the first five months. By using one of several mathematical line equations, Microsoft Excel can create a *trendline* for a data series that shows the trend of the existing data. You can extend that trendline into a forecast for as many periods as you want.

Forecast future sales based on current data trends

In preparation for a company-wide sales meeting, your manager asks you to create a chart that will help her forecast the projected company sales for the next six months. In this exercise, you create a chart with a trendline and six-month forecast for total company sales.

Chart Wizard

1   Select the Forecast worksheet.

2   Select cells A1 through B6, and then click the Chart Wizard button.

3   In the Chart Wizard Step 1 dialog box, click Finish.

     A default column chart is created.

4   Use the right mouse button to click any data marker in the chart.

     The entire data series is selected.

5   On the shortcut menu, click Add Trendline.

     The Add Trendline dialog box appears.

6   On the Type tab, click Linear.

7   On the Options tab, under Forecast, in the Forward box, click the up arrow until it shows 6, and then click OK.

     A trendline with a six-month forecast is inserted in the chart. You might want to try different trendlines to decide which type best displays a logical forecast based on your data.

8   Save your work.

NOTE   If you'd like to build on the skills you learned in this lesson, you can do the One Step Further. Otherwise, skip to "Finish the Lesson."

One Step Further: Creating a Chart with a Secondary Axis

After reviewing the six-month forecast you created in the previous exercise, your manager requests a chart of sales volume vs. average price, to see if changing prices affect the volume sold. The two series in your chart, sales volume and price per pound, have very different number scales: the volume will be in thousands, and the average price will be less than 15. This means that when both series are displayed in the same chart using the same value axis, only the volume series will be visible. The solution is to show each series on a different value axis. This way you can see how the volume and price change relative to each other over time, and then estimate how changing the price affects the volume sold.

Use a secondary axis to display data series that have different value scales

To make the chart as useful as possible, you decide to add a second axis to display each data series at the appropriate scale. In this exercise, you create a chart of sales volume vs. average price, and then add a secondary axis so that the average price series can be seen in the chart.

1 Select the Price Vs. Quantity sheet.

2 Select cells A1 through C7, click the Chart Wizard button, and then, in the Step 1 dialog box, click Finish.

A default chart is created on the worksheet.

If the Chart toolbar is not displayed, use the right mouse button to click any toolbar, and then click Chart.

3 On the Chart toolbar, click the Chart Objects down arrow, and then select Series "price."

4 On the Format menu, click Selected Data Series.

The Format Data Series dialog box appears.

5 On the Axis tab, under Plot Series On, click the Secondary Axis option button, and then click OK.

A secondary axis is added to the right side of the chart. The Price data markers are visible because they have an axis that is scaled to their values.

6 Use the right mouse button to click the Price series, and then click Chart Type.

7 In the Chart Type dialog box, click the Standard Types tab, verify that the Apply To Selection check box is selected, click the Line icon, and then click OK.

The Price data is displayed by line markers instead of by column markers, which makes it easier to distinguish.

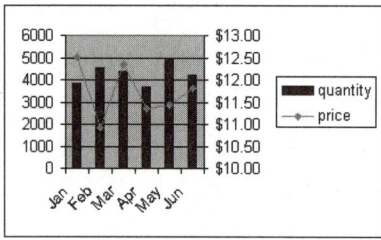

8 Save the workbook.

Finish the lesson

1 To continue to the next lesson, on the File menu, click Close.

2 If you are finished using Microsoft Excel for now, on the File menu, click Exit.

Lesson Summary

To	Do this	Button
Create a chart	Select the data you want to chart, and then click the Chart Wizard button. Follow the steps in the Chart Wizard to create the chart.	![button]
Customize a chart	Double-click the chart element you want to customize, and then select the desired colors, patterns, and effects in the Format dialog box.	
Add picture markers to a series	Double-click a marker in the series you want to add picture markers to, and then, in the Format Data Series dialog box, click Fill Effects. Click the Picture tab, click Select Picture, and then locate a picture you want. Double-click the picture you want, click OK to close the Fill Effects dialog box, and then click OK to close the Format Data Series dialog box.	

To	Do this	Button
Replace series markers with a drawn object	Use the right mouse button to click a toolbar, and then select Drawing. In the Drawing toolbar, click a shape button and draw an object in the worksheet or chart. Select the object, and then, on the Standard toolbar, click the Copy button. Click a marker in the series you want to replace. On the Standard toolbar, click the Paste button. Select the object you drew, and then press DELETE.	
Make a drawn object a 3-D object	Select the drawn object. On the Drawing toolbar, click 3-D, and then select a 3-D shape from the shortcut menu.	
Make an embedded chart into a chart sheet	Use the right mouse button to click in the chart area, and then, on the shortcut menu, click Location. In the Chart Location dialog box, select the As New Sheet option button, and then click OK.	
Create a custom chart type	On the Chart menu, click Chart Type, and then click the Custom Types tab. Click User Defined, and then click Add. Type a name and description for the new custom chart type, and then click OK.	
Create a trendline	Use the right mouse button to select the series you want a trendline for, and then, on the shortcut menu, click Add Trendline. On the Type tab, select a trendline type. If you want a forecast, on the Options tab, select a number of forecast periods, and then click OK.	

For online information about	On the Help menu, click Contents And Index, click the Index tab, and then type
Creating charts	**chart creation**
Customizing charts	**chart editing; chart formatting**
Trendlines	**trendlines**

Printing Reports to Distribute Information Offline

Estimated time
30 min.

In this lesson you will learn how to:

- Print a multiple-page worksheet.
- Set print titles to easily identify data on all pages.
- Change the page printing order.
- Print only selected data from a worksheet.
- Define print areas to print the same data repeatedly.
- Fit information onto a specific number of printed pages.
- Print charts with or without a worksheet.

As the office manager for the Island Tea & Coffee Company, you keep a current list of the company's orders. Different members of the sales staff often ask you for a printed copy of this data—sometimes the entire list, sometimes just portions of it.

In this lesson, you will learn a variety of methods for printing worksheet data depending on the requirements.

IMPORTANT In order to perform the exercises in this lesson, your computer will need to be connected to a printer.

Open an existing file

You keep the current orders in a workbook named 1997 Orders. In this exercise, you open the 1997 Orders workbook.

Open

1   On the Standard toolbar, click the Open button.

2   In the Open dialog box, click the Look In Favorites button.

3   In the file list, double-click the Excel SBS Practice folder.

4   Double-click the 1997 Orders file.

Save the file with a new name

In this exercise, you save the 1997 Orders file as Printing Lesson.

1   On the File menu, click Save As.

The Save As dialog box opens. Be sure the Excel SBS Practice folder appears in the Save In box.

2   In the File Name box, type **Printing Lesson**, and then click Save.

Printing an Entire Worksheet

The 1997 Orders list is a very large worksheet that will extend over several pages when printed. A common problem encountered while printing large worksheets is that each identifying column or row label is printed only on the first page. Another common problem relates to the default layout of the printed pages. For example, the default layout may print six columns on one page and a single column on the next page; or it may print the left side of a long worksheet followed by the right side, when you would rather print the top of the worksheet followed by the bottom. You can remedy these problems easily by changing some print settings for the worksheet.

First, you will preview the worksheet using two different preview methods, and then you will change print settings so that the 1997 Orders list prints out the way you want it to.

Preview the worksheet

You usually preview a worksheet before printing it so that you can determine the optimal way to lay out the printed pages. In this exercise, you use two different methods of previewing: Print Preview and Page Break Preview. Print Preview shows you what the printed page will look like, page by page; Page Break Preview shows you how the worksheet is broken up into pages, and allows you to easily alter the page layout.

Print Preview

1 Be sure that the Orders worksheet is active, and then, on the Standard toolbar, click the Print Preview button.

Page 1 appears in Print Preview mode. Only four columns are printed on page 1, and the status bar message tells you that there are 16 pages in the worksheet.

2 On the button bar, click Page Break Preview.

3 If you see a Welcome To Page Break Preview dialog box, select the Do Not Show This Dialog Again check box, and then click OK.

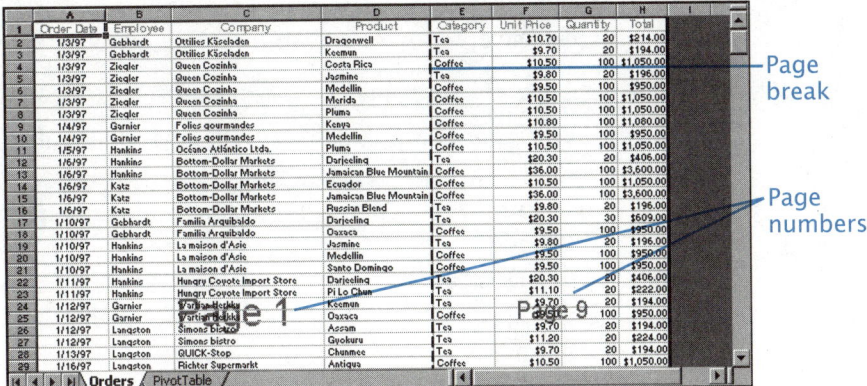

Page Break Preview shows you how the entire worksheet is broken into pages. The dotted lines show where the page breaks are, and the page numbers show the order in which the worksheet will be printed (in this case, the pages on the left side of the worksheet will be printed first, from the top down, and then the right side will be printed from the top down). This printing order is called *Down, Then Over*.

4 Point to the vertical page break line, and then, when the mouse pointer becomes a two-headed arrow, drag the line to the left by one column.

The vertical page break is reset so that only three columns print on the first eight pages. The page break line becomes a solid line after you move it to indicate that it is now a manual page break instead of an automatic page break.

5 On the Standard toolbar, click the Print Preview button.

6 On the button bar, click Next, and then click near the top of the page.

		Orders
1/27/97	Hankins	Split Rail Beer & Ale
1/30/97	Hankins	Folk och fä HB
1/30/97	Hankins	Folk och fä HB
1/30/97	Hankins	Princesa Isabel Vinhos
1/31/97	Garnier	Consolidated Holdings
1/31/97	Garnier	Consolidated Holdings

159

Page 2 is magnified, and there are no labels at the top of the page to identify the data in the columns. In the next exercise, you will fix this by adding *print titles*, labels that are automatically printed at the top of each page.

7 On the button bar, click Close.

Set print titles

While previewing the worksheet you saw that the identifying column labels appear only on pages 1 and 9, and the identifying order dates appear only on pages 1 through 8, so the data on every page except page 1 is not adequately identified. In this exercise, you set print titles so that no matter where the page breaks are, the order dates and column labels will be printed on each page.

1 On the File menu, click Page Setup.

2 In the Page Setup dialog box, click the Sheet tab.

3 Under Print Titles, click in the Rows To Repeat At Top box, and then click a cell in row 1. You might have drag the dialog box out of the way to click in row 1.

The row reference $1:$1 is entered in the Rows To Repeat At Top box.

4 Click in the Columns To Repeat At Left box, and then click a cell in column A.

The column reference $A:$A is entered in the Columns To Repeat At Left box.

5 Click OK.

6 On the Standard toolbar, click the Print Preview button, and then, on the button bar, click Next until you can see page 10.

Print Preview

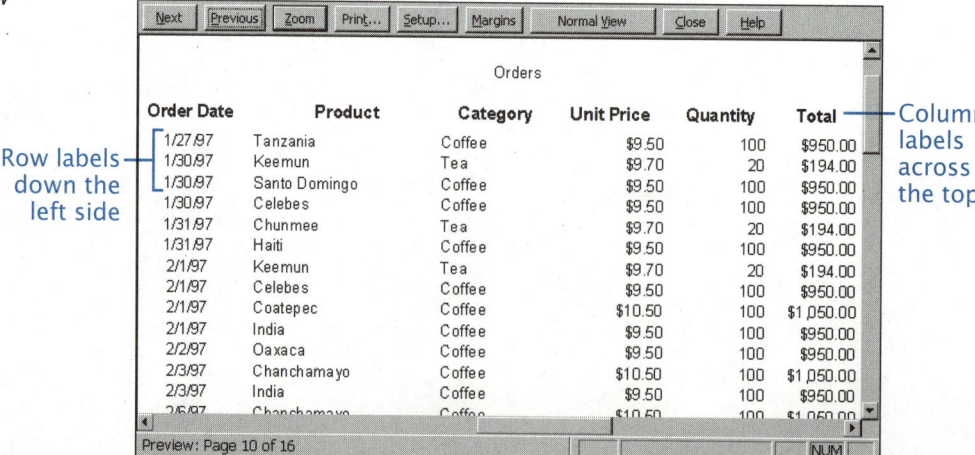

Column labels and order dates now appear on every page. Magnify the page to read the headings, if necessary.

7 On the button bar, click Close.

Change the page layout

Your list of current 1997 orders is wide as well as long, and you need to define whether to print the pages "Over, Then Down" or "Down, Then Over." In this exercise, you look at page printing order layouts to determine which is most effective.

1 If you are not in Page Break Preview, on the View menu, click Page Break Preview.

The default page layout is "Down, Then Over."

2 On the File menu, click Page Setup.

The Page Setup dialog box appears.

3 On the Sheet tab, click the "Over, Then Down" option button under Page Order, and then click OK.

	A	B	C	D	E	F	G	H	I
1	Order Date	Employee	Company	Product	Category	Unit Price	Quantity	Total	
2	1/3/97	Gebhardt	Ottilies Käseladen	Dragonwell	Tea	$10.70	20	$214.00	
3	1/3/97	Gebhardt	Ottilies Käseladen	Keemun	Tea	$9.70	20	$194.00	
4	1/3/97	Ziegler	Queen Cozinha	Costa Rica	Coffee	$10.50	100	$1,050.00	
5	1/3/97	Ziegler	Queen Cozinha	Jasmine	Tea	$9.80	20	$196.00	
6	1/3/97	Ziegler	Queen Cozinha	Medellin	Coffee	$9.50	100	$950.00	
7	1/3/97	Ziegler	Queen Cozinha	Merida	Coffee	$10.50	100	$1,050.00	
8	1/3/97	Ziegler	Queen Cozinha	Pluma	Coffee	$10.50	100	$1,050.00	
9	1/4/97	Garnier	Folies gourmandes	Kenya	Coffee	$10.80	100	$1,080.00	
10	1/4/97	Garnier	Folies gourmandes	Medellin	Coffee	$9.50	100	$950.00	
11	1/5/97	Hankins	Océano Atlántico Ltda.	Pluma	Coffee	$10.50	100	$1,050.00	
12	1/6/97	Hankins	Bottom-Dollar Markets	Darjeeling	Tea	$20.30	20	$406.00	
13	1/6/97	Hankins	Bottom-Dollar Markets	Jamaican Blue Mountain	Coffee	$36.00	100	$3,600.00	
14	1/6/97	Katz	Bottom-Dollar Markets	Ecuador	Coffee	$10.50	100	$1,050.00	
15	1/6/97	Katz	Bottom-Dollar Markets	Jamaican Blue Mountain	Coffee	$36.00	100	$3,600.00	
16	1/6/97	Katz	Bottom-Dollar Markets	Russian Blend	Tea	$9.80	20	$196.00	
17	1/10/97	Gebhardt	Familia Arquibaldo	Darjeeling	Tea	$20.30	30	$609.00	
18	1/10/97	Gebhardt	Familia Arquibaldo	Oaxaca	Coffee	$9.50	100	$950.00	
19	1/10/97	Hankins	La maison d'Asie	Jasmine	Tea	$9.80	20	$196.00	
20	1/10/97	Hankins	La maison d'Asie	Medellin	Coffee	$9.50	100	$950.00	
21	1/10/97	Hankins	La maison d'Asie	Santo Domingo	Coffee	$9.50	100	$950.00	
22	1/11/97	Hankins	Hungry Coyote Import Store	Darjeeling	Tea	$20.30	20	$406.00	
23	1/11/97	Hankins	Hungry Coyote Import Store	Pi Lo Chun	Tea	$11.10	20	$222.00	
24	1/12/97	Garnier	Wartian Herkku	Keemun	Tea	$9.70	20	$194.00	
25	1/12/97	Garnier	Wartian Herkku	Oaxaca	Coffee	$9.50	100	$950.00	
26	1/12/97	Langston	Simons bistro	Assam	Tea	$9.70	20	$194.00	
27	1/12/97	Langston	Simons bistro	Gyokuro	Tea	$11.20	20	$224.00	
28	1/13/97	Langston	QUICK-Stop	Chunmee	Tea	$9.70	20	$194.00	
29	1/16/97	Langston	Richter Supermarkt	Antigua	Coffee	$10.50	100	$1,050.00	

Orders / PivotTable /

Page 2 now appears on the right of page 1, which means that the pages will print from left to right instead of top to bottom.

4 On the View menu, click Normal.

Page Break Preview is replaced by the worksheet view.

Print

5 On the Standard toolbar, click the Print button.

Printing Selected Areas on a Worksheet

As keeper of the Island Tea & Coffee Company list of current orders, you receive many requests for printouts of different kinds: selected data for a specific month; a segment of data that needs to fit on a single page; or a summary report for a management meeting.

Print only selected data

In addition to a printout of the entire list of 1997 orders, your manager would like a printout of the orders data for March 1997. Because you have already set print titles, all you have to do is select the month's data; the column labels will be included automatically. In this exercise, you print the March orders data.

1 Select cells A121 through H182 (the March data).

2 On the File menu, click Print.

3 In the Print dialog box, under Print What, click the Selection option button.

4 In the Print dialog box, click Preview.

   The pages for your selected data are previewed. Because of the settings you defined in earlier exercises, the pages will print "Over, Then Down," and correct column and row labels will print on every page.

5 On the button bar, click Print.

   The worksheet is printed and Microsoft Excel returns to the worksheet view.

Define a print area

Co-workers regularly ask you for printouts of the list of orders for previous completed months, not including the orders for the current month. Since you do this several times each month, you can save time by defining a *print area*, an area of the worksheet that will be printed automatically when you click the Print button on the Standard toolbar. In this exercise, you define a print area that includes data for completed months only.

To set a print area from the worksheet view, select the print range, and then, on the File menu, point to Print Area and click Set Print Area.

1 On the View menu, click Page Break Preview.

2 In Page Break Preview, select the cells A1 through H356 (the records for January through June).

3 Use the right mouse button to click the selected range, and then click Set Print Area.

4 On the View menu, click Normal to return to worksheet view.

   Now that you have set a print area, only that area of the worksheet will be printed when you click the Print button on the Standard toolbar.

Print a worksheet on a specific number of pages

In preparation for a meeting, your manager has asked you if you can reduce the size of the completed months' data so that it will fit on a single page width and won't be longer than 5 pages. In this exercise, you make the print area 1 page in width by 5 pages in length.

1   On the File menu, click Page Setup.

2   On the Page tab, under Scaling, click the Fit To option button, and set the spinner boxes to show 1 Page(s) Wide By 5 Tall.

3   Click Print Preview.

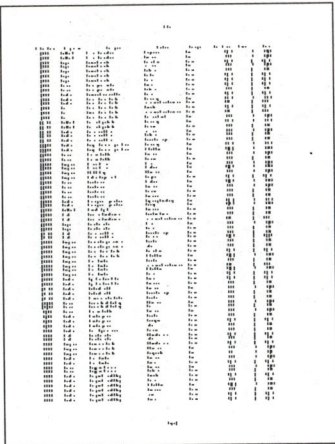

The status bar message indicates that the data fits on 5 pages, and you can see that it has been reduced in width so that all columns fit on a single page.

4   On the button bar, click Print.

The Print dialog box appears.

5   Click OK.

Center data on the printed page

The data on the printed page is left-aligned, but your manager wants it centered on the page. In this exercise, you center the data horizontally on the pages.

Print Preview

1   On the Standard toolbar, click the Print Preview button, and then click the page to zoom out if you need to so that you can see the whole page.

2   On the button bar, click Margins.

Margin lines appear around the edges of the page, and column breaks appear across the top of the page. The margin lines help you see whether the data looks centered.

You can drag margin lines and column breaks to change margins and column widths.

3   On the button bar, click Setup.

4   In the Page Setup dialog box, click the Margins tab.

5   Under Center On Page, select the Horizontally check box, and then click OK.

     The data on every page is centered horizontally.

6   On the button bar, click Print.

     The Print dialog box appears.

7   Click OK.

8   Save your workbook.

Printing Charts

As the office manager, you keep the Island Tea & Coffee Company workbooks arranged so that you can get to any type of data you want as quickly and efficiently as possible. This usually means that the worksheets and charts aren't arranged for instant printing. For example, you keep your charts embedded in worksheets because it's often more convenient to use an embedded chart than to flip back and forth between a worksheet and a chart; however, you sometimes need to print the worksheet without its embedded chart, or the chart without its source worksheet. You can easily do both without changing your workbook setup.

When you print a chart separately from its worksheet, you might notice that the chart's proportions are changed so that the printed chart is not in *scale* (not the same relative height and width) with the chart you created on the worksheet. If this presents a problem, you can easily re-scale the printed chart so that it retains the same relative proportions as the embedded chart.

Print a worksheet without printing the embedded chart

You can use the procedure in this exercise to prevent any graphical object on a worksheet from being printed with the worksheet.

Sometimes a chart covers up the data it is based on—for example, a large PivotTable might be covered by its embedded chart—and you need to print the data but don't want to print the chart. In this exercise, you print a worksheet without printing its embedded chart.

1   On the PivotTable sheet, point to an empty part of the chart background so that the ChartTip reads Chart Area, and then click with the right mouse button.

2   On the shortcut menu, click Format Chart Area.

3   In the Format Chart Area dialog box, click the Properties tab.

4   Clear the Print Object check box, and then click OK.

5   Click a cell in the worksheet, and then click Print Preview.

     The Print Preview window appears showing you that the worksheet will be printed without the embedded chart.

6   On the button bar, click Close.

Print Preview

Print an embedded chart without printing the worksheet

Your manager has asked you to present your charted data at a company meeting. In order to create a clear overhead slide, you want to print the chart without the extra clutter of the worksheet data. In this exercise, you print an embedded chart without printing its source worksheet.

1 Click anywhere on the chart, and then click the Print Preview button.

The Print Preview window opens, showing you that the chart will be printed separately.

2 On the button bar, click Print.

The Print dialog box appears.

3 Click OK.

Re-scale a printed chart

When you print a chart on its own page, by default the chart is scaled (its proportions are changed) to fill up the entire page. Your PivotTable chart is a short, wide rectangle, but when you print it, its scale changes so that it is taller and narrower. In this exercise, you re-scale the chart to print it with its original proportions.

1 Click anywhere on the chart.

2 On the File menu, click Page Setup, and then click the Chart tab.

3 On the Chart tab, click the Scale To Fit Page option button, and then click Print Preview.

The Print Preview window appears showing you that the chart will be printed with the proportions it has in the worksheet.

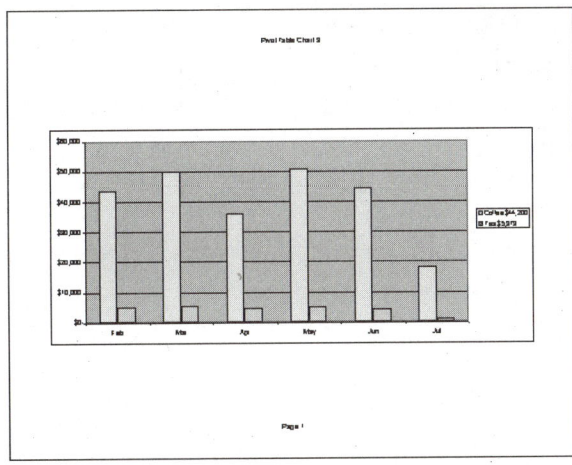

4   On the button bar, click Print.

The Print dialog box appears.

5   Click OK.

6   On the File menu, click Save.

> **NOTE**   This lesson has covered various ways to print data in a single worksheet, but you can also print all the worksheets in a workbook with one step. Be sure that a worksheet cell (not a chart) is selected, and then on the File menu, click Print; under Print What, click the Entire Workbook option button, and then click OK.

> **NOTE**   If you'd like to build on the skills you learned in this lesson, you can do the One Step Further. Otherwise, skip to "Finish the Lesson."

One Step Further: Setting Multiple Print Areas in a Worksheet

One of the Island Tea & Coffee Company's sales people has asked for printouts of March and June data. In this exercise, you set two print areas in one worksheet.

1   Select the Orders sheet, and then, on the View menu, click Page Break Preview.

2   Select cells A121 through H182 (the March records), and then hold down CTRL and select cells A302 through H356 (the June records).

3   Use the right mouse button to click in one of the selected ranges, and then, on the shortcut menu, click Set Print Area.

Two print areas are set.

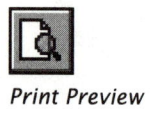

Print Preview

4   On the Standard toolbar, click the Print Preview button.

Each print area prints on its own page, and since your settings from previous exercises are still in place, each print area is centered on a single page.

5   On the button bar, click Print.

The Print dialog box appears.

6   Click OK.

7   On the File menu, click Save.

Finish the lesson

1 To continue to the Review & Practice section, on the File menu, click Close.

2 If you are finished using Microsoft Excel for now, on the File menu, click Exit.

Lesson Summary

To	Do this	Button
See a preview of printed pages	On the Standard toolbar, click the Print Preview button.	
See a preview of the page layout	On the View menu, click Page Break Preview.	
Change page breaks	On the View menu, click Page Break Preview. Drag page break lines to reposition page breaks.	
Set print titles	On the File menu, click Page Setup, and then click the Sheet tab. Click in the Rows To Repeat At Top box, and then click a cell in the row you want to appear at the top of each page. Click in the Columns To Repeat At Left box, and then click a cell in the column you want to appear down the left side of each page. Click OK.	
Change the page printing order	On the File menu, click Page Setup, and then click the Sheet tab. Under Page Order, click the "Over, Then Down" option button or the "Down, Then Over" option button, and then click OK.	
Print only selected data on a worksheet	Select the range to print, and then, on the File menu, click Print. Under Print What, click the Selection option button, and then click OK.	
Define a print area	On the View menu, click Page Break Preview. Select the range you want to set as a print area, and then use the right mouse button to click the selection. On the shortcut menu, click Set Print Area.	

To	Do this	Button
Print a worksheet on a specific number of pages	On the File menu, click Page Setup, and then click the Page tab. Under Scaling, click the Fit To option button, and set the number of pages wide by number of pages tall, and then click OK.	
Center data on a printed page	On the File menu, click Page Setup, and then click the Margins tab. Under Center On Page, select the Horizontally or Vertically check box, or both, and then click OK.	
Print a worksheet with an embedded chart	On the Standard toolbar, click the Print button.	
Print a worksheet without its embedded chart	Use the right mouse button to click an empty part of the chart, and then, on the shortcut menu, click Format Chart Area. Click the Properties tab, clear the Print Object check box, and then click OK. Click a cell in the worksheet, and then, on the Standard toolbar, click the Print button.	
Print an embedded chart without its worksheet	Select any part of the chart, and then, on the Standard toolbar, click the Print button.	
Print a chart sheet	Select the chart sheet, and then, on the Standard toolbar, click the Print button.	
Re-scale a printed chart	Select the chart, and then, on the File menu, click Page Setup. Click the Chart tab, select the Scale To Fit Page option button, and then click OK.	

For online information about	On the Help menu, click Contents And Index, click the Index tab, and then type
Printing worksheets	**printing, page setup**

Review & Practice

Estimated time
20 min.

You will review and practice how to:

- Import a text file.
- Create a PivotTable and group dates in the PivotTable by quarter.
- Create a chart.
- Format a chart.
- Print a PivotTable and a chart.

Before you move on to Part 4, in which you will learn techniques for finding answers and sharing your workbooks with co-workers, you can practice the skills you learned in Part 3 by working through the steps in this Review & Practice section. You will import a text file, create a PivotTable, create a chart from the PivotTable, and then print the PivotTable and the chart.

Scenario

The State University Alumni Association (SUAA) is planning a meeting to discuss ways to reduce expenses. One of the items on the agenda is a discussion of last year's expenses and how they might be reduced and managed more efficiently. You've been asked to create a summary of last year's expenses and print copies for everybody. The expense records for last year are stored in a text file that you will need to import into Microsoft Excel.

Step 1: Import a text file

You've been asked to create a PivotTable and a chart of last year's expense records. In this step, you start the process by importing the text file, in which the records are contained, into a Microsoft Excel worksheet.

1 Open the text file 1996exp.txt from the Excel SBS Practice folder.

2 In the Text Import Wizard, select the Tab Delimiter and use the default General format for each column.

3 After you import the data, apply the Currency format, with 2 decimal places, to column C (Amount).

4 Save the new file as a Microsoft Excel workbook, and name it 1996 SUAA Expenses.

For more information about	See
Importing data	Lesson 8

Step 2: Create a PivotTable

Now that you have imported the expenses data, you are ready to display it in the form of a summary. In this step, you create a PivotTable that shows expenses by category and by quarter.

1 Create a PivotTable from the list of data.

2 Place the Category field in a row orientation, the Date field in a column orientation, and the Amount field in the data area. (Hint: The field button should say Sum of Amount.) Create the PivotTable in a new worksheet.

3 Group the dates by quarter.

4 Apply the Currency format, with 2 decimal places, to the numbers in the data area.

If a warning message appears, click Cancel. Use the right mouse button to click the selection, point to Enable Selection, and then repeat step 4.

5 Name the new PivotTable sheet Data Summary.

Your PivotTable should look similar to the following illustration.

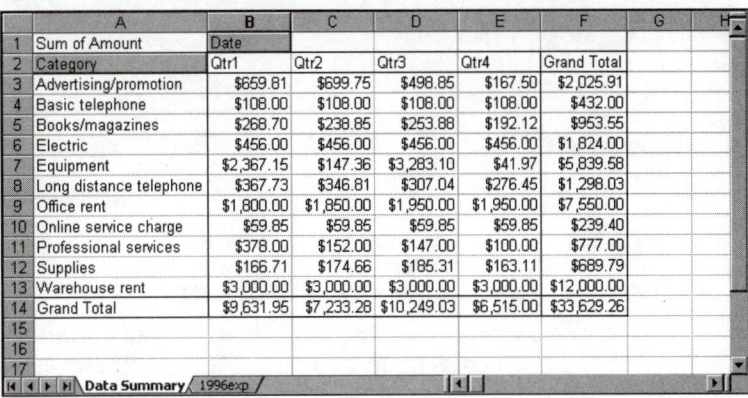

	A	B	C	D	E	F	G	H
1	Sum of Amount	Date						
2	Category	Qtr1	Qtr2	Qtr3	Qtr4	Grand Total		
3	Advertising/promotion	$659.81	$699.75	$498.85	$167.50	$2,025.91		
4	Basic telephone	$108.00	$108.00	$108.00	$108.00	$432.00		
5	Books/magazines	$268.70	$238.85	$253.88	$192.12	$953.55		
6	Electric	$456.00	$456.00	$456.00	$456.00	$1,824.00		
7	Equipment	$2,367.15	$147.36	$3,283.10	$41.97	$5,839.58		
8	Long distance telephone	$367.73	$346.81	$307.04	$276.45	$1,298.03		
9	Office rent	$1,800.00	$1,850.00	$1,950.00	$1,950.00	$7,550.00		
10	Online service charge	$59.85	$59.85	$59.85	$59.85	$239.40		
11	Professional services	$378.00	$152.00	$147.00	$100.00	$777.00		
12	Supplies	$166.71	$174.66	$185.31	$163.11	$689.79		
13	Warehouse rent	$3,000.00	$3,000.00	$3,000.00	$3,000.00	$12,000.00		
14	Grand Total	$9,631.95	$7,233.28	$10,249.03	$6,515.00	$33,629.26		
15								
16								
17								

Data Summary / 1996exp /

For more information about	**See**
Creating PivotTables	Lesson 8
Grouping dates	Lesson 8
Formatting PivotTable numbers	Lesson 8

Step 3: *Create a chart of the PivotTable*

Now that you have a summary of the data, you need to present it graphically. In this step, you create a chart to display the data visually.

1 Select cells E13 through A2 without including the grand totals in the chart. (Hint: Type **E13:A2** in the Name box.)

2 Create an embedded chart using the Chart Wizard.

3 Plot the data series in rows so that the legend lists categories and the horizontal axis shows quarters.

4 Add the text "1996 SUAA Expenses" to the chart as a title, and then complete the chart by formatting the chart so that it looks similar to the following illustration.

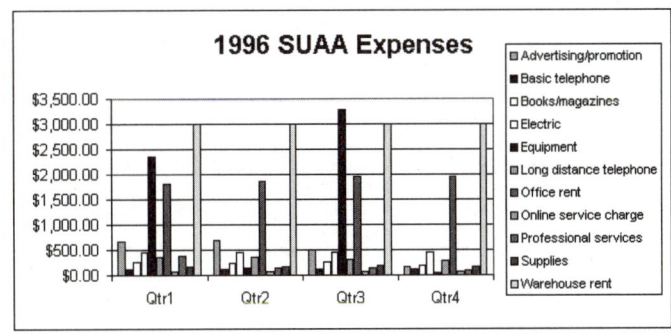

5   Save the workbook.

For more information about	See
Creating a chart	Lesson 9
Formatting a chart	Lesson 9
Adding a chart title	Lesson 9

Step 4:   Print the chart and the PivotTable

To complete your presentation for the meeting, you need to print the two documents you created. In this step, you print the PivotTable and the chart separately.

1   Move the chart down on the worksheet so that it does not cover the PivotTable.

2   Set a print area that consists only of the PivotTable.

3   Apply the AutoFormat named Classic 3 to the PivotTable.

4   Center the PivotTable horizontally on the printed page.

5   Print the worksheet.

6   Select the chart and scale it to fit the page with its original proportions. (Hint: Open the chart in Print Preview mode, and then click the Setup button on the button bar.)

7   Print the chart.

8   On the File menu, click Save.

For more information about	See
Setting a print area	Lesson 10
Applying an AutoFormat	Lesson 8
Centering on the printed page	Lesson 10
Scaling a chart for the printed page	Lesson 10
Printing an embedded chart without the worksheet	Lesson 10

Finish the Review & Practice

1   To continue to the next lesson, on the File menu, click Close.

2   If you are finished using Microsoft Excel for now, on the File menu, click Exit.

Analyzing and Sharing Your Data

Comparing Alternatives for Better Decisions

In this lesson you will learn how to:

■ Use Goal Seek to find a mathematical answer.

■ Create scenarios to compare alternative situations.

In this lesson, you will learn how to analyze data efficiently by using Goal Seek and Scenario Manager. Suppose you want to know by how much sales would have to increase to reach a specific operating income goal. When you know the answer (in this case, the desired operating income), Goal Seek can help you determine what the other side of the equation (sales) needs to be.

Goal Seek can give you a specific answer to a specific question, but often you need to determine which of several different scenarios is the best. Scenario Manager can help you set up a number of scenarios, each slightly different, to see how changing different figures in a situation can affect the outcome. By using Scenario Manager, you can make more informed business decisions.

At the Island Tea & Coffee Company, the management team is attempting to determine how much monthly sales need to increase to reach a monthly operating income of $10,000. A question of this nature can be complicated by the fact that other numbers in the budget also change when the sales volume changes. For example, each sales person gets a 50% commission; so, when sales go up, so do commissions, which affect the operating income.

You can also use Scenario Manager to set up various Island Tea & Coffee Company budget scenarios and compare the outcomes. Scenario Manager creates sets of values to use in different scenarios. Each scenario represents a set of "what-if" assumptions that you can use to view the outcome of a worksheet model. For example, you can ask "What if I change the COGs value?" or "What if I reduce the advertising expense?" With Scenario Manager, you can make these changes, and then view the results side-by-side for easy comparison and sound decision-making.

Open an existing file

You keep the current budget in a workbook named 1997 Budget. In this exercise, you open the 1997 Budget file.

Open

1 On the Standard toolbar, click the Open button.

2 In the Open dialog box, click the Look In Favorites button.

3 In the file list, double-click the Excel SBS Practice folder.

4 Double-click the 1997 Budget file.

Save the file with a new name

In this exercise, you save the 1997 Budget file as Analysis.

1 On the File menu, click Save As.

The Save As dialog box opens. Be sure the Excel SBS Practice folder appears in the Save In box.

2 In the File Name box, type **Analysis**, and then click Save.

Using Goal Seek to Determine the Best Price

At the beginning of the new fiscal year, the Island Tea & Coffee Company management is reviewing the projected operating budget, and looking for a way to increase monthly operating income to $10,000 a month. For example, based on the current budget model, sales need to increase by $2,358 in order to increase the operating income to $10,000 for the month of July. However, the question is more complex than that, since the sales staff commission needs also to be taken into account.

This type of problem can be resolved efficiently by using Goal Seek. Goal Seek substitutes different values into the *changing cell* (in this case, the sales cell) until the value in the *goal cell* (operating income) is equal to the value you want ($10,000).

Use Goal Seek to determine the optimal sales level

With the July data at hand, you need to start the analysis process by determining by how much the July sales need to increase in order for the Island Tea & Coffee Company to reach a monthly operating income of $10,000. In this exercise, you use Goal Seek to answer this question.

1 Click cell B26 (Operating Income).

2 On the Tools menu, click Goal Seek.

3 Verify that the Set Cell box reads B26, and then, in the To Value box, type **10000**

4 Press TAB to place the insertion point in the By Changing Cell box, and then click cell B6 (Sales).

5 Click OK.

The Goal Seek Status dialog box appears containing the answer to the question you asked. To reach a monthly operating income of $10,000, the Island Tea & Coffee Company will have to increase sales to $54,298, a difference of $4,717.

6 Click OK to keep the new values in your worksheet.

Return the worksheet to original values

You will use Scenario Manager in the next section to compare different budget possibilities, so you want to return your worksheet to the values it contained before you changed them with Goal Seek.

Undo

➤ On the Standard toolbar, click the Undo button.

The Goal Seek changes are removed and the original values appear in the worksheet.

Creating Multiple Scenarios to Compare Alternatives

The management team believes that there are additional ways to increase the operating income, and they want to look at alternative changes to the budget. To provide a summary of alternatives, you can use Scenario Manager to create different budget scenarios. When you finish creating multiple scenarios, you can create a scenario summary that can then be presented to the management team members for their review and analysis.

Before you create any scenarios, you should name all the cells that you might use in each scenario; this way, when you generate a scenario summary, the cell names you defined are used and the readability is improved.

Name input cells

To generate the clearest scenarios and summary possible, you name the cells that you will be using. In this exercise, you name all possible input cells.

1 Select cells A6 through B26.

2 On the Insert menu, point to Name, and then click Create.

The Create Names dialog box appears.

3 Verify that the Left Column check box is selected, and then click OK.

The cells are named using the labels in column A.

Create a scenario of changed costs

Before experimenting with different scenarios, you decide to create a scenario documenting the current budget so that you can refer back to it when you compare the alternatives. In this exercise, you create a first scenario based on your current budget.

1 On the Tools menu, click Scenarios.

The Scenario Manager dialog box appears.

2 Click the Add button.

The Add Scenario dialog box appears.

3 In the Scenario Name box, type **Current Budget**, and then press TAB to highlight the entry in the Changing Cells box.

4 Click cell B6, and then hold down CTRL and click cells B7, B10, B11, and B16.

The cell references are entered in the Changing Cells box and are separated by commas. These are the cells that you will change in different scenarios.

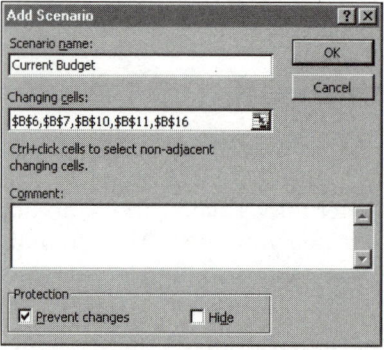

5 Click OK.

The Scenario Values dialog box appears containing the cell names.

6   Click OK.

The Scenario Manager dialog box appears with your first scenario listed in the Scenarios list.

7   Click Close.

8   Save your workbook.

Create additional scenarios

Now that you have created a scenario based on your current budget, you're ready to start experimenting. In this exercise, you create different scenarios by changing the values in the Changing Cells box and saving each scenario.

1   On the Tools menu, click Scenarios.

The Scenario Manager dialog box appears.

2   Click Add.

3   In the Add Scenario dialog box, in the Scenario Name box, type **Low COGs**, and then click OK.

The Scenario Values dialog box appears.

4   Double-click in the Goods box to highlight the Goods value, type **15000**, and then press TAB.

5   In the Freight box, type **200**, and then click OK.

The Scenario Manager dialog box appears again. The new scenario, Low COGs, is added to the Scenarios list.

6   Click Add to add another scenario.

The Add Scenario dialog box appears.

7   In the Scenario Name box, type **High Shipping**, and then click OK.

8   Press TAB to highlight the Shipping box, type **8000**, and then click OK.

The Scenario Manager dialog box appears.

9   Click Add.

The Add Scenario dialog box appears.

10   In the Scenario Name box, type **Low Advertising**, and then click OK.

11   Double-click in the Advertising box, type **400**, and then click OK.

All the scenarios have been added.

View the scenarios

Now that you have created different scenarios, you're ready to take a closer a look at them. In this exercise, you view each scenario and the changes it creates in your worksheet.

1 In the Scenario Manager dialog box, click Low COGS in the Scenarios list, and then click Show.

The values in the worksheet change to reflect the changes produced by the Low COGS scenario, but because the Scenario Manager dialog box is still open, you cannot scroll down to see how the operating income has been affected.

2 In the Scenario Manager dialog box, click Close, and then scroll down to see the change in the operating income.

Create a scenario summary

It is difficult to assess the impact of different scenarios in your worksheet because you can only see one scenario at a time. A better way to compare the results of your scenarios is to create a summary that lays out all the scenarios side-by-side in a single worksheet. In this exercise, you make your budget scenarios more useful to the management team by creating a scenario summary.

1 On the Tools menu, click Scenarios.

2 In the Scenario Manager dialog box, click Summary.

The Scenario Summary dialog box appears.

3 Verify that the Scenario Summary option button is selected and that the Result Cells box reads B26, and then click OK.

A new worksheet named Scenario Summary is added to your workbook. It shows the changes and results for each scenario, and has outline symbols on the left and across the top that operate like outline symbols in a subtotaled worksheet.

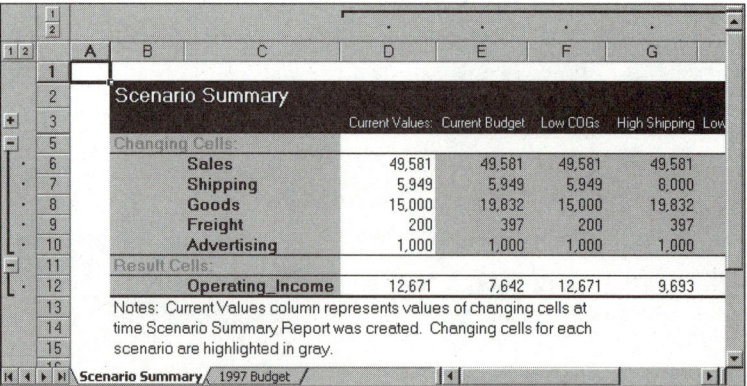

4 Save the Analysis workbook.

NOTE If you'd like to build on the skills you learned in this lesson, you can do the One Step Further. Otherwise, skip to "Finish the Lesson."

One Step Further: Editing a Scenario

While reviewing the scenarios before handing them off to the management team, you notice a mistake in the Low Advertising scenario: the advertising value should be $500 instead of $400. In this exercise, you edit the scenario appropriately, and then create a new Scenario Summary worksheet.

1 Delete the Scenario Summary worksheet. (Hint: Use the right mouse button to click the sheet tab, and then click Delete.)

2 On the Tools menu, click Scenarios.

3 Select the Low Advertising scenario, and then click Edit.

   The Edit Scenario dialog box appears.

4 Under Protection, clear the Prevent Changes check box, and then click OK.

   The Scenario Values dialog box appears.

5 Change the Advertising value to 500, and then click OK.

   The Scenario Manager dialog box appears.

6 Click Summary.

   The Scenario Summary dialog box appears.

7 Verify that the Scenario Summary option button is selected and that the Result Cells box reads B26, and then click OK.

   A new Scenario Summary worksheet is added to your workbook.

8 Save your work.

Finish the lesson

1 To continue to the next lesson, on the File menu, click Close.

2 If you are finished using Microsoft Excel for now, on the File menu, click Exit.

Lesson Summary

To	Do this
Use Goal Seek to determine a specific value	Select the cell that contains the formula in which you want to produce a desired result, and then, on the Tools menu, click Goal Seek. In the To Value box, type a goal value, and then, in the By Changing Cell box, specify the cell containing the value you want to change to reach the goal. Click OK.
Create a scenario	On the Tools menu, click Scenarios. Click Add. In the Scenario Name box, type a name; in the Changing Cells box, click cells to specify the cells that will change; and then, click OK. In the Scenario Values dialog box, type the values that you want, click OK, and then click Close.
View a scenario using the Scenario Manager dialog box	On the Tools menu, click Scenarios. Select the scenario you want, and then click Show.
Create a scenario summary	On the Tools menu, click Scenarios. In the Scenario Manager dialog box, click Summary. In the Scenario Summary dialog box, verify that the Scenario Summary option button is selected and that the Result Cells box reads the appropriate result cell reference, and then click OK.

For online information about	**On the Help menu, click Contents And Index, click the Index tab, and then type**
Finding answers with Goal Seek	**goal seeking**
Creating scenarios	**scenario manager**

Sharing a Workbook with Others

Lesson

12

In this lesson you will learn how to:

- Allow others to share and edit a workbook simultaneously.
- See who is currently looking at or working on a workbook.
- Review workbook revisions made by others.
- Update a shared workbook, resolve conflicting changes, and accept or reject revisions.

Estimated time
30 min.

In this lesson, you will learn how to share a workbook with other users on a network. A shared workbook can be edited simultaneously by multiple users. For example, you might enter formulas into a workbook at the same time as other users are entering data for those formulas into the same workbook. This saves time because users do not have to wait for a workbook to become available. Each user can see the changes that other users make in the workbook, and can resolve conflicts by choosing one entry.

To do this lesson, you will need to enlist the help of a co-worker on your network; you will also need to save the practice file in a shared folder on your network so that your co-worker can open it.

As the Island Tea & Coffee Company office manager and "keeper" of the inventory files, you have tried managing them using different techniques such as consolidation, subtotaling, and templates, but you have come to the conclusion that it would make more sense to keep the monthly inventories in a single workbook, and have everyone who works on the inventory enter their data directly into it. To make it an efficient process for everyone, you will make the inventory workbook a shared workbook; this will allow everyone involved to enter their part of the data when they are ready, without having to wait for other users to close the workbook.

In the following exercises, you will open the Shared Inventory List workbook and save it as a practice file with the name Shared Workbook Lesson.

Open an existing file

Open

1   On the Standard toolbar, click the Open button.

2   In the Open dialog box, click the Look In Favorites button.

3   In the file list, double-click the Excel SBS Practice folder.

4   Double-click the Shared Inventory List file.

Save the file with a new name

1   On the File menu, click Save As.

The Save As dialog box opens. If the Excel SBS Practice folder is not a shared folder on your network, locate a shared folder and be sure its name appears in the Save In box.

2   In the File Name box, type **Shared Workbook Lesson**, and then click Save.

Sharing a Workbook and Using it Simultaneously

You have decided to keep the Island Tea & Coffee Company inventory in a single workbook, and all of your co-workers who participate in the inventory count will enter their data in that workbook. When you *share* the workbook, each user can open it and enter data at any time, instead of having to wait for others to finish using the workbook. For example, one or several of your co-workers can enter monthly inventory data at the same time as you enter formulas to determine the average monthly inventory counts.

Before you and your co-workers can open and enter data in the Shared Workbook Lesson file, you need to make it a shared workbook.

Share a workbook so that multiple users can use it simultaneously

In this exercise, you make the Shared Workbook Lesson file a shared workbook.

1   On the Tools menu, click Share Workbook.

The Share Workbook dialog box appears.

2   On the Editing tab, select the Allow Changes By More Than One User At The Same Time check box, and then click OK.

3   When prompted to confirm that you want the workbook to be saved, click OK.

The workbook is shared and accessible to any other users on your network who have access to this folder.

 IMPORTANT   In order to complete the following exercises, you will need to enlist the help of a partner. You must both open the Shared Workbook Lesson file on your respective computers.

Enter data—you

In this exercise, you enter monthly inventory data (while your partner is entering formulas).

1   On the Tools menu, click Share Workbook.

The Share Workbook dialog box appears. The Editing tab shows that both you and your partner have the shared workbook open.

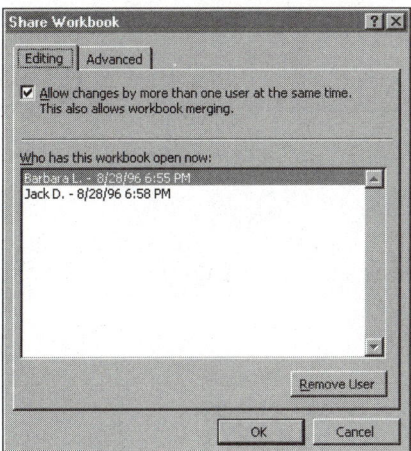

2   Click OK.

The Share Workbook dialog box closes.

3 Enter the following data in cells M12 through M25:

Cell	Entry
M12	200
M13	700
M14	600
M15	600
M16	1100
M17	800
M18	800
M19	600
M20	700
M21	600
M22	300
M23	300
M24	500
M25	800

Enter formulas—your partner

In this exercise, your partner enters formulas that average the monthly inventory data (while you are entering the remaining inventory data).

1 In cell N3, type **=average(g3:m3)**, and then press ENTER.

2 Drag the fill handle on cell N3 to copy the formula down to cell N39.

3 Use the right mouse button to click the column N header, click Format Cells, click the Number tab, and then select the Number format and 0 decimal places.

4 Click OK.

5 Enter the text **Average** in cell N2, click the Bold button on the Formatting toolbar, and then press ENTER.

Bold

Save the workbook—you and your partner

In this exercise, you and your partner save the file and see each other's entries. Each user should do this exercise on his or her own machine.

IMPORTANT Be sure that your partner has saved his or her changes before you save yours.

1   Save the Shared Workbook Lesson file.

   If a message box appears, click OK. Each changed cell is highlighted with a colored border and a colored triangle in the upper-left corner. The highlighting color identifies the user who made the change.

2   Point to a highlighted cell.

   A revision comment appears that indicates who made the change and what the change was.

   NOTE   You might both have to save again to guarantee that you can each see each other's changes.

Reviewing Changes in a Workbook

In a shared workbook, you can also make changes to the same data simultaneously with your co-workers, even if the changes conflict. The workbook maintains a change history so that you can see what changes have been made to the data and who made them. You can then resolve conflicting changes by choosing which changes to keep.

A co-worker helped perform the Island Tea & Coffee Company inventory count in July, and he wrote down an incorrect number for Haiti coffee: instead of 200, the entry should be 300. When he realized his error, he contacted both you and your partner with the change, but your partner misunderstood the message and changed the number from 200 to 100, while you entered the correct number, 300. In the following exercises, you will change the Haiti entry, and then resolve the conflict between the changes.

Make revisions in the workbook—your partner

In this exercise, your partner changes the Haiti count to 100.

1   Change the entry in cell M12 to 100.

2   Save the workbook.

Make revisions in the workbook—you

In this exercise, you change the Haiti count to 300.

1 Change the entry in cell M12 to 300.

2 Save the workbook.

The Resolve Conflicts dialog box appears.

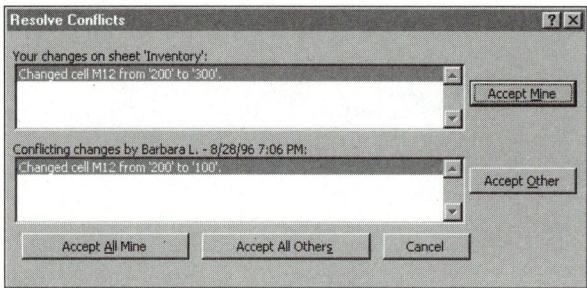

Resolve conflicts in a workbook

In this exercise, you resolve conflicting changes in the workbook.

1 In the Resolve Conflicts dialog box, click Accept Mine (which corresponds to the change from 200 to 300).

If a message box appears that says "Save Resulted In Some Changes From Other Users," click OK.

2 Your partner can save and close the shared workbook.

Accept or reject revisions in a shared workbook

1 On the Tools menu, point to Track Changes, and then click Accept or Reject Changes.

If a message box appears asking you to confirm that you want to save the workbook, click OK. The Select Changes To Accept Or Reject dialog box appears.

2 Be sure that the When check box is selected and that the When list box reads Not Yet Reviewed, and then click OK.

The Accept Or Reject Changes dialog box appears.

Undo

3 Click Accept All.

All of the changes in the worksheet are accepted, and the Undo button on the Standard toolbar is dimmed so that you cannot undo the changes that you accepted.

NOTE There are several things you cannot do in a shared workbook, such as delete worksheets; create or change the layout of PivotTables; and create conditional formats and data validation. In order to do any of these things, you will first need to remove the workbook from shared use. To do this, on the Tools menu, click Share Workbook, and then click the Editing tab. Clear the Allow Changes By More Than One User At The Same Time check box, and then click OK. When prompted to confirm your action, click Yes.

NOTE If you'd like to build on the skills you learned in this lesson, you can do the One Step Further. Otherwise, skip to "Finish the Lesson."

One Step Further: Printing a Change History

Your manager wants to know when and by whom a specific change was made in the inventory count. In this exercise, you create and print a change history worksheet.

1 On the Tools menu, point to Track Changes, and then click Highlight Changes.

2 Clear the When, Who, and Where check boxes if any are selected, select the List Changes On A New Sheet check box, and then click OK.

A new worksheet, named History, is inserted in the workbook. It lists the changes saved in the shared workbook and information about the changes.

The History worksheet is temporary and is not saved when the workbook is saved. To generate a new History worksheet, repeat step 2.

The History sheet lists all saved changes, according to your When, Who and Where selections, whereas Change Highlighting highlights all unsaved changes.

Action Number	Date	Time	Who	Change	Sheet	Range	New Value
1	8/28/96	7:03 PM	Barbara L.	Cell Change	Inventory	N3	=AVERAGE(G3:M3)
2	8/28/96	7:03 PM	Barbara L.	Cell Change	Inventory	N4	=AVERAGE(G4:M4)
3	8/28/96	7:03 PM	Barbara L.	Cell Change	Inventory	N5	=AVERAGE(G5:M5)
4	8/28/96	7:03 PM	Barbara L.	Cell Change	Inventory	N6	=AVERAGE(G6:M6)
5	8/28/96	7:03 PM	Barbara L.	Cell Change	Inventory	N7	=AVERAGE(G7:M7)
6	8/28/96	7:03 PM	Barbara L.	Cell Change	Inventory	N8	=AVERAGE(G8:M8)
7	8/28/96	7:03 PM	Barbara L.	Cell Change	Inventory	N9	=AVERAGE(G9:M9)
8	8/28/96	7:03 PM	Barbara L.	Cell Change	Inventory	N10	=AVERAGE(G10:M10)
9	8/28/96	7:03 PM	Barbara L.	Cell Change	Inventory	N11	=AVERAGE(G11:M11)
10	8/28/96	7:03 PM	Barbara L.	Cell Change	Inventory	N12	=AVERAGE(G12:M12)
11	8/28/96	7:03 PM	Barbara L.	Cell Change	Inventory	N13	=AVERAGE(G13:M13)
12	8/28/96	7:03 PM	Barbara L.	Cell Change	Inventory	N14	=AVERAGE(G14:M14)
13	8/28/96	7:03 PM	Barbara L.	Cell Change	Inventory	N15	=AVERAGE(G15:M15)
14	8/28/96	7:03 PM	Barbara L.	Cell Change	Inventory	N16	=AVERAGE(G16:M16)
15	8/28/96	7:03 PM	Barbara L.	Cell Change	Inventory	N17	=AVERAGE(G17:M17)

Inventory \ History

3 Print the History sheet.

Finish the lesson

1   On the File menu, click Save.

2   To continue to the next lesson, on the File menu, click Close.

3   If you are finished using Microsoft Excel for now, on the File menu, click Exit.

Lesson Summary

To	Do this
Share a workbook	On the Tools menu, click Share Workbook. On the Editing tab, click the Allow Changes By More Than One User At The Same Time check box, and then click OK. When prompted, click OK to confirm your action.
See who is currently looking at or working on a workbook	On the Tools menu, click Share Workbook, and then look at the list of names on the Editing tab.
Enter data in a shared workbook	Enter the data you want, and then save the workbook.
Resolve conflicts between changes	In the Resolve Conflicts dialog box, click the button corresponding to the change you want to accept.
Accept or reject changes	On the Tools menu, point to Track Changes, and then click Accept or Reject Changes. In the Select Changes To Accept Or Reject dialog box, select the changes to review, and then click OK. In the Accept Or Reject Changes dialog box, click the Accept or Reject button to review changes one by one, or click the Accept All or Reject All buttons to accept or reject all changes.

For online information about	On the Help menu, click Contents And Index, click the Index tab, and then type
Sharing workbooks	**workbooks, shared**

Integrating Microsoft Excel with Other Programs

Estimated time
30 min.

In this lesson you will learn how to:

- Link information from another program.
- Edit linked information.
- Embed information from another program.
- Edit embedded information.
- Convert a Microsoft Excel worksheet into a Microsoft Access database.
- Connect documents with hyperlinks.

Reports usually consist of several different types of information; for example, numerical data and charts from Microsoft Excel might be presented along with an analysis of the data written in Microsoft Word. A report can be composed of a worksheet with part of a Microsoft Word document in it, or a Word document containing an Excel table or chart.

There are three ways to integrate information from different programs: pasting, linking, and embedding. *Pasting* means that you simply copy a picture of the information you want to include in a document, and then paste the picture into another program. The information in a pasted picture cannot be edited or formatted. *Linking* means that the information you copy into your worksheet is connected to the *source*, or original, document or worksheet that you copied it from. Linked information can be edited and formatted; when you edit or format linked information, you make changes to the source file from which the information came. *Embedding* means the information is connected to the program in which it was created (the source program), but not to the source file, so you can edit and format the information using the source program, but changes you make will not affect the source file.

In this lesson you will learn how to link and embed information between Microsoft Excel and Microsoft Word, and you will practice editing both embedded and linked information. You will also practice pasting a picture into a Microsoft PowerPoint slide. Finally, you will learn how to convert a Microsoft Excel worksheet into a Microsoft Access database.

As the Island Tea & Coffee Company office manager, you have been asked to generate two reports: an electronic report in which a sales analysis from a Microsoft Word document is included in a worksheet, and a printed report in which a Microsoft Excel chart is included in a Microsoft Word document.

In the following exercises, you will open and then save the two documents necessary to complete this lesson.

IMPORTANT   You will need to have Microsoft Word 97 installed on your computer to perform the following exercises.

Open and save a Microsoft Excel file

Open

1   On the Standard toolbar, click the Open button.
2   In the Open dialog box, click the Look In Favorites button.
3   In the File list box, double-click the Excel SBS Practice folder.
4   Double-click the Sales Report file.
5   On the File menu, click Save As.

The Save As dialog box appears. Be sure that the Excel SBS Practice folder appears in the Save In box.

6   In the File Name box, type **Integration Lesson**, and then click Save.

Open and save a Microsoft Word file

1   Click Start. Point to Programs, and then click Microsoft Word.

Microsoft Word opens.

2 Open the Sales Analysis file located in your Excel SBS Practice folder, and then save it as **Integration Lesson**

Your window should look similar to the following illustration.

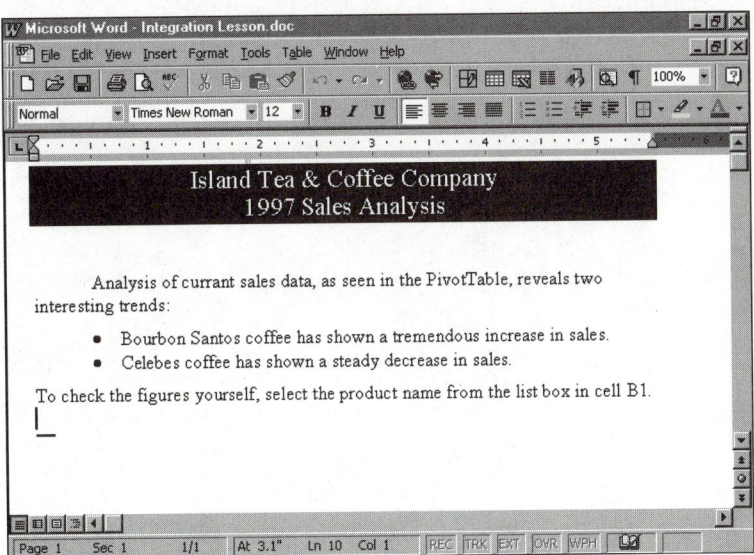

Linking Information Between Programs

The two files you have opened are related parts of an Island Tea & Coffee Company sales report for 1997: the workbook contains raw data and a PivotTable, and the document contains an analysis of the data. You've been asked to combine the two by pasting information from the Microsoft Word document into the Microsoft Excel worksheet that contains the PivotTable.

You will link the information from the Microsoft Word document so that any changes you might need to make to the analysis will also be made to the source Microsoft Word document. This way, any changes you make, such as correct spelling or grammar, will need to be made only once; all linked copies of the Microsoft Word document will be automatically updated when changes are made to the source document.

Paste a linked Microsoft Word document into a worksheet

In this exercise, you combine the Island Tea & Coffee Company's 1997 sales data and analysis into a complete report by copying and then pasting linked information from the Microsoft Word document into your Microsoft Excel worksheet.

1 In Microsoft Word, on the Edit menu, click Select All.

   The entire document is selected.

2 On the Edit menu, click Copy.

3 On the taskbar, click the Microsoft Excel button.

   The Microsoft Excel window appears.

4 On the Sales Report sheet, select cell D3.

5 On the Edit menu, click Paste Special.

   The Paste Special dialog box appears.

6 Click the Paste Link option button.

7 Verify that Microsoft Word Document Object is selected in the As list, and then click OK.

   A linked copy of the document is pasted into your worksheet, and when the linked object is selected, the path to the source file appears in the formula bar. Your worksheet should look similar to the following illustration.

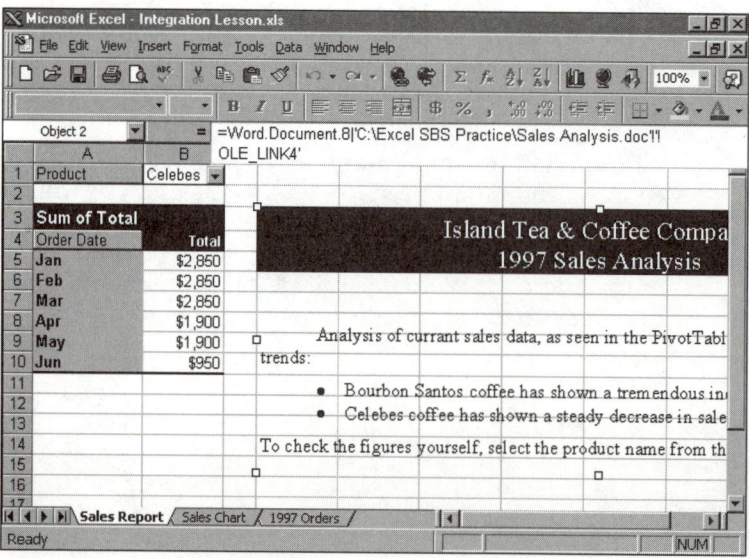

Edit a linked Microsoft Word document from within Microsoft Excel

When you double-click a linked object, the source program and file will open automatically.

While taking a quick look at the pasted Microsoft Word object, you noticed a misspelling in the first sentence. You need to correct the mistake in the source document as well as in the copy you pasted into your worksheet. In this exercise, you make the correction by editing the information from within Microsoft Excel.

1 Double-click the linked Microsoft Word object in your Microsoft Excel worksheet.

   The source file opens in Microsoft Word.

2 Change the spelling of the word "currant" to "current."

3 Save the Microsoft Word document.

4 On the taskbar, click the Microsoft Excel button.

   The object in your worksheet is updated to reflect the change in the Microsoft Word document.

5 Save the workbook.

Embedding Information Between Programs

You have been asked to create an Island Tea & Coffee Company sales report that contains an analysis report and a chart. You have elected to embed the chart into your Microsoft Word report because it will allow you to change the information and the formatting in the object using Microsoft Excel functionality without changing the pasted object. This is advantageous when you want to make changes to the object without changing the source, or when you need to be able to change the object but you don't have access to the source file (for instance, if the file you are working in is on your laptop computer and the source file is back at the office, on the Island Tea & Coffee Company network).

Embed a Microsoft Excel chart into a Microsoft Word document

Your Microsoft Excel file contains a chart sheet named Sales Chart. You will create an integrated report by embedding this chart into the Microsoft Word analysis document.

To go to the end of a document quickly, press CTRL+END.

1 Switch to Microsoft Word, and then place your pointer at the end of the document.

2 Switch to Microsoft Excel, and then select the Sales Chart sheet.

195

3 On the Edit menu, click Copy.

4 Switch to Microsoft Word, and then, on the Edit menu, click Paste Special.

5 Be sure that the Paste option button is selected and that Microsoft Excel Chart Object is selected in the As list, and then click OK.

The chart is embedded in the Microsoft Word document. You can resize the chart object by dragging the corner handles.

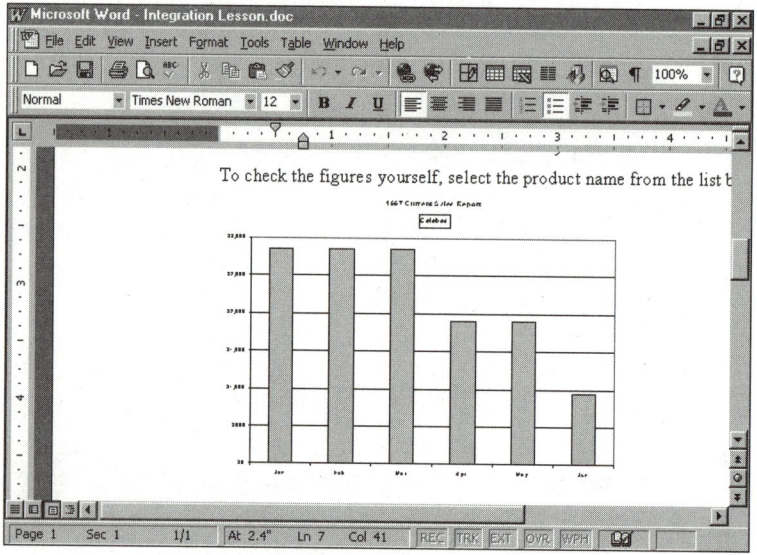

Edit an embedded chart from within Microsoft Word

Your manager has asked you to format the data markers in the report's chart with a pattern fill, without modifying the source chart. Because you embedded the chart rather than linking it, you can change the chart object in the document without affecting the source chart sheet. In this exercise, you edit the embedded object only.

1 In the Microsoft Word document, double-click the chart object.

The Microsoft Excel menu bar and toolbars appear. A hatched border appears around the chart object.

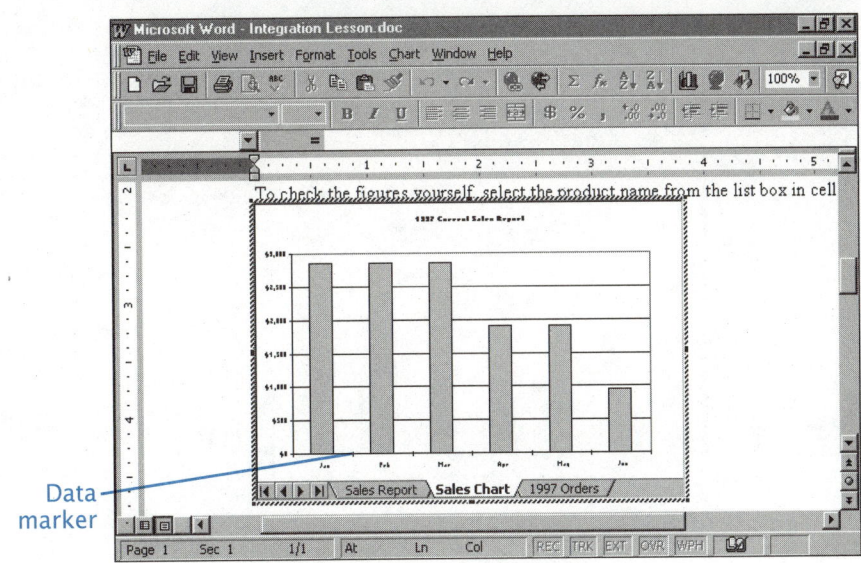

Data marker

2   In the chart object, double-click any data marker.

The Format Data Series dialog box appears.

3   On the Patterns tab, click the Fill Effects button.

The Fill Effects dialog box appears.

4   On the Texture tab, click Purple Mesh (the third texture down in the third column from the left—the name of the texture, "Purple mesh," appears in the box below the textures), click OK, and then click OK again.

The Format Data Series dialog box closes.

5   Click the Microsoft Word document (outside of the embedded chart) to return to Microsoft Word.

Your document should look similar to the following illustration. The source chart has not been changed.

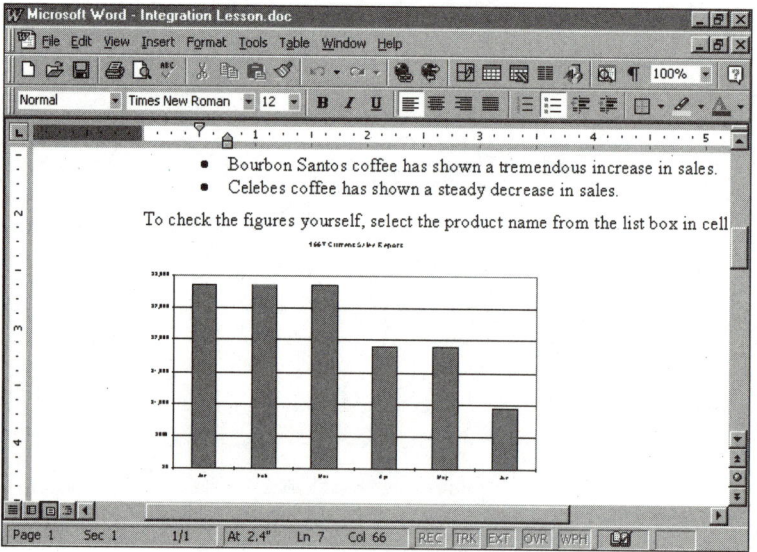

6   Save and then close the Integration Lesson document and Microsoft Word.

7   In Microsoft Excel, save the Integration Lesson workbook.

Pasting a Microsoft Excel Chart into a PowerPoint Slide

You have been asked to create a Microsoft PowerPoint slide containing a chart for a sales meeting. You will paste a picture of the chart into the slide, rather than linking or embedding it, because the slide will be presented from a laptop computer that only has Microsoft PowerPoint loaded.

 IMPORTANT   You will need to have Microsoft PowerPoint 97 installed on your computer to complete this exercise.

Paste a chart into a slide

In this exercise, you paste a picture of the Microsoft Excel chart into a blank Microsoft PowerPoint slide.

1   In the Microsoft Excel Integration Lesson workbook, select the Sales Chart sheet.

2 Click Start. Point to Programs, and then click Microsoft PowerPoint. Microsoft PowerPoint starts, and the PowerPoint dialog box appears.

3 Click the Blank Presentation option button, and then click OK.

4 Click in the Click To Add First Slide box, and then click the Chart AutoLayout (the second layout down in the rightmost column).

5 Click OK.

A blank slide appears that contains a text box at the top, and a picture box below the text box.

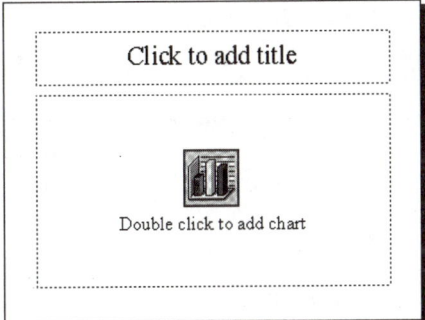

6 On the taskbar, click the Microsoft Excel button.

7 Be sure that the Sales Chart sheet is selected, and then, on the Edit menu, click Copy.

8 On the taskbar, click the Microsoft PowerPoint button.

9 Click in the picture box to select it, and then, on the Edit menu, click Paste Special.

10 Be sure that the Paste option button is selected, select Microsoft Excel Chart Object, and then click OK.

A picture of your Sales Chart is pasted into the slide. Your slide should look similar to the following illustration.

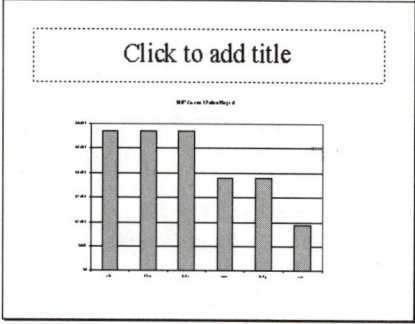

11 Save the presentation as Sales Chart, and then close the presentation and Microsoft PowerPoint.

12 Save the Integration Lesson workbook, but keep it open for a later exercise.

Converting a Worksheet into a Microsoft Access Table

For more information about Microsoft Access, see the Microsoft Access 97 Step by Step book.

The Island Tea & Coffee Company sales manager has decided to keep the customer list in Microsoft Access, where he can easily store large numbers of records and pull out, or extract, only those records that he needs. He has asked you to convert the customer list workbook into a Microsoft Access table.

IMPORTANT You will need to have Microsoft Access 97 installed on your computer to complete this exercise. You will also need to have the AccessLink add-in installed in Microsoft Excel. To do so, on the Tools menu, click Add-Ins, select AccessLinks Add-In, and then click OK.

Convert a worksheet to a Microsoft Access table

In this exercise, you will open the Island Tea & Coffee Company customer list in Microsoft Excel and convert it to a Microsoft Access table. The Integration Lesson workbook is still open from previous exercises, and you will use it again in later exercises; it can remain open while you open the customer list for this exercise.

1 Open the Customer List file located in the Excel SBS Practice folder, and then select a cell in the worksheet list.

2 On the Data menu, click Convert To MS Access. (If you do not see the Convert To MS Access command on your Data menu, you need to install the AccessLinks add-in.)

The Convert to Microsoft Access dialog box opens.

3 Under Convert To, be sure that the New Database option button is selected, and then click OK.

The Microsoft Access Import Spreadsheet Wizard appears.

4 Follow the steps in the wizard to convert the customer list into a Microsoft Access table.

5 Close Microsoft Access, and then close the Customer List workbook.

Connecting Documents with Hyperlinks

When co-workers read your Sales Analysis workbook, they are often curious about the current prices for various Island Tea & Coffee Company products. You can make it easy for your co-workers to open and examine the current price list by creating a *hyperlink* (sometimes also called a jump) in the workbook that will open the price list file when clicked. Hyperlinks are another method of integrating the information contained in different Microsoft Office programs.

Create hyperlinks that open other documents

In this exercise, you create a hyperlink in the Integration Lesson workbook that opens the Price List file.

1 In the Integration Lesson workbook, click the Sales Report sheet, select cell A12, and then type **Price List**

2 Select cell A12, and then, on the Insert menu, click Hyperlink.

The Insert Hyperlink dialog box appears.

3 Click the first Browse button, locate your Excel SBS Practice folder, and then double-click the Price List workbook file.

The path to the Price List file is automatically entered in the Link To File Or URL box.

4 Click OK.

The text in cell A12 is colored blue and underlined, indicating that it is a hyperlink. When you point to the cell, the pointer becomes a pointing-hand icon, indicating that it is positioned over a hyperlink.

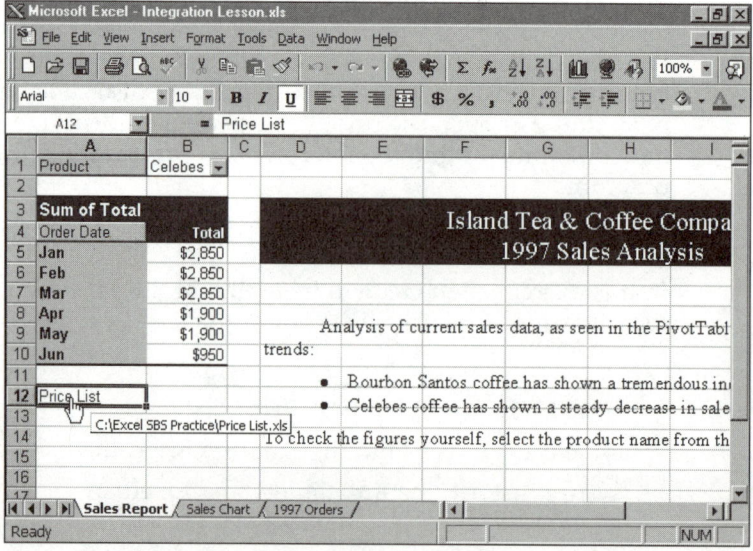

5 Save the workbook.

Test the hyperlink

In this exercise, you use the hyperlink you just created to open the Price List file.

1 Point to cell A12, and then click the hyperlink.

The Price List file opens.

2 Close the Price List file.

 NOTE If you'd like to build on the skills you learned in this lesson, you can do the One Step Further. Otherwise, skip to "Finish the Lesson."

One Step Further: Editing a Hyperlink to Open a Different File

You decide to change the hyperlink so it opens the inventory file instead of the price list.

1 Use the right mouse button to click the hyperlink.

A shortcut menu appears.

2 Point to Hyperlink, and then click Edit Hyperlink.

The Edit Hyperlink dialog box appears.

3 Delete the text in the Link To File Or URL box, click Browse, locate and double-click the Lesson 6 Inventory file in the Excel SBS Practice folder, and then click OK.

The hyperlink points to the inventory instead of the price list, but the hyperlink text still reads Price List.

4 Use the right mouse button to click the hyperlink.

A shortcut menu appears.

5 Point to Hyperlink, and then click Select Hyperlink.

6 Type **Inventory**, and then press ENTER.

The hyperlink text now correctly identifies the file it points to.

7 On the File menu, click Save.

Finish the lesson

1 To continue to the Review & Practice, on the File menu, click Close.

2 If you are finished using Microsoft Excel for now, on the File menu, click Exit.

Lesson Summary

To	Do this
Paste linked information from Microsoft Word into a Microsoft Excel worksheet	Copy the information in Microsoft Word, click in the worksheet where you want to paste it, and then, on the Edit menu, click Paste Special. Select the Paste Linked option button, select Microsoft Word Document Object, and then click OK.
Edit a linked Microsoft Word object from within Microsoft Excel	Double-click the linked object. The source file opens in Microsoft Word. Edit the document, save it, and then click the Microsoft Excel button on the taskbar to return to the Microsoft Excel workbook.
Paste an embedded chart from Microsoft Excel into Microsoft Word	Copy the chart in Microsoft Excel. Click in the Microsoft Word document where you want to paste the chart, and then, on the Edit menu, click Paste Special. Select the Paste option button, select Microsoft Excel Chart Object, and then click OK.
Edit a chart object embedded in a Microsoft Word document	Double-click the chart object. Microsoft Excel opens "within" Microsoft Word. Edit the chart object, and then click on the Microsoft Word document to return to Microsoft Word.

To	Do this
Paste a chart from Microsoft Excel into a Microsoft PowerPoint slide	Copy the chart in Microsoft Excel. In the Microsoft PowerPoint slide, select a picture box, and then, on the Edit menu, click Paste Special, select Microsoft Excel Chart Object, and then click OK.
Convert a worksheet into a Microsoft Access table	Select a cell in the worksheet. On the Data menu, click Convert To MS Access. In the Convert To Microsoft Access dialog box, select new Database or Browse to locate an existing database, and then click OK. Follow the steps in the Microsoft Access Import Spreadsheet Wizard.
Connect files with hyperlinks	Select the cell in which you want your hyperlink to appear, and then enter text to label the hyperlink. On the Insert menu, click Hyperlink. Browse to locate the file you want the hyperlink to open, double-click the filename, and then click OK.

For online information about	On the Help menu, click Contents And Index, click the Index tab, and then type
Linking	**linked objects**
Embedding	**embedded objects**
Microsoft PowerPoint slides	**Microsoft Powerpoint**
Microsoft Access database	**Microsoft Access Import Spreadsheet Wizard**
Hyperlinks	**hyperlinks**

Part

4

Review & Practice

You will review and practice how to:

■ Use scenarios to analyze data.

■ Integrate documents created using different programs.

■ Share a workbook.

Estimated time
20 min.

Now that you have finished Part 4, you can practice the skills you learned by working through the steps in this Review & Practice section. You will practice analyzing data using scenarios, integrating Microsoft Excel with Microsoft Word, and sharing a workbook.

Scenario

The State University Alumni Association quarterly expenses are entered in a list in a shared workbook so that all SUAA employees and volunteers have access to the workbook whenever they need to enter expenses; all the details in the list are then consolidated on another worksheet at the end of the quarter. The commentary is done in Microsoft Word and paste-linked into the consolidated worksheet so that an updated version is always ready to print for the newsletter. At the end of each quarter, you use scenarios to analyze the consolidated expenses list. When this process is complete, the workbook is shared again so that SUAA staff can continue to enter expenses.

207

Step 1: Analyze an expense list using scenarios

The shared status of the expense workbook has been removed and the detailed list has already been consolidated so that you can analyze the consolidated expenses using scenarios. In this step, you create three scenarios.

1 Open the practice file R&P 4, and then save it as Association Expenses.

2 On the Consolidated Expenses worksheet, create a scenario called 2nd Quarter Expenses that shows actual current expenses with no changes.

3 Create a scenario called Minimum Advertising that shows the advertising/promotion expense reduced to $200.00.

4 Create a scenario called Minimum Personal Expenses that shows the following expenses reduced to the specified amounts: basic telephone $75.00, books/magazines $0, and equipment $100.00.

5 Create a scenario summary so you can compare the scenarios easily. (Hint: Be sure the result cell is B14, the Total cell.)

For more information about	See
Creating scenarios	Lesson 11

Step 2: Paste a linked Microsoft Word document into the worksheet

One of the SUAA staff members has updated the Microsoft Word document that contains the expenses commentary, and it is ready to be paste-linked into the worksheet. In this step, you link the Microsoft Word document with the Microsoft Excel worksheet.

1 Open the Microsoft Word file named SUAA Newsletter Commentary, and then select and copy the entire text.

2 On the Microsoft Excel worksheet named Consolidated Expenses, paste a linked copy of the Microsoft Word text into cell A17.

3 Save the workbook.

For more information about	See
Pasting linked objects from other programs	Lesson 13

Step 3:   *Share the workbook*

Now that you have set up the scenarios, you need to share the workbook again so that other staff members can add their expenses for the next quarter. In this step, you make the Association Expenses workbook a shared workbook.

1   Make the workbook a shared workbook.

2   Click OK when prompted to save the workbook.

For more information about	See
Sharing a workbook	Lesson 12

Finish the Review & Practice

1   On the File menu, click Close.

2   If you are finished using Microsoft Excel for now, on the File menu, click Exit.

Appendixes

If You're New to Windows 95, Windows NT, or Microsoft Excel

If you are new to Microsoft Windows 95, Microsoft Windows NT version 4.0, or Microsoft Excel 97, this appendix will show you all the basics you need to get started. You'll get an overview of Windows 95 and Windows NT features, and you'll learn how to use online Help to answer your questions and find out more about using these operating systems. You'll also get an introduction to Microsoft Excel.

If You're New to Windows 95 or Windows NT

Windows 95 and Windows NT are easy-to-use computer environments that help you handle the daily work that you perform with your computer. You can use either Windows 95 or Windows NT to run Microsoft Excel 97—the explanations in this appendix apply to both operating systems. The way you use Windows 95, Windows NT, and programs designed for these operating systems is similar. The programs have a common look, and you use the same kinds of controls to tell them what to do. In this section, you'll learn how to use the basic program controls. If you're already familiar with Windows 95 or Windows NT, skip to the section titled "What is Microsoft Excel?"

Start Windows 95 or Windows NT

Starting Windows 95 or Windows NT is as easy as turning on your computer.

1   If your computer isn't on, turn it on now.

In Windows 95, you will also be prompted for a username and password if your computer is configured for user profiles.

2 If you are using Windows NT, press CTRL+ALT+DEL to display a dialog box asking for your username and password. If you are using Windows 95, you will see this dialog box if your computer is connected to a network.

3 Type your username and password in the appropriate boxes, and then click OK.

If you don't know your username or password, contact your system administrator for assistance.

Close

4 If you see the Welcome dialog box, click the Close button.

Your screen should look similar to the following illustration.

Using the Mouse

Although you can use the keyboard for most actions, many of these actions are easier to do by using a mouse. The mouse controls a pointer on the screen, as shown in the previous illustration. You move the pointer by sliding the mouse over a flat surface in the direction you want the pointer to move. If you run out of room to move the mouse, lift it up and then put it down in a more comfortable location.

NOTE In this book we assume that your mouse is set up so that the left button is the primary button and the right button is the secondary button. If your mouse is configured the opposite way, for left-handed use, use the right button when we tell you to use the left, and vice versa.

You'll use five basic mouse actions throughout this book.

When you are directed to	Do this
Point to an item	Move the mouse to place the pointer on the item.
Click an item	Point to the item on your screen, and quickly press and release the left mouse button.
Use the right mouse button to click an item	Point to the item on your screen, and then quickly press and release the right mouse button. Clicking the right mouse button displays a shortcut menu from which you can choose from a list of commands that apply to that item.
Double-click an item	Point to the item, and then quickly press and release the left mouse button twice.
Drag an item	Point to an item, and then hold down the left mouse button as you move the pointer.

Using Window Controls

All programs designed for use on computers that have Windows 95 or Windows NT installed have common controls that you use to scroll, size, move, and close a window.

To	Do this	Button
Move, or *scroll*, vertically or horizontally through the contents of a window that extends beyond the screen	Click a scroll bar or scroll arrow, or drag the scroll box. The previous illustration identifies these controls.	
Enlarge a window to fill the screen	Click the Maximize button, or double-click the window's title bar.	
Restore a window to its previous size	Click the Restore button, or double-click the window title bar. When a window is maximized, the Maximize button changes to the Restore button.	
Reduce a window to a button on the taskbar	Click the Minimize button. To display a minimized window, click its button on the taskbar.	
Move a window	Drag the window title bar.	
Close a window	Click the Close button.	

Using Menus

Just like a restaurant menu, a program menu provides a list of options from which you can choose. On program menus, these options are called *commands*. To select a menu or a menu command, you click the item you want.

 NOTE You can also use the keyboard to make menu selections. Press the ALT key to activate the menu bar, and press the key that corresponds to the highlighted or underlined letter of the menu name. Then press the key that corresponds to the highlighted or underlined letter of the command name.

In the following exercise, you'll open and make selections from a menu.

Open and make selections from a menu

1 On the Desktop, double-click the My Computer icon.

The My Computer window opens.

You can also press ALT+E to open the Edit menu.

2 In the My Computer window, click Edit on the menu bar.

The Edit menu appears. Some commands are dimmed; this means they aren't available.

Command is not available

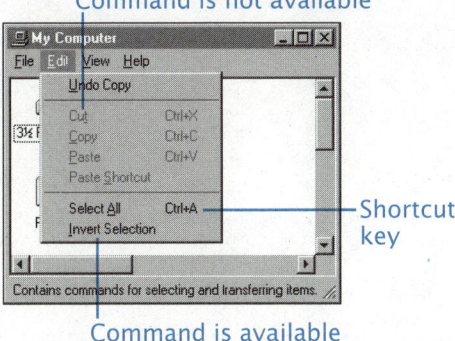

Shortcut
key

Command is available

3 Click the Edit menu name to close the menu.

The menu closes.

On a menu, a check mark indicates that multiple items in this group of commands can be selected at one time. A bullet mark indicates that only one item in this group can be selected at one time.

4 Click View on the menu bar to open the View menu.

5 On the View menu, click Toolbar.

The View menu closes, and a toolbar appears below the menu bar.

Toolbar

6 On the View menu, click List.

The items in the My Computer window now appear in a list, rather than as icons.

Large Icons

7 On the toolbar, click the Large Icons button.

Clicking a button on a toolbar is a quick way to select a command.

8 On the View menu, point to Arrange Icons.

A cascading menu appears listing additional menu choices. When a right-pointing arrow appears after a command name, it indicates that additional commands are available.

9 Click anywhere outside the menu to close it.

10   On the menu bar, click View, and then click Toolbar again.

The View menu closes, and the toolbar is now hidden.

11   Click the Close button in the upper-right corner of the My Computer window to close the window.

TIP   If you do a lot of typing, you might want to learn the key combinations for commands you use frequently. Pressing the key combination is a quick way to perform a command by using the keyboard. If a key combination is available for a command, it will be listed to the right of the command name on the menu. For example, CTRL+C is listed on the Edit menu as the key combination for the Copy command.

Using Dialog Boxes

When you choose a command name that is followed by an ellipsis (…), a dialog box will appear so that you can provide more information about how the command should be carried out. Dialog boxes have standard features, as shown in the following illustration.

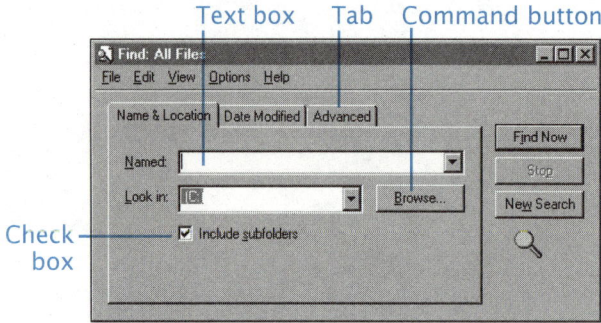

To move around in a dialog box, you click the item you want. You can also use the keyboard to select the item by holding down ALT as you press the underlined letter. Or, you can press TAB to move between items.

Display the Taskbar Properties dialog box

Some dialog boxes provide several categories of options displayed on separate tabs. You click the top of an obscured tab to make it visible.

1   On the taskbar, click the Start button.

The Start menu appears.

2   On the Start menu, point to Settings, and then click Taskbar.

3   In the Taskbar Properties dialog box, click the Start Menu Programs tab.

On this tab, you can customize the list of programs that appears on your Start menu.

4   Click the Taskbar Options tab, and then click the Show Small Icons In Start Menu check box to select it.

When a check box is selected, it displays a check mark.

Click here. When you click a check box that is selected, you turn the option off.

5   Click the check box a couple of times, and watch how the display in the dialog box changes.

Clicking any check box will turn the option off or on.

6   Click the Cancel button in the dialog box.

The dialog box closes without changing any settings.

Getting Help with Windows 95 or Windows NT

When you're at work and you want to find out more information about how to do a project, you might ask a co-worker or consult a reference book. To find out more about functions and features in Windows 95 or Windows NT, you can use the online Help system. For example, when you need information about how to print, the Help system is one of the most efficient ways to learn. The Windows 95 or Windows NT Help system is available from the Start menu. After the Help system opens, you can choose the type of help you want from the Help Topics dialog box.

To find instructions about broad categories, you can look on the Contents tab. Or, you can search the Help index to find information about specific topics. The Help information is short and concise, so you can get the exact information you need quickly. There are also shortcut icons in many Help topics that you can use to directly go to or to perform the task you want.

Viewing Help Contents

The Contents tab is organized like a book's table of contents. As you choose top-level topics, called *chapters*, you see a list of more detailed subtopics from which to choose. Many of these chapters have Tips and Tricks sections to help you work more efficiently as well as Troubleshooting sections to help you resolve problems.

Find Help about general categories

Suppose you want to learn more about using Calculator, a program that comes with Windows 95 and Windows NT. In this exercise, you look up information in the online Help system.

1 Click Start. On the Start menu, click Help.

The Help Topics: Windows Help dialog box appears.

2 If necessary, click the Contents tab to make it active.

3 Double-click "Introducing Windows" or "Introducing Windows NT."

A set of subtopics appears.

4 Double-click "Using Windows Accessories."

5 Double-click "For General Use."

6   Double-click "Calculator: for making calculations."

A Help topic window opens.

7   Read the Help information, and then click the Close button to close the Help window.

Finding Help About Specific Topics

You can find specific Help topics by using the Index tab or the Find tab. The Index tab is organized like a book's index. Keywords for topics are organized alphabetically. You can either scroll through the list of keywords or type the keyword you want to find. You can then select from one or more topic choices.

With the Find tab, you can also enter a keyword. The main difference is that you get a list of all Help topics in which that keyword appears, not just the topics that begin with that word.

Find Help about specific topics by using the Help index

In this exercise, you use the Help index to learn how to change the background pattern of your Desktop.

1   Click Start, and on the Start menu, click Help.

The Help Topics dialog box appears.

2   Click the Index tab to make it active.

3   In the text box, type **display**

A list of display-related topics appears.

4   Click the topic named "background pictures or patterns, changing," and then click Display.

The Topics Found dialog box appears.

5   Be sure that the topic named "Changing the background of your desktop" is selected, and then click Display.

6   Read the Help topic.

7   Click the shortcut icon in step 1 of the Help topic.

Shortcut

The Display Properties dialog box appears. If you want, you can immediately perform the task you are looking up in Help.

8   Click the Close button in the Display Properties dialog box.

9   Click the Close button in the Windows Help window.

 NOTE   You can print any Help topic if you have a printer installed on your computer. Click the Options button in the upper-right corner of any Help topic window, click Print Topic, and then click OK. To continue searching for additional topics, you can click the Help Topics button in any open Help topic window.

Find Help about specific topics by using the Find tab

In this exercise, you use the Find tab to learn how to change your printer's settings.

1   Click Start, and then click Help to display the Help dialog box.

2   Click the Find tab to make it active.

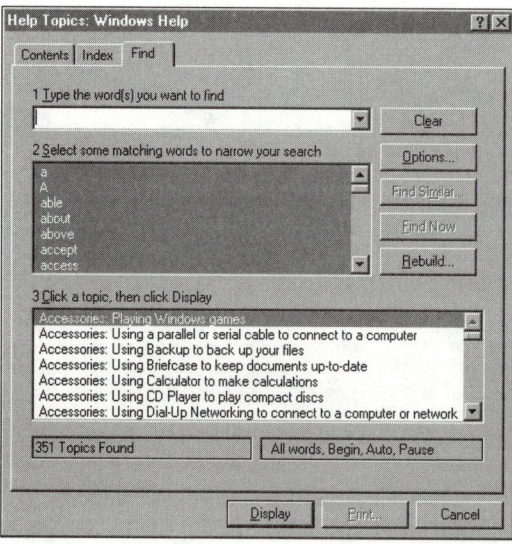

3 If you see a wizard, click Next, and then click Finish to complete and close the wizard.

The wizard creates a search index for your Help files. This might take a few minutes. The next time you use Find, you won't have to wait for the list to be created. The Find tab becomes active.

4 In the text box, type **print**

All topics that have to do with printing appear in the list box at the bottom of the tab.

5 In area 3 of the Help dialog box, click the "Changing printer settings" topic, and then click Display.

The Help topic appears.

6 Read the Help topic, and then click the Close button in the Windows Help window.

Find Help in a dialog box

Almost every dialog box includes a question mark Help button in the upper-right corner of its window. When you click this button and then click any dialog box control, a Help window appears that explains what the control is and how to use it. In this exercise, you'll get help for a dialog box control.

1 Click Start, and then click Run.

The Run dialog box appears.

Help

2 Click the Help button.

The mouse pointer changes to an arrow with a question mark.

3 Click the Open text box.

A Help window appears, providing information about how to use the Open text box.

4 Click anywhere on the Desktop to close the Help window.

The mouse pointer returns to its previous shape.

5 In the Run dialog box, click Cancel.

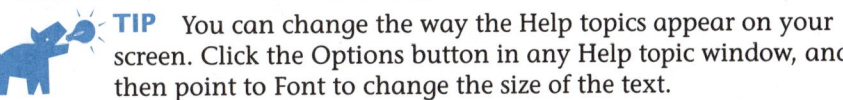

TIP You can change the way the Help topics appear on your screen. Click the Options button in any Help topic window, and then point to Font to change the size of the text.

What Is Microsoft Excel?

Microsoft Excel is an electronic spreadsheet that does a lot more than replace the accountant's paper ledger with its neat columns and rows—Microsoft Excel can perform just about any mathematical calculation you want, and changes can be made to your numbers and calculations without having to painstakingly rewrite the entire spreadsheet. A spreadsheet is essentially a large grid that aligns entries into rows and columns so that it is easy to see which numbers you are working with.

Microsoft Excel can also create charts from your numbers much more easily than you can create them by hand, and can exchange information easily with other programs such as Microsoft Word, Microsoft PowerPoint, and Microsoft Access so that your information can be presented to others in nearly any form you choose.

Quit Windows 95 or Windows NT

1   If you are finished using Windows 95 or Windows NT, close any open windows by clicking the Close button in each window.

2   Click Start, and then click Shut Down.

The Shut Down Windows dialog box appears.

3   Click Yes.

A message indicates that it is now safe to turn off your computer.

WARNING   To avoid loss of data or damage to your operating system, always quit Windows 95 or Windows NT by using the Shut Down command on the Start menu before you turn your computer off.

Matching the Exercises

Microsoft Excel has many optional settings that can affect either the screen display or the operation of certain functions. Some exercise steps, therefore, might not produce exactly the same result on your screen as shown in this book. For example, if your screen does not look like the illustration at a certain point in a lesson, you can turn to this appendix for guidance. Or, if you do not get the outcome described in the lesson, you can use this appendix to determine whether the options you have in effect are the same as the ones used in this book.

 NOTE Each computer system is configured with different hardware and software; therefore, your screen display of icons, folders, and menu options might not exactly match the illustrations in this book. These system differences should not interfere with your ability to perform the exercises in the book.

Installing Windows 95, Windows NT, or Microsoft Excel 97 Components

The exercises in this book assume that a "Typical" setup was used to install Windows 95 or Windows NT on your computer. If a "Portable," "Custom," or "Compact" setup was used, you might not have all the components necessary to complete the lessons. In addition, it is assumed that a "Typical" setup was used to install Microsoft Excel 97.

If you are missing a component, such as an accessory, you can easily add it. If the component is necessary to complete an exercise, a note precedes the exercise to help guide you to install or add the component.

Using the Default Windows 95 or Windows NT Settings

In Windows 95 or Windows NT, it is easy to configure your Desktop to suit your working style and preferences. However, the exercises and corresponding illustrations in this book assume that all Windows options are at their default settings. If you change option settings while working through the exercises, you will restore the default settings by the end of a lesson.

You can easily change your Windows 95 or Windows NT options to match the illustrations in the exercises by using the following procedures.

Show or hide the toolbar

You can show or hide the toolbar in most windows, including the My Computer, Windows Explorer, and Windows NT Explorer windows. The toolbar setting can be different for each window that you open. You can show or hide the toolbar on your screen as appropriate to match the illustrations in this book.

1   In the window, click the View menu.

    If there is a check mark next to the Toolbar command, the toolbar is currently showing; if there is no check mark, the toolbar is hidden.

2   On the View menu, click Toolbar to show or hide the toolbar.

Change window sizes

If the size of your window appears to be different from that of the illustrations in the exercises, you can adjust the window.

1   Position your mouse pointer on any edge of the window until the mouse pointer changes to a double-headed arrow.

2   Drag the edge or corner of the window in or out to make the window smaller or larger.

    You can change the window size horizontally by dragging on a side edge or vertically by dragging on the top or bottom; you can change the height and the width of a window simultaneously by dragging on a corner.

Restore window sizes

If a window fills the entire screen and you want to see other parts of the Desktop, you can restore the window to its previous size.

1   On the taskbar, click the window name button to make it the active window.

2   In the upper-right corner of the maximized window, click the Restore button.

    The window is restored to its previous, smaller size.

Restore

Change views

If the way files appear in a window are different from the illustrations in this book, you can easily change the view. The views can be different for each window you open.

▶   In the window, click the View menu, and then click the view you want: Large Icons, Small Icons, List, or Details.

Arrange icons on the Desktop

If your Desktop icons are jumbled or in a different order than what you want to see, you can arrange them.

1   Use the right mouse button to click an empty area of the Desktop.

    A shortcut menu appears.

2   Point to Arrange Icons, and then click Auto Arrange.

    The icons are aligned in a horizontal and vertical format on the left side of your Desktop.

3   Use the right mouse button to click an empty area of the Desktop again.

4   On the shortcut menu, point to Arrange Icons, and then click By Name.

    After the default Windows icons on your Desktop, the icons are first arranged by file type, and then in alphabetical order.

Arrange icons in a window

If the icons in a window are jumbled or in a different order than what you want to see, you can arrange them. The icons for each window that you open can have a different arrangement.

1   In a window, click the View menu, point to Arrange Icons, and then click Auto Arrange.

    The icons are arranged by name in your window.

2   On the View menu, point to Arrange Icons again, and then click By Name.

Open cascading My Computer windows

You can set up your display so that a new window appears every time you open a new folder, or you can browse through folders using a single window that changes each time you open a new folder.

1   Double-click the My Computer icon.

2   In the My Computer window, on the View menu, click Options.

     The Options dialog box appears.

3   Be sure that the Folder tab is active, and then click the Browse Folders By Using A Single Window That Changes As You Open Each Folder option button.

4   Click OK.

Matching the Screen Display to the Illustrations

Microsoft Excel makes it easy for you to set up the program window to suit your working style and preferences. If you share your computer with others, previous users might have changed the screen setup. You can easily change it back so that your screen matches the illustrations in the lessons. The following methods can help you control the screen display.

If you change the screen display as part of a lesson and leave Microsoft Excel, the next time you open Microsoft Excel, the screen looks the way you left it in the previous session.

Display toolbars

If toolbars are missing at the top of the screen, previous users might have hidden them to make more room for text. You can easily display the toolbars that contain the buttons you need in the lessons.

1   On the View menu, click the Toolbars command.

2   In the Toolbars dialog box, click the check boxes for the toolbars you need.

     Most of the lessons require that the Standard and Formatting toolbars appear.

Hide extra toolbars

To use specific features in some of the lessons, additional toolbars appear in the program window. If, after completing the lesson, you no longer want these toolbars to appear, you can use the Toolbars shortcut menu to hide toolbars you do not want to see. However, most of the lessons require that the Standard and Formatting toolbars appear.

1 Use the right mouse button to click any toolbar.

2 On the shortcut menu, click the name of the toolbar you do not want to see.

If the vertical or horizontal scroll bars do not appear

If you do not see the vertical or horizontal scroll bars, a previous user might have hidden the scroll bars to make more room for data. You can easily display them again.

1 On the Tools menu, click Options.

The Options dialog box appears.

2 Click the View tab to display the view options in the dialog box.

3 In the Window Options area, select the Vertical Scroll Bar and Horizontal Scroll Bar check boxes.

If either or both of these check boxes were previously selected, skip to step 4.

4 Click the OK button.

If the Microsoft Excel program window does not fill the screen

A previous user might have made the Microsoft Excel program window smaller to allow quick access to another program. You can enlarge the document window by doing the following.

Maximize

▶ Click the Maximize button.

If the right edge of the Microsoft Excel window is hidden so that you cannot see the Maximize button, point to "Microsoft Excel" in the title bar at the top of the screen, and then drag the title bar to the left until you see the Maximize button.

If your chart on a chart sheet does not fill the window

A previous user might have displayed charts at a smaller size. To see your chart at full size, use the Sized With Window command on the View menu.

▶ On the View menu, click Sized With Window.

If the document does not fill the space that Microsoft Excel allows

A previous user might have displayed the workbook in a smaller size to get an overview of a worksheet. To see your workbook at the normal size, use the Zoom Control down arrow on the Standard toolbar.

➤ Click the Zoom Control down arrow, and then select 100%.

If the sheet tabs do not appear in your workbook

A previous user might have hidden the sheet tabs to see more of the worksheets. To view the sheet tabs, you use the Options command on the Tools menu.

1 On the Tools menu, click Options.
2 In the Options dialog box, click the View tab.
3 In the Window Options area, select the Sheet Tabs check box, and then click OK.

If you see number signs rather than numbers in your practice files

If you see number signs (#) instead of numbers in your practice files, your column width might not be wide enough. To display the numbers, you resize the columns.

➤ Select the affected columns, and then double-click the column header border between two of the selected columns.

If gridlines do not appear in your workbook

A previous user might have hidden the gridlines to see a cleaner view of the data. To view the gridlines again, you use the Options command on the Tools menu.

1 On the Tools menu, click Options.
2 In the Options dialog box, select the View tab.
3 In the Window Options area, click the Gridlines check box, and then click OK.

If your columns are identified by numbers instead of letters

A previous user might have changed the reference style to R1C1. To change to the A1 reference style, you use the Options command on the Tools menu.

1 On the Tools menu, click Options, and then click the General tab.

2 In the Reference Style area, click the A1 option button, and then click OK.

If the File Properties dialog box does not open when you save a document

A previous user might have turned off the File Properties option. To turn the Prompt For File Properties option on again, use the Options command on the Tools menu.

1 On the Tools menu, click Options, and then click the General tab.

2 Select the Prompt For File Properties check box, and then click OK.

Changing Other Options

If you are not getting the results described in the lessons, you can follow the instructions in this section to verify that the options set in your program are the same as the ones used in this book.

Review each of the following dialog boxes to compare settings for those options that users change most often and that are most likely to account for different results. You can view these dialog boxes by clicking the Options command on the Tools menu. Then click the tab corresponding to the options you want to see. The following illustrations show the option settings used in this book.

View options

Click the View tab to change options that affect the appearance of the document window.

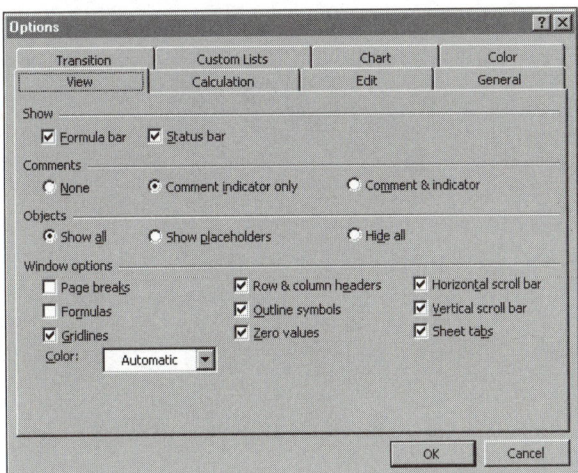

Calculation options

Click the Calculations tab to change options that affect the calculations of your formulas.

Edit options

Click the Edit tab to change options that affect how editing operations are performed.

General options

Click the General tab to change options that affect the operation of Microsoft Excel in general.

Chart options

Click the Chart tab to change options that affect how charts appear in Microsoft Excel. (Chart tab options are available only when a chart is active.)

Customizing Your Workspace

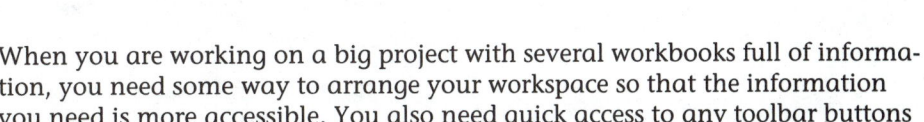

When you are working on a big project with several workbooks full of information, you need some way to arrange your workspace so that the information you need is more accessible. You also need quick access to any toolbar buttons you might want to use.

In this appendix, you'll learn how to customize your Microsoft Excel screen to meet your needs, and how to change your toolbars so that the buttons you need most are easy to find. In addition, you'll find out how to view and arrange worksheets so that you can see the information you need on all of your sheets. You'll also view your sheets at different magnifications and split your window into panes to display different parts of your sheet in each pane.

Making Your Toolbars Work for You

Microsoft Excel comes with several built-in toolbars containing buttons that can save you time and effort. When you first start the program, you'll see two toolbars by default, the Standard and Formatting toolbars.

In addition to these toolbars, there are several others that you can use as you work with Microsoft Excel. If you use scenarios often, you'll probably find it convenient to use the Workgroup toolbar. If you work with graphic elements, you'll become familiar with the Drawing toolbar.

You can customize your toolbars to make them work better for you. For example, if you rarely use the sorting buttons on the Standard toolbar or use only the Sort Descending (and not the Sort Ascending) button, you can easily remove the buttons you don't need from the toolbar. Or, if you often need to turn worksheet gridlines on and off, you can add the Gridlines button to the

Some toolbar buttons, such as the Sort buttons, are multi-functional—for example, to perform an ascending sort, hold down SHIFT and click the Sort Descending button.

Standard toolbar so it is within easy reach. You can create your own customized toolbars that contain only the buttons that you need to use. You can also move buttons around on your existing toolbar to make them easier to use or move the entire toolbar to a new location.

In the following exercises, you'll move toolbars around on your screen, hide and then show a toolbar, change the buttons on a built-in toolbar, and create a new toolbar.

Move a toolbar around on your screen

You can move your toolbars to any position on your screen. When you move a toolbar to the top, bottom, or either side of your window, it will *dock* at that location. When your toolbar docks, it changes its shape to a single vertical row of buttons (on either side of your screen) or a single horizontal row of buttons (at the top or bottom of your screen). If you move a toolbar anywhere near the center of your window, it will *float* there.

NOTE Drop-down lists, such as the Font box or Font Size box on the Formatting toolbar, will not appear on a toolbar if you dock the toolbar on either side of your screen, because the boxes will not fit.

In this exercise, you move your Formatting toolbar around on your screen to see how it docks in some positions and floats in others. Then, you dock it at the top of your screen, in its original position.

1 Click on the raised double bar on the left end of the Formatting toolbar, and then drag to the center of your worksheet.

Drag this bar. →

The Formatting toolbar floats in the center of your worksheet, and the toolbar name appears in the toolbar's title bar.

2 Drag the Formatting toolbar by its title bar all the way to the left, until the shape changes from a square to a vertical rectangle, and then drop it.

The toolbar is docked on the left side of your screen.

3 Click on the dark horizontal bar at the top of the Formatting toolbar and drag upward until the toolbar shape changes from vertical to horizontal, and then drop it below the Standard toolbar.

The Formatting toolbar is docked below the Standard toolbar.

Hide and show toolbars

You've seen how certain toolbars automatically appear when you perform a certain action or choose a particular command. For example, when you created a chart, and then clicked it to make changes, the Chart toolbar automatically appeared. When you created a PivotTable in Lesson 8, the Query And Pivot toolbar appeared so that you could make changes to the PivotTable easily. But what if you need to use a button located on a toolbar that isn't displayed or if you want to hide a toolbar that is displayed?

In this exercise, you practice hiding and showing different toolbars.

1 Use the right mouse button to click on a toolbar.

A shortcut menu appears with a list of toolbar names. Toolbars that are currently displayed have a check mark next to their names.

Toolbars currently displayed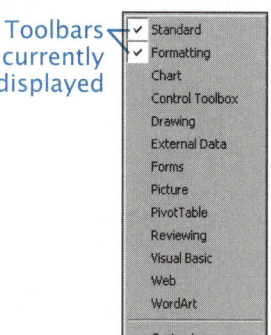

2 On the shortcut menu, click Formatting.

The Formatting toolbar is hidden.

3 Use the right mouse button to click the Standard toolbar, and then, on the shortcut menu, click Formatting.

The Formatting toolbar appears again.

4 Use the right mouse button to click a toolbar, and then, on the shortcut menu, click Customize.

The Customize dialog box appears. The Toolbars tab contains a list of all the available toolbars.

5 On the Toolbars tab, scroll down, and then click Picture.

The Picture toolbar appears.

6 Click Close.

7 On the Picture toolbar, click the Close button.

Change the buttons displayed on the Formatting toolbar

The default Formatting toolbar contains an assortment of buttons that are useful to most users, but you might have different needs, and therefore, there might be several buttons on the Formatting toolbar that you don't want to show constantly. You can easily remove buttons that you don't use and add buttons that you would like to have available on any toolbars.

In this exercise, you remove the Percent Style and the Currency buttons from the Formatting toolbar and add the Style button.

Percent Style

1 Hold down ALT and drag the Percent Style and Currency buttons away from the Formatting toolbar, and then drop them on the worksheet.

The buttons are removed from the toolbar.

Currency

238

2   Use the right mouse button to click a toolbar, and then, on the shortcut menu, click Customize.

The Customize dialog box appears.

3   Click the Commands tab, and then, in the Categories list, click Format.

4   In the Commands list, select Style.

5   Drag the Style command out of the dialog box, and then drop it on the right end of the Formatting toolbar.

The Style command is added to the Formatting toolbar. Your toolbar should look similar to the following illustration.

6   Click Close.

TIP   To reset a toolbar to its default configuration, use the right mouse button to click a toolbar, and then click Customize on the shortcut menu. On the Toolbars tab, select the appropriate toolbar, and then click Reset.

Create a new toolbar

As you share your computer with other employees of the Island Tea & Coffee Company, it might be inconvenient to change the configuration of the built-in toolbars to suit your needs. You might also find that there are a few buttons on several toolbars that you use often, but displaying all of these toolbars takes up too much of your screen area. In either case, you can easily resolve these problems by creating a new toolbar that contains only the buttons you want. In this exercise, you create a custom toolbar, and then add some buttons to it.

1   Use the right mouse button to click a toolbar, and then, on the shortcut menu, click Customize.

2   Click the Toolbars tab, and then click New.

The New Toolbar dialog box appears.

3   Type **My Tools** in the Toolbar Name box, and then click OK or press ENTER.

The name My Tools is added to the list of available toolbars, and a new, empty toolbar appears on top of the Customize dialog box.

4   Drag the new My Tools toolbar onto the worksheet.

5   In the Customize dialog box, click the Commands tab, and then be sure that Insert is selected in the Categories list.

A list of the buttons contained in the Insert category appears.

6   In the Commands list, select the Worksheet button, and then drag it onto the My Tools toolbar.

The new button appears on the My Tools toolbar. Your toolbar should look similar to the following illustration.

7   Repeat steps 5 and 6 to add the Style button (in the Formatting category) to the My Tools toolbar.

8   Repeat steps 5 and 6 to add the Button and Toggle Grid buttons (in the Forms category) to the My Tools toolbar.

9   Repeat steps 5 and 6 to add the Select Current Region button (in the Edit category) to the My Tools toolbar.

You can rear-range the tools on the toolbar by holding down ALT and drag-ging them to a new location.

10 Close the Customize dialog box.

Your new toolbar should look similar to the following illustration. You can dock it, float it, close it, and open it the same way you would any other toolbar.

Optimizing Your Screen Display

There might be some screen elements that you don't use frequently. For example, if you find that you don't use the formula bar and status bar often, and you want to see more of your data at one time, you can hide them easily. The Full Screen command on the View menu hides everything except your sheet, sheet tabs, menu bar, and scroll bars.

In order to perform the following exercises, you'll need to open a practice file so that you'll have data with which to practice optimizing your screen display.

Open a file

The practice file you will be using to perform the following exercises is a list of Island Tea & Coffee Company products and price information. You won't make any changes to the practice file, so there is no need to save it with a different name.

Open

1 On the Standard toolbar, click the Open button.

2 In the Open dialog box, locate and open the file named Price List.

The Open dialog box closes and the Price List file appears in the document window.

Hide and display on-screen elements

In this exercise, you practice hiding and showing different elements of your worksheet.

1 On the View menu, click Formula Bar.

The Formula bar is hidden, and a bigger portion of your worksheet is visible.

2 On the View menu, click Status Bar.

The Status bar is hidden, and a bigger portion of your worksheet is visible.

3 On the View menu, click Formula Bar.

The Formula bar appears again.

4 On the View menu, click Status Bar.

The Status bar appears again.

Show a full-screen view for maximum worksheet display

In this exercise, you invoke a full screen view of your worksheet, and then you restore the hidden screen elements to view.

1 On the View menu, click Full Screen.

Everything except the menu bar, row and column headers, scroll bars, and sheet tabs is hidden, and the Full Screen toolbar appears.

	B	C	D	E	F	G	H
1	Category	Source Country	Price $/lb	Warehouse location			
2	Coffee	Guatemala	10.50	S1			
3	Coffee	Jamaica	36.00	S1			
4	Coffee	Brazil	9.50	S1			
5	Coffee	Indonesia	9.50	S2			
6	Coffee	Peru	10.50	S2			
7	Coffee	Mexico	10.50	S2			
8	Coffee	Guatemala	9.50	S3			
9	Coffee	Costa Rica	10.50	S3			
10	Coffee	Ecuador	10.50	S3			
11	Coffee	Haiti	9.50	E1			
12	Coffee	Ethiopia	9.90	E1			
13	Coffee	India	9.50	E1			
14	Coffee	Indonesia	10.50	E2			
15	Coffee	Kenya	10.80	E2			
16	Coffee	Hawaii	10.50	E3			
17	Coffee	Columbia	9.50	E3			
18	Coffee	Venezuela	10.50	W1			
19	Coffee	Yemen	11.50	W1			
20	Coffee	Mexico	9.50	W2			
21	Coffee	Mexico	10.50	W2			
22	Coffee	Dominican Republi	9.50	W3			
23	Coffee	Indonesia	11.50	W3			
24	Coffee	Tanzania	9.50	W3			
25	Tea	India	9.70	N1			

Sheet1 / Sheet2 / Sheet3 /

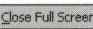

2 Click the Close Full Screen button on the Full Screen toolbar.

The previously hidden screen elements appear again.

Zooming In or Out to View a Worksheet

You've seen how to make more space to display your worksheet by hiding the screen elements, but what if you need to see even more data? For example, the Island Tea & Coffee Company price list is a long worksheet that contains more than one screenful of information. If you want to see the worksheet in its entirety on one screen, you can zoom out to display more cells in the window; if you want to take a closer look at a specific group of cells, you can zoom in.

Zoom in or out on your worksheet

In this exercise, you zoom out to see the entire price list in the window, and then zoom in and out at different magnifications to see the price list from different perspectives.

Select Current Region

1   Click cell A1, and then, on the My Tools toolbar, click the Select Current Region button.

The entire price list table is selected.

2   On the Standard toolbar, click the Zoom down arrow, and then click Selection.

Your view is zoomed out enough to display the entire selection in the available window area.

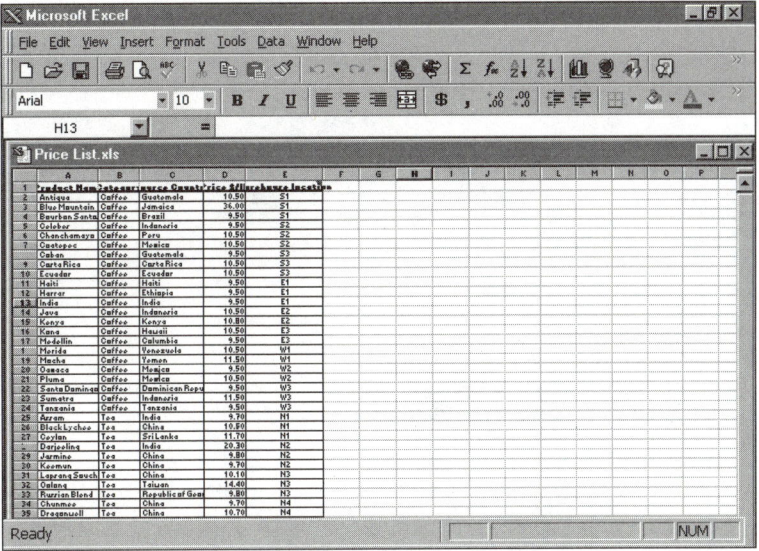

3   Click the Zoom down arrow, and then click 75%.

The view is zoomed to a magnification of 75% of the normal size.

4 Click the Zoom down arrow, and then click 100%.

The view is returned to normal magnification.

Splitting Your Worksheet into Panes

When you work in a large worksheet, you usually have headings at the top and/or the left of your worksheet, with data extending to the right and downward. When you have scrolled past the point where the headings are visible, it can be difficult to remember what they were. One way to keep the headings in view while you work is to freeze panes, as you did in Lesson 1. Another way is to simply split the worksheet into panes without freezing them—this way, you can scroll around in each pane independently.

Split your worksheet into panes

In this exercise, you split the Price List worksheet into two panes, and then remove the split.

1 Point to the small bar at the top of the vertical scroll bar, and when your pointer becomes a two-headed arrow, drag downward, and then drop the split in the middle of the screen.

The worksheet is split horizontally by a *split bar*. You can scroll the entire length of the worksheet in either pane.

2 Double-click the split bar.

The split is removed.

Customizing Your Workbooks

If you find that there are changes you consistently make to your new work-books, such as changing the font for the entire workbook or inserting five new worksheets, you can change the Microsoft Excel default settings so that your new workbooks always open looking just the way you want.

Change the default font and number of worksheets in all new workbooks

One of your co-workers in the Island Tea & Coffee Company Accounting de-partment has asked you to use a specific font for all of your worksheets, because he finds it easier to read. In the following exercise, you change the default font that will be used with all your new worksheets; this change won't affect existing workbooks.

1 On the Tools menu, click Options.

The Options dialog box appears.

2 In the Options dialog box, click the General tab.

3 Click the Standard Font down arrow, and then select Times New Roman.

4 Change the Sheets In New Workbook number to 8.

5 Click OK.

All new workbooks you open from now on will have eight worksheets and Times New Roman font.

Changing gridline color

If you would prefer another gridline color in your worksheets, such as a pale blue instead of gray, you can change the gridline color for the active worksheet.

1 On the Tools menu, click Options, and then click the View tab.

2 Click the Color down arrow, select a new gridline color, and then click OK.

The gridlines in the active worksheet are the color that you selected.

absolute cell reference A cell address in a formula that does not change when copied to another cell. An absolute reference has the form $A$1.

active cell The selected cell in a worksheet. The active cell is surrounded by a heavy border and is identified by the cell address.

active window In a multiple-window environment, the window that is currently selected and whose contents will be affected by all mouse actions, commands, and text entry.

alias A name or label that is used as an alternative means of referring to a file or person. For example, the group alias "Marketing" could be used to send an e-mail message to all the employees in the Marketing department.

alignment The horizontal position of text within the width of a column or between tab stops.

AND function A function used to perform multiple tests on the content of cells in a spreadsheet and display a value or text based on whether the overall test is true or false.

application *See* program.

argument The information that a function uses to produce a new value or perform an action. For example, a new value is displayed when the SUM function adds the argument (A6:A12). An argument consists of numbers, references, text, operators, arrays, or error values.

arithmetic operator A symbol used for simple math calculations. For example, the operators for addition and subtraction are the plus sign (+) and the minus sign (–).

arrow keys The UP ARROW, DOWN ARROW, LEFT ARROW, and RIGHT ARROW keys that are used to move the insertion point or to select from a menu or a list of options.

ascending A method of ordering a group of items from lowest to highest, such as from A to Z. *See also* sort.

AutoFormat A feature used to format a range of cells with a predefined set of attributes.

axis title Text that identifies the horizontal plot line.

binary file A file type that is encoded using only the binary digits 0 and 1. Binary files are usually programs, graphics, or complex documents, and are readable only by a computer.

bit A binary digit. The smallest unit of information a computer can handle. A bit can have the value 0 or 1, and is represented physically as a single pulse sent through a circuit, or a single spot on a disk. A group of 8 bits is called a byte.

bitmap   A collection of bits that make up a dot pattern or graphic image. Bitmaps with a BMP extension are the default file type for the Paint accessory.

border   A line that goes around text or tables. You can assign a variety of widths to a border.

browser   Software that can display information found in files posted on the World Wide Web. A browser can also play sound or video files if you have the necessary hardware.

bullet   A mark, usually a round or square dot, often used to add emphasis or to distinguish between items in a list.

byte   A unit of information consisting of 8 bits. The equivalent of a single character, number, or punctuation mark.

cascading menu   A submenu that branches off or cascades from another menu. A command name followed by an arrow indicates that a submenu appears when the command is pointed to.

cell   The basic unit of a table or worksheet. The intersection of a row and a column forms one cell. You type text, numbers, or formulas into cells. Each cell is named by its position in the row (1, 2, 3) and column (A, B, C). For example, cell A1 is the first cell in column A, row 1.

cell note   A note that explains, identifies, or comments on the information in a specific cell or range of cells.

central processing unit (CPU)   The microprocessor chip that interprets and carries out instructions.

character   An individual letter, number, or symbol corresponding to a key or key combination. Each character can be formatted individually.

chart   A graphic representation of worksheet data. Values from worksheet cells are displayed as bars, lines, or other shapes. Common chart types are pie, bar, line, and area.

chart sheet   A chart placed on a separate worksheet instead of on the worksheet where the chart data is stored.

check box   A dialog box option that is not mutually exclusive. Clicking a check box inserts or removes an "X."

click   To press the primary mouse button once.

Clipboard   A temporary holding area in computer memory that stores the last set of information that was cut or copied (such as text or graphics). You transfer data from the Clipboard by using the Paste command. The information remains on the Clipboard until you cut or copy another piece of information, which then replaces the current contents of the Clipboard.

collapse   To reduce the number of rows displayed in a view by showing only categories or by eliminating responses.

column   A vertical section of a worksheet. In Microsoft Excel, there are 256 columns in a worksheet. Columns are usually identified by letters (A–Z, AA–AZ, BA–BZ, IA–IV).

column heading   The lettered gray area at the top of each column that identifies the letter of the column, such as column B.

command   An instruction issued by a user that causes an action to be carried out by the computer program.

comment   A note that explains, identifies, or comments on the information in a specific cell or range of cells.

comparison operators   The flexible criteria used to search for records that are equal to, less than, or greater than a specific value, or for records that are between two values.

context-sensitive help   A type of online help used to identify any screen element in a window or to provide relevant information about the current operation.

Control menu   A menu that appears in each window when you click the Control-menu icon in the upper-left corner of the window.

Control Panel   The set of Windows 95 programs that you can use to change system, hardware, software, and Windows 95 settings.

conventional memory   The memory used to run software under MS-DOS. It is the lowest 640K of the memory.

coprocessor   A separate processor designed to assist in specific functions, such as handling complex mathematics or graphics, and to temporarily reduce the workload of the microprocessor.

copy   To duplicate information from one location to another, either within a file, to another file, or to a file in another program. The copied information is stored on the Clipboard until you cut or copy another piece of information.

criteria   The conditions that control which records to display in a query; the words or values used to determine the data that appears in a data list.

cursor   The pointer on the screen that indicates where characters appear in response to keyboard or mouse input.

cut   To remove selected information from a document so you can paste it to another location within the file, to another file, or to a file in another program. The cut information is stored on the Clipboard until you cut or copy another piece of information.

data points   The individual values plotted in a chart and represented by bars, lines, pie slices, dots, and other shapes.

data series   One row or column of values (data points) that appears on a chart, such as bars, lines, or pie slices. The orientation of the data series, either in rows or in columns, determines how the data is plotted on the chart.

data type   The attribute of a field that determines the kind of data the field can contain.

database   A collection of data related to a particular topic or purpose, such as a database of customer information. Can also refer to a type of program, such as Microsoft Access, that you can use to organize and manipulate detailed lists of information.

datasheet   A spreadsheet view of rows and columns. A chart is created from the values in a datasheet. Each new datasheet contains a set of default data that you modify to create the chart.

default   A predefined setting that is built into a program and is used when you do not specify an alternative setting. For example, a document might have a default setting of one-inch page margins unless you specify another value for the margin settings.

delete   To remove information such as a file or text. The user can choose the Delete command, press the DELETE key, or press the BACKSPACE key.

demote   In Outline view, an action that changes a heading to body text or a higher heading level to a lower heading level.

descending   A method of ordering a group of items from highest to lowest, such as from Z to A. *See also* sort.

Desktop   The entire Windows 95 screen that represents your work area. Icons, windows, and the taskbar appear on the Desktop. You can customize the Desktop to suit your preferences and working requirements.

destination   A document or program receiving information that was originally generated in another program. *See also* source.

dialog box   A window that displays additional options when a command is chosen from a menu.

disk   A round, flat piece of flexible plastic (floppy disk) or inflexible metal (hard disk) that stores data. The disk is coated with a magnetic material on which digital information can be recorded. To protect this material, disks are enclosed in plastic or metal casings.

disk drive   A hardware mechanism that reads information from a disk and writes information to a disk.

document   Any independent unit of information, such as a text file, worksheet, or graphic object, that is created with a program. A document can be saved with a unique filename by which it can be retrieved.

document window   A rectangular portion of the screen in which you view and edit a document. A document window is typically a window inside another window. For example, documents in Microsoft Word or Microsoft Excel are displayed in their own window, inside the program window.

double-click   To press the primary mouse button twice rapidly. Double-clicking an object performs the default action.

double-density disk   Common type of floppy disk for IBM-compatible computers. Capacity is 360K for 5.25-inch disks and 720K for 3.5-inch disks.

download   To transfer a file from a remote computer to your local computer. This type of transfer can be performed by using computers on a network or through telecommunication.

drag-and-drop   A mouse technique for directly moving or copying a set of information from one location to another. To drag an object, position the pointer over the object, hold down the mouse button while you move the mouse, and then release the mouse button when the object is positioned where you want it.

drive   *See* disk drive.

edit   To add, delete, or change information, such as text or graphics.

electronic mail   Notes, messages, or files sent between different computers using telecommunication or network services. Also referred to as e-mail.

embed   To insert an object from a source program into a destination document. When you double-click the object in the destination document, the source program opens and you can edit the object. *See also* link.

embedded chart   A chart that exists on a worksheet instead of on a separate chart sheet.

embedded object   Data (such as text or graphics) that you can edit using the full resources of its source program while it is in a destination document. *See also* embed.

expand   To display all subordinate entries in an outline or in a folder.

expanded memory   The additional memory above 640K. Expanded memory exists separately from conventional memory and extended memory. Most personal computers can accommodate expanded memory.

export   The process of converting and saving a file to be used in a another program. *See also* import.

field   In a list or database, a column of data that contains a particular type of information, such as Last Name or Phone Number or Quantity.

file   A document that you create or save with a unique filename.

file format   The format in which data is stored in a file. Usually, different programs, such as Microsoft Word or Microsoft Excel, have different file formats.

filter   A set of criteria you can apply to records to show specific tasks, records, or resources. The tasks, records, or resources that match your criteria are listed or highlighted so that you can focus on just the information you want.

floating palette   A palette that can be dragged away from its toolbar. *See also* palette.

floating toolbar   A toolbar that appears in a window with a title bar, stays on top of the other windows, and is not fixed in position.

floppy disk   *See* disk.

folder   A container in which documents, program files, and other folders are stored on your computer disks. Folders can help you organize your documents by grouping them into categories, as you would organize paper documents into file folders. Formerly referred to as a *directory*.

font   A family of type styles, such as Times or Arial. Effects, such as bold or italic, are possible within one font, and various point sizes can be applied to a font.

footer   The text or graphics printed at the bottom of every page in a document.

footnote   An explanation or comment reference inserted at the bottom of the page on which the reference mark is located or at the end of the document.

format   The way text and cells appear on a page. Types of formats include character, number, cell border, color, and more. Styles can contain any of these formats. Format can also refer to preparing a disk to record or retrieve data. Formatting usually erases any information previously stored on the disk.

formula   A sequence of values, cell references, names, functions, or operators that produces a new value from existing values. A formula always begins with an equal sign (=).

function   A built-in formula; a named and stored procedure that performs a specific operation and returns a value. Functions begin with a function command and are followed by a set of parentheses. Inside the parentheses is the argument, which can be a set of cell references, a range, numbers, text, or other functions. Some functions do not use an argument.

gridlines   The horizontal and vertical lines on a chart that help relate a plotted point to a value.

handles   Small black squares located in the lower-right corner of selected cells or around selected graphic objects, chart items, or text. By dragging the handles, you can perform actions such as moving, copying, filling, sizing, or formatting on the selected cells, objects, chart items, or text.

hard disk   *See* disk.

hardware   The physical parts of a computer system, such as the monitor, keyboard, and printer.

header   The text or graphics printed at the top of every page in a document.

high-density disk   A type of floppy disk. A high-density 3.5-inch disk has a capacity of 1.44 MB, and a high-density 5.25-inch disk has a capacity of 1.2 MB.

hyperlink   An object, such as a graphic or colored or underlined text, that represents a link to another location in the same file or in a different file, and that, when clicked, brings up a different Web page. Hyperlinks are one of the key elements of HTML documents.

icon   A small graphic that represents an object, such as a program, a disk drive, or a document. When you double-click an icon, the item the icon represents opens.

IF function   A function that tests the content of the cell, performs a calculation, and displays a value or text based on whether the test is true or false.

import   The process of converting and opening a file that was created in a another program. *See also* export.

indent   The distance between the left or right edge of a block of text and the page margin. A paragraph can have a left, right, and first-line indent. Indents can also be measured relative to columns in a section, table cells, and the boundaries of positioned objects.

index   A table that lists page numbers for topics in a document. The topics are usually listed alphabetically and the index is placed near the end of the document.

input   The information conveyed to a computer using a keyboard or a mouse.

insert   To enter text, data, or a graphic into a document, cell, or dialog box. You can also insert cells, rows, and columns into a worksheet. You insert information at the insertion point. *See also* insertion point.

insertion point   The blinking vertical bar that marks the location where text is entered in a document or a dialog box. You can move the insertion point by clicking the mouse in another location or by using the keyboard arrow keys.

install   To prepare equipment or software for use for the first time.

interface A point of connection between two elements so that they can work with one another. The connection can be at many levels, including between two types of hardware, between hardware and software, or between software and user.

Internet A worldwide "network of networks," made up of thousands of computer networks and millions of commercial, education, government, and personal computers, all connected to each other. You connect to the Internet using an Internet service provider, an online service such as CompuServe, or through a corporate network. Also known as the Net.

intranet A self-contained network that uses the same communications protocols and file formats as the Internet. An intranet can, but doesn't have to, be connected to the Internet. Many businesses use intranets for their internal communications. *See also* Internet.

kilobyte (K) A unit of measure for computer memory or storage capacity. One kilobyte equals 1024 bytes.

label A descriptive name that identifies a group of cells, a named value, or a formula.

landscape The horizontal orientation of a page; opposite of *portrait*, or vertical, orientation.

laser printer A high-quality printer that uses a laser beam to generate an image and has a resolution of 300 dots per inch (dpi) or higher.

legend A box containing the name of each data series in a chart.

link To copy an object, such as a graphic or text, from one file or program to another so that there is a dependent relationship between the object and its source file. *Link* also refers to the connection between a source file and a destination file. Whenever the original information in the source file changes, the information in the linked object is automatically updated. *See also* embed.

margin The absolute boundary of text and graphics on a page.

marquee *See* moving border.

megabyte (MB) A unit of measure for memory or storage. One megabyte equals 1024 kilobytes, or 1,048,576 bytes.

megahertz (MHz) A measurement of frequency equivalent to 1 million cycles per second; commonly used to measure the clock speed of a computer.

memory The primary storage in a computer, which is measured in bytes, kilobytes (K), and megabytes (MB).

menu A list of commands or options available in a program.

merge   To combine items, such as lists, without changing the basic structure of any item.

microprocessor   The central processing chip in a personal computer. Common microprocessors for IBM and IBM-compatible computers include the Intel 386, 486, and Pentium processors.

Microsoft Office 97   An integrated family of business programs. Microsoft Office 97 Standard includes Word, Excel, PowerPoint, and Outlook. Microsoft Office 97 Professional adds Access to the package.

minimize   To contract a window to an icon. This can be reversed by double-clicking the icon, or by using the Restore command or the Maximize command on the Control menu.

move   To transfer information from one location to another, either within a file, to another file, or to a file in another program.

moving border   A moving dotted line that surrounds a cell or range of cells. A moving border appears around a cell or range that has been cut or copied, or around a cell or range you are inserting into a formula.

network   A group of computers and associated devices that are connected with communication links.

object   A table, chart, graphic, equation, or other form of information you create and edit. An object can be inserted, pasted, or copied into any file.

OLE   A Microsoft programming standard that allows a user or a program to communicate with other programs, usually for the purpose of exchanging information. Drag-and-drop and linking and embedding are examples of OLE features. *See also* link *and* embed.

operating system   The software used to control application processing and hardware resources, such as memory, disk space, and peripheral devices.

options   The choices you have in a dialog box.

output   The results of processing that can be sent to a screen or printer, stored on disk as a file, or sent to another computer over a network.

Page Break Preview   A view that displays your document with preset page breaks or allows you to change page breaks by dragging page boundaries.

palette   A dialog box containing choices for color and other special effects that you use when designing a form, report, or other object. A palette appears when you click a toolbar button, such as Border or Fill Color. *See also* floating palette.

paragraph   Any text, graphics, tables, frames, or black lines followed by a paragraph mark. The paragraph mark is treated as part of a paragraph.

password   A unique series of characters that you type to gain entry into a restricted network system, messaging system, or protected file or folder.

paste   To insert cut or copied text into a document from the temporary storage area called the Clipboard.

path   The location of a file within a computer file system. The path indicates the filename preceded by the disk drive, folder, and subfolders in which the file is stored. If the file is on another computer on a network, the path also includes the computer name.

pattern   A graphic style that can be used to fill an object.

PivotTable   An interactive worksheet table that summarizes data using a selected format and calculations. It is called a pivot table because you can rearrange the table structure around the data.

pointer   The representation of the mouse position on the Desktop. You move the pointer on the Desktop by moving the mouse on a smooth, horizontal surface. The pointer changes shape depending on the action.

port   A channel for transferring electronic information between the CPU and peripheral devices. The system unit can have several physical ports.

portrait   A term used to refer to vertical page orientation; opposite of *landscape*, or horizontal orientation.

Print Preview   A view that displays your document as it will appear when you print it. Items, such as text and graphics, appear in their actual positions.

print range   A set area of the worksheet to be printed.

printer   A peripheral device that produces a paper copy of output. Different types of printers include dot matrix, ink jet, and laser printers.

program   A computer software program, such as a word processor, spreadsheet, presentation designer, or relational database, that is designed to do a specific type of work.

promote   In Outline view, an action that changes body text to a heading or a lower heading level to a higher heading level.

properties   The information about an object, including settings or options for that object. For example, you can look at the properties of a file for information such as the file size, file type, and file attributes.

protocol   A communications standard—such as TCP/IP, used on the Internet and intranets, or NETBEUI, used in Microsoft networks—that ensures reliable transmission among the computers and other components on a network.

random access memory (RAM)   The computer's memory, which can be accessed randomly rather than sequentially. RAM allows the computer to store and retrieve information without searching sequentially from the beginning of a location.

range   Two or more adjacent cells on a sheet. You identify a range by the upper-left corner and lower-right corner cell addresses, separated by a colon or by two dots, for example, A1:B10 or A1..C5.

read-only memory (ROM)   Memory containing instructions or data that can be read but not modified. Permanent startup programs and other essential information are stored in ROM.

record   A set of information that belongs together, such as all the information on one job program or one magazine subscription card. A record can also refer to one row in a database. The first row of the database contains the field names. Each additional row of the database is one record. Each record contains the same categories of data, or fields, as every other record in the database.

reference   A cell address used in a formula.

relative cell reference   In formulas, a reference to the address of another cell in relation to a cell that contains a formula.

report   A formatted collection of information that is organized to provide project data related to a specific area of concern.

restore   To expand a minimized application by double-clicking it or to return a window to its previous size.

row   A horizontal section of a worksheet. There are 65,576 rows in a worksheet.

save   To transfer data from temporary memory to a floppy disk or a hard disk.

scroll   To move vertically or horizontally in a window so you can view objects that are not currently visible. You can scroll through a window by clicking the scroll arrows, by dragging the scroll box, or by clicking the scroll bar.

scroll arrow   A button or box with an arrow that appears at each end of a scroll bar. You can scroll through a window in small increments by clicking the scroll arrows. The arrow indicates the direction the document moves when scrolled.

scroll bar   The bar that appears at the right side or the bottom of a window that contains more information than can be displayed. The scroll bar is used to scroll an object or parts of a document into view when the entire object or document does not fit in the window.

scroll box   The rectangle in a scroll bar that indicates the relative position of the current screen to the beginning or end of the file.

select To point to a button, phrase, icon, menu choice, or other object on the screen with the pointer, and then click the primary mouse button once.

shortcut An object that acts as a pointer to a document, folder, Internet address, or program. If you double-click the shortcut, the object opens.

shortcut menu A menu of commands that appears when you click the right mouse button while your mouse pointer is on a toolbar, property sheet, control, or other screen element. The menu of commands depends on the element you click.

software Internal computer programs that instruct the computer to do work. There are two basic categories of software: operating systems and programs.

sort To automatically reorder text or numbers in ascending or descending order, alphabetically, numerically, or by date.

source The document or program in which the data was originally created. *See also* destination.

split bar The double line that indicates where a window is split.

split box The solid box at the end or top of a scroll bar that users drag to split a document window in two, so that each half can be scrolled independently. Users can split a window vertically, horizontally, or both.

spreadsheet A collection of data organized into rows and columns.

status bar A bar at the bottom of the screen that displays information about the currently selected command, the active dialog box, the standard keys on the keyboard, or the current state of the program and the keyboard. You can turn the display of the status bar off and on.

style A named collection of text formatting choices, such as font, size, leading, spacing, and alignment, that can be applied to change the appearance of text. Body Text, Headline, and Subhead are examples of styles that are often used. Styles are also common to word-processing programs. Styles are stored in a document or template.

tab A horizontal setting used to determine the position of text on a line.

table One or more rows of cells commonly used to display numbers and other items for quick reference and analysis. Items in a table are organized into rows (records) and columns (fields).

taskbar The rectangular bar usually located across the bottom of the Windows 95 Desktop. The taskbar includes the Start button as well as buttons for any programs and documents that are open. Its location, size, and visibility can be modified to fit your preferences.

template   A special kind of document that provides basic tools and text for shaping a final document. Templates can contain the following elements: text, styles, glossary items, macros, and menu and key assignments.

text attributes   The characteristics of text, including the font, font style, font size, and color of text.

text box   A box within a dialog box where you type information needed to carry out a command. A text box can also refer to a graphic element that you can use to label parts of a worksheet or chart.

title bar   The horizontal bar at the top of a window that displays the name of the document or program that appears in that window.

toolbar   A bar at the top of Windows-based programs that displays a set of buttons used to carry out common menu commands. The buttons displayed on a toolbar change depending on which window or view is currently selected. Toolbars can be moved, or docked, at any edge of a program window. *See also* floating toolbar.

trendline   A graphic used to study problems of predictions such as future sales. Also called a regression analysis.

view   A set of criteria used to display items in a folder. By applying a different view to a folder, you can change the way the folder contents appear. Views can include specific groups, filters, and sort orders.

Web page   A document, formatted in HTML, that usually contains links that you can use to jump from one page to another or from one location to another. *See also* hyperlink.

widow   The last line of a paragraph forced to the top of the next page of text.

wildcard   Special character used in place of any other characters. An asterisk (*) takes the place of one or more characters; a question mark (?) takes the place of one character.

window   A separate rectangular part of the screen identified by a border. A window represents an open object and displays information. Multiple windows can be open at the same time.

wizard   A tool that guides you through a complex task by asking you questions, and then performing the task based on your responses.

workbook   A Microsoft Excel document in which you can store other documents. A workbook can include multiple worksheets and chart sheets.

worksheet   A set of rows, columns, and cells in which you store and manipulate data. Several worksheets can appear in one workbook, and you can switch among them easily by clicking their tabs with the mouse.

x-axis   A line, usually horizontal, along the bottom of a chart. The x-axis shows the labels for the data series. Also called the horizontal axis.

xy chart   A chart type that represents one data series. Xy charts include vertical bar, horizontal bar, line, area, high/low/close, and scatter charts.

y-axis   A line, usually vertical, along the left side of a chart. The y-axis shows the values for the data series.

Index

formulas, *continued*
    creating, 22–23, 46–54, 104–6
    defined, 52
    editing, 23
    functions in, 22, 52, 53–54, 104–6
    IF function in, 52, 53–54
    labels in, 51
    overview, 21–22
    SUBTOTAL function in, 104–5
    SUMIF function in, 105–6
    vs. functions, 52
    writing, 22–23, 46–54, 104–6
freezing panes, 13
FrontPage, 72
full screen view, 242
functions
    AVERAGE, 104
    defined, 22, 52
    entering, 54
    in formulas, 22, 52, 53–54, 104–6
    vs. formulas, 52
    IF, 52, 53–54
    nested, 52, 54
    SUBTOTAL, 104–5
    SUM, 48, 52, 53
    SUMIF, 105–6

G

Goal Seek, 175, 176–77
graphic objects
    3-D, 148–49
    adding to worksheets, 39–40
    as data markers, 147–49
    deleting, 149
    drawing, 148–49
graphs. *See* **charts**
gridlines
    changing default color, 245
    displaying/hiding, 230
grouping, in PivotTables, 130–31, 133–35

H

handles, defined, 145
headers and footers
    creating, 68–70
    dates in, 69
    fonts in, 68
    modifying, 68–70

headers and footers, *continued*
    page numbers in, 70
    row/column, 9
    standard, 68
Help
    in dialog boxes, 223
    Office Assistant, 8–9
    with practice files, xxv
    printing Help topics, 222
    Windows Help system, 219–23
hiding
    gridlines, 230
    outline details, 115
    scroll bars, 229, 242
    sheet tabs, 230
    toolbars, 217–18, 226, 237–38
history, shared worksheet changes, 189
hyperlinks
    adding to worksheets, 201–2
    editing, 203
    testing, 203

I

icons
    arranging, 227
    changing size, 227
    large, 217, 227
IF function, 52, 53–54
importing text files, 126–28
installing practice files, xxii–xxiii
intranet
    hyperlinks in worksheets, 201–3
    making templates available on, 72

K

keyboard
    shortcuts, 216, 217, 218
    vs. mouse, 214
keywords
    assigning to files, 29–30
    searching for, 44–45
    using to open files, 84–85

L

labels
    aligning text, 34–35
    entering, 32–33

Index

O

Office Assistant, 8–9
online Help. *See* Help
opening
    files, 4, 84–86
    new workbooks, 28
    practice files, 4
    template copies, 71–72
    text files, 126–28
operators
    for conditional number formatting, 90
    in formulas, 22
orientation, PivotTable, 136–37
outlines
    applying to worksheets, 116
    hiding details, 115, 116
    overview, 114–15
    removing, 116
    showing details, 115–16

P

page breaks, 161
page fields, 135–36
page layout, changing, 161
page numbers, 70
panes
    freezing, 13
    splitting worksheets into, 244–45
passwords, 214
pasting
    defined, 191
    Excel charts into PowerPoint slides, 198–200
    linked data, 194
    Word documents into Excel worksheets, 194
    worksheet data into Word documents, 117
patterns, adding to charts, 146–47
picture markers, adding, 147–49
PivotTables
    adding data to, 133–35, 137–38
    applying AutoFormat, 132
    charting, 144–50
    creating, 129–30
    creating page reports, 140
    dates in, 130–31
    drilling down, 139
    fields, 129–30, 133–35, 137–38

PivotTables, *continued*
    formatting, 132–33
    grouping data, 130–31, 133–35
    modifying, 133–37
    orientation of data, 136–37
    overview, 125–26
    refreshing data in, 138–39
    removing data from, 137
    showing all data, 139
    showing underlying details, 139
    view options, 136–37
PMT function, 22
pointers, mouse, 214
practice files
    copying to hard disk, xxii–xxiii
    corrections for, xxv
    installing, xxii–xxiii
    listing, xxiii–xxv
    opening, 4
    renaming, 5
    saving, 5
    starting, 4–5
    using, xxi, xxiii–xxv
previewing worksheets, 38–39, 158–60
print area, 162, 166
printing
    centering on page, 163–64
    charts, 149, 164, 165–66
    to fit, 162–63
    Help topics, 222
    order of pages, 159, 161
    partial worksheets, 161–64
    previewing, 39–39, 158–60
    shared change history, 189
    whole workbooks, 166
    worksheets, 161
    worksheets without charts, 164
print titles, 160–61
programs
    linking data between, 193–95
    sharing data among, 193–203

Q

QuattroPro, switching from, xvi
quitting Windows 95, 224

Get quick, easy answers— anywhere!

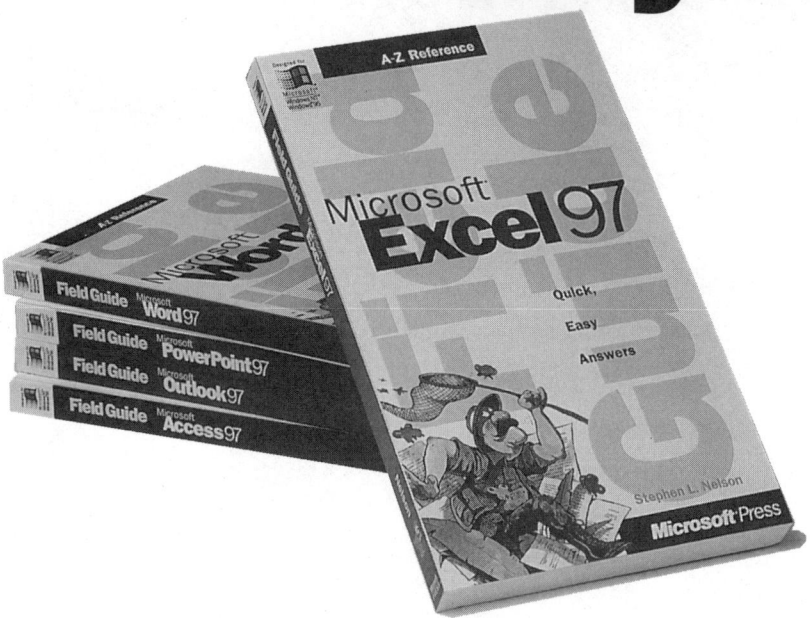

Microsoft® Excel 97 Field Guide
Stephen L. Nelson
U.S.A. **$9.95**   ($12.95 Canada)
ISBN 1-57231-326-9

Microsoft® Word 97 Field Guide
Stephen L. Nelson
U.S.A. **$9.95**   ($12.95 Canada)
ISBN 1-57231-325-0

Microsoft® PowerPoint® 97 Field Guide
Stephen L. Nelson
U.S.A. **$9.95**   ($12.95 Canada)
ISBN 1-57231-327-7

Microsoft® Outlook™ 97 Field Guide
Stephen L. Nelson
U.S.A. **$9.99**   ($12.99 Canada)
ISBN 1-57231-383-8

Microsoft® Access 97 Field Guide
Stephen L. Nelson
U.S.A. **$9.95**   ($12.95 Canada)
ISBN 1-57231-328-5

Microsoft Press® Field Guides are a quick, accurate source of information about Microsoft Office 97 applications. In no time, you'll have the lay of the land, identify toolbar buttons and commands, stay safely out of danger, and have all the tools you need for survival!

Microsoft Press® products are available worldwide wherever quality computer books are sold. For more information, contact your book or computer retailer, software reseller, or local Microsoft Sales Office, or visit our Web site at mspress.microsoft.com. To locate your nearest source for Microsoft Press products, or to order directly, call 1-800-MSPRESS in the U.S. (in Canada, call 1-800-268-2222).

Prices and availability dates are subject to change.

***Microsoft**·Press*

Keep things running smoothly around the Office.

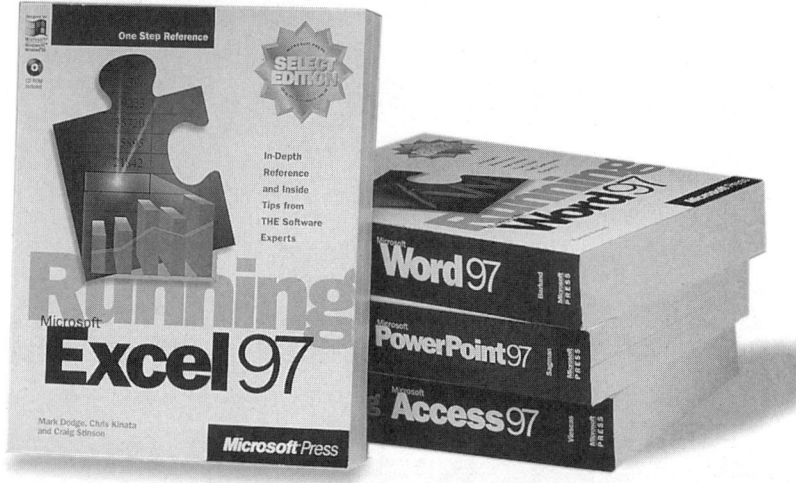

These are *the* answer books for business users of Microsoft Office 97 applications. They are packed with everything from quick, clear instructions for new users to comprehensive answers for power users. The Microsoft Press® *Running* series features authoritative handbooks you'll keep by your computer and use every day.

Running Microsoft® Excel 97
Mark Dodge, Chris Kinata, and Craig Stinson
U.S.A. $39.95   ($54.95 Canada)
ISBN 1-57231-321-8

Running Microsoft® Word 97
Russell Borland
U.S.A. $39.95   ($53.95 Canada)
ISBN 1-57231-320-X

Running Microsoft® PowerPoint® 97
Stephen W. Sagman
U.S.A. $29.95   ($39.95 Canada)
ISBN 1-57231-324-2

Running Microsoft® Access 97
John L. Viescas
U.S.A. $39.95   ($54.95 Canada)
ISBN 1-57231-323-4

Running Microsoft® Office 97
Michael Halvorson and Michael Young
U.S.A. $39.95   ($53.95 Canada)
ISBN 1-57231-322-6

Microsoft *Press*

Take
productivity
in
stride.

Microsoft Press® *Step by Step* books provide quick and easy self-paced training that will help you learn to use the powerful word processor, spreadsheet, database, desktop information manager, and presentation applications of Microsoft Office 97, both individually and together. Prepared by the professional trainers at Catapult, Inc., and Perspection, Inc., these books present easy-to-follow lessons with clear objectives, real-world business examples, and numerous screen shots and illustrations. Each book contains approximately eight hours of instruction. Put Microsoft's Office 97 applications to work today, *Step by Step.*

Microsoft® Excel 97 Step by Step
U.S.A. $29.95   ($39.95 Canada)
ISBN 1-57231-314-5

Microsoft® Word 97 Step by Step
U.S.A. $29.95   ($39.95 Canada)
ISBN 1-57231-313-7

Microsoft® PowerPoint® 97
 Step by Step
U.S.A. $29.95   ($39.95 Canada)
ISBN 1-57231-315-3

Microsoft® Outlook™ 97 Step by Step
U.S.A. $29.99   ($39.99 Canada)
ISBN 1-57231-382-X

Microsoft® Access 97 Step by Step
U.S.A. $29.95   ($39.95 Canada)
ISBN 1-57231-316-1

Microsoft® Office 97 Integration
 Step by Step
U.S.A. $29.95   ($39.95 Canada)
ISBN 1-57231-317-X

***Microsoft*®*Press*

IMPORTANT—READ CAREFULLY BEFORE OPENING SOFTWARE PACKET(S). By opening the sealed packet(s) containing the software, you indicate your acceptance of the following Microsoft License Agreement.

MICROSOFT LICENSE AGREEMENT

(Book Companion CD-ROM)

Register your Microsoft Press® book today, and let us know what you think.

At Microsoft Press, we listen to our customers. We update our books as new releases of software are issued, and we'd like you to tell us the kinds of additional information you'd find most useful in these updates. Your feedback will be considered when we prepare a future edition; plus, when you become a registered owner, you will get Microsoft Press catalogs and exclusive offers on specially priced books.
Thanks!

I used this book as
- ⬤ A way to learn the software
- ⬤ A reference when I needed it
- ⬤ A way to find out about advanced features
- ⬤ Other_____

I consider myself
- ⬤ A beginner or an occasional computer user
- ⬤ An intermediate-level user with a pretty good grasp of the basics
- ⬤ An advanced user who helps and provides solutions for others
- ⬤ Other_____

I purchased this book from
- ⬤ A bookstore
- ⬤ A software store
- ⬤ A direct mail offer
- ⬤ Other_____

I will buy the next edition of the book when it's updated
- ⬤ Definitely
- ⬤ Probably
- ⬤ I will not buy the next edition

The next edition of this book should include the following additional information:
1•_____
2•_____
3•_____
The most useful things about this book are_____
_____
This book would be more helpful if_____
_____
My general impressions of this book are_____
_____

May we contact you regarding your comments? ⬤ Yes ⬤ No
Would you like to receive a Microsoft Press catalog regularly? ⬤ Yes ⬤ No

Name_____
Company (if applicable)_____
Address_____
City_____State_____Zip_____
Daytime phone number (optional) (_____)_____

Please mail back your feedback form—postage free! Fold this form as described on the other side of this card, or fax this sheet to:
Microsoft Press, Attn: Marketing Department, fax 425-936-7329

NO POSTAGE
NECESSARY
IF MAILED
IN THE
UNITED STATES

BUSINESS REPLY MAIL

FIRST-CLASS MAIL   PERMIT NO. 53   BOTHELL, WA

POSTAGE WILL BE PAID BY ADDRESSEE

MICROSOFT PRESS
MICROSOFT® EXCEL 97 STEP BY STEP,
COMPLETE COURSE
PO BOX 3019
BOTHELL   WA   98041-9946

Microsoft® EXCEL 97

Advanced Topics

Step by Step

Other titles in the *Step by Step* series:

*Microsoft Access 97 Step by Step

*Microsoft Excel 97 Step by Step

*Microsoft FrontPage 97 Step by Step

  Microsoft Internet Explorer 3.0 Step by Step

  Microsoft Office 97 Integration Step by Step

*Microsoft Outlook 97 Step by Step

*Microsoft PowerPoint 97 Step by Step

  Microsoft Team Manager 97 Step by Step

  Microsoft Windows 95 Step by Step

  Microsoft Windows NT Workstation version 4.0 Step by Step

*Microsoft Word 97 Step by Step

*Microsoft Word 97 Step by Step, Advanced Topics

Step by Step books are also available for the Microsoft Office 95 programs.

* These books are approved courseware for Certified Microsoft Office User (CMOU) exams. For more details about the CMOU program, see page xi.

Microsoft®

EXCEL 97
Advanced Topics

Step by Step

Microsoft Press

PUBLISHED BY
Microsoft Press
A Division of Microsoft Corporation
One Microsoft Way
Redmond, Washington 98052-6399

Library of Congress Cataloging-in-Publication Data pending.

Printed and bound in the United States of America.

1 2 3 4 5 6 7 8 9   WCWC   2 1 0 9 8 7

Distributed to the book trade in Canada by Macmillan of Canada, a division of Canada
Publishing Corporation.

British Cataloging-in-Publication Data pending.

Microsoft Press books are available through booksellers and distributors worldwide. For further
information about international editions, contact your local Microsoft Corporation office. Or
contact Microsoft Press International directly at fax (425) 936-7329.

For Siechert & Wood, Inc.
Project Editor: Stan DeGulis
Technical Editors: Carl Siechert, Blake Wesley Whittington
Production/Layout: Paula J. Kausch

For Microsoft Press
Acquisitions Editor: Casey D. Doyle
Project Editor: Laura Sackerman

Part No. 097-0001851

Table of Contents

Table of Contents

*Quick*Look Guide

Using auditing arrows, see Lesson 2, page 38

Using functions in formulas, see Lesson 3, page 64

Using conditional formatting to highlight a cell based on its value, see Lesson 6, page 185

Making labels appear at an angle, see Lesson 6, page 179

Using labels in formulas, see Lesson 1, page 5

Using the Formula Palette, see Lesson 3, page 63

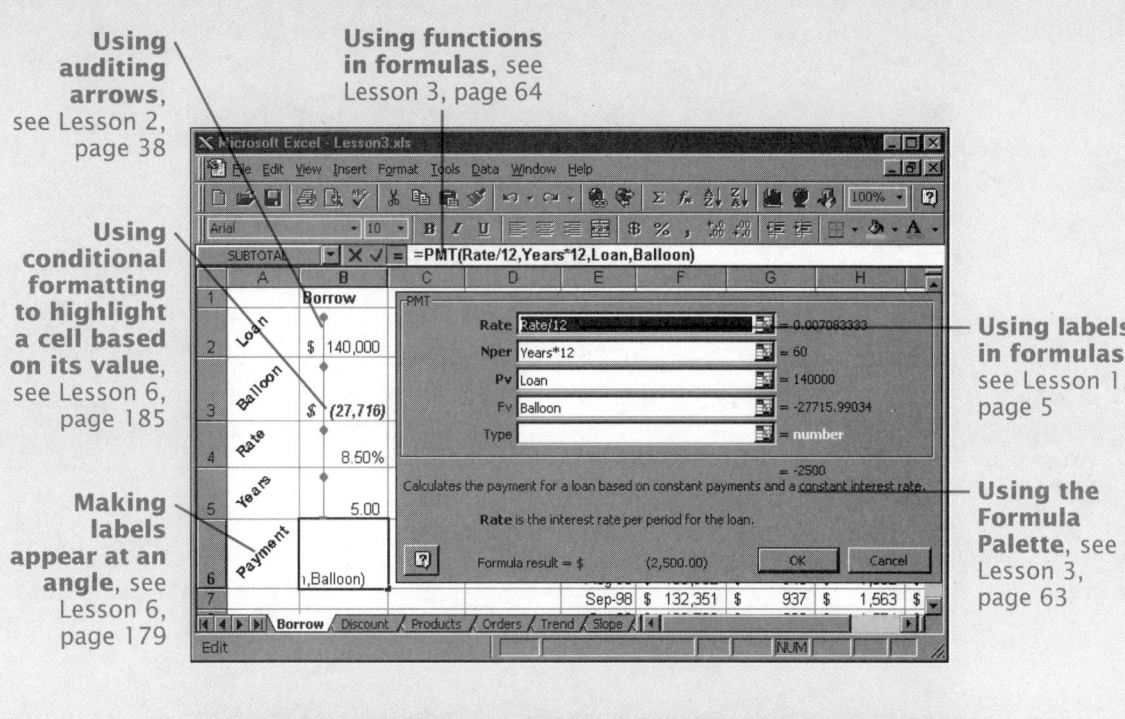

Importing data from an external data source, see Lesson 8, page 250

Creating a PivotTable to analyze data, see Lesson 5, page 128

Adding comments to cells, see Lesson 8, page 238

Creating 3-D shapes, see Lesson 6, page 195

Using WordArt to create a custom logo, see Lesson 6, page 193

Creating custom chart types, see Lesson 7, page 213

Adding OfficeArt graphics, see Lesson 6, page 187

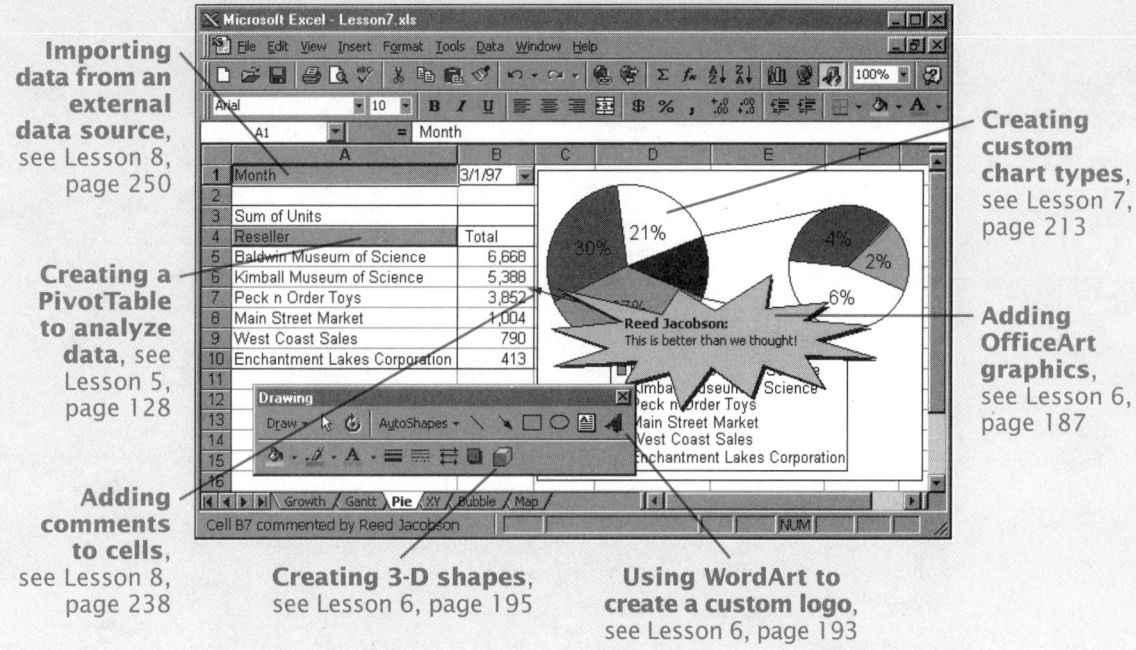

QuickLook Guide

Using AutoFilter,
see Lesson 4, page 109

Sorting a list,
see Lesson 4, page 100

Outlining to show and hide parts of a list,
see Lesson 4, page 105

Validating data,
see Lesson 8, page 234

Inserting subtotals in a list,
see Lesson 4, page 104

Adding a check box to a worksheet,
see Lesson 8, page 240

Creating a custom toolbar button,
see Lesson 10, page 296

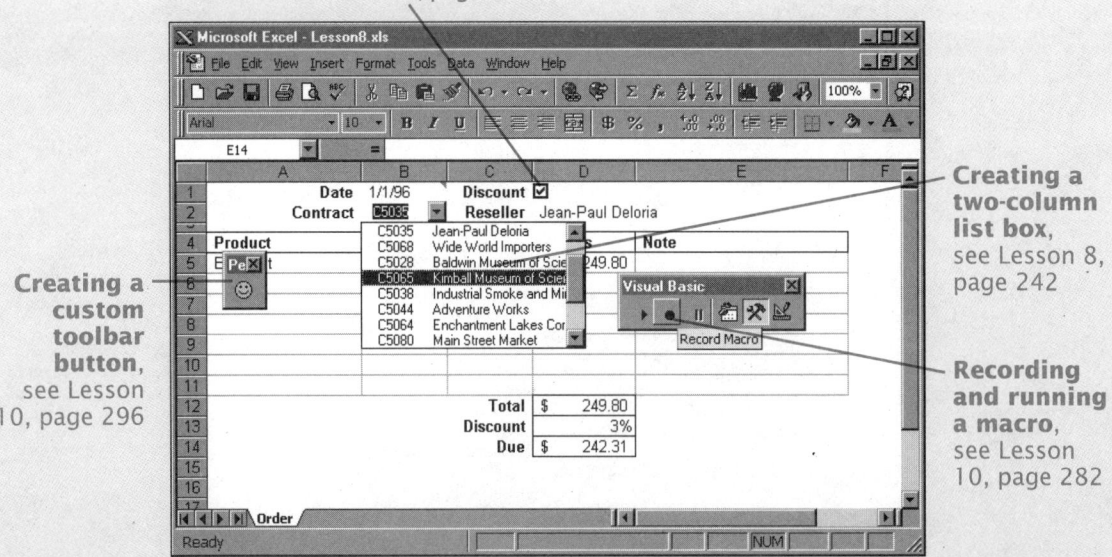

Creating a two-column list box,
see Lesson 8, page 242

Recording and running a macro,
see Lesson 10, page 282

Finding Your Best Starting Point

Microsoft Excel 97 is a powerful spreadsheet program that you can use to efficiently calculate, sort, chart, analyze and present text and numbers. With *Microsoft Excel 97 Step by Step, Advanced Topics*, you'll quickly and easily learn how to use advanced features of Microsoft Excel 97 to get your work done.

IMPORTANT This book is designed for use with Microsoft Excel 97 for the Windows 95 and Windows NT version 4.0 operating systems. To find out what software you're running, you can check the product package or you can start the software, click the Help menu at the top of the screen, and click About Microsoft Excel. If your software is not compatible with this book, a Step by Step book for your software is probably available. Many of the Step by Step titles are listed on the second page of this book. If the book you want isn't listed, please visit our World Wide Web site at http://mspress.microsoft.com/ or call 1-800-MSPRESS for more information.

Finding Your Best Starting Point in This Book

This book is designed for readers who are already comfortable using the basic features of Microsoft Excel and who want to become more proficient, or who want to learn to use powerful new features in the new release of Microsoft Excel. Use the table on the following page to find your best starting point in this book.

If you are	Follow these steps

New...

to computers

to graphical (as opposed to text-only) computer programs

to Windows 95 or Windows NT

1 Start with *Microsoft Excel 97 Step by Step* rather than this book.

2 Become acquainted with the Windows 95 or Windows NT operating system and how to use the online Help system by working through Appendix A, "If You're New to Windows 95, Windows NT, or Microsoft Excel," in *Microsoft Excel 97 Step by Step*.

3 Learn basic skills for using Excel 97 by working through Lessons 1 through 4 of *Microsoft Excel 97 Step by Step*. Then you can work through the remaining lessons in *Microsoft Excel 97 Step by Step* and the lessons in this book in any order.

Switching...

from Lotus 1-2-3

from Quattro Pro

1 Install the practice files as described in "Installing and Using the Practice Files."

2 Work through the lessons in this book in any order. If you need help with any of the basic skills required, start with *Microsoft Excel 97 Step by Step* rather than this book.

Upgrading...

from a previous version of Microsoft Excel for Windows

1 Learn about the new features in this version of the program that are covered in this book by reading through the following section, "New Features in Microsoft Excel 97."

2 Install the practice files as described in "Installing and Using the Practice Files."

3 Complete the lessons that cover the topics you need. Use the table of contents and the *Quick*Look Guide to locate information about general topics. Use the index to find information about a specific topic or a feature from a previous version of Excel.

Referencing...

this book after working through the lessons

1 Use the index to locate information about specific topics, and use the table of contents and the *Quick*Look Guide to locate information about general topics.

2 Read the Lesson Summary at the end of each lesson for a brief review of the major tasks in the lesson. The Lesson Summary topics are listed in the same order as they are presented in the lesson.

Certified Microsoft Office User Program

The Certified Microsoft Office User (CMOU) program is designed for business professionals and students who use Microsoft Office 97 products in their daily work. The program enables participants to showcase their skill level to potential employers. It benefits accountants, administrators, executive assistants, program managers, sales representatives, students, and many others. To receive certified user credentials for a software program, candidates must pass a hands-on exam in which they use the program to complete real-world tasks.

The CMOU program offers two levels of certification: Proficient and Expert. The following table indicates the levels available for each Microsoft Office 97 program. (You can find out more about the certification levels by visiting the CMOU program World Wide Web site at http://www.microsoft.com/msoffice/train_cert/)

Software	Proficient level	Expert level
Microsoft Word 97	✔	✔
Microsoft Excel 97	✔	✔
Microsoft Access 97		✔
Microsoft PowerPoint 97		✔
Microsoft Outlook 97		✔
Microsoft FrontPage 97		✔

Microsoft Press offers the following books in the *Step by Step* series as approved courseware for the CMOU exams:

Proficient level:
Microsoft Word 97 Step by Step, by Catapult, Inc. ISBN: 1-57231-313-7
Microsoft Excel 97 Step by Step, by Catapult, Inc. ISBN: 1-57231-314-5

Expert level:
Microsoft Word 97 Step by Step, Complete Course, by Catapult, Inc., and Russell Borland. ISBN: 1-57231-579-2
Microsoft Excel 97 Step by Step, Complete Course, by Catapult, Inc., and Reed Jacobson. ISBN: 1-57231-580-6
Microsoft Access 97 Step by Step, by Catapult, Inc. ISBN: 1-57231-316-1
Microsoft PowerPoint 97 Step by Step, by Perspection, Inc. ISBN: 1-57231-315-3
Microsoft Outlook 97 Step by Step, by Catapult, Inc. ISBN: 1-57231-382-X
Microsoft FrontPage 97 Step by Step, by Catapult, Inc. ISBN: 1-57231-336-6

Candidates may take exams from any participating CMOU-Approved Certification Test Center, or participating schools, corporations, or employment agencies. To find the CMOU Test Center nearest you, call 1-800-933-4493.

To become a candidate for certification, or for more information about the certification process, please visit the CMOU program World Wide Web site at http://www.microsoft.com/msoffice/train_cert/ or call 1-800-933-4493 in the U.S.

New Features in Microsoft Excel 97

The following table lists the major new features in Microsoft Excel 97 that are covered in this book. The table shows the lesson in which you can learn how to use each feature. You can also use the index to find specific information about a feature or a task you want to perform.

To learn how to	See
Use labels to create a formula	Lesson 1, Lesson 2
Use the Range Finder to analyze a formula	Lesson 1
Use the Formula Palette to create a formula	Lesson 3
Format a PivotTable	Lesson 5
Sort and filter a PivotTable	Lesson 5
Show all items in a PivotTable	Lesson 5
Add calculations to a PivotTable	Lesson 5
Review reports with Page Break Preview	Lesson 6
Make labels appear at an angle	Lesson 6
Change the format of a cell based on the value it contains	Lesson 6
Add WordArt and other OfficeArt graphics	Lesson 6
Use new preformatted chart layouts	Lesson 7
Create Pie of Pie charts, Bubble charts, and other new chart formats	Lesson 7
Validate the data entered into a cell	Lesson 8
Add custom controls such as check boxes and list boxes to a worksheet	Lesson 8
Allow multiple users to simultaneously edit a workbook saved on a network	Lesson 9
Merge changes from a distributed workbook	Lesson 9
Use the Visual Basic Editor to create and edit macros	Lesson 10
Add a custom macro to a toolbar button or a menu command	Lesson 10

Corrections, Comments, and Help

Every effort has been made to ensure the accuracy of this book and the contents of the practice files disk. Microsoft Press provides corrections and additional content for its books through the World Wide Web at

http://mspress.microsoft.com/mspress/support/

If you have comments, questions, or ideas regarding this book or the practice files disk, please send them to us.

Send email to

mspinput@microsoft.com

Or send postal mail to

Microsoft Press
Attn: Step by Step Series Editor
One Microsoft Way
Redmond, WA 98052-6399

Please note that support for the Excel software product itself is not offered through the above addresses. For help using Excel, you can call Microsoft Excel Technical Support at (425) 635-7070 on weekdays between 6 A.M. and 6 P.M. Pacific time.

Visit Our World Wide Web Site

We invite you to visit the Microsoft Press World Wide Web site. You can visit us at the following location:

http://mspress.microsoft.com/

You'll find descriptions for all of our books, information about ordering titles, notice of special features and events, additional content for Microsoft Press books, and much more.

You can also find out the latest in software developments and news from Microsoft Corporation by visiting the following World Wide Web site:

http://www.microsoft.com/

We look forward to your visit on the Web!

Installing and Using the Practice Files

The CD-ROM included with this book contains practice files that you'll use as you perform the exercises in the book. For example, when you're learning how to sort lists, you'll open one of the practice files—a partially completed product list—and then use the sorting feature. By using the practice files, you won't waste time creating the samples used in the lessons—instead, you can concentrate on learning how to use Excel. With the files and the step-by-step instructions in the lessons, you'll also learn by doing, which is an easy and effective way to acquire and remember new skills.

 IMPORTANT Before you break the seal on the practice CD package, be sure that this book matches your version of the software. This book is designed for use with Microsoft Excel 97 for the Windows 95 and Windows NT version 4.0 operating systems. To find out what software you're running, you can check the product package or you can start the software, and then on the Help menu at the top of the screen, click About Microsoft Excel. If your program is not compatible with this book, a Step by Step book matching your software is probably available. Many of the Step by Step titles are listed on the second page of this book. If the book you want isn't listed, please visit our World Wide Web site at http://mspress.microsoft.com/ or call 1-800-MSPRESS for more information.

Install the practice files on your computer

Follow these steps to install the practice files on your computer's hard disk so that you can use them with the exercises in this book.

NOTE: The setup program installs practice files for both books included with Microsoft Excel 97 Step by Step, Complete Course. If you already ran Setup to install files for the other book, you don't need to run it again.

1 Remove the Microsoft Excel 97 Step by Step Complete Course CD-ROM from its envelope.

2 Insert the CD-ROM in your computer's CD drive.

3 On the taskbar at the bottom of your screen, click the Start button, point to Settings, and then click Control Panel.

4 In Control Panel, double-click the Add/Remove Programs icon.

5 On the Install/Uninstall tab, click Install, and then follow the directions on the screen.

   The setup program window appears with recommended options preselected for you. For best results in using the practice files with this book, accept these preselected settings.

6 When the files have been installed, remove the CD-ROM from your drive and replace it in its envelope.

   A folder called Excel AT Practice has been created on your hard disk, and the practice files have been put in that folder.

Microsoft
Press
Welcome

Excel
Camcorder
Files

NOTE In addition to installing the practice files, the Setup program has created two shortcuts on your Desktop. If your computer is set up to connect to the Internet, you can double-click the Microsoft Press Welcome shortcut to visit the Microsoft Press web site. You can also connect to this web site directly at http://mspress.microsoft.com/

You can double-click the Excel Camcorder Files shortcut to display a workbook with links to audiovisual demonstrations of how to do a number of tasks in Excel. You can also copy these demonstration files from the *Microsoft Excel 97 Step by Step, Advanced Topics* Camcorder files Web page. You can connect to this Web site at http://mspress.microsoft.com/mspress/products/1244/

Using the Practice Files

Each lesson in this book explains when and how to use any practice files for that lesson. When it's time to use a practice file, the book will list instructions for how to open the file. The lessons are built around project tasks that simulate a real work environment, so you can easily apply the skills you learn to your own work. For the scenarios in this book, imagine that you're the resident Excel expert at Tailspin Toys, a company that manufactures and distributes model toys.

The screen illustrations in this book might look different than what you see on your computer, depending on how your computer has been set up.

For those of you who like to know all the details, here's a list of the files for this book included on the CD-ROM:

Filename	Description
Lesson 1	
Start1	An empty workbook you will use for creating new formulas
Lesson 2	
No practice file	This lesson begins with a new workbook
Lesson 3	
Start3	Several partially completed worksheet models that you will complete
Lesson 4	
Start4	A list with prior year orders that you will modify, sort, and filter
Lesson 5	
Start5	A list containing the complete monthly order history for Tailspin Toys, along with a separate list of Product Line information
Lesson 6	
Start6	Worksheets that you can format as reports
Lesson 7	
Start7	Sample data that you can use in charts
Lesson 8	
Start8	An order form that you will make easy for others to use
Tailspin.mdb	A sample database from which you will retrieve information
Lesson 9	
Start9	A planning workbook that you will protect and share
Lesson 10	
Start10	A sales log that you will write macros to enhance

Need Help with the Practice Files?

Every effort has been made to ensure the accuracy of this book and the contents of the practice files CD-ROM. If you do run into a problem, Microsoft Press provides corrections for its books through the World Wide Web at

http://mspress.microsoft.com/mspress/support/

We also invite you to visit our main Web page at

http://mspress.microsoft.com/

You'll find descriptions for all of our books, information about ordering titles, notices of special features and events, additional content for Microsoft Press books, and much more.

Deleting the Practice Files

Use the following steps when you want to delete the shortcuts added to your Desktop and the practice files added to your hard drive by the Step by Step Setup program.

1   If any windows are covering the shortcuts on your Desktop, use the right mouse button to click an unoccupied area of the taskbar at the bottom of your screen, and then click Minimize All Windows.

2   On the Desktop, click the Microsoft Press Welcome shortcut icon, hold down CTRL, and click the Excel Camcorder Files shortcut icon. Press DELETE.

If you are prompted to confirm the deletion, click Yes. The Desktop shortcut icons are removed from your computer.

3   Click the Start button, point to Settings, and click Control Panel.

4   In Control Panel, double-click the Add/Remove Programs icon.

5   To remove the practice files for *Microsoft Excel 97 Step by Step*, on the Install/Uninstall tab, select Excel 97 Step By Step.

6   Click Add/Remove, and then click Yes.

7   To remove the practice files for *Microsoft Excel 97 Step by Step, Advanced Topics*, on the Install/Uninstall tab, select Excel 97 Step By Step, Advanced Topics.

8   Click Add/Remove, and then click Yes.

9   To remove the Camcorder files, on the Install/Uninstall tab, select Excel 97 Step By Step, Camcorder Files.

10   Click Add/Remove, and then click Yes.

All practice files on your computer are now deleted.

 IMPORTANT   When you delete the practice files as described above, your Excel SBS Practice and Excel AT Practice folders and all the files they contain are deleted. Therefore, all files you've saved in those folders—including files you create while following the exercises in this book—are also deleted.

Conventions and Features in This Book

You can save time when you use this book by understanding, before you start the lessons, how instructions, keys to press, and so on are shown in the book. Please take a moment to read the following list, which also points out helpful features of the book that you might want to use.

Conventions

- Hands-on exercises for you to follow are given in numbered lists of steps (1, 2, and so on). An arrowhead bullet (▶) indicates an exercise that has only one step.

- Text that you are to type appears in **bold**.

- A plus sign (+) between two key names means that you must press those keys at the same time. For example, "Press ALT+TAB" means that you hold down ALT while you press TAB.

The following icons identify the different types of supplementary material:

Notes labeled	Alert you to
Note	Additional information or alternative methods for a step.
Tip	Suggested additional methods for a step or helpful hints.
Important	Essential information that you should check before continuing with the lesson.
Troubleshooting	Possible error messages or computer difficulties and their solutions.
Demonstration	Skills that are demonstrated in audio-visual files available on the Microsoft Excel 97 Step by Step Complete Course CD-ROM and on the World Wide Web.

Other Features of This Book

- You can learn about options or techniques that build on what you learned in a lesson by trying the optional "One Step Further" exercise at the end of the lesson.

- You can get a quick reminder of how to perform the tasks you learned by reading the Lesson Summary at the end of a lesson.

- You can quickly determine what online Help topics are available for additional information by referring to the Help topics listed at the end of each lesson. The Help system provides a complete online reference to Microsoft Excel.

- You can view audiovisual demonstrations of how to perform some of the more complicated tasks in Excel. Double-click the Excel Camcorder Files shortcut that was created on your Desktop when you installed the practice files for this book, or use your Web browser to connect to http://mspress.microsoft.com/mspress/products/1244/. The page that opens contains full instructions for viewing the demonstration files.

Part 1

Arranging Text and Graphics

Building a Worksheet

In this lesson you will learn how to:

Estimated time
30 min.

- Add numbers, labels, and formulas to a worksheet.
- Format numbers and labels.
- Work with multiple copies of a worksheet.

You are by far the luckiest person at Tailspin Toys. It is your distinct privilege to come up with a proposed pricing and discount policy for the new line of plastic model toys. If you set the prices too high, no one will buy the models, the company will have excess inventory, and you will be in trouble. If you set the prices too low, profits will be low, the company will have capacity problems, and you will be in trouble. Well, that's why they pay you the big bucks.

You get to propose the selling prices for the models, but of course you don't get any say in calculating the manufacturing costs. The production analyst has just given you the manufacturing costs for three new models: an airplane will cost $28, a train will cost $20, and an automobile will cost $14. Your job is to come up with an appropriate *suggested retail price* (SRP) for each model, along with a *reseller discount* (the amount of the suggested retail price that the dealer gets to keep), and an estimate of the profit Tailspin Toys will make.

Start the lesson

To begin the lesson, start Microsoft Excel. Then follow the steps below to open the practice file named Start1 and save the file with the new name Lesson1.

3

IMPORTANT If you have not yet installed the Excel AT Practice files, refer to "Installing and Using the Practice Files" earlier in this book.

Open

1 On the Standard toolbar, click the Open button.

2 In the Open dialog box, click the Look In Favorites button, and then double-click the Excel AT Practice folder.

3 In the list of files, double-click the Start1 file.

Look In Favorites

The Open dialog box closes, and the Start1 workbook appears in the document window.

Start1 is really just an empty workbook with two blank sheets. You'll save it in the Excel AT Practice folder with a new name so that the original practice file will remain unchanged.

4 On the File menu, click Save As.

5 In the File Name box, type **Lesson1** as the new name for the workbook and then click the Save button.

Creating Formulas in a Grid

It costs Tailspin Toys half as much to build a model automobile as it does to build a model airplane. So, do you charge half as much for an automobile? Or do you simply make a killing each time you sell an automobile? Of course, if you get too greedy, maybe you won't sell any automobiles at all. These questions are too hard to answer without the benefit of tangible numbers. It's time to create a Microsoft Excel worksheet.

Enter numbers and labels on a worksheet

Remember, SRP stands for suggested retail price.

Start by entering the numbers for the manufacturing cost of the model airplane, a possible SRP, and a possible reseller discount.

1 On Sheet1, enter **28** in cell A1, **49.95** in cell A2, and **21** in cell A3.

	A	B
1	28	
2	49.95	
3	21	
4		
5		

— Numbers without labels are hard to interpret.

Unfortunately, it's hard to tell by looking at the worksheet which of these numbers is which. You really should add labels to make the numbers more meaningful.

You can make room for the labels by inserting a blank row above the numbers and a blank column to the left of them.

2   Select cell A1. Then, on the Insert menu, click Rows.

Excel inserts a blank row at the top of the worksheet.

3   On the Insert menu, click Columns.

Excel inserts a blank column at the left of the worksheet. Now that you have cells at the top and the left, you can add the labels.

4   Enter **Airplane** in cell B1, **Cost** in cell A2, **SRP** in cell A3, and **Discount** in cell A4.

	A	B	
1		Airplane	— Labels show what the
2	Cost	28	numbers mean.
3	SRP	49.95	
4	Discount	21	
5			
6			

You now have numbers on the worksheet, supported by labels that tell you which number is which.

Speaking of labels, you should change the worksheet label from Sheet1 to something more meaningful, so that if you add additional worksheets to the workbook, you'll be able to find this worksheet again.

5   At the bottom of the worksheet, double-click the Sheet1 tab. Then type **Pricing** as the new name, and press ENTER.

Your worksheet looks very nice. You have some very nice numbers there. But the worksheet doesn't yet tell you anything about the implications of those numbers. For that, you need to calculate some new numbers.

Use formulas to calculate new values

Start by figuring out how much money Tailspin Toys will get for each airplane. Tailspin gets the difference between the SRP and the reseller discount. This is the *net price* of the product. Of course, you could get out your calculator, subtract 21 from 49.95, and enter the result into cell B5, but you're far too clever for that—you will instead create a formula.

In a formula, you can refer to a value in a cell by using the label next to the cell, rather than the value itself.

Excel formulas always begin with an equal sign.

1   Select cell B5, and then type the formula **=SRP–Discount** and press ENTER.

B5		▾	=	=SRP-Discount
	A	B	C	D
1		Airplane		
2	Cost	28		
3	SRP	49.95		
4	Discount	21		
5		28.95		
6				

You can use labels to refer to cells in formulas.

Excel puts the value 28.95 into cell B5. This is the net price, or difference between the $49.95 SRP and the $21 reseller discount.

An Excel formula recalculates whenever one of the input values changes. For example, if you change the SRP or the discount, Excel changes the net price for the model.

2 In cell B4, enter **21.5**

Cell B5 changes to 28.45.

Every value on a worksheet deserves a label—especially if you might use that value in a formula later. So add a label for the new net price value.

3 In cell A5, enter the label **Net**

You probably don't want to have to calculate in your head how much money Tailspin will actually make on each airplane. You can create a formula that subtracts the cost from the net price.

4 In cell B6, enter the formula **=Net–Cost**

B6		▾	=	=Net-Cost
	A	B	C	D
1		Airplane		
2	Cost	28		
3	SRP	49.95		
4	Discount	21.5		
5	Net	28.45		
6		0.45		
7				

Excel displays 0.45 in cell B6—the difference between what you get for an airplane and what the airplane costs to build. At least you aren't losing money. The difference between the net price and the cost for a product is often called the *margin*. If that doesn't sound like a cue for entering a label for the number, I don't know what would.

5 In cell A6, enter **Margin**

Given this particular price and discount scenario, you will make only 45 cents on each airplane. Is that good or bad? That depends on how many you sell. Assume that you will sell 20,000 model airplanes.

6 In cell A7, enter **Quantity**, and in cell B7, enter **20000**

Now that you have numbers (and labels) for the margin and the quantity, you can create formulas (and labels) for total revenue and total profit.

Excel uses an asterisk (*) to indicate multiplication.

7 In cell A8, enter **Revenue**, and in cell B8, enter the formula **=Net*Quantity**

Excel displays 569000 in cell B8 as the revenue. That's a lot of money. Unfortunately, most of it will go to build the models.

8 In cell A9, enter **Profit**, and in cell B9, enter the formula **=Margin*Quantity**

B9		=	=Margin*Quantity		Each formula uses labels to refer to cells.
	A	B	C	D	E
1		Airplane			
2	Cost	28			
3	SRP	49.95			
4	Discount	21.5			
5	Net	28.45			
6	Margin	0.45			
7	Quantity	20000			
8	Revenue	569000			
9	Profit	9000			
10					

In Lesson 2, you will learn how to create formulas without using labels.

Excel displays 9000 in cell B9 as the profit. That doesn't look too bad. Besides, your car pool leaves in less than an hour, and you still need to create proposals for the model trains and automobiles.

When you create a worksheet, you enter labels next to cell values for two reasons—one for the humans, and one for the formulas. The labels make it easier for humans to understand the numbers in the cells, and they allow formulas to refer to the numbers in the cells. Using labels to make cells easy to understand also allows you to make formulas easy to understand. Is that what they call a "win–win" situation?

Copy cells

All you have left is to do the same analysis for the model trains and automobiles. Trains and automobiles have different costs than airplanes, but, for starters, you can try the same SRP and discount values for them. Rather than retype all the numbers and formulas, you can copy what you have. Excel's *AutoFill* feature copies formulas and values, but AutoFill also tries to increment numbers when it can. If you use the right mouse button, you can get precise control over how AutoFill works.

1 Above the word *Airplane,* click the letter "B."

	A	B	C
1		Airplane	
2	Cost	28	
3	SRP	49.95	
4	Discount	21.5	
5	Net	28.45	
6	Margin	0.45	
7	Quantity	20000	

Use the right mouse button to drag the AutoFill handle in order to control how Excel fills the range.

Use the secondary mouse button. If you have reversed your mouse buttons from the default, use the left mouse button.

Excel selects the entire column. At the top right corner of the selection is a small, square dot. This is the *AutoFill handle*. Normally, to extend the selection, you use the left mouse button to drag the AutoFill handle. However, if you use the right mouse button, you can control how AutoFill works.

2 Using the right mouse button, drag the AutoFill handle to the right of column D.

Copy Cells
Fill Series
Fill Formats
Fill Values
Fill Days
Fill Weekdays
Fill Months
Fill Years
Linear Trend
Growth Trend
Series...

The Copy Cells command does not increment numbers.

A shortcut menu appears, asking how you want to extend the selection.

3 Click Copy Cells.

Excel extends the selection with an exact copy of column B.

4 In cell C1, enter the label **Train**, and in cell C2, enter **20**

5 In cell D1, enter the label **Automobile**, and in cell D2, enter **14**

	A	B	C	D	E
1		Airplane	Train	Automobile	
2	Cost	28	20	14	
3	SRP	49.95	49.95	49.95	
4	Discount	21.5	21.5	21.5	
5	Net	28.45	28.45	28.45	
6	Margin	0.45	8.45	14.45	
7	Quantity	20000	20000	20000	
8	Revenue	569000	569000	569000	
9	Profit	9000	169000	289000	
10					

Formulas with labels still calculate correctly in the new columns.

If you really could sell 20,000 units of each product regardless of price, you could make $169,000 on the trains and $289,000 on the automobiles. Unfortunately, the real world is probably more price-sensitive than that.

6 In cell C7, enter **1000**, and in cell D7, enter **100**

The profit drops to $8,450 for trains and $1,445 for automobiles. Painfully, these dramatically reduced sales for the overpriced items are probably a more realistic scenario. The good news, however, is that the formulas for each of the cloned columns calculate correctly. Take a look at what happened when you copied the formula =Net*Quantity to a new column.

7 Select cell D8. Then double-click the cell.

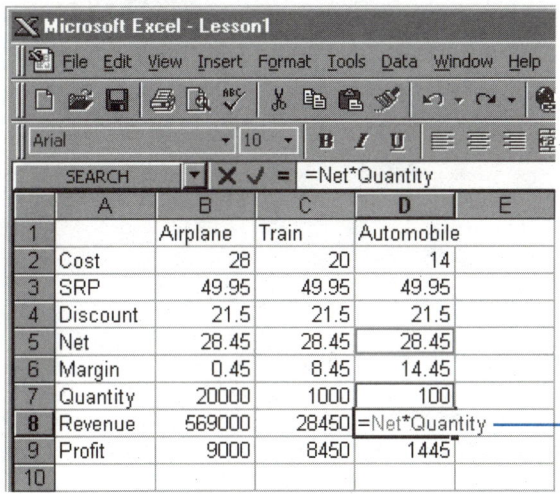

Double-click a cell, and Range Finder will show you which cells the formula uses. Excel intersects the row containing the label with the column containing the formula.

When you select the cell, you can see the formula in the formula bar. When you double-click the cell, you *edit* the formula. That means that you can see the formula in the cell itself, with colored boxes showing which part of the formula refers to which cell. The colored box that shows which cell (or range) is used in a formula is called a *Range Finder*. The word *Net* in the formula turns blue, and cell D5 gets a blue Range Finder border. Likewise, the word *Quantity* in the formula turns green, and cell D7 gets a green Range Finder border.

8 Press ESC to stop editing the formula.

Whenever you copy a formula that contains a label to a new column, Excel assumes that you want the corresponding cell from the new column. It's a simple rule—intersect the row containing the label with the column containing the formula—but this simple rule makes Excel very smart at copying formulas.

Format numbers

You now have a simple model that calculates the profitability of each of the new model toys, given certain pricing and volume assumptions. Maybe it's time to give it to your boss. Or maybe it's not. Maybe it looks, well, dumpy. The decimal places don't line up, and it's hard to read the large numbers. You'd like to spruce it up a little. At least make the numbers easier to read.

To start with, the SRP number is a dollar amount, so it would be easier to read if it looked the way that dollars and cents are normally written.

Currency Style

1 Select cell B2. Then, on the Formatting toolbar, click the Currency Style button.

	A	B	C	D	E
1		Airplane	Train	Automobile	
2	Cost	$ 28.00	20	14	
3	SRP	49.95	49.95	49.95	
4	Discount	21.5	21.5	21.5	

The Currency Style button adds a dollar sign, decimal places, and spaces.

Cell B2 changes to a currency format—a dollar sign at the left of the cell, two decimal places, and slightly more space to the right of the number. (The extra space on the right allows negative numbers—which the currency format always encloses in parentheses—to line up with positive numbers.)

Format Painter

Most of the rest of the numbers in this column should be formatted as currency too. You can copy the formatting from one cell to another cell or cells by using the Standard toolbar's Format Painter button.

2 Click the Format Painter button, and then click in cell B3 and drag to the middle of cell B9.

	A	B	C	D	E
1		Airplane	Train	Automobile	
2	Cost	$ 28.00	20	14	
3	SRP	$ 49.95	49.95	49.95	
4	Discount	$ 21.50	21.5	21.5	
5	Net	$ 28.45	28.45	28.45	
6	Margin	$ 0.45	8.45	14.45	
7	Quantity	########	1000	100	
8	Revenue	########	28450	2845	
9	Profit	########	8450	1445	
10					

Numbers appear as number signs
when the column is too narrow.

The cells change to a currency format, but the contents of cells B7, B8, and B9 change to number signs, indicating that, with their dollar signs, commas, cents, and spaces, the revenue and profit numbers are too wide to fit in their cells.

You can make a column wide enough to fit the longest value it contains by double-clicking the right edge of the column heading.

3 Double-click the right edge of the column B heading.

	A	B	C	D	E
1		Airplane	Train	Automobile	
2	Cost	$ 28.00	20	14	
3	SRP	$ 49.95	49.95	49.95	
4	Discount	$ 21.50	21.5	21.5	
5	Net	$ 28.45	28.45	28.45	
6	Margin	$ 0.45	8.45	14.45	
7	Quantity	$ 20,000.00	1000	100	
8	Revenue	$569,000.00	28450	2845	
9	Profit	$ 9,000.00	8450	1445	
10					

Double-click the
column heading
border to make the
column fit the cells.

The number signs change to formatted numbers.

The formatted cells look very good. Except for the Quantity number. It should not be currency. You want a format that doesn't have a dollar sign, but does keep the comma. That's the format you get with the Formatting toolbar's Comma Style button.

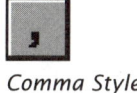

Comma Style

4 Select cell B7. Then click the Comma Style button.

The dollar sign disappears, but the cell still shows a comma, and also shows the two decimal places. You don't need to show hundredths of units because you sell only whole airplanes. The Formatting toolbar's Decrease Decimal button decreases the number of decimal places that are shown in a cell.

*Decrease
Decimal*

5   Select cell B7. Then click the Decrease Decimal button twice.

This gets rid of the two decimal places. You don't need to show cents for the Revenue and Profit values, either.

6   Click cell B8 and drag the mouse pointer to cell B9. This selects the range B8:B9. Then click the Decrease Decimal button twice.

The Decrease Decimal button can reduce the number of decimals for either the Currency style or the Comma style, but not at the same time.

The column of numbers now looks very good, except that the *Airplane* label at the top is closer to the edge of the cell than the dollar signs. It's a little thing, but your boss would probably notice it. To format a text label so that it lines up with a number formatted with the Currency style, simply format the text with the Currency Style button too.

Currency Style

7   Select cell B1. Then click the Currency Style button.

The left side of the label now lines up precisely with the left side of the dollar signs. Now, all you have to do is copy the format to the other two columns. You can extend the formatting of a column in the same way that you extend the contents of a column—with a customized AutoFill.

8   Above the Airplane label, click the letter "B." Then, use the right mouse button to drag the AutoFill handle to the right of cell D1. From the shortcut menu that appears when you release the mouse button, click Fill Formats.

Add formatting to the table

You can make the table look even more impressive by formatting the background and the fonts. It's easy, too. All you have to do is apply an AutoFormat.

1   Select cell A1 (or any single cell in the grid). On the Format menu, click AutoFormat, and from the Table Format list, select Classic 2.

An AutoFormat adds several formatting attributes to the block of cells surrounding the active cell. As you click a format name in the list on the left, you can see an example of the formatting on the right. AutoFormats make each column as wide as the widest value in that column. You don't want the Automobile column to be wider than the Train column, so you can turn off that part of the formatting.

2   Click the Options button, clear the Width/Height check box, and click OK. Then click cell A1 so you can see the formatting.

3 Save the Lesson1 workbook.

The worksheet is ready to give to your boss, and you still have twelve minutes to catch your car pool. Too bad you spent all your time working on airplanes and didn't take a particularly close look at trains and automobiles. That's all right. Maybe the high-price approach really is the best anyway.

Creating Formulas in a List

Management finally agreed on the pricing for the new model toys, and they will be available to order starting March 13, 1998. That's a Friday. That would make it Friday the 13th. (Who schedules these introductions, anyway?) At any rate, your next assignment is to make daily revenue projections for each of the three new products. You'll start by creating a projection for the model airplanes.

Create a list

Worksheets typically come in one of two forms: a grid or a list. A grid has labels in the left column and along the top. A list has labels only across the top. Earlier, you created a worksheet to compare pricing strategies. That worksheet is a grid, because there are labels on the left side as well as in the top row. Now you can create a worksheet to show daily order projections for the first couple of weeks. This worksheet is a list, so you start by creating labels in the top row.

1 At the bottom of the worksheet, click the Sheet2 tab to activate Sheet2.

Press TAB instead of ENTER to move right.

2 In cells A1 through E1, enter the labels, **Date**, **Product**, **Net**, **Quantity**, and **Revenue**

	A	B	C	D	E
1	Date	Product	Net	Quantity	Revenue
2					
3					

Press TAB instead of ENTER when entering values in a row.

The Date column should contain dates starting with March 13, the introduction date of the product.

3 In cell A2, enter the starting date, **3/13/98**

The list of dates should skip weekends. Luckily, one of the AutoFill options is to extend a series using only weekdays.

For a demonstration of how to create a list, double-click the Excel Camcorder Files shortcut on your Desktop or connect to the Internet address listed on page xvi.

4 Select cell A2, and then use the right mouse button to drag the AutoFill handle down to the bottom of cell A11. In the shortcut menu that appears when you release the mouse button, click Fill Weekdays.

This creates a list of days, excluding weekends.

This whole list consists of projections for airplanes, but it's a good idea to include the name in each row, in case you eventually combine the lists for the three products. You want to enter the product name into all the cells of column B that are part of the list (cells B2:B11). If you enter the product name into the top cell, you can use the AutoFill handle to copy the value down to the rest of the cells in the list.

5 In cell B2, enter Airplanes. Then double-click the AutoFill handle in the bottom right corner of cell B2.

	A	B	C	D	E
1	Date	Product	Net	Quantity	Revenue
2	3/13/98	Airplanes			
3	3/16/98	Airplanes			
4	3/17/98	Airplanes			
5	3/18/98	Airplanes			
6	3/19/98	Airplanes			
7	3/20/98	Airplanes			
8	3/23/98	Airplanes			
9	3/24/98	Airplanes			
10	3/25/98	Airplanes			
11	3/26/98	Airplanes			
12					

Double-click the AutoFill handle to fill rows to match the column to the left.

Excel automatically fills just the right rows. Double-clicking the AutoFill handle automatically extends the value to the rest of the cells in a list.

Column C contains the net price for the model. Once again, you can use the AutoFill handle to quickly enter the value in the list.

6 In cell C2, enter **28.45**—the amount you will receive for each model airplane.

Currency Style

7 Select cell C2, click the Currency Style button, and then double-click the AutoFill handle.

Excel fills the appropriate rows with copies of the formatted number.

The next column is for Quantities. Your expectations are that you will sell 100 units the first day, and then 5 additional units each following day. You can get AutoFill to enter this series for you if you give it the first two numbers.

8 In cell D2, enter **100**, and in cell D3, enter **105**

9 Select the range D2:D3, and then double-click the AutoFill handle at the bottom right corner of the range.

	A	B	C	D	E
1	Date	Product	Net	Quantity	Revenue
2	3/13/98	Airplanes	28.45	100	
3	3/16/98	Airplanes	28.45	105	
4	3/17/98	Airplanes	28.45	110	
5	3/18/98	Airplanes	28.45	115	
6	3/19/98	Airplanes	28.45	120	

Enter two values before using the AutoFill handle to establish a series.

Excel fills the appropriate rows, extrapolating the pattern of the first two cells.

Add a formula to a list

For the Revenue column, you need to enter a formula that multiplies the net amount by the quantity. You can use column labels to enter the formula, and then use AutoFill to copy the formula to all the correct cells.

Currency Style

Decrease Decimal

1 In cell E2, enter **=Net*Quantity**

2 Select cell E2, and then click the Currency Style button once and the Decrease Decimal button twice. Then double-click the AutoFill handle.

Excel calculates the correct value for each row in the list. When you use column labels in a list, Excel retrieves the value from the cell where the column containing the label intersects with the row containing the formula.

You just decided that you don't like the label Quantity. It seems too long. You would rather use the word *Units* as the label for the column. If you change a label that is used in a formula, Excel will automatically change the formula.

3 Change the label in cell D1 to **Units**, and then select cell E2 to look at the formula.

In a list, the formula intersects the column containing the label with the row containing the formulas.

	A	B	C	D	E	F
1	Date	Product	Net	Units	Revenue	
2	3/13/98	Airplanes	$ 28.45	100	$ 2,845	
3	3/16/98	Airplanes	$ 28.45	105	$ 2,987	
4	3/17/98	Airplanes	$ 28.45	110	$ 3,130	
5	3/18/98	Airplanes	$ 28.45	115	$ 3,272	

E3 = =Net*Units

Excel automatically changed the formula from =Net*Quantity to =Net*Units. Pretty cool, huh?

Since you will be creating worksheets for all three of the new products, you should name the worksheets to match the product name.

4   At the bottom of the worksheet, double-click the Sheet2 tab, type **Airplanes** as the name, and press ENTER.

You now have a list containing revenue projections for the model airplane's first two weeks. Creating a list is very similar to creating a grid. In both cases, you add labels, not only to make the worksheet easy to understand, but also to make formulas easy to write.

Total the list with a formula

Sometimes you might want to get a total for an entire column in a list. For example, suppose you want to see the total estimated revenue for these first two weeks. Your first impulse might be to put the total at the bottom of the list. But if you put the total at the bottom, any new rows you add to the list will destroy the total. Also, if the list gets long, you might not be able to see the total at the bottom. Instead, insert some rows above the list, and put the total there.

1   Select the range E1:E3. Then, on the Insert menu, click Rows.

You now have a place to put the summary information. Start by adding a label.

2   In cell E1, enter **Total**

Then create a formula that sums all the values in the Revenue column. You can use a label from the top of a column in a list to summarize the entire column.

3   In cell E2, enter the formula =**SUM(Revenue)**

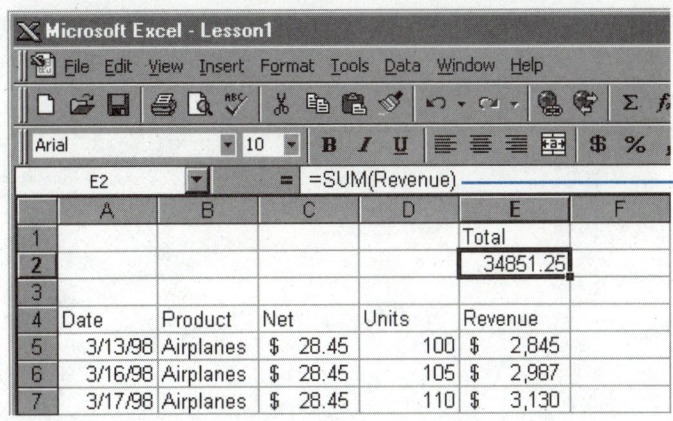

Use a column label with the SUM function to total all the items in a list.

The cell shows the total revenue, but it doesn't look like currency.

Currency Style

4 Select cell E2, and then click the Currency Style button once and the Decrease Decimal button twice.

Cell E2 now shows the total revenue as Currency with no decimal places.

Decrease Decimal

Excel is smart about how it interprets a range. In a formula like *=Net*Units*, it knows that Net and Units need to be single values, so it looks for that single value in the same row that contains the formula. On the other hand, in a formula like *=SUM(Revenue)*, it knows that the SUM function can handle multiple values, so it retrieves all the values from the Revenue column.

Freeze the heading of a list

Your list is still short; however, in time it may grow longer. When it does, it would be nice to always see the column labels and the total as you scroll up and down the list. In Excel, rows and columns that don't move are called *panes*. In order to freeze panes, you select the first cell that you are willing to let scroll away, and then you tell Excel to freeze the panes.

1 Select cell A5, and then on the Window menu, click Freeze Panes.

17

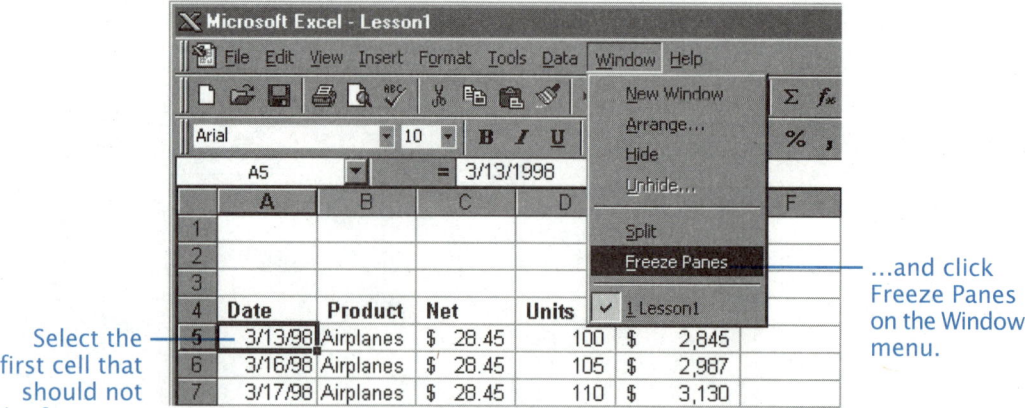

Select the first cell that should not be frozen ...

...and click Freeze Panes on the Window menu.

Now, when you scroll up and down in the worksheet, rows 1 to 4 will always be visible.

2 Save the Lesson1 workbook.

 TIP In a list, you typically freeze only the rows at the top. In a grid, you typically freeze rows at the top and also columns at the left. When you freeze panes, always select the first cell that you are willing to let scroll away.

Working with Multiple Worksheets

You have now created a startup sales projection for the model airplanes. You still need to create one for the trains and one for the automobiles. Of course, you could just follow the same steps, and create each worksheet from scratch, but you are the type of personality that compulsively seeks for a more effective way.

Clone a worksheet

One way to copy a worksheet is to use the Edit menu's Move Or Copy Sheet command. But the easiest way is to clone the worksheet by dragging the worksheet tab with the mouse while holding down CTRL.

1 At the bottom of the worksheet, click the Airplanes tab, but do not release the mouse button.

The mouse pointer acquires a small icon that looks like a worksheet and a small black triangle appears above left corner of the tab.

2 Drag the sheet tab to the right until the small black triangle moves to the right corner of the tab.

3 While still holding down the mouse button, press CTRL.

The mouse pointer icon acquires a small plus sign.

Hold down CTRL while dragging a sheet tab to make a copy of that sheet.

4 Release the mouse button, and then release the CTRL key.

Excel creates a copy of the Airplanes worksheet with a tab just to the right of the original.

5 Double-click the new worksheet tab, and type **Trains** to change its name.

CTRL+dragging a worksheet tab is the fastest and easiest way to copy a worksheet.

Modify a list

The Trains worksheet is now a clone of the Airplanes worksheet. You still need to change the values in the list. You need a new series of unit projections for this product. To enter a series of numbers, you enter the first two values and let AutoFill do the rest, as you did for the Airplanes worksheet.

1 In cell D5, enter **122**, and in cell D6, enter **125**

2 Select the range D5:D6, and then double-click the AutoFill handle at the bottom right corner to extend the new series.

In addition to the AutoFill handle, Excel has some keyboard techniques that can be very efficient when you want to replace values in cells that are already filled. For example, you can replace the entire list of product names at one time if you first select all the cells you want to change. The key to selecting a range is to hold down SHIFT as you move to a new cell.

3 Select cell B5. Hold down SHIFT as you press END and then the DOWN ARROW key. Release the SHIFT key.

This selects all the cells that currently contain the label *Airplanes*. You can now change them all at once by holding down CTRL as you enter the new value.

4 Type **Trains** and then hold down CTRL as you press ENTER.

Excel fills all the selected cells with the new label.

You can use the same technique to change the values in the Net column.

5 Press the RIGHT ARROW key to move to the next column. Then hold down SHIFT as you press END and the DOWN ARROW key.

6 Type **22.5** and press CTRL+ENTER.

The cells all change: the revenue cells change, and the total at the top changes. Filling multiple cells at once is a very fast way to customize a cloned worksheet.

Now you need to create another clone for the model automobiles.

7 Hold down CTRL as you drag the Trains tab to the right to clone the worksheet. Then change the name of the new worksheet to **Automobiles**

8 In cell D5, enter **200**, and in cell D6, enter **201**

9 Select the range D5:D6, and then double-click the AutoFill handle to replace all the unit values.

Using CTRL+ENTER allows you to fill multiple cells with a single value. But what if you have two columns, each of which needs a different value? If you select the entire range, and then enter the first value in each column, you can fill all the columns at once.

10 Select cell B5. Hold down SHIFT as you press the RIGHT ARROW key, END, and then the DOWN ARROW key. Release the SHIFT key.

This selects all the cells in both columns that you want to change, while leaving cell B5 as the active cell.

Pressing CTRL+D is the same as clicking Down on the Edit menu's Fill submenu.

11 Type **Automobiles**, press TAB, type **15.25**, press TAB, and then press CTRL+D.

	A	B	C	D	E	F
1					Total	
2					$ 44,563	
3						
4	Date	Product	Net	Units	Revenue	
5	3/13/98	Automobile	15.25	200	$ 3,050.00	
6	3/16/98	Trains	22.5	201	$ 4,522.50	
7	3/17/98	Trains	22.5	202	$ 4,545.00	
8	3/18/98	Trains	22.5	203	$ 4,567.50	

Enter new values in the top row of a range and press CTRL+D to fill the values down.

This fills the values from the top row into all the selected cells. The Automobile worksheet now has the appropriate projections.

Modify multiple worksheets

You now have three worksheets containing projections. As you look over the projections, however, you come to the sinking realization that there are some enhancements you wish you had made to the first worksheet before you copied it. You want to make the labels bold, and format them so that they align better. You want to format the units with the Comma style so that the numbers are not tight against the right side of the column. You might even want to add another summary formula to the top that calculates the average number of units.

You seem to be faced with two alternatives, both of which are unpleasant. Either you can make the changes three times (hoping you make the same changes to all three worksheets), or you can delete two of the worksheets, make the changes, and then re-create the clones. Wouldn't it be nice if you could just change all three worksheets at the same time? You can, as long as you select all three worksheets first, turning them into a *group*.

1   Click the Airplanes worksheet tab. Then hold down SHIFT as you click the Automobiles worksheet tab.

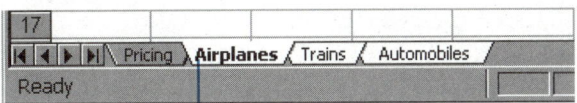

Click a sheet tab, hold down SHIFT, and click another sheet tab to create a *group*. Any changes you make will happen to all the sheets in the group.

This selects all three worksheet tabs, leaving the Airplanes tab on top. It also adds the word *[Group]* to the window title bar. When worksheets are in a group, any changes you make to the active worksheet also happen to the other worksheets in the group.

TIP   You can also group nonadjacent worksheets. Click the tab of the first worksheet, and then hold down CTRL as you click the tab of each of the other worksheets that you want to include in the group. If you want to select all the worksheets in the workbook, use the right mouse button to click a worksheet tab, and click Select All Sheets on the shortcut menu that appears.

You want to apply the Currency style and a bold font to all the cells in both row 1 and column A. (It's a good idea to format the entire rows and columns, in case you add additional entries to the list later.) You can use CTRL with the mouse to select both ranges before you apply the formatting.

2   Click the number 1 to the left of row 1, and then hold down CTRL as you click the number 4 to the left of row 4.

Hold down CTRL as you click to select separate ranges.

	A	B	C	D	E	F
1					Total	
2					$ 34,851	
3						
4	Date	Product	Net	Units	Revenue	
5	3/13/98	Airplanes	28.45	100	$ 2,845.00	
6	3/16/98	Airplanes	28.45	105	$ 2,987.25	

This selects both of the rows that contain titles.

Currency Style

3 Click the Currency Style button, and then click the Bold button.

That formats all the labels. You can activate another sheet to make sure the changes really did happen to all the sheets.

Bold

You can also press CTRL+PAGE DOWN to activate the next worksheet.

4 Click the Trains worksheet tab.

The labels are selected and formatted, the same as on the Airplanes worksheet.

> **NOTE** If you group all the visible worksheets in a workbook, activating a new worksheet in the group dissolves the group. If, on the other hand, you exclude at least one sheet when you create a group, you can activate a new worksheet in the group without dissolving the group.

Even though the Trains worksheet became the active sheet, the worksheets are still in a group, because the workbook includes one worksheet (Pricing) that's not part of the group. You can change the formatting of the Units column and have the change apply to all three worksheets.

Comma Style

5 Click the letter "D" above the Units column, click the Comma Style button once, and the Decrease Decimal button twice.

You can also add new labels and formulas to all the sheets simultaneously. For example, try adding a formula to calculate the average units for each sheet.

Decrease Decimal

6 In cell D1, enter **Average**, and in cell D2, enter **=AVERAGE(Units)**

After you make all the changes that apply to all the worksheets, be sure to dissolve the group.

7 Using the right mouse button, click the Trains worksheet tab, and then click Ungroup Sheets on the shortcut menu.

Right-click a sheet tab
and click Ungroup Sheets
to dissolve a group.

8 The *[Group]* label disappears from the title bar, and only the Trains
worksheet tab is highlighted.

 ⚡ **WARNING** Always be sure to ungroup worksheets after you make
the changes you want. Remember that any changes you make to
the active sheet will happen to all the grouped worksheets. You can
cause serious damage to other worksheets if you forget to ungroup
the worksheets.

One Step Further: Using Multiple Windows

You might at some time want to compare the worksheet data for the three
products. To do that with three separate worksheets, it appears you have to
keep switching back and forth. You would like to be able to see the data for
all three products at once, side by side. Fortunately, Excel has a solution.
Normally, each workbook has a single window for viewing worksheets. But if
you want to see multiple worksheets, you can create additional windows.

Create new windows

1 On the Window menu, click New Window.

A new window gets a new number in the title bar.

Nothing seems to happen, but the title bar changed the title of the
workbook from *Lesson1* to *Lesson1:2*. Create one more window before
continuing.

2 Once again, on the Window menu, click New Window.

The title of the workbook changes to *Lesson1:3*.

In order to see the windows side by side, you *arrange* them.

3   On the Window menu, click Arrange. In the Arrange Windows dialog box, select Horizontal and click OK.

The three windows now appear stacked in Excel's workspace. Initially, they all show the same worksheet, but you can activate a different worksheet in each window.

4   Click in the top window, and activate the Airplanes tab. Click in the middle window, and activate the Trains tab. Then click in the bottom window, and activate the Automobiles tab.

Arrange windows to see sheets in a workbook next to each other.

You can now see the summary rows at the top of each worksheet, but what if you want to compare values in columns, such as the daily unit and revenue projections? You simply arrange the windows vertically.

Manipulate windows

1 On the Window menu, click Arrange. Select Vertical and click OK. Then, in each window, scroll until you can see the Units and Revenues columns. Also, scroll the navigation arrows (to the left of the sheet tabs) until you can see the active tab in each window.

You normally look at the products in the order Airplanes, Trains, and Automobiles. But the order of the worksheet tabs are reversed. When you arrange windows, Excel always positions the currently active window first, followed by the next most recently activated window, and so forth. To control the order of the windows, click each window in the reverse order from the way you want them to appear. You want the windows in the order Airplanes, Trains, Automobiles, so click backwards through the list.

2 Click the Automobiles window (probably window 1), then click the Trains window (probably window 2), and then click the Airplanes window (probably window 3). Then click the Arrange command on the Windows menu and click OK. (The Arrange Windows dialog box remembers the most recent option.)

The windows are now in the correct arrangement.

Close Window

After you finish looking at the three worksheets, you may want to get back to a single window. You close windows by clicking the Close Window button. If you close the last window for a workbook, you will close the workbook itself.

3 Click the Close Window button at the top of any two of the three windows. Then maximize the remaining window by double-clicking its title bar.

4 Save and close the Lesson1 workbook.

Lesson Summary

To	Do this
Enter a formula into a worksheet	Add labels next to the cells you will use in the formula. Type an equal sign, followed by the label next to the cell you want to refer to. Use standard arithmetic operators between labels.
Use the mouse to copy formulas and values, without allowing the values to increment	Drag the AutoFill handle with the right mouse button and click Copy Cells on the shortcut menu.

To	Do this
See which cells are used in a formula	Double-click the cell containing the formula. The labels that refer to cells will change colors, and the cells that they refer to will appear with borders of corresponding colors.
Format cells to look like money	Select the cells you want to format, and click the Currency Style toolbar button.
Copy the format from one range to another	Select the range you want to copy the format from. Click the Format Painter button, and then select the range you want to copy the format to.
Make a column wide enough to show all the values in the column	Double-click the right border of the heading for the column you want to change.
Format a cell with commas and spaces on the edges, but without dollar signs	Select the cells you want to format and click the Comma Style toolbar button.
Format a label so that it has a small amount of padding on the right or left side	Select the cells you want to format and click the Currency Style toolbar button.
Copy the formats from a range of cells to an adjacent range of cells	Select the source cells, and use the right mouse button to drag the AutoFill handle over the cells you want to change. On the shortcut menu, click Fill Formats.
Create a series of dates that skips weekends	Enter the first date into a cell. Select the cell and use the right mouse button to drag the AutoFill handle to the new cells. On the shortcut menu that appears, click Fill Weekdays.
Fill a new column in a list with values or formulas	Enter the formula or value in the top cell. Select that cell and double-click the AutoFill handle.
Fill a range with a series of numbers	Enter the first two values of the list, select the two cells, and then drag or double-click the AutoFill handle.
Change a label that you use in a formula without breaking the formula	Change the label. The formula will adjust automatically.
Add all the values from a column in a list	Put the label from the top of the column inside the parentheses after a SUM function.

To	Do this
Lock the headings of a list so they don't scroll	Select the first cell that you are willing to have scroll away. On the Window menu, click Freeze Panes.
Make a copy of a worksheet	Hold down CTRL as you drag the worksheet tab.
Rename a worksheet	Double-click the worksheet tab, type a new name, and press ENTER.
Select a column of values in a list	Select the top value, hold down SHIFT, press END, and then the DOWN ARROW key.
Enter the same value or formula into all the selected cells	Type the value or formula and then press CTRL+ENTER.
Select multiple columns of values in a list	Select the top left cell, and while holding down SHIFT, press END, the DOWN ARROW key, and then the RIGHT ARROW key as many times as needed. Then release the SHIFT key.
Fill the values from the top row of the selected range into all the other selected rows	Press CTRL+D.
Select multiple worksheets in a workbook	Click the tab for the first worksheet. Then hold down SHIFT and click the tab for the last worksheet.
Select multiple worksheets that are not adjacent	Click the tab for the first worksheet. Then hold down CTRL as you click the tab for each of the other worksheets you want.
Select rows that are not adjacent	Click the row heading for the first row you want. Then hold down CTRL as you click the row heading for each additional row you want.
Make changes to multiple worksheets simultaneously	Select all the worksheets you want to change. Any changes you make to the active sheet will happen to all the other selected sheets.
Change from multiple selected worksheets to a single selected worksheet.	Use the right mouse button to click the worksheet tab. On the shortcut menu that appears, click Ungroup Sheets.

To	Do this
See two or more worksheets side by side	On the Window menu, click New Window. Do this once more for each additional worksheet you want to see. Then, on the Window menu, click Arrange, and select the way you want the windows arranged. Activate a different worksheet in each new window.
Control the order in which windows will appear as you arrange them	Select each window in turn, in the reverse order in which you want them to appear. Then, on the Window menu, click Arrange.
Close windows that you don't want to see.	Click the Close Window button at the top of the window. Closing the final window for a workbook closes the workbook file.

For online information about	On the Help menu, click Contents And Index, click the Index tab, and then type
Formatting cells	**formatting cells, overview**
Using the AutoFill handle	**AutoFill**
Using keyboard shortcuts	**shortcut keys, Microsoft Excel**
Selecting worksheets	**worksheets, selecting sheets**
Using workbook windows	**windows,**

Working with Formulas

Estimated time
45 min.

In this lesson you will learn how to:

- Create formulas using cell addresses, labels, and named ranges.
- Audit formulas.
- Manage names in a workbook.

I am not a particularly sophisticated woodworker. When I need a nail, I rummage around in a box on the shelf above the washing machine and try to find something long and skinny, made of metal, with one end pointed and the other end flat. I know people, however, who actually know the difference between a box nail and a casing nail, and whether a 6d nail is bigger than a 16d nail (and who even know how to pronounce 16d). If the world contained only one kind and size of nail, I would be happy. But someone who wants to build a picture frame or a house would not. The advantage of having a variety of nails is that it becomes possible to build strong and beautiful objects. The disadvantage is that you need to learn how to use them in order to take advantage of the advantage.

So it is with Microsoft Excel. In Excel, you have three different ways to create a *reference*—that is, make a formula refer to the value in another cell. You can refer to the other cell by address, by label, or by name. The advantage of having three ways to create references is that you can build extremely powerful and readable formulas—formulas that keep working even after you copy them to new cells. The disadvantage is that you need to learn how to use them in order to take advantage of the advantage.

Coincidentally, your manager asked you last week to calculate the revenue for various price and quantity combinations. The task is a simple one, but it requires you to navigate around common pitfalls in creating and copying formulas. In this lesson you will create worksheets that calculate revenue possibilities using each of Excel's three ways of creating references. When you are finished, you will have a clear understanding not only of how the three methods work, but also of their respective strengths.

Start the lesson

The first step is to save the new, blank workbook that appears when you start Excel.

New

 NOTE If you've already been working in Microsoft Excel, you need to open a new, blank workbook. On the Standard toolbar, click the New button.

Save

1 Start Microsoft Excel. On the Standard toolbar, click the Save button.

The Save As dialog box appears.

2 In the Save As dialog box, click the Look In Favorites button, and then double-click the Excel AT Practice folder.

Look In Favorites

3 In the File Name box, type **Lesson2** as the new name for the workbook, and click Save.

Using Cell Addresses

Your manager just called to see how that revenue comparison is coming. You need to get busy. You want to do a revenue calculation using *cell addresses*. Cell addresses are what you get when you point at a cell as you create a formula. Cell addresses are easy to use, but they're hard to read, and when you copy formulas, they sometimes produce different answers than what you expect—unless, of course, you know how to control them.

Create lists of prices and quantities

Your task is to compare the revenue from various price and quantity combinations. Why don't you start by using the AutoFill handle to create a grid with a list of prices across the top and a list of quantities down the left side?

To delete a worksheet, use the right mouse button to click its tab, and then click Delete.

1 Rename Sheet1 to **Addresses** and delete the other worksheets in the Lesson2 workbook.

2 In cell B1, enter **$5**, and in cell C1, enter **$10**

3 Select the range B1:C1, and drag the AutoFill handle (the small black square at the bottom right corner of the selection) to the right side of cell E1.

This creates a list of prices in increments of $5.

4 In cell A2, enter **10**, and in cell A3, enter **20**

5 Select the range A2:A3, and drag the AutoFill handle down to the bottom of cell A6.

Start with prices across the top...

	A	B	C	D	E	F
1		$5	$10	$15	$20	
2	10					
3	20					
4	30					
5	40					
6	50					
7						

...and quantities down the side.

This creates a list of quantities in increments of 10.

These lists are static. If you change the price in cell B1 to $100, the other prices will not automatically change.

Use relative addresses in a formula

If you want to create lists that change when you change the first value in the list, you need to replace all the values except the first with formulas. Each price formula should add five to the value in the cell on its left, and each quantity formula should add ten to the value of the cell above it. To accomplish this, you will use a formula for each value except the first.

1 Change cell B1 to 50, and cell A2 to 100.

To create a formula that refers to a cell, you can type an equal sign, and then click the cell.

2 Select cell C1, type =, then click cell B1, and type +5. Then press ENTER. This creates the formula *=B1+5*.

SEARCH		✗ ✓ =	=B1+5			
	A	B	C	D	E	F
1		$50	=B1+5	$15	$20	
2	100					
3	20					
4	30					

Enter a formula that points one cell to the left.

The value in cell C1 changes to $55. When you are creating a formula and point at a cell—either by clicking or by pressing an arrow key—Excel puts the cell address into the formula. Once you have a formula in one cell, you can use the AutoFill handle to copy it to adjacent cells.

3   Select cell C1, and drag the AutoFill handle to the right side of cell E1.

Cells D1 and E1 each get appropriate new values.

4   Select cell D1 and look at the formula in the formula bar.

When you copy a formula, the cell that the formula refers to changes. Even though you typed =B1+5 into cell C1, this copy shows the formula as =C1+5. This is because the formula contains a *relative address*. The cell address *B1* in the formula in cell C1 doesn't really mean "cell B1." It means "one cell to the left"—which, for cell C1, happens to be cell B1. When you copy the formula to cell D1, the relative address changes to C1—one cell to the left of cell D1.

You create formulas to increment the quantity values in the same way.

5   In cell A3, enter the formula =**A2+10**, select the cell, and drag the AutoFill handle down to the bottom of cell A6.

The values in cells A3 to A6 each become 10 greater than the value in the cell above. The relative address *A2* in the formula in cell A3, for example, means "one cell above," and changes as you copy the formula.

When you enter a cell address into a formula, either by typing the address, by clicking a cell, or by moving the selection with the arrow keys, the address is *relative* to the cell that contains the formula. Relative addresses make formulas easy to copy—most of the time. That's because most of the time you want addresses to adjust when you copy the formula. But occasionally, you do not want the addresses to change when you copy the formula. For these times, you want an *absolute address*.

Use absolute addresses in a formula

Suppose that you want to be able to change the amount of the increment for the lists of prices and quantities. All you need to do is put the increment amounts in a couple of cells at the top of the worksheet, and then adjust the formulas to use those cells. Start by inserting new rows at the top of the worksheet.

1   Select the range A1:A3, and on the Insert menu, click Rows.

If you put the increment amounts at the top of the worksheet, they will be easy to see and to change. Even though you won't use labels in the formulas (this time), adding labels makes the values easy for you to read.

2 In cell B1, enter **Quantity**, and in cell B2, enter **20**. Then in cell C1, enter **Price**, and in cell C2, enter **$15**

Enter increment values for price and quantity.

	A	B	C	D	E	F
1		Quantity	Price			
2		20	$15			
3						
4		$50	$55	$60	$65	
5	100					

Next, you modify the first price formula to refer to the increment cell at the top. To modify a formula, double-click the cell that contains it.

Enter

3 Double-click cell C4. Then double-click the number *5* in the formula, and click cell C2 to replace the 5 with a reference to cell C2. Then click the Enter button next to the formula bar.

	A	B	C	D	E
1		Quantity	Price		
2		20	$15		
3					
4		$50	=B4+C2	$60	$65
5	100				

Replace the constant with a cell reference.

The value of cell C4 changes to $65, which is $15 more than the cell to its left. But what happens if you copy the formula to the right?

4 Select cell C4 and drag the AutoFill handle to the right edge of cell E4.

Cells C4 and D4 change to $65, because the reference to cell C2 (which really meant "two cells above") adjusted to D2 and E2, both of which are empty. Not good. To keep a cell address from adjusting, you make it an absolute address by using the F4 key.

5 Double-click cell C4. Then double-click the address *C2* to select it, and press the F4 key. Then click the Enter button.

	A	B	C	D	E
1		Quantity	Price		
2		20	$15		
3					
4		$50	=B4+$C$2		$65
5	100				

Press F4 to add dollar signs and make the reference absolute.

33

Nothing changes in cell C4, but when you pressed F4, the address *C2* changed to *$C$2*. The dollar signs change the address from a relative address to an absolute address. This address no longer means "two cells above." Now it means "cell C2," period, and it doesn't change when you copy the formula to a new cell.

6 With cell C4 selected, drag the AutoFill handle to the right of cell E4.

	A	B	C	D	E	F
1		Quantity	Price			
2		20	$15			
3						
4		$50	$65	$80	$95	
5	100					

An absolute reference points to the same cell even when you copy the formula.

Each price is now $15 more than the price to its left. You now make an analogous change to the quantity values.

Enter

7 Double-click cell A6. Then double-click the number *10,* and click cell B2. Press F4, and then click the Enter button. Then double-click the AutoFill handle.

Each quantity is now 20 more than the quantity above it. You can now adjust both lists by changing either the starting value or the increment value.

Excel gives you the option of whether you want a cell address to be shorthand for the relative relationship between two cells, or to be the absolute, unchanging, address of a cell.

For a demonstration of how to use mixed references, double-click the Excel Camcorder Files shortcut on your Desktop or connect to the Internet address listed on page xvi.

Use mixed references in a formula

Of course, just as neither heredity nor environment can exclusively explain behavior, so neither relative nor absolute references can exclusively handle the possible uses for Excel addresses—as you will discover as soon as you quit playing around with lists and get on to the real task of making formulas to calculate revenue values. Start by making the price and quantity values small.

1 Change cells A5 and B2 (the initial quantity value and increment) to **1.** Change cells B4 and C2 (the initial price value and increment) to **$2**

Change the increment values.

Change the initial values.

Next, create a formula to calculate the first revenue value, using the default relative cell address.

2   In cell B5, enter the formula **=B4*A5** and press ENTER.

The value $2 appears in cell B5. This is correct. If you sell 1 unit at $2 each, you will get $2. Of course, as you surely suspect, merely copying this formula to the other cells in the grid will probably not provide consistently correct answers. But do it anyway, just for fun.

3   Select cell B5 and drag the AutoFill handle to the bottom of cell B9. Release it momentarily, and then drag it to the right of cell E9.

All the revenue numbers except the first are wrong, as you correctly predicted. You also know why. The cell addresses in the formula really meant "one cell above" and "one cell to the left," neither of which is appropriate in this context.

You can vividly see which cells each formula refers to by double-clicking a cell.

Cancel

4   Double-click cell B5 to see the blue and green Range Finder boxes correctly linking to cells B4 and A5. Double-click cell D7 to see the blue and green Range Finder boxes incorrectly linking to cells D6 and C7. Try other cells if you like, and click the Cancel button next to the formula bar when you are done.

	A	B	C	D	E	F
1		Quantity	Price			
2		1	$2			
3						
4		$2	$4	$6	$8	
5	1	$2	$8	$48	$384	
6	2	$4	$32	$1,536	$589,824	
7	3	$12	=C6*B7	$589,824	########	
8	4	$48	$18,432	########	########	
9	5	$240	########	########	########	
10						

When you double-click the cell, the Range Finder shows that the references changed.

Relative addresses are obviously inappropriate in this context, but absolute addresses would be too. If you changed the formula in cell B5 to =$B$4*$A$5 and filled the grid with that formula, then all the values would be $2. You need to create *mixed* addresses—part relative and part absolute. You use the F4 key to convert a cell address to a mixed address that has a relative column and an absolute row.

5 Double-click cell B5. Then double-click the address *B4* in the formula, and press the F4 key twice. The cell address changes to B$4.

	A	B	C	D
1		Quantity	Price	
2		1	$2	
3				
4		$2	$4	$6
5	1	=B$4*A5	$8	$48
6	2	$4	$32	$1,536

Press F4 twice to make the row absolute.

The address B$4 is a *mixed address*. The column portion does not have a dollar sign; so in the formula, it really means "the same column." The row portion does have a dollar sign, so it means simply "row 4." You can also use the F4 key to convert a cell address to a mixed address that has an absolute column and a relative row.

6 Double-click the address *A5* in the formula, and press the F4 key three times. The cell address changes to $A5.

This time, the column portion is the absolute address, "column A," while the row portion is the relative address that means "the same row."

Enter

7 Click the Enter button, and then drag cell B5's AutoFill handle down through cell B9 and then right through cell E9.

All the revenue numbers are now correct.

8 Double-click various cells in the grid. The Range Finder boxes show which cells each formula refers to. As you click each cell, one Range Finder box is always in row 4, and the other is always in column A.

	A	B	C	D	E	F
1		Quantity	Price			
2		1	$2			
3						
4		$2	$4	$6	$8	
5	1	$2	$4	$6	$8	
6	2	$4	=C$4*$A6	$12	$16	
7	3	$6	$12	$18	$24	
8	4	$8	$16	$24	$32	
9	5	$10	$20	$30	$40	
10						

The Range Finder shows that the references are partially relative and partially absolute.

Mixed references are most useful when you copy a formula into a two-dimensional grid. When you copy a formula within a single row or column, you can use either relative or absolute references.

Find inconsistent cells

After you copy a formula, you end up with multiple cells that all contain the same formula. At least, they all start out with the same formula. But because each cell is independent of each other cell, it is frighteningly easy to make a "temporary" change to one cell—a change that you forget about until you make a presentation to upper management and somebody asks why a number is wrong.

Just looking at a worksheet doesn't tell you whether a cell contains a formula or a value, or which cells a formula refers to, or whether a formula is correct. However, Excel provides some useful tools for helping you validate formulas. Suppose that you made a few changes to the grid of formulas on the Addresses worksheet as a "temporary" analysis. How would you find the inconsistencies? Start by creating a few inconsistent cells.

1 In cell D4, enter **$7**, in cell B7, enter the formula = **B$6*$A7**, and in cell E8, enter **$36**

	A	B	C	D	E	F
1		Quantity	Price			
2		1	$2			
3						
4		$2	$4	$7	$9	
5	1	$2	$4	$7	$9	
6	2	$4	$8	$14	$18	
7	3	$12	$12	$21	$27	
8	4	$8	$16	$28	$36	
9	5	$10	$20	$35	$45	
10						

When you change some formulas, how do you find which ones are different?

37

Three weeks later, you forget that you made those changes. You now want to double-check the formulas before presenting the results in a meeting. Excel provides the Auditing toolbar for looking at multiple relationships. The Auditing toolbar is not on the "short list" of toolbars that appears when you right-click a toolbar. You have to use the Customize dialog box to turn it on.

2 Right-click any toolbar, and click Customize on the shortcut menu that appears. In the Customize dialog box, click the Toolbars tab (if it is not already selected), and then click the check box next to the Auditing toolbar, and click Close.

Use the Customize dialog box to display the Auditing toolbar.

One important tool on the Auditing toolbar is the Trace Dependents button, which lets you see which cells use the value from a cell.

Trace Dependents

3 Select cell A5. Then, on the Auditing toolbar, click the Trace Dependents button.

Dependent arrows show which cells point to the active cell.

	A	B	C	D	E	F
1		Quantity	Price			
2						
3						
4		$2	$4	$7	$9	
5		1	$2	$4	$7	$9
6		2	$4	$8	$14	$18
7		3	$12	$12	$21	$27

Blue arrows appear, showing every cell that uses the value in this cell. As you can see, this first quantity value is used to calculate all the revenues in the first row, and also to calculate the remaining quantity values. Each time you click the Trace Dependents button, Excel shows you one more generation of dependents.

4 Click the Trace Dependents button five more times—until it beeps when you click it.

	A	B	C	D	E	F
1		Quantity	Price			
2						
3						
4		$2	$4	$7	$9	
5	1	$2	$4	$7	$9	
6	2	$4	$8	$14	$18	
7	3	$12	$12	$21	$27	
8	4	$8	$16	$28	$36	
9	5	$10	$20	$35	$45	
10						

The second time you click the Trace Dependents button, you see all the "grandchildren" of the active cell. These are cells that refer to the cells that refer to the active cell. Each successive click traces an additional generation, until there are no more dependents.

You can quickly see that the arrows associated with cells B7 and E8 are "unusual." Ordinarily, you would fix the inconsistent cells, but leave them alone for now so that you can try out some of Excel's other tools for analyzing a worksheet.

Remove All Arrows

5 On the Auditing toolbar, click the Remove All Arrows button, and then close the Auditing toolbar by clicking the Close button in its title bar.

Another tool that is invaluable for analyzing a worksheet is the *Go To Special* dialog box. This dialog box helps you detect whether cells contain values or formulas.

Close

6 With any single cell selected, press CTRL+G to display the Go To dialog box, and then click Special to display the Go To Special dialog box. Select the Constants option, and click OK.

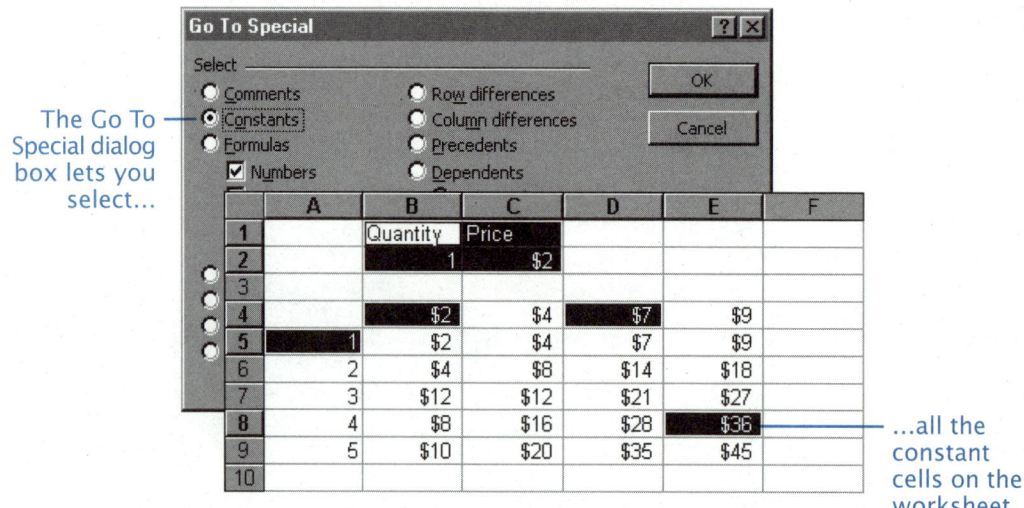

The Go To Special dialog box lets you select...

...all the constant cells on the worksheet.

Excel selects all the cells on the worksheet that contain constants, rather than formulas. The labels and values at the top are selected. That is appropriate. The first price and the first quantity are also selected. That is also appropriate. Cells D4 and E8, however, are also selected. These are cells that contain constants, but should contain formulas.

TIP If you start with only a single cell selected, the Go To Special dialog box selects all the constants on the entire worksheet. However, if you start with two or more cells selected, the Go To Special dialog box selects constants only in the selected cells.

Using the Go To Special dialog box to select constants can help you find places where you "temporarily" replaced a formula with a value. An additional option in the Go To Special dialog box can show you whether a copied formula has been changed.

7 Select the range B5:E9. These cells should all share a single formula. Press CTRL+G and click the Special button. In the Go To Special dialog box, select the Column Differences option and click OK.

You can also use the Row Differences option to look for inconsistencies in a row of formulas.

	A	B	C	D	E
1		Quantity	Price		
2		1	$2		
3					
4		$2	$4	$7	$9
5	1	$2	$4	$7	$9
6	2	$4	$8	$14	$18
7	3	$12	$12	$21	$27
8	4	$8	$16	$28	$36
9	5	$10	$20	$35	$45

The Column Differences option shows formulas that don't match that of the top cell in the range.

Excel selects cells B7 and E8. Neither of these cells matches the top cell in its respective column. Even though these cells are supposed to contain copies of the same formula, the Column Differences option shows that these have been changed.

8 Copy the formula from cell C4 and paste it into cell D4. Copy the formula from cell B5 and paste it into cells B7 and E8. Then save the Lesson2 workbook.

Inconsistencies sometimes happen in worksheets. Tracing references using the Auditing toolbar, searching for constants, and comparing copied formulas are all tools that Excel provides for finding inconsistencies.

Using Labels

In addition to using cell addresses to get the value from a cell into a formula, Excel can also use the labels on the worksheet. When you create a simple list (with labels at the top) or a standard grid (with labels on the top and the left), using labels in formulas is an intuitive process, as you saw in Lesson 1.

Some worksheet relationships are slightly more complex. For example, your current project is to multiply various prices times various quantities. In this situation, the grid does not have text labels on the top and left. The top row and left column contain numbers that are actually used in calculations. Meanwhile, the increment values at the top of the worksheet do have labels next to them, but how would you use those labels in formulas?

In this section, you will see how to convert the formulas you created on the Addresses worksheet to use labels. The process for creating these formulas may not seem as intuitive as using labels with simple lists and grids, but it does makes sense. And the formulas you end up with can be much easier to read than are those that use cell addresses alone.

Add labels to the worksheet

In order to use labels in formulas, you need labels on the worksheet. The price and quantity values in the top row and left column of the grid won't work as labels because they are numbers. Excel can use text labels and dates as labels. To use labels in formulas, you must first add labels to the grid.

1 Hold down CTRL as you drag the Addresses worksheet tab to the right to create a clone of the worksheet. Give the copy the name **Labels**

Next, you need to create a place to put new labels.

2 On the Labels worksheet, select cell A4. On the Insert menu, click Rows. Click the Insert menu again, and click Columns.

You can use the AutoFill handle to create incrementally numbered labels that you can use in formulas.

AutoFill will increment a numeric suffix that you add to any word.

3 In cell C4, type **Price1**. Then drag the AutoFill handle to the right of cell F4. In cell A6, type **Qty1**. Then drag the AutoFill handle to the bottom of cell A10.

You will also eventually need a couple of other labels. Add them now, and you'll see why later.

4 In cell B2, enter **Increment** and in cell B5, enter **Projection**.

Add labels to the worksheet so you can use labels in formulas.

	A	B	C	D	E	F	G
1			Quantity	Price			
2		Increment	1	$2			
3							
4			Price1	Price2	Price3	Price4	
5		Projection	$2	$4	$6	$8	
6	Qty1	1	$2	$4	$6	$8	
7	Qty2	2	$4	$8	$12	$16	
8	Qty3	3	$6	$12	$18	$24	
9	Qty4	4	$8	$16	$24	$32	
10	Qty5	5	$10	$20	$30	$40	
11							

Use relative labels

In the list of prices in row 5, each price adds an incremental value to the previous price. You can use the label from row 4 to refer to the price.

Enter

1 Double-click cell D5, and then double-click the address *C5* in the formula. Replace C5 with **Price1** and click the Enter button.

	A	B	C	D	E	F
1			Quantity	Price		
2		Increment	1	$2		
3						
4			Price1	Price2	Price3	Price4
5		Projection	$2	=Price1+$D$2		$8
6	Qty1		1	$2	$4	$6	$8

Replace the cell address with a label.

The result of the formula stays the same. Excel retrieves the value from the cell where the column that contains the Price1 label and the row that contains the formula intersect.

When you copy the formula, Excel will adjust the label because it is *relative*.

2   Drag the AutoFill handle to the right of cell F5. Then click cell E5.

The label in the formula shifted to Price2, because Excel interpreted the label in a relative way—as "one column to the left."

Excel automatically determines whether to refer to the cell below a label or to the cell to the right of a label. In the same way that you converted the list of prices, you can use labels in the formulas that create the list of prices in column B.

3   In cell B7, replace the cell address *B6* with **Qty1**. Then double-click the AutoFill handle to fill the formula down the column, and select cell B9 to look at the copied formula.

The formula in cell B9 is =Qty3+$C$2. The label in the formula shifted to Qty3. Excel interpreted the Qty1 label in a relative way—as "one row above."

Use absolute labels

The formulas in row 5 that increment the prices all refer to cell D2. Cell D2 has the label *Price* above it. If you use that label to refer to cell D2, you will create a *circular reference* that Excel can't calculate. The formula would be circular because Excel finds the cell where the column that contains the Price label (column D) intersects the row that contains the formula (row 5). That cell is D5, which happens to be the same cell that contains the formula. You don't want the value from cell D5; you want the value from cell D2.

When Excel automatically (or "implicitly") uses the row that contains the formula, that's called *implicit intersection*. Instead, you can manually (or "explicitly") tell Excel which row to use. That's called *explicit intersection*. To use explicit intersection, you use two labels—one for the row and one for the column—and leave a space between them.

Enter

1   Double-click cell D5. Replace the reference *$D$2* with **Price**, followed by a space, followed by **Increment**. Then click the Enter button.

	A	B	C	D	E	F
1			Quantity	Price		
2		Increment	1	$2		
3						
4			Price1	Price2	Price3	Price4
5		Projection	$2	=Price1+Price Increment		
6	Qty1	1	$2	$4	$6	$8

Put a space between labels to explicitly intersect the row and column.

The formula retrieves the increment value from cell D2, rather than creating a circular reference. But what happens when you copy it to the right?

2 Drag the AutoFill handle to the right of cell F5.

	A	B	C	D	E	F	G
1			Quantity	Price			
2		Increment	1	$2			
3							
4			Price1	Price2	Price3	Price4	
5		Projection	$2	$4	#NAME?	#NAME?	
6	Qty1	1	$2	$4	#NAME?	#NAME?	

The Price label was relative but had no label to the right.

Cells E5 through F10 display the #NAME? error value. This means that Excel could not figure out what to do with the Price label. As you copied the formula to the right, Excel tried to find labels to the right of the Price label, but there aren't any. This is the same problem you had when you tried to copy a relative cell address to the right. The solution is also the same: you use the F4 key to make the label absolute.

3 Double-click cell D5. In the formula, double-click the word *Price* and drag the mouse to the right to select both *Price* and *Increment*. Press the F4 key once. Click the Enter button, and drag the AutoFill handle to the right of cell F5.

This time the new formulas work properly. When you press F4, the reference *Price Increment* changes to *$Price $Increment*. This is equivalent to adding dollar signs to make cell addresses absolute.

Enter

4 Double-click cell B7. Replace the address *$C$2* with **$Quantity $Increment** and click the Enter button. Fill the formula down to cell A10.

You decide which is easier to read: the formula *=B6+$C$2* or the formula *=Qty1+$Quantity $Increment*.

If you want the column that contains a label to intersect with the row that contains the formula (or, conversely, the row that contains a label to intersect with the column that contains the formula), just use the label by itself, and let Excel do the intersection implicitly. If you want to control both the row and the column of the intersection, use two labels, separated by a space. It doesn't matter which label comes first, so use the order that makes the formula easier to read.

Labels, just like cell addresses, are relative by default, but you can make them absolute by adding a dollar sign.

Use mixed labels

The cells that make up the body of the revenue grid require mixed references. When referring to the prices, the column must be relative and the row absolute. When referring to quantities, the reverse must be true. Using explicit intersection, along with judicious use of the F4 key, you can convert these mixed formulas to use labels.

1 In cell C6, type the formula **=Price1 Projection*Qty1 Projection**, and press ENTER. Then double-click the cell to see that the colored Range Finder boxes refer to the correct cells.

	A	B	C	D	E	F
1			Quantity	Price		
2		Increment	1	$2		
3						
4			Price1	Price2	Price3	Price4
5		Projection	$2	$4	$6	$8
6	Qty1		1	=Price1 Projection*Qty1 Projection		
7	Qty2		2	$4	$8	$12	$16

Use a space to make the prices and quantities intersect explicitly with the Projecton label.

The formula calculates the correct revenue. Of course, if you copied it to the rest of the range, you know what would happen. For both parts of the formula, you want to make the Projection part absolute.

You could also select Projection and press the F4 key once.

2 While still editing the formula in cell C6, select *Price1 Projection* and press the F4 key twice.

	A	B	C	D	E	F
1			Quantity	Price		
2		Increment	1	$2		
3						
4			Price1	Price2	Price3	Price4
5		Projection	$2	$4	$6	$8
6	Qty1		1	=Price1 $Projection*Qty1 Projection		
7	Qty2		2	$4	$8	$12	$16

Press F4 to make one label relative and the other label absolute, the same as with cell addresses.

The Projection label gets a dollar sign.

3 Select *Qty1 Projection* and press the F4 key three times.

Once again, the Projection label gets a dollar sign.

 NOTE When you use labels, you can put them in any order, but the F4 key always cycles from *both relative* to *both absolute* to *row absolute* to *column absolute*, regardless of the order of the labels.

Enter

4 Click the Enter button, and use the AutoFill handle to fill the formula into the entire range. Then save the Lesson2 workbook.

The formulas with labels give the same answers as the formulas with cell addresses. Once again, you must decide whether the formula **=Price1 $Projection*Qty1 $Projection** is sufficiently clearer than **=C$5*$B6** to warrant adding the labels and converting the formulas.

Perhaps you like the readability of the formulas, but don't like the clutter of extra labels on the worksheet. Coincidentally, Excel has a third method for referring to cells that allows you to create readable formulas without the clutter of extra labels.

NOTE Most auditing tools work the same with cell addresses and with labels. Regardless of which method you choose, you can double-click a cell and see the Range Finder outline cells, or you can use the Auditing toolbar to trace dependents, or you can search for constants or formulas. However, the Column Differences and Row Differences options in the Go To Special dialog box do not recognize that the formulas are functionally identical when you use relative labels.

Using Named Ranges

When you use a column label such as *Price* in a formula, you never actually tell Excel which cell you want to use; Excel just figures it out automatically. On the one hand, that's good, because you can often create readable formulas just by using labels that you already have on the worksheet. On the other hand, that's not so good, because if Excel thinks you meant a different cell than you thought you meant, there's not a lot you can do about it. With names, you have complete control over what the name refers to. The cost of that control is that you must explicitly define the name.

In this section, you will convert the formulas you created in the Addresses worksheet to make them readable by using names. You might expect that the tasks would be similar to the tasks for using addresses and labels: create relative, absolute, and mixed references with names. You are right, but names have some interesting twists of their own.

Use absolute names

References you create with cell addresses and labels are relative references, unless you specify otherwise. Names are different. References you create with names are absolute references, unless you specify otherwise. You will start, therefore, by converting the increment values to use names.

1 Hold down CTRL as you drag the Addresses (not the Labels) worksheet tab to the right, creating a clone of the worksheet. Give the new copy the name **Names**

The easiest way to name a cell is to type the name into the Name Box. Rather than use the name *Quantity* to refer to cell B2 (you will use that name later), use the name *QtyAdd*, to represent the amount you want to add to each new quantity. You can use almost any word as a name, but the name can contain only letters, numbers, underscores, and periods. The name must begin with a letter or an underscore.

2 On the Names worksheet, select cell B2. Click the Name Box (the place that shows the B2 address), type **QtyAdd** to replace the cell address, and then press ENTER.

Name the selected range by entering a name in the Name Box.

WARNING If you don't press ENTER after you type a new name in the Name Box, Excel does not assign the name.

Now that the cell is named, you can use the Name Box to jump directly to the cell.

3 Select cell B10. Then click the arrow next to the Name Box, and select QtyAdd from the list.

Excel selects cell B2, the cell named QtyAdd.

NOTE If you select cell B10, click the Name Box, and type the name of a previously defined name, Excel does not change the name to refer to cell B10. Rather, it selects the named range, just as if you selected the name from the list.

Once the cell is named, you can use the name in a formula. As you are entering a formula, if you click a cell that has a name, Excel automatically uses the name in the formula.

Enter

4 Double-click cell A6, double-click the cell address *$B$2* in the formula, click cell B2, and click the Enter button.

The formula in cell A6 is now *=A5+QtyAdd*. The formula does not have any dollar signs in it. The name QtyAdd appears to be a relative reference—it doesn't have a dollar sign—but if you copy the formula to new cells, the name will keep referring to the same cell.

5 Double-click the AutoFill handle on cell A6. Then select cell A8 to look at the formula.

The formula for cell A8 is now *=A7+QtyAdd*. The cell address shifted, because it is a relative address, but the name reference still refers to the QtyAdd cell, because names are absolute by default.

Now you need to define the name for the price increment.

Excel provides several ways to name a range. One way that is very useful if you want to name several cells at the same time is to use the label from an adjacent cell. If you change the labels in cells B1 and C1 to match the names you want to give to the cells, you can name both cells B2 and C2 at the same time, using the Create Names dialog box.

6 Change cell B1 to **QtyAdd** and cell C1 to **PriceAdd**

7 Select the range B1:C2 (the range that includes the labels in the top row). On the Insert menu, point to Name, and then click Create.

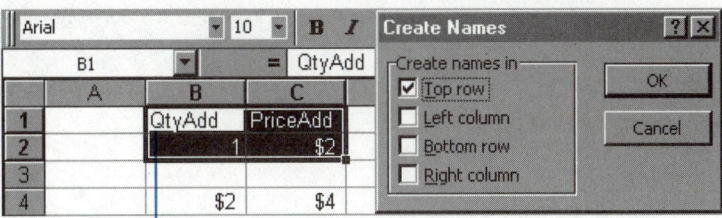

The Create Names dialog box uses the label from the first row or column to name the other cells in the selected range.

The Create Names dialog box appears, with the Top Row check box selected. Excel guessed (correctly) that you wanted to use the labels from the top row of the selected range.

8 Click OK.

This gives the name QtyAdd to cell B2, and PriceAdd to cell C2. (If you had not already given the name QtyAdd to cell B2, this step would have named it.)

9 Change the formula in cell C4 to **=B4+PriceAdd**, and then copy that formula to cells D4 and E4.

Excel continues to calculate the correct prices.

One valuable use for defining a name is to make it easy to create absolute references. If you use either cell addresses or labels, you must include a dollar sign if you want to prevent Excel from shifting the reference when you copy the formula to a new cell. If you define a name—regardless of whether you use the Name Box or the Create Names dialog box—you can use the name, without bothering with a dollar sign, as an absolute, unmoving reference.

Create relative names

Defining a name creates an absolute reference. But what if you want to have a relative reference in a formula, so the reference will shift as you copy the formula? Does that mean that you can't use a defined name?

For example, in this revenue calculation example, the formulas in cells C4:E4 each increment the cell to the left. Is there a way to define a name that refers to "one cell to the left"? There is, but you can't use either of the shortcut methods for defining a name—the Name Box and the Create Names dialog box. Rather, you must use the Define Name dialog box, which gives you complete control over how to define a name.

1 Select cell C4. On the Insert menu, point to Name, and then click Define.

The Define Name dialog box gives you complete control over the names in the workbook.

The Define Name dialog box appears. You see the PriceAdd and QtyAdd names. You can use the Define Name dialog box to manage all the names on the worksheet, regardless of how you originally created the name. To create a new name, you type the name into the Names In Workbook box.

2 Type **PrevPrice** as a new name in the Names In Workbook box. (Do not press ENTER.)

You will define a name to refer to the "previous" price cell. The Refers To box at the bottom of the dialog box contains =*Names!$C$4*. This is the complete, absolute address of the active cell: cell C4 of the Names worksheet. You want to refer to the relative address of cell B4.

3 Click in the white space after the cell address in the Refers To box.

4 Click cell B4 on the worksheet.

The contents of the Refers To box changes to =*Names!$B$4*. As on the worksheet, you use the F4 key to cycle between different relative and absolute options.

5 Press the F4 key three times.

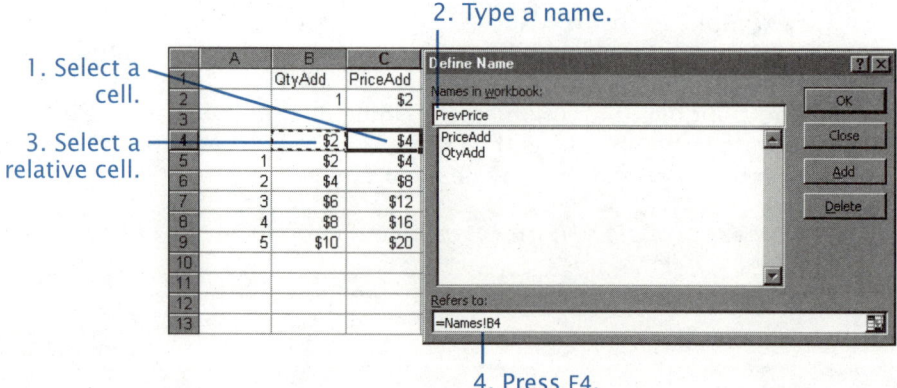

2. Type a name.

1. Select a cell.

3. Select a relative cell.

4. Press F4.

The address changes to =*Names!B4*. The name PrevPrice will now refer to the relationship between cell B4 and the currently active cell, cell C4. That relationship is "one cell to the left."

 TIP In the Refers To box, pressing the arrow keys changes the selection on the worksheet. This is called *Enter mode*. The status bar at the bottom of the window contains the word *Enter*. If you want to use the arrow keys to move around in the Refers To box, press the F2 key. The status bar changes to *Edit*, and you can use the arrow keys to navigate within the cell address. To return to Enter mode, press the F2 key again.

6 Click OK to define the name and close the dialog box.

The formula in cell C4 did not change to refer to the new name. It still says =*B4+PriceAdd*. Excel has an Apply Names dialog box that can convert the formulas to use the new name for you.

7 On the Insert menu, point to Name, and then click Apply.

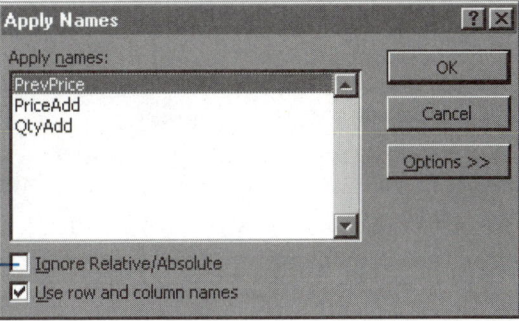

To apply a relative name, clear this check box, and click OK.

The Apply Names dialog box appears, showing a list of all the names defined for this worksheet. The name PrevPrice is selected. The Apply Names dialog box automatically preselects the newest name. It will search the entire worksheet (as long as only a single cell is active) and replace any cell references it can with the selected defined name. The only formulas that should change to the new name are those that point "one cell to the left"—that is, formulas that have the same relative reference as the name.

8 Clear the Ignore Relative/Absolute check box. Click OK, and then look at the formulas in cell C4, D4, and E4.

All the cells now contain the same formula: =*PrevPrice+PriceAdd*. In the formula, the two names appear similar. PriceAdd, however, is defined as an absolute address; it refers to a specific cell. PrevPrice is defined as a relative address; it refers to a relationship to the cell with the formula.

51

Excel names are actually extremely flexible. They can be relative or absolute, at your complete discretion.

Create mixed name references

Inside the body of the revenue grid, each formula multiplies one price by one quantity. To refer to the price, each formula uses row 4 for the row part of the address and its own column for the column part of the address. Likewise, to refer to the quantity, each formula uses column A for the column part of the address and its own row for the row part of the address. One part of the address is fixed, the other part is relative—relative to the same row or column that contains the formula.

Because each formula retrieves a value from its own row or column, you can take advantage of implicit intersection with named ranges to achieve an incredibly elegant formula. First give names to some ranges.

1   Select the range B4:E4, click the Name Box, type **Price**, and press ENTER.

2   Select the range A5:A9, click the Name Box, type **Quantity**, and press ENTER.

This defines both input ranges. When you use the Apply Names dialog box to use those names in existing formulas, Excel will demonstrate for you how implicit intersection works with named ranges.

3   Select cell A4 (or any single cell in the worksheet). On the Insert menu, point to Name, and then click Apply.

In the dialog box, only the Quantity name is selected, because it is the newest name. You want to apply both Quantity and Price.

4   Click the Price name in the Apply Names list.

Both names are now highlighted. Excel will search the entire worksheet for cell addresses that it can replace with either of these names.

5   Leave the Ignore Relative/Absolute check box selected, and click OK. Then look at several of the revenue formulas.

All 20 cells contain the formula =Price*Quantity. There are no dollar signs. The names are both absolute. The formulas behave as if they contained mixed references. This is what happens when you ignore absolute references. This is implicit intersection at work.

Here's how Excel interprets the copy of the formula in cell C8:

"I am supposed to multiply Price by Quantity. In order to do the multiplication, I want a single price and a single quantity. But Price and Quantity both refer to ranges with multiple cells. Can I intersect the column I am in (column C) with one of those ranges? Yes. Column C intersects with the Price range in a single cell, cell C4. I will use that for the price. Next, can I intersect the row I'm in (row 8) with one of those ranges? Row 8 intersects with the Quantity range in a single cell, cell A8. I will use that for the quantity. Great! I will interpret this formula as =C4*A8."

Excel says that whole speech to itself for each of the 20 cells in the grid. Fortunately, Excel is a very fast talker.

Extend named ranges

What happens if Excel is unable to find an intersecting cell? If Excel cannot intersect the current row or column with the range, the formula returns an error.

1 Click the column E heading, and drag the AutoFill handle to the right of column F.

	A	B	C	D	E	F	G
1		QtyAdd	PriceAdd				
2		1	$2				
3							
4		$2	$4	$6	$8	$10	
5		1	$2	$4	$6	$8	#VALUE!	
6		2	$4	$8	$12	$16	#VALUE!	

When you extend the formulas that intersect with a name, you get error values.

The revenue formulas all produce the #VALUE! error value. You can use the Range Finder boxes to graphically see how Excel interprets the formulas.

2 Double-click cell D7, look at the Range Finder boxes, and then press ESC. Then double-click cell F5 and do the same.

	A	B	C	D	E	F	G
1		QtyAdd	PriceAdd				
2		1	$2				
3							
4		$2	$4	$6	$8	$10	
5		1	$2	$4	$6	$8	=Price*Quantity	
6		2	$4	$8	$12	$16	#VALUE!	
7		3	$6	$12	$18	$24	#VALUE!	

Excel can't intersect with the range if it doesn't include the column containing the formula.

When you double-click a cell that calculates a number, the Range Finder boxes each show single cells within the Price and Quantity named ranges. When you double-click one of the cells that contain an error, the blue Range Finder box for Price selects the entire range. The Price range does not intersect column F, the column containing the formula.

53

You can easily avoid this problem by defining the Price and Quantity ranges much larger than you need. Since each formula intersects with only a single cell, extra cells in the formula don't hurt anything. In fact, the easiest way to make sure you never go past the end of the named range is to name the entire row or column. The easiest way to change what a name refers to is to delete the name and start over.

3   On the Insert menu, point to Name, and then click Define. In the Names In Workbook list, select Quantity and click the Delete button. Then select Price and click Delete. Click OK to close the dialog box.

This deletes the names. The formulas that use those names all change to the #NAME? error value. Now you can redefine the names to refer to the entire column or row.

4   Click the *A* heading at the top of column A, click in the Name Box, type **Quantity**, and press ENTER.

5   Click the *4* heading at the left of row 4, click in the Name Box, type **Price**, and press ENTER. Then save the Lesson2 workbook.

The errors disappear from all the revenue cells, including those in column F. You can now extend the formulas in either direction without getting any errors.

TIP   Consider the following suggestions for when to use each of the three kinds of references:

- Use labels whenever you create a list or a grid that already has labels on the worksheet.

- Use names when you refer to a range on a different worksheet, or to create readable formulas when labels are not convenient.

- Use cell addresses for simple formulas that are easy to decipher.

As you decide which type of reference to use, always think of how easy the formula will be to read, either by someone else, or by yourself after you haven't looked at it for six months.

One Step Further: Using Names on Different Sheets

When you define a name, it becomes global to a workbook. In other words, if you define a name on one worksheet, you can still refer to it on another. For example, if you activate the Addresses worksheet and enter the formula =QtyAdd into a cell, the formula would return the number 1, or whatever the current value of the QtyAdd cell is.

Create duplicate names in a workbook

What happens if you define the same name on two different worksheets? For example, what if you want to calculate two different revenue scenarios simultaneously, and you create a clone of the Names worksheet? What happens to the names?

Excel will create special versions of the name that are specific·to the new worksheet. If you copy the Names worksheet, you will see what Excel does to the names.

1 Hold down CTRL as you drag the Names worksheet tab to the right. Give the new sheet the name **Alternate**. Look at various formulas to verify that they look the same on this new worksheet as they did on the Names worksheet.

2 On the Alternate worksheet, change the QtyAdd amount from 1 to 10, and the starting quantity amount from 1 to 10.

The formulas calculate properly with the new numbers, but the formulas on the Names worksheet are still using the original named ranges.

3 Activate the Names worksheet. Change the QtyAdd amount from 1 to 2, and the starting quantity amount from 1 to 2.

Each worksheet uses its own copy of the name.

Delete a local name

You can use the Define Name command to see the difference between global names and names that are local to a worksheet.

1 Select the Names worksheet. On the Insert menu, point to Name, and then click Define.

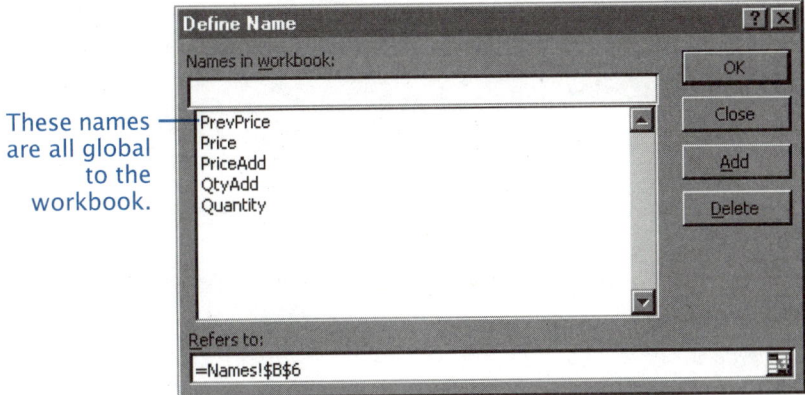

These names are all global to the workbook.

All the names appear on the left of the Names In Workbook list, with nothing on the right side of the list. These are all global names, because this is the worksheet where you originally created the names. On the Alternate worksheet, the names will look different.

2   Click Close. Activate the Alternate worksheet. On the Insert menu, point to Name, and then click Define.

These names —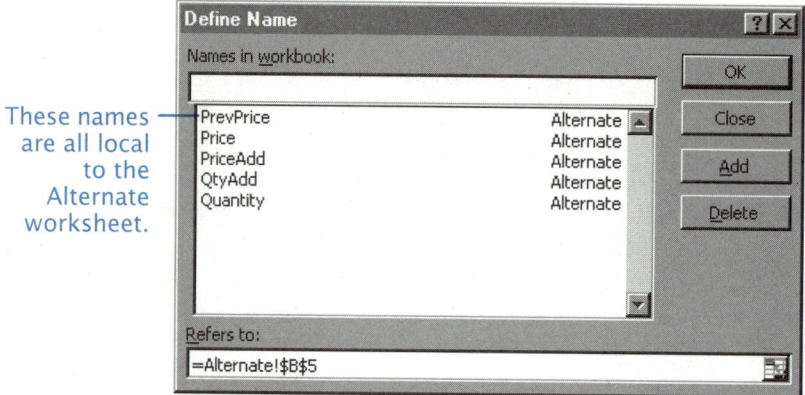
are all local
to the
Alternate
worksheet.

Each of the names has the word *Alternate* on the right side of the list. Each of these names is a local name, visible only to the Alternate worksheet. When you cloned the Names worksheet, Excel saw that the names already existed at the workbook level, so it created new worksheet level names. The new names are visible only on the Alternate worksheet, and the local names "hide" the global names from the formulas on this worksheet.

3   Select QtyAdd from the list and click Delete.

When you —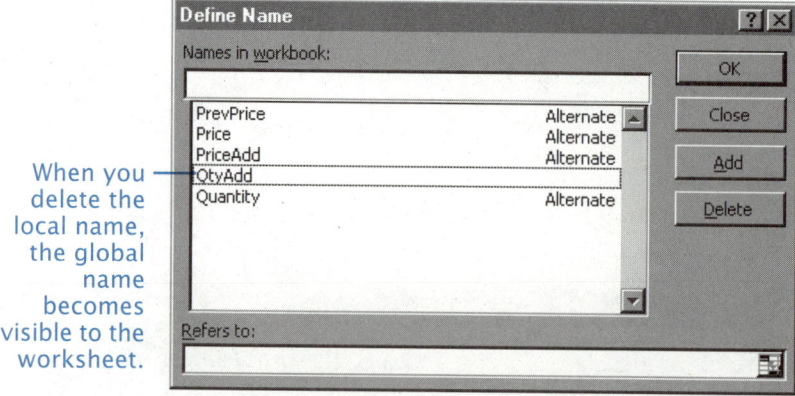
delete the
local name,
the global
name
becomes
visible to the
worksheet.

The name stays, but the word *Alternate* disappears. You just deleted the local version of the name, allowing the global version (the one on the Names worksheet) to become visible to this worksheet. When you close the dialog box, the formulas will recalculate using 2 instead of 10 as the value of QtyAdd.

4 Click Close.

The numbers all recalculate using the global value of QtyAdd.

To define a local name manually, you include the sheet name as part of the name. Type the worksheet name, then an exclamation mark, and then the name.

5 On the Alternate worksheet, select cell B2. On the Insert menu, point to Name, and then click Define. Type **Alternate!QtyAdd** in the Names In Workbook box, and click OK.

Once again, the worksheet recalculates using the local version of the name.

6 Save and close the Lesson2 workbook.

Names in a workbook are global—unless you specifically make them visible to a single sheet. When you clone a worksheet, Excel converts any names that are defined on that worksheet to local names on the copy. You can use local names either to use the same name on two or more worksheets, or to keep a name from appearing in the Name Box drop-down list when any other worksheet is active.

Lesson Summary

To	Do this
Create a relative reference to "the cell above" from a formula in cell C4	Use the address of the cell above the one with the formula (in this case, C3). Do not use dollar signs before any part of the address.
Create an absolute reference to cell B3	Enter the address B3, and then press the F4 key once to change the address to $B$3. (Or simply type the address with the dollar signs.)
Create a mixed reference to a cell in row 2 of the current column, from a formula in cell C4	Enter the address C2, and then press the F4 key twice to change the address to C$2.
Create a mixed reference to a cell in column A of the current row, from a formula in cell C4	Enter the address A4, and then press the F4 key three times to change the address to $A4.

To	Do this
Display the Auditing toolbar	Right-click any toolbar, and click Customize. On the Toolbars tab, select the Auditing toolbar, and click OK.
Display blue arrows showing all the cells with formulas that refer to cell C4	Select cell C4 and click the Trace Dependents button on the Auditing toolbar.
Remove auditing arrows from the worksheet	Click the Remove All Arrows button on the Auditing toolbar.
Display the Go To Special dialog box	Press CTRL+G, and click the Special button.
Select all the cells on the worksheet that contain constants	In the Go To Special dialog box, select the Constants option, and click OK.
Select all the cells within a given range that contain constants	Select the range you want to examine before selecting the Constants option in the Go To Special dialog box.
Select all the cells in a range where the formula does not match that of the top cell in the range	Select the range you want to examine. Display the Go To Special dialog box. Select the Column Differences option, and click OK.
Enter a series of labels with the form *Label1, Label2, Label3*, and so forth	Enter the first label, along with its numeric suffix. Drag the AutoFill handle to create a series of labels with incrementing suffixes.
Refer to a value in a column with the label *Price1* at the top, in the same row as the formula	In the formula, type **Price1** (the label from the top of the column). If you copy the formula to the right, Excel will look for a label to the right of the original label.
Refer to a value from a cell with the label *Price* at the top of the column and the label *Increment* at the left of the row	In the formula, type **Price Increment** or **Increment Price**. In other words, enter both labels (in either order) with a space in between.
Make a formula reference keep referring to a column labeled *Price*, even when you copy the formula to a new column	When you type the label *Price*, press the F4 key once to change the label to $Price.

To	Do this
Create a formula in the Price1 column of a grid with a row labeled *Projection*, and columns labeled *Price1, Price2, Price3*, that will always refer to the Projection row, but will shift to the appropriate column as the formula is copied	In the formula, type **Price1 $Projection**, with a dollar sign in front of the label you don't want Excel to shift when you copy the formula.
Give a name to a cell	Select the cell, click the Name Box (at the left end of the formula bar), type the name, and press ENTER. The name will automatically refer to an absolute cell address.
Use labels from adjacent cells to name several cells at once	Select the range that includes both the labels and the cells that you want to name. On the Insert menu, point to Name and click Create. Verify the location of the labels in the selection, and click OK.
Create a name that refers to "the cell to the left" on a worksheet named Sheet1	Select cell B1. On the Insert menu, point to Name and click Define. Type the name in the Names In Workbook box. Click the right half of the Refers To box, and then click cell A1 (the cell to the left of the active cell). Press the F4 key three times to convert the reference to =*Sheet1!A1*. Then click OK.
Convert existing formulas that use cell addresses to use defined names	Select any single cell on the worksheet. On the Insert menu, point to Name and click Apply. Select any names you want to apply, and click OK.
Use names to refer to the cell in row 4 (assume that row 4 contains prices), and the column containing the formula.	Give the name *Price* to all of row 4. (Click the heading 4, click the Name Box, type **Price**, and press ENTER.) In the formula, type **Price**.
Change the reference for an existing name	Display the Define Name dialog box. (On the Insert menu, point to Name and click Define.) Delete the name and click OK. Select the new range, click in the Name Box, type the name, and press ENTER.

To	Do this
Use arrow keys to move around in the Refers To box of the Define Name dialog box	After you click in the Refers To box, press the F2 key to switch to Edit mode. Press the F2 key again to return to Enter mode.
Create the name *Begin* on a worksheet named Prices that is visible only to formulas on that worksheet	In the Define Name dialog box, type **Prices!Begin** as the new name in the Names In Workbook box.
Create a worksheet where all the names are local names	Clone a worksheet. (CTRL+drag the worksheet tab.) All the names on the new copy will have local names.

For online information about	On the Help menu, click Contents And Index, click the Index tab, and then type
Naming cells	cells, naming
Cell references	references (cell), absolute/relative/mixed
Cell labels	labels, in formulas
Auditing tools	precedents and dependents, auditing formulas
Selecting special cells	cells, selecting

Lesson

3

Using Functions

Estimated time
45 min.

In this lesson you will learn how to:

- Use functions to manipulate time and money.
- Use functions to lookup values in lists.
- Use functions to calculate trends.
- Use functions to manipulate text strings.

A few years ago, I was teaching a group of engineers at a nuclear power plant how to write Microsoft Excel macros. One morning, one of the engineers came in very excited and showed me a very complex macro that he had written to calculate some obscure relationship. I, very innocently, asked if he had checked to see whether Excel had a built-in function that would calculate that number. We launched Excel and looked through the list of available engineering functions—I can't even pronounce the names of most of them—and he discovered, with a mixture of delight and horror, that Excel included a function that would completely replace this macro that he had spent days creating.

A function is a calculation machine that produces a result. In the same way that one of your production machines at Tailspin Toys produces a colorful new model when you provide it with the appropriate chemicals, a *function* produces a shiny new number or text value after you provide it with the appropriate input values, or *arguments*. Many people use Excel for years and never use any functions beyond the SUM function generated by the AutoSum button. That is most unfortunate, because Excel has well over 200 different functions that you can use to calculate new values from old.

In this lesson, you will not learn how to use obscure engineering functions. But you will learn how to use some of the most useful functions, and you will become familiar with using functions and the Formula Palette. You can then browse Excel's list of functions to find others that can save you days of work.

Start the lesson

> Start Microsoft Excel, change to the Excel AT Practice folder, and open the Start3 workbook. Save a copy of the workbook as **Lesson3**

Working with Time and Money

Your boss just walked up to your desk with a pile of folders. He tells you that since you are the in-house Excel expert, he wants to see whether you can help people from departments all around the company. These are people who were trying to use Excel to solve problems, but got stuck. If you can help all of them, he will be impressed, which might have favorable ramifications in your next performance evaluation. You interpret this as a highly motivational opportunity, and plunge into the folders.

The first folder that your boss gave you came from the people in Finance. They are working on a project to purchase a new machine. The machine is going to cost $140,000. Apparently, there is some disagreement about how much the loan payments will be. You get to provide the financial analyst with the correct formulas.

Calculate a savings amount

The financial analyst created the Borrow sheet of the Lesson3 workbook. It contains everything you need to calculate the loan payment amounts—except the correct formula.

When dealing with loans, always enter money you receive as a positive number, and money you pay as a negative number.

	A	B	C
1			
2	Loan	$ 140,000	
3	Balloon	$ (10,000)	
4	Rate	8.50%	
5	Years	5.00	
6	Payment		
7			

You will need to calculate the monthly loan payment.

The company needs $140,000, and wants to be able to pay off the loan in five years. The bank is willing to lend the money at 8.5 percent interest, compounded monthly. An extra $10,000 balloon payment at the end would be acceptable. Your task is to figure out what the monthly payments will be. Excel's Formula Palette can help you create a formula that calculates the loan payment amount.

Edit Formula

1 Select cell B6 and click the Edit Formula button next to the formula bar. (If the Assistant offers to help you, politely decline.)

The Formula Palette appears when you click the Edit Formula button.

The Formula Palette appears. The Name box changes to a list box of common functions. One of those functions will help you calculate the payments you will need to make. It is the PMT (short for "Payment") function. You give the PMT function information about the interest rate, the time periods, and the amount of money, and it gives you the monthly amount you need to pay.

2 Click the arrow next to the list of functions, and click PMT.

NOTE If PMT does not appear in the list of functions, select More Functions. In the Paste Function dialog that appears, select Financial as the Function Category, select PMT as the Function Name, and click OK.

A bold name means the argument is required.

An expanded version of the Formula Palette box appears, showing the information you need to give the PMT function. These are the *arguments* for the function. If the argument name is bold (like Rate, Nper, and Pv), then you must provide a value for the argument. If the name is not bold (like Fv and Type), then the argument is optional. As you click in an argument's box, the description at the bottom explains that argument.

3   Click the background of the Formula Palette and drag it to the side so you can see the values on the worksheet.

The Rate argument is the interest rate per period. The rate the bank wants is 8.5 percent, but that is an annual rate. To turn the annual rate into a monthly rate, you divide it by 12.

4   Type **Rate/12** in the Rate box, and press TAB to move to the Nper box.

The name *Nper* stands for "Number of Periods." The worksheet shows the time period in years, but you will be making the payments monthly. This time, you multiply the number of years by 12 to get the number of months.

5   Type **Years*12** in the Nper box, and press TAB to move to the Pv box.

The name *Pv* stands for "Present Value." This is the amount of money that you either put in or take out at the present time.

6   Type **Loan** in the Pv box, and press TAB to move to the Fv box.

The name *Fv* stands for "Future Value." This is the extra money, or balloon payment, that you will make at the end. This is money you pay, so it is a negative number.

7   Type **Balloon** in the Fv box, and click OK.

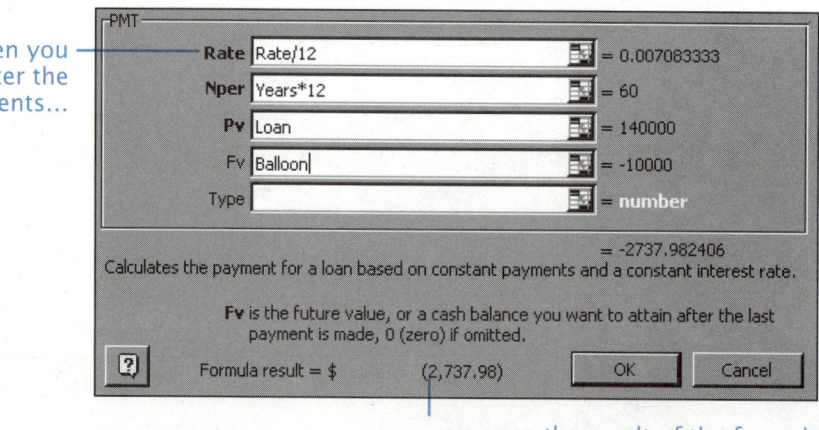

When you enter the arguments...

...you see the result of the formula.

The function calculates that you will need to pay about $2,738 each month in order to pay off $130,000 in five years. (You still need to pay the final $10,000 at the end.)

In case you are a profoundly analytical type who wants to know the formula for how Excel calculates the payment, you can look in Help under the topic for the PV function (which uses the same mathematical formula as the PMT function). Perhaps it will be enough to say that one of the steps in the underlying calculation (for this example) involves raising the number 1.007083 to the 60th power. That's enough to make me grateful for the PMT function.

Change the result of a formula

You show the calculations to the analyst in finance. She tells you that this is totally unworkable. The payment cannot be more than $2,500. She wants you to find out how much the balloon payment would have to be in order to get the payment down to $2,500.

If you were not in public, you might be tempted to say a naughty word at this time. The payment amount is the result of a formula. How do you change the result of a formula? You envision an entertaining evening of typing various random numbers in for the Balloon payment until you get the "correct" payment. Fortunately, you decided to take a break and read this lesson. Excel has a tool called *Goal Seek* that changes the value of a cell of your choice until the value of a formula of your choice reaches a goal of your choice. Goal Seek allows you a lot of choices. Start by selecting the cell with the formula.

1 Select cell B6.

2 On the Tools menu, click the Goal Seek command.

The Goal Seek dialog box appears, with cell B6 already entered in the Set Cell box. You enter the goal you want for cell B6 into the To Value box.

3 In the To Value box, type **–2,500**

You want to find a new balloon payment amount that will give you the desired payment amount. The Balloon payment goes into cell B3, so that's what you type in the By Changing Cell box.

You can't type labels into the Goal Seek dialog box.

4 In the By Changing Cell box, type **B3**, and click OK.

Excel madly types various random numbers into cell B3. (You can watch the worksheet calculating wildly.) After a few tries, it finds an acceptable number and displays the Goal Seek Status dialog box. You can see in the background that the new Balloon payment is about $28,000.

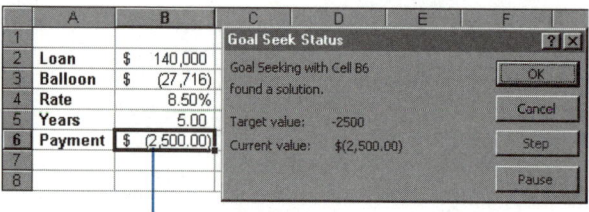

Goal Seek allows you to specify the result of a formula.

5   Click OK to accept the changes.

For only $18,000 more at the end of five years, you can get the loan payment down to the $2,500 limit.

I hope you don't take this personally, but Excel is much faster at plugging random numbers into a cell than you are. Of course, with Goal Seek, Excel only tries a few random numbers before figuring out how to quickly home in on the goal. Whenever you have a formula that you wish you could change, use Goal Seek.

Make an amortization schedule

The analyst in finance now says that she needs to know how much of each payment will go towards paying off the loan, and how much will be interest. It has something to do with calculating tax benefits. A report that shows the details of each payment of a loan is called an *amortization* schedule, from the French word *mort*, which means "death." You are detailing how you will kill off the loan.

Columns E through I of the Borrow worksheet already have some headings and five years worth of dates ready for you to add formulas. Some of these formulas will refer to the values in columns A and B. In order to use the labels from that part of the sheet, you need a column label for column B.

1   In cell B1, enter the label **Borrow**

Now you can refer to any cells on the left part of the worksheet by intersecting the row label with the word *Borrow*.

2   In cell F2, the first month's start value, type **=Borrow Loan** and press ENTER.

	A	B	C	D	E	F	G
		Borrow			Month	Start	Interest
1							
2	Loan	$ 140,000			Apr-98	$ 140,000	
3	Balloon	$ (27,716)			May-98		

Start the amortization schedule
with the original loan amount.

You will not copy this formula, so you don't need to worry about making anything absolute.

For the interest part of the loan, you will multiply the monthly interest rate (the annual rate divided by 12) by the current loan balance. The first interest calculation is in cell G2, so that's where you will enter the formula.

3   In cell G2, type =**Start*(Borrow $Rate/12)** and press ENTER.

This retrieves the value from the column labeled Start, and multiplies it by the value where the Borrow column and the Rate row intersect. Since you will be copying this to other rows, you need a dollar sign in front of Rate. The parentheses make sure that you divide the rate by 12 before multiplying it by the current balance.

The portion of the payment that goes to pay off the loan goes in the Principal column. This is simply whatever is left from the payment after you pay the interest. The payment to the left is a negative value, so you will need to convert it to a positive number before you subtract the interest.

You can include extra spaces between words in a formula to make it easier to read.

4   In cell H2, type = – **Borrow $Payment – Interest** and press ENTER.

To calculate the ending value for a month, you simply subtract the amount from the principal column from the starting balance.

5   In cell I2, type =**Start–Principal** and press ENTER.

The end value from the first month is actually the start value for the next month.

6   In cell F3, the second value in the start column, type =**Apr-98 End** and press ENTER.

	F3		▼	=	=4/1/1998 End				
	D	E	F		G	H	I	J	
1		Month	Start		Interest	Principal	End		
2			Apr-98	$ 140,000	$ 992	$ 1,508	$ 138,492		
3			May-98	$ 138,492					
4			Jun-98						

Each month starts where the previous month ended.

If you look at the formula in cell F3, you will see that Excel changed what you typed to =*4/1/1998 End*. I think it's easier to type *Apr-98* than *4/1/1998*. As you copy this formula down, Excel will convert each date label to refer to the next month.

You now have all the formulas you need. You just need to copy the formulas down to the proper rows.

7   Select cell F3, and double-click the AutoFill handle.

8   Select the range G2:I2, and double-click the AutoFill handle.

67

You want to see how final payments work out. Double-clicking the bottom border of a range jumps to the last cell in the list.

9 Select cell E2, and double-click the bottom border of the cell.

59		Jan-03	$	34,530	$	245	$	2,255	$	32,275
60		Feb-03	$	32,275	$	229	$	2,271	$	30,003
61		Mar-03	$	30,003	$	213	$	2,287	$	27,716
62									

The ending balance equals the balloon payment.

The ending balance is $27,716, precisely the balloon amount you planned in the original model.

An amortization schedule is not only useful for determining tax benefits, it also confirms that the PMT function really did calculate the correct payment amount.

See Lesson 2 for more details about names and labels.

TIP If you put the amortization schedule on a different sheet from the loan information, define names for the loan information values. You can use names from any worksheet in the workbook, but you can use labels only from the same sheet as the formula.

Calculate the last day of a month

That most charming financial analyst just called you back, pleading for one more favor. The dates on the amortization table you made are all for the first of the month. In order to make sure that the payments are on time, she wants to know the last date of each preceding month. Since the months all have different lengths, that is not trivial. Is there any way…?

For dates, Excel simply enters a number that counts the days since the beginning of the twentieth century. Because those numbers come in a series, this kind of date is often called a *serial date*, or a *serial number*. Excel's DATE function allows you to construct a serial date.

1 On the Borrow worksheet, in cell J1, enter the label **PayDate**

2 Select cell J2, and click the Edit Formula button. Click the arrow next to the list of functions and select More Functions.

Edit Formula

3 In the Paste Function dialog box, select Date & Time from the Function Category list, select DATE from the Function Name list, and click OK.

The Formula Palette box now shows the arguments for the DATE function. This function has three arguments, all required: Year, Month, and Day. Start by typing constants as the arguments. If you use constants from the beginning of the century, you can see how the DATE function works. Later, you will replace the constants with calculated values.

If you do press ENTER, click the Edit Formula button.

4 As the Year argument, type **1900**. As the Month argument, type **12**. As the Day argument, type **31**. Do not press ENTER.

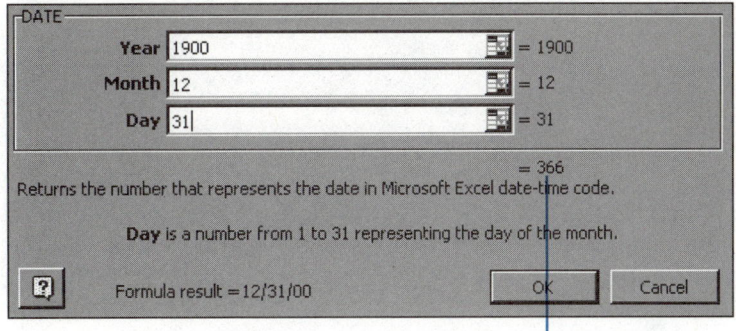

A serial date counts the days since January 1, 1900.

Excel does not use dates be- fore January 1, 1900.

At the bottom, the dialog box shows the Formula result as =*12/31/00*, the last day of the year 1900. In the middle of the box, just below the arguments, you can see the number =*366*. This number is the actual value returned by the DATE function. This is the number of days since January 1, 1900. (The year 1900 was a leap year, so it had 366 days.)

You really don't want to use a constant for the Year argument. What you want is to look at the month number on the current row and calculate its year. Excel has another date function, YEAR, that will extract the year portion of a date.

5 Double-click the number 1900 in the Year box. Then click the arrow next to the list of functions and select More Functions. In the Function Name list, select YEAR, and then click OK.

Excel now displays a new Formula Palette box for the new function. This function is nested inside the DATE function, as you can see in the formula bar. You want to extract the year portion of the date that is in the Month column.

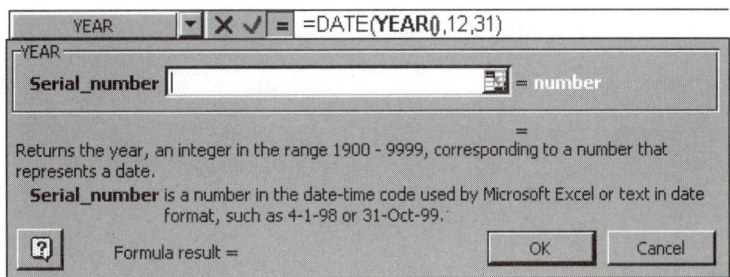

6 In the Serial_number box, type **Month** (the label for the column that contains the dates), but do not click OK. Rather, click in the formula bar, in the white area to the right of the formula.

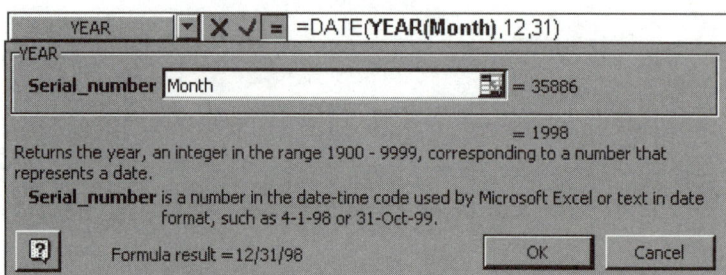

You are now back in the Formula Palette box for the main formula. The YEAR function is in its place in the Year box. Next you want to replace the constant for the month with the month portion of the date in the Month column. Excel's MONTH function extracts the month from a serial date.

7 Double-click the number 12 in the Month box. Then click the arrow next to the list of functions and select More Functions. In the Function Name list, select MONTH, and then click OK.

You are now in the Formula Palette for the MONTH function.

8 In the Serial_number box, type **Month**. Once again, click the white space in the Formula Box.

You can see at the bottom of the Formula Palette that the function displays the date 4/1/98. This is the first day of the month in the Month column. What you want is the last day of the previous month. The DATE function does not restrict you to "legal" values for the argument. If using 1 for the Day gives you the first day of the month, what do you suppose that using 0 for the Day would give you?

9 Replace the number 31 in the Day box with **0**, and click OK.

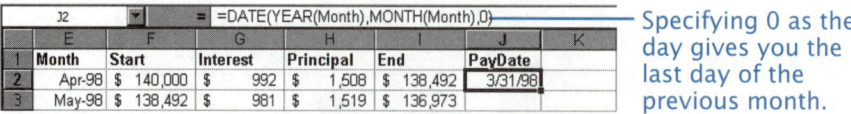

Specifying 0 as the day gives you the last day of the previous month.

The date *3/31/98* appears in the cell. Regardless of which day of the month was in the Month column, this formula would calculate the last day of the preceding month.

Let's see how the formula does with months of different lengths.

10 Double-click the AutoFill handle at the bottom of cell J2. Then look at various months in the column to see how the formula did, and save the Lesson3 workbook.

	E	F	G	H	I	J	K
1	Month	Start	Interest	Principal	End	PayDate	
2	Apr-98	$ 140,000	$ 992	$ 1,508	$ 138,492	3/31/98	
3	May-98	$ 138,492	$ 981	$ 1,519	$ 136,973	4/30/98	
4	Jun-98	$ 136,973	$ 970	$ 1,530	$ 135,443	5/31/98	
5	Jul-98	$ 135,443	$ 959	$ 1,541	$ 133,902	6/30/98	
6	Aug-98	$ 133,902	$ 948	$ 1,552	$ 132,351	7/31/98	

Regardless of the length of the month, the formula calculates the correct date for the last day of the preceding month.

Excel's date functions are powerful tools for manipulating dates. You can deconstruct a date by using the YEAR, MONTH, and DAY functions, change the values, and then construct a new date by using the DATE function. You can also add integers to dates, or subtract one date from another, all because dates are really serial numbers, starting at the beginning of the twentieth century.

NOTE You may have heard of the impending computer crisis coming at the year 2000. Many computers store dates in the form YYMMDD. Programs that work with those dates will have a hard time differentiating between the year 1900 and the year 2000. Microsoft Excel's serial dates completely avoid this problem, since January 5, 1900 is stored as 5, and January 5, 2000 is stored as 36530, regardless of how either one is formatted.

Finding a Value from a List

The next folder your manager passed on to you is from Marketing. They are renewing some contracts with stores and chains that sell your models, and need help calculating the appropriate discount rates. Your company actually provides two types of discounts to resellers. One discount is based on the total minimum dollar volume that a reseller commits to order during the year. An additional discount is for the products themselves; products belong to groups and each group of products gets a different discount rate. The Marketing analyst started creating the worksheets, but was having trouble getting the formulas correct.

Create random sample numbers

The Discount sheet of the Lesson3 workbook contains the reseller discount analysis as the Marketing analyst left it.

	A	B	C	D	E	F	G
1	Contract	Commitment	Discount		Level	Discount	
2	C5001				$ -	0%	
3	C5004				$ 10,000	1%	
4	C5011				$ 20,000	2%	
5	C5015				$ 40,000	3%	
6	C5017				$ 80,000	5%	

You will need to calculate sample commitment levels and appropriate discounts.

On the right is a table of discount rates. On the left is the list of contracts, along with the commitment amount. Unfortunately, the analyst informed you, the commitment dollars aren't finalized yet. Could you put in some sample numbers until the real ones arrive? The commitment levels will be anywhere from $0 to $100,000, and are always rounded to the nearest $5,000. (Because of the Currency formatting, zero values appear as dashes.)

1 Activate the Discount sheet, and select cell B2.

This is where the first random number will go. Excel has a function, RAND, which generates a random number between 0 and 1.

Edit Formula

2 Click the Edit Formula button, click the arrow next to the list of functions, and select More Functions. In the Function Category list, select Math & Trig, and in the Function Name list, select RAND. Then click OK.

RAND	▼	✕ ✓ =	=RAND()

RAND

= Volatile

Returns an evenly distributed random number greater than or equal to 0 and less than 1 (changes on recalculation).

This function takes no arguments.

Formula result = Volatile

[OK] [Cancel]

A *volatile* function recalculates whenever anything on the worksheet changes.

The Formula Palette explains that this function returns a number greater than or equal to zero, and less than one, and that the function does not require any arguments. As the return value of the function, it shows *Volatile*. This means that the function will recalculate anytime any other formula on the worksheet recalculates.

 TIP You can recalculate the RAND function at any time by pressing the F9 key.

You don't want random numbers between 0 and 1. You want random numbers between 0 and 100,000. The trick is to multiply the result of the RAND function by 100,000.

Enter

3   In the formula bar, click after the function's parentheses, type ***100000** and click the Enter button. Then double-click the AutoFill handle.

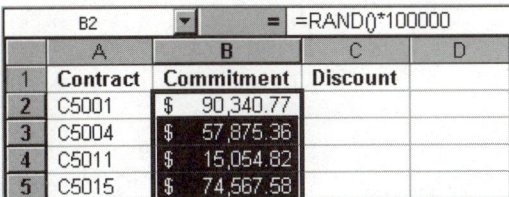

The range fills with random numbers between 0 and 100,000. These numbers, however, are not rounded to the nearest 5000, or even to the nearest 1.

As you might guess, Excel has a function that will round a number. It's named ROUND.

Cut

4   Double-click cell B2, and then select the entire formula except for the equal sign. On the Standard toolbar, click the Cut button.

You need to get the RAND function temporarily out of the way so that you can add the ROUND function.

Paste

5   Click the arrow next to the function list, and select More Functions. Select Math & Trig in the Function Category list, and ROUND in the Function Name list. Click OK. With the insertion point in the Number box, click the Paste button on the Standard toolbar.

The number that you want to round is the number that you get after you multiply the result of the RAND function by 100,000.

A negative number of digits rounds to the left of the decimal point.

6   In the Num_digits box, type **–3**. Click OK, and then double-click the AutoFill handle.

The numbers are all rounded to the nearest 1000. (If you had wanted to round to the nearest ten cents, you would have used 1 for the Num_digits argument.)

The ROUND function only rounds to a power of ten. You want to round to the nearest 5000. The secret is to divide by 5 before rounding, and then multiply by 5 after rounding.

Enter

7 Double-click cell B2. In the formula, click between the number *100000* and the comma. Type */5* and click after the final closing parenthesis. Type **5* and click the Enter button. Then click the AutoFill handle.

B2		=	=ROUND(RAND()*100000/5,-3)*5		
	A	B	C	D	E	F
1	Contract	Commitment	Discount		Level	Discount
2	C5001	$ 5,000.00			$ -	0%
3	C5004	$ 75,000.00			$ 10,000	1%
4	C5011	$ 5,000.00			$ 20,000	2%
5	C5015	$ 70,000.00			$ 40,000	3%
6	C5017	$ 25,000.00			$ 80,000	5%

The final formula is *=ROUND(RAND()*100000/5,-3)*5*. This calculates a random number between 0 and 1, multiples the result by 100,000, divides that result by 5, rounds that result to the nearest 1000, and finally multiplies that result by 5.

> **TIP** If you want to round up or down to the next multiple of a given number, you can use the CEILING or FLOOR functions.

You don't need to show cents when you round to thousands.

Decrease Decimal

8 Select column B by clicking the "B" at the top of the column, and click the Decrease Decimal button twice.

You now have random numbers that simulate the type of commitments the resellers will make. Because the formula is *volatile*, you can calculate new random numbers at any time.

9 Press the F9 key.

Each time you press F9, Excel calculates a new set of random numbers.

Random numbers are often useful when you need to prepare a worksheet before the actual numbers are available. Even when actual numbers are available, random numbers can help you make sure that your formulas will handle extreme cases that may occur in the future.

Find a number range in a lookup table

Now that you have sample order commitment levels, you can create a formula that finds the correct discount percent from a table. Excel has a function, VLOOKUP, that will "look up" a value in a vertical list, a list where the value you want to match is in a column. Before you use the function, give a name to the lookup table.

1 Select cell E1, a cell inside the lookup table. Press CTRL+SHIFT+* to select the entire table. Click in the Name Box, type **ResellerDiscounts**, and press ENTER.

Naming the lookup table provides at least four benefits: It makes the lookup formula easier to read; it simplifies referring to the table as an absolute reference; it allows you to easily move the table to a different worksheet; and it eliminates the need to change formulas if you change the size of the lookup table.

Edit Formula

2 Select cell C2, click the Edit Formula button, click the arrow next to the list of functions, and select More Functions. In the Function Category list, select Lookup & Reference, in the Function Name list, select VLOOKUP, and click OK.

Use the VLOOKUP function to find a value in a list.

The VLOOKUP function has three required arguments, and one optional argument.

3 In the Lookup_value box, type **Commitment**, the label at the top of the column containing the value you want to look up.

4 In the Table_array box, type **ResellerDiscounts**, the name you gave to the lookup table.

5 In the Col_index_num box, type **2**, the number of the column that contains the value you want to retrieve from the table.

6 Click OK, and then click the AutoFill handle to create a column of random numbers.

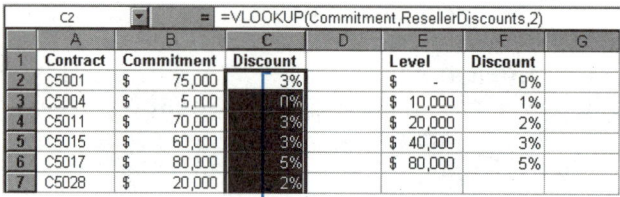

Each reseller gets an appropriate discount based on the dollar range.

7 Check the discount when the commitment is at $0, $5,000, $10,000, and so on. If the list does not show a reseller with a commitment level of $0 (indicated by a dash), press F9 repeatedly until one appears.

In each case, the discount percent comes from the row in the table where the level in the first column is less than or equal to the value from the commitment column.

This type of lookup, where you search to find which range a value falls into, is sometimes called a *range lookup*. The instructions in the Formula Palette box say that the function returns "the closest match." That's not quite accurate.

Here's what the VLOOKUP function does with a range lookup, searching for the appropriate discount for a $15,000 commitment: It starts with the top value in the first column of the list ($0), and asks, "is this value greater than $15,000?" It is not, so the function moves down to the next value ($10,000), and asks, "is this value greater?" It is not, so the function moves down to the next value ($20,000), and asks the same question. This time, $20,000 is greater than $15,000. The function then backs up one row, and retrieves the discount from column 2. So, technically, a range lookup finds "the last value that is not greater." I wonder why they didn't put that in the Formula Palette box.

Find a product group in a lookup table

The Products worksheet contains the analyst's preparations for the product discount analysis.

Product discounts are based on the product line.

	A	B	C	D	E	F	G
1	Product	Line	Discount		Line	Discount	
2	Elephant	Animal			Animal	50%	
3	Giraffe	Animal			Vehicle	43%	
4	Zebra	Animal			Dinosaur	40%	
5	Aardvark	Animal					
6	Brontosaurus	Dinosaur					
7	Pteradon	Dinosaur					
8	Tyranosaurus	Dinosaur					
9	Airplane	Vehicle					
10	Train	Vehcle					
11	Automobile	Vehicle					

The list on the right shows the appropriate discount for each of three product lines. The list on the left shows several products, along with the product line for each product. You need to add formulas to column C to calculate the appropriate discount for each product. Once again, begin by naming the lookup table.

1   Activate the Products worksheet, select cell F1, press CTRL+SHIFT+*, click in the Name Box, type **ProductDiscounts**, and press ENTER.

This lookup appears to be essentially the same as the reseller discount lookup. You remember how the formula worked in that worksheet and decide to type a similar formula here.

2   Select cell C2, type the function **=VLOOKUP(Line,ProductDiscounts,2)**, and press ENTER.

The function returns the value 50%. That is correct. The formula appears to work properly.

3   Select cell C2, double-click the AutoFill handle, and check the discount percents.

	A	B	C	D	E	F	G
1	**Product**	**Line**	**Discount**		**Line**	**Discount**	
2	Elephant	Animal	50%		Animal	50%	
3	Giraffe	Animal	50%		Vehicle	43%	
4	Zebra	Animal	50%		Dinosaur	40%	
5	Aardvark	Animal	50%				
6	Brontosaurus	Dinosaur	50%				
7	Pteradon	Dinosaur	50%				
8	Tyranosaurus	Dinosaur	50%				
9	Airplane	Vehicle	43%				
10	Train	Vehcle	50%				
11	Automobile	Vehicle	43%				
12							

The dinosaur discounts are incorrect. A range lookup did not work.

Something is wrong. All the Dinosaur products show 50% discount, when they should be 40%. Cell C10 also has 50%, but it is a Vehicle. No, someone mistyped the product line as *Vehcle*. But shouldn't the formula display an error, rather than give a Train the Animal discount?

The lookup formula is treating this as a range lookup. When the function tries to find the discount for Dinosaur, it searches down the first column in the lookup table for the first value that is alphabetically greater than Dinosaur. Vehicle is. Then it backs up a row and gives 50% as the discount. Is there some way to tell the VLOOKUP function that you want to match only exact values?

Edit Formula

4   Select cell C2 and click the Edit Formula button, and click in the Range_lookup box.

The Range_lookup argument lets you search for an exact match.

VLOOKUP

Lookup_value	Line	= "Animal"
Table_array	ProductDiscounts	= {"Line","Discount";"A
Col_index_num	2	= 2
Range_lookup		= logical

= 0.5

Searches for a value in the leftmost column of a table, and then returns a value in the same row from a column you specify. By default, the table must be sorted in an ascending order.

Range_lookup is a logical value: to find the closest match in the first column (sorted in ascending order) = TRUE or omitted; find an exact match = FALSE.

Formula result =50%   [OK]   [Cancel]

The instructions say that in order to find an exact match, you must enter FALSE as the value of this argument.

5 In the Range_lookup box, type **FALSE**, click OK, and double-click the AutoFill handle.

	A	B	C	D	E	F	G
1	Product	Line	Discount		Line	Discount	
2	Elephant	Animal	50%		Animal	50%	
3	Giraffe	Animal	50%		Vehicle	43%	
4	Zebra	Animal	50%		Dinosaur	40%	
5	Aardvark	Animal	50%				
6	Brontosaurus	Dinosaur	40%				
7	Pteradon	Dinosaur	40%				
8	Tyranosaurus	Dinosaur	40%				
9	Airplane	Vehicle	43%				
10	Train	Vehcle	#N/A				
11	Automobile	Vehicle	43%				
12							

With Range_lookup set to FALSE, the VLOOKUP function produces the proper answers.

The discounts are all correct. Even cell C10 is correct in showing an error.

6 Change cell B10 to **Vehicle**.

There are two different types of lookups that you can do. On the one hand, if you are searching for a range, such as a volume discount or a tax rate or a card catalog grouping, you want a range lookup. On the other hand, if you are searching for a product number, or a telephone number, or a ZIP Code, you need an exact match. You can use the VLOOKUP function for either kind of lookup. Just use the Range_lookup argument to control which you want. For a range lookup, the lookup table must be sorted, but for an exact match lookup, the lookup table can be in any order you want.

Calculating a Trend

The final project is one you received from an analyst in the Planning department. The worksheet as you received it is on the Orders worksheet in the Lesson3 workbook.

	A	B	C	D	E
1	Day	Airplane	Train	Automobile	
2	1	132	105	161	
3	2	138	108	145	
4	3	105	114	171	
5	4	186	156	198	
6	5	153	137	172	
7	6	154	159	200	
8	7	181	151	204	
9	8	220	170	227	
10	9	285	201	218	
11	10	275	194	226	
12	11	221	201	240	
13	12	272	206	233	
14					

You need to project trends based on the early orders.

The planning analyst has daily order units for the first 12 days for each of three new projects. He wants to use the values from those first 12 days to extrapolate a trend for the next 6 days.

Use AutoFill to calculate a trend

You decide to show the analyst the easiest possible way to extrapolate a trend. If this is good enough, you may get to go home early. First create a simple chart so you can see whether the trend works correctly.

1 Activate the Orders tab in the Lesson3 workbook, and select cell A1.

2 On the Standard toolbar, click the Chart Wizard button. In the Chart Type list, select XY (Scatter), and select the last option in the Chart Sub-type palette (lines without markers). Then click Finish, and drag the top left corner of the chart to cell F1.

Chart Wizard

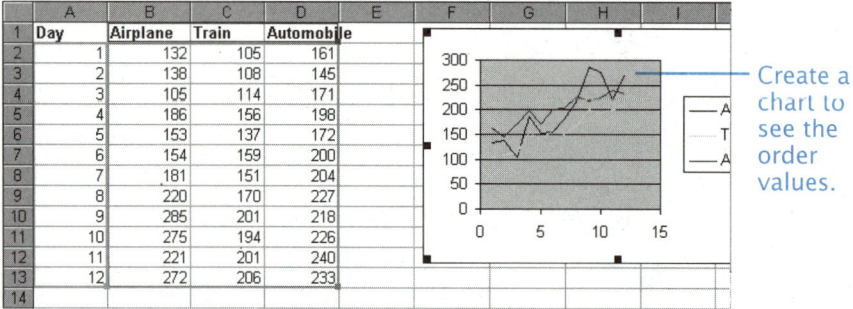

Create a chart to see the order values.

Excel creates a chart. When you use an XY chart, Excel spaces the numbers across the bottom based on their values, and not based on their position in the list.

Before continuing, why don't you make a copy of the worksheet?

3 Copy the Orders worksheet. (Hold down CTRL as you drag the sheet tab to the right.) Give the name **Trend** to the copy.

Now you can create the trend.

4 On the Trend worksheet, select the range A2:D13. Then drag the AutoFill handle down to the bottom of cell D19.

Excel fills the new cells in column A with incrementally numbered days, and the cells in columns B, C, and D with a straight-line extrapolation of the original numbers in each series.

You can adjust the chart to include the trend.

5 Click the chart. Drag the AutoFill handle at the lower right corner of the blue Range Finder box down to the bottom of cell D19.

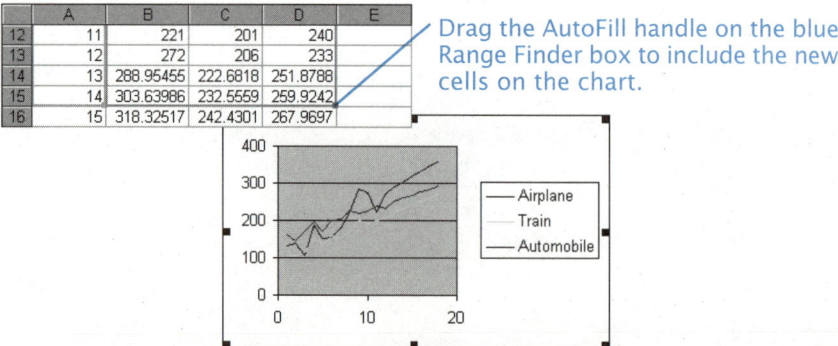

Drag the AutoFill handle on the blue Range Finder box to include the new cells on the chart.

The chart now includes the newly extrapolated trend values.

If all you need is a simple linear extrapolation of a trend, the easiest way to create it is by using the AutoFill handle to extend a range. You can also use the AutoFill handle of a Range Finder box to adjust the range that a chart plots.

Use a formula to calculate a trend

The planning analyst was exuberant when you showed him how easy it is to create a trend. Unfortunately, he explained, he would really like to be able to see the trend values not only for the future, but also for the period covered by the actual values. Fortunately, Excel has a function that will calculate a trend. This function is interesting, however, because it doesn't return a single value, the way most functions do, but it returns a whole series of values.

1   In cell E1, enter **Trend** as a label for a new column.

2   In cell E2, type the formula **=TREND(Airplane)** and press ENTER.

Excel calculates the number 112.7308. If you were to take the trend line calculated for days 13 to 18, and extend it back, this is what the value for day 1 would be.

3   Select cell E2, and double-click the AutoFill handle.

	A	B	C	D	E	F
1	Day	Airplane	Train	Automobi	Trend	
2	1	132	105	161	112.7308	
3	2	138	108	145	112.7308	
4	3	105	114	171	112.7308	
5	4	186	156	198	112.7308	

When you copy the formula, each cell gets the first value.

Excel fills all the cells from E2 to E19 with the number 112.7308. Each cell contains a new copy of the TREND function. Each cell independently calculates all the values of the trend, but then displays only the first value.

 TIP You can verify that each copy of the formula calculates multiple values. Select cell E2, click in the formula bar, and press F9. You see multiple values, separated by semicolons, and surrounded by braces. Each copy of the formula calculates all these numbers. Press ESC to restore the formula.

You need to give the formula enough cells to display all the answers it calculates. You need several cells to share a single formula. You share a formula between multiple cells by holding down CTRL and SHIFT as you press ENTER.

4 With cells E2:E19 selected, click in the formula bar, and then, while holding down both CTRL and SHIFT, press ENTER.

	E2	▼		= {=TREND(Airplane)}		
	A	B	C	D	E	F
14	13	288.95455	222.6818	251.8788	288.9545	
15	14	303.63986	232.5559	259.9242	303.6399	
16	15	318.32517	242.4301	267.9697	318.3252	
17	16	333.01049	252.3042	276.0152	333.0105	

To share the multiple values among multiple cells, enter the formula using CTRL+SHIFT+ENTER.

Excel fills the range with different values. The values for days 13 to 18 match the numbers in column B. All 18 cells share a single formula. If you look at the formula bar, you can see that the entire formula is enclosed in braces. Excel puts the braces there when you use CTRL+SHIFT+ENTER to enter a formula. This kind of formula is called an *array formula*.

NOTE Once you share a single formula among several cells by entering it as an array formula, you must then deal with the entire block of cells as a unit. You can delete all the cells at once, but not one at a time. If you try to clear, say, cell E5, Excel informs you that you cannot change part of an array.

Unfortunately, this TREND function is cheating just a little bit. If you clear cells B14:B19 (the cells that contain the trend values created by AutoFill), the TREND function will return an error. Let's see how to modify the TREND function so that it will create the proper answers even if cells B14:B19 are empty.

Edit Formula

5 Select cell E2 and click the Edit Formula button.

The TREND function's optional arguments let you control the input and output ranges.

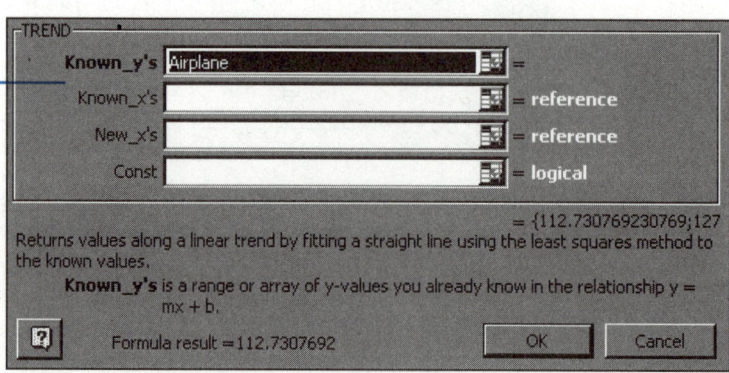

Excel displays the Formula Palette for the TREND function. The function accepts four arguments, only the first of which is required. When you use the TREND function with a single argument, the output series contains the same number of values as the input series. If you want the output series to contain more values than the input series, you use the first three arguments.

6 Drag the Formula Palette to the right so you can see the worksheet. The word Airplane should already be selected in the Known_y's box. Replace it by selecting the range B2:B13.

These are the order values for the first 12 days.

A trend calculates how much an output value (a *y* value) will change when an input value (an *x* value) changes. In this example, trying to estimate how much orders (the *y* value) will change when the number of days since introduction (the *x* value) changes.

7 Click in the Known_x's box. Select the range A2:A13.

These are the day numbers that correspond to the order values in the first argument.

8 Click in the New_x's box. Select the range A2:A19. Then click OK.

> **NOTE** Because you had already used CTRL+SHIFT+ENTER to enter the array formula once, the Formula Palette knows to reenter the formula as an array formula. If you were creating the TREND formula for the first time, you would need to hold down CTRL and SHIFT as you click OK to create the array formula.

The new *x* values are the days you want to calculate orders for. The new *x* values can overlap the original *x* values, or they can be completely distinct. The TREND function will return one value for each of the values in this range.

The final revised formula is =TREND(B2:B13,A2:A13,A2:A19). When you see it in the formula bar, it has braces around it to remind you that several cells are sharing it. The numbers returned by this revised formula are the same as the ones from the =TREND(Airplane) formula you originally entered, but this one will keep working even if you clear cells B14:B19.

If you don't need to see the trend numbers, you can add a trend line directly on the chart.

Now you can make the chart include the new column.

9 Click the edge of the chart. Drag the AutoFill handle of the blue Range Finder box to the right of cell E19. Then save the Lesson3 workbook.

The Trend line extends through all the data points.

When you use the TREND function to calculate a trend, you can control which values to use as the known *x* and *y* values, and which to use as the new *x* values. Because the TREND function produces multiple values, you must share the formula between several cells by using CTRL+SHIFT+ENTER.

 TIP You may want to reduce the number of cells that share an array formula, without simply deleting the formula. Select all the cells that share the formula, then click in the formula bar, and press CTRL+ENTER. (Using CTRL+ENTER copies the formula into all the cells at one time, thus avoiding the error message that comes from changing a single cell in an array formula.) Clear the cells you don't want to include. Select the remaining cells, click in the formula bar, and press CTRL+SHIFT+ENTER to reenter the formula as an array formula.

Calculate a slope and intercept

Once again, the planning analyst is most grateful for your work. Once again, however, he suggests that there really is one more, surely trivial, improvement he would like to see. He would like to tinker with the slope of the trend line. "I'm a little concerned the trend may not continue quite that strong. Is there a way I can see what the slope is and be able to adjust it?"

When the TREND function calculates a line, it really calculates two numbers—a *slope* and an *intercept*—and then uses those two numbers to calculate the line. The slope tells you how much the output *(y)* value changes for each single unit change in the input *(x)* value. The intercept tells you the output value when the input value is zero. Excel has a different function that will tell you the slope and intercept values, and you can then use those values to calculate the line on your own.

You figure that this "trivial" enhancement might warrant working on a new copy of the worksheet.

1 Create a copy of the Orders worksheet (not the Trend worksheet) and give the name **Slope** to the new copy.

You need a place to store the slope and intercept values for each of the three products.

2 On the Slope worksheet, select the range A1:A3. On the Insert menu, click Rows. Enter **Slope** in cell A1 and **Intercept** in cell A2.

The function that calculates the slope and the intercept is called *LINEST*, which is short for *linear estimation*, the mathematical technique that Excel uses to calculate a trend.

Enter

3 Select cell B1, type the formula =**LINEST(Airplane)** and click the Enter button.

To calculate the slope of a range use the LINEST function.

	A	B	C	D	E
	B1		=	=LINEST(Airplane)	
1	Slope	14.685315			
2	Intercept				

For a demonstration of how to enter the LINEST array formula, double-click the Excel Camcorder Files shortcut on your Desktop or connect to the Internet address listed on page xvi.

Excel calculates the number 14.685315. This is the slope. This is how much, on average, each day's orders exceed those of the previous day.

The LINEST function also produces the intercept, but you must share the formula between two cells in order to see both the slope and the intercept. But should the cells be side-by-side, or up-and-down? The easiest way to find out, when you are using an unfamiliar function, is to try both.

	A	B	C	D	E
1	Slope	14.685315	98.04545	#N/A	
2	Intercept	14.685315	98.04545	#N/A	
3		14.685315	98.04545	#N/A	
4					

The LINEST function produces two numbers in a single row. Excel can duplicate values from a single row into multiple rows.

4 Select the range B1:D3. Click in the formula bar and press CTRL+SHIFT+ENTER.

The number in cell B1 is the slope, and the number in cell C1 is the intercept. (According to this calculation, on day zero you would have sold 98 airplanes.)

85

The LINEST function returns an array that is two cells wide and one cell tall. When you share an array over too many cells, Excel follows a simple rule: If a dimension contains a single item, repeat the item to fill all the available cells; if a dimension contains more than one item, fill the additional cells with the #N/A error value. The array returned by LINEST has a single row, so that row is repeated through all three rows of the range. Conversely, the array has two columns, so the third column is filled with #N/A.

The values would fit much better at the top of the worksheet if they were flipped, or transposed. Believe it or not, Excel has a TRANSPOSE function that swaps the rows and columns of an array.

Undo

5 Click the Undo button to restore the formula to a single cell. Select the range B1:B2. In the formula bar, click immediately after the equal sign and type **TRANSPOSE(**. Click after the closing parenthesis and type **)**, and then press CTRL+SHIFT+ENTER.

Use the TRANSPOSE function to convert columns to rows.

The final formula is *=TRANSPOSE(LINEST(Airplane))*. This calculates the slope and the intercept, based on the numbers in the Airplane column, transposes the resulting two values, and shares them into cells B1 and B2.

6 Drag the AutoFill handle from cell B2 to the right of cell D2.

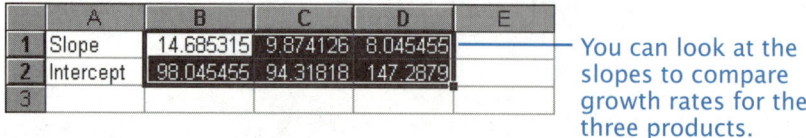

You can look at the slopes to compare growth rates for the three products.

The formulas calculate the slope and intercept for trains and automobiles. Just by looking at the slopes and intercepts, you can see that automobiles got off to a better start than airplanes (the intercept for automobiles is much higher than for airplanes), but that sales for airplanes have been growing faster than sales for automobiles (the slope for airplanes is higher than for automobiles).

The LINEST function is like the TREND function in that both calculate a straight line based on pairings of *x* and *y* values. Both also return multiple values and must be shared over multiple cells with CTRL+SHIFT+ENTER. The

TREND function calculates the new trend values directly, and the LINEST function gives you the tools to calculate a trend on your own.

Use a slope to create a trend

You now need to create the formulas that calculate a line based on a slope and intercept. The standard formula for a straight line is $y=ax+b$, where a is the slope, b is the intercept, x is the input value, and y is the calculated value. In other words, multiply the day number by the slope, and add the intercept.

First you need to create some new day numbers. Since you used column labels as arguments to the LINEST function, you must leave a blank row in the worksheet, so the LINEST function won't try to extend the list of input values past the 12th.

1   In cell A18, enter **13**, and in cell A19, enter **14**. Select A18:A19, and drag the AutoFill handle down to the bottom of cell A23.

This creates a new list of output days. If you think closely about what just happened, you'll realize that AutoFill just calculated a trend based on the numbers 13 and 14.

Now you can add the formula, using absolute labels so you can copy it to other cells.

2   Select cell B18, type **=$Day*$Slope+$Intercept** and press ENTER.

The formula calculates 288.95455. This is the same number you got when you used AutoFill and TREND to calculate the trend.

3   Double-click the AutoFill handle on cell B18, and then drag the AutoFill handle to the right of cell D23.

The formula calculates correct trend values for each of the cells.

You can add the new values to the chart.

4   Click the chart, and drag the AutoFill handle on the blue Range Finder box to the bottom of cell D23.

A blank row on the worksheet produces a gap on the chart.

The chart now shows both the actual and the projected values, with a gap between the two.

TIP If you want to get rid of the gap caused by a blank cell, click the chart. Then on the Tools menu, click Options, and select the Chart tab. Select the Plot Empty Cells As Interpolated option, and click OK.

Suppose you want to change the Train projection to have a much lower rate of increase. Before you can manipulate the slope and intercept values, you must convert the formula to values. Copying a range, and then using Paste Special to paste just the values converts the formulas into values. Pressing the ESC key removes the copy border.

Copy

5 Select cells C1:C2. Click the Copy button. Then right-click cell C1 and click Paste Special. In the dialog box, select the Paste Values option, and click OK. Then press the ESC key.

To convert formulas to values, use the Paste Special command.

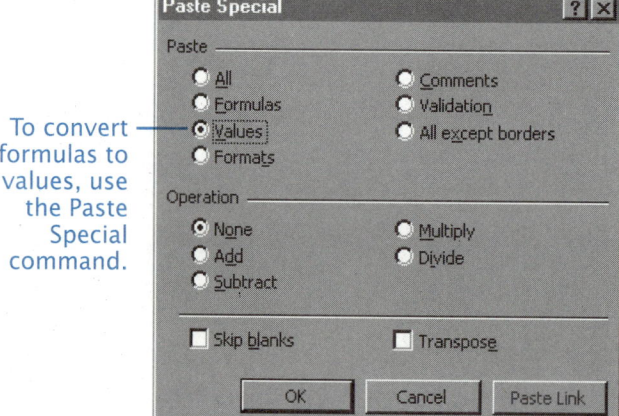

You can now modify the slope and intercept to create the trend you want.

6 In cell C1, enter **2**, and in cell C2, enter **180**

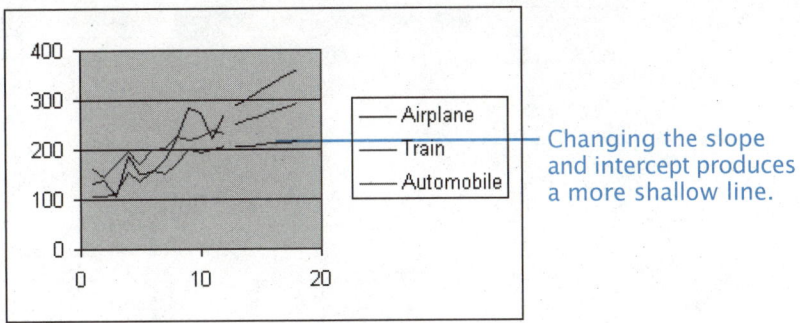

Changing the slope and intercept produces a more shallow line.

The line for Train slopes much more gradually. To visualize what is happening, project the trend line back to the left edge of the graph and imagine a pivot pin stuck right there. As you change the slope, the pivot pin does not move, and the whole line tilts to the new slope. To slide the pivot pin up or down, you change the intercept.

7 Save the Lesson3 workbook.

You can now give the worksheet to the Planning analyst. He can either use the trend generated by the TREND function, or he can fiddle with the slope and intercept to get just the effect that managers want to see.

You made it through the whole stack of projects. You were able to come up with an effective solution for each one. You deserve to have a plaque over your desk proclaiming you the Office Excel Expert.

One Step Further: Manipulating Text

Your boss just came to your desk and thanked you for the great work. He hesitates as he prepares to leave and then informs you that your labors have earned you a new plaque over your desk. Actually, one of the human resource management persons in the Personnel department has just created a new motivational program. One of the rewards is a personalized plaque bearing the name of one of the current justices of the United States Supreme Court. He would like to give you one of the plaques, but the people in Personnel are having a hard time getting the names right. You will get your reward as soon as you help them create formulas to manipulate the names of the judges. In the Lesson3 workbook, the Judges worksheet shows the worksheet as you received it from the person in Personnel.

You need to convert the names so that the first name comes first.

	A	B	C	D	E
1	Name	LastName	FirstName	FullName	
2	Breyer, Steven				
3	Ginsburg, Ruth Bader				
4	Kennedy, Anthony M.				
5	O'Conner, Sandra Day				
6	Rehnquist, William Hubbs				
7	Scalia, Antonin				
8	Souter, David Hackett				
9	Stevens, John Paul				
10	Thomas, Clarence				
11					

The source list of the justices' names has the last name first—presumably so the list could be sorted. The plaques should have the first name first. Rather than have someone retype all the names, they want you to come up with formulas to convert the names into the proper form. First, you must split the names from the list into separate first and last names. Then you can recombine the names in the appropriate order.

Find a comma in a name

The comma is the key to splitting the name. The last name is everything in front of the comma. The first name (which may include a middle name) is everything after the comma. First, insert a new column where you can put a formula to find where the comma is in each name.

1   Activate the Judges worksheet and select cell B1. On the Insert menu, click Columns, and enter **Comma** in cell B1. Then double-click the border between the headings of columns B and C to shrink column B.

Excel has a function named SEARCH that will search for one or more characters within a text string.

Edit Formula

2   Select cell B2 and click the Edit Formula button. Click the arrow next to the list of functions and select More Functions. In the Function Category list, select Text, and in the Function Name list, select SEARCH. Then click OK.

The Formula Palette appears. The SEARCH function has two required arguments: what you want to search for, and where you want to search for it.

3   In the Find_text box, type a comma (,) and press TAB.

Excel adds quotation marks around the comma. You could have typed the quotation marks, but if Excel will do it for you, why bother?

4   In the Within_text box, type **Name**—the label at the top of the column of names—and press TAB.

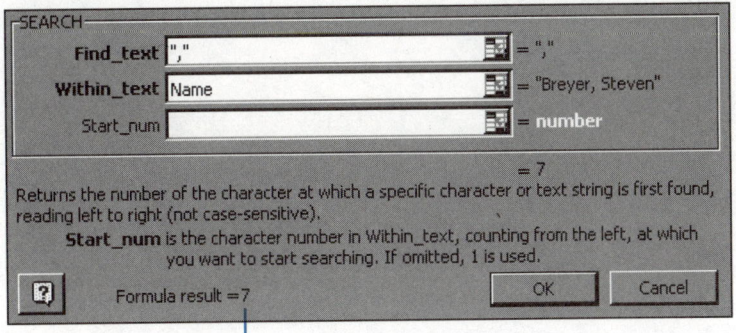

Use the SEARCH function to find the location
of one or more characters within a text string.

The Start_num box is for when you want to search for, say, the second comma in a cell. In this case, you want to find the first comma, so you can leave this box empty.

5   Click OK to enter the formula in cell B2, and then double-click the AutoFill handle to find the commas for the rest of the judges.

NOTE   Excel has a function named FIND that is almost identical to the SEARCH function. The only difference is that FIND searches for an exact match of uppercase and lowercase letters, whereas SEARCH ignores case. When you search for something like a comma, the functions are interchangeable.

Edit Formula

If you know the name of a function, but want help with the arguments, you can type the function name before clicking the Edit Formula button.

Extract the pieces of a name

Once you know where the comma is in a name, you can extract everything to the left of the comma into the LastName column, and everything to the right of the comma into the FirstName column. To extract characters from the left of a cell, you use the LEFT function.

1   In cell C2, the first cell in the LastName column, type =**LEFT** and click the Edit Formula button.

Excel displays the Formula Palette.

2   As the Text argument, type **Name** and press the TAB key.

3   As the Num_chars argument, type **Comma** and do *not* press ENTER.

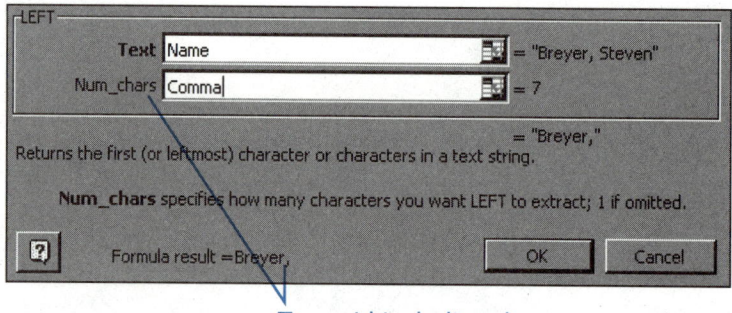

To avoid including the comma, subtract
1 from the Num_chars argument.

To the right of the argument box, the Formula Palette shows you that the current value of the Comma column is 7. Just below that, you can see that the result of the function is "Breyer," including the comma. Since the comma is in the seventh position, extracting seven letters includes the comma.

4 Type **-1**, watch the comma disappear in the function result, and click OK.

To extract the right portion of the name, you could use Excel's RIGHT function, but then you would also have to use the LEN function and subtract the position of the comma. An easier approach is to use the MID function to start extracting from the middle of the cell.

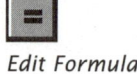

Edit Formula

5 Select cell D2, type **=MID**, and click the Edit Formula button.

You tell the MID function the text you want to dissect, the position of the first character that you want, and the number of characters that you want. If you want more characters than are in the text, the function simply stops when it gets to the end anyway. It is highly unlikely that a Supreme Court justice would have a name with more than a thousand characters, so using 1000 as the third argument is safe.

6 Type **Name** in the Text box, type **Comma** in the Start_num box, and type **1000** in the Num_chars box, but do not click OK.

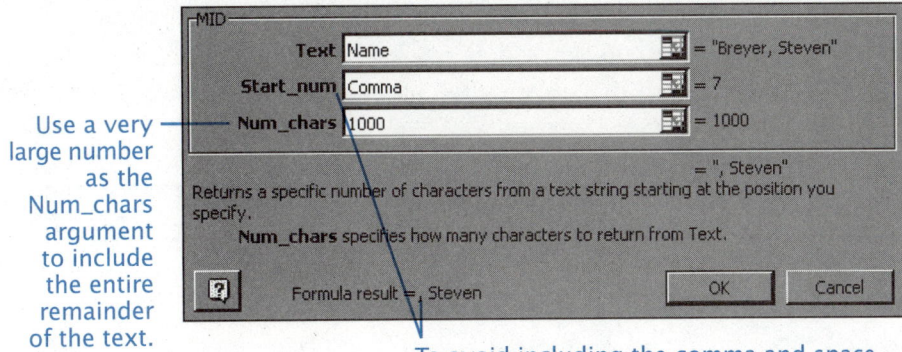

Use a very large number as the Num_chars argument to include the entire remainder of the text.

To avoid including the comma and space, add 2 to the Start_num argument.

The result of the formula, however, is ", Steven". It includes the comma and the space. You don't want to start extracting until two characters after that.

7   After the word *Comma* in the Start_num box, type **+2** and click OK.

8   Select cells C2:D2, and double-click the AutoFill handle.

You now have the names of all the justices, split into first and last names.

Between the SEARCH function, the LEFT function, and the MID function, you have the tools to split up the text in any cell by any fragment. This process is almost exactly identical to that used by molecular biologists as they use enzymes to split a DNA molecule into fragments. You should write and tell your mother that you are a virtual genetic engineer.

Reconstruct a name

The representative in the Personnel department wants complete names to put onto the plaques. You still need to combine the fragmented names into a complete whole.

Edit Formula

1   Select cell E2 and click the Edit Formula button.

Even without a function, the Formula Palette can help you see the result of a function before you actually enter it into a cell.

Combining two words is very similar to combining two numbers, except that instead of using a plus sign, you use an ampersand (&).

2   Type **FirstName&LastName**, but do not press ENTER. First, look at the result of the formula.

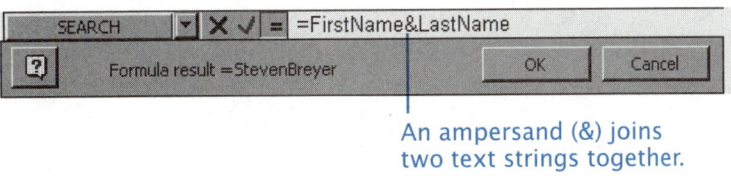

An ampersand (&) joins two text strings together.

The formula result is =StevenBreyer, with no space between the names. You need to insert a space, once again adding an ampersand as the glue.

3   Click after the ampersand, and type " "&

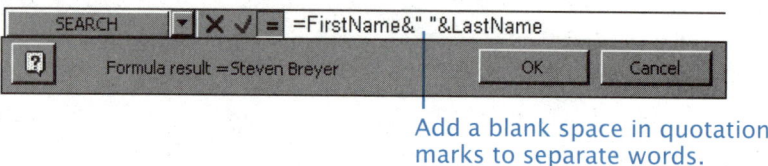

Add a blank space in quotation marks to separate words.

The final formula should be =FirstName&" "&LastName.

4   Click OK, and then double-click the AutoFill handle.

You now have a beautiful list of names to give to your contact in Personnel. The list can be sorted either by first name or by last name.

You are concerned, however, that the Comma column may be distracting.

5   Select cell B1. On the Format menu, point to Column, and then click Hide.

6   Save and close the Lesson3 workbook.

The list is finished, and the formulas are ready to do their work, in case the Supreme Court should happen to add additional justices. You will get your plaque in 6 to 8 weeks. Today, you get to go home.

Lesson Summary

To	Do this
Enter a function into a cell	Click the Edit Formula button. Select a function from the list of common functions, or click More Functions and select a function from the list.
Move the Formula Palette so you can see worksheet cells	Click the background of the palette and drag it.
Calculate the monthly payment for a loan	Select the PMT function.
Change the result of a formula to a desired goal	On the Tools menu, click Goal Seek, and follow the instructions in the dialog box.
Calculate the interest for a specific period	Multiply the starting balance for that period times the interest rate for that period.
Calculate the principal payment for a specific period	Subtract the interest amount for the period from the total loan payment.

To	Do this
Move to the bottom cell in a list	Double-click the bottom border of a cell.
Calculate a date, given the year, month, and day	Use the DATE function.
Calculate the year portion of a date	Use the YEAR function.
Calculate the month portion of a date	Use the Month function.
Calculate the last day of the previous month	Use the DATE function, specifying 0 as the day.
Create random numbers between 0 and 100	Use the formula =RAND()*100.
Round numbers to the nearest thousand	Use the ROUND function with –3 as the value of the Num_digits argument.
Use a function as an argument to another function (nest functions)	Click in the argument box of the Formula Palette. Then click the list of functions.
Return to the main function in the Formula Palette after entering a nested function	Click in the white area of the formula bar.
Look up a value within a range	Use the VLOOKUP function with True as the value of the Range argument.
Look up the exact match for a value	Use the VLOOKUP function with False as the value of the Range argument.
Calculate a trend continuing from a series of numbers	Select the numbers and drag the AutoFill handle down.
Calculate a trend that automatically recalculates	Use the TREND function.
When a formula returns multiple values, share that formula between multiple cells	Hold down CTRL and SHIFT as you enter the formula.
Calculate the slope and intercept for a series of numbers	Use the LINEST function.
Transpose a range of numbers	Use the TRANSPOSE function.
Calculate a trend for values in a Day column, given slope and intercept values	Use the formula =Day*Slope+Intercept.

To	Do this
Convert formulas to values	Copy the cells and use the Paste Special command to paste the values.
Find the location of a text string within another text string	Use the SEARCH function.
Extract characters from the left part of a text string	Use the LEFT function.
Extract characters from the middle or right part of a text string	Use the MID function.
Join two text strings together	Use an ampersand (&) to join the text.

For online information about	On the Help menu, click Contents And Index, click the Index tab, and then type
Worksheet functions	functions, overview
Nesting functions	functions, using as arguments

Enhancing the Look of a Page

Part 2

Manipulating Lists

Estimated time
35 min.

In this lesson you will learn how to:

- Sort lists in both alphabetical and custom orders.
- Summarize lists using Subtotals.
- Filter lists using AutoFilters.
- Filter lists using Advanced Filters.

It's quarterly planning time. Each quarter the Manufacturing and Marketing departments request projections of how many of each of Tailspin Toys' products will be ordered by each of the resellers. The Order Processing department has provided you with a list of resellers and products, along with the average number of units of each product that each reseller ordered each quarter for the past year. These averages will form the basis of the fourth quarter plans. You need to review the list, convert the numbers to monthly projections, and adjust quantities for different resellers based on information the resellers have sent you.

Start the lesson

➤ Start Microsoft Excel, change to the Excel AT Practice folder, and open the Start4 workbook. Save a copy of the workbook as **Lesson4**

Sorting and Subtotaling a List

Before you start manipulating numbers in the list, you want to look over the numbers that are already there. Sorting and subtotaling the list can help you get a sense of how the resellers and the products compare.

Sort multiple columns

The list you received is on the Plan worksheet of the Lesson4 workbook.

The original list is unsorted.

	A	B	C	D	E	F
1	Product	Line	Reseller	Channel	Contract	QtrAvg
2	Pteradon	Dinosaur	Hiabuv Toys	Toys	C5055	7,650
3	Elephant	Animal	West Coast Sal	Distrib	C5017	1,650
4	Tyranosaurus	Dinosaur	Wide World Imp	Distrib	C5068	300
5	Aardvark	Animal	Baldwin Museur	Museums	C5028	7,350
6	Brontosaurus	Dinosaur	West Coast Sal	Distrib	C5017	4,050
7	Elephant	Animal	Industrial Smoke	Retail	C5038	-
8	Pteradon	Dinosaur	Wide World Imp	Distrib	C5068	450
9	Giraffe	Animal	Main Street Mar	Retail	C5080	900

It's hard to tell how the list as you received it is sorted. For all you know, the list is in random order. You can start by sorting by the reseller name. The easiest way to sort a column in a list is to use the Sort Ascending button.

Sort Ascending

1 Click the *Reseller* heading (cell C1), and then click the Sort Ascending button.

	A	B	C	D	E	F
1	Product	Line	Reseller	Channel	Contract	QtrAvg
2	Automobile	Vehicle	Adventure Work	Retail	C5044	2,250
3	Pteradon	Dinosaur	Adventure Work	Retail	C5044	10,650
4	Tyranosaurus	Dinosaur	Adventure Work	Retail	C5044	1,950
5	Brontosaurus	Dinosaur	Adventure Work	Retail	C5044	4,350

You select a single cell and Excel figures out the list boundaries and the heading row.

As long as blank cells (or the edge of the worksheet) surround the list, Excel can figure out the list that you want to sort. In most cases, Excel guesses correctly whether or not the list has a row of headings.

TIP If you have a row of headings and want to ensure that Excel will interpret the row as headings, format the cells bold.

Now the list is sorted by resellers, but Retail resellers are intermixed with Museums and other resellers. Perhaps the list would be easier to understand if all the resellers for a single channel were sorted together. When you sort by channel, the resellers remain sorted within a given channel.

2 Click the Channel heading (cell D1), and then click the Sort Ascending button.

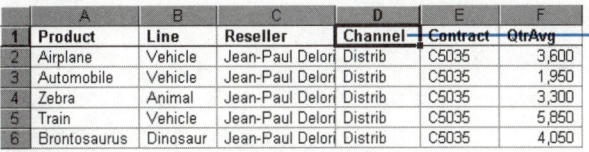

	A	B	C	D	E	F
1	Product	Line	Reseller	Channel	Contract	QtrAvg
2	Airplane	Vehicle	Jean-Paul Delori	Distrib	C5035	3,600
3	Automobile	Vehicle	Jean-Paul Delori	Distrib	C5035	1,950
4	Zebra	Animal	Jean-Paul Delori	Distrib	C5035	3,300
5	Train	Vehicle	Jean-Paul Delori	Distrib	C5035	5,850
6	Brontosaurus	Dinosaur	Jean-Paul Delori	Distrib	C5035	4,050

Sorting by Channel leaves Resellers sorted within each Channel.

Now all the Distrib (distributor) resellers are at the top, sorted alphabetically within the channel. The Jean-Paul Deloria reseller is at the top of the list, but the products and product lines for that reseller are in random order.

You can sort by as many columns as you want, as long as you start with the most detailed column and end with the most general column. If you want the products sorted by line for each reseller, you sort four times.

3 Sort by Product, then by Line, then by Reseller, and finally by Channel.

TIP To sort multiple columns quickly, use one hand to press the arrow keys to change the active cell, and the other hand to click the Sort Ascending button. A two-handed combination of keyboard and mouse can be much more efficient than either the keyboard or the mouse on its own.

	A	B	C	D	E	F
1	Product	Line	Reseller	Channel	Contract	QtrAvg
2	Aardvark	Animal	Jean-Paul Delori	Distrib	C5035	4,200
3	Elephant	Animal	Jean-Paul Delori	Distrib	C5035	1,050
4	Giraffe	Animal	Jean-Paul Delori	Distrib	C5035	1,650
5	Zebra	Animal	Jean-Paul Delori	Distrib	C5035	3,300
6	Brontosaurus	Dinosaur	Jean-Paul Delori	Distrib	C5035	4,050
7	Pteradon	Dinosaur	Jean-Paul Delori	Distrib	C5035	6,000

To sort multiple columns, sort the major column last.

Once again, Jean-Paul Deloria is at the top of the list, but now all the animals, properly sorted, are together at the top.

The column that you sort last is called the *major key*. Columns that you sort earlier are called *minor keys*.

Sort in a custom order

When you use the Sort Ascending button, Excel sorts in alphabetical order. That makes the product lines appear in the order *Animal*, *Dinosaur*, and *Vehicle*. The owner of the company, however, is very partial to dinosaurs. Because of that, official publications always show the product lines in the order *Dinosaur*, *Animal*, and *Vehicle*. That sequence is not alphabetical at all. You can create a list of words in whatever order you want, and make Excel sort using your custom sort order. Start by creating the sample list.

1 Enter **Dinosaur** into cell I2, **Animal** into cell I3, and **Vehicle** into cell I4.

2 Select the range I2:I4.

3 On the Tools menu, click Options. Then select the Custom Lists tab.

To create a custom sort list, put the list on the worksheet...

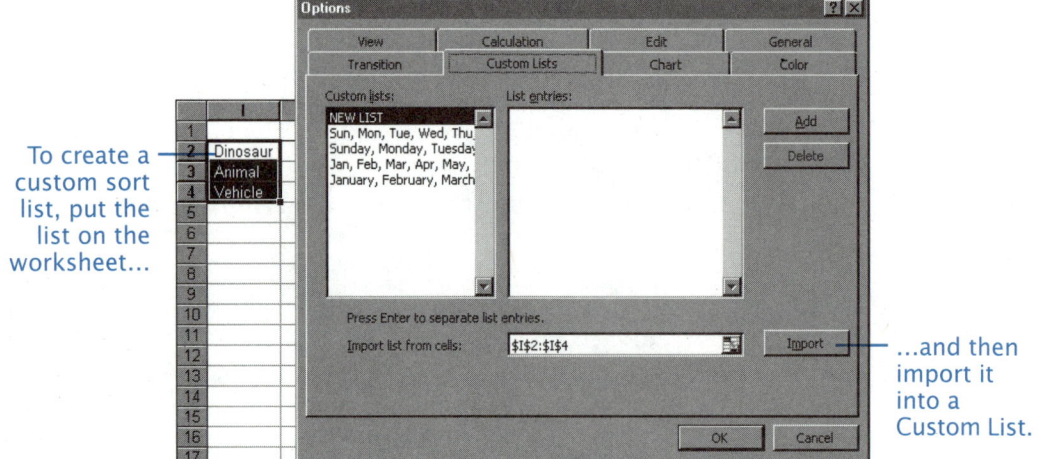

...and then import it into a Custom List.

Excel comes with custom lists for the names of weeks and months already included. You can also add any lists of your own that you want. If you had not typed the list items into the worksheet, you could type them directly into the List Entries box, pressing ENTER after each item. But because you entered the items into the worksheet, you can simply import the list by clicking the Import button.

You can also click Cancel to close the dialog box.

4 Click the Import button. Then click OK.

You now have a custom list built into your working environment. When you exit, Excel stores the list on your computer. The list will be available until you delete it, regardless of which workbook is open.

5 Press DELETE to clear the range I2:I4.

You can't use a toolbar button to sort using a custom list. You must use the Sort dialog box.

6 Select cell A1 (or any single cell within the list). On the Data menu, click Sort.

The Sort dialog box lets you sort in ascending or descending order by up to three keys.

But you can specify a custom sort order only for the first key. You must be sure that you specify the column that contains the custom sort values for the first key in the Sort dialog box.

7 In the Sort By list, select Line.

To specify a custom sort, you must use the Sort Options dialog box.

8   Click Options. In the First Key Sort Order list, select Dinosaur, Animal, Vehicle. Then click OK twice.

To sort by a custom list, use the Sort dialog box to specify the column...

...and then click the Options button to select the sort order.

Excel sorts the list by product line, with dinosaurs at the top. The resellers and channels are now spread out. To put them back on the top, you must once again go through the remaining keys.

9   Sort by the Reseller column, and then by the Channel column.

The custom sort order puts Dinosaur before Animal.

	A	B	C	D	E	F
1	Product	Line	Reseller	Channel	Contract	QtrAvg
2	Brontosaurus	Dinosaur	Jean-Paul Delori	Distrib	C5035	4,050
3	Pteradon	Dinosaur	Jean-Paul Delori	Distrib	C5035	6,000
4	Tyranosaurus	Dinosaur	Jean-Paul Delori	Distrib	C5035	2,400
5	Aardvark	Animal	Jean-Paul Delori	Distrib	C5035	4,200
6	Elephant	Animal	Jean-Paul Delori	Distrib	C5035	1,050

The list is now sorted with Jean-Paul Deloria, the first reseller in the distributor channel, at the top. Within each reseller, the product lines are in the company standard order, and within each product line, the products are in alphabetical order.

Creating a custom list is not difficult. If you frequently need to sort a list in a particular way, create a custom list. However, if you give the workbook to someone else, the custom list will not go with it. A custom list is a part of your working environment, not the workbook.

TIP After you create a custom list, you can use the AutoFill handle to extend the list. With the list *Dinosaur, Animal, Vehicle* created on your computer, if you type **Dinosaur** into a cell and then drag the AutoFill handle, Excel will extend the list with the custom items, in the correct order.

Subtotal a sorted list

Now that your list is sorted by reseller and by product line, you might want to see how big each reseller is. Excel can add subtotals each time the value in a column changes. To add subtotals, you first sort the list by the column you want to use to group the subtotal, and then use the Subtotal command on the Data menu. In this case, you've already sorted the list.

1 Select cell A1 (or any single cell in the list). On the Data menu, click Subtotals.

2 In the Subtotal dialog box, select Reseller from the At Each Change In list. Leave the default value for all the other options, and click OK.

Excel adds a new row after each reseller and includes a total of the units for that reseller. Just below the Name Box, the numbers 1, 2, and 3 appear. These correspond to different levels of detail. Level 1 is for the grand total of all rows. Level 2 is for the reseller totals. Level 3 is for the detail.

Outline numbers appear for each level of summary...

		A	B	C	D	E	F
	1	Product	Line	Reseller	Channel	Contract	QtrAvg
	2	Brontosaurus	Dinosaur	Jean-Paul Delori	Distrib	C5035	4,050
	3	Pteradon	Dinosaur	Jean-Paul Delori	Distrib	C5035	6,000
	4	Tyranosaurus	Dinosaur	Jean-Paul Delori	Distrib	C5035	2,400
	5	Aardvark	Animal	Jean-Paul Delori	Distrib	C5035	4,200
	6	Elephant	Animal	Jean-Paul Delori	Distrib	C5035	1,050
	7	Giraffe	Animal	Jean-Paul Delori	Distrib	C5035	1,650
	8	Zebra	Animal	Jean-Paul Delori	Distrib	C5035	3,300
	9	Airplane	Vehicle	Jean-Paul Delori	Distrib	C5035	3,600
	10	Automobile	Vehicle	Jean-Paul Delori	Distrib	C5035	1,950
	11	Train	Vehicle	Jean-Paul Delori	Distrib	C5035	5,850
	12			**Jean-Paul Deloria Total**			34,050
	13	Brontosaurus	Dinosaur	Lakes & Sons	Distrib	C5004	900
	14	Pteradon	Dinosaur	Lakes & Sons	Distrib	C5004	2,700

...along with new total rows.

3   Click the number 2 under the Name Box.

Click the outline number to show only the totals.

		A	B	C	D	E	F
	1	Product	Line	Reseller	Channel	Contract	QtrAvg
	12			**Jean-Paul Deloria Total**			34,050
	23			**Lakes & Sons Total**			17,400
	34			**West Coast Sales Total**			35,700
	45			**Wide World Importers Total**			3,300

Excel hides all the detail rows, leaving only the reseller totals and the grand total. To show the detail for only one reseller, click the plus sign to the left of the total for that reseller.

4   Click the plus sign to the left of row 23, Lakes & Son.

Click the plus sign next to the total row to show the detail. Click the minus sign to hide the detail.

		A	B	C	D	E	F
	19	Zebra	Animal	Lakes & Sons	Distrib	C5004	2,100
	20	Airplane	Vehicle	Lakes & Sons	Distrib	C5004	1,350
	21	Automobile	Vehicle	Lakes & Sons	Distrib	C5004	750
	22	Train	Vehicle	Lakes & Sons	Distrib	C5004	3,750
	23			**Lakes & Sons Total**			17,400
	34			**West Coast Sales Total**			35,700

Excel unhides the detail rows. To show all the detail rows, click the number for the lowest level of detail.

5   Click the number 3 under the Name Box.

Suppose you want to see how Jean-Paul Deloria is doing for each product line. Since the list is sorted by product line within the reseller, you can add an additional level of totals.

6   Select any single cell within the list. On the Data menu, click Subtotals. In the At Each Change In list, select Line. Clear the Replace Current Subtotals check box. Click OK.

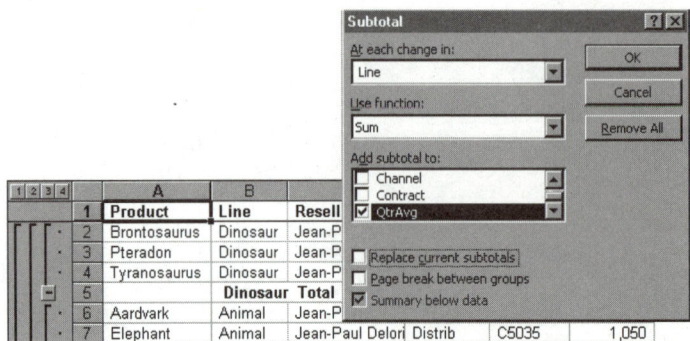

Excel adds total rows each time the product line name changes. You end up with several totals for Dinosaur, one for each reseller. If you didn't sort the list before adding a subtotal, the Subtotal command would add a new total row each time the value in the list changed.

When you add a second set of totals, Excel adds another number below the Name Box, representing another level of detail.

The list with subtotals is sorted in a particular order. What if you decide that you want to sort it differently, say, by Product? Excel will let you sort the list, but it first removes all the subtotals.

Totals Without Double-Counting

The totals that appear in a subtotaled list are all formulas. If you change one of the detail rows, the total changes. If the total formula used the SUM function, the grand total would sum up not only the detail rows, but also the intermediate subtotals. Instead, Excel uses a special function that avoids double counting: the SUBTOTAL function. As the SUBTOTAL function adds the numbers in a range, it ignores any cell that itself contains the SUBTOTAL function.

The one SUBTOTAL function can be used for several different types of aggregation: summing, counting, averaging, and so forth. When you use the Subtotal dialog box, the item you select in the Use Function list determines which kind of aggregation Excel will use for the SUBTOTAL functions.

The Subtotal command creates formulas for you, but you can create formulas using the SUBTOTAL function yourself, any time you want to avoid double counting. The function's first argument specifies the kind of aggregation. The most common arguments are 9 (SUM), 1 (AVERAGE), and 2 (COUNT).

7 Select cell A1, the Product heading, and click the Sort Ascending button. Click OK when Excel warns you that this will remove the subtotals.

The list is now back to the way it was before you added the subtotals.

8 Save the Lesson4 workbook.

 TIP To remove subtotals without the cautionary message, on the Data menu, select Subtotals, and click the Remove All button in the Subtotal dialog box.

Excel has another tool for subtotaling a list—the PivotTable dynamic views report, which you will learn about in Lesson 5. For complex analyses, the PivotTable report is easier to use than the Subtotals command. But if all you need is a quick way to see the totals in a list, you can easily add a subtotal, zoom in and out on the numbers, and then remove the subtotals from the list.

Filtering a List

You have looked at the list long enough. It's time to start changing some numbers. You need to create monthly numbers for the company's fourth fiscal quarter, June, July, and August. For most of the resellers, the future plan will be based on the previous year's average orders. Some resellers, however, have given you specific information.

Add columns to the list

The list you received has a single column with quantities. The QtrAvg column contains the average quarterly units of a particular product that a particular reseller bought in the previous twelve months. You need to create additional columns for the three months of the coming fiscal quarter. You can start by using AutoFill to create column headings for the months.

1 Enter **Jun** in cell G1. Then drag the AutoFill handle to the right of cell I1 to create Jun, Jul, and Aug headings.

As a starting point for the plan, you want to fill the three new columns with the average orders for a single month. In other words, you want to divide the QtrAvg column by 3.

You need to select all the values in the QtrAvg column (not including the heading), so that you can use the AutoFill handle to copy them to the new columns. You already know that you can double-click the bottom border of a cell to jump to the last cell in the list. But if you hold down SHIFT as you double-click, Excel selects all the cells down to the last cell in the list.

For a demonstration of how to divide a block of cells by a number, double-click the Excel Camcorder Files shortcut on your Desktop or connect to the Internet address listed on page xvi.

2 Select cell F2. Hold down SHIFT, and double-click the bottom border of the cell.

Excel selects all the cells from F2 to F141, the bottom of the list.

3 Drag the AutoFill handle to the right of cell I141.

Drag the AutoFill handle to make copies of the quarter totals.

Excel fills all the cells with a copy. You still need to divide the new cells by 3. You can divide a range of cells by a constant by putting the constant into a cell, copying the cell, and using the Paste Special dialog box to paste it on top of the range. The Paste Special dialog box allows you to divide by the value of the copied cell.

Copy

4 Enter **3** into cell K1, select cell K1, and click the Copy button.

5 Select cell G2. Hold down SHIFT, and double-click the bottom border of the cell. Keep holding down SHIFT, and double-click the right border of the selection.

You can also find the Paste Special command on the Edit menu.

6 Right-click in the selected range, and select Paste Special from the shortcut menu that appears.

7 In the Paste group, select Values. In the Operation group, select Divide. Then click OK.

The selected cells all now contain a value one third as large as it was five seconds ago.

8 Clear the contents of cell K1.

The Paste Special dialog box is a very effective way to modify a large range of cells without creating large blocks of temporary formulas.

Filter for a specific value

Before you begin adjusting quantities, you get a note that one of the resellers, Industrial Smoke and Mirrors, has decided to stop selling directly to customers as a retail store, and will become a distributor to smaller outlets. Before you forget, you should change the channel in all the rows for that reseller. The list is currently sorted by product, but the sort order doesn't matter when you filter the list.

1 Click any single cell in the list. On the Data menu, point to Filter, and then click AutoFilter.

	A	B	C	D	E	F	G
1	Product	Line	Reseller	Channe	Contrac	QtrAvg	Jun
2	Aardvark	Animal	Jean-Paul Delori	Distrib	C5035	4,200	1,400
3	Aardvark	Animal	Lakes & Sons	Distrib	C5004	2,700	900
4	Aardvark	Animal	West Coast Sal	Distrib	C5017	6,600	2,200

Arrows appear at the top of each column, turning each of the column headings into drop-down lists. You filter the list by selecting an item from one of the lists.

2 From the Reseller list, select Industrial Smoke and Mirrors.

	A	B	C	D	E	F	G
1	Product	Line	Reseller	Channe	Contrac	QtrAvg	Jun
10	Aardvark	Animal	Industrial Smoke	Retail	C5038	150	50
24	Airplane	Vehicle	Industrial Smoke	Retail	C5038	450	150
38	Automobile	Vehicle	Industrial Smoke	Retail	C5038	150	50
52	Brontosaurus	Dinosaur	Industrial Smoke	Retail	C5038	-	-

Excel hides all the rows except the ones for the reseller you selected and turns the row numbers blue. (You can tell that rows are hidden because there are gaps in the row number sequence.) First, change the channel for the first row.

3 Select the first cell below the Channel row heading (probably D10, depending on how your list is sorted), type the letter **D** and press ENTER.

Excel changes the cell to *Distrib*, because that is a value that begins with a *D* and is already in the list. Now you can fill the channel down using the AutoFill handle. Because intermediate rows are hidden, you might be nervous about whether all the hidden rows will change along with the visible rows. Watch closely as you fill the list. You can see how Excel selects only the visible cells before extending the value.

4 Select cell D10 and double-click the AutoFill handle.

Excel briefly flashes borders around the visible cells. To confirm that only Industrial Smoke and Mirrors changed, you can redisplay the entire list. To show all the items from a filtered column, select *(All)* from the drop-down list for the column.

5 Select *(All)* from the list of resellers.

	A	B	C	D	E	F	G
1	Product ▼	Line ▼	Reseller ▼	Channe ▼	Contrac ▼	QtrAvg ▼	Jun ▼
8	Aardvark	Animal	Adventure Work	Retail	C5044	9,750	3,250
9	Aardvark	Animal	Enchantment La	Retail	C5064	3,000	1,000
10	Aardvark	Animal	Industrial Smok	Distrib	C5038	150	50
11	Aardvark	Animal	Main Street Mar	Retail	C5080	2,100	700
12	Aardvark	Animal	Hiabuv Toys	Toys	C5055	5,850	1,950
13	Aardvark	Animal	Mightyflight Toy	Toys	C5011	7,200	2,400

The channel changed to Distrib for only the one reseller.

Most changes you make while a list is filtered automatically apply to only the visible rows. Later in this lesson you will learn about one of the few exceptions.

Summarize filtered values

One of the resellers, Main Street Market, has indicated to you that for this next quarter they want to change their marketing strategy. Rather than purchase a few of one model and several of a different one, they want to purchase the same quantity for each product. They want you to use approximately the average of the monthly units from the previous year.

You can use the AutoFilter feature to display only the rows for that one reseller, but the AVERAGE function will calculate the average of all resellers, regardless of whether they are visible or not. The SUBTOTAL function—in addition to avoiding double counting—also ignores any cells that are hidden in a filtered list. Start by creating a place to calculate the average.

1 Select cells A1:A2. On the Insert menu, click Rows.

To calculate an average, you will use 1 as the SUBTOTAL function's first argument, and the label at the top of the column as the second argument.

2 Select cell F1. Type the formula **=SUBTOTAL(1, QtrAvg)** and press ENTER. Select cell F1 and drag the AutoFill handle to the right of cell I1.

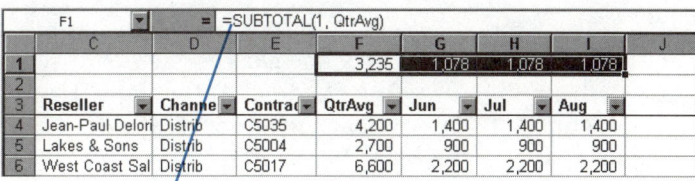

The SUBTOTAL function summarizes much the same as the SUM or AVERAGE functions. Use 1 for average. Use 9 for sum.

These cells calculate the average for each column for the entire list. When you filter the list, the formulas will ignore everything except the visible cells.

 NOTE If the AutoFilter arrows are not visible, on the Data menu, point to Filter, and then click AutoFilter.

3 From the Reseller drop-down list, select Main Street Market.

	C	D	E	F	G	H	I	J
1				1,365	455	455	455	
2								
3	Reseller	Channel	Contrac	QtrAvg	Jun	Jul	Aug	
13	Main Street Mar	Retail	C5080	2,100	700	700	700	
27	Main Street Mar	Retail	C5080	2,250	750	750	750	
41	Main Street Mar	Retail	C5080	750	250	250	250	

The SUBTOTAL function ignores rows that are hidden by filtering.

This hides all the other resellers. The average for the quarter changes to 1365, and the average for each month becomes 455.

You decide to suggest that they order 460 units of each of the products each month. If you enter that value into a cell, you can use copy and paste to replace all the existing values.

Paste

4 In cell J1, enter **460**. Copy cell J1. Select the range G13:I139. Click the Paste button.

	D	E	F	G	H	I	J	K
1			1,365	460	460	460	460	
2								
3	Channe	Contrac	QtrAvg	Jun	Jul	Aug		
13	Retail	C5080	2,100	460	460	460		
27	Retail	C5080	2,250	460	460	460		
41	Retail	C5080	750	460	460	460		

When you paste onto a filtered list, Excel selects only the visible rows before pasting the cells.

The white stripes that appear between each row show you that Excel deselected all the hidden cells so that you pasted the number into only the visible rows. The averages at the top of the worksheet change to show that the new average is also 460.

5 Clear cell J1.

The SUBTOTAL function is an effective way to summarize numbers from a filtered list. Once again you see that common operations, such as pasting values, automatically apply only to the visible rows.

Manually select visible rows

The Hiabuv Toys company asked that you give them 120 percent of their previous average. The Paste Special dialog box is an effective way to multiply a whole range of cells by a constant. Unfortunately, the Paste Special dialog box pastes a value onto both visible and hidden rows. Rather than give up this extremely useful tool, you can manually select only the visible rows before using the Paste Special command.

1 From the list of Resellers, select Hiabuv Toys.

In order to use Paste Special, you must first enter the constant into a cell and copy it.

2 Enter **120%** into cell D1 (or any convenient empty cell). Then copy that cell.

Next, you select the range where you want to paste the value.

3 Select the range G14:I140.

Next, you need to change the selection to include only the visible cells. The Go To Special dialog box can help you out.

You can also find the Go To command on the Edit menu.

4 Press CTRL+G to display the Go To dialog box. Then click Special. Select the Visible Cells Only option, and click OK.

Before using the Paste Special command on a filtered list, you must manually select only the visible cells.

You see the distinctive white lines between the rows, confirming that only the visible cells will be affected by the next command.

5 Right-click in the selected range, and select Paste Special from the shortcut menu that appears. In the Paste Special dialog box, select the Values option and the Multiply option. Then click OK.

The average units for the three months change from 1315 to 1578, a 20 percent increase.

6 Clear the cell containing the temporary 120% value.

Most of the time, Excel applies changes only to the visible rows in a filtered list. But when you use Paste Special you can manually select only the visible cells by using the Go To Special dialog box.

Delete rows from a list

You can manually select only visible cells any time you don't want to take chances.

One of the resellers, Wingtip Toys, has decided to no longer sell Tailspin Toys' models. That is unfortunate. But you no longer need to plan for them. To delete rows from a list, simply filter the list to show the rows you want to delete, and then delete them. Excel will take care of preserving all the hidden rows.

1 From the list of resellers, select WingTip Toys.

2 Select the range from C17:C143. (You can select rows 17 to 143 from any column in the list.)

When a list is filtered, the Delete command changes to Delete Row.

3 On the Edit menu, click Delete Row. When Excel asks if you really want to delete the entire row, click OK.

All the rows for WingTip Toys disappear.

 TIP To avoid the confirmation dialog box when deleting rows from a filtered list, select the row numbers at the left of the list. This selects the entire row. If the entire row is selected when you click the Delete Row command, Excel does not ask for confirmation.

Customize a filter

All the other resellers have agreed to a default order quantity where the first month is the same as the average for the previous year, the second month is 10 percent greater, and the third month is 20 percent greater. You need to hide the two resellers you already changed, while leaving all the other resellers visible. Each of the AutoFilter drop-down lists contains a Custom option. The Custom option allows you to create more complex criteria for a filter.

1 From the Reseller drop-down list, select Custom.

The Custom AutoFilter dialog box shows you the current filter, where the Reseller equals Wingtip Toys. The first box gives you a list of comparison operators. The second box gives you a list of values.

You want to exclude a reseller. You can exclude a value by choosing a new option from the list of operators.

2 In the list of operators, select Does Not Equal. In the second box, select Hiabuv Toys.

This will hide Hiabuv Toys. You also need to hide Main Street Market. The Custom dialog box lets you combine two options. The two lower boxes serve the same purposes as the two upper boxes.

3 In the lower list of operators, select Does Not Equal. In the lower list of reseller names, select Main Street Market.

Because you want to hide both of these resellers, leave the combination option with the default And.

 NOTE If you wanted to display only two resellers, you would use Equals for each of the comparison operators, and select Or to combine the two criteria.

4 Click OK.

All the resellers are visible except for the two you excluded. Now you can use Paste Special to multiply the values in the second month by 110 percent and the values in the third month by 120 percent. Enter the percentages into some convenient blank cells.

5 Enter **110%** into cell D2, and **120%** into cell E2. Select the two cells and copy them.

Next you will select the range that you want to change.

6 Select cell H4, and then hold down SHIFT as you double-click the bottom edge of the cell. Continue holding down SHIFT as you click cell I143, the bottom right cell.

Before you can use Paste Special, you must select only the visible cells.

7   Press CTRL+G and click Special. Select Visible Cells Only and click OK.

8   Right-click in the selection, and click Paste Special. In the Paste Special dialog box, select the Values option and the Multiply option, and click OK.

The second and third month values are appropriately larger.

9   Clear the temporary values from cells D2:E2.

Most of the time, you can use AutoFilter to select a simple value. Every now and then, however, you need a slightly more complex filter. The Custom dialog box gives you a few more options, while still being very easy to use.

Select top items from a list

The people in Marketing like to keep up to date on which resellers and which products are the most popular. To filter the list to show the 5 percent of the rows with the greatest values in the August column, you select the item named Top 10 from the AutoFilter drop-down list. First, redisplay all the hidden rows.

1   On the Data menu, point to Filter, and then click Show All.

This removes all the filters from the list, but leaves the drop-down lists.

2   In the drop-down list for the Aug column, select Top 10.

The Top 10 AutoFilter dialog box lets you select from either the top or the bottom, and allows you to specify the number of items. (It doesn't have to be 10, in spite of the name on the dialog box.) It allows you to choose between specifying the actual number of rows to show and specifying a percentage of the total rows. You want to show the top 5 percent of the rows.

3   Leave Top selected in the leftmost list. Click the down arrow to select 5 in the middle list. Select Percent in the list on the right. Then click OK.

Since the list contains 140 rows, displaying the top 5 percent gives you seven rows.

To see the top 5 percent of each product line, you can use a Pivot-Table report. See Lesson 5.

Unfortunately, the Top 10 filter always looks at the entire list. You can't see the top 5 percent of the rows for the Dinosaur product line. If you select Dinosaur from the Line filter, you will see only one row, since there is only one Dinosaur product in the top 5 percent list.

When you are ready to return the worksheet to its original state, you can simply turn off AutoFilter.

4 On the Data menu, point to Filter, and then click AutoFilter.

5 Save the Lesson4 workbook.

With AutoFilters, you can easily show just the rows you want in a list. You can then edit the visible rows, paste new values into them, delete them, or just look at them.

Using Advanced Filters

AutoFilters are easy to use, but they are also limited in what you can do with them. For example, you can't extract a part of the list to a new location, you can't see the criteria you used to filter the list, and you can't create a list of unique values. Advanced Filters are slightly more complex than AutoFilters, but they give you much more control over the filtering process.

Create a list of unique values

You have made some changes to the list of resellers, and would now like to have a clean list of the resellers. Extracting a list of unique values is a perfect task for an Advanced Filter. Start by selecting just the portion of the list that you want to extract from—the Reseller column.

For a demonstration of how to extract unique values from a list, double-click the Excel Camcorder Files shortcut on your Desktop or connect to the Internet address listed on page xvi.

1 Select cell C3. While holding down SHIFT, double-click the bottom edge of the cell.

Excel selects all the values in the Reseller column, from cell C3 through C133. This is the range you will extract from. Excel calls this the *filter database*. Now you can use the Advanced Filter to extract a list of unique values from this filter database.

2 On the Data menu, point to Filter, and then click Advanced Filter.

3 In the Action group, select the Copy To Another Location option. The List Range box should contain $C$3:$C$133, which is the range you selected.

If you select a subset of the list, such as a single column, before you use the Advanced Filter command, Excel uses the current selection as the filter database.

4 In the Copy To box, type **K3**, which is a cell off to the side of the list. Select the Unique Records Only checkbox. Then click OK and scroll up to see cell K3.

Excel created a list of unique resellers, starting in cell K3.

Looking at the extract, however, you realize that you really wanted not just the list of reseller names, but also their respective channel assignments—since you changed the channel for at least one reseller. Delete this extracted list and try again.

5   Select cell K3, press CTRL+SHIFT+* to select the entire list, and press DELETE.

After you have used a subset of the list as the filter database, Excel remembers that subset and ignores the current selection the next time you use the Advanced Filter command. You could, of course, select the range while in the dialog box, but then you wouldn't be able to double-click the bottom of the cell to extend the range. If you want to reset the Advanced Filter command, the easiest way is to turn AutoFilter on and back off.

6   On the Data menu, point to Filter, and then click AutoFilter to turn on the AutoFilter arrows. Choose AutoFilter again to turn off the arrows.

Now you can select both columns C and D as your filter database.

7   Select cell C3. While holding down SHIFT, double-click the bottom edge of the cell. Still holding down SHIFT, press the RIGHT ARROW key.

8   On the Data menu, point to Filter, and then click Advanced Filter. Select the Copy To Another Location option. (Make sure the List Range box contains $C$3:$D$133.) Type **K3:L3** in the Copy To box. Select the Unique Records Only check box. Then click OK and scroll to cell K3. Widen column K to fit the reseller names.

	K	L	M
1			
2			
3	**Reseller**	**Channel**	
4	Jean-Paul Deloria	Distrib	
5	Lakes & Sons	Distrib	
6	West Coast Sales	Distrib	
7	Wide World Importers	Distrib	
8	Baldwin Museum of Science	Museums	
9	Kimball Museum of Science	Museums	

The unique list includes the columns you selected in the input list.

This time Excel extracted the unique values from both the Reseller and the Channel lists.

Remember that if you ever try to use the Advanced Filter command with a portion of the list, and the dialog box does not recognize the current selection, simply turn AutoFilter on and off to reset the list.

 NOTE Excel uses the range name *Extract* to remember the range you specify as the Copy To range in the Advanced Filter dialog box. To remember the filter database, Excel uses a hidden name *_FilterDatabase* (complete with an underscore character as the first letter). To see the current filter database, click in the Name Box, type **_FilterDatabase**, and press ENTER.

Filter using a criteria range

You may have noticed an extra box in the middle of the Advanced Filter dialog box with the label *Criteria Range*. A criteria range works like the drop-down AutoFilter lists, except that you type the value you want to match in a cell, rather than select it from a list. A criteria range requires a little more preparation than turning on AutoFilter lists, but it also has a couple of advantages. For one thing, you can easily see what you used as the criteria. Create a criteria range for the plan and see what you can do with it.

A criteria range consists of two rows on the worksheet. The top row contains column labels from the list. The second row contains the criteria you want to use. A good place to put a criteria range is at the top of a worksheet, above the list.

Copy

1 Select the range A1:A2. On the Insert menu, click Rows.

This is the place where you will put the criteria range.

Paste

2 Select cell A5, the label for the first column. Hold down SHIFT and double-click the right edge of the cell. Click the Copy button. Then select cell A1, click the Paste button, and press ESC.

These are the labels for the criteria range. The criteria range also needs to include one blank row below the labels. Hold down SHIFT and press the DOWN ARROW key to extend the selection to include one additional row.

Create a range with labels above a blank row as a criteria range.

	B	C	D	E	F	G	H	I	J
1	Line	Reseller	Channel	Contract	QtrAvg	Jun	Jul	Aug	
2									
3					3,474	1,179	1,297	1,414	
4									
5	Line	Reseller	Channel	Contract	QtrAvg	Jun	Jul	Aug	
6	Animal	Jean-Paul Delori	Distrib	C5035	4,200	1,400	1,540	1,680	
7	Animal	Lakes & Sons	Distrib	C5004	2,700	900	990	1,080	

See Lesson 2 for more information about local names.

If you name the range *Criteria*, Excel will automatically know what you want to use. Use a name that is local to the Plan worksheet, in case you some day add a criteria range to another worksheet in this workbook.

3 On the Insert menu, point to Name, and then click Define. Type **Plan!Criteria** and click OK.

Your criteria range is now ready. Suppose that you want to see all the resellers in the Retail channel who sell Elephant models. You enter the value you want to match under each of the labels.

4 Type **Elephant** in cell A2, and **Retail** in cell D2.

5 Reset the filter list range by turning AutoFilter on and then off again.

6 Select cell A5 (or any single cell in the list). On the Data menu, point to Filter, and then click Advanced Filter. Leave all the options with their default values, and click OK.

	A	B	C	D	E	F	G
1	Product	Line	Reseller	Channel	Contract	QtrAvg	Jun
2	Elephant			Retail			
3						1,600	637
4							
5	Product	Line	Reseller	Channel	Contract	QtrAvg	Jun
64	Elephant	Animal	Adventure Work	Retail	C5044	3,300	1,100
65	Elephant	Animal	Enchantment La	Retail	C5064	1,050	350
67	Elephant	Animal	Main Street Mar	Retail	C5080	450	460

The criteria range lets you see how the list was filtered.

You can see the three Retail resellers who sell Elephants. You can also easily see the criteria that you used. By defining the range names, you enabled Excel to correctly fill in all the dialog box options for you.

What if you want to see all the resellers who ordered at least 2000 Elephants each quarter last year? You can use comparison operators at the beginning of any criteria field.

7 Clear cell D2. Enter **>=2000** in cell F2. Select cell A5. On the Data menu, point to Filter, and then click Advanced Filter. Then click OK.

	A	B	C	D	E	F	G
1	Product	Line	Reseller	Channel	Contract	QtrAvg	Jun
2	Elephant					>2000	
3						3,150	1,050

You can use inequalities in the criteria range.

Three resellers sold the most Elephants. And once again, you can easily see what the criteria was that gave you these three resellers.

Suppose that you want to see all the resellers whose contract number begins with a C and ends with a 1. You can use wildcard characters to specify criteria. Use a question mark (?) to match any single character, or an asterisk (*) to match one or more characters.

8 Clear cell F2. Enter **C???1** in cell E2. Select cell A5. On the Data menu, point to Filter, and then click Advanced Filter. Then click OK.

	A	B	C	D	E	F
1	Product	Line	Reseller	Channel	Contract	QtrAvg
2	Elephant				C???1	
3						3,075
4						
5	Product	Line	Reseller	Channel	Contract	QtrAvg
6	Elephant	Animal	Mightyflight Toy:	Toys	C5011	2,850
7	Elephant	Animal	Peck n Order Tc	Toys	C5001	3,300

You can use wildcard characters in the criteria range.

Two resellers meet the criteria.

9 On the Data menu, point to Filter, and then click Show All.

Once you set up the criteria range, the Advanced Filter command is not much more difficult to use than the AutoFilter command, and it has the advantage of letting you see what the filter was that you used. If you are going to print a copy of the filtered list and show it to people in a meeting, you might be grateful for the reminder.

NOTE Whenever you enter a value in the criteria range, Excel treats it as if you typed an asterisk at the end of the value. For example, if you type C50 in the Contract column of the criteria range, Excel would interpret that as C50* and show you all the rows that begin with the letters C50. To force Excel to match only cells that have exactly C50 as the contract, you must enter the formula =″=C50″ (with two equal signs) into the criteria range. The result of this formula is =C50.

This applies only to the Advanced Filter command. When you use the AutoFilter command's Custom option, you can use wildcard characters, but AutoFilter never assumes that there is an asterisk at the end of the item.

Extract a portion of a list

Suppose that you want to create a list showing the Reseller name, the Contract number, and the June plan for all resellers who sell Aardvarks. You do not want all of the columns from the original list, only Reseller, Contract, and Jun. You can use the Advanced Filter command to create an extract. First set the criteria range to select every reseller who sells Aardvarks.

1 Clear all the cells in row 2. In cell A2, enter **Aardvark**

If you want to extract only certain columns, you can create an extract range that includes only the column labels that you want. The easiest way to make sure the labels are correct is to copy them from the original list. Holding down CTRL allows you to select cells that are not adjacent.

2 Select cell C5. Hold down CTRL and click cell E5. Keep holding down CTRL and click cell G5. (Use the scroll bar if you need to scroll to the right.)

These are the labels that you want to copy. You can put them off to the right side of the other lists.

Copy

3 Click the Copy button. Select cell N5, and click the Paste button.

You will use N5:P5 as the Copy To range in the Advanced Filter dialog box.

Paste

4 Select cell A5. On the Data menu, point to Filter, and then click Advanced Filter.

5 Select the Copy To Another Location option. In the Copy To box, type **N5:P5**. Then click OK, scroll to see N5:P5, and widen column N to fit the reseller names.

	N	O	P
1			
2			
3			
4			
5	Reseller	Contract	Jun
6	Jean-Paul Deloria	C5035	1,400
7	Lakes & Sons	C5004	900
8	West Coast Sales	C5017	2,200
9	Wide World Importers	C5068	200

To extract only certain columns, put the column headings into the extract area.

You see just the columns you want for the selected rows.

The Advanced Filter command allows you to filter by both rows and columns. You use the criteria range to control which rows you will get, and you use column labels in the extract area to control which columns you get.

One Step Further: Using a Calculated Criterion

The person in Marketing who is in charge of promotions just sent you an email message. She has come up with a crazy idea for a random reward system, and needs you to randomly select 5 percent of the rows in your list. (It's alright for the same reseller to appear more than once.)

Select random rows

One way to select a random 5 percent of the rows would be to add a column that contains the formula =RAND()<5%. Since the RAND function returns random values between 0 and 1 (which is equivalent to 0 percent and 100 percent), the formula would generate the value TRUE approximately 5 percent of the time. You could then use AutoFilter to select all the rows with the value TRUE. You can, however, accomplish the same result using the Advanced Filter command, without having to add an extra column to the list.

Normally, when you create a criteria range, you fill the top row with the column labels from the list. If instead, you use a label that does not appear in the list, you create what is called a *calculated criterion*. A calculated criterion adds a *virtual* column of formulas to the list. You put the "sample" formula in the cell below the label. Excel then, in effect, puts an exact copy of that formula into a cell in the first row of the list and copies the formula to the rest of the list. Each row where the formula returns a TRUE value meets the criterion.

One way to create a calculated criterion is to replace one of the labels in a regular criteria range with a word like *Calc*.

1 Enter **Calc** in cell A1.

Because the word *Calc* does not match any of the column labels, cell A2 is now a calculated criterion.

2 Enter **=RAND()<5%** in cell A2. Clear any other cells in row 2.

This is the formula that Excel will "virtually copy" to each row of the list. The Advanced Filter command will display any row where the formula returns TRUE.

3 Select cell A5. On the Data menu, point to Filter, click Advanced Filter, and then click OK.

Excel displays approximately 5 percent of the rows. If you repeat the Advanced Filter command, you will get different rows.

Compare columns

Suppose that you want to see the rows where the June plan is more than three times the quarter average. You could add a new column with the formula *=June*3>QtrAvg*, or you could use that formula as a calculated criterion.

1 In cell A2, type the formula **=Jun*3>QtrAvg** and press ENTER.

 NOTE If you want to use cell addresses rather than column labels, enter the addresses as if you were typing them into a cell on the first row of the database. For this example, where the list begins on row 5, you could enter *=G6*3>F6* as the formula.

You can also make a calculated criterion refer to a cell that is not in the list. Just use dollar signs to make the cell reference absolute.

2 Select cell A5. On the Data menu, point to Filter, click Advanced Filter, and then click OK.

Excel displays the matching rows, all of which happen to be from Main Street Market and Hiabuv Toys.

3 Save and close the Lesson4 workbook.

Many people are not aware of calculated criteria. In fact, this feature is not even mentioned anywhere in Excel's Help files. You can always avoid calculated criteria simply by adding additional columns to your list. But once you understand the secret of calculated criteria, they are really not hard at all.

Lesson Summary

To	Do this
Sort by multiple columns	Sort by the most detailed column first; sort by the most general column last.
Make sure Excel recognizes the top row as headers	Format the top row bold.
Create a custom sort list	Create the list on the worksheet. On the Tools menu, select Options and select the Custom Lists tab. Click the Import button.
Sort using a custom list	On the Data menu, select Sort. Select the column you want to sort and click Options. Select the custom sort order you want.
Add labels from a custom list on the worksheet	Enter one label from a custom list on the worksheet. Drag the AutoFill handle.
Add subtotals to a list	Sort the list by the column you want to use to group the subtotals. On the Data menu, select Subtotals, set the desired options, and click OK.
Show only the totals for a subtotaled list	Click one of the outline numbers to the left of the column headings.
Show or hide the detail for a total row on a subtotaled list	Click the plus sign (to show the detail) or the minus sign (to hide the detail) to the left of a total row.
Create a second level of subtotals	On the Data menu, select Subtotals. Clear the Replace Current Subtotals check box.
Remove subtotals from a list	On the Data menu, select Subtotals. Click the Remove All button. Or, use the Sort Ascending button to sort the list.
Jump to the bottom of a list	Double-click the bottom border of a cell.
Select the range down to the bottom of a list	Hold down SHIFT as you double-click the bottom border of a cell.
Divide a range of cells by a constant	Enter the constant into a cell and copy the cell. Select the range, click with the right mouse button, and select Paste Special. Select the Values and the Divide options.
Filter a list by the value in a column	On the Data menu, point to Filter and click AutoFilter. Click the drop-down arrow on the column and select the filter value.

To	Do this
Replace the value in a column for only some selected rows in a list	Use AutoFilter to show only the rows you want to change. Change the value in the first visible row. Double-click the AutoFill handle. Only the visible rows will change.
Show the average of a column for only the visible rows in a filtered list	Use the SUBTOTAL function with 1 as the first argument and a column heading for the second argument. (Use 9 for Sum and 3 for Count.)
Select only visible rows in a filtered list	Press CTRL+G and click the Special button. Select the Visible Cells Only option.
Affect only the visible cells in a filtered list when you use the Paste Special command	Manually select the visible rows before you use Paste Special.
Delete selected rows from a list	Use AutoFilter to show only the rows you want to delete. Select the range you want to delete. On the Edit menu, click Delete.
Use AutoFilter to select a range of items, or to specify two different comparison items	In the AutoFilter list for a column, select Custom.
Select the top or bottom items in a list	In the AutoFilter list, select Top 10.
Show all the rows in a filtered list	On the Data menu, point to Filter and click Show All.
Turn off AutoFilters	On the Data menu, point to Filter and click AutoFilter.
Extract unique values from one or more columns in a list	Select the columns you want to extract. On the Data menu, point to Filter and click Advanced Filter. Select the Copy To Another Location option, type a destination cell in the Copy To box, and select the Unique Values option.
Reset the default Advanced Filter range	Turn AutoFilter on and then back off.
Create a criteria range to use with Advanced Filters	Copy the headings from a list to a new range. Select the range containing the copy of the headings plus a blank row. Name the range Criteria.

To	Do this
Enter an exact match criteria	Type the criteria value in the blank row beneath the column heading. (This matches all rows with a value that begins with the same as the value you type.)
Create an exact match comparison that must match the entire cell (for example, match the text *xx*)	Create a formula in the criteria range that looks like this: ="=xx", which produces =xx as the criteria value.
Enter comparison criteria	Enter a comparison operator followed by the comparison value in the blank row beneath the column heading.
Use wildcards in a comparison	Use a question mark (?) to match any single character and an asterisk (*) to match text of any length.
Extract only selected columns from a list	Copy the column headings you want to extract to a new range. Specify the range containing the headings in the Copy To box of the Advanced Filter dialog box.
Create a calculated criterion	Change one of the headings in the criteria range to something that does not match any column label. Enter a formula which, when copied to any row in the list, will produce TRUE for the rows you want to see and FALSE for the rows you don't want to see.

For online information about	On the Help menu, click Contents And Index, click the Index tab, and then type
Sorting a list	**sorting, overview**
Subtotaling a list	**subtotals, multiple-level**
Filtering a list	**lists, filtering**

Summarizing Lists

Estimated time
55 min.

In this lesson you will learn how to:

■ Calculate summaries using a PivotTable.

■ Format numbers and patterns in a PivotTable.

■ Show and hide detail in a PivotTable.

■ Calculate new values in a PivotTable.

A PivotTable is a powerful tool for dynamically summarizing and browsing a list. Microsoft first introduced PivotTables in Excel version 5. Soon after version 5 came out, I tried to persuade a reluctant client to upgrade. She was adamant in her refusal, because upgrading at that time would also have required her to change operating systems. Then one day when I arrived at the job, she told me that she was changing her entire computer system so that she could switch to Excel 5. My perplexed look elicited an explanation: The previous day, a coworker had demonstrated to her some of the wonders of PivotTables. I like to think that my weeks of fruitless persuasion had at least primed her for the final decision.

PivotTables are unquestionably one of the most useful tools in Excel. If you are new to PivotTables, prepare yourself to enter a whole new world. If you have already been using PivotTables, prepare to discover some hidden vistas and valleys you didn't know were there.

Start the lesson

➤ Start Microsoft Excel, change to the Excel AT Practice folder, and open the Start5 workbook. Save a copy of the workbook as **Lesson5**

Creating a PivotTable

Now that Tailspin Toys has completed two full fiscal years of operations, the top-level managers have decided that they want your department to publish a quarterly report showing them how the company is doing. The first report, which "doesn't have to be fancy," is due on the president's desk in two days. Your manager, impressed with your rapidly escalating abilities with Microsoft Excel, has bequeathed this major new project to you. By tomorrow morning, she wants a proposal for some analyses that might be put into the report: a comparison between product lines, quarterly growth rates—that sort of thing.

Fields and Items: Some Definitions

Thankfully, the Information Systems department has provided you with a list containing order information for the past two years. That list is on the Orders sheet of the Lesson5 workbook. You can use a PivotTable to summarize the data in the list. However, a PivotTable does not work with rows and columns; instead, it works with fields and items.

A *field* corresponds to a column.

	A	B	C	D	E
1	Reseller	Product	Month	Units	Dollars
2	Baldwin Museum of Science	Elephant	9/1/96	363	$ 8,884.61
3	Enchantment Lakes Corporation	Elephant	9/1/96	352	$ 8,351.64
4	Kimball Museum of Science	Elephant	9/1/96	1,204	$ 29,167.80
5	Baldwin Museum of Science	Giraffe	9/1/96	1,552	$ 29,620.70
6	Enchantment Lakes Corporation	Giraffe	9/1/96	425	$ 7,863.03
7	Kimball Museum of Science	Giraffe	9/1/96	1,305	$ 24,652.43

An *item* corresponds to a unique value in a column.

A *field* in a PivotTable corresponds to a column in a list. The name of the field is the label from the top of the column. For example, when you create a PivotTable from this list, *Reseller* and *Units* will become field names in the PivotTable.

An *item* in a PivotTable is a unique value in a field. The word *Elephant* in the Product column will become an item in the Product field. Even though the word *Elephant* appears in multiple rows in the list, it is a single item in the PivotTable.

Define a PivotTable report

The list of orders is quite large. You decide that you'd like to work first with a subset of the list, just to get comfortable with manipulating the PivotTable. You can use a named range to control how much of the list the PivotTable uses. The PivotTable Wizard looks for a range named *Database*, so if you use that name, you can avoid some typing later.

1 On the Orders worksheet, select the range A1:E7.

These are the orders from Tailspin Toys' first month of business.

2 Click the Name Box, type **Database**, and press ENTER.

Now you can create the PivotTable using the PivotTable Wizard.

3 On the Data menu, click PivotTable Report.

4 In Step 1 of the PivotTable Wizard, accept the default option, Microsoft Excel List Or Database, and click Next.

The PivotTable Wizard guesses that you want to use the range named *Database* as the source for the PivotTable. If you had used a different range name for the list, you could type it here.

5 In Step 2 of the PivotTable Wizard, accept *Database* as the name of the source list, and click Next.

Step 3 of the PivotTable Wizard allows you to specify an initial layout for the PivotTable report. On the right are five field buttons, one for each column label in the list. In the center of the dialog box is a schematic diagram of the *pivot area*.

PivotTable fields can contain text (such as the Reseller and Product fields), dates (such as the Month field), or numbers (such as the Units and Dollars fields). Typically, you use text or date fields in the row and column heading areas, and number fields in the data area.

6 Drag the Reseller field button to the row area, drag the Product field button to the column area, and drag the Units field button to the data area.

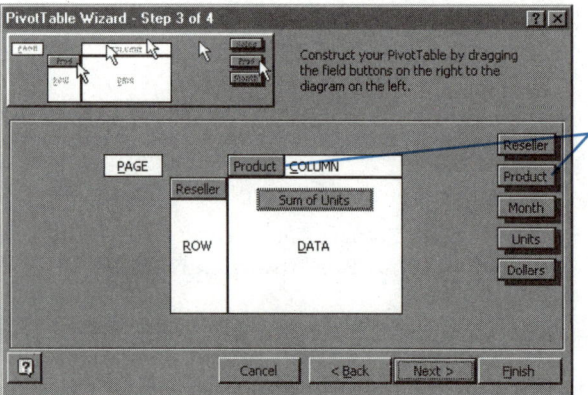

Drag the field buttons from the right to the pivot area in the middle.

When you drag the Units field button to the data area, the label on the field button changes to *Sum Of Units*. This is a new type of field, a *data field*. It is a derived field that consists of summarized values from the original column in the database.

The final step of the PivotTable Wizard allows you to control where the new PivotTable will go. Since the active cell was not blank when you started (you selected the range to give it a name), the PivotTable Wizard suggests creating a new worksheet for the PivotTable. That is an acceptable option.

7 Click Finish.

	A	B	C	D	E
1	Sum of Units	Product			
2	Reseller	Elephant	Giraffe	Grand Total	
3	Baldwin Museum of Science	363	1552	1915	
4	Enchantment Lakes Corporation	352	425	777	
5	Kimball Museum of Science	1204	1305	2509	
6	Grand Total	1919	3282	5201	
7					

Unique item labels become row and column headings.

The PivotTable report appears on a new worksheet. A field button for the Product field is in cell B1, with each item from the Product field appearing as a column heading. A field button for the Reseller field is in cell A2, with each item from the Reseller field appearing as a row heading. The summarized units for each reseller and product combination appear in the grid, along with grand totals at the right and at the bottom.

The worksheet has a name like Sheet1. You could name the sheet to indicate that this is your very first PivotTable.

8 Double click the worksheet tab, type **First Pivot** and press ENTER.

You started with a list with labels only at the top. The PivotTable created a grid with labels both at the top and down the left side.

Pivot the PivotTable

See Lesson 4 for more information about the Subtotal command.

Another use of a PivotTable is to allow you to quickly try different arrangements of the numbers and labels in the PivotTable. You can *pivot* the PivotTable, simply by dragging the field buttons. Suppose that you want to see the data in a summarized list, much as the Subtotal command would give you, with totals for each reseller. You can simply drag a field button to rearrange the PivotTable. As you drag a field button, the mouse pointer changes, and Excel displays an I-shaped dotted outline on the table to show you where the item labels for that field will move.

1 Drag the Product field button down to the border between cell A4 and cell B4.

	A	B	C
1	Sum of Units		
2	Reseller	Product	Total
3	Baldwin Museum of Science	Elephant	363
4		Giraffe	1552
5	Baldwin Museum of Science Total		1915
6	Enchantment Lakes Corporation	Elephant	352
7		Giraffe	425

Drag the field button to "pivot" the column headings into row headings.

The PivotTable now has two row fields. The items in the Product field show the detail for each reseller, and each reseller has a total row in addition to the detail.

Suppose that you would rather see the totals for the products, with reseller information as the detail. To rearrange the PivotTable, simply drag a field, watching the I-shaped dotted outline to see where the field's item labels will go.

2 Drag the Product field button onto cell A4.

Drag the field button to control which field is on the left.

	A	B	C
1	Sum of Units		
2	Product	Reseller	Total
3	Elephant	Baldwin Museum of Science	363
4		Enchantment Lakes Corporation	352
5		Kimball Museum of Science	1204
6	Elephant Total		1919
7	Giraffe	Baldwin Museum of Science	1552

The Product items are now on the left, and the resellers are details.

131

You can also use a PivotTable to filter the data that is displayed in the table. To filter data so that the PivotTable shows data for only a single item, you drag the field to the *page area*, above the column field.

3 Drag the Product field button above cell A1.

When a field becomes a page field, the list of items collapses into a single cell that initially shows the value *(All)*. The PivotTable now shows the total of all products ordered by each reseller.

You can make the PivotTable show the total for only Giraffes by selecting Giraffe from the Product page field list box.

4 Select Giraffe from the Product page field list box.

	A	B	C
1	Product	Giraffe ▾	
2			
3	Sum of Units		
4	Reseller	Total	
5	Baldwin Museum of Science	1552	
6	Enchantment Lakes Corporation	425	
7	Kimball Museum of Science	1305	
8	Grand Total	3282	
9			

Drag a field button to the top left corner of the PivotTable to create a *page field* for filtering data.

Now the body of the PivotTable shows units for only the Giraffe product.

When you pivot the PivotTable by dragging a field, you can make only one change at a time. Suppose you want to make several changes—say, make Product the row field, Reseller the page field, and Dollars the data field. Rather than make the changes one at a time, you can go back to Step 3 of the PivotTable Wizard and make the changes all at once.

PivotTable Wizard

5 On the PivotTable toolbar, click the PivotTable Wizard button. In the PivotTable Wizard dialog box, drag the Product button to the row area, drag the Reseller button to the Page area, drag the Sum Of Units button away from the pivot area, and drag the Dollars button into the data area. Then click Finish.

	A	B	C
1	Reseller	(All) ▾	
2			
3	Sum of Dollars		
4	Product	Total	
5	Elephant	46404.05	
6	Giraffe	62136.16	
7	Grand Total	108540.21	
8			

The PivotTable appears with all the changes.

A PivotTable allows you to control how the data from the source appears. You can pivot the table one field at a time by dragging the field buttons on the worksheet itself, or you can make several changes at once by using the PivotTable Wizard button.

Add a second data field

What exactly is a data field? When you drag the Dollars field button into the data area, it changes to Sum Of Dollars. When you click Finish to display the PivotTable, you don't see a field button for Dollars or for Sum Of Dollars anywhere. Rather, the label Sum Of Dollars appears as the top left corner of the data portion of the PivotTable.

What if you want to see more than one data field? For example, suppose you want to show both units and dollars. You can do that. When you have more than one data field, each data field behaves like an item in a new, tempo-rary field named *Data*. The Data field does not exist in the source list on the Orders worksheet, but it behaves much like the fields that do come from the column headings. Try adding a second data field and see how this temporary Data field works.

PivotTable Wizard

For a demon-stration of how to add a second data field to a PivotTable, double-click the Excel Camcorder Files shortcut on your Desktop or connect to the Internet ad-dress listed on page xvi.

1 On the PivotTable toolbar, click the PivotTable Wizard button. Drag the Units field button above the Sum Of Dollars field button in the data area. Also, drag the Product field button to the page area and the Reseller field button to the row area. Then click Finish.

	A	B	C
1	Product	(All)	▼
2			
3	Reseller	Data	Total
4	Baldwin Museu	Sum of Units	1915
5		Sum of Dollars	38505.31
6	Enchantment L	Sum of Units	777

— When you have more than one data field, a new *Data* field button appears.

A new field button, labeled *Data*, now appears to the right of the Reseller field button. The labels Sum Of Units and Sum Of Dollars appear under the Data field button, the same as if they were items in an ordinary field. You also see an extra grand total row at the bottom of the entire PivotTable.

You can change the position of the Data field, much the same as you can that of any other field.

2 Drag the Data field button to the middle of cell A4.

	A	B	C	D
1	Product	(All)		
2				
3	Data	Reseller	Total	
4	Sum of Units	Baldwin Museum of Science	1915	
5		Enchantment Lakes Corporation	777	
6		Kimball Museum of Science	2509	
7	Sum of Dollars	Baldwin Museum of Science	38505.31	
8		Enchantment Lakes Corporation	16214.67	
9		Kimball Museum of Science	53820.23	
10	Total Sum of Units		5201	
11	Total Sum of Dollars		108540.21	
12				

Totals for data fields all appear at the bottom of the PivotTable.

The two items in the Data field behave almost the same as items in a regular field. But the totals all appear at the bottom, rather than below each item, the way the total would for a regular field.

You can also move the Data field to the Column area.

3 Drag the Data field button to cell C3.

	A	B	C
1	Product	(All)	
2			
3		Data	
4	Reseller	Sum of Units	Sum of Dollars
5	Baldwin Museum of Science	1915	38505.31
6	Enchantment Lakes Corporation	777	16214.67

Drag the Data field button to the column area to put dollars and units side-by-side.

The data items now serve as separate columns. Having the dollars and units side-by-side is a good way to compare them.

When you have multiple data fields, you get a new Data field. You can use that Data field almost the same as a regular field from the original list. You can't move it to the page area, but you can move it around in the row and column areas.

For a demonstration of how to format portions of a PivotTable, double-click the Excel Camcorder Files shortcut on your Desktop or connect to the Internet address listed on page xvi.

Format numbers in a PivotTable

You have been looking intently at the PivotTable for some time, aware that something is not right, but trying to figure out what it could be. Suddenly you realize what is wrong with the PivotTable. The numbers are hard to read. The dollars should be formatted as currency. Before you format the dollars, change the layout of the PivotTable so that you can see how the PivotTable formats cells.

1 Drag the Product page field button down to cell B3, the cell containing the Data field button.

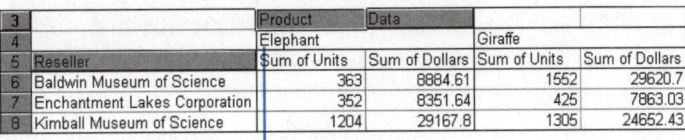

3		Product	Data		
4		Elephant		Giraffe	
5	Reseller	Sum of Units	Sum of Dollars	Sum of Units	Sum of Dollars
6	Baldwin Museum of Science	363	8884.61	1552	29620.7
7	Enchantment Lakes Corporation	352	8351.64	425	7863.03
8	Kimball Museum of Science	1204	29167.8	1305	24652.43

If you add a second layer of column labels, the data fields become interleaved.

This adds products as a second layer of column titles. One of the effects is to split the data values into distinct columns, with dollars and units interleaved. Now you can format the dollars.

2 Click cell C5, which is one of the Sum Of Dollars item cells.

3		Product	Data		
4		Elephant		Giraffe	
5	Reseller	Sum of Units	Sum of Dollars	Sum of Units	Sum of Dollars
6	Baldwin Museum of Science	363	8884.61	1552	29620.7
7	Enchantment Lakes Corporation	352	8351.64	425	7863.03
8	Kimball Museum of Science	1204	29167.8	1305	24652.43

Click the data field label to select all the cells that belong to that field.

NOTE If Excel does not select all the dollar amounts, on the PivotTable toolbar, click the PivotTable menu. Point to Select, and then click Enable Selection.

Excel selects all the dollar amounts in the entire PivotTable, even if the cells are not contiguous. The PivotTable shows you all the cells that will be affected if you reformat the dollar amounts.

Currency Style

3 On the Formatting toolbar, click the Currency Style button.

Excel formats the dollars. Even if you change the layout of the PivotTable, Excel will remember to format all the dollars as currency.

4 Drag the Data field button to cell B7.

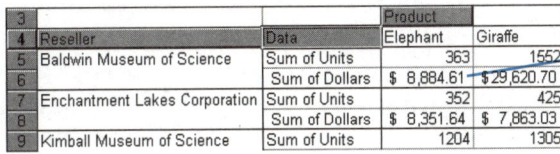

3			Product	
4	Reseller	Data	Elephant	Giraffe
5	Baldwin Museum of Science	Sum of Units	363	1552
6		Sum of Dollars	$ 8,884.61	$ 29,620.70
7	Enchantment Lakes Corporation	Sum of Units	352	425
8		Sum of Dollars	$ 8,351.64	$ 7,863.03
9	Kimball Museum of Science	Sum of Units	1204	1305

Even if you rearrange the PivotTable, the data field retains its formatting.

Excel swaps the data fields, but still formats all the dollar values as currency.

The units still need to be formatted as well.

Comma Style

Decrease Decimal

5 Click cell B5 (one of the Sum Of Units item labels). On the Formatting toolbar, click the Comma Style button, and then click the Decrease Decimal button twice.

The units—and the Sum Of Units label—now look consistent with the dollars.

When you select a data field, Excel selects all the values for that item. When you format the selection, Excel assigns that format to that data field and applies the format properly, regardless of how you pivot the table.

Format portions of a PivotTable

Suppose that you want to focus on the Enchantment Lakes reseller. It seems to have the lowest orders for that first month of any of the three resellers. Even as you rearrange the PivotTable, you would like to highlight that one reseller. In the same way that you can apply a format to a specific data field, you can format a specific item from a regular field as well. You simply select the item before applying the format.

Fill Color

1 Click cell A7, the cell containing Enchantment Lakes Corporation. On the Formatting toolbar, click the arrow next to the Fill Color button, and select Light Green (the fourth color on the bottom row).

The Enchantment Lakes cells change to light green. Even if you rearrange the PivotTable, all the Enchantment Lakes cells will stay green.

2 Drag the Data field button to cell A5.

3			Product	
4	Data	Reseller	Elephant	Giraffe
5	Sum of Units	Baldwin Museum of Science	363	1,552
6		Enchantment Lakes Corporation	352	425
7		Kimball Museum of Science	1,204	1,305
8	Sum of Dollars	Baldwin Museum of Science	$ 8,884.61	$29,620.70
9		Enchantment Lakes Corporation	$ 8,352.00	$ 7,863.00
10		Kimball Museum of Science	$29,167.80	$24,652.43

You can format all the cells that relate to a specific item, regardless of where they appear in the PivotTable.

The Enchantment Lakes cells are no longer together, but they are still highlighted light green.

You are also concerned about how Baldwin Museum of Science may be doing, but in this case you only want to monitor the Elephant orders. You can narrow down the selection by clicking multiple times.

3 Drag the Product field button to cell B5.

This puts the Product field between the Data field and the Reseller field. Now you can select Baldwin Museum of Science, and then narrow the selection to include only Elephants.

4 Click cell C4, which contains Baldwin Museum of Science. (Excel selects every occurrence of the museum.) Then click cell C4 again.

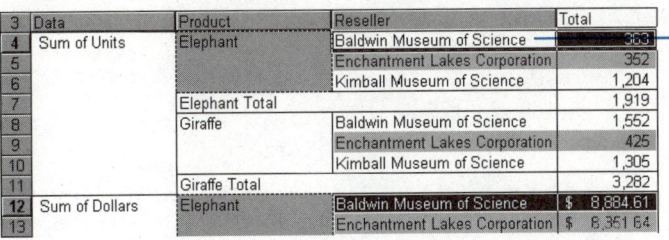

Click the Reseller label a second time to include only the items that relate to the Elephant product.

The Elephant boxes turn gray, and the selection now includes only the Baldwin Museum of Science cells that also happen to be Elephant cells. (If you click cell C4 again, you will get only the Baldwin Museum of Science cells that are Elephant cells and also are units. Each time you click cell C4, Excel narrows the selection one more level, finally returning the selection back to include everything, which restarts the cycle.)

5 On the Formatting toolbar, click the arrow next to the Fill Color button, and select Light Yellow (the third color in the bottom row).

Excel colors the cells. Now you can rearrange the PivotTable and still keep track of these items.

6 Drag the Product field button to cell C3, and then drag the Data field button to cell C3.

Even as you rearrange the PivotTable, Excel highlights every cell that applies to Baldwin Museum of Science and also Elephants.

The ability of a PivotTable to select all the cells that relate to a particular item—and to remember the formatting that you applied to that item—is called *structured selection*. Even though you select a single cell, the PivotTable utilizes the underlying structure of the data to select all the related values.

NOTE Structured selection applies to page fields as well. If you have a page field with a single item selected, then any formats that you apply will affect only the currently selected item. If you want to want to apply a format to all the cells of a PivotTable, make sure that any page fields are set to All.

Manipulating a PivotTable

You are now probably comfortable with the basics of PivotTables. You are ready to expand your PivotTable to include the entire list. Because you gave a name to the range for the PivotTable, you can simply change the range that the name refers to and refresh the PivotTable.

Refresh the data source

1   Activate the Orders worksheet. Select cell A1 and press CTRL+SHIFT+*.

    This is the entire list. You can now redefine the Database range name to refer to this entire range.

2   On the Insert menu, point to Name, and then click Define. In the Names In Workbook box, type **Database** (don't select the name from the list), and click OK.

    The name Database should now appear in the Name Box. You can now refresh the PivotTable to look at the new range.

Refresh Data

You can also select Refresh Data on the Data menu.

3   Activate the First Pivot worksheet. On the PivotTable toolbar, click the Refresh Data button. Click OK when Excel informs you that you changed the PivotTable.

    Excel changes the PivotTable to include all the data from the list. (Items you had previously formatted retain their formatting.)

    Before continuing, remove the Sum Of Units data field.

4   Right-click the Sum Of Units label in cell C4. Then click Delete.

    The Sum Of Units rows disappear, and since there is only a single data field remaining in the PivotTable, the Data column and field button disappear as well.

When Excel creates a PivotTable, the PivotTable reads all the data from the source list into a special storage area called a *cache*. (It sounds like a kind of money.) The data in the cache is organized to allow Excel to summarize values very fast. When you use the Refresh Data command, the PivotTable rereads the data from the list into the cache.

Sort and filter PivotTable items

When you add additional data to a PivotTable, the PivotTable automatically adds any new items that are now in the list. The new items, however, are not sorted alphabetically. For example, the items that were originally in the Product field—Elephant and Giraffe—still come before the Aardvark item. One way to adjust the order of items is to manually move them. To move an item in a field, you simply drag its border.

1   Select cell B7, the cell that contains the Aardvark item label. Drag the border of the cell to cell B4. (The I-shaped outline should appear between rows 4 and 5.)

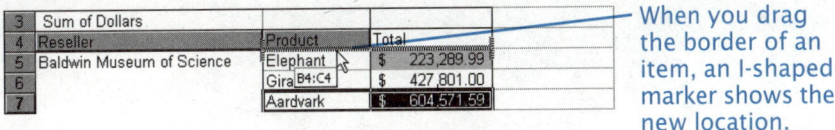

When you drag the border of an item, an I-shaped marker shows the new location.

When you want complete control over the order of items, moving them manually is the most effective way to do it. But if you simply want the items sorted, you can tell the field to always sort them for you.

2 Double-click cell B4, the cell that contains the Product field button. In the PivotTable Field dialog box that appears, click the Advanced button.

The PivotTable Field Advanced Options dialog box contains a group of options that allow you to control how the items in that field are sorted. The default option is Manual, which allows you to rearrange the items by dragging the border. You can make the field sort the items by selecting one of the other options.

3 In the AutoSort Options group, select the Ascending option and click OK twice.

Select an AutoSort option to let the PivotTable sort the items.

The products now appear in alphabetical order.

You can also sort based on the totals for a data field. Suppose that you want to sort the resellers in descending order, based on the total order dollars. First move the Product field up to the page area to get it out of the way. Then you can use the PivotTable Field Advanced Options dialog box to sort the resellers based on the Sum Of Dollars field.

4 Drag the Product field button up to cell A1. Double-click the Reseller field button and click the Advanced button. In the AutoSort Options group, select the Descending option. In the Using Field list, select Sum Of Dollars, and then click OK twice.

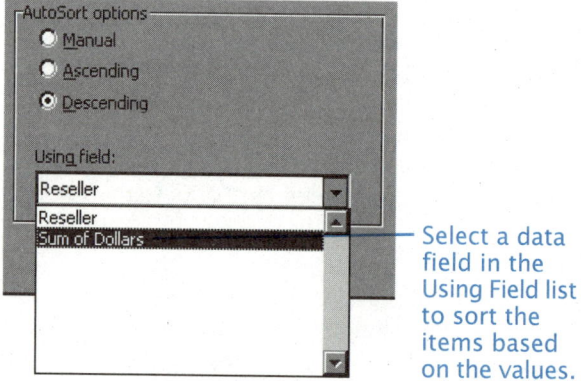

Select a data field in the Using Field list to sort the items based on the values.

The resellers are sorted by order dollars over the entire two-year period, from highest to lowest.

If you want to rank the resellers using only the most recent month, August 1998, you can use the PivotTable Wizard to add the Month field as a page field to filter the PivotTable.

5   Right-click any cell in the PivotTable and click Wizard on the shortcut menu that appears. Drag the Month field button above the Product field button in the page area and click Finish. Select 8/1/98 from the Month field's list of items.

The order of a few of the resellers changes.

You next ask yourself whether the order varies from product to product. If you move the Product field to the left of the Reseller field, Excel will sort the resellers independently for each product.

6   Drag the Product field button to cell A5.

The orders for Aardvarks and Airplanes are dramatically different. But there are too many resellers to be able to see easily which are the top resellers for each product.

You can use the PivotTable Field Advanced Options dialog box to automatically show only the top three resellers for each product.

7   Double-click the Reseller field button and click the Advanced button. In the AutoShow Options group, select the Automatic option. Then leave Top selected in the Show list and change the value in the number box to 3. In the Using Field box, select Sum Of Dollars, and click OK twice.

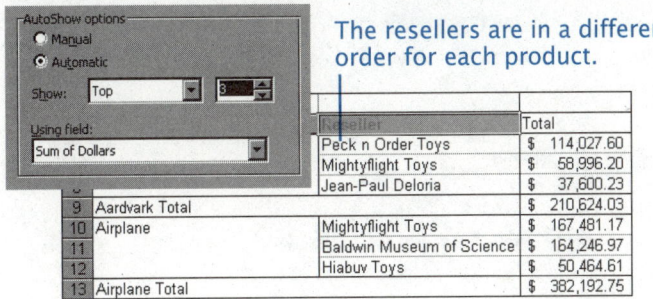

The resellers are in a different order for each product.

It is now much easier to compare the top resellers for each product. The PivotTable changes the label in the Reseller field button to blue to remind you that the list is filtered. When you filter a field, the totals include only the values that made it through the filter.

The PivotTable Field Advanced Options dialog box is very useful for controlling how the items in a field are sorted. You can sort the values in ascending or descending order, either alphabetically, or based on the totals in one of the data fields. You can also automatically filter the list to show just the top or bottom items.

Show and hide detail for items

The list of products is long. Even showing only the top three resellers for each product, it is hard to keep track of all the numbers. In the same way that the Subtotal command (see Lesson 4) allows you to show and hide detail in a list by using outline symbols, a PivotTable allows you to show and hide detail by using the Show Detail and Hide Detail buttons on the PivotTable toolbar. Showing and hiding detail is not the same as filtering. When you filter, you pretend that the rows that are filtered out don't exist—even in totals. When you hide detail, you choose to see only the totals.

Hide Detail

1 Click the Product field button, and then on the PivotTable toolbar, click the Hide Detail button.

Because you selected the field button, the Hide Detail button hid the detail for all the items in the field. Now you can easily see the entire list of products. You can also show or hide detail for individual items.

Show Detail

2 Click the Giraffe item label in cell A11, and then click the Show Detail button on the PivotTable toolbar.

To show ⟶
detail for a
single item,
double-click
the item.

9	Brontosaurus		$	295,277.47
10	Elephant		$	155,336.51
11	Giraffe	Adventure Works	$	100,725.48
12		Peck n Order Toys	$	56,302.23
13		Hiabuv Toys	$	44,870.01
14	Giraffe Total		$	201,897.72

The PivotTable shows the three top resellers for that one product. In addition to using the Show Detail and Hide Detail toolbar buttons, you can simply double-click an item label to show or hide details.

3 Double-click the Pteradon label in cell A15 to show its resellers. Then double-click it again to hide the detail.

Before continuing, reshow all the resellers.

4 Select the Product field button in cell A5, and click the Show Detail button.

When you have two or more fields in either the row area or the column area, you can show and hide the items for the inner fields. If you want to show or hide detail for all the items at once, the easiest way is to select the field button and use the buttons on the PivotTable toolbar. If you want to show or hide detail for a single item, the easiest way is to double-click the one item label.

Drill down to show detail for values

The numbers in the data area of a PivotTable summarize the values from a field in the original list. The PivotTable gets the values in the Sum Of Dollars field, for example, by summing the values from the Dollars column of the original list for those rows that match the current item in the row, column, and page fields. What if you want to see which rows actually went into making any particular value in the PivotTable? In the same way that you can double-click an item label to see the detail for that item, you can double-click a value to see the rows from the original list that were used to calculate that value.

Cell C9 contains the total dollars for the Aardvark product for the month of August 1998. If you want to see the detail that went into that number, you can double-click the cell.

1 Double-click cell C9.

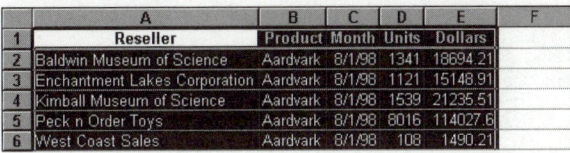

A new worksheet appears, containing copies of the 14 rows that contributed to that summary total. Double-clicking a value to see the detail rows that went into it is called *drilling down* into the detail.

Because the detail is a copy that was created on a new worksheet, you can simply delete the worksheet to get rid of it after you finish reviewing the detail.

2 Right-click the sheet tab of the new worksheet, and click Delete. Click OK when asked to confirm the deletion.

You should be careful when drilling down not to select a cell with more summary than you would like. If you double-click the grand total cell at the bottom of an unfiltered PivotTable, you will get a new worksheet with a copy of the entire original list!

You can use the PivotTable Options dialog box to tell the PivotTable that you would prefer not to drill down when you double-click a value cell.

3 Right-click any cell in the PivotTable, and click Options on the shortcut menu. Clear the Enable Drilldown check box near the bottom of the dialog box, and click OK.

4 Double-click cell C9.

Nothing happens.

Even if you disable the drilldown option, you can still double-click cells containing item labels to show and hide the detail within the PivotTable.

Remove group totals and grand totals

Because the PivotTable shows only the top three resellers for each product, you would rather not see the totals for either the product or the grand total. To remove the subtotals for a field, you can use the PivotTable Field dialog box.

1 Double-click the Product field button.

2 In the Subtotals group, select None and click OK. Scroll down to see the bottom of the PivotTable.

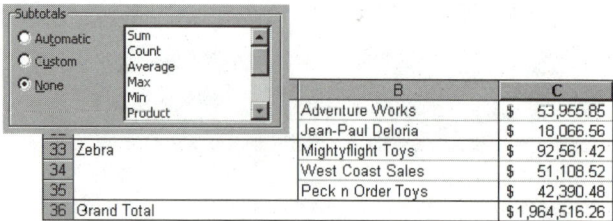

The totals have disappeared at the bottom of each product group, but the grand total row is still visible at the bottom of the PivotTable. To get rid of the grand total row at the bottom of the columns, you must change an option for the PivotTable as a whole.

3   Right-click any cell in the PivotTable and click Options. Clear the Grand Totals For Columns check box, and click OK.

The PivotTable now has no extra totals anywhere, so you can focus on the actual numbers.

A PivotTable has two different types of totals. The totals that appear at the end of each item when the item has detailed items below it is a *subtotal;* you turn it on or off by double-clicking the field button. The totals that appear at the bottom or right side of the PivotTable are *grand totals;* you turn them on or off using the PivotTable Options dialog box.

Hide items

In addition to hiding detail for an item, you can actually hide an item itself. Hiding is like using AutoFilter—the hidden items don't appear in totals—but you choose which items to hide.

For the time being, you want to focus your attention on just three products: Airplanes, Giraffes, and Pteradons—the top-selling models in each of Tailspin Toys' three product lines. You can use the PivotTable Field dialog box to manually hide specific items from a field.

1   Double-click the Product field button.

2   In the Hide Items list, select Aardvark.

You can hide as many items as you want (as long as you leave at least one visible.)

If you accidentally hide an item you want to retain, click it again to unhide it.

3   Select all the items in the Hide Items list except Airplane, Giraffe, and Pteradon. Then click OK.

The PivotTable now shows only the three items you want to focus on.

 TIP To quickly hide and unhide many items in the list, you can use the keyboard. Press the SPACEBAR to toggle the hidden status, and use the UP ARROW and DOWN ARROW keys to move between items.

Create additional PivotTables

You have a PivotTable that shows the top resellers for the three products, but only for a single month, August 1998. Now that you are looking at only three products, you'd like to see the entire list of resellers for each one, and compare the order of resellers now to what it was six months ago. Rather than radically change the PivotTable you already have, you would like to leave this one intact and create a copy to work with.

Because a PivotTable copies all the data from the original list into a cache, creating a PivotTable can significantly increase the size of a workbook. Therefore, you might be reluctant to create additional PivotTables. But because multiple PivotTables can share a single cache, you can actually add as many PivotTables as you want without increasing the size of the cache. You just need to make sure all the PivotTables do share the same cache.

You can create a new PivotTable that shares a cache with an existing PivotTable using several different methods. You can use the PivotTable Wizard (the same as you did to create the original PivotTable), and select the Another PivotTable option when asked for the location of the data in Step 1.

Or, you can clone the worksheet. Cloning the worksheet creates an exact copy of the original PivotTable.

1 Hold down CTRL as you drag the First Pivot worksheet tab to the right. Double-click the new worksheet tab, type **Compare Months** as the new name, and press ENTER.

You now have a copy of the original PivotTable, and both copies share the same cache. You want to change this PivotTable to show all the resellers for each product, and to show only the dollars.

2 On the Compare Months worksheet, double-click the Reseller field button, and click the Advanced button. In the AutoShow Options group, select the Manual option, and click OK twice.

The PivotTable now shows all the resellers for the three products. You want to compare the list of resellers for each product with what the resellers were back in February. Rather than keep switching the page field and trying to remember which reseller is where, you would rather have two PivotTables side by side.

A third way to create an additional PivotTable is to copy a rectangular range that contains the PivotTable. Before copying the PivotTable, hide the detail for the products so that you will have a smaller range to copy.

Hide Detail

3 Click the Product field button, and then on the PivotTable toolbar, click the Hide Detail button.

To copy a PivotTable, you select a rectangular range that bounds the entire PivotTable. You can select the bounding rectangle by using CTRL+SHIFT+* to select the current region, but if you are not careful about which active cell you start with, you will get just the page area or just the data area, rather than the entire PivotTable.

4 Select cell A3, the cell just below the page field.

Pressing CTRL+SHIFT+* selects the *current region*—that is, the rectangular block of cells that includes the active cell, and is completely surrounded by blank cells (or the edge of the worksheet). By selecting a cell between the page field and the data portion of the PivotTable, the first rectangle that meets the definition of a current region is the one that bounds the entire PivotTable.

Copy

5 Press CTRL+SHIFT+* to select the current region around the PivotTable.

Now you can copy and paste the PivotTable.

Paste

6 On the Standard toolbar, click the Copy button. Select cell E2, click the Paste button, and then press ESC.

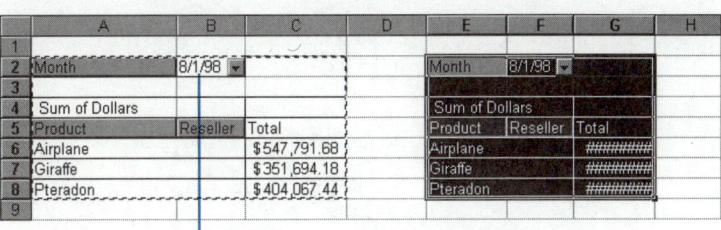

To copy a PivotTable, select the range that includes the entire table.

The columns in the new PivotTable are not the proper width, but making a change to the PivotTable, such as selecting a new month, will cause the PivotTable to reformat itself.

7 From the Month list in cell F2, select 2/1/98—six months ago.

2	Month	8/1/98			Month	2/1/98		
3								
4	Sum of Dollars				Sum of Dollars			
5	Product	Reseller	Total		Product	Reseller	Total	
6	Airplane		$ 547,791.68		Giraffe		$318,287.71	
7	Giraffe		$ 351,694.18		Pteradon		$226,775.26	
8	Pteradon		$ 404,067.44					

The column widths adjust themselves, but the items in the August and February PivotTables do not line up. You didn't start getting orders for Airplanes until April, so the Airplane item does not appear in the February PivotTable.

Show empty items

Typically, a PivotTable shows only those items that actually have values. When you are making side-by-side comparisons, however, you might want the PivotTable to display all the items, even if they don't have values. You can use the PivotTable Field dialog box to control whether the field displays items that have no data.

1 Double-click the Product field button in cell E5. Then select the Show Items With No Data check box, and click OK.

Now all three products appear in both PivotTables. If you show the detail for both PivotTables, you can compare the ranked resellers for the two months.

Show Detail

2 Click the Product field button in cell A5, and then click the Show Detail button. Click the Product field button in cell E5, and click the Show Detail button again. (If necessary, make the column widths narrower so you can see both PivotTables side by side.)

3   Scroll down to row 20 so you can see the lists of resellers for the Giraffe product.

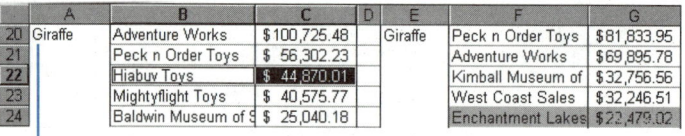

To compare two PivotTables side-by-side, use the Show Items With No Data options.

If you want a PivotTable to be as compact as possible, leave the Show Items With No Data check box unselected. If you want to compare two PivotTables, or print reports that all have the same layout, or accentuate missing values, select the Show Items With No Data check box.

Calculating with a PivotTable

You have now tried various standard permutations of a PivotTable: summing up the values from the numeric columns, and grouping by the unique items in the label and date columns. But you want to show your manager more. You want to compare product lines, not just products. You want to see the orders grouped by years, or even better, by fiscal quarters. You want to see growth rates. You want to compare the volume of large orders against the volume of small orders. All these analyses require items or numbers that don't exist in the original source list.

Count items

The Marketing department puts a lot of work into signing resellers to what they call "big deals," where the reseller orders a lot of products in a single month. You are curious how much of the company's business comes from those big deals, as opposed to smaller, "bread and butter" orders.

Most of the time when creating a PivotTable, you use columns containing text as row, column, and page fields, and columns containing numbers as data fields. You can reverse the roles and use the order size as the row label. This is particularly useful for grouping the order sizes into ranges. See what happens when you create a new PivotTable using Units for the row field and Product for the data field. To avoid problems with other PivotTables that share the same cache, create a new cache for this PivotTable.

1   Activate the Orders sheet and select cell A1. On the Data menu, click PivotTable Report. In Step 1, click Next. In Step 2, click Next. When Excel suggests that you use the existing data, click No to create a new cache.

2 In Step 3, drag the Units field button to the row area, and drag the Product field button to the data area.

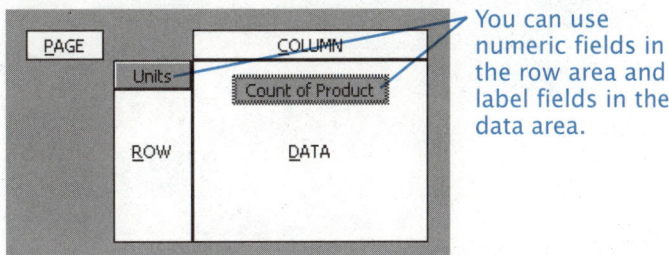

You can use numeric fields in the row area and label fields in the data area.

The data field label is *Count Of Product*. When you drag a numeric field to the data area, the PivotTable suggests summing the numbers. When you drag a text field or a numeric field that has some blank cells to the data area, the PivotTable suggests counting the rows. That is exactly what you need for this analysis. (You could have used any text field as the data field, since each row counts as one, regardless of what text happens to be in the field.)

3 Click Finish. Rename the new worksheet **Count**

	A	B
1	Count of Product	
2	Units	Total
3	1	4
4	2	4
5	3	5
6	4	6

You get a new row for each different quantity level.

You now have a new worksheet with a new PivotTable that shows all the different quantity levels on the left, and the number of times that quantity occurs on the right.

There are over a thousand different order quantity levels. You can get the PivotTable to group the quantities into useful ranges.

Group

4 Click cell A2, and then on the PivotTable toolbar, click the Group button.

The Grouping dialog box suggests starting with the smallest value, ending with the largest value, and grouping by 1000s. First try using the defaults.

5 Click OK.

Group the numbers...

...to count orders in ranges.

It appears that the vast majority of the business is in smaller orders. However, you don't think your manager will like the way these units are grouped. You would rather group by 2000 units, adjust the groups down one unit to 0–1999, 2000–3999, and so on, and list everything above 9999 as >10000. You can adjust the buckets using the Grouping dialog box.

6   Click cell A2, and then click the Group button. Type **0** in the Starting At box, type **9999** in the Ending At box, type **2000** in the By box, and click OK.

	A	B	C
1	Count of Product		
2	Units	Total	
3	0-1999	1245	
4	2000-3999	199	
5	4000-5999	73	
6	6000-7999	25	
7	8000-9999	7	
8	Grand Total	1549	
9			

The list looks better, except that you are sure that there used to be at least some items greater than 9999. The PivotTable always makes the assumption that you don't want show items above the value in the Ending At box, so it hides that item. You can override that decision by unhiding the item.

7   Double-click the Units field button, click the >10000 item to unhide it, and click OK.

This report really shows that it is small orders that account for the bulk of the business.

> **TROUBLESHOOTING** As soon as you group the units, the PivotTable thinks of them as text labels, and all the other PivotTables that share the same cache will have problems doing calculations with units. If you have a workbook with multiple PivotTables and you plan to group a numeric field, create a separate cache for the PivotTable that has the groups.

Calculate percent of total

The more you look at the report that shows the number of orders based on the order size, the more you think something is missing. A large order will, by definition, provide more dollars than a small order. What if the large orders really do account for more of the dollar volume of the business? You better be ready to answer the question before your manager asks it.

PivotTable Wizard

1 Click any cell in the PivotTable, and click the PivotTable Wizard button. Drag the Dollars field button into the data area, below the Product field button. Then click Finish.

2 Drag the Data field button to cell C1.

	A	B	C
1		Data	
2	Units	Count of Product	Sum of Dollars
3	0-1999	1245	12633850.01
4	2000-3999	199	9322287.1
5	4000-5999	73	5722076.18
6	6000-7999	25	3189804.89

You can now see that the smaller orders do still account for the bulk of the dollars. But you can't tell how much by just looking at the dollar totals. In order to see the percent of the dollar total for each level of units, you can add an additional data field to calculate that.

3 Click any cell in the PivotTable, and click the PivotTable Wizard button. Drag the Dollars field button into the data area, below the Sum Of Dollars field button.

You now have a Sum Of Dollars field button and a Sum Of Dollars2 field button. You can change the way the new one calculates by double-clicking it.

4 Double-click the Sum Of Dollars2 field button.

This is where you control whether the PivotTable sums or counts the item. You can also choose to average or multiply or find the smallest or largest value, or any of several other options. In this case, you still want to sum the dollars, but then you want to find out what percent of the total the sum is.

151

Calculating a percent of total is a secondary calculation, because you first have to sum the numbers before you can determine the percent of the total. In order to specify a secondary calculation, you enlarge the PivotTable Field dialog box by clicking the Options button.

5 Click the Options button. From the Show Data As list, select % Of Column. Click OK, and then click Finish.

The percent of total is a *derived* calculation. Click the Options button to see it.

It is true that the small orders still account for over a third of the total order dollars, but the 2000–3999 group is surprisingly strong, considering how few orders are in this group.

You still need to format the table.

Currency Style

Decrease Decimal

6 To format the Sum Of Dollars column, click cell C2, click the Currency Style button, and then click the Decrease Decimal button twice. To format the Sum Of Dollars2 column, click cell D2, and then click the Percent Style button. To replace the Count Of Product label, click cell B2, type **Number**, and press ENTER. To replace the Sum Of Dollars2 label, click cell D2, type **Percent**, and press ENTER.

You want to replace the Sum Of Dollars label with simply *Dollars*, but that label already exists as a field name, so you can't use it for the summary name. However, a computer is inherently stupid. You can trick the PivotTable by adding a space after the illegal name.

Percent Style

7 Click cell C2, type **Dollars**, press the SPACEBAR, and then press ENTER.

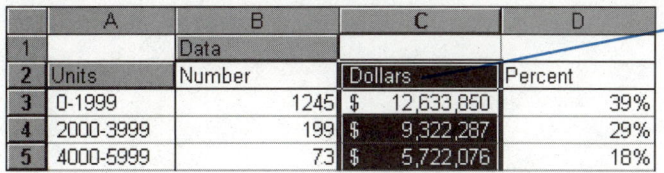

	A	B	C	D
1		Data		
2	Units	Number	Dollars	Percent
3	0-1999	1245	$ 12,633,850	39%
4	2000-3999	199	$ 9,322,287	29%
5	4000-5999	73	$ 5,722,076	18%

To use the same name for a data field as for the source field, add a space after the name

As far as you are concerned, the label appears the way you want. As far as the PivotTable is concerned, the label *Dollars* (with a space) is completely different from the label *Dollars* (without a space).

Your manager will like this analysis. She will be able to argue that the Marketing department is wasting time and money chasing after those few big deals.

NOTE In addition to grouping numeric fields, you can also group text fields and date fields. When you group text fields, the Grouping dialog box does not appear. Before you click the Group button, select the items you want to group. (If the items are not adjacent, hold down CTRL as you click each one.) When you group date fields, a different version of the Grouping dialog box allows you to group by years, quarters, months, days, or even intervals of days.

When you group text or date fields, however, you create new *virtual fields* in the PivotTable. These virtual fields appear in every PivotTable that shares the same cache. Changing the grouping in one PivotTable affects—sometimes with unpleasant consequences—related fields in other PivotTables. Rather than use groups to add virtual fields to text and date fields, you may prefer to add new fields to the source list itself.

Add a grouping field to the data source

You wrote a report explaining that the "big deal" orders are a relatively small part of the company's business. Just before distributing the report, you realize that you looked at only the total business. Your analysis may not be valid for all the product lines. Unfortunately, the list you were given does not have a column for the product line. You could use the PivotTable's grouping command to group the labels, but that might affect other PivotTables that share the same cache. Fortunately, the Lesson5 workbook contains a table listing the product line for each product. You can add a formula to the original list that will give you the product lines. Before you create the lookup formula, you should give a name to the list of products.

1 Activate the Products worksheet and select cell A1. Press CTRL+SHIFT+* to select the entire table. Click in the Name Box, type **Products**, and press ENTER.

Now you can use the name to refer to the list.

2   Activate the Orders worksheet and select cell C1. On the Insert menu, click Column.

3   In cell C1, type **PL** and press ENTER.

You can use the VLOOKUP function to find the product line. In order to find out the product line, you must provide the function with the product, the table, the column from the table, and whether you want a range lookup.

*For more infor-
mation on look-
up formulas,
see Lesson 3.*

4   In cell C2, type the formula **=VLOOKUP(Product,Products,2,False)** and press ENTER.

5   Select cell C2, and double-click the AutoFill handle in the bottom right corner of the cell.

This new column can now become a field in the PivotTables. Because you created the PivotTable using a range name, and because you inserted the column in the middle of the range, all you need to do is refresh the PivotTable.

Refresh Data

6   Activate the Count worksheet. Click any cell in the PivotTable, and then on the PivotTable toolbar, click the Refresh Data button. Click the PivotTable Wizard button, drag the PL field button to the page area, and click Finish.

*PivotTable
Wizard*

Refreshing any of the PivotTables that share a cache refreshes the cache itself, which refreshes all the PivotTables.

When looking at the company as a whole, small orders account for 39 percent of the dollars. Now you can see whether the ratio of big deals to base business is the same for Dinosaurs as it is for all the products.

7   From the PL list, select Dinosaur.

You're in luck. Small orders account for 37 percent of the dollars for the Dinosaur product line. Narrowing the selection to a single product line did not significantly change the analysis. You don't need to rewrite the report.

Add fiscal dates to the data source

Tailspin Toys started business in September, 1996. Because of that, the company chose to have a fiscal year from September to August. You want to create a report that shows orders for the past two years based on fiscal quarters rather than calendar quarters.

The grouping function in a PivotTable can group dates by year and quarter, but it doesn't take fiscal dates into consideration. The easiest way to show fiscal years and quarters in a PivotTable is to add formulas to the original list.

1   Activate the Orders worksheet. Select cell E1, insert a new column, and enter **FY** in cell E1 as the heading for the column.

You want to create a formula that will display the fiscal year for each date in the Month column. For example, the fiscal year for the first date, 9/1/96, should be *FY97*.

Excel's TEXT function allows you to format a date (or any other number) any way you want. You give the TEXT function two arguments: the first is the date you want to format, the second is the formatting instructions. To display a two-digit year, you use *yy* as the formatting instructions. To add the prefix, you use an ampersand (&). So putting the formula *="FY"&TEXT(Month,"yy")* into cell E2 results in the date *FY96*.

Unfortunately, the TEXT function always works with calendar years. Fortunately some simple arithmetic can convert the calendar dates to fiscal dates. Tailspin Toys fiscal year is offset from the calendar year by exactly four months, or about 120 days. If you add 130 to the calendar date, you will always end up in the correct fiscal year.

2   In cell E2, enter the formula **="FY"&TEXT(Month+130,"yy")** and press ENTER.

The result is *FY97*, which is what you want. After you copy the formula to the rest of the column, you can make sure that each month gets its correct fiscal year.

3   Select cell E2 and double-click the AutoFill handle. Scroll down the column, making sure that 8/1/97 is FY97, and 9/1/97 is FY98.

	E230	▼	=	="FY"&TEXT(Month+130,"yy")		
	A		B	C	D	E	F
229	Main Street Market		Zebra	Animal	8/1/97	FY97	1,032
230	Peck n Order Toys		Aardvark	Animal	9/1/97	FY98	1,680
231	Mightyflight Toys		Aardvark	Animal	9/1/97	FY98	206

Next you need a formula to calculate the fiscal quarter. First create a new column.

4   Select cell F1, insert a new column, and enter **FQtr** in cell F1.

Unfortunately, the TEXT function does not have a formatting code for displaying even a calendar quarter. The arithmetic for calculating the calendar quarter is a little tricky, but you don't need to understand it if you don't want to. Just copy and use the formula.

The basic idea is to subtract one from the month number, resulting in a number between 0 and 11. Then divide that number by three and discard the remainder, resulting in a number between 0 and 3. Then add one to that number. The function to discard the remainder is INT, so the formula for calculating the calendar quarter of a date in the Month column is *=INT((MONTH(Month)–1)/3)+1*.

155

To calculate a fiscal quarter, you once again add 130 to the month. To calculate a fiscal date with the format *FY96Q2*, you join the value in the FY column with the letter Q with the calculation for the quarter. Are you ready?

5 Select cell F2, type the formula **=FY&"Q"&INT((MONTH(Month+130)–1)/3)+1** and press ENTER.

	A	B	C	D	E	F	G
					F2	=FY&"Q"&INT((MONTH(Month+130)-1)/3)+1	
1	Reseller	Product	PL	Month	FY	FQtr	Units
2	Baldwin Museum of Science	Elephant	Animal	9/1/96	FY97	FY97Q1	363
3	Enchantment Lakes Corporation	Elephant	Animal	9/1/96	FY97		352

The text *FY97Q1* should appear in the cell. If it didn't, make sure the Month column contains 9/1/96, and the FY column contains FY97. Then very carefully check the formula.

6 Select cell F2, and double-click the AutoFill handle.

Now that the calculated date fields are in the list, you can use them in a PivotTable. Before you base a new PivotTable on the existing cache, you need to refresh the cache so it will contain the new fields.

Refresh Data

7 Activate the First Pivot worksheet, select any cell in the PivotTable, and click the Refresh Data button.

You can make a new PivotTable that shows the order dollars by product line for each fiscal quarter.

PivotTable Wizard

8 Select a cell outside of the PivotTable, and click the PivotTable Wizard button. In Step 1, select Another PivotTable, and click Next. In Step 2, select the PivotTable on the First Pivot sheet (or on any sheet except the Count sheet), and click Next. In Step 3, drag the PL field button to the row area, drag the FQtr field button to the column area, drag the Dollars field button to the data area, and click Next. In Step 4, select New Worksheet, and click Finish.

Currency Style

9 Click any cell other than A1, and then click the Sum Of Dollars label in cell A1. Click the Currency Style button, and click the Decrease Decimal button twice. Rename the worksheet **Quarters**

Decrease Decimal

	A	B	C	D	E	F
	C12					
1	Sum of Dollars	FQtr				
2	PL	FY97Q1	FY97Q2	FY97Q3	FY97Q4	FY98Q1
3	Dinosaur					$ 1,189,436
4	Animal	$ 258,943	$ 206,925	$ 1,478,656	$ 2,511,183	$ 2,634,284
5	Vehicle					
6	Grand Total	$ 258,943	$ 206,925	$ 1,478,656	$ 2,511,183	$ 3,823,720

You can now see the progression of orders from quarter to quarter. Now the report is ready to give to your manager.

One Step Further: Creating a Computed Field

Before Excel 97, you could add formulas to a source list, and you could create data fields that used a secondary calculation such as percent of total, but you could not create a formula to create a new field or a new item. You can now create both calculated fields and calculated items. You may wonder about the difference between adding a new column of formulas to the source list and adding a calculated field. The difference has to do with an arithmetic concept you learned in fifth grade. Consider the following simple grid of numbers.

	A	B	C	D
1	2	4	8	
2	2	5	10	
3	4	9	???	
4				

If you multiply across and add down, you get a different answer depending on the order.

Column C is equal to column A times column B. Row 3 is equal to row 1 plus row 2. What value should go into cell C3? If C3 is the product of A3 and B3, then the result is 36. But if C3 is the sum of C1 and C2, then the result is 18. Whenever you combine multiplication (or division) with addition (or subtraction), you have this choice.

Do you multiply values in each detail row and then add the result? If so, add a new column of formulas to the source list. Or do you add each column of values and then multiply the result? If so, use a calculated field.

Calculate the average of prices

Your manager has just left you an urgent voice mail message that one of the reports the president definitely wants included in the presentation is something that shows the actual average price of the products, taking discounts into consideration. The list already contains dollars and units, so you can easily calculate the price for each row in the list.

Currency Style

1 Activate the Orders worksheet. In cell I1, enter **Price**. In cell I2, enter **=Dollars/Units**. Select cell I2, click the Currency Style button, and then double-click the AutoFill handle.

2 Press CTRL+SHIFT+* to select the list, including the new Price column. On the Insert menu, point to Name, and then click Define. Type **Database** in the Names In Workbook box, and click OK.

PivotTable Wizard

3 On the First Pivot worksheet, refresh the data in the PivotTable. Select a cell outside the PivotTable, and click the PivotTable Wizard button. In Step 1, select Another PivotTable, and click Next. In Step2, click Next.

4 In Step 3, drag the PL field button to the row area. Drag the Units field button, the Dollars field button, and the Price field button to the data area. Double-click the Sum Of Price field button, select Average from the Summarize By list, and click OK.

5 Click Next. Select the New Worksheet option, and click Finish.

6 Drag the Data field to cell C2. Select the range C2:D2, and click the Currency Style button.

Currency Style

7 Rename the worksheet **Prices**

You now have a report that shows the units, dollars, and average price for each product line over the past two years. You quickly save the file on the network and leave a message for your manager that the price analysis is finished.

Calculate an average total price

In less than five minutes, you get a call back from an irate manager who asserts that the price numbers are incorrect and unacceptable. All she did—and she assures you that the president personally will do just this sort of double-check—was to divide the dollars column by the units column on the worksheet. The numbers don't match yours. Your first step is to replicate the problem.

1 Select cell E3. Enter the formula =C3/B3. Drag the formula down to fill the remaining cells.

	A	B	C	D	E	F
1		Data				
2	PL	Sum of Units	Sum of Dollars	Average of Price		
3	Dinosaur	601817	$ 7,478,702.25	$ 12.48	$ 12.43	
4	Animal	998786	$18,084,362.51	$ 19.55	$ 18.11	
5	Vehicle	287867	$ 6,774,246.05	$ 21.59	$ 23.53	
6	Grand Total	1888470	$32,337,310.81	$ 17.72	$ 17.12	
7						

Adding a formula to the data source divides before adding. If you add before dividing, you get a different answer.

Your manager was correct. The average prices shown in the report do not match the new calculations. Of course not. You call your manager back and give her a short course on the associative property of division. She replies with some unkind words about your fifth grade teacher and makes it clear that the kind of price she wants is the other one.

This is where a calculated field comes in. A calculated field is a new data field (you can't create a new calculated row or column field) that calculates based on the results already calculated by other data fields. Before creating a calculated field, you should move the double-check formulas to make room for the new field on the worksheet.

2 Select cell E1. Then, on the Insert menu, click Columns.

You can now create a new calculated data field.

3 Select any cell in the PivotTable. On the PivotTable toolbar, click the PivotTable menu, point to Formulas, and then click Calculated Field.

To create a calculated data field, you give the field a name, and then create a formula that includes other data fields.

4 Type **AvgPrice** in the Name box, and **=Dollars/Units** in the Formula box. Then click OK.

A calculated field operates after the PivotTable summarizes the numbers.

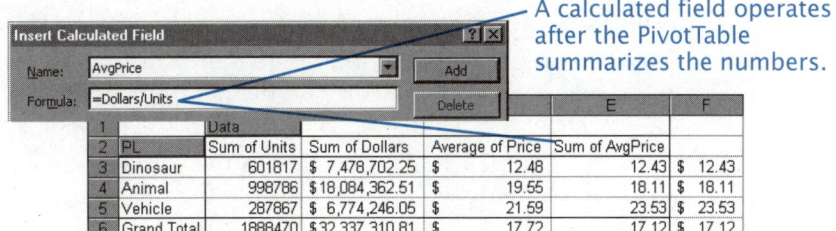

The new Sum Of AvgPrice data field automatically appears in the PivotTable.

NOTE   The label *Sum Of AvgPrice* is slightly deceptive. The word *Sum* in the label really means that the formula is operating on the sum of each field in the formula. In other words, the formula *=Dollars/Units* really means *=Sum Of Dollars/Sum Of Units*. You cannot create a calculated field that uses Averages or any other operation other than Sum.

The numbers in the new column are what the managers want to see, so you can format them, delete the other versions of the price calculation, and be done.

Currency Style

5 Click cell E2, and then click the Currency Style button. Right-click the letter "F" at the top of column F, and click Delete. Right-click cell D2, and click Delete.

6 Save and close the workbook, leave a voice mail message for your manager, and sneak home quickly.

Lesson Summary

To	Do this
Name the range that contains a list so that the PivotTable Wizard will automatically use that list	Assign the name *Database* to the range.
Create a PivotTable using a list named Database as the data source	On the Data menu, click PivotTable Report and click Next for the first two steps.
Assign fields from the database to the row, column, page, or data areas of a PivotTable	In Step 3 of the PivotTable Wizard, drag the field buttons from the right side into the appropriate area of the dialog box.
Rearrange the fields of a PivotTable interactively	On the worksheet containing a PivotTable, drag the field button from one part of the PivotTable to another.
Filter the PivotTable so that it shows only some of the available data	Drag a field to the page area of the PivotTable, and select an item from the drop-down list.
Change multiple data fields that appear on separate rows so that they appear in separate columns	On the worksheet (not in the PivotTable Wizard), drag the Data field to the column area of the PivotTable.
Format the numbers in a PivotTable so that they retain their formatting even when you change the PivotTable	If Excel does not select the data when you click a label, you need to enable the selection. On the PivotTable toolbar, click the PivotTable menu. Point to Select, and then click Enable Selection.
Format the data for a single item in a group	Click the detail item label once to format the item every time it appears. If you have more than one row or column field, click the detail item label again to format only the item in the current summary group. Select All for each page field to avoid formatting only a single item.
Change the data source range to include additional rows	If you named the source range, redefine the range to include additional rows or columns. Then, on the PivotTable menu, click Refresh Data.
Manually rearrange pivot items on a worksheet	Click the item label. Then drag the border of the cell to the new location.

To	Do this
Automatically sort item labels for a pivot field	Double-click the pivot field, and click the Advanced button. In the AutoSort Options group, choose Ascending or Descending.
Sort item labels based on the value in a data field	Specify the sort order for the field in the PivotTable Field Advanced Options dialog box, and then select a data field from the Using Field list box.
Show only the top few items from a field	In the PivotTable Field Advanced Options dialog box's AutoShow group, click Automatic, and then specify how many items you want to see.
Hide or show the detail rows for all items in a field	Click the field button, and then click the Hide Detail button on the PivotTable toolbar. To show the detail, click the Show Detail button.
Hide or show the detail rows for a single item in a field	Double-click the item label.
Show the detail rows that contributed to a data cell in the PivotTable	Double-click the cell whose detail you want to see.
Prevent double-clicking a cell from showing detail rows	Use the right mouse button to click the PivotTable and click Options. Clear the Enable Drilldown check box.
Remove group totals from a pivot field	Double-click the field button, and select None from the Subtotals group.
Remove grand totals from the rows or columns of a PivotTable	Use the right mouse button to click the PivotTable and click Options. Clear the Grand Totals For Columns or the Grand Totals For Rows check box.
Hide an item from a pivot field	Double-click the field. In the Hide Items list, click each item you want to hide.
Create a second PivotTable that shares the same data cache as an existing PivotTable	In Step 1 of the PivotTable Wizard, select Another PivotTable. In Step 2 of the PivotTable Wizard, select the PivotTable whose cache you want to share.
Copy an existing PivotTable	Hold down CTRL as you drag the worksheet tab to the right. Or, copy the entire range containing the PivotTable, and paste it into a new range.

To	Do this
Show items in a pivot field, even if the items do not have any data	Double-click the field. Select the Show Items With No Data check box.
Count the number of items in each range of a numeric field	Move the numeric field to the row area. Select the field, click the Group button on the PivotTable toolbar, and specify the size of the ranges you want.
Calculate an item as a percent of the entire column	Create a data field. In Step 3 of the PivotTable Wizard, double-click the data field and click Options. In the Show Data As list, select % Of Column.
Use the same name for a data field as the name of the original source field	On the worksheet, select the cell containing the field name. Type the new name, and then press the SPACEBAR to make the name unique.
Add a calculated field to a PivotTable that calculates for each row of the source list	Insert a column with a formula in the source list.
Calculate the fiscal year for an arbitrary date in a column labeled Month—assuming a fiscal year beginning in September, approximately 120 days before the end of the calendar year	Use the formula =*"FY"&TEXT(Month+130,"yy")*
Calculate the fiscal quarter for an arbitrary date in a column labeled Month—assuming a fiscal year beginning in September	Use the formula =*"Q"&INT((MONTH(Month+130)–1)/3+1*
Add a calculated field that calculates based only on the totals that appear in the PivotTable	On the PivotTable toolbar, click the PivotTable menu, select Formulas, and then Calculated Field. Type a name in the Name box and a formula in the Formula box.

For online information about	On the Help menu, click Contents And Index, click the Index tab, and then type
Creating PivotTables	**PivotTables**
Using functions to format numbers as text	**text functions**

Combining Documents

Publishing a Document

**Estimated time
55 min.**

In this lesson you will learn how to:

- Control how documents print.
- Control the formatting of cells.
- Create formats that change based on the contents of a cell.
- Add graphics to a worksheet.

Microsoft Excel was the first major spreadsheet program to use a graphical user interface. One benefit of a graphical user interface is that you can manipulate objects directly on the screen, which makes the program easier to use. With Excel, for example, the graphical user interface lets you click toolbar buttons and drag AutoFill handles. Another equally important benefit of a graphical user interface is that it allows you to see on the screen something very similar to what you can get from a printer. You can use different fonts, borders, and colors in a document, and the printed document will look the same as what you see on the screen—provided you have a suitable printer.

Excel has always been a pioneer in providing tools for creating visually stimulating documents. Whether you are trying to create a document that is filled with graphical images, or whether you are simply trying to get a large report to print properly, Excel provides tools that give you a remarkable amount of control.

Start the lesson

> Start Microsoft Excel, change to the Excel AT Practice folder, and open the Start6 workbook. Save a copy of the workbook as **Lesson6**

Printing Documents

Printing in Microsoft Excel is easy. All you have to do is click the Print toolbar button—that is, as long as you are printing a small document that all fits on one page. When you want to print a large document, you need more control over the result. Fortunately, Excel provides you with many tools for making the printed version of your document appear just the way you want.

In order to help the marketing representatives better understand the customers, you want to publish a document that shows the monthly unit orders for each reseller and each product for the most recent fiscal year. The FY98 worksheet in the Lesson6 workbook contains the report that you want to print.

For a demonstration of how to add print titles to a report, double-click the Excel Camcorder Files shortcut on your Desktop or connect to the Internet address listed on page xvi.

	A	B	C	D	E
1	FY	FY98			
2					
3	Sum of Units			FQ	Month
4				Q1	
5	Reseller	Line	Product	9/1/97	10/1/97
6	Adventure Works	Dinosaur	Brontosaurus		223
7			Pteradon		2,869
8			Tyranosaurus		28
9		Dinosaur Total			3,120
10		Animal	Aardvark	83	875
11			Elephant	118	1,252
12			Giraffe	66	1,437

Repeat headings on each page

The first step is to see how the document will appear if you just click the Print button. To save time (and paper) you can use the Print Preview feature to see how the report will look.

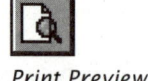

Print Preview

1 Activate the FY98 worksheet and click the Print Preview button.

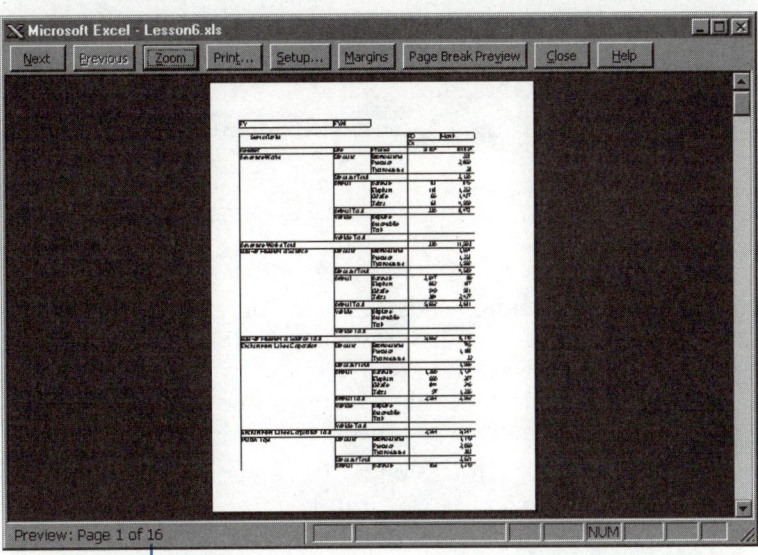

The status bar in Print Preview shows
you how many pages the report will be.

You see the first page of the report. At the bottom of the preview
window, the status bar indicates that the total report is 16 pages. That
is a large report. The top couple of rows show the quarter and month.
The first few columns on the left show the reseller and product. You can
use the Next button to see what later pages look like.

2   Click Next to display page 2. Then click Next four more times to
display page 6.

Page 1 is the only page that displays the labels for both rows and
columns. On succeeding pages, you can't tell what the numbers are
supposed to mean. On a large report, you often need Excel to repeat
the heading rows and columns on each page. To repeat row and
column headings, you use the Page Setup command.

3   Click Close to close print preview. On the File menu, click Page Setup.
Click the Sheet tab. Click in the Rows To Repeat At Top box, and then
click in the middle of cell A4 and drag to the middle of cell A5.

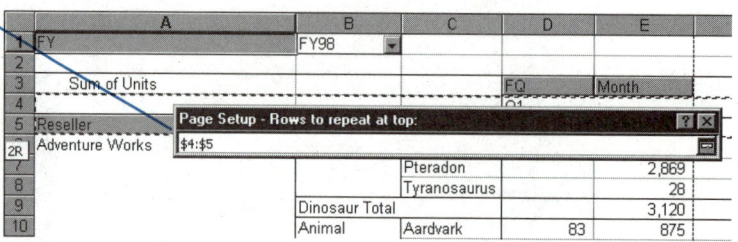

While you select the rows to repeat, the dialog box collapses so you can see the worksheet.

The address $4:$5 appears in the box. Since you must always specify entire rows, Excel automatically selects the entire row when you click in a cell. You don't have to include the top rows on the worksheet, but the rows that you do select must be adjacent to each other. You can specify the columns to repeat in the same way.

4   Click in the Columns To Repeat At Left box, drag from cell A3 to cell C3, and click the Print Preview button. In print preview, drag the scroll bar at the right down until the status bar indicates Page 8 of 36.

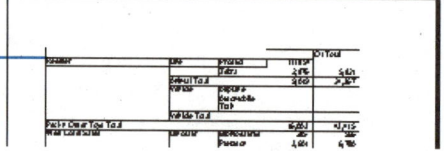

Each page now has row and column headings.

Each page now shows the headings both at the top and the left that you need to identify what the numbers mean.

Adjust margins and orientation

However, the report now extends to 36 pages! You would like to make the report fit on fewer pages. The report currently prints vertically on a page, in *portrait* orientation. You can try changing it to sideways, or *landscape* orientation.

1   Click the Setup button at the top of the print preview window. Click the Page tab, select the Landscape option, and click OK.

The status bar shows that the report now takes only 24 pages.

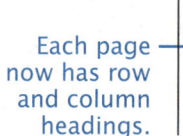

Zoom

If you are not in print preview, you can open the View menu and select Page Break Preview.

You want to see how the report is spread across those 24 pages, and where you can make changes to get the report to fit better. Excel has a Page Break Preview mode that allows you to see how the report fits onto pages.

2   Click the Page Break Preview button at the top of the print preview window. On the Standard toolbar, click the arrow next to the Zoom box, and select 25%.

Page Break Preview mode shows you which
part of the worksheet will print on each page.

The portion of the worksheet that will print is white, the remainder of
the worksheet is gray, and blue dashed lines show where the page
breaks occur. The second and third columns of pages appear narrower
than the first one because extra copies of the row headings will appear
on them.

The fourth column contains only two months. If you can fit even slightly
more of the report onto a page, you can eliminate six whole pages.
One way to fit more onto a page is to reduce the size of the margins.

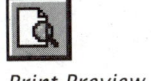

Print Preview

3 Click the Print Preview button, and then click the Margins button.

Print preview displays lines to show where the current margins are. The
black boxes, or *handles*, allow you to drag the margins to new locations.

4 Drag the left margin farther to the left, until the status bar shows that it
is approximately 0.5 inches. Drag the right margin farther to the right,
until the status bar shows that it is approximately 0.5 inches.

Drag the
margin
indicator...

...until the status bar shows you it is 0.5 inches.

There is a wider gap at the right of the report, but that wasn't enough
to fit a whole new column onto the page. If you make the Reseller
column narrower, the report might fit. You can change the width of a
column in print preview by dragging the black handle at the top right
corner of the column.

5 Drag the column width of the Reseller column until the status bar
indicates that the width is approximately 26.5.

Drag the column marker to change the column width.

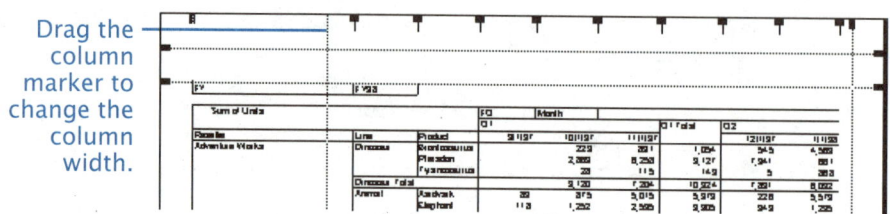

The status bar now shows that the report will fit in only 18 pages. That is good progress.

Adjust the size of the report

But the report still shows about one and a half quarters on each page. It would be easier to read the report if you could fit two quarters evenly onto a single page. In other words, you want to fit the whole report on two pages across, rather than three.

Excel has a *Shrink To Fit* option that can shrink a report to fit the number of pages you specify. The Shrink To Fit option does not work perfectly, particularly when you have columns that repeat on each page, but with some minor manual adjustments, it can help you adjust the size of the report.

1 Click the Setup button, and click the Page tab. In the Scaling group, select the Fit To option. Change the Pages Wide box to 2, and clear the Tall box completely. Click OK to return to the print preview window, and then click Close to return to Page Break Preview.

The report is now only two pages wide. Excel shrunk the report a little more than necessary. But that's all right, because you need to make the second page wider than the first so it can include the grand totals. The dashed lines in Page Break Preview show you where Excel automatically places the breaks between pages. You can reduce the amount that Excel puts onto a page by dragging the page break line to the left.

2 Click the dashed line separating the two columns of the pages, and drag it to the left until it is just to the right of the second quarter totals.

To put less on a page, drag the page break indicator to the left.

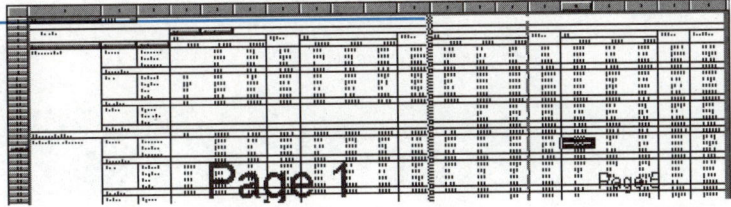

The blue line becomes solid to remind you that this is a manual page break. Now you can go back into print preview mode to fine-tune the amount that Excel shrinks the report.

Print Preview

3 Click the Print Preview button, and drag the scroll bar down to show page 5.

The second half of the year still has extra room to the right.

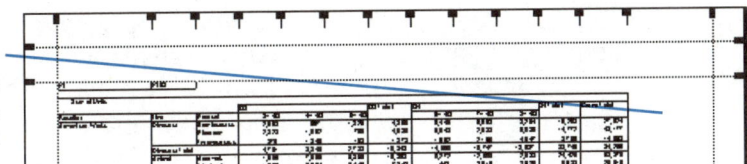

This is the first page that shows the second half of the year. Since this page shows the year total, it is wider than the first page. However, it is still too narrow. You can enlarge the report and it will still fit on the two pages.

4 Click the Setup button, and click the Page tab.

The Scaling option is set to Adjust To 70% Of Normal Size. The 70% is the amount that Excel calculated when you set the option to fit to two pages wide. You don't need to shrink the report quite this much.

5 Change the Adjust To percent to 75%, and click OK. Then click Close to return to Page Break Preview.

The report still fits on two pages across, with the first half of the year on the first page, and the second half (plus the year total) on the second page.

Add headers and footers

Rows 4 and 5 repeat at the top of each page. Rows 1 through 3, which show the fiscal year, appear only on the top page, and they don't look very good at that. You would prefer to have a big, bold heading at the top of each page, and not include the first three rows of the worksheet at all.

Page Break Preview displays the printable area in white, surrounded by a blue border. You can change the printable area by dragging the blue border.

Zoom

1 Change the Zoom box to show 100%. Then move the mouse pointer between the column headings and row 1 until it turns into a double-headed arrow, and drag the border down to the bottom of row 3.

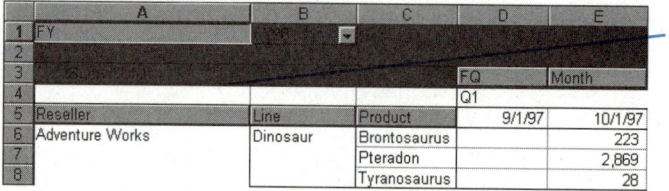

— To exclude part of the worksheet from the report, drag the blue border of the print area.

The blue border moves, and rows 1 to 3 become gray. Now you can use the Page Setup command to add headers and footers to the report.

2 On the File menu, select Page Setup, and click the Header/Footer tab.

Excel includes several predefined headers and footers. Since the information in the report is very sensitive information, you can select one of these to warn the recipient to keep the report confidential.

3 Click the arrow next to the Footer box, and select the fifth item in the list, the one that includes your company name and Confidential.

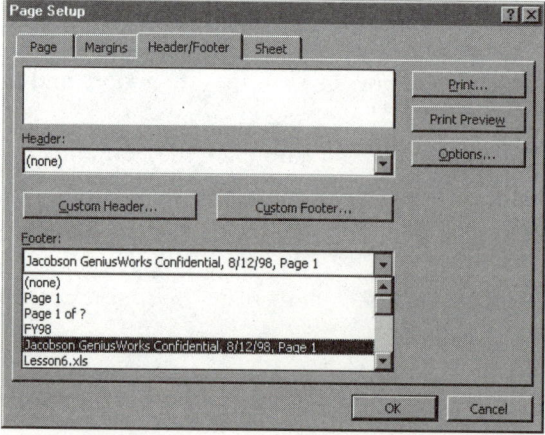

The predefined footer also shows the date and the page number. Because the report is long, you would also like to show the total number of pages on each report. You can use the Custom Footer button to modify the footer you selected.

Total Pages

4 Click the Custom Footer button. Click at the very end of the Right Section box, after the page number. Press the SPACEBAR, type **of**, and press the SPACEBAR again. Then click the Total Pages button and click OK.

You also want to add a header that displays a large, bold title for the report, along with the name of the workbook and the sheet tab. You can use the Custom Header button to create a header completely from scratch.

Font

5 Click the Custom Header button. In the Left Section box, type **FY98 Order Units by Reseller**. Select everything you just typed, and click the Font button. In the Font Style list, select Bold, and in the Size list, select 24. Then click OK.

File Name

6 Click in the Right Section box. Click the File Name button, press ENTER, and then click the Sheet Name button. Then click OK.

Sheet Name

Change the font.

Press ENTER to create multiple lines.

7 Click the Print Preview button to see the report. Click Next to see additional pages. Then click Close to return to Page Break Preview.

Finish adjusting the report

The Page Break Preview shows you the page number for each page of the report. The top left sheet is naturally page 1. Page 2 is immediately below it. That means that you see the first half of orders for the first reseller on page 1, but you don't see the second half of orders for that same reseller until several pages later. You can control the order in which the pages appear.

1 On the File menu, click Page Setup, and click the Sheet tab. Select the Over, Then Down option. Then click OK.

Use the Page Setup dialog box to control the print order of the sheets.

An entire year for any reseller will now appear on adjacent pages. If you scroll to the bottom of the Page Break Preview, you can see that the bottom pages contain only a few rows. If you adjust the top and bottom margins of the report, you can probably eliminate those pages.

In addition to changing the margins by dragging lines on the print preview screen, you can also change them by entering specific numbers into the Page Setup dialog box.

2 On the File menu, click Page Setup, and click the Margins tab.

The Header and Footer boxes control how close to the top and bottom of the page the header and footer will go. The Top and Bottom boxes control how close to the top and bottom of the page the actual worksheet contents will go.

3 Change the Header and Footer values to **0.4**, and change the Top and Bottom values to **0.75**. Then click Print Preview to see how the report will appear.

The status bar shows that the report is now 8 pages long.

You can zoom in to get a closer look at the positions of the margins.

4 Click the top left corner of the worksheet.

Zoom to make sure the header doesn't overlap the body of the report.

FY98 Order Units by Reseller

			Q1		
Reseller	Line	Product	9/1/97	10/1/97	11/1/97
Adventure Works	Dinosaur	Brontosaurus		223	831
		Pteradon		2,869	6,258
		Tyranosaurus		28	115
		Dinosaur Total		3,120	7,204

The portion of the worksheet near where you clicked appears, close to the size it will actually print. The worksheet does not overlap the header, and the header does not appear too close to the edge of the page. The header is indented farther than the edge of the report. The header and footer always begin three-quarters of an inch from the left edge of the page. You can't control that distance.

5 Click Normal View to close print preview without returning to Page Break Preview. Save the Lesson6 workbook.

Amazingly, you were able to get the report down from 36 pages to 8, while still keeping the repeating rows and columns, and even adding page headers and footers.

Formatting Ranges

Ever since you distributed the reseller reports, you have been receiving a lot of new requests for a report showing the number of stores that each reseller operates. That's because some of the resellers have only a single outlet, while others have several or even dozens of outlets. The marketing representatives want to be able to compare the number of units for a reseller to the number of stores that reseller has.

Convert labels into dates that you can format

The Stores sheet in the Lesson6 workbook contains a table showing the number of stores for each reseller by month over the past two years.

	A	B	C	D	E	F	G	H
1	Reseller	96/09	96/10	96/11	96/12	97/01	97/02	97/03
2	Baldwin Museum of Science							
3	Kimball Museum of Science	4	4	5	5	5	6	6
4	Enchantment Lakes Corporation	1	1	1	1	1	1	2
5	West Coast Sales							

The dates on the report are hard to read. You need to improve the formatting.

Unfortunately, the table is not formatted suitably for distribution. The first problem is that the origin of this report was an older computer system and the dates appear as labels in a YY/MM format that is difficult for most people to understand. Because the dates are labels (and not Excel date values), you can't simply reformat them the way you want.

Excel does have a Text To Column feature that will convert labels into one or more columns of cells. That feature can interpret a variety of date formats. However, in order to use the Text To Column feature, the labels must be in a column, and the dates on the Stores worksheet are in a row. You can transpose the row of dates, convert them to Excel dates, and then transpose them back to their original position.

1   Activate the Stores worksheet. Click cell B1, and then hold down SHIFT as you double-click the right border of the cell to select all 24 dates.

In order to transpose the cells, you need to copy them, and then use the Paste Special command to paste the transposed version in a new location.

Copy

2   Click the Copy button to copy the selected range. Then right-click cell AA1, and click Paste Special on the shortcut menu that appears. In the Paste Special dialog box, select the Transpose check box, and click OK.

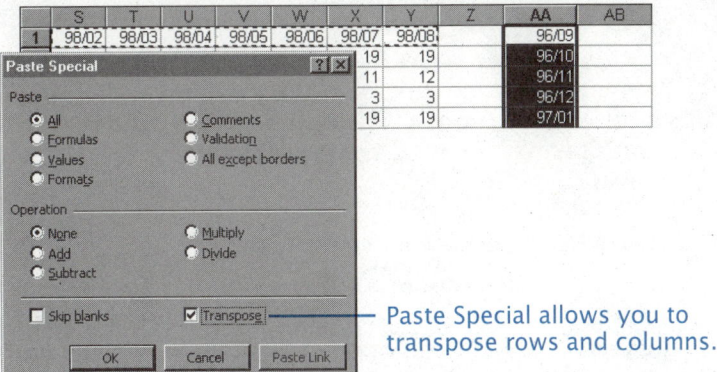

Paste Special allows you to transpose rows and columns.

Now that the dates are in a column, you can use the Text To Columns command to convert the YY/MM dates into Excel dates. Because you are converting from a single column of labels to a single column of dates, you can skip through steps 1 and 2 of the Convert Text To Columns Wizard.

3 With cells AA1:AA24 still selected, on the Data menu, click Text To Columns. Click Next twice to get to step 3 of the wizard.

4 In the Column Data Format group, select the Date option, select YMD from the list of date formats, and then click Finish.

The Text To Columns Wizard allows you to convert dates of various formats.

Excel converts the labels into dates that you can format. You can now transpose these dates to replace the original labels.

Copy

5 Click the Copy button. Right-click cell B1, and click Paste Special. Select the Transpose check box and click OK. Select cells AA1:AA24 and press the DELETE key.

177

When you have a column of labels that you would like to divide into separate columns, you can use the Text To Columns command. You can also use that command to translate any of several different possible date formats into dates that Excel can format. If the values you need to convert are in a row, use the Paste Special command to transpose them into a column temporarily to convert the values.

Create a custom date format

The default date format for months uses a three-letter abbreviation for the name of the month, followed by a two-digit year number. You are sending this report to Marketing representatives. You would like it to be as easy to interpret as possible. You would like to format the dates with the full name of the month, followed by the full four-digit year. The Format Cells dialog box contains a built-in format that is close to the one you want.

1 Select the dates in cells B1:Y1. On the Format menu, click Cells, and then click the Number tab.

2 In the Type list, select the March-97 item.

This is the closest built-in format to the one that you want. You can now customize this format to get exactly what you want.

3 In the Category list, select Custom.

First select a standard format, and then click Custom to refine it.

The Type box contains the formatting code for the format you previously selected. The letters *mmmm* tell Excel to use the full month name. The letters *yy* tell Excel to use a two-digit year abbreviation. As you might guess, you can replace the hyphen with a space and add two more *y*'s to the year code. You can watch the contents of the Sample box change as you make the changes in the Type box.

4   In the Type box, replace the hyphen with a space and change *yy* to *yyyy*

The Sample label changes to *September 1996*. This is the format that you want.

5   Click OK to apply the format to all the selected cells.

	A	B	C	D	E	F	G	H
1	Reseller	######	######	######	######	######	######	######
2	Baldwin Museum of Science							
3	Kimball Museum of Science	4	4	5	5	5	6	6
4	Enchantment Lakes Corporation	1	1	1	1	1	1	2

Numbers and dates that are too wide for the cell result in number signs.

The cells all change to show number signs. If a number (or a date) cannot fit in a cell, Excel does not truncate the number because that could give you invalid information. Instead, it displays number signs. You can adjust the column widths to make the dates fit.

6   On the Format menu, point to Column, and then click AutoFit Selection.

The labels make the report too wide.

	A	B	C	D	E
1	Reseller	September 1996	October 1996	November 1996	December 1996
2	Baldwin Museum of Science				
3	Kimball Museum of Science	4	4	5	5
4	Enchantment Lakes Corporation	1	1	1	1

Now you can see all the formatted dates, but the columns are very wide, particularly since the store numbers in the cells below are very narrow.

Format oversized labels

Excel has a number of tools for making long labels fit better on a report. The Stores worksheet does not have very many rows, but it is wide. Even if you change the printed report to a landscape orientation, the report is short but wide. If you can make cells take up less horizontal space, but more vertical space, the report will fit better on a page. You can orient the dates at an angle so that they will take up very little horizontal space.

For a demonstration of how to rotate text at an angle, double-click the Excel Camcorder Files shortcut on your Desktop or connect to the Internet address listed on page xvi.

1   With cells B1:Y1 still selected, right-click cell B1, then click Format Cells on the shortcut menu, and click the Alignment tab.

2   Drag the red dot in the Orientation box up until the Degrees box shows 45. Then click OK.

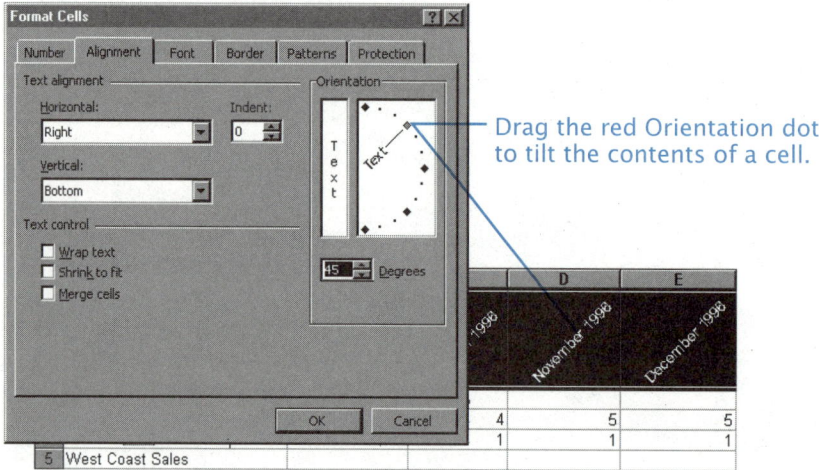

Drag the red Orientation dot to tilt the contents of a cell.

The date labels are now tilted up, but the columns are all still just as wide as they were before. The dates also happen to be right aligned. (The Align Right button is indented on the toolbar.) Before you change the column width, turn off the alignment.

Align Right

3   Click the Align Right button.

Now you can change all the columns to the same width.

4   On the Format menu, point to Column, and then click Width. Type **3.4** for the new column width, and click OK.

A	B	C	D	E	F	G	H	I	J	K	L	M	N
1 Reseller													
2 Baldwin Museum of Science									9	10	11	11	12
3 Kimball Museum of Science	4	4	5	5	5	6	6	6	7	7	7	8	8
4 Enchantment Lakes Corporation	1	1	1	1	1	1	2	2	2	2	2	2	2
5 West Coast Sales									10	11	11	12	13

Reduce the column width to overlap angled text.

The date labels now take up very little horizontal space on the report.

The reseller names still take up a lot of horizontal space. Since this is a single column, you can make the column narrower by dragging the column heading.

5   Drag the line between the A and B column headings to the left until the Width indicator shows that the width is 12.00.

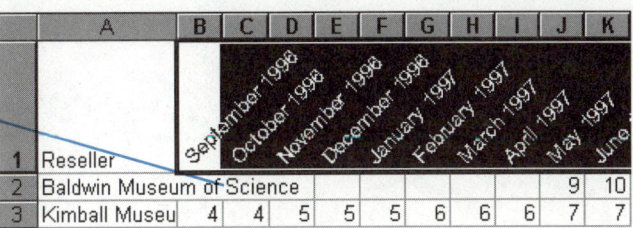

If text is too wide, it spills over into adjacent empty cells.

The column is now narrower, but the labels spill over into blank cells to the right. You can use the Alignment tab of the Format Cells dialog box to allow the labels to take up more than one row, or *wrap*.

6 Right-click the column A heading. On the shortcut menu, click Format Cells. Select the Wrap Text check box, and click OK.

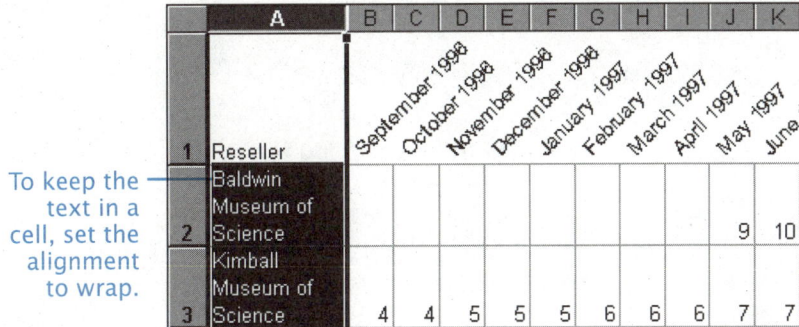

To keep the text in a cell, set the alignment to wrap.

Now that the month and the reseller name columns are narrower, the whole report may fit on a single page—as long as you make the orientation landscape.

7 On the File menu, click Page Setup. Click the Page tab. Select the Landscape option, and click Print Preview. After inspecting the report, click Close to close print preview.

Use borders to group columns

The dates at the top of the report seem to flow on endlessly. If you group the months by fiscal quarter, it might be easier to interpret the report. One way to group the months is to add a border around every three months. Start by adding a box around the first three month labels.

Border

1 Select the range B1:D1. (Ignore the part of the cell that overlaps the cell to the right.) Click the arrow next to the Border button, and select the thin box border (the third border on the bottom row).

181

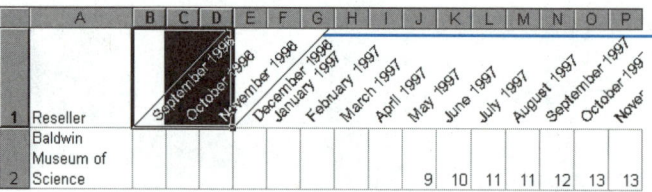

Borders follow the angle of the labels, regardless of what the selecton seems to show.

You can add a single box around all the numbers for the first three months. The Border button remembers the most recent border you used, so you don't need to click the arrow again.

2 Select the range B2:D15. Click the Border button.

Now you can copy the format of this block of columns to the rest of the columns.

Format Painter

3 Select columns B:D. Click the Format Painter button. Drag through the headings for columns E:Y. Then press CTRL+HOME to select cell A1.

Create labels in merged cells

In addition to grouping the columns, you would also like to show the quarter for each group of columns. Start by inserting a new row for quarter labels under the month labels.

1 Click cell A2. On the Insert menu, click Rows.

2 Select cell B2, type **Q197**, and press ENTER.

When you insert a row, it copies the format of the row above.

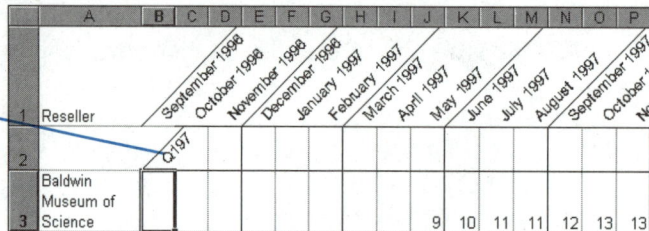

The label rotates to a 45-degree angle. When you insert a row in a worksheet, the new row copies the formatting of the row above it. You can clear the formatting of a range without affecting the contents of the cells.

3 Click the number 2 at the left of row 2 to select the entire row. On the Edit menu, point to Clear, and then click Formats.

The quarter label should apply to three columns. You can actually merge the three cells into a single cell for the quarter label.

4 Select the range B2:D2. On the Format menu, click Cells. Click the Alignment tab. In the Horizontal Text Alignment list, select Center. Then select the Merge Cells check box and click OK.

Merge And Center

 TIP Using the Merge And Center button on the Formatting toolbar is a shortcut for displaying the Format Cells dialog box, and then selecting the Merge Cells and Center Horizontal options.

Cell B2 now takes up the space of all three cells. (Cells C2 and D2 no longer officially exist; if you refer to them from formulas, they are treated as empty cells.) Before copying the cell to the other columns, add a border around it.

Border

5 Select the enlarged cell B2, and click the Border button.

Now you can use AutoFill to extend the quarter labels to the right.

6 Drag cell B2's AutoFill handle to the right until you get to the right edge of cell Y2, just below the August 1998 label.

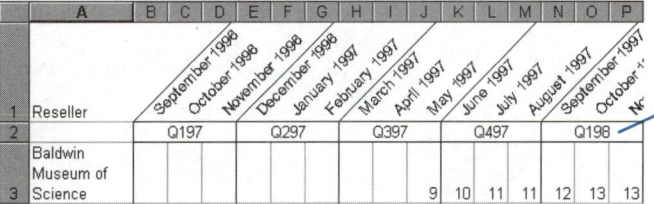

AutoFill extends a series, even after you merge cells.

Excel fills the cells with the appropriate year and quarter values.

Merging cells is a useful way of dealing with labels that apply to multiple rows or columns. After you merge cells, you can format the resulting cell the same as any ordinary cell.

Create and modify styles

You would like to improve the way that the numbers appear. For example, the numbers are all snug against the right side of the cell. You know that the Comma Style button will add a little bit of space to the right side of a cell. Before you do any more formatting, you should name the range that contains the units.

1 Click cell B3. Scroll until you can see cell Y16, then hold down SHIFT and click cell Y16. In the Name Box, type **Stores** and press ENTER.

Rather than format the entire Stores range at once, start by formatting a small section of the range. You can then apply the format to the entire range.

Comma Style

2   Select the range K3:M6. Click the Comma Style button. Then click the Decrease Decimal button twice.

The Comma Style button formats the cells almost the way you want. It always uses two decimal places, and you almost never want two decimal places. As the name of the button implies, the Comma Style button actually changes the *style* of the selected cells to a style named *Comma*. If you redefine the style, the Comma Style button will apply a different format.

*Decrease
Decimal*

3   Select cell K3. On the Format menu, click Style.

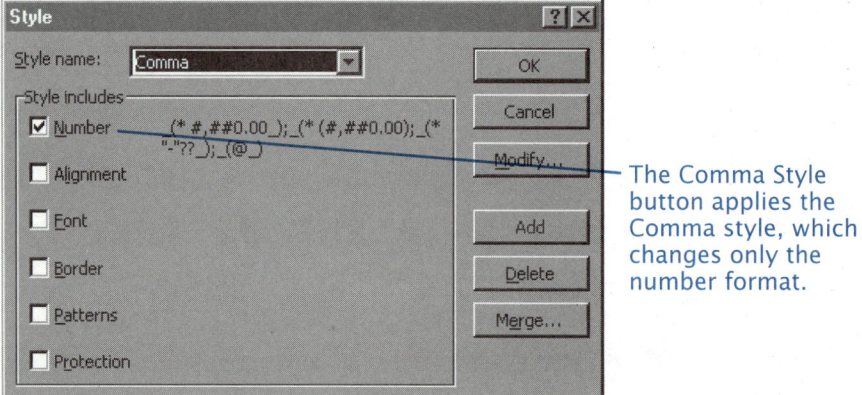

The Comma Style button applies the Comma style, which changes only the number format.

The Style Name box at the top says *Comma*, because that is the style assigned to the active cell. In the Style Includes group, there are six check boxes, one for each tab in the Format Cells dialog box. For the Comma style, only the Number check box is selected, because that style changes only the number format of a cell. You can use the Modify button to change the number format that it applies.

4   Click the Modify button, and click the Number tab. Change the Decimal Places option to 0.

While you're at it, why not change the Comma style to make the background of the cell pale yellow?

5   Click the Patterns tab. In the second group of colors, select the pale yellow in the top row. Then click OK to return to the Style dialog box.

The Style dialog box now has both the Number and the Patterns check boxes selected. You can still apply the Comma style to cells without affecting the alignment, font, border, or protection.

6 Click OK to close the Style dialog box.

All the cells from K3 to M6 change to the new style. These are the cells that you previously formatted with the Comma style. One of the advantages of using a style is that if you change the definition of the style, all the cells assigned to that style change automatically. Now you can apply the style to the rest of the cells in the Stores range.

7 From the Name Box list, select Stores. Then click the Comma Style button and press CTRL+HOME.

NOTE When you redefine a style, the style changes for the entire workbook. The Normal style applies to all unformatted cells, so modifying the Normal style changes all unformatted cells in the workbook.

You can't undo modifying a style, but you can restore the styles in a workbook to the default by merging the styles from an unmodified workbook. To restore the styles in Book1, create a new workbook (Book2), activate Book1 and display the Styles dialog box. Click Merge. In the Merge Styles From list, select Book2, and click OK.

Create conditional formats

As you look at the report of the number of stores, you think of an idea for a way to make the report even more useful. If you calculate the average number of stores, you can format the cells that significantly deviate from the average. You can make text red for all the cells that are less than half the average, and green for all the cells that are more than one and one-half times the average. Rather than manually format each cell, you can use Excel's conditional formatting to format the cells for you. Start by formatting a single cell that appears to be significantly lower than average.

1 Select cell B4. On the Format menu, click Conditional Formatting. (Excuse the Office Assistant if it offers to help.)

The Conditional Formatting dialog box allows you to specify a condition, and then designate what format to use if that condition is true. You want to make the text of the cell red if the value of the cell is less than half the average for the entire Stores range.

2 Leave the first box alone. In the second box, select Less Than. In the third box, type the formula **=AVERAGE(Stores)*0.5**. Then click the Format button.

You can use formulas as part of conditional formatting.

A modified version of the Format Cells dialog box appears. You can change some attributes of the font, the border, and the patterns. You just want to change the color of the font.

3 On the Font tab, click the arrow next to the Color box. Click Red (the first box in the third row). Then click OK twice.

Conditional formatting can change the font color and style, but not the font name or size.

The font changes to red, because the cell is much lower than the average. Now you can apply the same format to the entire Stores range. Because in all the cells of the Stores range there is only a single conditional format, the Conditional Formatting dialog box assumes that you want to apply that same format to the entire range.

4 In the Name Box list, select Stores. On the Format menu, click Conditional Formatting. The format you previously defined still appears in the dialog box. Click OK to apply the format to the entire range.

The cells with small values become red. (Because the range is selected, the "red" cells appear light blue instead of red.) Now you can add a second condition to format the cells containing large values green.

5   On the Format menu, click Conditional Formatting. Click the Add button. In the Condition2 area, change the value of the second box to Greater Than and the value of the third box to =**AVERAGE(Stores)*1.5**, and click Format. Select Green from the Color list, and click OK twice.

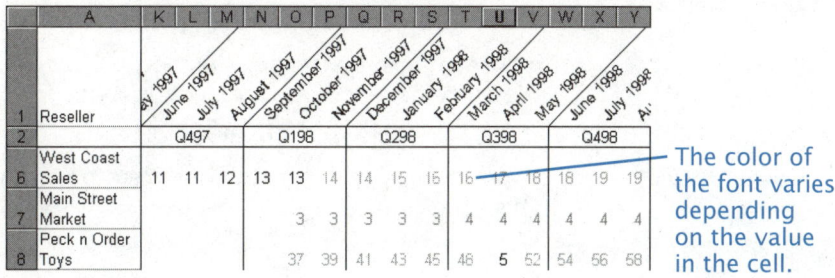

The color of the font varies depending on the value in the cell.

Now the cells with a number of stores greater than average are green. You have a report that not only fits nicely on the page, but also provides some useful analysis.

Formatting can serve several purposes. You can format to make a report fit on a single page, you can format to group related items, and you can format to accentuate important information. Excel provides many tools for formatting ranges.

Adding Graphics

Marketing managers have been looking closely at the reseller reports you created. They have been discussing ways to minimize the costs of supporting a growing number of resellers, and recently decided to encourage smaller resellers to order from distributors. They came up with guidelines for determining which resellers should order from a distributor, and would like you to create a simple flowchart to communicate the new rules.

Create and format a text box

Microsoft Excel shares a new set of drawing tools with all the Office 97 components. These new tools are called *OfficeArt*, and allow you to use Excel as if it were a drawing program. The easiest way to use the OfficeArt tools is to display the Drawing toolbar.

1   Right-click any toolbar. On the shortcut menu, click Drawing.

You want to add a new worksheet for the flowchart. You won't be putting formulas into the cells on the worksheet, but you can use the cell borders as a grid to help you align objects.

187

2 On the Insert menu, click Worksheet, and rename the worksheet **Flow**. Press CTRL+A to select all the cells on the worksheet, and then drag the border between any two column headings to set the width to 2.00. Press CTRL+HOME to select cell A1.

Next you can add a title to the worksheet. A text box allows you to add text to a worksheet without fitting the text into a cell.

Text Box

3 On the Drawing toolbar, click the Text Box button, and then click anywhere on the worksheet to create a text box.

You can type directly into the text box.

4 Type **Who do you order from?** and then press ESC to stop entering text and select the container box.

Font Size

Use the gridlines to format AutoShape drawing objects.

Bold

You can drag the corners to resize the box. If you hold down ALT as you move or size the box, the corner of the box will precisely align with, or snap to, the cell borders.

Center

5 Hold down ALT as you drag the top left corner of the text box to the top left corner of cell A1. Keep holding down ALT as you drag the bottom right corner of the text box to the bottom right corner of cell AD2. Then release the ALT key.

Fill Color

With the container of the text box selected, you can use the buttons on the Formatting toolbar to change the entire text string.

6 From the Font Size list, select 18. Click the Bold button. Click the Center button. From the Fill Color palette, select Tan (the second box in the fifth row). From the Font Color palette, select Dark Red (the first box in the second row).

Font Color

Now you are ready to create the flowchart.

Create a flowchart by using AutoShapes

In addition to basic rectangles, circles, and lines, OfficeArt comes with a collection of elaborate shapes called AutoShapes. These shapes are grouped into categories. One of the categories contains Flowchart shapes. An AutoShape rectangle seems very similar to an ordinary rectangle, but it has some special capabilities that you will discover shortly.

*Flowchart:
Process*

1 On the Drawing toolbar, click the AutoShapes menu, point to Flow-chart, and then click the Flowchart: Process button (the first button in the top row). Then click the worksheet.

A rectangle appears, complete with sizing handles. You can add text to the rectangle by typing, just as with a text box. This box will represent the first question of the flow chart, asking whether the reseller sells more than 5000 units per month.

2 Type **Sell > 5000 units each month?** and press ESC to finish editing the text. Then hold down ALT as you fit the rectangle to the range B5:L6.

	A B C D E F G H I J K L M N O P Q R S T U V W X Y Z AA AB AC AD AE
1	**Who do you order from?**
2	
3	
4	
5	Sell > 5000 units each month?
6	
7	

You can use the Center toolbar button to center the text horizontally, but in order to center it both horizontally and vertically, you must use a dialog box.

3 On the Format menu, click AutoShape, and click the Alignment tab. Select Center in both the Horizontal and Vertical boxes. Click the Colors And Lines tab, and in the Fill Color box, select Light Yellow (the third box in the fifth row). Then click OK.

You will need another box to ask whether the reseller has more than 10 stores. If you clone the box, you won't need to format the new box. To clone an AutoShape object, you hold down CTRL as you drag the box.

4 Hold down CTRL (to make a clone) and ALT (to snap to the grid). Then drag the rectangle down to the range B10:L11. Release the mouse and the keys. Type **Have > 10 stores or outlets?** and press ESC.

In addition to the two questions in the flow chart, you will have two final options. You can create the first answer by cloning one of the questions.

5 Hold down CTRL and ALT and drag one of the rectangles to the range T5:AD6. Type **Order Direct** and press ESC. Hold down ALT and shrink the rectangle to fit the range W5:AD6.

Rather than use a rectangle for this final option, you can use a rounded rectangle, or *terminator*, in flowchart terminology. The Drawing toolbar has a command that allows you to convert an AutoShape to a new shape.

*Flowchart:
Terminator*

Fill Color

*Flowchart:
Decision*

6 On the Drawing toolbar, click the Draw menu, point to Change AutoShape, point to Flowchart, and then click the Change Shape To Flowchart: Terminator button (the first button on the third row). Click the arrow next to the Fill Color button and select Light Turquoise (the fifth box on the fifth row) from the palette.

7 Hold down CTRL and ALT and drag the blue oval down to the range W10:AD11. Type **Use Distributor** and press ESC.

In a flowchart, you use a diamond shape to indicate a decision.

8 On the Drawing toolbar, click the AutoShapes menu, point to Flowchart, and then click the Flowchart: Decision button (the third button in the first row). Click in the vicinity of cell N4. Then click the arrow next to the Fill Color button and select Light Green (the fourth box in the fifth row).

Who do you order from?

Sell > 5000 units each month?

Order Direct

Have > 10 stores or outlets?

Use Distributor

Add flowchart connectors

The flowchart needs arrows to connect the shapes. Connectors are one place where AutoShape objects differ greatly from ordinary rectangles. Each AutoShape object has *connection points* around its perimeter. When you draw an AutoShape connection line, you can make the ends of the line link to the connection point on an object. Then, even if you move the objects around, the connector will stay connected.

*Elbow Arrow
Connector*

1 On the Drawing toolbar, click the AutoShapes menu, point to Connectors, and click the Elbow Arrow Connector button (the second button on the second row). Move the mouse over the first question box until you see four blue connection point dots appear. Click the blue dot on the right side of the box. Then click the blue dot on the left point of the diamond.

Once you connect both ends of a connector, the ends turn red, indicating that they are locked into place.

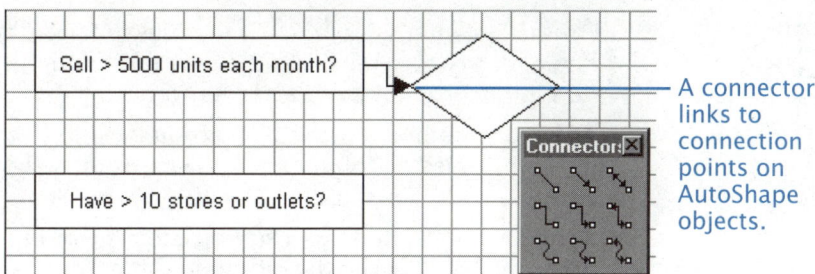

A connector links to connection points on AutoShape objects.

TIP Some drop-down menus can become toolbars. If a menu has a gray bar at the top, you can drag the bar onto the worksheet to turn the menu into a toolbar. The AutoShapes menu and all the AutoShape submenus can become toolbars.

2 Draw another Elbow Arrow Connector from the bottom of the diamond to the top of the second question box. Draw a third Elbow Arrow Connector from the right of the diamond to the left of the Order Direct oval.

The diamond is now fully connected. You can position the diamond and the connectors will move with it. You can't use ALT to align the points of a diamond with the worksheet grid, but you can use the arrow keys to move the object very slightly.

3 Select the diamond. (Click while the mouse pointer shows four arrows, not when it looks like the letter I. If you see a blinking vertical line, you are editing nonexistent text; press ESC to select the diamond.) Press the arrow keys until the left point of the diamond is at the point where cells M5 and N6 touch.

The decision diamond needs indicators for Yes and No. Unfortunately, you can't add text to the connectors. The best alternative is to arrange the letters *Y* and *N* in the diamond using spaces.

Center

4 Press the SPACEBAR eight times and type **Y**. Press ENTER and type **N**. Press ESC and click the Center button.

(If you don't like the Y and N letters, you can wait until you complete the flowchart, and then add text boxes for Yes and No next to the connector lines.)

You need a similarly connected decision diamond for the second question. You can copy the first diamond along with its three connectors by first selecting the four objects. To select multiple objects, use the Select Objects button.

191

Select Objects

5 On the Drawing toolbar, click the Select Objects button. Drag a rectangle that entirely encloses the decision diamond and all three connection lines. (From E3 to Y11 should work.)

As usual, you hold down CTRL as you drag to clone the objects. To move the objects straight down as you drag, without drifting off to the side, you hold down SHIFT as well.

6 Hold down CTRL and SHIFT as you drag the group of objects down. Make the left point of the diamond touch the line between rows 10 and 11. Release the mouse button and then release the keys.

The ends of the connectors that touch the diamond are still red—meaning they are linked to the object, but the loose outer ends of the connectors are green—meaning they are free-floating. To link the connectors, you drag the green dots over blue connection points.

7 Link the connector on the left of the diamond to the right of the second question box. Link the connector on the right of the diamond to the Order Direct oval. Link the connector on the bottom of the diamond to the Use Distributor oval. Then press ESC to deselect the objects.

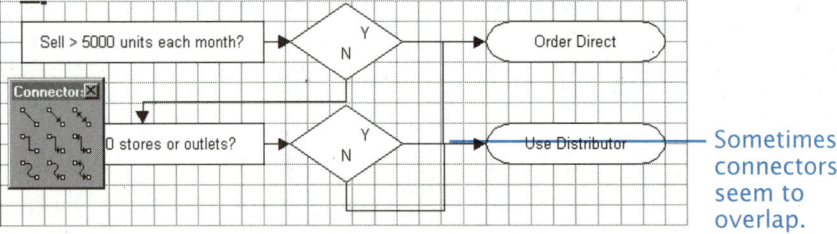

Sometimes connectors seem to overlap.

The two connection lines at the right touch each other, making it hard to see which line goes where. Many AutoShapes have a yellow diamond-shaped *adjustment handle* that you can use to modify the object. Angle connectors have adjustment handles to control where the lines bend.

8 Click the connector that is close to cell U8. Drag the adjustment handle to the line between columns S and T.

Your flow chart is finished. As a final touch, you can turn off the gridlines on the worksheet.

9 On the Tools menu, click Options. Click the View tab, clear the Gridlines check box, and click OK. Then save the Lesson6 workbook.

AutoShapes allow you to create adjustable objects and add connectors that dynamically link the objects. You can even switch an object to a new shape, without losing the formatting or text you have already added to it.

TIP If you want to create an organization chart, don't use AutoShapes. Rather, use the MS Organization Chart 2.0 tool that comes bundled with Microsoft Office. To install Organization Chart, run Setup and look in the Shared Tools group. To add an organization chart, on the Insert menu, click the Object command, and select MS Organization Chart 2.0 from the list of objects.

Create an instant WordArt logo

Your manager is getting very excited about the report you're putting together. She wants it to have a nice cover page and has been hinting that you should make some kind of logo using the Tailspin Toys company name that will help people instantly recognize this quarterly report. You have neither the time nor the inclination to learn a new graphics program. But OfficeArt has a WordArt feature that can create an instant logo for you.

1 Insert a new worksheet and name it **Logo**

Insert WordArt

2 On the Drawing toolbar, click the Insert WordArt button.

The WordArt Gallery dialog box appears. You can instantly make your text look like any of these sample styles. You want something dramatic, yet sophisticated.

3 Select the third item in the fourth row, and click OK. In the Text box, type **Tailspin Toys** and click OK.

193

Your instant logo appears, along with a new WordArt toolbar. Don't look at the buttons on the toolbar, because they may stir up an unhealthy curiosity.

Customize a WordArt logo

Even though you can create an instant logo using WordArt's gallery, the creative, inquisitive artist inside you wants to know what control you have over WordArt. You decide to replicate the instant logo, but without using the gallery. First you need to create a copy of the WordArt logo, and strip all its formatting.

WordArt Gallery

1 With the logo selected, hold down CTRL and drag the logo up to row 2, making a new copy directly above the original. On the WordArt toolbar, click the WordArt Gallery button, and double-click the top left item in the gallery.

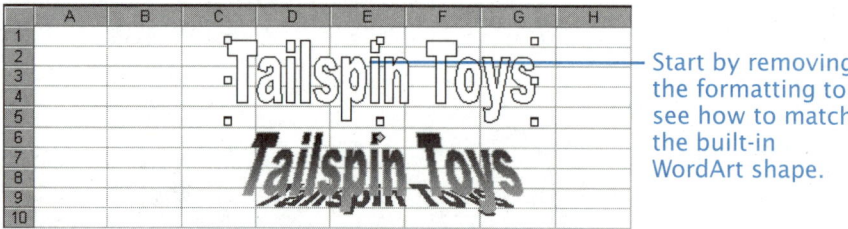

Start by removing the formatting to see how to match the built-in WordArt shape.

This is an unformatted WordArt object. Your task is to make it look very similar to the object below it. Start by changing the general shape of the object.

WordArt Shape

2 On the WordArt toolbar, click the WordArt Shape button, and click the Fade Up button (the third button in the bottom row).

Fade Up

Drag the adjustment marker to control how much the text fades up.

The default Fade Up shape fades up too much for what you want. The yellow adjustment handle lets you adjust how much the text fades.

3 Drag the adjustment handle to the left, approximately half way between its original position and the sizing handles on the left.

Next, you change the fill color of the letters to a brown shaded pattern.

Fill Color

4 On the Drawing toolbar, click the arrow next to the Fill Color button, and click Fill Effects. In the Fill Effects dialog box, select the Two Colors option. Click the arrow next to the Color 1 box and click More Colors. Select the fourth color from the left on the third row from the bottom, and click OK. Click the arrow next to the Color 2 box, click More Colors, and then click the Custom tab. Type **82** in the Red box, **4** in the Green box, and **2** in the Blue box, and click OK. Back in the Fill Effects dialog box, select the top right variant, and click OK.

> **TIP** To find the numbers you need to match a color in an existing object, select the object and carry out the commands you would use to set the color. Click the More Colors option, select the Custom tab, and write down the numbers in the Red, Green, and Blue boxes.

The new fill pattern matches that of the target. In the original, however, the border around the letters is gray.

Line Color

5 On the Drawing toolbar, click the arrow next to the Line Color button. Select the Gray-25% box (the rightmost box in the fourth row).

All that is left is to add and color the shadow.

Shadow

6 On the Drawing toolbar, click the Shadow button. Click the Shadow Style 19 button (the third button on the bottom row).

To change the color of the shadow, you need to use the Shadow Settings toolbar.

Shadow Style 19

7 On the Drawing toolbar, click the Shadow button, and then click Shadow Settings. On the Shadow Settings toolbar, click the arrow next to the Shadow Color button, and click More Shadow Colors. On the Custom tab, type **135** in the Red box, type **91** in the Green box, type **13** in the Blue box, and click OK.

Shadow Color

Your custom logo is now essentially indistinguishable from the instant logo you created from the gallery. All the styles in the WordArt gallery are created using OfficeArt formatting features. Once you use custom features, you can create formats that don't exist in the WordArt gallery. For example, you can create a clone of the logo and add 3-D perspective to it.

3-D

8 Hold down CTRL and drag a copy of one of the logos. On the Drawing toolbar, click the 3-D button, and click the 3-D Style 6 button (the second button on the second row).

3-D Style 6

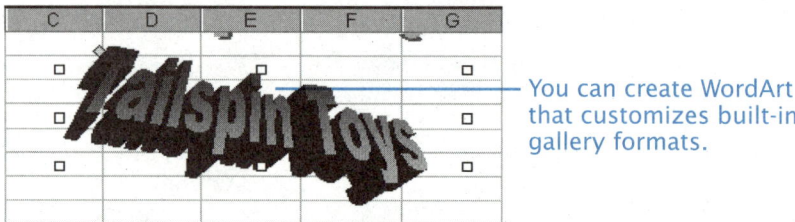

You can create WordArt that customizes built-in gallery formats.

The new logo has a style that you will not find in the gallery. The gallery is useful for giving you instant logos and for helping you come up with creative ideas, but you are never limited to the actual formats in the gallery.

9 Save the Lesson6 workbook.

One Step Further: Formatting a Picture of a Range

You can't use OfficeArt formatting, such as gradient fills, on the cells in a worksheet. However, you can create a picture of a range on a worksheet and format that picture, giving the appearance of formatting a worksheet.

Create a linked picture

The first step is to create a drawing object that is a picture of a worksheet range. The Facts worksheet in the Lesson6 workbook contains a simple list of the total order dollars by product line for FY98.

Copy

1 Activate the Facts worksheet, select the range A1:B6, and click the Copy button.

To create a picture, you must use the Paste Picture Link command. This command does not appear on any menu—unless you know the secret. The secret is to hold down SHIFT as you select the Edit menu.

2 Select cell A9. Hold down SHIFT as you click the Edit menu, and then click Paste Picture Link.

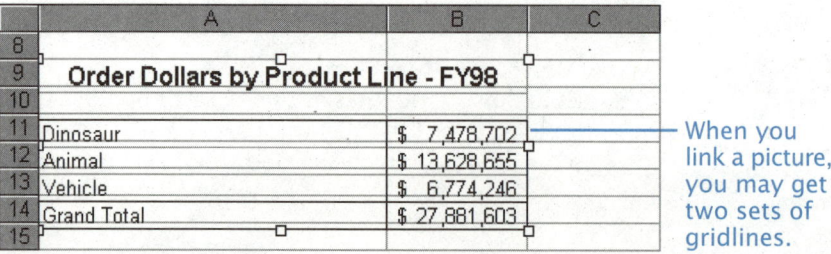

When you link a picture, you may get two sets of gridlines.

A visual copy of the original range appears. This copy is a picture object, and it precisely copies the visual appearance of the original, including such things as the worksheet gridlines. If you don't want gridlines in the picture, you must remove them from the original sheet.

3 On the Tools menu, click Options, and click the View tab. Clear the Gridlines check box, and click OK.

You can format the picture using all the OfficeArt tools. For example, you can change the background of the picture to a gradient fill, even though you can't use a gradient fill with a worksheet range.

Fill Color

4 With the picture selected, click the arrow next to the Fill Color toolbar button, and click Fill Effects. On the Gradient tab, select the Preset option. From the Preset Colors list, select Late Sunset. Select the top left variant, and click OK.

A dark background makes black text hard to read.

The background is beautiful, but it is so dark that you can't see the text. One option would be to change the original text to white, but then you wouldn't be able to see it on the worksheet. A better solution is to change the original text to dark gray—which is hardly distinguishable from black, but can be turned to white in the picture by using controls on the Picture toolbar.

Font Color

5 Select the range A1:B6. On the Formatting toolbar, click the arrow next to the Font Color button. Select the Gray-80% box (the rightmost box in the first row).

More Brightness

6 Select the picture object. On the Picture toolbar, click the More Brightness button repeatedly until it reaches its maximum level and becomes disabled (about 16 times).

The brightness control can't change black into white, but it can change dark gray to white.

You can also add a finished look to the picture report by giving it a multiline border.

Line Style

7 On the Drawing toolbar, click the Line Style button, and click the bottom style.

Order Dollars by Product Line - FY98

Dinosaur	$ 7,478,702
Animal	$ 13,628,655
Vehicle	$ 6,774,246
Grand Total	$ 27,881,603

You now have a worksheet table that does not look anything like a worksheet table. It is still, however, linked to the original cells. If the numbers in the original cells change, the formatted table will change as well.

8 Save and close the Lesson6 workbook.

 TIP The linked picture does not need to be on the same worksheet, or even in the same workbook as the original object. Simply cut the object and paste it where you want it to be. If you decide you want to break the link to the cells, leaving an unchangeable picture, select the picture object, and then clear the reference from the formula bar.

Lesson Summary

To	Do this
Print a document	Click the Print button.
Preview how a printed document will look	Click the Print Preview button.
See how many pages a printed document will be	Look at the status bar at the bottom of the Print Preview window.
Make selected rows and columns print at the top or left of each page of a document	On the File menu, click Page Setup and select the Sheet tab. Enter row and column references in the Rows To Repeat At Top and Columns To Repeat At Left boxes.
Adjust the size of the margins	In the Print Preview window, click the Margins button and drag the margin markers on the edge of the screen. Or click Setup, select the Margins tab, and type the desired value for each margin.
Control whether a report prints vertically or horizontally on a page.	In the Page Setup dialog box, select the Page tab and select the Orientation option that you want.

To	Do this
See which portion of a document will print on each page of a report	In the Print Preview window, click the Page Break Preview button. Or, on the View menu, click Page Break Preview.
Adjust the width of a column in Print Preview	Click the Margins button and drag the column width marker.
Reduce a report to fit on a specified number of pages	In the Page Setup dialog box, select the Page tab. In the Scaling group, select the Fit To option and enter values in the Pages Wide and the Pages Tall boxes. You can leave one of the boxes empty.
Change where a page break occurs	While in Page Break Preview, drag the dashed blue line for a page break up or to the left.
Control how much Excel enlarges or shrinks a report	In the Page Setup dialog box, select the Page tab. In the Scaling group, select the Adjust To option and enter a percentage in the box.
Change how much of the worksheet will print	While in Page Break Preview, drag the dark blue border around the edge of the document. The portion of the document that will not print becomes gray.
Add Headers or Footers to each page of a report	In the Page Setup dialog box, click the Header/Footer tab. Select a predefined header or footer from one of the lists, or click the Custom Header or Custom Footer button to design your own.
Control whether page two of a large report is from the right of page one or below page one.	In the Page Setup dialog box, select the Sheet tab. In the Page Order group, select one of the two options.
Transpose a row of cells into a column	Right-click an empty cell and click Paste Select the range and click the Copy button. Special. Select the Transpose check box.
Convert a column of date labels to true dates	Select the column you want to convert. On the Data menu, click Text To Columns. On the third page, select the date format, and click Finish.
Create a custom number or date format	On the Format menu, click Cells, and select the Number tab. Select a format that is close to the format you want, and then click Custom. Modify the codes in the Type box to customize the format.

To	Do this
Make labels tilt at an angle	On the Format menu, click Cells and click the Alignment tab. Drag the red dot in the Orientation box to the desired angle.
Make angled labels overlap one another	On the Format menu, point toColumn, and then click Width. Type a desired width in the Column Width box.
Make long text in a cell wrap to another row in the same cell	On the Format menu, click Cells, and select the Alignment tab. Select the Wrap Text check box.
Put a border around a group of cells	Select the range you want to put the border around. Click the thin box border from the Border palette on the Formatting toolbar.
Copy the format from one range to another	Select the range whose format you want to copy, and click the Format Painter button. Then select the range you want to format.
Merge multiple cells into one	On the Formatting toolbar, click the Merge And Center button. Or, on the Format menu, click Cells, and select the Alignment tab. Select the Merge Cells check box.
Adjust the formatting applied by the Comma Style button	On the Format menu, click Style. Select the Comma Style, and click Modify. Change the values on the formatting tabs. (You can also modify the Currency Style and the Percent Style buttons.)
Change the formatting of a cell based on the value in the cell	On the Format menu, click Conditional Formatting. Enter the condition and click Format. Adjust the format and click OK twice.
Add text that does not fit into a cell	On the Drawing toolbar, click the Text Box button. Then click on the worksheet and type the text. Press ESC to select the container text box.
Move or resize a drawing object so that it aligns precisely with cell borders	Hold down ALT as you drag the object (to move it) or the object handles (to resize it).
Create a rectangle that has connection points	On the Drawing toolbar, click the AutoShapes menu, point to Flowchart, and click a shape.
Center text both horizontally and vertically in a cell or a drawing object	On the Format menu, click Cells and select the Alignment tab. Select Center from both the Horizontal and the Vertical lists.

To	Do this
Create a copy of a drawing object	Hold down CTRL as you drag the object.
Add a connector between two AutoShape objects	On the Drawing toolbar, click the AutoShape menu, point to Connectors, and click a connector. Click a blue connection dot on one shape. Then click another blue connection dot.
Select multiple OfficeArt objects	On the Drawing toolbar, click the Select Objects button. Then drag a rectangle around the objects you want to select. Click the Select Objects button again to return to normal selection mode.
Adjust where connection lines bend	Drag the yellow adjustment markers on the connection line.
Change an AutoShape into a different shape	Select an AutoShape. On the Drawing toolbar, click the Draw menu, point toChange AutoShape, and click the new AutoShape you want to use.
Force a drawing object to move in only one direction (either vertical or horizontal, but not both)	Hold down SHIFT as you drag the object.
Create an instant logo	On the Drawing toolbar, click the Insert WordArt button. Double-click the design you want. Type the new text.
Change the basic shape of a WordArt object	On the WordArt toolbar, click the WordArt Shape button. Double-click the new shape you want.
Adjust the shape of a WordArt object	Drag the yellow adjustment handle on the WordArt object.
Apply a gradient fill to an OfficeArt object	Click the arrow next to the Fill Color button and click Fill Effects. Select options on the Gradient tab, and click OK.
Add a shadow to a drawing object	On the Drawing toolbar, click the Shadow button and select a shadow style.
Change the color of a shadow	Click the Shadow button and click Shadow Settings. On the Shadow Settings toolbar, click the arrow next to the Shadow Color button, and select a new color.

To	Do this
Add a 3-D effect to an OfficeArt object	On the Drawing toolbar, click the 3-D button and select a 3-D style.
Format a range of cells as if it were an OfficeArt object	Copy the range and select an empty cell. Hold down SHIFT as you click the Edit menu, and then click Paste Picture Link. Format the linked picture object.
Unlink a picture of a worksheet range	Select the picture and clear the contents of the Formula Bar.

For online information about	On the Help menu, click Contents And Index, click the Index tab, and then type
Printing a document	printing
Formatting cells	formatting cells, overview
Formatting dates and numbers	dates, formatting
Using styles	styles
Using conditional formats	conditional formats
Adding graphics	graphics, overview

Creating Charts and Maps

Estimated time
40 min.

In this lesson you will learn how to:

- Create and format a line chart.
- Create a Gantt chart.
- Create complex charts.
- Create maps that represent data.

Baby chicks become hysterical and dart for cover when a sharp-edged moving shadow passes overhead. Presumably, the chicks' brains are wired to respond instinctively to hawks. Our brains too respond directly to edges, slopes, and movement. Identifying physical objects requires the brain to work harder, and interpreting printed words and numbers is a monumental task for overworked and underpaid neurons. (What would a chicken do if the words "a hawk is coming" appeared in the sky?) Is it any wonder we first browse the graphics in an annual report?

Microsoft Excel has always had extremely strong tools for creating charts. Recently, Excel added the ability to display information using maps as well.

Start the lesson

➤ Start Microsoft Excel, change to the Excel AT Practice folder, and open the Start7 workbook. Save a copy of the workbook as **Lesson7**

Creating and Formatting Charts

Tailspin Toys is a dynamic company. It is growing so fast that the issues its managers must deal with change frequently. You would like to provide the company managers with some charts to help them understand various issues regarding the company.

Use the chart gallery

Tailspin Toys has been in business for only two years, but its growth has been dramatic. A chart that represents that growth should help everyone in the company understand why life always seem to be filled with chaos. In the Lesson7 workbook, the Growth sheet has a PivotTable showing the order dollar totals for each month. First, use the Chart Wizard to create a line chart of the order dollars.

Chart Wizard

1 Select cell A1, which selects the entire PivotTable. On the Standard toolbar, click the Chart Wizard button. In step 1 of the Chart Wizard, select Line as the Chart Type, and click Finish.

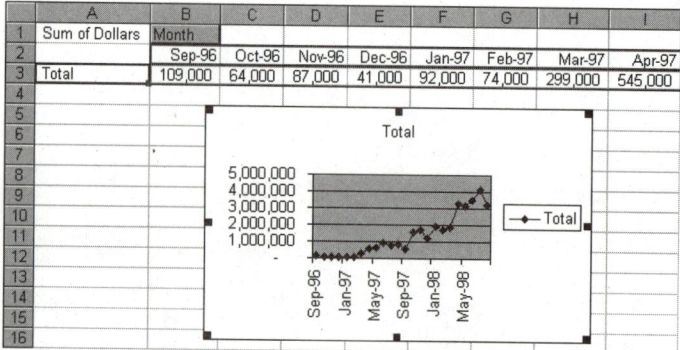

Excel correctly interpreted which part of the PivotTable should be included in the chart. The chart shows the growth in orders, but the appearance is not as striking as you want. Excel has a gallery of predefined chart formats that allow you to create a dramatic chart with very little work.

Once you have created a chart, the first four commands on Excel's Chart menu correspond to the four steps in the Chart Wizard, allowing you to modify any decisions you made while creating the chart. The Chart menu's Chart Type command is the exact equivalent of Step 1 of the Chart Wizard.

2   On the Chart menu, click Chart Type, and then click the Custom Types tab. Make sure that the Built-In option at the bottom of the dialog box is selected.

Built-in Custom Types provide instant designer chart options.

The Chart Type list contains all the predefined chart formats. As you select an item in the Chart Type list, the Sample area to the right of the list shows you how your chart will appear with that formatting.

3   Select B&W Line - Timescale, and click OK. Drag the left edge of the chart to the middle of column A, and then drag the sizing handle on the right edge to the right side of column K.

The chart has a much more dramatic look about it. Your manager will like this.

Customize labels on the chart

There appears to be a lot of wasted space at the top of the Growth chart's chart area. The *chart area* is the gray rectangle that includes the title and axis labels (the labels that go across the bottom and up the side). The *plot area* is the rectangle that contains the grid lines. You can resize the plot area to fill as much of the chart area as possible.

For a demon-stration of how to format a chart title and subtitle, double-click the Excel Camcorder Files shortcut on your Desktop or connect to the Internet ad-dress listed on page xvi.

1   Move the mouse pointer between the grid lines of the chart. When you see a ScreenTip that says *Plot Area*, click. Then drag the sizing handle at the top of the plot area box up as close to the top of the chart area as it will go.

Drag the top of the Plot Area up to increase the size of the chart.

The plot area becomes larger, but so do the axis labels. Axis labels change to fit the room available. You can manually set the size of all the labels on the chart at the same time by first selecting the chart area.

Font Size

2   Move the mouse pointer over the gray area of the chart. When the ScreenTip says *Chart Area*, click. In the Font Size list on the Formatting toolbar, select 8.

Now you can move the title down onto the chart and change it to a more appropriate title. To make the title take two lines, you can hold down ALT as you press ENTER.

3   Drag the chart title (the word *Total*) down to the center of the grid lines. If the sizing handles disappear and you see a vertical bar, press ESC. Type **Tailspin Toys Growth**, hold down ALT and press ENTER, type **(in Dollars)**, and press ENTER.

Next you can format the title box so that it stands out against the gridlines.

4   On the Format menu, click Selected Chart Title, and click the Patterns tab. Select Automatic for both the border and the area, and click OK.

You would like the first line of the title to be large and bold. If you select only a part of the title, any formatting that you do applies only to the selected portion.

206

Bold

5 Double-click the word *Tailspin* in the title, and then drag the mouse to the right to select the rest of the first line. On the Formatting toolbar, click the Bold button, and then select 14 from the Font Size list.

Select the part of the title that you want to format.

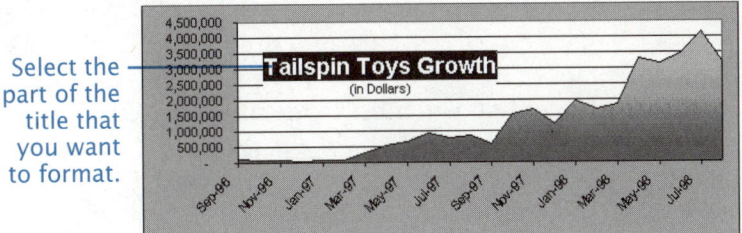

6 Press ESC three times to deselect the text, the title box, and the chart. Then save the Lesson7 workbook.

Customize chart number formats

Since the numbers represented on the chart are in millions of dollars, the labels on the axis are very long. You would like the numbers to be more compact. Perhaps you could format the numbers as thousands with K as a suffix. If you format the numbers on the worksheet, the chart will change automatically. The numbers in the PivotTable have the format that you get when you click the Comma Style button and then click the Decrease Decimal button twice. Before customizing the format, return the format to the standard Comma style.

Comma Style

The Currency formatting category puts the dollar sign next to the number.

1 Click cell A3, which selects all the totals, and click the Comma Style button. On the Format menu, click Cells, and click the Number tab.

207

The Format Cells dialog box has a list of predefined formatting categories on the left. The Comma Style button formats the cells using a format from the Accounting category. The Currency Style button also uses the Accounting category, but with a dollar symbol added. To format numbers as percentages, fractions, scientific, or other predefined formats, simply select the category you want.

Excel does not have a predefined format for printing numbers as thousands. To do that, you must create a custom format.

2 In the Decimal Places box, select 0. Then click the Custom category.

The dialog box shows a custom number format. The custom format in the Type box has four parts, separated by semicolons. The first part controls the format of positive numbers, the second formats negative numbers, the third formats zeros, and the fourth formats text.

Without worrying too much about all the symbols in the formatting code, you can make the format divide a number by 1000 by adding an extra comma after the final zero. You only need to change the positive and negative number portions. While you're at it, you can add the letter "K" after the comma to make it clear that the number represents thousands of dollars.

3 In the Type box, click after the first 0. Type ,**K** (a comma and the letter "K"). Click after the second 0, and type ,**K** again. Then click OK.

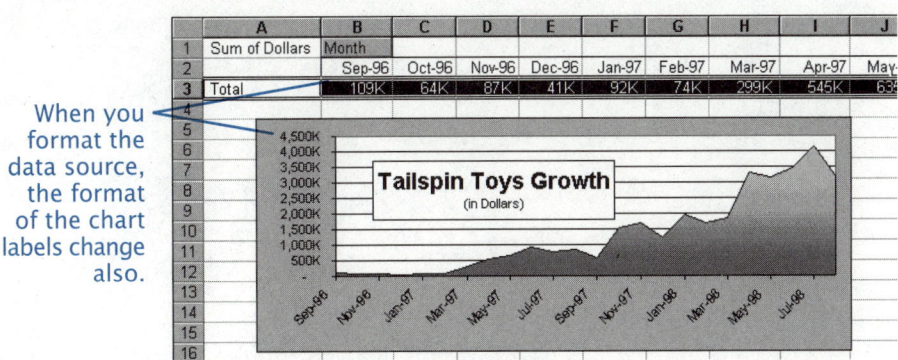

When you format the data source, the format of the chart labels change also.

Both the PivotTable and the chart axis are formatted as thousands of dollars. This will be a good chart to submit to your manager.

Creating a Gantt Chart

The company has been trying to analyze the process of getting new products ready to sell. The Planning department came up with a table that shows the target start date and duration for each of the four phases for the next round of products: Design, Build, Test, and Distribute. The planning table is on the Gantt sheet of the Lesson7 workbook.

	A	B	C	D
1		Start	Duration	
2	Design	Mar-98	80	
3	Build	May-98	55	
4	Test	Jul-98	30	
5	Distribute	Aug-98	65	
6				

You want to create a Gantt chart displaying this project information.

The Design phase began in March and is estimated to last 80 days. The Build phase begins when the Design phase completes and so forth. You would like to create a Gantt chart with bars to show each phase.

Chart Wizard

1 Activate the Gantt worksheet, select cell A1, and click the Chart Wizard button. In step 1, click the Custom Types tab, make sure the Built-In option is selected, select Floating Bars, and click Finish. Move the chart so its top left corner is close to the top left corner of cell D1.

209

The Floating Bars built-in chart type creates a Gantt chart.

The Floating Bars built-in type is essentially a Gantt chart. The first series of bars (which corresponds to the starting date for each phase) is formatted as invisible, with no area fill and no border.

The fonts on the chart are too large. That's because they are set to automatically change size, or *scale*, if you change the size of the chart. The easiest way to turn off automatic scaling is to set any one attribute of the font. If you change the color of the font to match the ivory color of the bars, the font will change to the default size.

Font Color

2 On the Formatting toolbar, click the arrow next to the Font Color button, and select Ivory (the third box in the second row from the bottom).

Changing the color of the font disables automatic scaling and lets the size of the font return to normal.

The bars on the chart start from the bottom and move up. You would rather have the first phase of the project appear at the top. You can make the axis display the categories in reverse order.

3 Double-click one of the category labels (Distribute, Test, and so on) to display the Format Axis dialog box, and click the Scale tab. Select the Categories In Reverse Order check box, and click OK.

The first bar in the chart does not begin until almost halfway across the chart. That's because Excel rounds the dates down about 150 days, or half a year. You would like the first bar to begin right on the axis. In order to do that, you must find out the number that corresponds to the first date in the table. Dates in Excel are really numbers that count the days since the beginning of the century, and then they are formatted to look like dates. To find out the underlying number for a date, clear the formatting of the cell.

Undo

4 Select cell B2. On the Edit menu, point to Clear, and then click Formats. Note the number, and click the Undo button to restore the formatting.

The serial number for March 1, 1998, is 35855. You can now tell the chart to use this number as the minimum scale. You can also tell it to display labels every 62 days so that the labels will appear every other month.

The default Major unit value will vary depending on the resolution of your screen.

5 Double-click one of the dates along the bottom of the chart to display the Format Axis dialog box. On the Scale tab, replace the default 35700 in the Minimum box with 35855. Replace the default value in the Major unit box with 62. Then click OK.

You have a very nice, professional Gantt chart.

Interact with the chart

The Gantt chart gives you a clear vision of what the project flow will be. As you show the chart to the Planning analyst, you decide together that the Build phase is not long enough. Rather than change the numbers on the worksheet, you can change the numbers interactively on the chart. In order to interact with a chart, you must get rid of the 3-D formatting.

For a demonstration of how to modify data directly on a chart, double-click the Excel Camcorder Files shortcut on your Desktop or connect to the Internet address listed on page xvi.

1 Click the chart area on the chart. On the Chart menu, click Chart Type, and click the Standard Types tab. With Bar as the Chart Type, select the Stacked Bar option (the second type on the first row). Then click OK.

The chart no longer has its 3-D formatting. Now you can interact with the chart by selecting a single bar.

2 Click the Build box to select the series of points. Then click the Build box again to select only the one marker.

Once you select a single marker on a bar, column, line, or XY chart, you can drag that marker to change the value on the worksheet.

3 Move the mouse over the right edge of the Build box until the mouse pointer becomes a two-headed arrow. Then drag the right edge to the right until the ScreenTip is approximately 100.

Drag the end of the bar to change a constant on the worksheet.

The value of cell C3 on the worksheet changes to 100. When you drag a chart item that is linked to a cell containing a constant, the constant value changes. If you drag a chart item linked to a cell containing a formula, Excel uses the Goal Seek tool to ask you what to change.

For example, you want to start distribution by the first of September. How many days could you spend testing in order for distribution to start that soon? You need to drag the invisible bar to the left of the Distribution box. The easiest way to select that bar is to use the arrow keys.

4 Click the chart area, and then click the Distribute box to select the entire series of boxes. Then press the LEFT ARROW key to select the box representing the distribution start date.

5 Drag the right edge of the invisible box until the mark at the top aligns with the Sep-98 tick mark.

The Goal Seek dialog box asks you which cell to change.

6 Click cell C4, the Test Duration box, and click OK. When the Goal Seek Status box announces success, click OK again.

If you drag a bar that is linked to a cell containing a formula, the Goal Seek dialog box asks which input cell you want to change.

You will need to reduce testing to about 8 days in order to start distribution at the first of September if the build phase takes 100 days.

7 Save the Lesson7 workbook.

An Excel chart can be more than a mechanism for displaying information; it can also be a tool for analyzing and manipulating numbers graphically.

Creating Complex Charts

Most business charts consist of pie charts, line charts, and bar charts. Excel can create these basic charts, but Excel can also create variations of these charts, variations that can help you understand the numbers that underlie the charts.

Create a pie of a pie

You have been thinking a lot about the resellers that Tailspin Toys works with. Several of the resellers have been with the company almost since the beginning. The Pie worksheet contains a PivotTable that shows the resellers who were selling back in March of 1997. You would like to show the relative size of those early resellers. A pie chart is a good way to show relative size.

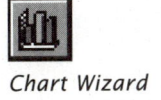

Chart Wizard

1   Activate the Pie worksheet, select cell A3, and click the Chart Wizard button. In Step 1, click the Standard Types tab, double-click Pie in the Chart Types list, and click Finish. Move the top left corner of the chart to the top of cell C1, and drag the bottom of the chart down to row 16.

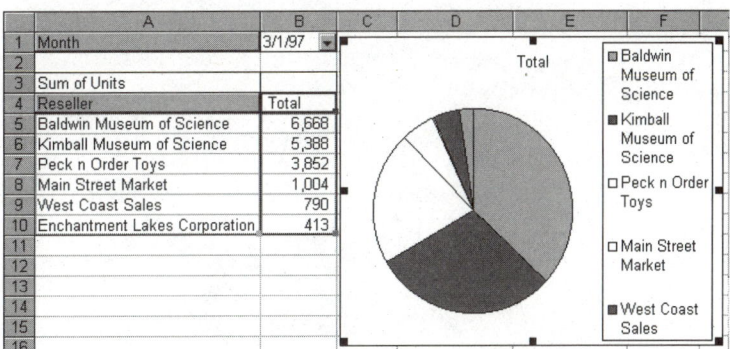

The legend is not large enough for all the resellers. If you put the legend at the bottom of the chart, the reseller names will each fit on a single line.

2   Double-click the legend and click the Placement tab. Select the Bottom option, and click OK. Drag the top of the legend down to the middle of the second reseller (Kimball Museum of Science).

213

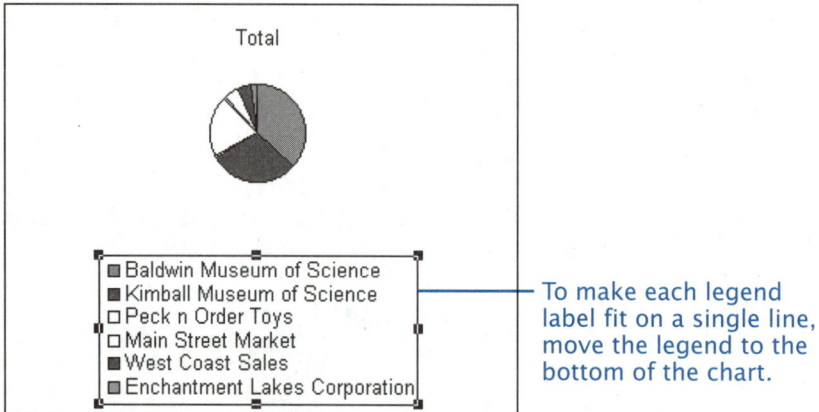

To make each legend label fit on a single line, move the legend to the bottom of the chart.

The title takes up valuable space and does not provide useful information, so you can remove it.

3 Right-click the title (Total) and click Clear.

Now you have room to enlarge the pie itself.

4 Click the plot area, and drag its top left corner up to the top of the chart. Drag its bottom right corner down until it almost touches the legend.

Labels showing the percent of each segment would clarify the relationship between the resellers.

5 Double-click the pie, and click the Data Labels tab. Select the Show Percent option and click OK.

Data labels may be hard to read.

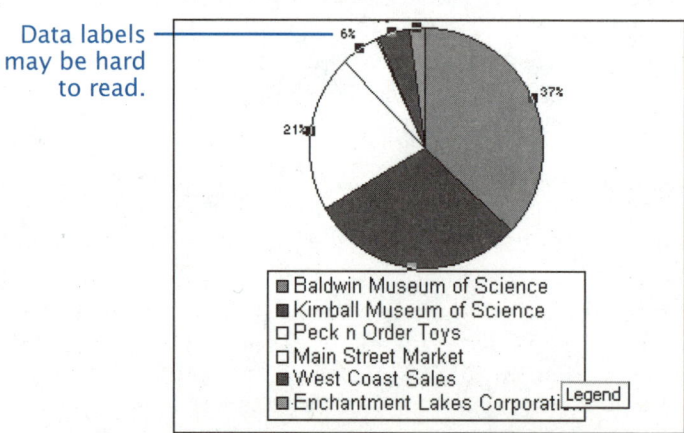

The labels appear, but they are hard to read because they are outside the pie. You can make the labels appear inside each segment.

6   Double-click one of the labels, and click the Alignment tab. In the
Label Position list, select Center, and click OK.

The labels all fit on the chart, but some of the segments are so small
that the labels are hard to read. Excel's new Pie Of Pie option allows
you to combine these small segments into a single segment, along with
a separate pie chart that shows just the small segments.

7   On the Chart menu, click Chart Type. Select the Pie Of Pie option (the
third chart on the top row), and click OK. Once again, enlarge the plot
area to fill the top portion of the chart area.

You can control how many segments go into the secondary pie.

8   Double-click either pie, and click the Options tab.

The Pie Of Pie chart
type lets you break the
small segments out
into a separate pie.

The Format Data Series dialog box lets you control how many segments
go into each pie. If you set the Second Plot Contains The Last box to 0,
then the chart on the left is the same as the original pie chart. If you set
the box to 6 or more (for this chart), then the chart on the right is the
same as the original pie chart. You can experiment with the optimal
setting for any given chart. For this chart, 3 is a good value.

9   Change the Second Plot Contains The Last box to 3, and click OK. Then
save the Lesson7 workbook.

The Pie Of Pie chart allows you to clearly see the relationship between the
resellers back in March of 1997. You can see that the smaller three resellers
combined accounted for only 12% of the orders that month, fewer dollars than
any of the other three resellers. But you can still see the detail for the small
resellers, without merely lumping them all into "other."

Create an XY chart

Four of the companies that sell Tailspin Toys' models are publicly traded on the stock market. The head of the Employee Benefits department has decided to allow employees to purchase stock in those resellers as retirement plan options. She came to you for help creating a chart that would help employees understand how the stock prices for those companies have done over the past three years. She has found information for each of the four companies on how much the end-of-month stock prices have grown (the *return*) and on how much the prices have fluctuated (the *risk*). These numbers are on the XY sheet in the Lesson7 workbook.

	A	B	C	D
1	Reseller	Risk	Return	
2	Adventure Works	3%	3.3%	
3	Lakes & Sons	12%	15.0%	
4	Hiabuv Toys	10%	5.5%	
5	Wingtip Toys	8%	17.0%	
6				

It is good for the price of a company's stock to have grown over the past few years, but it is not good if the price has fluctuated widely. She would like to create a chart that compares the risk with the return. An XY (Scatter) chart compares one value against another value. A line chart uses the X axis (the horizontal axis) for evenly spaced labels, and scales values only on the Y axis (the vertical axis). An XY (Scatter) chart scales values on both the X axis and the Y axis.

Chart Wizard

1   Activate the XY worksheet, select the range B1:C5, and click the Chart Wizard button.

Before creating the XY (Scatter) chart, you can see the difference between an XY (Scatter) chart and a line chart by previewing a line chart using these data values.

2   Select Line from the Chart Type list. Then click and hold down the button labeled Press And Hold To View Sample.

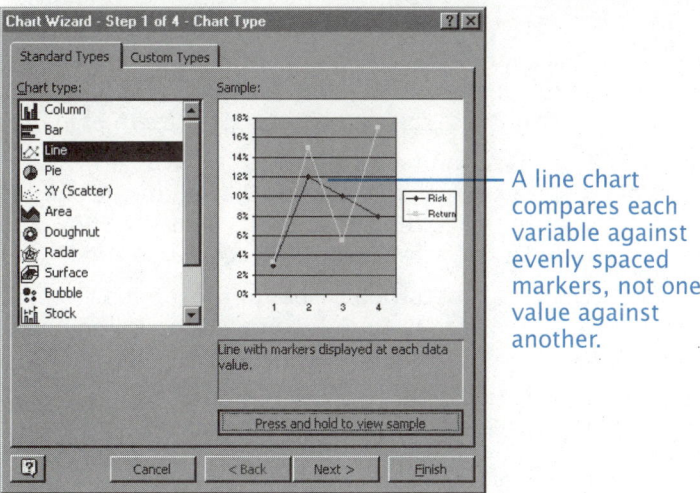

A line chart compares each variable against evenly spaced markers, not one value against another.

Ignore the lines on the chart; you can remove them later. The chart has four columns of evenly spaced numbers, one for each stock. Each column has two points, one for the Risk, and one for the Return. Now you can see what the same information looks like as an XY (Scatter) chart.

3 Select XY (Scatter) from the Chart Type list, and click Next (not Finish).

An XY (Scatter) chart can plot the return on one axis and the risk on the other axis.

The points on this chart are not evenly spaced along the X axis. The spacing on the X axis is controlled by the Risk values. The spacing on the Y axis is controlled by the Return values. In fact, you should add titles to these axes. You can add titles in Step 3 of the Chart Wizard.

4 Click Next and click the Titles tab. Clear the Chart Title box. In the Value (X) Axis box, type **Risk**, and in the Value (Y) Axis box, type **Return**. Click the Legend tab, clear the Show Legend check box, and click Finish. Move the top left corner of the chart to cell D1.

On this chart, a point close to the top left corner is good, and a point close to the bottom right corner is bad. It is hard, however, to identify which point represents which company. You should add labels to the points, showing the names of the companies.

Unfortunately (and unbelievably!), Excel does not have an easy way to link the list of company names to the chart. You must link the labels one at a time. You can simplify the task slightly by creating automatic labels for the points. Later, you will replace the automatic labels with the company names.

5 Double-click one of the points on the chart to display the Format Data Series dialog box. Click the Data Labels tab, select the Show Label option, and click OK.

To add the Reseller names as labels, you must first assign default labels to the points.

	A	B	C
1	Reseller	Risk	Return
2	Adventure Works	3%	3.3%
3	Lakes & Sons	12%	15.0%
4	Hiabuv Toys	10%	5.5%
5	Wingtip Toys	8%	17.0%
6			
7			
8			
9			
10			
11			
12			
13			

This adds the X axis value as a label for each point. Now you must replace each default label with a link to the company name.

Enter

6 Click the 3% label to select all the labels. Click the 3% label again to select that one label. Type an equal sign (=), click cell A2 (the reseller name next to the 3% value on the worksheet), and click the Enter button. Repeat for each of the other three labels: click the default label, type an equal sign, click the cell with the appropriate company name, and click the Enter button.

The labels might be easier to read if each one were centered around its data marker. You can format the alignment of all the labels at once.

7 Click the background of the chart (to deselect the data label), and then double-click any label. Click the Alignment tab, select Center from the Label Position list, and click OK.

The labels now surround the markers. The markers would be easier to identify if each one had a different color. Changing the markers is easy once you select the series of markers. But now that the labels surround the markers, clicking a marker will always select the label. You can use the Chart toolbar to select the series of markers.

8 On the Chart toolbar, click the arrow next to the Chart Objects list, and select Series "Return." On the Format menu, click Selected Data Series, and click the Options tab. Select the Vary Colors By Point check box, and click OK.

Then link each label individually to the appropriate cell.

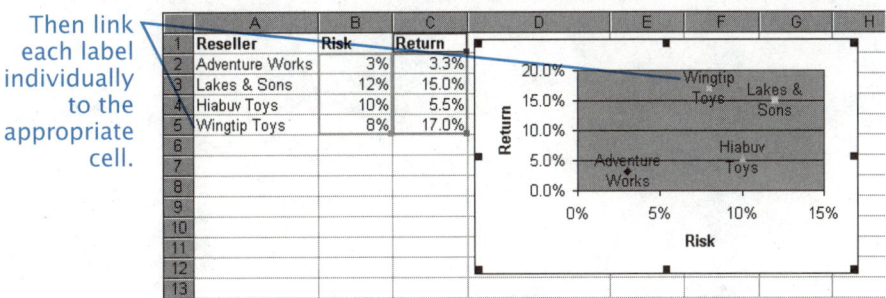

The XY (Scatter) chart can now give an accurate and informative picture of how the companies' stock prices have performed over the past few years. Of course, past performance is no guarantee of future results.

Create a bubble chart

It has been two days since you gave the XY chart to the Employee Benefits department manager. Just when you were feeling safe that the project was finished, she sent you an urgent message. She is very happy with the XY chart, except that she just thought of something new. She would like to also show the size of each company on the chart. The size of the company (its *valuation*) is the dollar amount of the shares currently outstanding. The Bubble worksheet in the Lesson7 workbook contains the valuation of each company. Is there some way that you could include the size of the companies on the chart?

Fortunately, Excel has a new kind of chart, called a *bubble chart*, that is just like an XY chart, except that it uses a third column of values to control the size of each marker. Unfortunately, the Chart Wizard does not seem to understand how to create a bubble chart properly. With a bubble chart, you need a legend that shows the name of each company, since text labels would clutter the chart. Ideally, you should be able to select a table of data and have the Chart Wizard create a bubble chart with an appropriate legend.

In order to have the company names appear as a legend, each company must be a separate series on the chart. The only way to make each company into a separate series is to add the companies one at a time.

Chart Wizard

1 Activate the Bubble worksheet, select the range B2:D2, and click the Chart Wizard button. In the Chart Type list, select Bubble, select the second chart in the Chart Sub-Type list, and then click Finish.

A bubble chart is an XY chart that also shows a third variable as the size of the bubble.

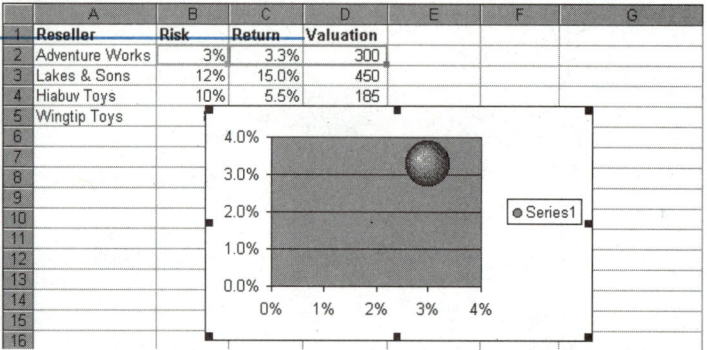

The marker for Adventure Works appears on the chart. It is in the same position as the Adventure Works marker on the XY (Scatter) chart, but the marker is a large ball, representing the size of the company. Excel used the word *Series1* as the legend for this series. It will be faster to add all the series first, and then change their legend names later.

2 Select the range B3:D3. Drag the border of the range onto the chart. Click OK in the Paste Special dialog box. Repeat for the ranges B4:D4 and B5:D5. Select each range, drag it onto the chart, and click OK.

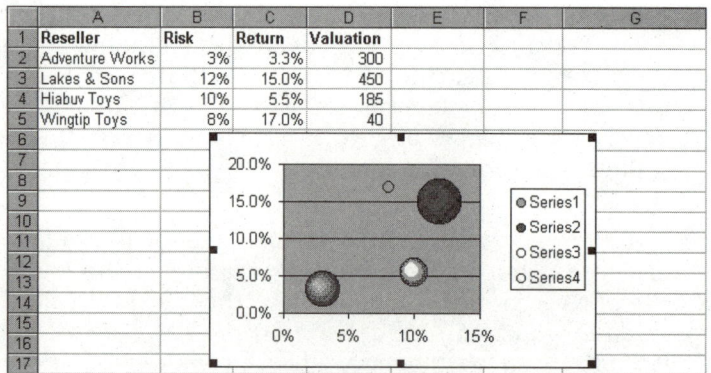

You now have all four series on the chart, each with its own color and its own legend entry. You can now use the Source Data dialog box to link the legends to the cells containing the names of the companies.

3 Click the chart. On the Chart menu, click Source Data, and click the Series tab.

To add the reseller names, select each series label and then link to the reseller name here.

This dialog box shows you each of the data series on the chart, and shows which cell or range is used for the X, Y, and size values. The Name box is blank. You can link the Name box for each series to the appropriate cell on the worksheet.

4 Select Series1, click the Name box, and click cell A2 on the worksheet. Select Series2, click the Name box, and click cell A3. Select Series3, click the Name box, and click cell A4. Select Series4, click the Name box, and click cell A5. Then click OK.

You can resize the chart to make the legend fit better.

5 Drag the top left corner of the chart close to the top left corner of cell A6. Extend the bottom right corner of the chart to the bottom right corner of cell E15. Save the Lesson7 workbook.

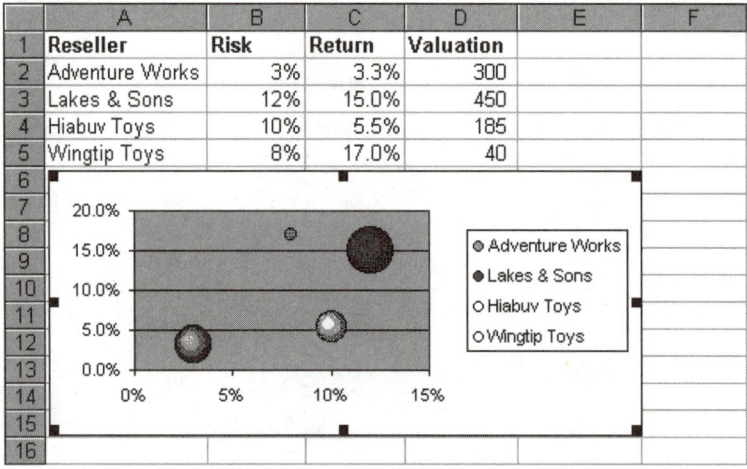

	A	B	C	D	E	F
1	Reseller	Risk	Return	Valuation		
2	Adventure Works	3%	3.3%	300		
3	Lakes & Sons	12%	15.0%	450		
4	Hiabuv Toys	10%	5.5%	185		
5	Wingtip Toys	8%	17.0%	40		

The bubble chart shows not only the risk and return relationship, as the XY (Scatter) chart does, but it also shows the sizes of the companies. And it even has a legend so you can tell which company is which.

Creating a bubble chart (with a legend) is a little more work than creating a simple line or column chart, but the bubble chart conveys a lot of information in a way that is easy to understand.

Creating Data Maps

When Tailspin Toys first started two years ago, all the resellers the company worked with were based in Los Angeles. Several months later, new resellers based in Chicago were added. A few months after that, resellers from New York began carrying the company's products. You would like to capture the progression of the company from state to state. You would like to display the numbers on a map.

IMPORTANT The Microsoft Map component of Excel is not included as part of the "typical" installation. If you didn't install Microsoft Map when you installed Excel, you need to install it to complete this exercise. Run the Excel setup program and select Add/Remove components. Under Microsoft Excel, select the Microsoft Map check box.

Map numbers from a worksheet

The Map worksheet in the Lesson7 workbook shows the total units sold to distributors based in each of three states. The numbers are also broken out by product line. You can create a map to show graphically how many units were sold by resellers based in each state. Because the numbers are in a PivotTable, you will need to disable automatic selection in order to select the range you want.

1 Activate the Map worksheet, and click cell A1. If the entire PivotTable becomes selected, then use the right mouse button to click cell A1, point to Select, and click Enable Selection. Then click cell E5 and drag the mouse up to cell A2.

To create a map, select a range with geographical names in the first column.

	A	B	C	D	E	F
1	Sum of Units	Line				
2	State	Dinosaur	Animal	Vehicle	Grand Total	
3	CA		315965	528960	147890	992815
4	IL		206570	396967	103418	706955
5	NY		79282	72859	36559	188700
6						

Once you have selected a range with geographic names in the leftmost column, you can use the Map button to create a map.

2 On the Standard toolbar, click the Map button and drag a rectangle from the middle of cell A1 to the middle of cell I14. When you are prompted for which map to use, select United States (AK & HI Inset), and click OK.

Map

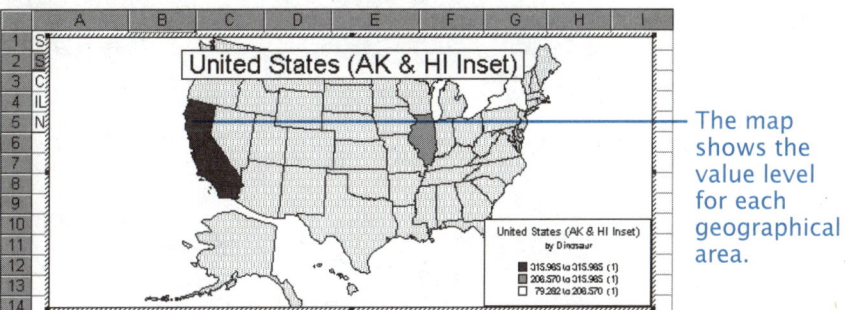

The map shows the value level for each geographical area.

A default map appears, with California, Illinois, and New York shaded with different levels of gray and white. The Microsoft Map Control also appears. The Map Control allows you to control how the map charts the data. The default chart is plotting the level of Dinosaur sales. You want it to plot the Grand Total sales instead. To change which column is plotted, drag the column button from the top part of the Microsoft Map Control window onto the format description in the bottom part of the window.

3 Drag the Grand Total column button onto the Dinosaur button.

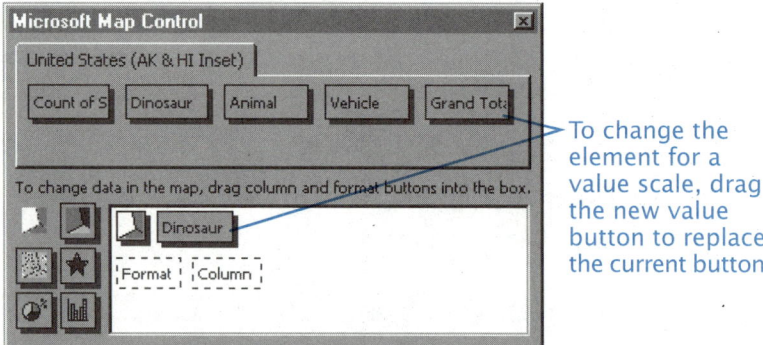

To change the element for a value scale, drag the new value button to replace the current button.

The default type of plot is called *value shading*, because the states have different colors depending on the value for that state. A value shading plot can display values for only a single column, so the Grand Total column button replaced the Dinosaur button.

You can also compare how product lines have done in each state, using a *column chart*. A column chart can display values for multiple columns.

4   Drag the Column Chart button into the white area. Then drag the Dinosaur button, the Animal button, and the Vehicle button down onto the Column Chart.

With a column chart, you can drag multiple buttons onto the same chart.

You now see a column chart for each state, as well as the shading for the state itself. You may be able to see the chart better if you remove the Map Control window.

5 On the View menu, click Microsoft Map Control.

The Map Control window disappears. The Microsoft Map Control command is a toggle, so if you need to use the Map Control window again, simply execute the same command again.

Format the map

Before you forward the map to your manager, you want to enhance its appearance. Start by replacing the default title with one that mentions the name of your company.

1 Double-click the title of the map, and then drag through the current title and type **Tailspin Toys Units by Region**, and press ENTER. If the title overlaps New York, drag it to the left.

You can also change the title on the column chart legend.

2 Double-click the column chart legend box, and click the Legend Options tab. Replace the default title with **Product Lines**, and click OK. Drag the column chart legend box until it is approximately centered over Texas.

You would like the value shading legend entries to be rounder numbers. You can replace the legend labels, and replace the title at the same time.

3 Drag the value shading legend box until it is approximately centered over Georgia. Then double-click the value shading legend, and click the Legend Options tab. Replace the default title with **Total Units**, and clear the default subtitle. Finally, click the Edit Legend Entries button.

You may need to change custom labels if the data values change.

4 In the Type New Legend Entry box, replace the default for the first entry with **750K to 1M**, and click the second entry. Replace the default label with **500K to 750K**, and click the third entry. Replace the default label with **100K to 500K**, and click OK twice.

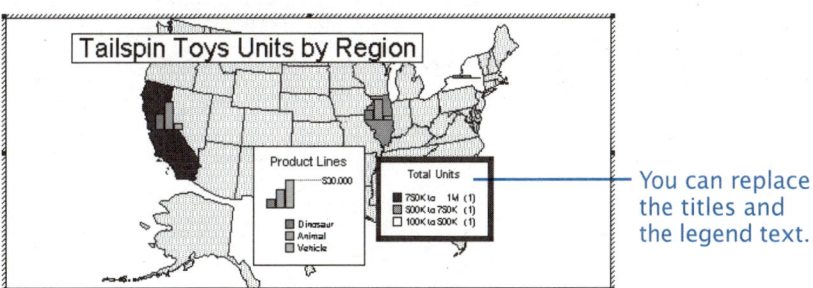

You can replace the titles and the legend text.

Since Tailspin Toys deals with resellers in only 3 states, it might be easier to see those states if the rest of the states were invisible. The state boundaries are a feature of the map that you can turn on or off.

5 On the Map menu, click Features. Clear the check box next to United States (AK & HI Inset), and click OK. Then click cell A15 to deselect the map.

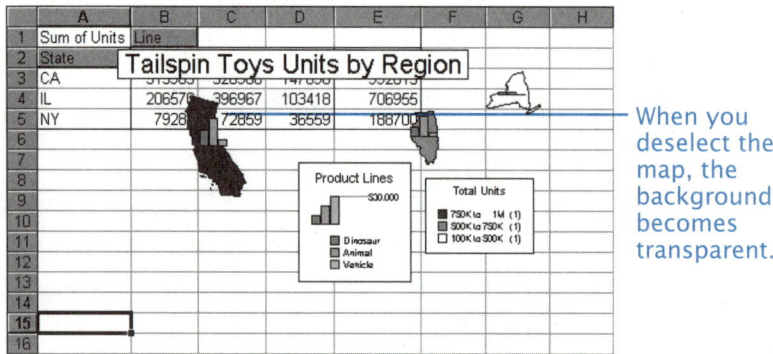

When you deselect the map, the background becomes transparent.

While you are editing the map, the background is white and opaque. When you stop editing the map, the background becomes transparent. This makes it possible for you to integrate a map into a worksheet. But what if you want the map to be enclosed in a white rectangle? The easiest way to do that is to draw a white rectangle and put it behind the map.

Drawing

6 Click the Drawing button to display the Drawing toolbar. Click the Rectangle button and drag a rectangle around the map, approximately from the center of cell A1 to the center of cell H14.

The rectangle appears, but it covers the map. You need to change the order of the objects so that the rectangle is behind the map.

Rectangle

7 On the Drawing toolbar, click the Draw menu, point to Order, and then click Send To Back. Then press ESC to deselect the rectangle.

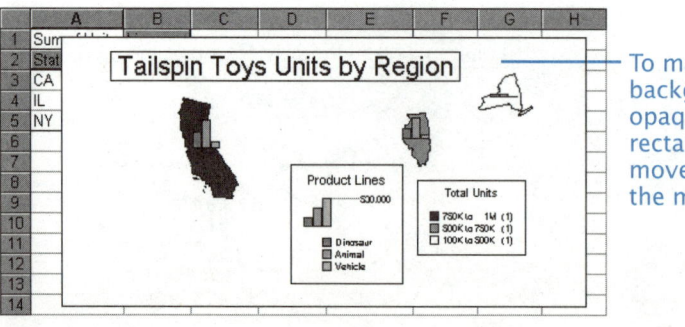

To make the background opaque, draw a rectangle, and move it behind the map.

The map now appears to have an opaque background. Since the rectangle is an OfficeArt object, you can apply gradient fills or textures to the rectangle. Of course, that means that you have to select the rectangle first, which you can no longer do with the mouse, since it is behind the map. Fortunately, you can use the keyboard to select the rectangle.

8 Click what appears to be the rectangle—in the area of cell B11. If the formula bar contains the formula =EMBED("MSMap.8",""), then press TAB to select the rectangle.

Now can apply a gradient fill to the rectangle.

Fill Color

9 Click the arrow next to the Fill Color button, and click Fill Effects. On the Gradient tab, leave the default gray colors, select the Diagonal Down option, select the top right variant, and click OK. Then press ESC, and save and close the Lesson7 workbook.

The shading not only gives a nice background, it also makes the white of New York stand out more than it did with the white background.

Maps are powerful tools for presenting information. Microsoft Map can link to data on your worksheet and present the information graphically, as long as you have geographic labels in the first column of data.

Lesson Summary

To	Do this
Add a designer look to a chart	In Step 1 of the Chart Wizard (or after clicking Chart Type on the Chart menu), click the Custom Types tab, select the Built-In option, and then select one of the chart designs.

To	Do this
Increase the size of the chart without enlarging the outer border of the chart frame	Click the plot area and drag its edges as close to the edges of the chart area as possible.
Simultaneously change the font attributes of all the parts of a chart	Select the chart area before making the changes.
Force the text in a title to extend to a new line	Hold down ALT as you press ENTER.
Format only part of a title	Select the part of the title you want and format it.
Format a number as thousands	On the Number tab of the Format Cells dialog box, click Custom. After the last zero in each part of the format string, type , (a comma).
Include a letter in a number format string, even if that letter has a special meaning (such as "M")	Type \ (a backslash) before the letter.
Create a Gantt chart from a table showing dates and durations	Use the Floating Bars built-in chart type.
Change automatically scaling fonts on a chart (that is, fonts that are oversized) to ordinary fonts	Change any attribute of the font. For example, set the Font Color.
Reverse the order of categories on a chart	Double-click the category labels, click the Scale tab, and select the Categories In Reverse Order check box.
Find out the number underlying a date in a cell	On the Edit menu, point to Clear, and then click Formats. Click Undo to restore the formatting.
Change the value on a worksheet by manipulating its position on a chart	Click a data marker to select the series. Click again to select a single point. Drag the marker.
Combine small segments of a pie chart into a single segment, while showing the individual segments as a separate pie chart	Select the Pie Of Pie chart type.

To	Do this
Adjust how many segments are in each part of a Pie Of Pie chart.	Double-click a series on the chart, and in the Format Series dialog box, click the Options tab. Change the value in the Second Plot Contains The Last box.
Compare one set of values against another (such as return against risk)	Use an XY (Scatter) chart.
Add labels to an XY chart showing the category name	Apply default labels that show the X value. Then click each default label, type an equal sign, and click the cell on the worksheet that contains the correct label.
On a chart with a single series, make each point in the series use a different color	Double-click the chart series, and click the Options tab. Select the Vary Colors By Point check box.
Compare three values on a chart, one as the x position, one as the y position, and one as the size of a circle	Select the three values for a single series and then create a Bubble chart. Add additional series, one at a time.
Add legend names to a Bubble chart	On the Chart menu, click Source Data, and click the Series tab. In the Name box for each series, click the cell containing the name for that series.
Create a map showing different colors for different geographic areas	Select a data range with geographic labels in the left column and titles in the first row. Click the Map toolbar button, and drag a rectangle on the worksheet.
Change the column whose value is used in a *value shading* map	Drag the new column button on top of the current button in the Microsoft Map Control.
Add a column chart showing multiple values for each geographic area	In the Microsoft Map Control, drag the Column Chart button onto the map area. Then drag the button for each column you want to include in the chart.
Change the legend labels for a value shading chart	Double-click the legend, and click the Legend Options tab. Click the Edit Legend Entries button. Select each legend entry, and type a new legend in the Type New Legend Entry box.
Turn off the borders of unused geographic areas.	On the Map menu, click Features. Clear the check box next to each feature you want to disable.

To	Do this
Create a solid background for a map so that it is not transparent	Click the Rectangle button on the Drawing toolbar and drag a rectangle that surrounds the map. On the Drawing toolbar, click the Draw menu, point to Order, and click Send To Back.
Select a graphical object that is behind another object (such as a map)	Click the front object and then press TAB until you select the object you want.

For online information about	On the Help menu, click Contents And Index, click the Index tab, and then type
Creating a chart	**chart creation**
Formatting a chart	**chart formatting**
Selecting parts of a chart	**chart components**
Selecting the right chart type	**chart types, examples**
Creating data maps	**maps**

Sharing Documents and Work

Sharing Data

In this lesson you will learn how to:

- Validate data entered into worksheet cells.
- Use controls to enter values into cells.
- Link to external workbooks.
- Retrieve a list from an external database.
- Attach a PivotTable to an external database.

An Excel spreadsheet always starts out empty. If you want text and numbers in cells, somebody needs to put them there. One way to get values into cells is to type them there yourself. When you created your first spreadsheet, you undoubtedly typed everything yourself. As you build spreadsheets that involve more people in an organization, you will most likely get information from other sources. For example, you might distribute spreadsheets for other people to type numbers into. You might transfer data from an existing spreadsheet into a new one. You might retrieve data from a corporate database. These are all ways of sharing data.

Excel has excellent tools for sharing data. In this lesson, you will learn how to get data into a worksheet from other people, from other workbooks, and from a database.

Start the lesson

▶ Start Microsoft Excel, change to the Excel AT Practice folder, and open the Start8 workbook. Save a copy of the workbook as **Lesson8**

Retrieving Data From Other People

The employees in the Order Processing department take orders from reseller representatives. They used to write down the order information on paper. But a couple of months ago, you created an Excel spreadsheet for entering order information. That spreadsheet is on the Order worksheet in the Lesson8 workbook.

	A	B	C	D	
1	Contract	C5017	Reseller	West Coast Sales	
2	Date	10/15/98	Discount	TRUE	
4	Product	Qty	Net Price	Dollars	Note
5	Elephant	50	$ 24.98	$ 1,249.00	
6	Airplane	10	$ 28.45	$ 284.50	
7	Tyranosaurus	22	$ 11.97	$ 263.34	
8					
9					
10					
11					
12			Total	$ 1,796.84	
13			Discount	3%	
14			Due	$ 1,742.93	
15					

The original order form requires correct spelling.

The person taking the order types the contract number and date at the top of the form. For each product, the order taker types the name of the product and the quantity. Formulas look up the reseller name and the product price, and calculate the dollars per item and the total for the order. The worksheet takes care of the calculations involved in taking an order, but the person using the form must still be very careful not to make typing mistakes. Excel offers you tools that not only minimize the chance for errors, but also make the task of entering data in the form easy and natural.

Validate a cell from a list

It is easy to make errors entering the product name on the order form. The person taking the order must type the name precisely as it appears on the list of products. Excel's new *data validation* feature not only allows you to control which values can go into a cell, but also makes it easy to enter the correct value. You want to require that the entries in the Product column come from the list of product names on the Products worksheet. Start by giving a name to the range that contains the list of valid products.

For a demonstration of how to validate data using a list, double-click the Excel Camcorder Files shortcut on your Desktop or connect to the Internet address listed on page xvi.

1 Activate the Products worksheet, select the range A2:A11, click the Name Box, type **ProductList**, and press ENTER.

Now you can link the cells on the Order worksheet to this range. When you link a cell to a list, data validation can automatically create a drop-down list to select a valid item.

2 Activate the Order worksheet, and select cell A5 (the first cell in the Product column). On the Data menu, click Validation. In the Allow list, select List. In the Source box, type **=ProductList**. (Don't forget the equal sign.) Leave both the Ignore Blank and the In-Cell Dropdown check boxes selected. Then click OK.

To select from a list, type an equal sign and then the name of a range that contains the list.

An arrow now appears next to cell A5. This arrow allows you to select a valid entry from a list.

3 Click the arrow next to cell A5, and click Pteradon.

The cell now contains a new valid product name. But if you click cell A6, there is no drop-down list, and no data validation. You can copy a cell and then use the Paste Special command to paste only the validation setting to additional cells.

Copy

4 Select cell A5 and click the Copy button. Select the range A5:A11. On the Edit menu, click Paste Special. Select the Validation option, and click OK. Press ESC to remove the border around cell A5.

5 Change the product in cell A6 to Automobile.

Linking a cell to a list is not merely an enforcement technique, it is also a way to make data entry easier. Selecting an item from a list is usually easier and faster than typing the item. Giving a name to the list range also has several benefits. It makes the data validation rule easy to understand. It makes it easy to change the range of the list if you add or delete items. And it also makes it possible to use a list that is not on the same worksheet as the cell with the validation rule. You cannot enter a range address for a list on a different worksheet or in a different workbook, but you can enter a range name that refers to a list on a different worksheet or in a different workbook.

Validate a date

The person taking an order needs to enter a date in cell B2 of the worksheet. According to company guidelines, orders can be dated anytime from the current date up to one month in the future. Exceptions are possible, but most orders should be dated within that framework. You can add a validation that warns the person entering the date about the company guideline.

1   Select cell B2. On the Data menu, click Validation. In the Allow list, select Date.

You can specify the type of data a cell can contain.

The default choice for the type of validation is *between*. You could select any of several other combinations, but *between* is appropriate to reflect the company policy. You now specify a start date and an end date. These dates will change depending on the current date, so you can enter formulas into the boxes to calculate the appropriate start and end dates.

2   In the Start Date box, type =TODAY(). In the End Date box, type =TODAY()+31

Normally, when you create a validation for a cell, Excel will not allow anyone to enter a value that breaks the rule. In this case, you only want to warn about the guideline, not enforce it. The Error Alert tab allows you to change the validation from a rule to a warning that displays a message and asks if you want to continue.

3 Click the Error Alert tab. In the Style list, select Warning. In the Title box, type **Corporate Guidelines.** In the Error Message box, type **The date is outside the recommended range.** Then click OK.

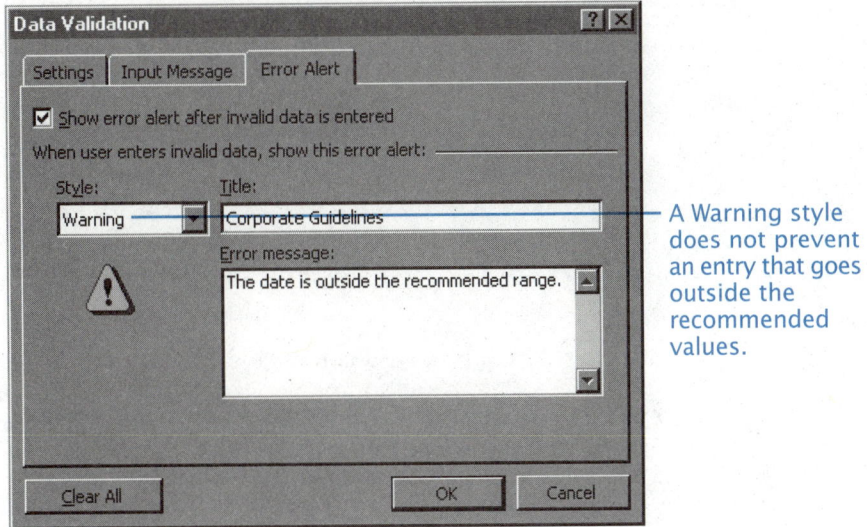

A Warning style does not prevent an entry that goes outside the recommended values.

You can test the validation rule by entering an old date.

4 In cell B2, type **1/1/96** and press ENTER. When the warning appears, click Yes to continue.

You can choose to ignore a warning.

When you are reviewing a worksheet that has validation rules that are not strictly enforced, you might want an easy way to tell if any cells contain violations of the rules. The Auditing toolbar contains a button to find cells that do not meet the data validation rules.

Circle Invalid Data

5 On the View menu, point to Toolbars, and then click Customize. Select the Auditing check box and click Close. On the Auditing toolbar, click the Circle Invalid Data button.

The Circle Invalid Data button puts a circle around cells that do not follow the validation rule.

The date gets a big red circle around it. The Auditing toolbar also allows you to remove the circles.

Clear Validation Circles

6 Click the Clear Validation Circles button and close the Auditing toolbar.

With Data Validation, you can decide whether to inform, warn, or require the value entered into a cell to follow a rule. You can even use formulas to dynamically calculate the limits for a rule using Excel functions or values from the cell on the worksheet.

Add comments to cells

You can insert a comment to create instructions for a cell. A comment acts like a ScreenTip: a message appears when you move the mouse pointer over the cell, and disappears as soon as you move the pointer away.

> **NOTE** The Input Message tab in the Data Validation dialog box allows you to create a message that appears whenever you select a cell with a Data Validation rule. However, unlike a comment or a ScreenTip, an input message does not disappear when you move the mouse pointer away. It remains visible until you select a different cell.

1 Right-click cell B2, and on the shortcut menu that appears, click Insert Comment.

You can add a comment to explain what should go into a cell.

	A	B	C	D	
1	Contract	C5017	Reed Jacobson:		Sales
2	Date	1/1/96			
4	Product	Qty			Note
5	Pteradon	50			
6	Zebra	10			
7	Tyranosaurus	22	$ 11.97	$ 263.34	
8					

A comment box appears with your name already entered. You can replace your name with the instructions for the cell.

 TIP If the name that appears in the comment is not yours, you might want to inform Excel who you are. On the Tools menu, click Options and select the General tab. Type your name in the User Name box, and click OK.

2 Select and delete your name from the comment box. Type **The order date should be between today's date and one month in the future.** Then click cell A1 to hide the comment box.

	A	B	C	D	
1	Contract	C5017	Reseller	West Coast Sales	
2	Date	1/1/96	Discount	TRUE	
4	Product	Qty	Net Price	Dollars	Note
5	Pteradon	50	$ 11.97	$ 598.50	

A triangle in the corner indicates that a comment will appear if you move the mouse over the cell.

A small red triangle appears in the top right corner of the cell, indicating that there is a comment available for that cell. The comment will now act like a ScreenTip for the cell.

3 Move the mouse pointer over cell B2, read the comment, and then move the mouse away.

Comments can be an effective tool for adding instructions, explanations, or documentation to a worksheet.

TIP A comment is really an AutoShape object attached to the cell by an arrow. You can format and modify the comment box the same as any AutoShape object. Right-click a cell with a comment, and, on the shortcut menu, click Edit Comment. Press ESC to select the comment box. While the comment box is selected, activate the Drawing toolbar and change the font or fill color. You can use gradient or pattern fills. You can add shadows or 3-D effects. You can even change the AutoShape to a star or other shape. See Lesson 6 for more details about working with AutoShapes.

Link a check box to a cell

Cell D2 on the Order worksheet allows you to control whether or not the reseller gets the standard discount for this order. The value of cell D2 should always be True or False. A True or False value is easy to select with a check box. The only control that data validation provides to help enter values into a cell is a list box, but Excel also has a *Control Toolbox* that allows you to add several different types of controls to a worksheet. First, you need to display the Control Toolbox toolbar.

1   Right-click any toolbar, and, on the shortcut menu, click Control Toolbox. Move or resize the toolbox as you wish.

The Control Toolbox lets you put dialog box controls onto a worksheet.

The Control Toolbox lets you add controls that you usually find in a dialog box, such as list boxes, check boxes, and spinner buttons, directly to a worksheet. You can then link the control to a cell. If you hold down ALT as you drag a control on the worksheet, the corners of the control will snap to the worksheet grid.

Check Box

2   Click the Check Box button. Hold down ALT as you drag from the top left to the bottom right corner of cell D2. Release the mouse and then the ALT key.

Change the appearance of the check box by changing the properties of the control.

	A	B	C	D	
1	Contract	C5017	Reseller	West Coast Sales	
2	Date	1/1/96	Discount	☐ CheckBox1	
4	Product	Qty	Net Price	Dollars	Note
5	Elephant		50	$ 24.98	$ 1,249.00	

The check box control appears in the cell. The gray background and the indented appearance of the check box are more appropriate to a dialog box than to a worksheet. You can change the formatting of a control by using the Properties window. To display the Properties window, you click the Properties button.

Properties

3 In the Control Toolbox, click the Properties button. Move and resize the Properties window as you wish.

The Properties window contains a list of attributes or *properties* that determine the appearance or the behavior of the control. You can ignore most of the properties, but you might want to remove the CheckBox1 caption (since the check box already has a label on the worksheet), make the background match the window background, and make the check box itself flat.

4 Select the BackColor property, click the arrow that appears, and select Window Background from the drop-down list. Select the word *CheckBox1* next to the Caption property, and press DELETE. Select the SpecialEffect property, click the arrow that appears, and select 0 - fmButtonEffectFlat from the drop-down list.

241

Next, you can link the check box to the value of cell D2.

5 Click the LinkedCell property, type **D2**, and press ENTER. Then close the Properties window.

Cell D2 contained the value TRUE, so as soon as you linked the control, the check box became selected. You still can't change the control's value by clicking it, however, because you are in what is called *design mode*. When you are in design mode, clicking the check box selects it so that you can change its properties. When you turn off design mode, clicking the check box changes its value.

Exit Design Mode

6 In the Control Toolbox, click the Exit Design Mode button to turn off design mode. Then click the check box repeatedly and watch the discount in cell D13 change between 0% and 3%.

 TIP If Excel leaves a partial border around the cell that contains the control, press the PAGE DOWN key and then press the PAGE UP key to refresh the display.

The formula in cell D13 is really linked to the value in cell D2, which you can't see because it's covered by the check box. Because the check box is also linked to cell D2, the effect is that the check box is linked to the discount in cell D13.

Clicking a check box control is much easier than typing TRUE or FALSE into a cell, and you are guaranteed that no one will accidentally type an invalid value into the cell.

Link a two-column list box to a cell

The order sheet also requires a contract number in cell B1. When you type a new contract number in cell B1, the name of the reseller appears in cell D1. You could use Data Validation to link the contract number to the list of contract numbers, but it would still be easy to pick the wrong contract number from the list. What you would really like to have is a list that displays both the Contract number and the Reseller name. The person entering the order could then look at the name to select the correct contract number.

The Control Toolbox contains a list box control that can display lists with multiple columns. In fact, it contains two list box controls: The List Box control shows the list on the worksheet, and the Combo Box control lets you create a dropdown list that appears only when you click the arrow. Before creating the control on the worksheet, you should name the range that contains the contract numbers and reseller names.

1 Activate the Resellers worksheet. Select the range A2:B15. Name this range **ResellerList**

Now you can put the combo box control onto cell B1 of the Order worksheet.

2   Activate the Order worksheet. Clear cell B1. In the Control Toolbox, click the Combo Box button. Hold down ALT as you drag from the top left to the bottom right corner of cell B1. Release the mouse button and the ALT key.

Combo Box

With a combo box, you can allow a user to type a value that is not in the list, or you can restrict the control to only values in the list. You determine which you want by setting the Style property. You can also make the control fit naturally on a worksheet by making it "flat."

3   In the Control Toolbox, click the Properties button. In the Properties window, change the Style property to 2 - fmStyleDropDownList. Change the SpecialEffect property to 0 - fmSpecialEffectFlat.

Properties

Now you are ready to tell the control what range to use as the source of the list, how many columns the list has, and which cell to put the contract number into.

4   Click the ListFillRange property and type **ResellerList**, the named range you created on the Resellers sheet. Click the ColumnCount property and type **2**. Click the LinkedCell property and type **B1**

The BoundColumn property specifies which column from the list should provide the value for the linked cell. The contract number is in the first column of the ResellerList range, and the default value of the BoundColumn property is 1, so you can leave it alone. Now you're ready to test the list.

5   In the Control Toolbox, click the Exit Design Mode button, and then click the drop-down arrow in cell B1.

Exit Design Mode

The list box contains two lists, but you see only one of them until you change the widths.

	A	B	C	D	
1	Contract		Reseller	#N/A	
2	Date	C5004	scount ☐		
3		C5017			
4	**Product**	C5035	t Price	Dollars	Note
5	Pteradon	C5068	11.97	$ 598.50	
6	Zebra	C5028	20.98	$ 284.50	
7	Tyranosaurus	C5065	11.97	$ 263.34	
8		C5038			
9		C5044			

A point is a measurement traditionally used in graphic design.

You see the list of contract numbers, but not the list of reseller names. There is, however, a horizontal scroll bar at the bottom of the list. The names are there; the list is just too narrow to display them. You can set properties to control the width of the columns in the list, and the width of the list itself. You specify widths in *points*, which are 1/72 inch. So if you want 1/2 inch for the first column you use 36 points. If you want 1½ inches for the second column, you use 108 points. You separate the widths for multiple columns with a semicolon.

Design Mode

6 Click the Design Mode button, and then click the list box in cell B1. In the Properties window, click the ColumnWidths property, and type **36; 108**

The total width of the list will now be 2 inches, or 144 points.

7 Click the ListWidth property, and type **144**

8 Turn off design mode, and select Enchantment Lakes Corporation from the list.

With two columns, you can select the name to enter the number.

	A	B	C	D	
1	Contract	C5064 ▾	**Reseller**	Enchantment Lakes Corp	
2	Date	C5038	Industrial Smoke and Mi ▲		
~		C5044	Adventure Works		
4	**Product**	C5064	Enchantment Lakes Cor	s	**Note**
5	Pteradon	C5080	Main Street Market	598.50	
		C5001	Peck n Order Toys		
6	Automobile	C5011	Mightyflight Toys	53.50	
7	Tyranosaurus	C5015	Wingtip Toys	263.34	
8		C5055	Hiabuv Toys ▼		

9 Close the Properties window and the Control Toolbox, and then save the Lesson8 workbook.

A two-column list box is an extremely sophisticated tool. It is not trivial to set up, but once you do, it makes entering valid customer numbers very easy to do.

Retrieving Data From Workbooks

On the Order worksheet in the Lesson 8 workbook, many formulas, validations, and controls link to the lists on the Resellers and the Products worksheets. Eventually, however you will create many copies of the Order worksheet, and you don't want each copy of the workbook to need its own copy of these two table worksheets. If you move the table worksheets into their own workbook, each new worksheet can link to a single copy of that workbook.

Link to a different workbook

Before moving the worksheets, take a look at the Define Name dialog box to see how the names currently appear.

1 Activate the Order sheet of the Lesson8 workbook. On the Insert menu, point to Name, then click Define, and select the ProductList name. Look at the contents of the Refers To box, and then click Close.

A range in the same workbook does not show the workbook name.

The reference for the name is =*Products!$A$2:$A$11*. Now move the worksheets into a separate workbook.

2   Click the Products sheet tab. Hold down SHIFT and click the Resellers sheet tab. Right-click one of the tabs, and, on the shortcut menu that appears, click Move Or Copy.

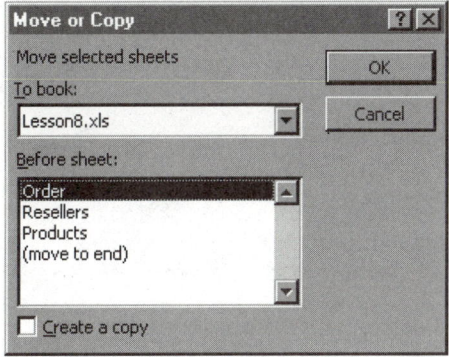

You can move the worksheets within the current workbook or move them to a new workbook.

3   In the To Book list, select New Book, and click OK.

The new workbook has a name like Book1. (The number may be different.) Now you can look again at the defined name in the Lesson8 workbook.

4   Activate the Lesson8 workbook (on Window menu, click Lesson8). Display the Define Name dialog box and select Product List. After looking at the reference, close the dialog box.

A range in a different workbook shows the workbook name in brackets.

This time the reference is *=[Book1]Products!$A$2:$A$11*. Excel automatically adjusted all the references in the Lesson8 workbook to refer to the new workbook. When a reference points to a different workbook, the workbook name appears in square brackets. Next, save the workbook with the tables and give it a name.

Save

5   Activate the Book1 workbook and click the Save button. Change to the Excel AT Practice folder if necessary. Type **Tables** as the name of the workbook, and click Save.

If you look at the ProductList name in the Lesson8 workbook, you will see that the reference is now *=[Tables.xls]Products!$A$2:$A$11*.

Now you can close both workbooks. The Close command on the File menu will change to a Close All command if you hold down SHIFT as you open the menu.

6   Hold down SHIFT and click the File menu. Click Close All. When prompted whether you want to save changes, click Yes.

To create a link to a separate workbook, you have several choices. You can create the link to a sheet in the same workbook and then move the worksheet to a new workbook. You can type an equal sign and then activate the other workbook and click a cell. Or you can type a cell reference, complete with the square brackets around the workbook name. As long as both workbooks are open when you move the worksheets or save a workbook with a new name, Excel can automatically adjust any links for you. If you change a file name when a workbook is not open, or if you use Windows Explorer or Windows NT Explorer to rename a file, you can end up with a broken link.

Fix a broken link

Suppose that you decide that you don't like the name Tables for the workbook that contains the lookup tables. You would rather use the name Lists. You can rename the file right in the File Open dialog box.

Open

1 Click the Open button. In the Excel AT Practice folder, right-click the Tables workbook, and click Rename. Type **Lists** as the new workbook name (type **Lists.xls** if you told Windows to show extensions), and press ENTER. Then double-click the Lists workbook to open it.

Now, when you try to open the Lesson8 workbook, it will still try to link to the old Tables workbook, which no longer exists.

2 Click the File menu, and click Lesson8 from the recent file list.

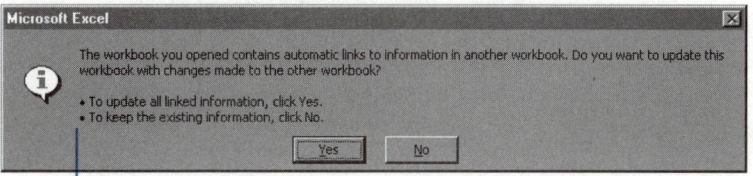

Anytime you open a workbook that has a link to another workbook, Excel asks if you want to update the links.

Excel asks if you want to update the workbook with changes made to the other document. It only asks if the other document is not open. The newly renamed Lists workbook is already open, but Excel is looking for the Tables workbook. Updating the links to that workbook would be futile.

3 Click No to close the warning dialog box, and then try to select a product from the list in cell A5.

The list doesn't work because the link is broken. To fix the broken list, you use the Links command on the Edit menu.

4 Click cell A1. On the Edit menu, click Links. Select the link you want to change (there is only one), and click Change Source. In the Change Links dialog box, select Lists, and click OK. Then click OK to close the Links dialog box.

5 Try again to select a product in cell A5.

This time the list works because the link is repaired. Some links require that you close and reopen the workbook. For example, you still can't select a Contract from the list in cell B1 without saving and reopening the Lesson8 workbook.

6 Save and close the Lesson8 workbook. Then reopen the Lesson8 workbook. Try selecting a new contract number in cell B1.

The list works. The link is now completely repaired. Excel didn't prompt to update values because the Lists workbook was already open, and all the lists and formulas work.

Links are valuable tools for sharing information between workbooks. If you rename or move a file, you can break the link. When you break a link, use the Links dialog box to adjust the link to the correct location.

Create a workbook template

Now that the Order sheet is the only worksheet in the Lesson8 workbook, you can create additional orders by making new copies of the workbook. One way to make copies of the workbook is to always open the most recent order, make the necessary changes, and then remember to use the Save As command to save the order with a new name. That approach, however, is dangerous. You might forget to change something about the order, or you might use the Save command instead of the Save As command and destroy a previous order.

A better approach is to create a workbook template. A template is identical to any other workbook, except that when you open it, Excel forces you to use the Save As command to save the file with a new name. Before you turn a workbook into a template, you should clear out any sample data so that it is ready to become a new workbook.

1   Make sure that both the Lists workbook and the Lesson8 workbook are open. Activate the Lesson8 workbook. Clear cell B1 (use the arrow keys to select the cell beneath the combo box control) and clear cell B2. Clear any cells in the range A5:B11. Then select cell A1.

	A	B		C	D		
1	Contract		▼	Reseller	#N/A		
2	Date	1/1/96		Discount ☑			
4	Product		Qty	Net Price	Dollars		Note
5							
6							

Before creating a template, make the workbook look the way you want each new workbook to appear.

The workbook is now ready to turn into a template. To make a workbook into a template you use the Save As command, and then tell Excel to save it as a template.

2   On the File menu, click Save As. Type **Order** in the File name box, and select Template (*.xlt) from the Save As Type list.

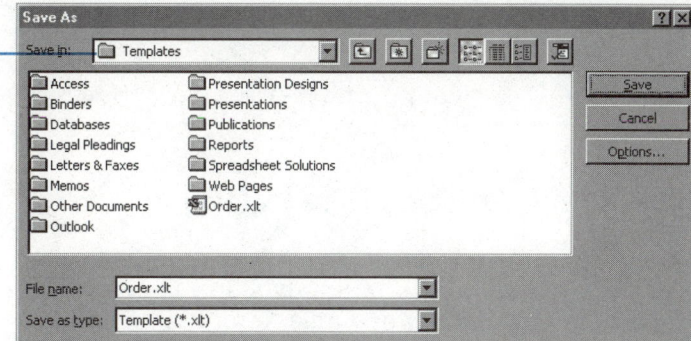

When you save a file as a template, Excel saves it in the Templates folder.

If file extensions are visible, the extension changes to .xlt. The folder also changes to the Microsoft Office Templates folder.

Close

3 Click the Save button to create the template workbook. Then click the Close button to close the workbook.

Now you can create a new workbook based on the template by using the New command on the File menu. When you click the New toolbar button, Excel always opens a standard workbook. When you use the New command on the File menu, Excel allows you to choose which template you want to use.

4 On the File menu, click New. Select the Order template and click OK.

A copy of the Order workbook opens. The workbook name in the title bar is *Order1*. In the same way that Excel uses the names *Book1*, *Book2*, and so forth when you create new standard workbooks, Excel adds incremental numbers to copies of a template that you create. You cannot use the Save command to save changes to the template file; the Save command prompts you for a new name for the new workbook file.

 NOTE If you put any workbook into the Templates folder, it becomes a template that you can open using the File New command, even if you did not select Template when you saved the file.

Save

5 Click the Save button. In the Save As dialog box, click Save to save the file with the name *Order1.xls*.

Now that you have named the file, you can make changes and use the Save button to save those changes to the new file.

6 Save and close both the Lists and the Order1 workbooks.

> **TIP** To make changes to the template file, open it (use the Open command, not the New command), make your changes, and then resave the file.

Retrieving Data From a Database

As Tailspin Toys has grown, the Information Technology manager wants more control over information that is available to people in the company. Rather than have order history and other information reside in Excel worksheets, she would like to store the information in a database. One of the database designers has created a test database containing the order history, and product and reseller information. You have been given the assignment to make sure that the information is still readily available to people who use Microsoft Excel.

> **TIP** It's easy to export a list from Excel so that it can be imported into a database program. Select the list and give it the name Database (which, as you learned in Lesson 5, is useful when creating a PivotTable from a list anyway). Then, on the File menu, click Save As. In the Save As Type list, select DBF 4 (dBase IV), and save the file. Excel saves only that portion of the file that was included in the range named Database. Once you save the file, a database administrator can import it into a Microsoft Access database, or into some other database program. Most database programs can import files in the dBase IV file format.

Create a new data source

The list of products is one of the lists that are in the new test database. Eventually the product list in the database will be the master list. Anyone who wants the list in a spreadsheet should retrieve a copy. You can create a new workbook to retrieve the product list from the database.

New

1   Click the New button to create a new workbook. Save the workbook as **Lesson8b**. Rename the active sheet to **QueryProducts**

Retrieving information from a database is called *querying* the database. To retrieve a list, you need to create a *query*. When you create a query, Excel launches the Microsoft Query application to communicate with the database.

2   On the Data menu, point to Get External Data, and then click Create New Query.

IMPORTANT The Microsoft Query component of Excel is not included as part of the "typical" installation. If you didn't install Microsoft Query when you installed Excel, you need to install it to complete this exercise. Run the Excel setup program and select Add/Remove components. Under Data Access, select the Microsoft Query check box.

Microsoft Query starts running. You can see its icon in the Windows 95 or Windows NT taskbar.

The first time you get data from an external data source, you must define the source.

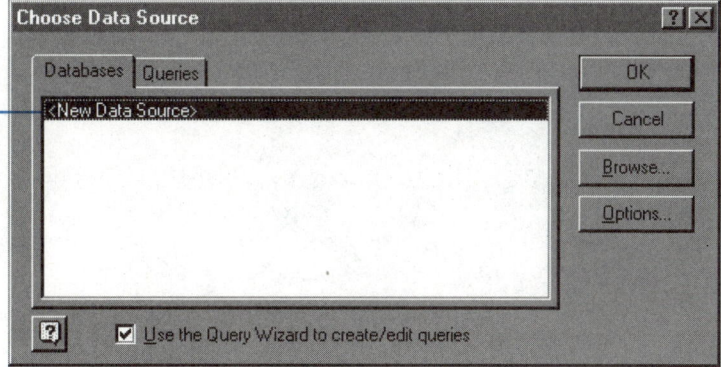

The database from which you retrieve the information is a *data source*. The first time you retrieve information from a database, you need to create a new data source.

3 In the Choose Data Source dialog box, select New Data Source, and click OK.

There are many vendors of databases. You can communicate with a database from any vendor as long as the vendor provides a *driver* that translates between the database and Microsoft Query. When you create a new data source, you give the data source a name so that you can use it again in the future. You must also specify which driver to use.

4 Type **Tailspin** as the name of the data source. From the Select A Driver list, select Microsoft Access Driver (*.mdb).

When you define a data source, you specify which driver to use.

Each driver has a different way of allowing you to identify the database you want to use. Some databases require a user login and password. Once you specify the driver, a dialog box specific to the driver appears in order to connect to the database.

5 Click the Connect button to display the ODBC Microsoft Access 97 Setup dialog box.

6 In the Database group, click the Select button. Change to the Excel AT Practice folder, and double-click the Tailspin.mdb file. Then click OK twice to finish defining the new data source.

You only need to create a new data source once.

Retrieve a list from a database

Once the data source exists, you can retrieve a list from the database.

1 In the Choose Data Source dialog box, select Tailspin. Make sure the Use The Query Wizard check box is selected, and click OK.

The Query Wizard shows the tables that are available in the database. If you double-click one of the table names, you can see a list of all the columns in that table. If you want to select all the columns from a table, you can simply select the entire table.

2 Select Products from the list of tables, and click the arrow pointing to the right.

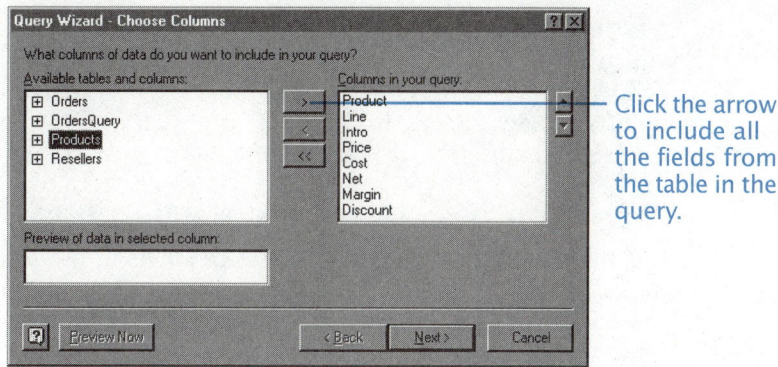

Click the arrow to include all the fields from the table in the query.

All the columns from the Product table appear in the Columns In Your Query list. That's all you really need to specify if you are going to retrieve the entire table into the worksheet.

3 Click Next three times, and then click Finish. When prompted where to put the list, click OK.

Excel puts the list from the data source onto the worksheet.

	A	B	C	D	E	F	G	H	I
1	Product	Line	Intro	Price	Cost	Net	Margin	Discount	
2	Elephant	Animal	8/30/96 0:00	49.95	25	24.975	0.45	0.5	
3	Giraffe	Animal	8/30/96 0:00	38.95	18	19.475	1.5	0.5	
4	Aardvark	Animal	2/17/97 0:00	28.45	12	14.225	2.25	0.5	
5	Zebra	Animal	2/17/97 0:00	41.95	20	20.975	0.9	0.5	
6	Brontosaurus	Dinosaur	9/8/97 0:00	23.95	12	14.37	2.45	0.4	
7	Pteradon	Dinosaur	9/8/97 0:00	19.95	9	11.97	2.85	0.4	
8	Tyranosaurus	Dinosaur	9/8/97 0:00	19.95	10	11.97	1.95	0.4	
9	Airplane	Vehicle	3/13/98 0:00	49.95	28	28.45	0.45	0.43043043	
10	Automobile	Vehicle	3/13/98 0:00	26.95	14	15.3499	1.3499	0.43043043	
11	Train	Vehicle	3/13/98 0:00	39.5	20	22.498	2.498	0.43043043	
12									

The list of products is now in the Excel worksheet. Some of the columns could have better formatting. For example, Microsoft Query always formats dates to include a time, even if the time is always midnight. You can adjust the format of the date column so that it shows only the day.

4 Right-click the letter "C" at the top of column C. On the shortcut menu, click Format Cells, and select the Number tab. In the Category list, select Date. In the Type list, select 4-Mar-97, and click OK.

Refresh Data

If you want, you can also format the dollar columns with the Currency style and the percent column with the Percent style. If you format the entire column, any new rows that are added to the table will get the correct format when you refresh the data. To refresh the table, you can either click the Refresh Data command on the Data menu, or click the Refresh Data button on the External Data toolbar.

The Query Wizard is an effective tool for creating a simple query. As long as you can define the data source, the Query Wizard can help you select the records you want. In addition to using the Query Wizard, you can design or modify a query directly in Microsoft Query. For certain types of requests, you must interact directly with Microsoft Query.

Retrieve a filtered list from a database

As Tailspin Toys develops additional products in the future, some people may not want to retrieve the entire list of products. You can add a filter, or *criteria*, to a query, limiting the rows retrieved to those that meet the criteria. In order to have as much control as possible over the definition of the query, you can bypass the Query Wizard and interact with Microsoft Query.

Edit Query

1 With the QueryProducts worksheet active, click the Edit Query button on the External Data toolbar. Click Next three times to get to the last step of the Query Wizard. Select the View Data Or Edit Query In Microsoft Query option, and click Finish.

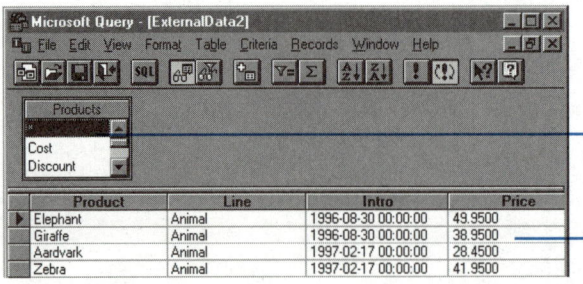

The top of the Microsoft Query window shows the table names.

The bottom part shows rows from the table.

The Microsoft Query window appears. This window shows the database table at the top, and a grid with the columns and rows in the query at the bottom. Microsoft Query has a third component that is initially hidden: the criteria area. To show the criteria area, you click the Show/Hide Criteria button.

Show/Hide Criteria

2 Click the Show/Hide Criteria button.

The criteria area allows you to specify a column, or *field*, in the table, and then identify a criteria value for that column. If you want to see only the products where the price is greater than $40, you select the Price field in the Criteria Field row, and type a greater than sign (>) followed by the amount, in the Value row.

3 Click the first box in the Criteria Field row. Click the arrow that appears. Select Price from the list. Click the first box in the Value row. Type >**40** and press ENTER.

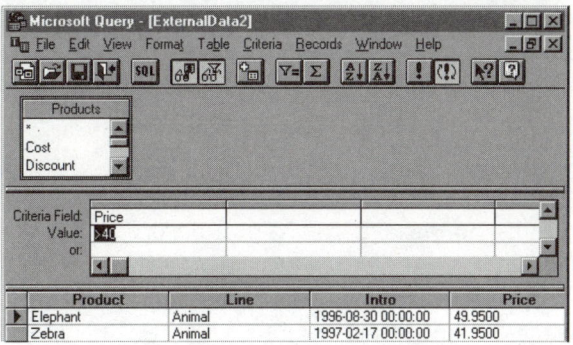

The grid at the bottom of the window changes to show only the three products with a price greater than $40. If you want to see all the products with a price greater than $30, you can change the 40 in the criteria area to 30. If you want to try several different price levels, you can replace the 40 in the criteria area with a *parameter*. A parameter is simply a prompt that allows you to enter a value at the time the query executes. To create a parameter, replace a value in the criteria area with a prompt surrounded by square brackets.

4   Select the number *40* in the criteria area (do not select the greater than sign), and replace it with **[Minimum Price]**. Then press ENTER.

Enter a prompt in brackets and Query will prompt you for the value.

As soon as you press ENTER, Microsoft Query executes the query and prompts you for a value for the parameter.

5   Type **30** as the value for the parameter and click OK.

The grid shows all the rows with a price greater than $30. When you close Microsoft Query, you will be able to enter a parameter value when you execute the query from Excel.

6   On the File menu, click Return Data To Microsoft Excel. When the Enter Parameter Value box appears, type **40** as the Minimum Price, and click OK.

The table in Excel shows only the three expensive products. To query again with a new parameter value, you can click the Refresh Data button.

Refresh Data

7 Click the Refresh Data button. Type **25** as the Minimum Price, and click OK.

A parameter query allows you to interactively adjust the criteria for a list that you retrieve from a database. You can even use the value of a cell to determine the parameter value for criteria.

Query Parameters

8 In cell J1, enter **40**, and then click cell G1 (or any cell in the query list). On the External Data toolbar, click the Query Parameters button. Select the Get The Value From The Following Cell option, click cell J1, and then click OK. Click the Refresh Data button to update the list.

Link a parameter to a cell to make a dynamic filter.

The list changes to show the three products.

9 Change cell J1 to **30**, click cell G1, and click the Refresh Data button to show the top five products.

Using criteria allows you to retrieve only part of a list. Adding parameters allows you to dynamically change the criteria. Linking parameters to cells allows you to avoid a dialog box, or to create formulas to calculate the appropriate value.

Retrieve data from a database into a PivotTable

A PivotTable is a great way to review and analyze numerical data. Whether the numbers are in a local Excel list or are in a corporate database, you can use a PivotTable to analyze them. Linking a PivotTable to a database is very similar to retrieving a list from a database. Once you specify that you want to use an external data source, you specify the source and then use the Query Wizard to define the data you will bring into the PivotTable.

1 In the Lesson8b workbook, activate Sheet2 and rename it to **PivotDatabase**. On the Data menu, click PivotTable Report. In step 1 of the PivotTable Wizard, double-click the External Data Source option. In step 2 of the wizard, click the Get Data button.

The Choose Data Source dialog box appears, precisely the same as when querying a list.

If the Tailspin data source is not available, see "Create a new data source," earlier in this lesson.

2 Double-click the Tailspin data source.

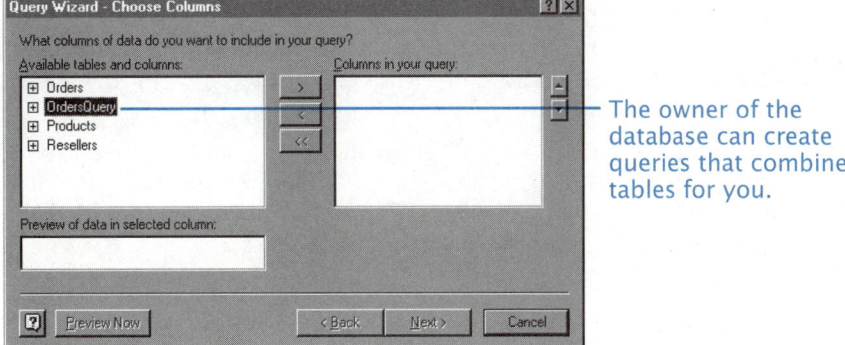

The owner of the database can create queries that combine tables for you.

Orders, Products, and Resellers are all tables in the database. The Orders table includes the Contract number, the Product name, the month, units, and dollars. But the Orders table does not include the Reseller name, channel, or discount percent. That information is in the Resellers table. Fortunately, the programmer who set up the database joined information from the Orders, Products, and Resellers tables into a query. A query in the database combines tables into a *virtual table*—something that appears to be a table, but really combines information from multiple tables. Microsoft Query can retrieve information from either an actual table or from a query.

3 Select OrdersQuery from the Available Tables And Columns list, and then click the arrow pointing to the right.

The Columns In Your Query list shows all the columns from the query. The Query Wizard is defining a query that the PivotTable can use to retrieve data from the database. As you continue, you will return the definition of the query to the PivotTable wizard.

4 Click Next three times, and then click Finish.

The PivotTable Wizard informs you when it has retrieved the field names.

You are back in step 2 of the PivotTable wizard, but now the message in the box says that Data fields have been retrieved. The PivotTable has not yet retrieved the data from the database, but it has retrieved the names of all the columns. You can now define the appearance of the PivotTable.

5 Click Next to go to step 3 of the PivotTable Wizard. Then drag the Product button to the page area, drag the Reseller button to the row area, and drag the Dollars button to the data area.

Normally, when you click Finish, the PivotTable Wizard retrieves all the data for the PivotTable and puts it into a *cache*, or holding place. When you have a large database, you may not want to retrieve all the information at one time. When a PivotTable links to an external data source, and you add a page field, you can tell the page field to retrieve only the rows from the database that match that one field.

6 Double-click the Product field button (in the page area). Click the Advanced button. In the Page Field Options group, select the second option, Query External Data Source As You Select Each Page Field Item (Requires Less Memory). Then click OK twice.

With large databases, you can retrieve only a part at a time with a page field.

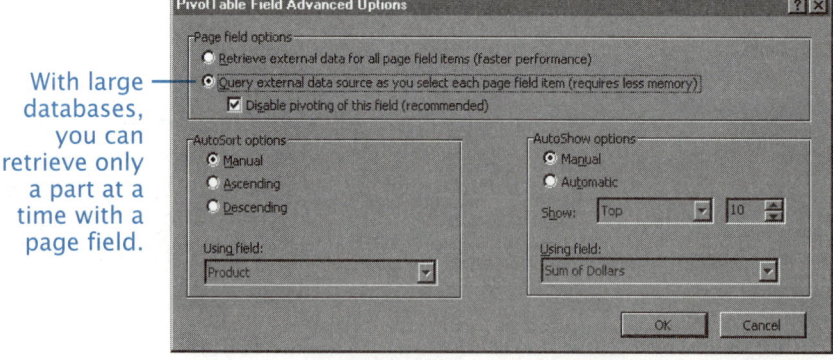

When you click Finish to create the PivotTable, Excel first retrieves the list of unique values for the product field. Then it arbitrarily selects the product and retrieves only the data for that one product. Watch the status bar as the PivotTable communicates with the data source, both as you create the PivotTable, and as you change the page field item.

7 Click Finish. Then change the page field from Aardvark to Airplane.

Each time you change the item in the page field, Excel reconnects to the data source and retrieves the new information, but the first time takes far longer than subsequent queries. If you have a large database and a single page field accounts for relatively few of the rows, you may want to link the page field to the database. However, if the data source is relatively small, you may find the PivotTable more responsive if you retrieve all the information into the cache at one time.

8 Double-click the Product field button, and click the Advanced button. Select the first of the page field options, Retrieve External Data For All Page Field Items (Faster Performance). Then click OK twice. Then try changing the page field to Tyrannosaurus.

Once the cache is filled, changing the PivotTable is almost instantaneous.

9 Save and close the Lesson8b workbook.

When retrieving data from an external database into a PivotTable, you have several options, depending on how large the database is and what kind of analysis you will do in the PivotTable. You can use the Query Wizard or Microsoft Query to filter the rows before they even get to the PivotTable. You can use page fields to retrieve only part of the rows at a time. Or you can import the entire data source into the PivotTable cache.

Lesson Summary

To	Do this
Require a cell to contain a value from a list	Give a name to the list. Select the cell. On the Data menu, click Validation. Select List in the Allow list. Type an equal sign plus the range name of the list in the Source box.
Copy a validation rule from one cell to another range of cells	Copy the cell with the validation. Select the range you want to apply the validation to. On the Edit menu, click Paste Special. Select Validation and click OK.
Require a cell to contain only a valid date	Select the cell. On the Data menu, click Validation. In the Allow box, select Date.

To	Do this
Use a formula to calculate the limit values for a data validation	In the Data Validation dialog box Minimum or Maximum box, type an equal sign and then type the formula.
Make a validation rule into a recommendation rather than a requirement	On the Data menu, click Validation. Click the Error Alert tab. In the Style list, select Warning. In the Error Message box, type a warning message.
Display the Auditing toolbar	On the View menu, point to Toolbars, and then click Customize. Click the check box next to Auditing and click Close.
Circle all cells on the worksheet that violate validation rules	On the Auditing toolbar, click the Circle Invalid Data button.
Clear validation circles on a worksheet	On the Auditing toolbar, click the Clear Validation Circles button.
Add a comment to a cell	Right-click the cell, and click Insert Comment.
Change the format of a comment	Right-click the cell, and click Edit Comment. Press ESC. Use buttons on the Drawing and Formatting toolbars to customize the comment.
Add a check box to a worksheet	In the Control Toolbox, click the Check Box button. Drag on the worksheet to create a place for the control.
Make a control line up with the gridlines on a worksheet	Hold down ALT as you drag the corners of the control.
Change the formatting of a control on a worksheet	Select the control, and in the Control Toolbox, click the Properties button. Change the BackColor, Caption, and SpecialEffect properties.
Link a check box control to a cell	Type the cell address as the value of the control's LinkedCell property.
Activate a control (so that you don't just select it when you click it)	In the Control Toolbox, click the Exit Design Mode button.
Create a two-column drop-down list box on a worksheet	In the Control Toolbox, click the Combo Box button and drag on the worksheet to create a place for the control. Enter the address of the source list as the control's ListFillRange property. Set the ColumnCount property to 2, and type a cell address in the control's LinkedCell property.

To	Do this
Adjust column widths for a multicolumn list box	In the ColumnWidths property, type the widths for the columns in points (1/72 inch), separated by semicolons. Enter the total width for the list in the ListWidth property.
Move a worksheet to a new workbook	Right-click the sheet tab, and click Move Or Copy. In the To Book list, select New Book and click OK.
Create a reference to cell A1 on the Sheet1 worksheet in the Book2.xls workbook	Use the reference *[Book2.xls]Sheet1!A1*.
Fix a broken link to another workbook	On the Edit menu, click Links. Select the link you want to change and click Change Source. Find the new source file and click OK.
Create a template—a workbook that must always be saved with a new name	On the File menu, click Save As. Type the name in the File Name box, select Template (*.xlt) from the Save As Type list, and click Save.
Open a workbook based on a template	On the File menu, click New. (Do not use the New toolbar button.) Select the template and click OK.
Create a data source for a query from an external database	On the Data menu, click Get External Data. Then click Create New Query. Select New Data Source and click OK. Type a name for the data source and select a driver type. Then click Connect and fill in information specific to that data source.
Create a new query	On the Data menu, point to Get External Data, and click Create New Query. Select the data source and click OK. Select the table or query you want to use and click the arrow to select all the fields from the table. Click Next three times and then click Finish.
Add a filter to a query	On the External Data toolbar, click Edit Query. Click Next three times. Select View Data Or Edit Query and click Finish. Click Show/Hide Criteria. Select a field name and type a criteria.
Add a parameter filter that prompts you for a value	In the Criteria row of Microsoft Query, replace the value with a prompt in square brackets.

To	Do this
Link a parameter to a cell	In Excel, click a cell in a query list. On the External Data toolbar, click Query Parameters. Select Get The Value From The Following Cell, and type the address of the cell.
Retrieve data from an external data source into a PivotTable	On the Data menu, click PivotTable Report. In Step 1 select External Data Source. In Step 2, click Get Data. Select a data source and define a query.
Retrieve data from the database for only a single page field item at a time	Create a page field. Double-click the page field button, and click Advanced. Select Query External Data Source As You Select Each Page Field.

For online information about	On the Help menu, click Contents And Index, click the Index tab, and then type
Validating data	**data validation**
Adding comments to cells	**comments**
Adding controls to worksheets	**controls**
Linking to external workbooks	**workbooks, references**
Retrieving lists from an external data source	**queries**
Importing data into a PivotTable from an external data source	**PivotTables, external data**

Sharing a Workbook

Estimated time
25 min.

In this lesson you will learn how to:

- Control who makes changes to a workbook.
- Allow multiple users to simultaneously edit a single workbook.

A few years ago, I learned vividly the power of a graphical user interface. File Manager had just been added to Windows. My company had just loaned me a computer to use at home. My son had just turned five. I got home from work one day to discover that my hard drive had been completely rearranged. Needless to say, I quickly added a password-protected screen saver to the computer.

As long as you are the only person who has access to your computer, you don't have to worry too much about protection. As long as you are the only person who uses an Excel workbook that you create, you don't have to worry too much about preventing changes. But as soon as you start to share your computer or your workbooks, you must think carefully about which changes you are willing to allow.

Microsoft Excel has powerful support for sharing workbooks. You might simply want to control what another person can see or do. You might want to actually edit a workbook at the same time as another user. Excel allows you to share as much or as little as you want. This lesson shows you how.

Start the lesson

▶ Start Microsoft Excel, change to the Excel AT Practice folder, and open the Start9 workbook. Save a copy of the workbook as **Lesson9**

Protecting a Workbook

It is time to begin the initial plans for fiscal year 1999. Your job is to distribute preliminary estimates for the dollar volumes of Tailspin Toys' three product lines for that year. Naturally, it's hard to predict what the future will be, so your first estimate includes best case and worst case estimates along with the actual targets. Your initial estimates appear on the FY99 sheet of the Lesson9 workbook.

You need to protect your projections for next year.

	A	B	C	D	E
1		Worst Case	Best Case	Plan	
2	Dinosaur	5,000	15,000	8,000	
3	Animal	10,000	20,000	15,000	
4	Vehicle	4,000	12,000	9,000	
5					

These initial projections are extremely sensitive information in the company. Management wants to be sure that only selected individuals have access to them. You can restrict access to the workbook by requiring a password to even open the file.

Add a password to a workbook

Adding a password to a workbook prevents anyone who does not know the password from opening the file. To add a password, you use the Options button in the Save As dialog box.

1 On the File menu, click Save As. Then click the Options button.

The Save Options dialog box appears.

Enter a password to prevent unauthorized access to the workbook.

2 In the Password To Open dialog box, type **abc** and click OK. In the Confirm Password dialog box, type **abc** again and click OK.

Excel returns to the Save As dialog box. You haven't yet saved the file.

3 Leaving Lesson9 as the name of the workbook, click the Save button. Then click Yes to confirm that you want to replace the earlier version.

The workbook is now saved with a password. You can try opening it to make sure the password works properly.

4 Close the Lesson9 workbook. On the File menu, click Lesson9 in the list of recently used files.

The Password dialog box appears.

You must enter the correct password, or you can't open the workbook at all.

5 Type **abc** and click OK to open the workbook.

Once a workbook is given a password, you must enter the password—using the correct combination of uppercase and lowercase letters—in order to open the workbook. Once you open the workbook, however, you have complete control, and can change anything about it you want. You can even remove the password.

Prevent changes to a workbook

Company managers have just changed their minds about how to handle the security of the FY99 planning worksheet. They have decided that protecting users from opening the workbook is unnecessary, since only authorized users can get to the file on the network anyway. Instead, they have begun to worry about who might make changes to the estimates. Therefore, your manager has asked you to allow anyone to open the workbook, but to prevent anyone but yourself from making changes to the estimates. To do that, you will use the Save Options dialog box, remove the password needed to open the file, and add a password to modify the file.

1 On the File menu, click Save As. Then click Options.

2 Clear the Password To Open box, type **abc** in the Password To Modify box, and click OK. Type **abc** in the Confirm Password dialog box, and click OK again to return to the Save As dialog box.

3 Click Save, and then click Yes to confirm.

You can now try opening the file as if you didn't know the password.

4 Close the Lesson9 workbook. On the File menu, click Lesson9 to reopen it.

The Password dialog box appears with a Read Only option for those who don't know the password.

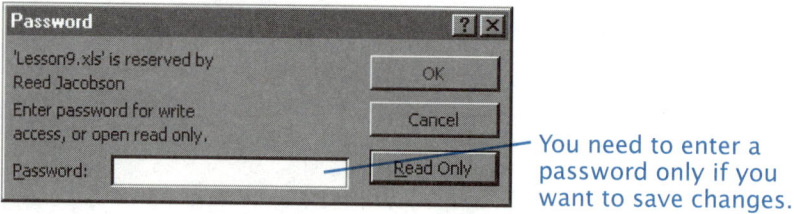

You need to enter a password only if you want to save changes.

5 Click the Read Only button.

The file opens with the words *Read-Only* in brackets in the title bar. When a workbook is open in *read-only* mode, you can still make changes to it, but if you want to save the workbook, you must give it a different name.

You can also make sure that the password gives you full access to the file.

6 Close the Lesson9 workbook. On the File menu, click Lesson9. In the Password box, type **abc** and click OK.

The file opens without the notice in the title bar.

When a workbook is available on a network, a user can attempt to open a workbook that another user has open. As long as each user opens the work-book in read-only mode, multiple users can open the file without even know-ing that anyone else has it open. However, only one person can open the file for modification at one time—unless you *share* the file, which you will learn about later in this lesson. Making a workbook read-only is an easy way to allow the workbook to be opened simultaneously by several people.

Change the Read-Only property of a file

Within two days of making the protected file available, you get several complaints about the Password dialog box. Everybody wants you to make the file open automatically in read-only mode. You talk with your manager about the problem, and she asks you to make a proposal.

In Microsoft Windows, every file has certain properties. One of those proper-ties is the Read-Only attribute. If you set the Read-Only attribute of a work-book file, Excel will open it in read-only mode automatically. First, remove the password from the workbook.

1 On the File menu, click Save As, and click Options. Clear the Password To Modify box and click OK. Then click Save and Yes to confirm.

2 Close the Lesson9 workbook.

3 In Windows Explorer, open the folder containing the practice files for this book, and select the Lesson9 workbook.

4 On the File menu, click Properties to display the Properties dialog box.

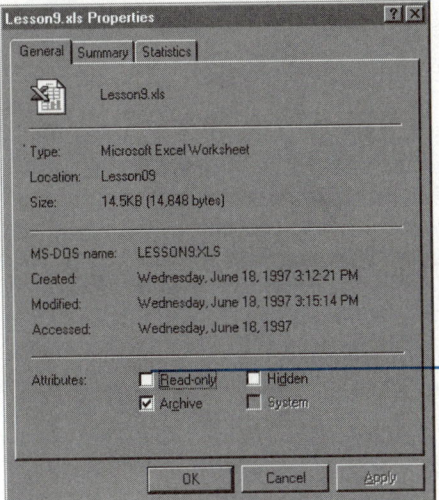

Click here to make a file read-only, but anyone can change it back.

5 Select the Read-Only attribute check box, and click OK.

6 Activate Microsoft Excel. On the File menu, click Lesson9.

The workbook automatically opens in read-only mode. When you are ready to make changes to the workbook, you simply turn off the Read-Only property before you open the workbook.

7 Close Lesson9. Activate Windows Explorer, and select the Lesson9 workbook. On the File menu, click Properties. Clear the Read-Only check box, and click OK. Activate Microsoft Excel and open Lesson9.

You discuss this option with your manager. The advantage is that the workbook automatically opens in read-only mode without any dialog box. Unfortunately, there are also several disadvantages:

■ You must turn off the Read-Only property to edit the workbook.

■ You must remember to turn on the Read-Only property when you finish.

■ There is no password protection for the Read-Only property; any user who knows how can turn it off.

Protect the contents of a workbook

Your manager quietly ponders the options for protecting the FY99 estimates. After a few minutes, she turns to you and says she knows the real problem. It is that once the workbook is open—whether read-only or not—users can change the values of cells in the workbook. She wants the workbook to act more like a report that just happens to be available online. Users should not be able to change the values of the cells.

You can protect the contents of a worksheet by enabling protection on that worksheet. You protect the contents of each worksheet separately. Since the Lesson9 workbook has only one sheet, you can protect everything in the workbook by protecting that one sheet.

1 The Lesson9 workbook should be open, with the FY99 worksheet active. On the Tools menu, point to Protection, and then click Protect Sheet.

The Protect Sheet dialog box appears.

Protect the sheet to prevent changes to cell content.

For specific in-formation about the three check boxes, press F1 to display the Assistant, and then click Con-trol Access To Workbooks And Worksheets.

2 Leave all three check boxes selected to protect everything about the worksheet. Type **abc** in the Password box and click OK. Type **abc** in the Confirm Password dialog box and click OK again.

The worksheet is now protected. You can test the protection by trying to change the value of a cell.

3 Select cell B2 and try to type **6**. Click OK to close the warning message.

With the worksheet protected, no one can make unauthorized changes to the worksheet, but anyone can still add a new worksheet or even delete the FY99 worksheet altogether. To prevent changes to the work-book structure, you must protect the workbook.

4 On the Tools menu, point to Protection, and then click Protect Work-book to display the Protect Workbook dialog box.

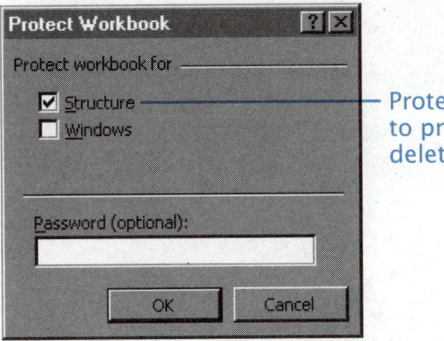

Protect the workbook to prevent adding or deleting sheets.

Selecting the Structure check box prevents a user from adding or deleting worksheets. Selecting the Windows check box prevents a user from resizing the workbook window or adding windows or freezing panes. You want to prevent any changes to the workbook.

5 Select both check boxes, type **abc** in the Password box, and click OK. Type **abc** again to confirm the password and click OK to return to the protected workbook.

Now, no one can make any changes to the workbook or its single worksheet without knowing the password. You may still want to set the file's Read-Only property in Windows, so that multiple users can easily open the file at the same time.

Allow changes to selected cells in a protected worksheet

Various managers have been able to review your initial proposal for FY99 order levels for a few days. It is now time for the product line managers to suggest adjustments to the plan levels. Your instructions are to allow changes to the Plan column of the worksheet, but leave the Worst Case and Best Case numbers protected.

For a demonstration of how to unlock cells on a protected worksheet, double-click the Excel Camcorder Files shortcut on your Desktop or connect to the Internet address listed on page xvi.

When you enable worksheet protection, you protect all the cells that are designated as *locked*. When you create a new worksheet, all the cells are locked. You can modify cells in a new worksheet because it is not protected. Protecting the worksheet causes Excel to take note of the locked setting for each cell. In order to allow users to change certain cells, while leaving others protected, you unlock those certain cells before enabling protection. Start by unprotecting the FY99 worksheet.

1 On the Tools menu, point to Protection, and then click Unprotect Sheet. Type **abc** as the password and click OK.

With the worksheet unprotected, you can change the locked status of specific cells.

2 Select the range D2:D4.

3 On the Format menu, click Cells, and click the Protection tab.

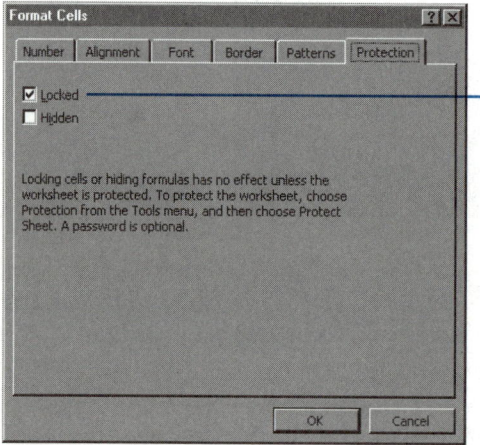

In a new workbook, all cells are locked. Before protecting the workbook, unlock cells you want to allow others to change.

4 Clear the Locked check box and click OK.

You can't see any difference between cells that are locked and cells that are not until you enable protection on the worksheet.

5 On the Tools menu, point to Protection, and then click Protect Sheet. Then click OK.

Enabling protection without using a password allows you to disable protection without entering the password. When you are dealing with employees in your own organization who are willing to follow the protection policies, you may not need to add a protection password.

6 Select cell B2 and try to type the number 6. Then click OK when Excel informs you that the cell is protected.

When some cells are unprotected, you can use the TAB key to jump quickly to the next unprotected cell.

7 Press TAB to select cell D2. Enter **9000** as the new plan value.

By selectively unlocking cells before you enable worksheet protection, you can protect most of a worksheet, while still allowing users to modify certain cells. Of course, if you are going to allow users to modify cells, then you must not make the workbook read-only. But only one person can edit it at a time—that is, unless you take advantage of Excel's capabilities for *sharing* a workbook.

Sharing a Workbook

Before you make the planning workbook available for managers to share, you are determined to test it thoroughly. However, it may seem difficult to test sharing a workbook by yourself. You could always evict your neighbor from his desk for an hour and run back and forth between offices. But an easier way to try out Excel's sharing tools is to run two copies of Excel.

Run two copies of Excel

When multiple users share a workbook, Excel identifies which user makes which change. To make it clear which copy of Excel is which, assume that this copy belongs to a person named *Boris*. You can change the user name in the Options dialog box (assuming your name is not Boris).

1 On the Tools menu, click Options, and click the General tab. In the User Name box, type **Boris**, and click OK. Then save the workbook.

The name you enter here will appear as the person editing the workbook.

If you reduce the size of the window, you can tell which copy of Excel belongs to Boris.

Restore

2 If the Excel window is maximized, click the Restore button at the top right corner of the window. Resize the window to fit the top half of the screen.

Now you're ready to start the second copy of Excel. You already have one copy of Excel running. If you double-click the name of a workbook in Windows Explorer, that workbook will open in the copy of Excel that is already running. To open a second copy of Excel, you must run it explicitly from the Start menu.

3 Click the Start menu, point to Programs, and click Microsoft Excel.

271

You now have two copies of Excel running. Assume that this copy belongs to a coworker of Boris named *Natasha*.

4 On the Tools menu, click Options, and click the General tab. In the User Name box, type **Natasha** and click OK.

You can put Natasha's copy of Excel below Boris's copy.

5 If necessary, click the Restore button for the Excel window. Resize the window to fit the bottom half of the screen, below the one for Boris.

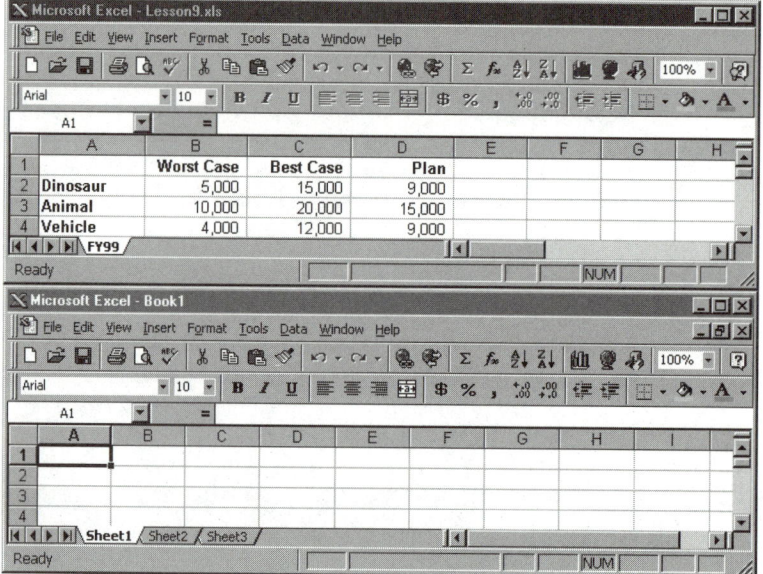

Share a workbook

Boris has the Lesson9 workbook open for editing. If Natasha tried to open it at this time, she would see a warning message.

Only one person can have a workbook open for editing at a time, unless that person chooses to *share* the workbook. When you share a workbook, more than one person can make changes at the same time. While a workbook is shared, most normal Excel functions are available, but certain actions that are difficult to share are disabled. For example, you can insert or rename a worksheet, but you can't delete one.

1 Activate Boris's copy of Excel. On the Tools menu, click Share Workbook, and click the Editing tab.

The dialog box shows that the workbook is currently being edited exclusively by Boris.

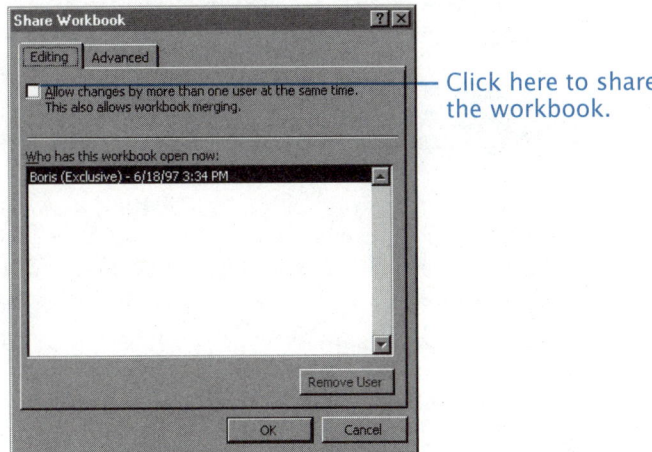

Click here to share the workbook.

2 Select the check box that allows changes by more than one user at the same time, and click OK. Click OK again when Excel informs you that this action will save the workbook.

The title bar shows that the workbook is being shared. Natasha can now open and edit the Lesson9 workbook.

3 Activate Natasha's copy of Excel. Switch to the folder containing the practice files for this book, and open the Lesson9 workbook.

Both Natasha and Boris can make changes to the workbook.

Synchronize shared workbooks

Natasha's changes get posted back to the shared copy on the network each time she saves the workbook. With a logic that might seem backward but is actually very convenient, Excel imports Natasha's changes from the network copy when Boris saves his copy of the workbook.

1 In Natasha's copy of the workbook, select cell D3. Change the value from 15,000 to 18,000. Then save the workbook.

2 Activate Boris' copy of Excel, and select cell D2. Change the value from 9,000 to 8,000 and save the workbook. Click OK when Excel notifies you that the workbook was updated with changes from another user.

Excel not only changed cell D3 to 18,000, it highlighted the change with a colored border along with a comment on the cell. You can see the history of the change by moving the mouse pointer over cell D3.

3   Move the mouse pointer over cell D3 to display the comment.

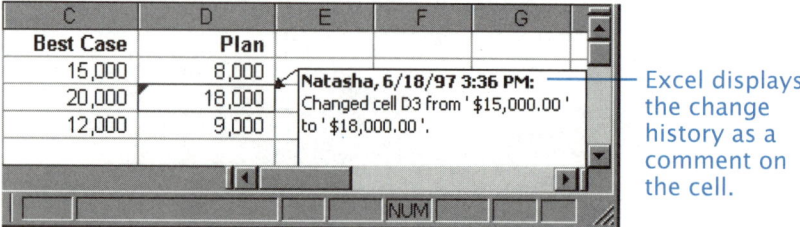

Excel displays the change history as a comment on the cell.

Boris's copy of the workbook includes both his and Natasha's changes. Natasha's copy, however, shows only her own changes. That is because she hasn't saved her workbook since Boris saved his changes. As soon as she saves her workbook, the two copies will be synchronized.

4   Activate Natasha's copy of Excel, save the workbook, and click OK when notified of the change.

Now both open workbooks contain all the changes.

Manage conflicts

As long as each person editing a shared workbook changes a different cell, Excel is able to smoothly integrate the changes. But when two or more users change the value of a single cell, someone must decide which value will "win." The first person who encounters the conflict is the one who gets to make the decision, but Excel does retain a history of all the changes, even the ones that "lost."

1   Activate Natasha's copy of Excel, change cell D4 to 6,000 and save the workbook.

2   Activate Boris's copy of Excel, change cell D4 to 10,000 and save the workbook.

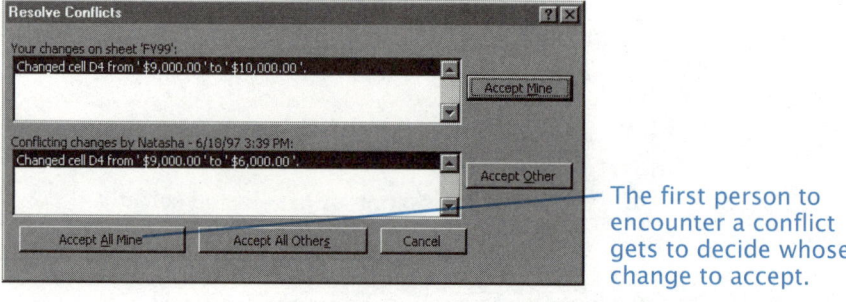

The first person to encounter a conflict gets to decide whose change to accept.

The Resolve Conflicts dialog box shows all the conflicting changes and allows Boris (who happened to be the one saving the workbook at the time the conflict was detected) to decide whose changes win.

3 Click the Accept All Mine button.

The next time Natasha saves her workbook, there will be no conflict. She will be merely notified that a change occurred.

4 Activate Natasha's copy of Excel, save the workbook, and click OK when notified of the change.

Natasha's previous value for cell D4 is gone, but Natasha still has an opportunity to reject Boris's change.

5 On the Tools menu, point to Track Changes, and then click Accept Or Reject Changes.

The Select Changes To Accept Or Reject dialog box allows Natasha to limit the types of changes to review. When only a few changes are involved, the default options are fine.

6 Click OK to show the Accept Or Reject Changes dialog box. Click Accept twice to accept the first two changes, which are uncontested.

Select the value you want and click Accept.

The dialog box now shows a history of the changes to cell D4. Natasha can see her earlier change, and she can see that Boris overwrote it. She can also reaffirm her previous decision.

7 Select the second entry in the list, Natasha's previous $6,000 entry, and click Accept. Then save the workbook.

Show a history of changes

Now it is Boris's turn to find his change rejected. Rather than go through the accept or reject process, he merely wants to see an audit trail of all the changes that have occurred.

1 Activate Boris's copy of Excel, save the workbook, and click OK when informed that someone made changes.

2 On the Tools menu, point to Track Changes, and then click Highlight Changes.

Click here to see a history of changes.

The Highlight Changes dialog box appears. This dialog box has the same choices as the Select Changes To Accept Or Reject dialog box that Natasha encountered, plus a few extra check boxes.

3 Clear the When check box. Select the List Changes On A New Sheet check box, and click OK. (You may want to enlarge the window for Boris's copy of Excel so that you can see more of the log.)

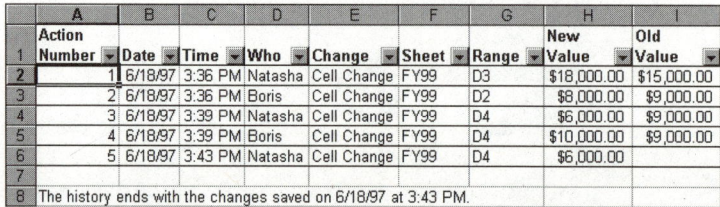

	A	B	C	D	E	F	G	H	I
1	Action Number	Date	Time	Who	Change	Sheet	Range	New Value	Old Value
2	1	6/18/97	3:36 PM	Natasha	Cell Change	FY99	D3	$18,000.00	$15,000.00
3	2	6/18/97	3:36 PM	Boris	Cell Change	FY99	D2	$8,000.00	$9,000.00
4	3	6/18/97	3:39 PM	Natasha	Cell Change	FY99	D4	$6,000.00	$9,000.00
5	4	6/18/97	3:39 PM	Boris	Cell Change	FY99	D4	$10,000.00	$9,000.00
6	5	6/18/97	3:43 PM	Natasha	Cell Change	FY99	D4	$6,000.00	
7									
8	The history ends with the changes saved on 6/18/97 at 3:43 PM.								

Excel displays a new worksheet that lists all the changes that have been made since the worksheet was shared. Boris can filter the value of any column. He can see that Natasha rejected his change. At this point, he may choose to place a strategic phone call, or stop by her desk to resolve their different opinions about how Vehicles will do next year.

The History worksheet is a special worksheet that is "owned" by Excel. You cannot make any changes to it. Because the History worksheet can change any time that you save a workbook, it hides itself when you save the workbook.

4 Save the workbook.

Clean up the second copy of Excel

Unless your name is Natasha, you don't want Excel to remember that as your user name.

1 Activate Natasha's copy of Excel. On the File menu, click Exit.

2 Activate the remaining copy of Excel. On the Tools menu, click Options, and click the General tab. In the User Name box, type your name, and click OK.

You can now turn off sharing, which will erase the history of changes from the workbook.

3 On the Tools menu, click Share Workbook. On the Editing tab, clear the Allow Changes check box, and click OK. Click Yes when asked if you want to make the workbook exclusive.

One Step Further: Sharing with Remote Users

Allowing multiple users to edit a workbook at the same time is a powerful feature for people who have access to a shared network folder. Sometimes, however, you want to "share" a workbook with people who do not have access to a network file. For example, you might distribute a workbook as an email attachment or on a floppy disk. The recipients make changes and send back the files. You need to integrate the changes and manage any conflicts the same as if the users were editing the file simultaneously.

When you share a workbook, that workbook retains a history of all the changes that have been made to it. If you make copies of the workbook, each copy retains a history of the changes.

Distribute shared workbooks

One of the managers who needs to provide input for the FY99 plans is leaving later this morning for a short business trip. He wants to edit the workbook while he is on the airplane. You can make a copy of the shared workbook to give to him.

1 With the Lesson9 workbook open, on the Tools menu, point to Track Changes, and then click Highlight Changes.

The Highlight Changes check box appears. Selecting the Track Changes check box in this dialog box has exactly the same effect as selecting the Allow Changes check box in the Share Workbook dialog box.

2 Select the Track Changes check box and click OK. Click OK again when asked if you are willing to save the workbook.

You can make a copy of the workbook either by copying the file in Windows Explorer (or File Manager), or by using the Save As command.

3 On the File menu, click Save As. If necessary, change to the folder containing the practice files for this book. Then type **Lesson9a** as the name for the copy, and click Save.

The Lesson9a workbook is the one that the travelling manager will copy to his notebook computer. Assume that you are now that manager, on the airplane, editing the workbook.

4 Change cell D2 to 5,000, and change cell D3 to 11,000. Save and close the workbook.

Merge shared workbooks

The manager has now returned and has copied the modified Lesson9a workbook back to its original location. You are ready to merge the changes into the original Lesson9 workbook.

1 Open the Lesson9 workbook.

This workbook has the same contents as the one the travelling manager originally took with him.

If you distributed multiple copies, you could hold down CTRL to select and merge multiple workbooks at this time.

2 On the Tools menu, click Merge Workbooks. Select the Lesson9a workbook, and click OK.

The changes are incorporated into the Lesson9 workbook.

3 Save and close the Lesson9 workbook.

Merging workbooks is identical to simultaneous sharing of a single workbook, except that you can integrate copies of the file that have different names or are in different folders. Otherwise, managing conflicts, accepting or rejecting changes, and reviewing history all work the same whether you are sharing a single file, or merging copies of the file.

Lesson Summary

To	Do this
Prevent anyone who does not know the password from opening a workbook	On the File menu, click Save As. Then click Options. Type a password in the Password To Open box and click OK. Confirm the password, and then click Save.
Prevent anyone who does not know the password from saving changes to a workbook	Follow the same steps as adding a password for opening the workbook, but type a password in the Password To Modify box.
Make a file automatically open in read-only mode	In Windows Explorer (or File Manager), select the workbook file. On the File menu, click Properties. Select the Read-Only check box and click OK.
Prevent a user from changing any cells on a worksheet once the workbook is open	On the Tools menu, point to Protection, and then click Protect Sheet. Type a password in the Password box (if you want), and click OK.
Allow a user to change specific cells on a protected worksheet	Before protecting the worksheet, select the cells you want to allow changes to. On the Format menu, click Cells, and select the Protection tab. Clear the Locked check box and click OK. Then protect the worksheet.
Prevent a user from making changes to a workbook, such as inserting or deleting worksheets	On the Tools menu, point to Protection, and then click Protect Workbook. Type a password in the Password box (if you want), and click OK.
Change the user name for your copy of Excel	On the Tools menu, click Options, and click the General tab. Type a new name in the User Name box, and click OK.

To	Do this
Share a workbook so that multiple users can edit it at the same time	On the Tools menu, click Share Workbook. Select the Allow Changes check box and click OK.
Send changes you made in a shared workbook back to the copy saved on the network	Save the workbook.
Update your open copy of a shared workbook with changes that others may have made	Save the workbook.
When you and another person have both changed the same cell, decide whose change to keep	Save the workbook. When the Resolve Conflict dialog box appears, select the change to keep.
Review changes already made in a shared workbook, deciding whether to save or reject each change	On the Tools menu, point to Track Changes, and then click Accept Or Reject changes. Click Accept or Reject for each change.
Show a history of all the changes to a shared workbook	On the Tools menu, point to Track Changes, and then click Highlight Changes. Select the type of changes you want to see. Select the List Changes On A New Sheet check box, and click OK.
Hide the History worksheet	Save the workbook.
Return a shared workbook to exclusive use	On the Tools menu, click Share Workbook. Clear the Allow Changes check box and click OK.
Prepare a workbook so that you can distribute copies and later merge all the changes	On the Tools menu, click Share Workbook, or, on the Tools menu, point to Track Changes, and click Highlight Changes.
Merge changes from another copy of a shared workbook	On the Tools menu, click Merge Workbooks. Select the copy of the workbook you want to merge (hold down CTRL to select multiple workbooks), and click OK.

For online information about	On the Help menu, click Contents And Index, click the Index tab, and then type
Protecting workbooks	protecting, worksheets and workbooks
Sharing workbooks	shared workbooks

Creating Macros

Estimated time
30 min.

In this lesson you will learn how to:

■ Record and run macros.

■ Create macros that select ranges.

■ Make macros easy to run.

There are more than 5,000 species of cockroaches on the earth, spread over the entire world, including the North and South poles. However, the only place I have seen humans dressed up as giant cockroaches was at a field day activity in Tokyo, Japan. It seems somehow fitting, then, that it would be Japanese scientists who would figure out how to automate a cockroach. They remove the wings and add a little harness that sends electrical signals directly into the roach's nervous system. (Is there some kind of Society for Prevention of Cruelty to Cockroaches?) Maybe someday wired roaches will be able to clean out clogged drainpipes.

I will admit that adding automation to a spreadsheet is not nearly as exotic as automating a cockroach, but it probably has more immediate practical applications. And it's also a lot easier to do. Not so easy that you don't need to read this lesson, mind you, but easy, fun, and practical.

Start the lesson

➤ Start Microsoft Excel, change to the Excel AT Practice folder, and open the Start10 workbook. Save a copy of the workbook as **Lesson10**

Recording Macros

Tailspin Toys recently started a promotional program to increase sales of the company's toy models. Because of your Excel expertise, you have been asked to create a log to record promotional expenditures. The Promotions sheet in the Lesson10 workbook contains the beginning of the promotion log.

You keep a log of promotions for each product.

	A	B	C	D	E	F	G
1	Month	Product	Line	Description	Amount	Cumulative	
2	Aug-98	Giraffe	Animal	Magazine Ad	$8,400	$8,400	
3	Aug-98	Brontosaurus	Dinosaur	Dealer Incentive	$6,000	$14,400	
4							

See Lesson 3 for more information about lookup formulas.

Column C contains a lookup formula that finds the product line for the product. Column F contains a formula that adds the current dollar amount to the previous one. You often adjust the value for a promotion, typically up or down $100. You would like to be able to touch a key and have the value increment by $100 or touch a different key and have the value decrement by $100. You know that Excel has the ability to create macros that automate routine tasks. You would like to create a pair of macros that will quickly adjust the value.

Record and run a macro

Macros in Excel use an automation language called Visual Basic, Applications edition, which is derived from Microsoft's popular Visual Basic programming language. Excel has a Visual Basic toolbar that is extremely useful if you are going to create macros.

1 Right-click any toolbar, and then click Visual Basic.

The Visual Basic toolbar appears. You can now use the toolbar to start recording a macro.

Record Macro

2 On the Visual Basic toolbar, click the Record Macro button. In the Record Macro dialog box, type **ValueUp** as the macro name and click OK.

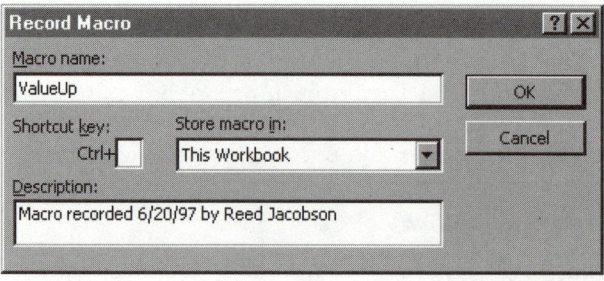

The word *Recording* appears in the status bar, and a new Stop Recording toolbar appears. You are now recording. Start by selecting the first value you want to change.

3 Select cell E2, the first value in the Amount column.

The current value in the cell is $8,400. If you add $100 to that, you get $8,500.

4 Type **8500** and press ENTER.

That's all you need in the macro. You can now turn off the recorder.

Stop Recording

5 On either the Stop Recording toolbar or the Visual Basic toolbar, click the Stop Recording button.

You have now recorded a macro. Before testing the macro, change cell E2 to $500.

6 In cell E2, enter **$500**

You can now try out your macro to see how it works. The Visual Basic toolbar has a button for running a macro.

Run Macro

7 On the Visual Basic toolbar, click the Run Macro button.

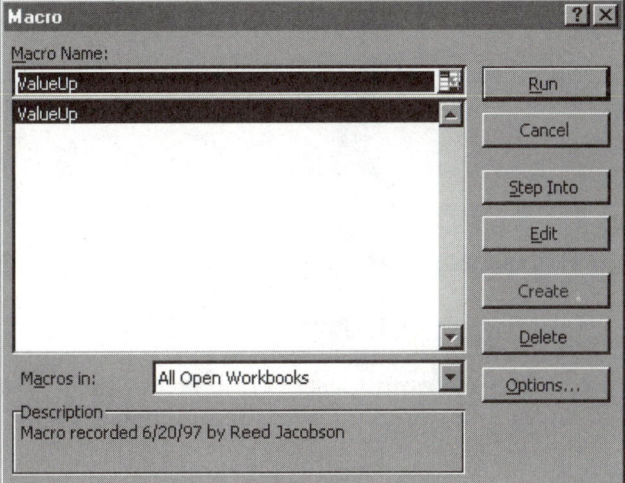

The Macros dialog box appears with the single macro, ValueUp, already selected in the list.

8 Click Run.

The value of cell E2 changes to $8,500.

As you probably expected, the macro didn't increment the current value of the cell; it simply put the same value into the cell that you did when you recorded the macro. In order to get a macro to take the existing value in a cell and adjust that value, you have to change the recorded macro. And in order to change the macro, you have to find it. Where is the macro you recorded?

Find a macro

Excel stores macros in the workbook, but they are in a hidden location. In order to see the macro, you must use the Visual Basic Editor. You can use the Run Macro button on the Visual Basic toolbar to display the Visual Basic Editor.

Run Macro

1   On the Visual Basic toolbar, click the Run Macro button.

2   In the Macro dialog box, click ValueUp, and click Edit.

Close these other windows.

The macro appears in the code window.

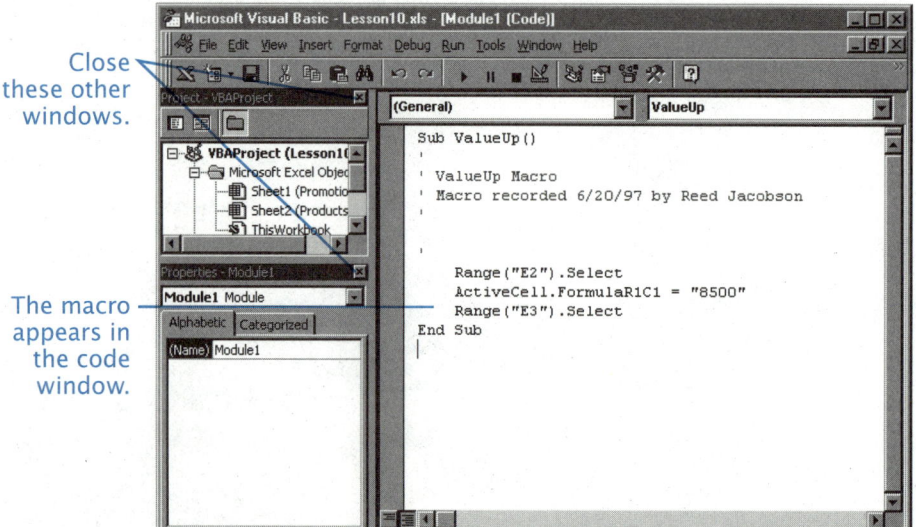

The Visual Basic Editor appears as a new application, with one main window and a couple of windows on the side. The main window—the one with the word *(General)* in a box at the top—is called the *code window* and contains your macro. If you close the other windows and shrink the Visual Basic Editor, you can see the Excel workbook behind the code window.

Close

3   Click the Close button for the Project window and for the Properties window. Reduce the size of the Visual Basic Editor until you can see the Excel window behind it.

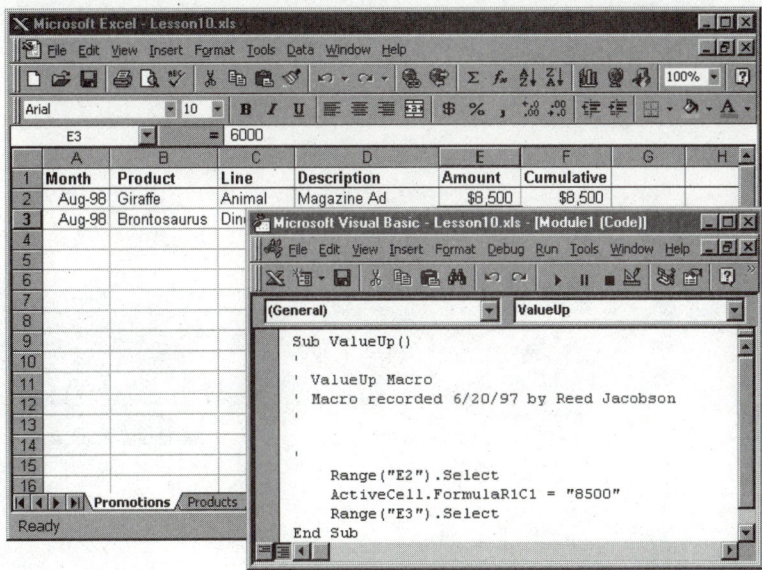

A macro begins with the word *Sub*, followed by the name of the macro, followed by empty parentheses. The macro ends with the words *End Sub*. The macro recorder puts a few *comment lines* at the beginning of the macro. A comment line begins with an apostrophe and is ignored by Visual Basic. Each line in the macro is called a *statement*, and carries out one action. The statements between the Sub statement and the End Sub statement are called the *body* of the macro.

Each statement in the body of a recorded macro consists of two parts separated by a period. Everything before the period is the *object*, which tells what part of Excel the statement will affect. I call the word after the period the *action word*. If the action word is followed by an equal sign, then it is called a *property*. If it is not followed by an equal sign, then it is called a *method*. Visual Basic always communicates with Excel by using the methods and properties of objects.

The best way to understand the statements in the body of a macro is to watch them work.

Step through a macro

You can watch the statements in a macro work by *stepping through* the statements one at a time. You start stepping through a macro the same way you run it: by using the Run Macro toolbar button.

1   Activate the Excel window. Change cell E2 to **$1,000**, and then select cell A2.

2   On the Visual Basic toolbar, click the Run Macro button. With the ValueUp macro selected, click Step Into.

Run Macro

285

The Visual Basic Editor appears again, but this time, the Sub statement at the beginning of the macro is highlighted yellow and has a yellow arrow in the left margin. The yellow arrow indicates the *next statement*, the statement that will execute next. You execute a single statement in a macro by pressing the F8 function key.

3 Press F8 to skip the comment lines and highlight the first statement in the macro: *Range("E2").Select*

The yellow highlight shows the next statement that will execute.

In this statement, the part before the period is the object and tells Excel that you want to do something to the range known as "E2." The word after the period is a method. (It is not followed by an equal sign.) It tells Excel what you want to do to cell E2—you want to select it.

4 Press F8 to select cell E2 and highlight the next statement in the macro: *ActiveCell.FormulaR1C1 = "8500"*

Once again, the part before the period is the object. This statement tells Excel that you want to do something to the cell that is currently active or, in other words, the cell that you just selected in the preceding statement. The word after the period is a property. (It is followed by an equal sign.) It apparently has something to do with the formula or contents of the cell. A statement modifies a property by assigning a new value to it. In this case, the new value is "8500."

5 Press F8 to assign the value to the cell and highlight the next statement in the macro: *Range("E3").Select*

You should be able to understand this statement. The object is cell E3, and the action is to select that cell.

6 Press F8 twice, once to select cell E3, and once to end the macro.

Each statement in the body of a macro follows the same general pattern: specify an object and then specify an action to do to it. By stepping through the macro, you can identify the statement that changes the value of the cell. You can now edit the macro to make that statement increment the current value of the cell.

Edit a macro

The action word in the statement you need to change is a property. Statements where the action word is a property are easy to modify. To get the current value of the property, simply put the property (along with its objects) on the right side of the equal sign.

Copy

Paste

1   In the ValueUp macro, select the words *ActiveCell.FormulaR1C1* and click the Copy button.

2   Select the value *"8500"* (in other words, everything after the equal sign) and click the Paste button.

The statement should now look like this: *ActiveCell.FormulaR1C1 = ActiveCell.FormulaR1C1*. This statement now takes the current value of the active cell and puts it back into the active cell. That is close to what you want, but it wouldn't be terribly useful. All you have left to do is to add 100 to the value before you reassign it.

3   After the word *FormulaR1C1* at the end of the statement, type **+100** and press the DOWN ARROW key.

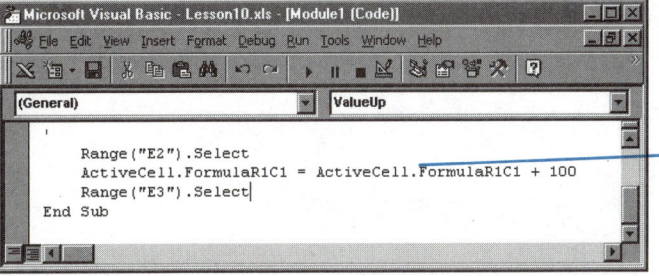

Move a property to the right side of the equal sign to get its current value.

As soon as you move the mouse pointer away from the statement, Visual Basic adds spaces around the plus sign. That means that Visual Basic was able to interpret the change you made.

The macro should now select cell E2, add 100 to its current value, and then select cell E3. Rather than switch back to Excel, you can test the macro right in the Visual Basic Editor, by clicking the Run Sub button.

Run Sub

4   Click the Run Sub button and watch the value of cell E2 change. Run the macro multiple times if you want.

The macro always changes cell E2, regardless of which cell is selected when you run it. If you delete the two statements that select cells, you can generalize the macro to increment whichever cell happens to be active.

5 Click to the left of the *Range("E2").Select* statement (just to the right of the gray margin) to select the entire statement, and press DELETE. Click to the left of the *Range("E3").Select* statement, and press DELETE.

In the worksheet, cell E3 should be the active cell. You can test the revised macro without leaving the Visual Basic Editor.

6 Click the Run Sub button to test the macro.

The value of cell E3 changes to $6,100.

Sometimes you want a macro to select a specific cell. Other times you want it to operate on whatever is selected when you run the macro. If you record a macro that selects specific cells, you can make it operate on the current selection by deleting the statements that selects the cells. (Later in the lesson you will learn more about selecting ranges with a macro.)

NOTE If you create a macro that operates on the active cell, be sure that you select an appropriate cell before you run the macro.

Add a shortcut key

You can now add 100 to the value of any cell by running your ValueUp macro. Unfortunately, running the macro when Excel is active requires almost as many keystrokes or mouse clicks as merely typing a new value in the cell. You can add a shortcut key to make the macro run at the touch of a key (or at least a key combination).

Run Macro

1 Activate Excel. On the Visual Basic toolbar, click the Run Macro button. With the ValueUp macro selected, click Options.

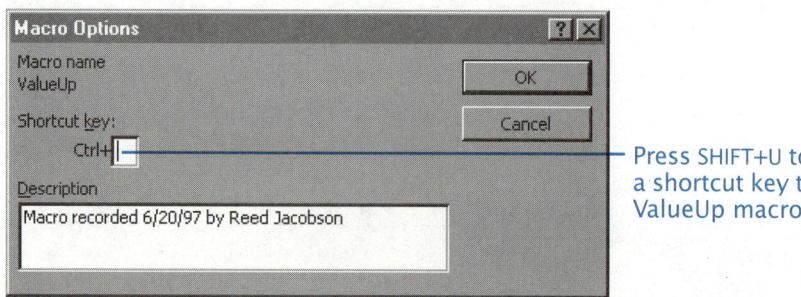

Press SHIFT+U to add a shortcut key to the ValueUp macro.

The Options dialog box allows you to specify a shortcut key for the macro. All shortcut keys consist of either CTRL plus a letter or

CTRL+SHIFT plus a letter. Many of Excel's built-in shortcut keys consist of CTRL plus a letter, and you usually don't want to replace those. By using CTRL+SHIFT combinations for your custom shortcut keys, you can avoid interfering with built-in shortcuts. For this macro, you can assign CTRL+SHIFT+U. ("U" for Up.) You don't need to press the CTRL key because that is already part of the shortcut.

2 Click in the shortcut box, and press SHIFT+U. Then click OK to get back to the Macro dialog box, and click Cancel to get back to Excel.

3 Select cell E2 and press CTRL+SHIFT+U.

The shortcut works fine.

Shortcut keys are very easy to use—provided that you can remember what they are. Later in the lesson you will learn how to attach a macro to a button or a menu command.

Write your own macro

To create the ValueUp macro, you started with the macro recorder and then made modifications to the recorded macro. You need a ValueDown macro that will subtract $100 from the active cell when you press CTRL+SHIFT+D. You should be able to create that macro without the help of the macro recorder. (If you are brave, you can create it without looking at the following steps!)

Visual Basic Editor

1 On the Visual Basic toolbar, click the Visual Basic Editor button.

2 Click below the End Sub statement, type **Sub ValueDown**, and press ENTER.

Visual Basic automatically adds the parentheses after the macro name and the *End Sub* statement at the bottom.

3 Press TAB to indent the body of the macro. Then type the statement **ActiveCell.FormulaR1C1 = ActiveCell.FormulaR1C1 – 100**

Select the property you want from the list.

TIP After you type each period, Visual Basic helps you by displaying a list of the methods and properties you can use with the object before the period. You can use the UP ARROW and DOWN ARROW keys to select the method or property name you want, and then press TAB to enter the word into the statement.

Run Macro

4 Activate Excel. On the Visual Basic toolbar, click the Run Macro button. Select ValueDown and click Options. Press SHIFT+D to create a shortcut key and click OK. Then click Cancel to close the Macros dialog box.

Your macro is now ready to test.

5 Select cell E3 and press CTRL+SHIFT+D.

The value decreases by $100.

6 Save the Lesson10 workbook.

You now have a pair of easy-to-run macros, one to increment a value and one to decrement a value. You can create a macro by using the macro recorder, by editing a recorded macro, or by typing a macro directly in the Visual Basic Editor.

NOTE When you open a workbook that contains a macro, Excel offers to disable the macros. This is in case you receive a workbook from an unknown source and want to avoid a macro that could damage your computer. Unfortunately, Excel cannot tell the difference between a workbook you created yourself and one you received from a stranger. If you use workbooks created only by trusted people (including yourself), you can safely select the option not to see the warning message in the future. When you disable the message, Excel tells you how to turn the warning back on.

Recording a Macro that Selects Ranges

Because the promotions log contains a mixture of constant values and formulas, you must be careful when you add a new entry to the log. In addition to entering appropriate values for the constants, you must correctly copy the formulas from columns C and F down to the new row. You would like to create a macro to add a new row for you. The easiest way to add a new row is to copy the bottom row in the list down to the first empty row.

Copy a range down one row

The bottom row of the list is currently the range A3:F3. You can turn on the recorder and copy the range A3:F3 down one row, to the range A4:F4. But when you play back the macro, it will always copy from A3:F3 to A4:F4, regardless of where the bottom row actually is.

Suppose that the active cell is A3 when you start recording a macro, and you then select the range A3:F3. How is the macro recorder to interpret that action? Do you want the macro to always select the range A3:F3 (an *absolute reference*)? Or do you want the macro to select columns A to F of whichever row currently contains the active cell (a *relative reference*)? The macro recorder has no way of automatically detecting your intentions.

When adding a row to the promotions log, you want to copy the bottom row of the list (whichever row that happens to be) to the next row down. At least some of the time, you will need to use relative references. The Stop Recording toolbar that appears when you start recording a macro has a Relative References button that allows you to precisely control how the recorder interprets your selections.

Record Macro

1 On the Visual Basic toolbar, click the Record Macro button. Type **CopyRow** as the name of the new macro and click OK.

In order to select the bottom row of the list, you must start in cell A1 and jump to the bottom. You always want to start with cell A1, so leave the Relative References button alone for the first part of the macro.

Relative References

2 Click cell A1. Press the END key, and then press the DOWN ARROW key to select cell A3.

You have now selected the first cell in the bottom row. You need to select all the cells in this row. Now, you need the selection to be relative.

Copy

3 On the Stop Recording toolbar, click the Relative References button. Then select the range A3:F3.

4 On the Standard toolbar, click the Copy button.

You will next select the corresponding cells in the next row down. This still needs to be a relative selection.

Paste

5 Select the range A4:F4, and click the Paste button. Press ESC to inform Excel that you won't need to paste the range anywhere else.

Now you can turn off the recorder and test the macro.

Stop Recording

6 On the Stop Recording toolbar, click the Stop Recording button.

7 On the Visual Basic toolbar, click the Run Macro button. Select CopyRow and click Run.

The macro creates a new bottom row.

Run Macro

The macro appears to work fine, even as the bottom row of the list moves down. The macro doesn't seem to need any modifications, but you may want to see how it works.

Watch relative references at work

Once again, the easiest way to understand how a macro works is to step through it, watching each action happen as you look at the statement that causes it.

Run Macro

1 On the Visual Basic toolbar, click Run Macro. Select CopyRow, and click Step Into.

The Visual Basic Editor appears, with the Sub statement highlighted.

2 Press F8 to skip the comment lines and highlight the first statement in the body of the macro: *Range("A1").Select*

This statement should look familiar. The part before the period is the object and the part after the period is a method. Often, it is easiest to read a macro statement by starting at the end and working your way to the front. You can read this statement as *Select the "A1" range.*

3 Press F8 to select cell A1 and highlight the next statement: *Selection.End(xlDown).Select*

This statement has two periods. Think of everything before the final period as the object for the Select method. Then mentally discard the action word and repeat the process. The part before the first period, *Selection,* is the object and the part after the first period, *End(xlDown),* is a property. The only action this embedded property does, however, is to calculate a new object.

NOTE Properties that are embedded in the middle of a statement are not followed by an equal sign and are actually indistinguishable from methods. You need to worry about the difference between a method and a property only when it occurs as the action word in the statement—that is, after the final period. Whenever you record a statement that has a property as the action word, the property will always have an equal sign after it.

Once again starting from the back, you can read this statement like this: *Select the down end from the selection.* The recorder creates a statement similar to this when you press the END key followed by an arrow key.

4 Press F8 to select the bottom cell in column A (probably cell A5), and highlight the next statement: *ActiveCell.Range("A1:F1").Select*

This is the first statement you recorded after turning on relative references. You can read this as *Select the range A1:F1 of the active cell.* But what does that mean? Think of the active cell (in this case cell A5) as the "A1" cell of a *virtual worksheet.* Select cells A1:F1 of that virtual worksheet. Which cells does that equate to in the real worksheet? Cells A5:F5, the range *relative* to the active cell.

5 Press F8 to select the entire bottom row and highlight the next statement: *Selection.Copy.*

This statement is easy: *Copy the selection*. This turns on what is called *copy mode*. You can tell when Excel is in copy mode because it displays a blinking border around the copied cells and puts a message in the status bar.

6 Press F8 to copy the range and highlight the next statement: *ActiveCell.Offset(1, 0).Range("A1:F1").Select*

This is another relative selection. Try reading it like this: *Select the range A1:F1 after offsetting by one from the active cell*. Once again, the address A1:F1 is relative to a virtual worksheet. This virtual worksheet starts not at the active cell, but shifted down one cell from the active cell.

NOTE Offset is a property that calculates a new range object based on another range object. The first number in parentheses tells Offset how much to shift the range down (or up if the number is negative). The second number tells Offset how much to shift the range to the right (or left if the number is negative). Fortunately, the macro recorder takes care of figuring out how to use Offset. All you have to do is read the finished statement.

The net effect of this statement is to select the first six cells in the row immediately below the active cell.

7 Press F8 to select the target cells and highlight the next statement: *ActiveSheet.Paste*

Read this statement as *Paste to the active sheet*. For some reason, Excel copies from a range but pastes to a worksheet. It always pastes to the selected cells on the worksheet.

8 Press F8 to paste the copied cells and highlight the next statement: *Application.CutCopyMode = False*

Read this as *Assign False as the CutCopyMode of the application*. This is the only action word in this entire macro that is a property. This statement cancels copy mode. The recorder created this statement when you pressed ESC.

9 Press F8 to turn off copy mode. Press F8 again to end the macro.

Some of the statements in this macro are a little complicated. But you can see how the recorder handles relative selections: by selecting cells on a virtual worksheet that begins with the active cell—sometimes shifted with the Offset property. The macro recorder will take care of the hard work of creating the relative reference statements. All you have to do is remember to click the Relative References button when you want a selection to be relative.

Select special cells

The new row that the macro appended to the promotions list contains a mixture of constants and formulas. You never want to change the formulas, only the constants. And you won't even change some of those very often. For example, you change to a new month relatively rarely. You can create a macro that will select only the constants in any row, making it easy to enter new constants without disturbing the formulas.

Record Macro

1 Activate Excel, and select cell C3, an arbitrary cell in the list. On the Visual Basic toolbar, click the Record Macro button. Type **SelectConstants** as the name of the macro and click OK.

First make the macro select the leftmost cell on the row. This will be a consistent starting place for a relative selection.

2 Press the END key and then press the LEFT ARROW key.

Then make sure that relative selection is turned on, and select all the cells in the row.

Relative References

3 Make sure the Relative References button on the Stop Recording toolbar is still pressed in. Then select cells A3:F3.

You can now use the GoTo Special dialog box to select just the constants.

4 Press CTRL+G to display the Go To dialog box, and click the Special button.

The Go To Special dialog box allows you to select cells based on a wide variety of attributes.

5 Select the Constants option and click OK.

Select the type of cell you want to select.

Excel selects the cells in columns A, B, D, and E. When multiple cells are selected, only one of them is the active cell. Pressing ENTER or TAB moves the active cell from one cell to the next within the selected cells.

Now you can enter the constants without disturbing the formulas. Since you don't change the month very often, you can even have the macro make the cell in column B the active cell.

6   Press TAB to activate the cell in column B.

7   Click the Stop Recording button to stop the recorder.

Stop Recording

Step through the macro

To examine the code that the macro created, test the macro by stepping through it.

Run Macro

1   Select cell E4 as an arbitrary starting cell.

2   On the Visual Basic toolbar, click the Run Macro button, select SelectConstants, and click Step Into to highlight the starting row of the macro.

3   Press F8 to skip the comment lines and highlight the first statement in the body of the macro: *Selection.End(xlToLeft).Select*

This statement selects the leftmost cell, starting from the original selection.

4   Press F8 to select cell A4 and highlight the next statement: *ActiveCell.Range("A1:F1").Select*

This makes a selection relative to the active cell, which is now the leftmost cell in the row.

5   Press F8 to select the range A4:F4 and highlight the next statement: *Selection.SpecialCells(xlCellTypeConstants, 23).Select*

Starting from the right, you can read this as *Select the constant special cells of the selection.* You don't need to worry about the details of the SpecialCells property; the macro recorder took care of that for you.

6   Press F8 to select cells A4, B4, D4, and E4, and to highlight the final statement in the body of the macro: *ActiveCell.Offset(0, 1).Range("A1").Activate*

Starting from the right, you can read this as *Activate the A1 cell of the virtual worksheet that starts offset one cell to the right of the active cell.* This statement shows the difference between the Select method and the Activate method: the Select method changes the entire selection; the Activate method changes which cell within the selection is the active cell.

7   Press F8 to make cell B4 the active cell. Then press F8 again to end the macro.

You do not need to make any modifications to the SelectConstants macro.

Make a macro run a macro

Sometimes, you want to run the SelectConstants macro by itself—for example, when you are modifying an existing row. You also want to run the SelectConstants macro every time you run the CopyRow macro. In fact, you can have the CopyRow macro run the SelectConstants macro for you. In the Visual Basic Editor, if you click the Run Sub button while the insertion point is inside a macro, Visual Basic will run the macro. If, on the other hand, the insertion point is not inside a macro, Visual Basic will display the Macros dialog box.

Run Sub

1 To get to the CopyRow macro, click below the End Sub statement of the SelectConstants macro (that is, outside of any macro), and click the Run Sub button. Select CopyRow from the list of macros, and click Edit.

   To make one macro run another macro, you simply type the name of the macro you want to run.

2 Insert a blank line at the bottom of the CopyRow macro, just before the End Sub statement. On that blank line, press TAB, and type **SelectConstants**

   Now you can try out both macros.

3 Activate Excel, select cell B5, and run the SelectConstants macro.

   The macro selects the constants on row 5.

4 Run the CopyRow macro.

   The macro copies the bottom row of the list and selects the constants on that row.

5 Save the Lesson10 workbook.

Making Macros Easy to Run

Clicking the Run Macro button to run the macros is more bother than you would like. You could add shortcut keys to make the macros easy to run, but your goal is to pass the promotional planning log on to someone else as soon as possible. You would like to make it easy to teach your successor how to use it. A toolbar button, or a menu command, or a button on the worksheet would be easy to show someone else how to use.

For a demonstration of how to add a macro to a toolbar button, double-click the Excel Camcorder Files shortcut on your Desktop or connect to the Internet address listed on page xvi.

Attach a macro to a toolbar button

Attaching a macro to a custom toolbar button is easy. You can either add the toolbar button to an existing toolbar, or you can create a new toolbar for it. In either case, you start by opening the Customize dialog box for toolbars.

1 Right-click any toolbar, and click Customize. Click the Toolbars tab.

2 Click the New button, type **Personal** as the name for a new toolbar, and click OK.

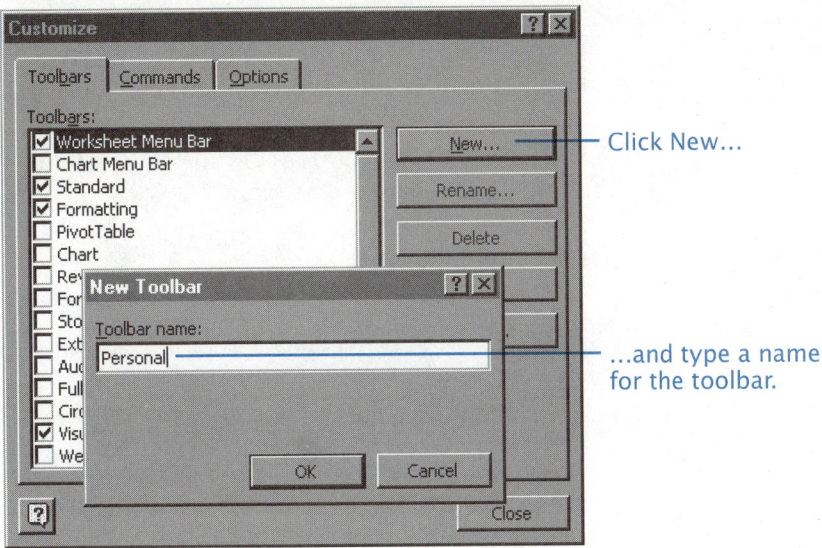

Click New...

...and type a name for the toolbar.

A new, empty toolbar appears.

3 In the Customize dialog box, click the Commands tab.

You can add any of the built-in toolbar buttons or menu commands to your new toolbar. You can also add a custom toolbar button that will run a macro.

4 From the Categories list, select Macros. Then from the Commands list, drag the Custom Button item onto the Personal toolbar.

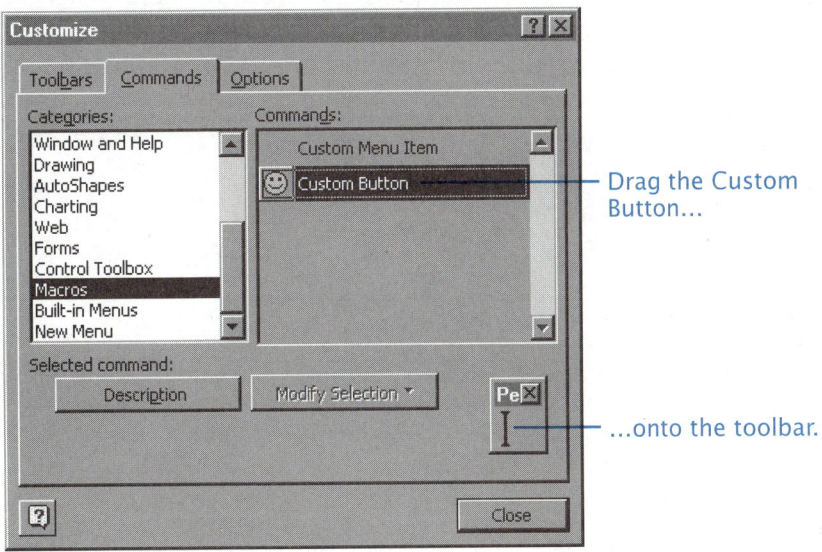

Drag the Custom Button...

...onto the toolbar.

Once the button is on the toolbar, you can customize it. You should give each toolbar button a *name*. (The name is what appears in the ScreenTip when you hold the mouse over the button.) And you should assign it to a macro.

5 Right-click the new button. On the shortcut menu, select the default name *Custom Button* and replace it with the name **Add Row**.

Change the name of the button to define the ScreenTip.

6 Click the Assign Macro command, select CopyRow, and click OK.

You can also change the icon associated with the toolbar button.

7 Right-click the new button and point to Change Button Image. Click the down arrow icon (the fourth icon on the fifth row).

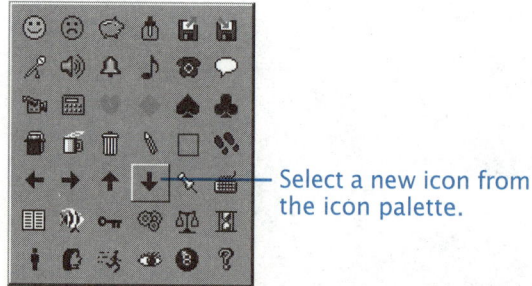

Select a new icon from the icon palette.

The icon on the button changes. In order to use the button, you must close the Customize dialog box.

8 In the Customize dialog box, click the Close button. Then move the mouse pointer over the new toolbar button.

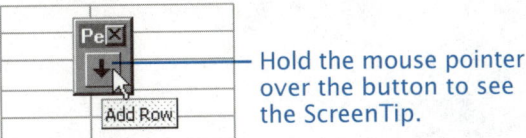

Hold the mouse pointer over the button to see the ScreenTip.

The ScreenTip showing the name of the button appears.

9 Click the Add Row button.

The macro runs, and you get a new row at the bottom of the worksheet.

Add Row

Attach a macro to a menu

A toolbar button can be very convenient, but it can also disappear easily. If the user chooses to close the toolbar, then the button is no longer available. Most toolbar buttons have an equivalent command on a menu. The user can then choose whether to use the toolbar button or the menu command. To modify a menu, you open the same Customize dialog box you used to customize a toolbar.

1 Right-click any toolbar and click Customize. Click the Commands tab.

If you intend to add several commands to a menu, you might want to add them to a submenu. Even though you have only one command right now, you might add more later, so you want to create a submenu for these custom items.

2 In the Categories list, select New Menu. In the Commands list, select New Menu, and drag it onto the Insert menu in the menu bar. Move the insertion point below the Columns command, and then release the mouse button.

Drag the new menu to the Insert menu.

Excel adds a new submenu where you released the mouse. Changing the name of a menu or command changes the label that appears on the menu.

3 Right-click the new submenu, select the default name *New Menu*, replace it with the name **Custom Items**, and press TAB.

The name on the menu changes. But all the other menu items have an underlined letter that makes it easy for users who like the keyboard to navigate a menu. The new Custom Items menu name does not have an underlined letter. To create an underlined letter, you add an ampersand (&) before the letter in the name that you want underlined.

4 Insert an ampersand (&) before the letter "u" of the name *Custom Items*, and press ENTER.

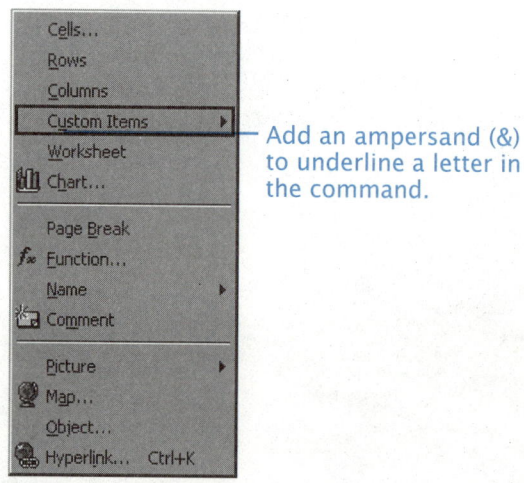

Add an ampersand (&) to underline a letter in the command.

The menu now has an underlined letter. You can now add the Add Row command. In fact, you can simply copy the toolbar button directly to your menu. Just hold down CTRL as you drag the button to make a copy.

5 On the Personal toolbar, click the Add Row button, and drag it onto the Insert menu, and the Custom Items submenu. Hold down CTRL as you release the mouse button.

The name you gave the toolbar button becomes the label for the command. However, the name does not have an underlined letter. You can add an ampersand before the first letter of the name.

6 Right-click the new Add Rows command. Insert an ampersand before the letter "A," and press ENTER. Then click the Customize dialog box's Close button.

The command is now ready to test. You can try out the keyboard shortcut while you test the command.

7 Press ALT. Then press I (for Insert), U (for Custom Items), and A (for Add Row).

The macro runs and a new row appears.

Toolbar buttons and menu commands are easy to modify. You can customize your personal workspace, using either built-in commands or buttons attached to macros. However, these buttons and commands are linked to your computer, not to the workbook. When you close the workbook, the buttons and commands remain visible. (They actually reopen the workbook if you use them.) On the other hand, if you open the workbook on another computer, the buttons and commands do not come with it.

 TIP To restore the menu and toolbar to their original conditions, right-click any toolbar and click Customize. Then activate the Toolbars tab. To restore the menu, click Worksheet Menu Bar, click Reset, and then click OK to confirm the action. To delete the Personal toolbar, click Personal, click Delete, and once again confirm the action.

Attach a macro to a button

See Lesson 1 for more information about freezing panes. If you want a button that is completely associated with one worksheet—a button that is available if and only if the worksheet is available—you can simply add a button directly to the worksheet. If the top row of the worksheet is part of a frozen pane, then you can include a button at the top of the sheet and it will be visible, even if you scroll the window. On the Promotions worksheet, you don't want to insert an extra row for a button, because the macro assumes that the list beings in cell A1. But you can increase the height of row 1 to make room for a button.

1 Click the border between the numbers 1 and 2 on the left edge of the worksheet. Drag the border down until the ScreenTip indicates that the height of row 1 is about 36.

Drag row 1 down until the height is about 36.

See Lesson 8 for more information about using the Control Toolbox.

You now have room to put a button above the column headings. Excel has two different types of controls you can put on a worksheet: controls from the Forms toolbar, and controls from the Control Toolbox toolbar. Controls from the Control Toolbox are new in Excel 97, and have many powerful capabilities. Controls from the Forms toolbar are older, but the button from the Forms toolbar is easy to use because it attaches to a macro in the same way as toolbar buttons and menu commands do. Start by displaying the Forms toolbar.

2 Right-click any toolbar and click Forms.

The Forms toolbar appears. As with any toolbar, you can move and resize the toolbar as you wish.

Button

3 On the Forms toolbar, click the Button button, and then drag a rect-angle from the top left corner of cell A1 to the middle of the right side of cell C1. (Hold down ALT while you start dragging, to get the button to align precisely with the corner of the cell.)

As soon as you release the mouse button, the Assign Macro dialog box appears.

4 Select CopyRow and click OK.

While the button is selected, you can replace the default caption with a more meaningful one.

5 Type **Add Row** and press ESC twice, once to stop editing the caption, and once to deselect the button.

You can now test the button.

6 Click the Add Row button to add a new row to the list.

You decide that you don't like the label *Add Row*. You would like to change it to *Add New Row*. If you click the button, you will run the macro. Forms controls do not have a *design mode* as controls from the Control Toolbox do. In order to select the button without running the macro, you must hold down CTRL as you click it.

7 Hold down CTRL and click the Add Row button. Click in front of the letter "R" and type **New**, followed by a space. Then press ESC twice.

8 Save the Lesson10 workbook.

One Step Further: Making a Macro Run Automatically

As you use the promotions list over time, you realize that every time you open the workbook, the first thing you do is click the Add New Row button to create a new row. If an Excel workbook contains a macro with the name *Auto_Open*, that macro will run every time you open the workbook. In order to run the CopyRow macro when you open the workbook, you can create an Auto_Open macro, and make that macro run the CopyRow macro.

A macro named Auto_Close will run each time that you close the workbook.

Create an Auto_Open macro

Before you create the Auto_Open macro, think about what would happen if you happened to save and close the workbook while the Products worksheet is active. The Auto_Open macro will run, regardless of which sheet is active, but the macro will not work properly if the Promotions worksheet is not active. If you activate the Products worksheet before you start recording the Auto_Open macro, the macro can activate the Promotions worksheet, just to be safe.

Record Macro

1 Activate the Products worksheet.

2 On the Visual Basic toolbar, click the Record Macro button. Type **Auto_Open** as the name of the macro, and click OK.

Stop Recording

3 Activate the Promotions worksheet, and click the Stop Recording button.

4 On the Visual Basic toolbar, click the Run Macro button. Select Auto_Open and click Edit.

Run Macro

5 In the Auto_Open macro, click after the word *Select* and press ENTER. Using all lowercase letters, type **copyrow** and press the DOWN ARROW key.

Use lowercase letters to type the macro name and Visual Basic will change it for you.

As you move the insertion point off the line, Visual Basic changes *copyrow* to *CopyRow*, which is how the name appears in its Sub statement.

 TIP Typing a predefined word in lowercase letters is a simple spelling checker in the Visual Basic Editor: if you spell the word correctly, Visual Basic will convert it to the appropriate uppercase and lowercase letters.

6 Close the Visual Basic Editor. Save and close the Lesson10 workbook.

When you open the workbook, the macro will automatically run. If you did not disable the warning message, you will have to enable the macros when you open the workbook.

7 On the File menu, click Lesson10 to open the workbook. Click the Enable Macros button if Excel prompts you.

As the workbook opens, the Auto_Open macro automatically runs.

 TIP If you want to learn more about Excel macros and Visual Basic, see *Microsoft Excel 97 Visual Basic Step by Step*, by Reed Jacobson, also published by Microsoft Press.

Lesson Summary

To	Do this
Display the Visual Basic toolbar	Right-click any toolbar and click Visual Basic.
Start recording a macro	On the Visual Basic toolbar, click the Record Macro button, type a name for the macro, and click OK.
Stop recording a macro	Click the Stop Recording button.
Run a macro	Click the Run Macro button, select the macro you want to run, and click OK.
Look at a macro	Click the Run Macro button, select a macro, and click Edit.
Watch a macro as it executes each statement	Click the Run Macro button, select a macro, and click Step Into. Press F8 to execute a single statement.
Retrieve the current value of a property in a macro statement	Move the property and its object to the right side of the assignment equal sign.
Delete a statement in a macro	Click to the left of the statement and press DELETE.
Add a shortcut key to an existing macro	Click the Run Macro button, select a macro and click Options. In the Shortcut box, press the letter (or SHIFT+letter) you want to use for the shortcut.
Activate the Visual Basic Editor	On the Visual Basic toolbar, click the Visual Basic Editor button.
Add a new macro	Type **Sub**, followed by a space, followed by a macro name, and press ENTER.
Record selecting a range relative to the current active cell	On the Stop Recording toolbar, click the Relative References button (so that the button is pressed in).
Record selecting an absolute range on the worksheet	Click the Relative References button (so that the button is not pressed in).
Select only cells that contain constants	Press CTRL+G to display the Go To dialog box. Click Special to display the Go To Special dialog box. Select the Constants option and click OK.
Run a macro from another macro	Type the name of the macro you want to run as a statement in the other macro.

To	Do this
Display the Customize dialog box for toolbars and menu bars	Right-click any toolbar, and click Customize.
Create a new toolbar	In the Customize dialog box, select the Toolbars tab. Click New, and type a name for the new toolbar.
Add a new button to an existing toolbar	In the Customize dialog box, click the Commands tab. In the Category list, select Macros. Drag the Custom Button item onto the toolbar.
Give a ScreenTip to a toolbar button	With the Customize dialog box open, right-click the toolbar button. In the Name box, select the existing name and replace it with the desired ScreenTip.
Select a new bitmap for a toolbar button	With the Customize dialog box open, right-click the button. Point to Change Button Image, and select a new button image.
Assign a macro to a toolbar button	With the Customize dialog box open, right-click a toolbar button. Select the name of the macro, and click OK.
Add a submenu to an existing menu	With the Customize dialog box open, select the Commands tab. In the Categories list, select New Menu, and drag it to where you want the new submenu to go.
Underline a shortcut letter in a menu command	In the name of the command, add an ampersand (&) before the letter you want to underline.
Copy a toolbar button onto a menu	With the Customize dialog box open, drag the toolbar button onto a menu. Hold down CTRL as you release the mouse in order to copy the command.
Make room for a button on a worksheet without inserting a new row	Drag the heading for a row to make the heading taller.
Display the Forms toolbar	Right-click any toolbar and click Forms.
Add a command button to a worksheet	On the Forms toolbar, click the Button button. Drag a place for the button on the worksheet. In the Assign Macro dialog box, select a macro and click OK.

To	Do this
Deselect a worksheet button so that the assigned macro runs when you click the button	Press ESC once or twice until the selection returns to a cell on the worksheet.
Select a worksheet button without running it	Hold down CTRL as you click the button.
Create a macro that runs each time you open a workbook	Name the macro *Auto_Open*.
Create a macro that runs each time you close a workbook	Name the macro *Auto_Close*.

For online information about	**On the Help menu, click Contents And Index, click the Index tab, and then type**
Creating macros	**macros**
Stepping through a macro	**Step Into command** (open Help from the Visual Basic Editor)
Customizing toolbars	**toolbars, buttons**
Customizing menus	**menus**
Adding buttons to a worksheet	**buttons, adding**

Index

Index

Index

square brackets ([]), 245, 255
statements, 285
stepping through macros, 285–86,
    292–93, 295
Stop Recording button, 283
structured selection, 137
styles, 183–85
SUBTOTAL function, 106, 110–11
subtotals. *See also* totals
    in lists, 104–7
    in PivotTables, 143–44
SUM function, 16–17, 106
Supreme Court justices, fixing
    names, 89–94
swapping rows and columns, 86
synchronizing shared workbooks,
    273–75

T

tables, lookup, 75–78
TAB versus ENTER, 13
technical support, xiii, xviii
templates, 248–50
text
    aligning with numbers, 12
    angled, 179–81
    centering, 189
    on charts, 206–7
    combining text strings, 93–94
    extracting from string, 91–93
    finding characters in string, 90–
        91
    in PivotTables, 148
    right aligned, 180
    swapping first name and last
        name, 89–94
    wrapping, 181
text boxes, 187–88
TEXT function, 155
Text To Column feature, 176–78
tilting text, 179–81
title bar
    [Group] in, 21
    numbers in, 23
    [Read-Only] in, 266
titles
    on charts, 206–7, 214, 218, 225
    at top of each page, 167–68,
        173
TODAY function, 236
toolbars
    Auditing, 38, 238
    Control Toolbox, 240
    converting drop-down menus
        to, 191
    creating new, 296–97
    customizing buttons, 297–98
    Drawing, 187, 226

toolbars, *continued*
    Forms, 302
    Visual Basic, 282
totals, 16–17. *See also* subtotals
Trace Dependents button, 38–39
tracking changes, 275–77
TRANSPOSE function, 86
TREND function, 81–84
trends
    calculating with AutoFill, 79–81
    calculating with TREND
        function, 81–84
    creating with slope, 87–89
True value, 240
two-column list boxes, 242–44

U

ungrouping worksheets, 22–23
unique values, creating list of,
    116–18
unlocking cells, 270
updating links, 247
user name, changing, 239, 271

V

validating entries, 234–38
ValueDown macro, 289–90
#VALUE! error value, 53
values, creating from formulas, 88
ValueUp macro, 282–88
virtual tables, 257
visible cells, selecting, 112
Visual Basic, Applications edition,
    282, 285
Visual Basic Editor, 284, 289
VLOOKUP function, 75–78, 154
volatile functions, 72

W

warnings, 237
weekdays, creating series, 14
width of columns, 11, 146, 169–
    70, 179–80, 243–44
wildcard characters, 120
windows, arranging, 23–25
WordArt, 193–96
WordArt Gallery button, 194
WordArt Shape button, 194
workbooks
    closing, 25
    linking to different, 244–48
    with macros, opening, 290, 303
    merging shared, 278–79
    opening by multiple users, 266
    preventing adding or deleting
        worksheets, 268–69

workbooks, *continued*
    printing name on each page, 173
    protecting, 264–66
    read-only, 266–67
    renaming, 247
    saving as templates, 248–49
    sharing, 272–79
    and styles, 185
worksheets
    adding to workbook, 188
    buttons on, 301–2
    changing multiple, 20–23
    copying, 18–19
    deleting, 30, 143
    finding inconsistencies, 37–41
    gridlines, 192, 197
    grouping, 21–23
    History, 277
    moving, 245
    names on different, 54–57
    preventing from adding or
        deleting, 268–69
    printing, 166
    printing name on each page, 173
    protecting, 267–70
    renaming, 5
    ungrouping, 22–23
World Wide Web sites
    Excel Camcorder Files, xvi
    Microsoft Press, xiii
wrapping text, 181

X

.xlt filename extension, 249
XY (Scatter) charts, 216–19

Y

year 2000, 71
YEAR function, 69–70

Z

Zoom box, 168. *See also* scaling

314

IMPORTANT—READ CAREFULLY BEFORE OPENING SOFTWARE PACKET(S). By opening the sealed packet(s) containing the software, you indicate your acceptance of the following Microsoft License Agreement.

MICROSOFT LICENSE AGREEMENT

(Book Companion CD-ROM)

This is a legal agreement between you (either an individual or an entity) and Microsoft Corporation. By opening the sealed software packet(s) you are agreeing to be bound by the terms of this agreement. If you do not agree to the terms of this agreement, promptly return the unopened software packet(s) and any accompanying written materials to the place you obtained them for a full refund.

MICROSOFT SOFTWARE LICENSE

1. GRANT OF LICENSE. Microsoft grants to you the right to use one copy of the Microsoft software program included with this book (the "SOFTWARE") on a single terminal connected to a single computer. The SOFTWARE is in "use" on a computer when it is loaded into the temporary memory (i.e., RAM) or installed into the permanent memory (e.g., hard disk, CD-ROM, or other storage device) of that computer. You may not network the SOFTWARE or otherwise use it on more than one computer or computer terminal at the same time. For the files and material referenced in this book which may be obtained from the Internet, Microsoft grants to you the right to use the materials in connection with the book. If you are a member of a corporation or business, you may reproduce the materials and distribute them within your business for internal business purposes in connection with the book. You may not reproduce the materials for further distribution.

2. COPYRIGHT. The SOFTWARE is owned by Microsoft or its suppliers and is protected by United States copyright laws and international treaty provisions. Therefore, you must treat the SOFTWARE like any other copyrighted material (e.g., a book or musical recording) except that you may either (a) make one copy of the SOFTWARE solely for backup or archival purposes, or (b) transfer the SOFTWARE to a single hard disk provided you keep the original solely for backup or archival purposes. You may not copy the written materials accompanying the SOFTWARE.

3. OTHER RESTRICTIONS. You may not rent or lease the SOFTWARE, but you may transfer the SOFTWARE and accompanying written materials on a permanent basis provided you retain no copies and the recipient agrees to the terms of this Agreement. You may not reverse engineer, decompile, or disassemble the SOFTWARE. If the SOFTWARE is an update or has been updated, any transfer must include the most recent update and all prior versions.

4. DUAL MEDIA SOFTWARE. If the SOFTWARE package contains more than one kind of disk (3.5", 5.25", and CD-ROM), then you may use only the disks appropriate for your single-user computer. You may not use the other disks on another computer or loan, rent, lease, or transfer them to another user except as part of the permanent transfer (as provided above) of all SOFTWARE and written materials.

5. SAMPLE CODE. If the SOFTWARE includes Sample Code, then Microsoft grants you a royalty-free right to reproduce and distribute the sample code of the SOFTWARE provided that you: (a) distribute the sample code only in conjunction with and as a part of your software product; (b) do not use Microsoft's or its authors' names, logos, or trademarks to market your software product; (c) include the copyright notice that appears on the SOFTWARE on your product label and as a part of the sign-on message for your software product; and (d) agree to indemnify, hold harmless, and defend Microsoft and its authors from and against any claims or lawsuits, including attorneys' fees, that arise or result from the use or distribution of your software product.

DISCLAIMER OF WARRANTY

The SOFTWARE (including instructions for its use) is provided "AS IS" WITHOUT WARRANTY OF ANY KIND. MICROSOFT FURTHER DISCLAIMS ALL IMPLIED WARRANTIES INCLUDING WITHOUT LIMITATION ANY IMPLIED WARRANTIES OF MERCHANTABILITY OR OF FITNESS FOR A PARTICULAR PURPOSE. THE ENTIRE RISK ARISING OUT OF THE USE OR PERFORMANCE OF THE SOFTWARE AND DOCUMENTATION REMAINS WITH YOU.

IN NO EVENT SHALL MICROSOFT, ITS AUTHORS, OR ANYONE ELSE INVOLVED IN THE CREATION, PRODUCTION, OR DELIVERY OF THE SOFTWARE BE LIABLE FOR ANY DAMAGES WHATSOEVER (INCLUDING, WITHOUT LIMITATION, DAMAGES FOR LOSS OF BUSINESS PROFITS, BUSINESS INTERRUPTION, LOSS OF BUSINESS INFORMATION, OR OTHER PECUNIARY LOSS) ARISING OUT OF THE USE OF OR INABILITY TO USE THE SOFTWARE OR DOCUMENTATION, EVEN IF MICROSOFT HAS BEEN ADVISED OF THE POSSIBILITY OF SUCH DAMAGES. BECAUSE SOME STATES/COUNTRIES DO NOT ALLOW THE EXCLUSION OR LIMITATION OF LIABILITY FOR CONSEQUENTIAL OR INCIDENTAL DAMAGES, THE ABOVE LIMITATION MAY NOT APPLY TO YOU.

U.S. GOVERNMENT RESTRICTED RIGHTS

The SOFTWARE and documentation are provided with RESTRICTED RIGHTS. Use, duplication, or disclosure by the Government is subject to restrictions as set forth in subparagraph (c)(1)(ii) of The Rights in Technical Data and Computer Software clause at DFARS 252.227-7013 or subparagraphs (c)(1) and (2) of the Commercial Computer Software — Restricted Rights 48 CFR 52.227-19, as applicable. Manufacturer is Microsoft Corporation, One Microsoft Way, Redmond, WA 98052-6399.

If you acquired this product in the United States, this Agreement is governed by the laws of the State of Washington.

Should you have any questions concerning this Agreement, or if you desire to contact Microsoft Press for any reason, please write: Microsoft Press, One Microsoft Way, Redmond, WA 98052-6399